MW00653909

BANKRUPTCY LAW
IN
CONTEXT

Editorial Advisors

Rachel E. Barkow
Segal Family Professor of Regulatory Law and Policy
Faculty Director, Center on the Administration of Criminal Law
New York University School of Law

Erwin Chemerinsky
Dean and Jesse H. Choper Distinguished Professor of Law
University of California, Berkeley School of Law

Richard A. Epstein
Laurence A. Tisch Professor of Law
New York University School of Law
Peter and Kirsten Bedford Senior Fellow
The Hoover Institution
Senior Lecturer in Law
The University of Chicago

Ronald J. Gilson
Charles J. Meyers Professor of Law and Business
Stanford University
Marc and Eva Stern Professor of Law and Business
Columbia Law School

James E. Krier
Earl Warren DeLano Professor of Law
The University of Michigan Law School

Tracey L. Meares
Walton Hale Hamilton Professor of Law
Director, The Justice Collaboratory
Yale Law School

Richard K. Neumann, Jr.
Alexander Bickel Professor of Law
Maurice A. Deane School of Law at Hofstra University

Robert H. Sitkoff
John L. Gray Professor of Law
Harvard Law School

David Alan Sklansky
Stanley Morrison Professor of Law
Faculty Co-Director, Stanford Criminal Justice Center
Stanford Law School

ASPEN CASEBOOK SERIES

BANKRUPTCY LAW IN CONTEXT

THERESA J. PULLEY RADWAN
Professor of Law
Stetson University College of Law

MARK D. BAUER
Professor of Law
Stetson University College of Law

ROBERTA K. FLOWERS
Interim Director, Center for Excellence in Advocacy and Professor of Law
Stetson University College of Law

REBECCA C. MORGAN
Boston Asset Management Chair in Elder Law, Interim Director Center for
Excellence in Elder Law and Professor of Law
Stetson University College of Law

JOSEPH F. MORRISSEY
Professor of Law
Stetson University College of Law

Wolters Kluwer

Copyright © 2020 CCH Incorporated. All Rights Reserved.

Published by Wolters Kluwer in New York.

Wolters Kluwer Legal & Regulatory U.S. serves customers worldwide with CCH, Aspen Publishers, and Kluwer Law International products. (www.WKLegaledu.com)

No part of this publication may be reproduced or transmitted in any form or by any means, electronic or mechanical, including photocopy, recording, or utilized by any information storage or retrieval system, without written permission from the publisher. For information about permissions or to request permissions online, visit us at www.WKLegaledu.com, or a written request may be faxed to our permissions department at 212-771-0803.

To contact Customer Service, e-mail customer.service@wolterskluwer.com, call 1-800-234-1660, fax 1-800-901-9075, or mail correspondence to:

Wolters Kluwer
Attn: Order Department
PO Box 990
Frederick, MD 21705

Printed in the United States of America.

1 2 3 4 5 6 7 8 9 0

ISBN 978-1-5438-1003-5

Library of Congress Cataloging-in-Publication Data

Names: Radwan, Theresa Pulley, author. | Bauer, Mark D., author. | Flowers,
   Roberta K., author. | Morgan, Rebecca C., author. | Morrissey, Joseph F.,
   author.
Title: Bankruptcy law in context / Theresa J. Pulley Radwan, Mark D. Bauer,
   Roberta K. Flowers, Rebecca C. Morgan, Joseph F. Morrissey.
Description: First edition. | New York : Wolters Kluwer, 2020. | Includes
   bibliographical references and index. | Summary: "Bankruptcy Law
   casebook that addresses other foundational topics/areas of the law that
   frequently arise in the bankruptcy context"– Provided by publisher.
Identifiers: LCCN 2019045872 (print) | LCCN 2019045873 (ebook) |
   ISBN 9781543810035 (hardcover) | ISBN 9781543817089 (ebook)
Subjects: LCSH: Bankruptcy–United States. | Debtor and creditor–United
   States. | LCGFT: Casebooks (Law)
Classification: LCC KF1524 .R315 2020 (print) | LCC KF1524 (ebook) | DDC
   346.7307/8–dc23
LC record available at https://lccn.loc.gov/2019045872
LC ebook record available at https://lccn.loc.gov/2019045873

About Wolters Kluwer Legal & Regulatory U.S.

Wolters Kluwer Legal & Regulatory U.S. delivers expert content and solutions in the areas of law, corporate compliance, health compliance, reimbursement, and legal education. Its practical solutions help customers successfully navigate the demands of a changing environment to drive their daily activities, enhance decision quality and inspire confident outcomes.

Serving customers worldwide, its legal and regulatory portfolio includes products under the Aspen Publishers, CCH Incorporated, Kluwer Law International, ftwilliam.com and MediRegs names. They are regarded as exceptional and trusted resources for general legal and practice-specific knowledge, compliance and risk management, dynamic workflow solutions, and expert commentary.

*To my amazing parents, who taught me to manage money
and to manage life. — TJPR*

To Jessica and Jim. — MDB

*To Mark, Kyle, Samee and Anna, for helping me know the value
of money is measured in memories. — RKF*

To J, thank you for yesterday, today, and tomorrow. — RCM

*To my sons, whom I hope to have shown that you can
always get a fresh start. — JFM*

Summary of Contents

Contents

Preface

This casebook approaches the study of bankruptcy law as a compendium of other subjects, mostly subjects studied in the first year of law school. While the Bankruptcy Code is itself federal law, the Code interacts with many areas of state law as well as other areas of federal law. It is impossible to understand the concept of "property of the estate"—truly a core concept in any bankruptcy course—without understanding its link to state property law. And a creditor cannot have a claim against the debtor in the bankruptcy case unless that claim stems from a typically state-law right, such as contracts or torts. Thus, the practice of bankruptcy law requires the ability to link the Bankruptcy Code to the core subject areas that most students learn in the first year of law school.

This casebook is different than other casebooks you may have used in your law school studies. Although the subject area is bankruptcy law, bankruptcy law can encompass a number of legal issues, such as contracts, torts, property, agency, evidence, criminal law, constitutional law, administrative law, professional responsibility, and more. We realize that many of these subject areas are the subject areas that are covered in a law school's required curriculum. The context of this book is this: We discuss bankruptcy law in the context of these various areas of law.

As do traditional casebooks, we relied heavily on cases to illustrate the various topics. But as you go through the cases, remember that the Bankruptcy Code is always the starting point for bankruptcy practice. The book will reference Bankruptcy Code sections, and you should read those sections in conjunction with the cases to understand how the courts use the statutory language, supplemented by other areas of law, to reach a conclusion.

Note that the cases and other excerpted materials have been edited for length and readability. We have indicated the omission of some text by using ellipses, but most deleted text, including original footnotes and citations, have been omitted without indication.

We also want to be sure you have an opportunity to apply what you have learned. To that end, you are provided with a hypothetical client who appears in each chapter. You will be given client facts as needed for the subject area, questions are posed to you, examples are offered, and at the end of most chapters we include a practical exercise that allows you to use what you have learned in answering a question from your client. You will want to refer back to the facts presented about your debtor in Chapter 1 throughout the course.

As you go through this book, keep in mind the practical knowledge you are obtaining about various areas of law and the skill of statutory interpretation developed throughout the course. Even if you don't plan to practice bankruptcy law, all of us are debtors and creditors, and the knowledge you gain will help you, your family, and your future clients.

This book, like any project, could not be possible without the help of many people. We would like to thank Stetson University College of Law, which supported the writing of this book. We also thank Stetson's amazing Faculty Support Services team, and particularly Janice Strawn, Derrick Morse, and Jessica Zook. Finally, many students have helped by providing research assistance, editing, or comments, but we would particularly like to thank super-research-assistant Kathryn Bondi (J.D., 2019) for all of her help on this project.

We hope you enjoy your course and this book.

Professors Radwan, Bauer, Flowers, Morgan, and Morrissey

July 2019

Acknowledgments

American Bar Association, Model Rules of Professional Conduct, Copyright © by The American Bar Association. All rights reserved.

American Law Institute:

Restatement (Second) of Contracts, Copyright © 1981
Restatement (Second) of Torts, Copyright © 1965
Restatement (Third) of The Law Governing Lawyers, Copyright © 2000
Restatement (Third) of Torts: Liability for Physical Harm, Copyright © 2010

Reprinted with permission by The American Law Institute. All rights reserved.

1

Introduction to Bankruptcy: Entering Bankruptcy and Bankruptcy Chapters

> It's easy to say you don't care about money when you
> have plenty of it.[1]

Merriam-Webster's Collegiate Dictionary defines *bankrupt* as "a person who has done any of the acts that by law entitle creditors to have his or her estate administered for their benefit; a person judicially declared subject to having his or her estate administered under the bankrupt laws for the benefit of creditors; a person who becomes insolvent." At the heart of this definition are laws—laws that provide for distribution of the assets of a debtor (the person or entity that owes money) to the creditors (the persons or entities owed debt). The current Bankruptcy Code was enacted by Congress and became effective in 1978—though it has seen significant modifications since that time.[2] Bankruptcy laws find their origin in the constitutional provision enabling Congress to create "uniform bankruptcy laws," U.S. Const. art. I, § 8, cl. 4. This book

---

1. Ransom Riggs, *Miss Peregrine's Home for Peculiar Children* (2016).

2. Federal bankruptcy laws existed prior to 1978. Several bankruptcy laws (the Bankruptcy Act of 1800, the Bankruptcy Act of 1841, and the Bankruptcy Act of 1867) were adopted by Congress but repealed shortly thereafter. The Bankruptcy Act of 1898, with significant amendments thanks to the Chandler Act of 1938, served as the basis for the modern-day Bankruptcy Code. The Bankruptcy Reform Act of 1978—known as the Bankruptcy Code—replaced the Bankruptcy Act; the most significant modifications to the Bankruptcy Code came from the Bankruptcy Reform Act of 1994 and the Bankruptcy Abuse Prevention and Consumer Protection Act of 2005. Federal Judicial Center, *The Evolution of Bankruptcy Law: A Timeline*, https://www.fjc.gov/sites/default/files/2012/BKTimeLine2012.pdf.

includes cases to help you understand the Code, as well as the inherent challenges involved in interpreting a code in light of different facts presented in each case. But regardless of the caselaw, a good bankruptcy practitioner always starts with the language of the Bankruptcy Code. For that reason, each section begins by identifying the most critical Code sections for that subject area. You should review the Code sections before diving into the reading—and keep them handy for reference as you read the narrative and cases.

While the Bankruptcy Code is federal law, most of the substantive rights of debtors and creditors arise from state and other non-bankruptcy laws. How does a creditor become a creditor? The creditor's claims against the debtor often arise as a matter of contract or tort law. What assets does the debtor have to pay creditors with? That is typically a matter of property law. Thus, a complete understanding of the bankruptcy system requires not only knowledge of the Bankruptcy Code but also of the myriad of other laws impacting the relationship between a debtor and creditors. This book seeks to examine bankruptcy laws through the lens of other subjects— primarily core subjects studied by most students in the first and second year of law school. While each chapter combines a substantive area of law with a bankruptcy concept in which that substantive area frequently arises, there are many more connections than are provided in this book. For example, Chapter 4 discusses contract law and claims of creditors. But contracts arise in bankruptcy outside of the claims context, and there are claims of creditors that arise outside of the contract context. The book helps provide some of the connections between bankruptcy law and other areas of law, and provides a capstone experience, connecting core subjects together in the context of a more detailed and typically upper-level doctrinal course. For those seeking a career in bankruptcy law, it allows consideration of a variety of subjects crucial to practice in the area. For those interested in other areas of practice, it provides knowledge of bankruptcy and the opportunity to reconnect with subjects studied at the beginning of law school.

Throughout this book, you will have the opportunity to apply the concepts you have learned to a fictional debtor in bankruptcy, Diana Detter. Debtors can be individuals or organizations, and they enter the bankruptcy system for a variety of reasons. Diana is a consumer debtor—an individual—who has faced several personal problems that have culminated in financial distress. As you work through the book, you will return to consider Diana's situation, adding facts to consider in each chapter to narrow the discussion to the concepts you have just learned.

MEET YOUR CLIENT: DIANA DETTER

You have a 10:00 A.M. meeting with a potential new client, Ms. Diana Detter. When you meet with Diana, you learn that she is a 35-year-old divorced mother of two—Will (age 12) and Catie (age 9). Diana's ex-husband, Bryan, has primary custody of the children, but they spend alternate weekends and most of the summer with Diana. She pays monthly child support and owes Bryan $10,000 from their divorce property settlement. Diana is a high school math teacher. She earns $5,000 per month on a 10-month contract (August through May); her take-home pay is roughly $4,000 per month.

Diana explains that she is having trouble making ends meet. Her daughter, Catie, has a heart defect, which has required several surgeries already and will require a few more over the next ten years. But she and Bryan were managing the medical expenses—fortunately, Bryan is a nurse and had managed Catie's at-home care himself—until work troubles set in. Diana's students have been underperforming on statewide math assessments, and Diana was put on probation at work. To make matters worse, one evening a few weeks ago, she was frustrated (and under the influence of some alcoholic beverages). She went to the principal's house with a baseball bat and began attacking his new car. When the principal heard noise outside, he came out to investigate. Unfortunately, he stepped between Diana and the car and was hit by the bat. He suffered a broken arm and rib and a concussion, requiring emergency room treatment. She has been placed on paid administrative leave at work pending an investigation, and the principal has filed a lawsuit against her. Even if she is not fired, she knows that she and the principal can never work in the same school again.

With all of the stress at work, Diana missed two child support payments. She has the money to pay them, but has decided not to at this time because she believes that Bryan has not been paying Catie's medical expenses. Part of the child support is supposed to go toward medical expenses, but Diana is receiving calls from debt collectors indicating that they have not been paid.

Diana has the type of assets that you might expect. She owns a $300,000 home, on which the bank has a $275,000 mortgage; she pays $2,000 per month on the home. Her car is leased; she pays $300 per month, and the lease expires in six months. As for debts, in addition to the ones mentioned above, Diana owes $20,000 on student loans incurred when she pursued (but did not complete) a master's degree. She also helps pay for her children's private-school education.

Throughout this book, you will interact with Diana. Some chapters may modify or add facts for you to consider in representing her. As you start to represent her and read through the following materials, consider the following:

1. Does Diana have any options outside the bankruptcy system?

2. Is bankruptcy a good option for Diana? What are the advantages or disadvantages of a bankruptcy filing?

3. Why might an individual debtor be reticent to file bankruptcy?

4. What factors will matter most in determining whether she is eligible to file for bankruptcy protection?

A. REMEDIES FOR CREDITORS

As you start to consider whether filing for bankruptcy protection provides Diana with the relief she seeks, you should start by considering how a creditor collects on debt outside of the bankruptcy system. These collections operate under state laws. Though each state passes its own laws, the systems from state to state are fairly similar. Key to a knowledge of collections is an understanding of the different rights of secured and unsecured creditors. Chapter 4 of this book will provide you with more depth on the various types of creditors and their rights in bankruptcy, but this section provides you with some basic information regarding secured and unsecured creditors.

Most creditors are "unsecured"; unsecured creditors are owed money, services, or other value by the debtor but do not have any specific assets or collateral to support repayment of the debt obligation. Tort creditors are generally unsecured because they lack the ability to contract for collateral. Most credit cards are unsecured; while the cardholder has an obligation to repay the debt, no specific collateral has been promised in the event that the cardholder fails to meet the payment obligation. Even your student loans are typically unsecured (at least those obtained through the federal government).

Unsecured creditors who are not paid by the debtor can seek to collect upon the debt. But what does an unsecured creditor do when the debtor simply will not pay? Creditors can seek to collect that debt in a variety of ways, and Chapter 11 of this book considers protections available to debtors when creditors go too far in those collection efforts. Within the judicial system, the creditor can seek a judgment of nonpayment against the debtor and, if the debtor still fails to pay, turn that judgment into a lien on the property of the debtor. A lien gives the creditor the right to a specific asset of the debtor. That lien can be turned over to the sheriff for execution, which involves the sheriff taking the property for the benefit of the creditor. These steps—filing a judgment lien and levying upon that judgment and sheriff's sale—are discussed in the following case.

Salminen v. Morrison & Frampton, PLLP

339 P.3d 602 (Mont. 2014)

MCGRATH, Chief Justice

* * *

[Don and Sue] Salminen[] commenced this action with a complaint filed in August 2011, alleging wrongful levy, abuse of process, conversion and other claims. . . . the following facts are taken from the allegations in the Salminens' complaint.

In November 2009 the defendants Centennial and Leonard obtained a judgment against the Salminens in the amount of $482,499.00. Defendant Morrison & Frampton law firm (Frampton) represented Centennial and Leonard in that litigation. On December 7, 2009, Frampton requested and the District Court issued a writ of execution and garnishment. In December 2009 Frampton levied against certain assets (a bank account and wages) belonging to the Salminens with modest results.

On January 14, 2010, Salminens filed a notice of claimed exemptions and request for a hearing, supported by affidavits and a description of property that they claimed to be exempt from execution. . . . On January 19, 2010, Frampton obtained a warrant of execution from the District Court based upon Frampton's supporting affidavit, and presented the warrant to the Flathead County Sheriff's Department. The affidavit in support of the warrant contained false statements of fact, including that the writ of execution had been returned unsatisfied; that there was no other property available to levy; that the judgment creditor was entitled to execute upon all of the Salminens' personal property, none of which was exempt from execution; that the warrant without notice to the Salminens was proper based upon a demand letter in 2007; and that the Salminens had paid nothing toward the judgment. Frampton did not file any copies of the application, affidavit or the warrant with the District Court.

On the morning of March 9, 2010, Frampton associate Joos met Flathead County Deputy Sheriff Tyler at the Salminen residence in Columbia Falls. Joos falsely told Tyler that the Salminens knew that a seizure would happen that morning but that he had no way to contact them. Deputy Tyler had a locksmith come to open a door and then entered the house with Joos, determining that no one was there. Joos then alerted a moving company waiting nearby and directed them to remove the contents of the house. Deputy Tyler asked Joos what property was to be seized. Joos called Frampton who gave the direction to "take everything that is not nailed down." The movers then began to pack up the contents of the house at the direction of Joos, while Deputy Tyler remained primarily outside.

Several hours later the Salminens' granddaughter arrived at the house. Deputy Tyler told her that there was a court-ordered seizure and asked if she could contact the Salminens. The granddaughter called Don Salminen, and Deputy Tyler informed him what was happening, confirming that the Salminens had no knowledge that the seizure was taking place. Don Salminen asked his daughter to go to the house, and when she arrived she saw a man in a suit in her parents' house directing people who were packing the contents. The man said that he worked for Frampton, but soon left in a vehicle.

Sue Salminen arrived shortly thereafter distressed and crying. She saw a mover packing the pantry of canned food, including open boxes of food such as crackers and cereal. The walls, countertops, drawers and shelves had been stripped almost bare. The movers had left a phone book but had taken the phone, shoveling everything into boxes. Sue Salminen begged to keep a photo of her son in his border patrol uniform, and Deputy Tyler told her she could keep it. He also allowed her to keep the grandchildren's Easter baskets, some family photos and movies, and some batteries. Everything else was packed.

The Salminens' son-in-law arrived and asked Deputy Tyler about their food, clothes and medications, and how they were supposed to eat or get ready for work the next day. Deputy Tyler stated that he had been instructed by Frampton to "take everything." When asked about food in a freezer, Deputy Tyler said that the "plan" was to take the appliances to a storage facility and plug them back in. Ultimately, Deputy Tyler convinced Frampton to allow the Salminens to take their food and game meat from the appliances. All of the furniture had been taken from the home, including the bed "and other medical equipment," forcing the Salminens to live with family members.

The next morning the Salminens' attorney went to the District Court to discover the circumstances of the seizure, but found that neither the District Court nor the Clerk of the Court had any information regarding Frampton's application, affidavit or the warrant. The Sheriff's Office knew about the seizure but did not have copies of the documents. At some point counsel obtained copies of the documents from Frampton and provided them to the District Court.

Frampton's movers placed all of the Salminens' property in a storage facility. The property included used and soiled clothing, dirty dishes from the kitchen sink; open boxes of perishable food; canned goods, plastic utensils, paper plates and Tupperware; the entire contents of the kitchen "junk drawer"; used toiletries, medications and eyeglasses; children's toys, crayons and coloring books; family heirlooms including the cremated ashes of Sue Salminen's aunt; and thousands of other articles of personal property that had no economic value and from which the judgment creditor could not realize any value. Frampton also took $5400 in cash that was not on the mover's inventory and was not given to the Sheriff's Office. Deputy Tyler counted the money and gave it to Joos, who took it with him when he left. Frampton put the money in the firm's trust account. Salminens allege that Frampton seized virtually everything in their house, knowing it to be exempt from execution, to leverage a settlement of the judgment so that they could get back their personal property and avoid future harassment.

On March 25, 2010, Salminens filed and served a revised notice of claimed exemptions and renewed their request for a hearing, which occurred on April 6, 2010. Frampton did not disclose the seizure of the $5400 in cash from the Salminens' house, nor the approximately $1000 levied from their bank account and wages. On April 21, 2010, Frampton filed a notice of partial satisfaction of the judgment reflecting the money levied from the bank account and wages. On May 7, 2010, Frampton filed another notice of partial satisfaction reflecting seizure of the $5400 found at the house.

The District Court did not rule on the Salminens' claim for exemptions until July 13, 2010. The District Court on that day held that *all* of the property seized in the March 9 event was exempt from execution and must be returned to the Salminens. Frampton's mover did not return the Salminens' property for another three weeks, until August 4, 2010.

* * *

In August 2011 the Salminens filed the present action against Morrison & Frampton, Centennial, and Leonard. The action asserted claims for violation of rights secured by Article II of the

Montana Constitution; for abuse of legal process; for conversion; for negligence, and for wrongful levy. . . .

* * *

Proof of a claim for conversion requires that plaintiff own the property; that plaintiff have the right to possess the property; that defendant exercise unauthorized control over the property; and that plaintiff suffer damages. The Salminens' claim for conversion incorporated the facts summarized above and alleged that they "owned and were in lawful possession of the subject personal property," and the defendants "exercised unauthorized dominion" over it. They alleged they had suffered damages as a result of unlawful conversion and that they would seek damages to be determined by a jury.

The District Court dismissed the Salminens' claim for conversion because Frampton "exercised authorized control over the Plaintiffs' property pursuant to a writ of execution and obtained the right to enter Plaintiffs' premises under a warrant of execution." . . .

The District Court erred in determining that the Salminens failed to state a claim for conversion. The process of executing upon a judgment debtor's assets is controlled by statute. A writ of execution is issued in the name of the State of Montana, and is directed to a "sheriff or levying officer." The writ allows a levy or seizure of assets, as was done in this case against the Salminens' bank account and wages. A judgment debtor can claim the right to certain exemptions from execution for personal property by filing a claim for exemption with the district court. The Salminens did so in this case, and just a few days later Frampton appeared at their house and seized their possessions. . . . [T]he Salminens were entitled to a hearing on the claims for exemption within ten days. In fact, although they requested a hearing, the District Court did not hold one for almost three months. The decision on their request for exemption was not rendered for several more months, but was ultimately in favor of the Salminens. This failure to conduct a hearing and to promptly render a decision on the exemption issue after the hearing clearly hampered the Salminens' efforts to regain their personal property.

* * *

A judgment creditor may enter a debtor's home to seize and execute upon personal property only by obtaining a warrant of execution as provided in § 25–13–213, MCA. The statute provides that if there is "reason to believe that there is personal property subject to execution" in the debtor's residence, the creditor may "file" an application for a warrant with the district court. The application must be supported by an affidavit stating that the writ of execution has been issued and returned unsatisfied in whole or in part; that the affiant has reason to believe that there is "property subject to execution" in the debtor's residence; that there is no other property available for levy and execution; and describing the property sought. If the "judge" determines that reasonable cause exists, the judge may issue a warrant authorizing entry into the residence and seizure of the property. In the present case the Salminens' claims that their property was wrongfully seized rely upon their allegations of Frampton's failure to follow these requirements and they allege that he falsified the affidavit supporting the warrant. They allege that Frampton procured the warrant of execution not because he had actual reason to believe that property in their home was subject to execution as required by the statute. Rather, they allege that Frampton procured the warrant with the plan to seize all of their personal property so that they would provide other assets to satisfy the judgment, and so that they would not have to endure future seizures of their property.

. . . At the time Frampton obtained the warrant and entered the Salminens' home they had filed their claim of exemption pursuant to the statute and had requested a hearing. Frampton knew or should have known that much of the property in the home was covered by the exemption claim.

If the Salminens can prove the allegations in their complaint, they may be able to establish that the entry into their home and seizure of the property was not authorized by law. Therefore there are facts which, if proven, could establish that there was conversion of the Salminens' property. The District Court erred in determining that as a matter of law the Salminens could not establish conversion and that claim should not have been dismissed.

. . . The complaint, after incorporating the facts noted above, alleges that there was an abuse of process because Frampton filed an affidavit containing false statements and had an ulterior purpose in taking the Salminens' property that Frampton knew was exempt. The ulterior motive was to "leverage [Salminens'] settlement position and coerce them to come up with the money to satisfy the civil judgment in order to get their exempt personal property back and avoid further judgment creditor harassment." The property that Frampton seized from the house, if sold, would have provided little if any actual money that could be applied to satisfy the large judgment against the Salminens.

A successful claim for abuse of process depends upon proof that the defendant made a "willful use of process not proper in the regular conduct of the proceeding, and that the process was used for an ulterior purpose." The legal process must be "put to a use perverted beyond its intended purpose." An abuse of process may occur when a party uses process to coerce another to "do some collateral thing [that he] could not be legally and regularly compelled to do.". . .

The District Court determined that as a matter of law the Salminens had not stated a claim for abuse of process. The District Court determined that there is nothing ulterior about seeking to satisfy a civil judgment; that Frampton was only pressing "valid legal claims" to a "regular conclusion," and that the Salminens' mere assertion that their property was exempt does not make it exempt. While it is certainly true that seeking to satisfy a valid judgment is not a basis for a claim of abuse of process, that is not the Salminens' contention in this case. As discussed above in regard to the conversion claim, the contention in this case is that Frampton wrongfully obtained a warrant that authorized entry into the Salminens' home, and that after entry he seized clearly exempt property of minimal value to essentially hold the property hostage. They contend that Frampton did this to force them to do something to pay the underlying judgment in order to get back their exempt property and to avoid Frampton's conducting such entries and seizures in the future.

The Salminens' claims of abuse of process and conversion are bolstered by Frampton's alleged conduct of seizing virtually everything in the home down to the bare walls with little or no thought of its probable exemption or value. Seizure of the cremated remains of a family member, used clothing, food, medications and such clearly has nothing to do with a genuine attempt to satisfy a very substantial judgment. . . . The abuse of process claim should not have been dismissed because there are facts that, if proved, would entitle the Salminens to relief. . . .

The District Court also dismissed the Salminens' claim of wrongful levy, concluding that Frampton "lawfully obtained" the writ of execution and that the claim turned upon whether the Salminens received advance notice of the seizure. Montana law recognizes a claim for "wrongful levy" where assets are wrongfully seized to satisfy a judgment.

As discussed above, the Salminens' allegation is that Frampton failed to comply with the requirements of § 25–13–213, MCA, in obtaining the warrant that was used to gain entry into their home. If they prove their allegations then the warrant may not have been "lawfully obtained" and the seizure may have been unauthorized. While it appears that a wrongful levy claim could be subsumed within the claims for conversion and abuse of process, the District Court erred in dismissing the claim at this early stage of the case.

* * *

(Citations omitted.)

NOTES AND COMMENTS

1. Would the filing of a notice of claimed exemptions always suffice as the basis for a claim of wrongful levy?

2. Why would a creditor seek to levy on a judgment before a determination is made as to the status of the assets?

3. If you represent the Salminen family as their attorney and they called while the sheriff was at their house and the moving company was seizing their property, what should you do?

Once a creditor has obtained property through the execution process, the creditor needs to find a way to use the value of the property to pay the obligation owed by the debtor. Rarely does a creditor want to keep the property itself. Instead, the creditor typically sells the property and uses the proceeds of sale to pay off the debt. But competing goals can arise in such a sale. On the one hand, the creditor wants to maximize the amount of money received (as does the debtor, who will continue to owe whatever amount of the debt is not paid off via the sale). But the creditor also wants to ensure that it does not spend too much time and effort with the sale—a quick resolution allows the creditor to get back to other matters. The following case navigates some of the issues that arise during the sale of property levied upon by a creditor.

Howard v. Adams

2016 Ark. App. 597 (Ark. App. 2016)

GLADWIN, Chief Judge

This is the fifth appeal in a dispute between appellant Gary Howard and appellee Lauren Adams over attorney's fees. In the most recent appeal, *Howard IV*, we affirmed the circuit court's decision to foreclose on forty-six acres of property in order to satisfy Adams's attorney-fee lien and other matters. While *Howard IV* was pending, the foreclosure sale took place and was confirmed by the circuit court. The court also awarded additional fees to Adams for the work of her attorney Tamra Cochran, who has represented her throughout this dispute. Gary now appeals from the order confirming the sale and the order awarding additional attorney's fees. We affirm.

I. Background

The lengthy history of this case is set forth in our earlier opinions. To summarize past events, Adams represented Gary in a lawsuit to recover forty-six acres of property that had been owned by Gary's late father, Odis Howard. Adams obtained a successful outcome, which resulted in the forty-six acres being placed into the Odis Howard estate. Gary was the administrator and sole beneficiary of the estate. . . .

Afterward, Adams sought a one-third contingency fee from Gary in accordance with her representation contract. When Gary refused to pay, Adams filed an attorney-fee lien on the forty-six acres and a claim against the estate for thirty-three percent of the property's value. Following a lengthy period in which the forty-six acres remained unsold, Adams began seeking foreclosure of her attorney-fee lien through a judicial sale of the property.

In November 2014, the circuit court ordered foreclosure and public sale of the forty-six acres. . . .

While the appeal in *Howard IV* was pending, the foreclosure sale was held, and Adams and her law partner bought the forty-six acres for $450,000. The circuit court confirmed the sale. . . . Gary appeals and raises five arguments for reversal.

II. Judicial Sale of the Property

Gary argues that three errors occurred in connection with the sale of the forty-six acres. As explained below, we find no error in the sale process.

We begin by recognizing that we accord great discretion to the circuit court in matters pertaining to judicial sales. The circuit court is the vendor in judicial sales, and, in the exercise of sound judicial discretion, it may confirm or refuse to confirm a sale made under its order. In determining whether the circuit court abused its discretion, we do not substitute our decision for that of the circuit court: instead, we merely review the case to see whether the circuit court's decision was within the latitude of decisions that it could make in the particular case.

Gary argues first that notice of the sale was not published the requisite number of times in the newspaper. The circuit court's foreclosure decree set forth the following requirement:

> That the Commissioner of this Court hereinafter appointed shall, after advertising the time, terms, and place of sale for twenty (20) or more days by publication in a newspaper published or circulated in Benton County, Arkansas, having a bona fide circulation therein, *by at least two insertions*, sell at the front door of the Benton County Courthouse . . . [the described property].

(Emphasis added.) The Commissioner complied with the decree by inserting notice of the sale in the Northwest Arkansas Democrat Gazette two times within twenty days of the sale. However, Gary contends that the notice should have been inserted three times.

He cites Arkansas Code Annotated section 28–51–304 (Repl. 2012), which reads in pertinent part:

> (a)(1) In all sales of real property at public auction, the personal representative shall give notice of the sale, particularly describing the property to be sold, and stating the time, place, and terms of sale.
> (2) The notice shall be printed one (1) time a week for three (3) consecutive weeks in a newspaper published or having a general circulation in the county in which the property is situated.

The circuit court refused to apply section 28–51–304 on the ground that it governs those situations in which the personal representative is selling the property. The court was correct. Section 28–51–304 imposes duties on the personal representative with regard to publication of notice, but it makes no such demand on the seller in a judicial sale. Here, as in all judicial sales, the court was the seller, not the personal representative.

Gary argues next that the $450,000 price paid for the property was inadequate. He cites Arkansas Code Annotated section 28–51–303(b)(2)(A), which provides that "if the sale [of the property] is to be at public auction, the property shall be sold for not less than three-fourths (3/4) of its appraised value." According to Gary, $450,000 was less than three-fourths of the property's appraised value.

Initially, we observe that section 28–51–303(b)(2)(A), like section 28–51–304 discussed above, is inapplicable because it is part of the Probate Code that governs the personal representative's sale of estate property. But, in any event, the proof taken by the circuit court does not bear out Gary's claim that the sale price was inadequate.

Gary testified that the forty-six acres had been appraised at $2 million, but subsequent testimony indicated that he may have been referring to a 2006 appraisal. He offered no qualified appraisal of the property's value at the time it was sold in 2015. Moreover, the property had been on the market for many years without being sold, and a realtor testified that she would list the property for $600,000 to $750,000 in order to sell it quickly. Under these circumstances, the $450,000 sale price was not inadequate and does not shock the conscience of the court.

For his third point, Gary argues that the sales notice contained a misleading description of the sale's location. The notice stated that the sale would take place "at the West Front Entrance of the Benton County Courthouse" on June 22, 2015, at 9:15 a.m. At the hearing below, Gary testified that he thought the sale would be held at the entrance, outside the courthouse. He said that he arrived at 8:30, waited on the steps, and intended to bid on the property. He further testified that, when nothing occurred, he entered the building about 9:30 but found no activity.

At the same hearing, court commissioner Brenda DeShields, who conducted the sale, testified that the sale was held in the courthouse's second-floor lobby, which may be considered inside the west, front entrance. According to DeShields, the west, front-entrance door is typically locked, and part of the stairs leading up to it are barricaded. She testified that she usually asks attorneys to modify their notices to state that the sale will take place in the lobby, but that was not done in this case. DeShields also testified that the usual practice was to look out the locked west-entrance door to see if anyone was waiting, but she could not recall if that had been done here. However, she said that she announced the sale so that anybody waiting inside the front doors would have heard it. DeShields also said that Gary's attorney, Harry McDermott, attended the sale and was waiting on his client. DeShields agreed to delay the sale but McDermott did not object to it continuing.

Appellee Lauren Adams attended the sale and testified that she and another person checked outside to see if anyone was there before the sale occurred. She said that she did not see anyone, in particular Gary Howard. Another witness testified similarly.

After hearing this evidence, the circuit court ruled that the entrance door had been checked: that Gary was not there: that McDermott was present at the sale and did not object to its location: and that Gary was familiar enough with the courthouse to find his way in. Given the deference we accord to the circuit court's credibility rulings, we affirm on this point.

* * *

(Citations omitted.)

NOTES AND COMMENTS

1. Though the requirements did not apply to the case at hand, why are the requirements for noticing the property sale three times and ensuring that the property sells for at least 75 percent of appraised value important in a foreclosure sale?

2. The case points out that the property was purchased by the attorney-creditor, and that the debtor sought to bid on the property at the sale. Why would the debtor or creditor want to bid on the property?

Secured creditors have collateral—assets specifically promised to them in order to protect the creditors' right to be paid—and are able to skip some of the steps required of unsecured creditors. This right to assets is also called a "security interest." Secured creditors do not need to obtain a judgment in order to take property on which they have a lien. And they record that lien in a statewide registry for personal property or a countywide registry in most states for real property. Once the debtor defaults, the creditor can then "repossess" the property as long as the creditor does so without breaching the peace. And, rather than selling through a sheriff's sale, the creditor can sell the collateral on its own in a commercially reasonable manner. A course in Secured Transactions, offered at most if not all law schools, will allow you to understand how a creditor becomes secured by personal property and establishes priority in collateral over other creditors, and will flesh out the foreclosure and sale process in more detail.

Giles v. First Virginia Credit Servs., Inc.

560 S.E.2d 557 (N.C. App. 2002)

McGEE, Judge

Richard Giles and Joann Giles (plaintiffs) appeal the trial court's order granting First Virginia Credit Services, Inc.'s (First Virginia) motion for summary judgment in part.

* * *

Joann Giles entered into an installment sale contract on or about 18 January 1997 for the purchase of an automobile. The contract was assigned to First Virginia, which obtained a senior perfected purchase money security interest in the automobile. The terms of the contract required Joann Giles to make sixty regular monthly payments to First Virginia. The contract stated that Joann Giles' failure to make any payment due under the contract within ten days after its due date would be a default. The contract contained an additional provision agreed to by Joann Giles that stated:

> If I am in default, you may consider all my remaining payments to be due and payable, without giving me notice. I agree that your rights of possession will be greater than mine. I will deliver the property to you at your request, or you may use lawful means to take it yourself without notice or other legal action. . . .
>
> . . .
>
> If you excuse one default by me, that will not excuse later defaults.

During the early morning hours of 27 June 1999, Professional Auto Recovery, at the request of First Virginia, repossessed the locked automobile from plaintiffs' front driveway. According to First Virginia, the account of Joann Giles was in arrears for payments due on 2 May 1999 and 2 June 1999, and pursuant to the terms of the contract, repossession was permitted.

In an affidavit filed by plaintiffs in opposition to First Virginia's motion for summary judgment, plaintiffs' neighbor, Glenn A. Mosteller (Mr. Mosteller), stated that he was awakened around 4:00 a.m.

> by the running of a loud diesel truck engine on the road outside my house. Evidentially [sic] the truck was stopped because I lay in bed for a while and did not get up. I then became concerned and went to the window to see what was going on. At this time I saw a large rollback diesel truck with a little pickup truck on the truck bed behind it. The truck only had its parking lights on. The truck . . . started going toward the Giles' yard. It still only had its parking lights on. About that time, a man jumped out of the truck and ran up the Giles' driveway. Their car was parked up at their house. Then the car came flying out back down the driveway making a loud noise and started screeching off. . . . At about the same time, the rollback also pulled off real fast making a real loud diesel noise and went down [the road]. . . . I got to the phone, called the Giles and told them someone was stealing their car. . . . My lights were on . . . and the Giles' lights were on and that portion of our neighborhood had woken up. Richard Giles came out in his yard and we hollared [sic] a few words back and forth and I jumped in my truck . . . to try to get the police. About 5 minutes later a police car came up

and pulled into the Giles' yard. Then another police car came then a Sheriff's Deputy car came. Then another police car came. . . . There was a great commotion going on out in the street and in our yard all to the disturbance of the quietness and tranquility of our neighborhood. . . . It scared me and it scared the Giles.

Joann Giles stated in a deposition that she was awakened by Mr. Mosteller's telephone call in which he told her that someone was stealing her car. She stated she ran to see if the automobile was parked outside and confirmed that it was gone. Joann Giles testified she woke up her husband and gave him the telephone; he ran outside into the yard and heard Mr. Mosteller "hollering" at him from across the street. Plaintiffs testified in their depositions that neither of them saw the car being repossessed but were only awakened by their neighbor after the automobile was gone. During the actual repossession, no contact was made between Professional Auto Recovery and plaintiffs, nor between Professional Auto Recovery and Mr. Mosteller.

* * *

By their first assignment of error, plaintiffs argue the trial court erred in granting in part First Virginia's motion for summary judgment dismissing plaintiffs' claim for wrongful conversion and/or repossession of their automobile. Plaintiffs specifically argue that (1) the determination of whether a breach of the peace occurred in violation of N.C. Gen.Stat. § 25–9–503 is a question for the jury and not one to be determined by summary judgment, and (2) there is a dispute as to whether plaintiffs were in default.

* * *

Our Courts have long recognized the right of secured parties to repossess collateral from a defaulting debtor without resort to judicial process, so long as the repossession is effected peaceably. . . .

The General Assembly did not define breach of the peace but instead left this task to our Courts, and although a number of our appellate decisions have considered this self-help right of secured parties, none have clarified what actions constitute a breach of the peace.

* * *

In a pre-UCC case, a defaulting debtor left his locked automobile on his front lawn. An agent of the mortgagee went to the debtor's home to repossess the automobile, saw the automobile parked on the lawn, found no one at home, and asked a neighbor where the debtor was. The agent was told no one was at home and he thereafter opened the automobile door with a coat hanger and removed the automobile on a wrecker. Our Supreme Court found that this evidence could not warrant a finding by a jury that the mortgagee's agent wrongfully took possession of the automobile because no breach of the peace occurred. . . .

. . . our Court [in another case] explained that "[o]f course, if there is confrontation at the time of the attempted repossession, the secured party must cease the attempted repossession and proceed by court action in order to avoid a 'breach of the peace.'" This indicates, as argued by First Virginia, that confrontation is at least an element of a breach of the peace analysis.

* * *

The phrase "breach of the peace" is defined in Black's Law Dictionary as the "criminal offense of creating a public disturbance or engaging in disorderly conduct, particularly by an unnecessary or distracting noise." Black's Law Dictionary 183 (7th ed. 1999). The phrase is also commonly understood to mean a "violation of the public order as amounts to a disturbance of the public tranquility, by act or conduct either directly having this effect, or by inciting or tending to incite such a disturbance of the public tranquility." 12 Am.Jur.2d *Breach of Peace* § 5 (1997).

* * *

The courts in many states have examined whether a breach of the peace in the context of the UCC has occurred. Courts have found a breach of the peace when actions by a creditor incite violence or are likely to incite violence.

* * *

Many courts have used a balancing test to determine if a repossession was undertaken at a reasonable time and in a reasonable manner, and to balance the interests of debtors and creditors. Five relevant factors considered in this balancing test are: "(1) where the repossession took place, (2) the debtor's express or constructive consent, (3) the reactions of third parties, (4) the type of premises entered, and (5) the creditor's use of deception." . . .

* * *

Based upon our review of our appellate courts' treatment of breach of the peace in pre-UCC and UCC cases, as well as in other areas of the law, the purposes and policies of the UCC, and the treatment other jurisdictions have given the phrase, we find that a breach of the peace, when used in the context of N.C. Gen. Stat. § 25–9–503, is broader than the criminal law definition. A confrontation is not always required, but we do not agree with plaintiffs that every repossession should be analyzed subjectively, thus bringing every repossession into the purview of the jury so as to eviscerate the self-help rights duly given to creditors by the General Assembly. Rather, a breach of the peace analysis should be based upon the reasonableness of the time and manner of the repossession. We therefore adopt a balancing test using the five factors discussed above to determine whether a breach of the peace occurs when there is no confrontation.

In applying these factors to the undisputed evidence in the case before us, we affirm the trial court's determination that there was no breach of the peace, as a matter of law. Professional Auto Recovery went onto plaintiffs' driveway in the early morning hours, when presumably no one would be outside, thus decreasing the possibility of confrontation. Professional Auto Recovery did not enter into plaintiffs' home or any enclosed area. Consent to repossession was expressly given in the contract with First Virginia signed by Joann Giles. Although a third party, Mr. Mosteller, was awakened by the noise of Professional Auto Recovery's truck, Mr. Mosteller did not speak with anyone from Professional Auto Recovery, nor did he go outside until Professional Auto Recovery had departed with the Giles' automobile. Further, neither of the plaintiffs were awakened by the noise of the truck, and there was no confrontation between either of them with any representative of Professional Auto Recovery. By the time Mr. Mosteller and plaintiffs went outside, the automobile was gone. Finally, there is no evidence, nor did plaintiffs allege, that First Virginia or Professional Auto Recovery employed any type of deception when repossessing the automobile.

* * *

(Citations omitted.)

NOTES AND COMMENTS

1. Confrontation is not always required to have a breach of the peace. Cases regularly agree that the use of a police officer (on- or off-duty) in a self-help repossession is a breach of the peace due to the coercive nature

of police presence. *See* Goard v. Crown Auto, Inc., 170 F. Supp. 3d 915, 920 (W.D. Va. 2016) (noting several opinions that have determined that police officers should not be involved in self-help repossessions); Ryan McRobert, *Defining "Breach of the Peace" in Self-Help Repossessions*, 87 Wash. L. Rev. 569 (June 2012) (discussing cases involving variety of ways that police may be involved in self-help repossessions and variety of resolutions of those cases). In addition, some courts have found that trickery or deception that causes a debtor to voluntarily surrender collateral may also constitute a breach of the peace. *See* Ford Motor Credit Co. v. Byrd, 351 So. 2d 557 (Ala. 1977) (tricking debtor into bringing car into dealership under guise of renegotiation constituted breach); *but see* Ivy v. General Motors Acceptance Corp., 612 S. 2d 1108, 1111 (Miss. 1992) ("Courts in other jurisdictions have generally held that the use of trickery or deceit to peaceably repossess collateral does not constitute a breach of peace.").

2. What can a secured creditor do if it cannot peaceably repossess? It can follow the requirements available to an unsecured creditor in order to have a sheriff levy upon the property.

3. Without judging the taste of the television viewing public, shows focused on the repossession of collateral have become popular. Perhaps you were coerced by a friend (or for some reason voluntarily decided) to watch *Operation Repo, Airplane Repo, Lizard Lick Towing, Bear Swamp Recovery*, or any of the alarming number of other repo business shows. Is there some aspect of these shows that you find difficult to believe (beyond the marginal acting) after reviewing repossession law?

B. ENTERING BANKRUPTCY (§§ 301, 303)

The decision to enter bankruptcy is complex. Studies seeking to capture the reason for bankruptcy filing have cited a variety of triggers for bankruptcy filings—excessive use of credit cards, job loss, medical problems, and more. As the National Bankruptcy Review Commission found in 1997:

> Why are so many Americans in financial trouble? The question haunts the economic prosperity of the 1990s. Answers for individual families depend on their own specific circumstances - layoffs, downsizing, moving from employee to independent contractor status, uninsured medical bills, car accidents, taking in a sister's children, gambling, failed businesses, job transfers, caring for elderly parents, divorce, kids' braces and school tuition. Answers for the country as a whole are far more difficult to determine.

The 1970 Commission noted the "tremendous rise" in consumer credit since World War II. In 1978, Congress initiated its discussion of consumer bankruptcy by observing that "[t]he result of the increase in consumer credit has been a corresponding increase in the number of consumers who have overburdened themselves with debt." Few would have expected that the debt levels and the bankruptcy filing rates of the 1970s would be viewed retrospectively as modest compared to the record levels achieved today.

Americans in the 1990s have unprecedented access to consumer credit, and the American economy has benefitted from that access. Consumer credit permits many Americans to buy what they need when they need it - cars, appliances, and clothing. It also enables them to make emergency purchases and to make long-term investments in homes and education. Greater access to credit has improved the quality of life for millions of American families. But the benefits of credit are not free. Between 1977 and 1997, consumer debt has grown nearly 700%. For generations, Americans have experienced divorces, illnesses and uninsured medical costs, and job layoffs. However, never before have so many families faced these setbacks with so much consumer debt. The ordinary and not-so-ordinary troubles that families weathered a generation ago can become unmanageable for a family that already has committed several paychecks to meet monthly bills.[3]

Bankruptcy filings occur at all income levels; one well-known study found bankruptcy to be primarily a middle-class phenomenon.[4] While concerns exist that debtors see bankruptcy as a "get out of jail free" card to avoid debt, others note that the decision to enter the bankruptcy system often follows months or years of financial hardship, and debtors feel stigmatized as a debtor in the bankruptcy system.[5] In short, bankruptcy debtors come from a variety of backgrounds and come to the court system with different points of view regarding the benefits and burdens of filing for bankruptcy protection.

If a debtor seeks to voluntarily enter the bankruptcy system, the debtor does so through the filing of a petition, followed by the filing of schedules. While the petition is a relatively simple document, schedules are detailed filings providing a variety of information about the debtor's financial situation—listing the debtor's assets, debts, contracts, etc. If the debtor voluntarily enters bankruptcy, an "order for relief" is issued by the court upon filing of the petition. Knowing the date for the *petition* and the *order*

3. National Bankruptcy Review Commission Final Report Chapter 1, *Bankruptcy: The Next Twenty Years*, http://govinfo.library.unt.edu/nbrc/report/01title.html (1997).

4. Teresa A. Sullivan, Elizabeth Warren, & Jay Lawrence Westbrook, *The Fragile Middle Class: Americans in Debt* (Yale Univ. Press 2001).

5. Teresa Sullivan, Jay Lawrence Westbrook, & Elizabeth Warren, *Less Stigma or More Financial Distress: An Empirical Analysis of the Extraordinary Increase in Bankruptcy Filings*, 59 Stan. L. Rev. 213, 216–18 (noting several statements by senators and government employees regarding decreased stigma of bankruptcy, but finding increased stigma in recent years for those actually filing for bankruptcy protection).

for relief (typically the same date in a voluntary case) is critical. As you will see throughout this book, many bankruptcy deadlines are measured from these two dates, and these dates provide a clear separation between the debtor's pre- and post-bankruptcy lives. In reading cases, you will want to make a note of the filing date for future reference.

In some cases, creditors seek to put the debtor into a bankruptcy case. Such cases, known as *involuntary* bankruptcy cases, require the court to make a determination after filing of the petition that the debtor should be in bankruptcy. If the court determines that bankruptcy is appropriate, it will then issue the order for relief. Section 303(b) provides the requirements for creditors to put a debtor into an involuntary bankruptcy case under Chapter 7 or 11, the only chapters for which an involuntary case is permitted. Those requirements mandate that a requisite number of creditors (usually three) holding a requisite value of claims petition the court for bankruptcy relief. It also notes that, to qualify, a creditor must have a non-contingent, undisputed claim—concepts that will be discussed in Chapter 9. The vast majority of cases enter the bankruptcy system as voluntary cases.

THE BANKRUPTCY COURT SYSTEM

In Chapter 2, you will learn that jurisdiction over bankruptcy cases lies with the U.S. district courts. However, the U.S. Code allows district courts to refer bankruptcy cases to a specialized court. Every district court now refers its bankruptcy cases to the U.S. bankruptcy courts. Appeals from the bankruptcy courts are then taken to the district court, sitting not as a trier of fact but as an appellate court. From there, appeals are generally taken to the U.S. circuit courts and then to the U.S. Supreme Court, which grants certiorari on a handful of bankruptcy cases every year.

While appeals from the district court presumably go to the circuit court, the bankruptcy system has an alternative appellate court option, the Bankruptcy Appellate Panel (commonly known as a "BAP"). Established under 28 U.S.C. § 158(b), a BAP consists of three bankruptcy judges sitting in an appellate capacity. Appeals from the district court only go to the BAP if (1) the circuit has established a BAP, and (2) both parties in the appeal consent to having the appeal heard by the BAP. BAPs exist in the First, Sixth, Eighth, Ninth, and Tenth Circuits, although not all district court cases in the Sixth Circuit are eligible to go to the BAP. https://www.uscourts.gov/news/2012/11/26/court-insider-what-bankruptcy-appellate-panel. Appeals from the BAP go to the circuit court. As a result, a bankruptcy matter could conceivably go through *three* levels of appeal—to the district court or the BAP, then the circuit court, and finally to the U.S. Supreme Court.

C. ELIGIBILITY FOR BANKRUPTCY CHAPTERS (§§ 109, 707)

Chapters 1, 3, and 5 of the Code are chapters of general applicability, meaning that they apply to any bankruptcy case. But Chapters 7, 9, 11, 12, 13, and 15 are filing chapters—every debtor files (or is involuntarily filed) under one of these chapters.

Chapter 7 is the most commonly used chapter; it liquidates (for the most part, sells) the debtor's assets and distributes the proceeds to the creditors. After distribution of the proceeds, the debtor's remaining debts are *discharged* (forgiven) and the case closes. As you will see, however, there are many details left out of that brief description. Not all assets are liquidated; not all remaining debts are discharged. But key to a Chapter 7 case is the idea of liquidation and a relatively quick means of using the debtor's current assets to pay creditors to the extent that there is value with which to pay them.

Cases under Chapters 11 (primarily for businesses) and 13 (for individuals) generally last longer than a Chapter 7 case. These chapters envision using the debtor's future income, rather than current assets, to pay creditors. Each of these chapters requires a plan for how future assets will be used to pay these claims. Though each chapter is based in a plan and each chapter uses future assets, the similarities between Chapters 11 and 13 end there.

The remaining chapters are less utilized and will not be discussed in depth in the book. Chapter 12 is a plan-based bankruptcy case focused on farmers and fishermen. Chapter 9 is also plan-based, but for municipalities and other governmental units. Finally, Chapter 15 cases involve transnational insolvency proceedings.

While the debtor may have some choice of the filing chapter, the debtor must meet the chapter's eligibility requirements. Section 109 of the Code provides the eligibility requirements:

Filing chapter	Subsection listing requirements	Debtors eligible to file within chapter
7	109(b)	a person (defined broadly to include entities per § 101(41)) other than railroads and certain other named entities
9	109(c)	insolvent municipalities that have already attempted negotiations with creditors

Filing chapter	Subsection listing requirements	Debtors eligible to file within chapter
11	109(d)	persons eligible to be a debtor in Chapter 7, as well as railroads and other named entities
12	109(f)	family farmers/fishermen with "regular annual income"
13	109(e)	individuals with regular income and limited debt
15	109(a) *See also* In re Barnet, 737 F.3d 238 (2d Cir. 2013); § 1501(b)	person with a connection (residence, business, property) in the United States and who is the subject of an insolvency proceeding in another country

For Chapter 7 filings, the Bankruptcy Abuse Prevention and Consumer Protection Act of 2005 ("BAPCPA") added another eligibility requirement. Chapter 7 allows a case to be dismissed or converted to another chapter if "granting of relief would be an abuse of the provisions of this chapter." 11 U.S.C. § 707(b)(1). BAPCPA added means testing; an individual debtor is *presumed* to abuse Chapter 7's provisions if the debtor fails the means test. The means test process is detailed in § 707(b)(2), and essentially involves these steps:

(1) Compare the debtor's income[6] to the state average income for similarly situated households; if the debtor makes the same or less than the state average income, the debtor passes the means test and may file under Chapter 7 absent another basis for denying relief.

(2) If the debtor's income exceeds the state average income, permitted deductions are reduced from the debtor's monthly income[7] to determine a net monthly amount that could, presumably, be paid to unsecured creditors.

(3) Multiply the net monthly amount left to pay unsecured creditors by 60, and compare it to the statutory amounts provided in § 707(b)(2)(A)(i) to determine if the debtor passes the means test or if the debtor is presumed to abuse the system by filing under Chapter 7.[8]

---

6. The debtor's annual income is calculated as the current monthly income multiplied by twelve. 11 U.S.C. § 707(b)(7). Current monthly income is the average income received by the debtor over the six full months prior to the bankruptcy filing. 11 U.S.C. § 101(10A).

7. Current monthly income, as determined by 11 U.S.C. § 101(10A).

8. Section 707(b)(2)(A)(i) can be complicated to read, especially for those new to Code interpretation. Section 707(b)(2)(A)(i)(II) provides an upper threshold—if the amount the debtor has remaining over 60 months after deducting allowed expenses exceeds that upper threshold, the debtor fails the

While calculators exist to determine whether a debtor passes or fails the means test, a debtor's attorney should understand how the calculation works in order to effectively argue in favor of a debtor if the means test calculation does not provide an accurate picture of the debtor's financial ability. The following case involves a dispute over the ability to take deductions from the debtor's income. Before reading the case, you may want to look at the bankruptcy schedules—documents filed when the debtor enters bankruptcy mentioned in the case. Relevant to the means test analysis are Schedules B22A and Schedules I and J. The schedules are available at https://www.uscourts.gov/forms/bankruptcy-forms, or by a simple search for "bankruptcy schedules."

THE ROLE OF THE TRUSTEE

The following case introduces you to the U.S. Trustee, a role within the U.S. Department of Justice. The U.S. Trustee oversees the bankruptcy system and can be involved in individual bankruptcy cases. Be careful to distinguish the U.S. Trustee from the trustee you will encounter more frequently in this course—the panel trustee. Panel trustees are not government employees, but instead are private persons (usually attorneys) appointed by the U.S. Trustee to oversee the administration of an individual case. It is these panel trustees who collect the property of the estate and make distributions to creditors.

Morse v. Rudler (In re Rudler)

576 F.3d 37 (1st Cir. 2009)

LIPEZ, Circuit Judge

* * *

The Bankruptcy Abuse Prevention and Consumer Protection Act of 2005 ("BAPCPA") was enacted in response to an upward trend

---

means test. Section 707(b)(2)(A)(i)(I) provides a lower threshold—if the amount the debtor has remaining over 60 months after deducting allowed expenses falls below that lower threshold, the debtor passes the means test. In the event that the amount the debtor has remaining over 60 months after deducting allowed expenses falls between the two thresholds, § 707(b)(2)(A)(i)(I) requires a comparison of the amount the debtor has remaining over 60 months to the value of general unsecured claims against the debtor. If the amount the debtor has remaining could pay at least 25 percent of the general unsecured claims, the debtor fails the means test; if the amount the debtor has remaining is insufficient to pay 25 percent of the general unsecured claims, the debtor passes the means test.

in consumer bankruptcy filings and concerns that bankruptcy relief was "too readily available" and "sometimes used as a first resort, rather than a last resort." H.R.Rep. No. 109–31(I), at 4 (2005), *reprinted in* 2005 U.S.C.C.A.N. 88, 90. Of particular concern was the pursuit of Chapter 7 liquidations instead of Chapter 13 debt repayment plans by consumer debtors who could afford to repay some of their debts.

. . . Previously, a showing of "substantial abuse" was required, and "[t]here was a presumption in favor of granting the relief sought by the debtor." As amended by the BAPCA [sic], section 707(b) drops the qualifying word "substantial," permitting a bankruptcy court to dismiss a Chapter 7 proceeding brought by an individual debtor who has mostly consumer debts "if [the court] finds that the granting of relief would be an abuse." 11 U.S.C. § 707(b)(1). In order to "ensure that debtors repay creditors the maximum they can afford," the BAPCPA established a mathematical formula, known as a "means test," by which some Chapter 7 cases are deemed presumptively abusive. . . .

Only those debtors whose monthly income exceeds the state median for their family size are subject to means testing. 11 U.S.C. § 707(b)(7). The formula calculates the debtor's average monthly disposable income, over a sixty-month period, by deducting statutorily prescribed expenses from current monthly income. If the resulting income figure exceeds a threshold amount specified in the statute—$167 per month at the time relevant here—the bankruptcy case is presumptively abusive. Upon motion by the United States Trustee, the bankruptcy court may either dismiss such a case or, with the debtor's consent, convert it into a Chapter 13 proceeding.

The deductible expenses under the means test include standard living expenses prescribed by the Internal Revenue Service, *see, e.g., id.* at § 707(b)(2)(A)(ii)(I); certain "reasonably necessary" actual expenses (such as for health and disability insurance), *id.;* and other actual expenses up to a maximum allowable deduction (for example, expenses for the education of a minor child "not to exceed" $1650 per year), *id.* at § 707(b)(2)(A)(ii)(IV). At issue here is the allowable deduction "on account of secured debts," such as mortgage or car payments. *Id.* at § 707(b)(2)(A)(iii)(I). The critical language describes the deductible amount of such debts to be "the total of all amounts scheduled as contractually due to secured creditors in each month of the 60 months following the date of the petition," divided by 60. The resulting amount is the debtor's average monthly expense for secured debt. Debtors submit their calculations under the means test on Form B22A. . . . Debtors also must file "a schedule of current income and current expenditures," known as Schedules I and J, respectively, and a Statement of Intention that discloses plans to retain or surrender the properties that are securing the debts listed on a separate schedule of assets and liabilities. . . .

The type of dispute that underlies this case arises when a debtor announces an intention to surrender certain property—here, a house that secures two mortgages—but includes future mortgage payments in calculating the amount of secured debt to be deducted from monthly income on Form B22A. Given that the property will be surrendered and the mortgage will no longer be paid, the question is whether such payments are "scheduled as contractually due . . . in each month of the 60 months following the date of the petition."

. . . Appellee Glen H. Rudler filed a Chapter 7 bankruptcy petition in August 2006. Since his monthly income at the time of the filing exceeded the applicable state median for his family size, Rudler was subject to the means test to determine if his bankruptcy case should be categorized as presumptively abusive. In a Statement of Intention, Rudler reported that he intended to surrender his home, which was secured by two mortgages with a combined monthly payment of approximately $4,000. Despite his plans to give up the house, Rudler deducted the $4,000 in mortgage payments when calculating his monthly disposable income on Form B22A. That calculation produced a monthly disposable income of negative $2,376, avoiding the presumption of abuse.

If Rudler were unable to deduct the mortgages, he instead could claim a statutorily prescribed housing allowance of $1,439. In that event, his monthly disposable income under the formula would be $1,461, far in excess of the $167 monthly amount that triggers the presumption of abuse. Based on these figures, the United States Trustee moved under section 707(b)(1) to dismiss Rudler's Chapter 7 case as abusive. . . .

The bankruptcy court denied the motion to dismiss. . . . The Trustee appealed the decision to the Bankruptcy Appellate Panel ("BAP") for the First Circuit, which affirmed. . . .

* * *

In arguing her view of section 707(b)(2)(A)(iii)(I), the Trustee relies heavily on Congress's purpose in enacting the BAPCPA, i.e., to ensure that individuals who are able to repay a portion of their debts do so. However, we must defer our consideration of Congressional intent because our examination of the statute must begin "where all such inquiries must begin: with the language of the statute itself." . . .

. . . Although the precedent runs both ways, the vast majority of bankruptcy courts to consider the issue have concluded that the plain language of section 707(b)(2) permits a Chapter 7 debtor to deduct payments on a secured debt even when the debtor plans to surrender the collateral underlying that debt. The courts have focused in particular on two aspects of the text: the significance of the phrase "scheduled as contractually due" and the forward-looking nature of the reference to the period "*following* the date of the petition." The Trustee asserts that, read in combination, the two phrases call for a projection of the *actual* payments the debtor will make on secured debts after the bankruptcy proceedings have ended. . . .

1. "Scheduled as Contractually Due"

At the time a debtor files a bankruptcy petition and completes Form B22A, which includes the means test calculation and the inquiry about secured debts that are "scheduled as contractually due," . . . the debtor will not yet have given up any secured property identified for surrender in his or her Statement of Intention. Thus, even if the debtor plans to surrender a house on which he is paying a mortgage, he will at that point still have "contractually due" payments that are "scheduled" to be paid during the upcoming months. This is so whether or not the debtor has already defaulted on the mortgage by failing to make such payments in previous months because the fact of default does not release him from the ongoing obligation.

The instructions on Form B22A confirm that the debtor is expected to provide *current* information for all secured debt. It identifies the "Future payments on secured claims" that must be listed on Line 42, pursuant to section 707(b)(2)(A)(iii), as follows:

> For each of your debts that *is secured* by an interest in property that you own, list the name of [the] creditor, identify the property securing the debt, and state the Average Monthly Payment. The Average Monthly Payment is the total of all amounts contractually due to each Secured Creditor in the 60 months following the filing of the bankruptcy case, divided by 60.

(Emphasis added.)

The form, like the statute itself, asks in the present tense for a list of debts secured by property. The list is not limited to debts on property the debtor plans to retain, nor does it exclude debts that recently have gone unpaid. . . .

The Trustee argues that "reading the phrase 'scheduled as contractually due' to include all current contractual obligations fails to give independent meaning to the words 'scheduled as.'" If that is what Congress meant, she asserts, it could simply have defined the relevant payments as those "contractually due . . . following the date of the petition." To give effect to the separate term "scheduled as," she maintains that the statute must be read as asking for a forward-looking assessment of whether the payments actually will be made.

The word "scheduled," however, does not connote the confirmation of payments to be made that the Trustee ascribes to it. Indeed, it implies the contrary recognition that such payments, although "scheduled," may in fact not be made; otherwise, the request would more logically have been for information about all payments that *will be made* to creditors during the targeted sixty-month period, or all payments the debtor expects or intends to make during that time frame. . . .

The Trustee points out fairly that, under this interpretation, the term "scheduled as" appears to play no role in defining the payments covered by section 707(b)(2)(A)(iii)(I). The same result would be achieved by referring only to payments that were, at the time of the bankruptcy filing, "contractually due." Still, we fail to see how that apparent surplusage warrants limiting the words "scheduled as"—which are stated in the present tense—to only those payments that will be made in the future. Although our construction of the statutory language cannot turn on the language of Form B22A—the official document on which debtors must report their means test calculations—we think it worth noting that the phrase "scheduled as" is omitted from the form's instructions for calculating secured debt. The absence of that language may reflect a recognition by those tasked with creating the document that the term adds nothing to the inquiry.

* * *

2. "[F]ollowing the date of the petition"

The Trustee argues that Congress, in using the word "following," contemplated a projection of future expenses—i.e., expenses that will exist "following" the bankruptcy proceedings—rather than a snapshot of current expenses. Again, however, that interpretation is not supported by the words themselves, which are forward-looking only in the sense that the required *current* calculation is for debts that are scheduled into the future. The Trustee attempts to change this plain meaning by analogy, asserting that other deductions allowed by the means test are forward-looking and that the deduction for secured debts should be treated consistently with the treatment of such other expenses.

As the Trustee acknowledges, however, the statute sets allowable expenses by means of several different methods, and, "[l]ike section 707(b)(2)(A)(iii), many other provisions of the means test appear to operate contrary to the goal of accurately determining the amount of income that would actually be available for payments to unsecured creditors in a Chapter 13 case." For example, the starting point for the means test, current monthly income, is calculated as the average income earned by the debtor in the six months preceding the bankruptcy filing. By the time of the filing, the amount of actual income could be dramatically different from the previous six-month average—for example, if the debtor has just lost his job or secured a new one.

Even on the expense side of the calculation, the means test relies on standard deduction amounts for certain types of expenses that may be "either significantly less than or greatly in excess of the debtor's actual expenses." For example, the IRS has prescribed standard amounts to be used in the means test calculation, instead of the individual debtor's actual costs, for certain categories of expenses (food, housekeeping supplies, and transportation). Thus, the future inaccuracy of the snapshot-in-time approach to the expense for secured debt does not help the Trustee's argument.

* * *

Our conclusion that the language of the statute is unambiguous allows us to consider Congressional intent only if literal application of the statute would lead to absurd results. That exception is not triggered here. As we shall explain, a "snapshot" approach to the deduction for secured debts fits rationally within the statutory scheme.

. . . The Trustee argues that allowing debtors to deduct only payments they will actually make, rather than all payments scheduled at the time of the bankruptcy filing, better serves the purpose behind the means test because it more accurately reflects the debtor's resources following the bankruptcy proceedings. This argument has force—but it misses the point. . . .

A test that relies on a snapshot of the debtors' circumstances at the time of the bankruptcy filing is not an "absurd" alternative. To the contrary, a fixed approach to the secured debt deduction makes sense because the actual amount the debtor will pay on secured debts in the relevant sixty-month period is subject to a number of variables. . . .

Although Congress could have chosen to give bankruptcy judges the discretion to address such uncertainties on a case-by-case basis, there is nothing absurd about Congress's choice to adopt a rigid formula. A number of courts have in fact concluded that a specific intent to limit the bankruptcy court's discretion underlies the means test and accounts for Congress's adoption of a "'mechanical formula' for presuming abuse of Chapter 7."

* * *

. . . BAPCPA's goals extend beyond increasing debtors' accountability for their debts. Still part of the Code is the longstanding objective to "provid[e] honest debtors with a fresh start, as well as encouraging financially responsible behavior and rehabilitation." If section 707(b)(2)(A)(iii)(I) were interpreted as the Trustee urges—excluding debts on property that will be surrendered—debtors might be inclined to unwisely reaffirm such debts to avoid triggering the presumption of abuse. Although other provisions of the Code may defeat such a strategy, see, e.g., 11 U.S.C. § 524(m) (giving the court authority to disapprove reaffirmation agreements), the possibility of manipulation—and the other uncertainties, noted above, surrounding the decision to reaffirm or surrender—further support a plain-language reading of the secured-debt deduction. A calculation that is more generous to the debtor, but has the advantage of certainty, is not inevitably at odds with Congress's intent.

. . . We thus conclude that, in calculating monthly income under the means test, the plain language of section 707(b)(2)(A)(iii)(I) allows debtors to deduct payments due on a secured debt notwithstanding the debtor's intention to surrender the collateral. That plain language is consistent with other provisions that rely on standardized estimates of expenses rather than the debtor's actual circumstances. The mechanical approach avoids the uncertainties that surround a debtor's announced, but not yet executed, plan to surrender property or reaffirm secured debts. Hence, allowing the deduction does not produce an "absurd" result and the plain language of section 707(b)(2)(A)(iii)(I) must govern.

* * *

(Citations omitted.)

NOTES AND COMMENTS

1. Since the *Rudler* decision was issued, the Supreme Court has decided two cases involving Chapter 13's "projected disposable income" requirement, which is modeled after the means test—and rejected a mechanical approach to calculating projected disposable income. Some courts have determined that those decisions also signify the end of the mechanical approach for means test calculations. *See, e.g.,* In re Fredman, 471 B.R. 540 (Bankr. S.D. Ill. 2012). However, in Lynch v. Jackson, 853 F.3d 116 (4th Cir. 2017), the court reaffirmed the use of a mechanical approach for means testing even after those Supreme Court decisions. As a result, the debtor was permitted to deduct mortgage and automobile payments in excess of the debtor's actual expenses in determining eligibility for a Chapter 7 bankruptcy case. The mechanics of the projected disposable income requirement and how it differs from the means test will be discussed further in Chapter 6.

2. Has means testing succeeded by funneling debtors with the means to pay more to creditors into Chapter 13 bankruptcy cases? *See* David W. Read & Robert J. Landry, III, *Religiosity and Consumer Bankruptcy: A State-Level Analysis*, 68 Cons. Fin. L.Q. Rep. 55, 58 (2014) (noting 70.34 percent rate of filing under Chapter 7 prior to BAPCPA and 68.59 percent rate of filing post-BAPCPA).

CANONS OF STATUTORY CONSTRUCTION

"EACH WORD GIVEN EFFECT"

A statute should be interpreted to ensure that each word is given effect, and none are rendered superfluous. 2A Sutherland Statutory Construction, § 46:6 (7th ed.).

Several other canons of construction fall under this general rule:

- The same word within a statute should be interpreted in the same way throughout the statute, and different words should be afforded different meanings.

- The use of a word or phrase in one section indicates that the legislature intended to exclude that word of phrase in other sections where it is missing, and that word or phrase should not be read into other sections where omitted (*"expressio unius est exclusio alterius"*).

See Dept. of Homeland Security v. MacLean, 135 S. Ct. 913 (2015). However, as with most of the canons of construction, they do not apply when the result would be absurd or against the legislature's clear language or intent. Lamie v. U.S. Trustee, 540 U.S. 526 (2004).

As the prior case noted, the means test involves a fairly rigid calculation to determine a debtor's eligibility for Chapter 7. Concerns that a rigid test can be manipulated to allow a debtor to use Chapter 7 when the debtor is capable of paying more to creditors under Chapter 13 are alleviated through another provision of § 707. Even if a debtor passes the means test, the case may be dismissed or converted if a court determines that use of chapter 7 is abusive, as discussed by the following case.

Witcher v. Early (In re Witcher)

702 F.3d 619 (11th Cir. 2012)

GILMAN, Circuit Judge

* * *

Robert Alan Witcher and Jennifer Witcher filed for chapter 7 bankruptcy in January 2010. The bankruptcy administrator moved to dismiss the case or convert it to chapter 13 on the ground that the Witchers' bankruptcy petition constituted an abuse of the chapter 7 process. In ruling on the motion, the bankruptcy court first found no presumption of abuse by the Witchers under the "means test" contained in 11 U.S.C. § 707(b)(2). . . . Next, the court considered the "totality of the circumstances" test set forth in 11 U.S.C. § 707(b)(3)(B) and found, under this second test, that the Witchers' bankruptcy petition demonstrated abuse.

The primary factor that the court relied upon to support its conclusion was its finding that the Witchers had kept certain luxury items—including a camper, a boat, a trailer, and a tractor—and had continued making payments on these items to their secured creditors. It determined that "the Debtors' ability to pay, as well as their reluctance to change their lifestyle in order to provide a distribution to creditors, together indicate that granting relief in this chapter 7 case would be an abuse." Because "a meaningful distribution to unsecured creditors could be made by simply surrendering those items that are being kept for merely recreational purposes," reasoned the court, the Witchers' decision to keep paying for these "unnecessary, luxury items" showed that they were not prepared to earnestly engage in the "give and take process" of bankruptcy. The court accordingly gave the Witchers 14 days to convert their case to chapter 13. When they failed to do so, the court dismissed the case.

The Witchers subsequently moved to amend or alter the order of conversion based on a change in their financial circumstances due to Mr. Witcher's loss of employment. After a hearing, the bankruptcy court found that the alleged change in circumstances was not material and therefore denied the motion, again giving the Witchers 14 days to convert.

* * *

Section 707 of the Bankruptcy Code, 11 U.S.C. § 707, sets forth the circumstances under which a court may dismiss a chapter 7 case or, with the debtor's consent, convert it into a chapter 11 or a chapter 13 case. One of the grounds justifying dismissal or conversion is a court's finding that "the granting of relief [i.e., bankruptcy discharge] would be an abuse of the provisions" of chapter 7. 11 U.S.C. § 707(b)(1).

* * *

Subsection 707(b)(3) comes into play when the presumption of abuse under 707(b)(2) does not arise or is rebutted. Under § 707(b)(3), the court shall consider "whether the debtor filed the petition in bad faith," § 707(b)(3)(A), or whether "the totality of the circumstances (including whether the debtor seeks to reject a personal services contract and the financial need for such rejection as sought by the debtor) of the debtor's financial situation demonstrates abuse," § 707(b)(3)(B).

. . . The sole question presented on appeal is whether consideration of the debtors' ability to pay their debts under § 707(b)(2) precludes consideration of their ability to pay under § 707(b)(3)(B).

The Witchers contend that ability to pay should not be considered under the totality-of-the-circumstances test because such a consideration would render the means test meaningless. They argue that there would be no point to the complex formula crafted by Congress in the means test if a court could take the same factors that are incorporated in that formula and plug them into the totality-of-the-circumstances test. . . .

We disagree with the Witchers' narrow reading of § 707(b)(3)(B). To begin with, the text of § 707(b)(3)(B) broadly refers to "the totality of the circumstances . . . of the debtor's financial situation," phrasing which is surely intended to include the debtor's ability to pay his or her debts.

Moreover, although the Witchers are correct that allowing each bankruptcy court to devise its own subjective means test under § 707(b)(3) would defeat the purpose of the congressionally enacted means test in § 707(b)(2), the same logic does not dictate that any factors that are considered under § 707(b)(2) are by implication precluded from consideration under § 707(b)(3). . . .

Our examination of the structure and textual evolution of § 707 further bolsters our reading of the statute. The current version of § 707 is largely a product of the Bankruptcy Abuse Prevention and Consumer Protection Act of 2005 (BAPCPA). BAPCPA made it harder to obtain chapter 7 relief by eliminating the "presumption in favor of granting the relief requested by the debtor" that had existed in the previous version of § 707(b), adding a means test that created a presumption of abuse, and lowering the standard from "substantial abuse" to "abuse."

The phrase "totality of the circumstances" was not in the pre-BAPCPA statute, but it was the pre-BAPCPA standard used by many courts across the country in determining whether there had been a substantial abuse of chapter 7. These courts uniformly took the ability to pay into account in examining the totality of the circumstances. . . .

Congress was doubtless aware when it codified the totality-of-the-circumstances standard that the relevant pre–BAPCPA jurisprudence took into consideration a debtor's ability to pay his or her debts. Accordingly, if Congress had intended to preclude such consideration, it presumably would have explicitly said so. . . .

* * *

Before concluding, we wish to emphasize the limited nature of our holding. We do not decide whether a debtor's ability to pay his or her debts can alone be dispositive under the totality-of-the-circumstances test. Nor do we decide how much weight a bankruptcy court may properly give to the debtor's ability to pay as compared with other factors making up the totality of the circumstances. . . .

* * *

(Citations omitted.)

NOTES AND COMMENTS

1. Courts often look at the debtor's true ability to pay creditors in determining actual abuse. Consider, for example, Calhoun v. U.S. Trustee, 650 F.3d 338 (4th Cir. 2011). The debtors passed the means test, despite having an annual salary of roughly $87,000 and Social Security income. While the debtors listed $7,330.19 in applicable and actual monthly expenses under § 707(b), they had managed to pay nearly $3,000 per month to creditors before the filing and did not have any significant change in circumstances. The Court also found that their expenses "border[ed]

on the extravagant"—particularly calling out expenses for "cable and internet, laundry and dry cleaning [and] excessive transportation."

2. Should a bad faith/abuse determination be based on the circumstances that led the debtor into a bankruptcy case? *See* In re Baum, 386 B.R. 649 (Bankr. N.D. Ohio 2008) (fact that debtor sought bankruptcy to eliminate debts that she could not repay due to gambling addiction did not constitute abuse of bankruptcy Chapter 7). In *Baum*, the Court adopted a standard from another Court, finding abuse in cases of "concealed or misrepresented assets and/or sources of income, and excessive and continued expenditures, lavish lifestyle, and intention to avoid a large single debt based on conduct akin to fraud, misconduct, or gross negligences." *Id.* at 653, *citing* Indus. Ins. Servs., Inc. v. Zick (In re Zick), 931 F.2d 1124, 1129 (6th Cir. 1990).

D. BANKRUPTCY IN PRACTICE

Earlier in the chapter, you met your new client, Diana Detter. She has come to you in anticipation of a bankruptcy filing. Consider what options Diana has, and whether bankruptcy is the best option for Diana. If she does file for bankruptcy protection, which bankruptcy chapters are available to her? Are there other facts that you would like to know in helping to advise Diana on her options?

2

Constitutional Law in Bankruptcy

. . . and still the suit "drags its weary length before the Court."[1]

Most decisions involving the intersection of constitutional law and bankruptcy fall within one of two categories. The jurisdiction of the bankruptcy courts has been the subject of several U.S. Supreme Court decisions over a span of nearly 40 years. Those jurisdictional decisions revolve around questions concerning the power of the bankruptcy courts and the balance between state and federal rights. The other notable category of decisions comes in the area of individual rights guaranteed by the First Amendment, including freedom of speech and freedom of religion. Thus, bankruptcy law gives the opportunity to revisit some core principles of constitutional law.

RECALL DIANA DETTER

As you work through this chapter, keep in mind that if our heroine, Diana Detter, files for bankruptcy protection, her creditors have claims that arise in part under state law. The interplay between federal bankruptcy law and state law may affect the rights of Diana and her creditors. Recall that Diana has a number of claims pending, including claims relating to child support, health insurance, and her boss's and his insurance company's claims against her for her attack. Consider also, if Diana were to file for bankruptcy, whether it would be permissible for her to make charitable donations either to religious or non-religious charities.

---

1. Chief Justice Roberts in a recent Supreme Court case challenging the jurisdiction of a bankruptcy court, Stern v. Marshall, 564 U.S. 462 (2011), excerpted below.

A. JURISDICTION

The Bankruptcy Code is federal law, and bankruptcy cases are filed with the federal courts. Every federal district has bankruptcy courts that have initial jurisdiction over the case. But bankruptcy courts are Article I courts, making them different from most of the federal courts that you studied in earlier courses. As a result, the jurisdiction of bankruptcy courts implicates both (1) the power granted to the various branches of the federal government, and also (2) the division of power between the federal government and state governments. This section will examine each of those in turn.

1. Separation of Powers

Questions of which branch of the federal government has power in a particular situation can be vexing. In considering the power of the federal government over bankruptcies, it is helpful to keep a general idea of what kinds of power each branch of the federal government has. The Constitution, of course, holds the answer. Article I details the power of the legislative branch. Article II governs the power of the executive branch. Article III grants power to the federal courts.

Separation of Powers

Articles I, II, and III of the Constitution are complicated and have been the subject of many cases to clarify the power of each branch of the federal government. Nonetheless, it is possible to generally summarize the power of each of the branches:

Legislative (Article I) — Legislative power includes the power of elected representatives to debate and enact legislation regulating their constituents.

Executive (Article II) — Executive power includes the power to execute and defend the laws and oversee the administration of the government.

Judicial (Article III) — Judicial power generally includes the power to finally decide cases and controversies, subject only to review of higher courts.

It would seem logical that Article III would be the source of the power of the federal bankruptcy courts. Indeed, Article III of the United States Constitution establishes the federal judiciary, providing that,

The judicial power of the United States, shall be vested in one Supreme Court, and in such inferior courts as the Congress may from time to time ordain and establish. The judges, both of the supreme and inferior courts, shall hold their offices during good behaviour, and shall, at stated times, receive for their services, a compensation, which shall not be diminished during their continuance in office."[2] It goes on to provide the jurisdiction of the federal courts over "all cases, in law and equity, arising under this Constitution, the laws of the United States, and treaties made, or which shall be made, under their authority. . . ."[3]

Though the U.S. bankruptcy courts are part of the federal court system, they were not established pursuant to Congress's powers under Article III of the Constitution. Instead, Congress created the bankruptcy courts pursuant to its specifically enumerated power under Article I to make laws on the subject of bankruptcies. Thus, bankruptcy courts are distinctly different than the other federal courts that were established pursuant to Article III of the Constitution.

Even bankruptcy judges are treated differently than judges presiding over federal courts established under Article III. For example, bankruptcy judges lack two primary protections given to Article III judges—lifetime tenure and salary protection. While those differences may seem to be most important to the bankruptcy judges themselves, failure to provide for such protections has significant implications for the jurisdiction of the bankruptcy courts.

BANKRUPTCY IN THE CONSTITUTION

While the Bankruptcy Code is located within the U.S. Code, its origins lie in Article I, Section 8, Clause 4 of the Constitution, which gives Congress the power "[t]o establish an uniform Rule of Naturalization, and uniform Laws on the subject of Bankruptcies throughout the United States."

In 1982, the U.S. Supreme Court considered the jurisdiction of the bankruptcy courts to hear cases and controversies arising under the Bankruptcy Code in Northern Pipeline Constr. Co. v. Marathon Pipe Line Co., 458 U.S. 50 (1982). Northern Pipeline Construction Co. filed for bankruptcy protection and filed suit against Marathon Pipe Line Co. in the bankruptcy court, alleging breach of contract and other claims. Marathon argued that the bankruptcy court could not render a determination on Northern Pipeline's claims because the Bankruptcy Code "unconstitutionally conferred Art. III judicial

2. U.S. Const. art. III, § 1.
3. U.S. Const. art. III, § 2.

power upon judges who lacked life tenure and protection against salary dimi-nution." In rendering its decision, the Supreme Court considered the need to maintain an independent judicial branch and how the protections for federal judges promote this goal. Congress cannot establish a court with the juris-dictional reach of a federal court but that lacks the constitutional protections designed to ensure independence of the court from the legislature, and thus Congress's jurisdictional grant to the bankruptcy courts exceeded its power.

The *Northern Pipeline* decision did not reject congressional authority to create a bankruptcy court. Rather, it required that the court's purpose and jurisdiction be limited:

> Together these cases establish two principles that aid us in determining the extent to which Congress may constitutionally vest traditionally judicial func-tions in non-Art. III officers. First, it is clear that when Congress creates a substantive federal right, it possesses substantial discretion to prescribe the manner in which that right may be adjudicated—including the assignment to an adjunct of some functions historically performed by judges. . . . Second, the functions of the adjunct must be limited in such a way that "the essential attributes" of judicial power are retained in the Art. III court. . . .

In the wake of *Northern Pipeline*, 28 U.S.C. § 157 was amended slightly to limit the bankruptcy courts' jurisdiction so that they do not interfere with "essential" functions of Article III courts. While § 157 still allows bankruptcy judges to "hear and determine all cases under title 11," it adds the concept of a core proceeding and provides an illustrative list of what constitutes core proceedings under 28 U.S.C. § 157(b)(2). Initially, courts deemed the modification to limit the bankruptcy court's authority to render final decisions to "core" proceedings sufficient to solve the jurisdictional problem. *See, e.g.,* Halper v. Halper, 164 F.3d 830, 836 (3d Cir. 1999); In re Guild and Gallery Plus, Inc., 72 F.3d 1171, 1178 (3d Cir. 1996).

But the issue arose again after lying dormant for nearly 30 years. Before reading the following opinion, review the list of "core proceedings" in § 157(b)(2). While you may not yet understand each type of proceeding listed, this course will cover many of these proceedings as critical parts of a bankruptcy case. Note in particular § 157(b)(2)(C), which deems "coun-terclaims by the estate against persons filing claims against the estate" core.

REFERRAL AND WITHDRAWAL OF BANKRUPTCY CASES

28 U.S.C. § 157(a) permits district courts to refer cases under Title 11 of the U.S. Code (the Bankruptcy Code) to bankruptcy courts. In practice, all district courts have done so. However, 28 U.S.C. § 157(d) also provides that the district court may withdraw the reference—taking a case under the Bankruptcy Code back to the district court for initial determination.

Stern v. Marshall

564 U.S. 462 (2011)

ROBERTS, Chief Justice

. . . This is the second time we have had occasion to weigh in on this long-running dispute between Vickie Lynn Marshall and E. Pierce Marshall over the fortune of J. Howard Marshall II, a man believed to have been one of the richest people in Texas. The Marshalls' litigation has worked its way through state and federal courts in Louisiana, Texas, and California, and two of those courts—a Texas state probate court and the Bankruptcy Court for the Central District of California—have reached contrary decisions on its merits. The Court of Appeals below held that the Texas state decision controlled, after concluding that the Bankruptcy Court lacked the authority to enter final judgment on a counterclaim that Vickie brought against Pierce in her bankruptcy proceeding. To determine whether the Court of Appeals was correct in that regard, we must resolve two issues: (1) whether the Bankruptcy Court had the statutory authority under 28 U.S.C. § 157(b) to issue a final judgment on Vickie's counterclaim; and (2) if so, whether conferring that authority on the Bankruptcy Court is constitutional.

* * *

Because we have already recounted the facts and procedural history of this case in detail, see *Marshall v. Marshall*, 547 U.S. 293, 300–305 . . . (2006), we do not repeat them in full here. Of current relevance are two claims Vickie filed in an attempt to secure half of J. Howard's fortune. Known to the public as Anna Nicole Smith, Vickie was J. Howard's third wife and married him about a year before his death. . . . Although J. Howard bestowed on Vickie many monetary and other gifts during their courtship and marriage, he did not include her in his will . . . . Before J. Howard passed away, Vickie filed suit in Texas state probate court, asserting that Pierce—J. Howard's younger son—fraudulently induced J. Howard to sign a living trust that did not include her, even though J. Howard meant to give her half his property. Pierce denied any fraudulent activity and defended the validity of J. Howard's trust and, eventually, his will. . . .

After J. Howard's death, Vickie filed a petition for bankruptcy in the Central District of California. Pierce filed a complaint in that bankruptcy proceeding, contending that Vickie had defamed him by inducing her lawyers to tell members of the press that he had engaged in fraud to gain control of his father's assets. . . . The complaint sought a declaration that Pierce's defamation claim was not dischargeable in the bankruptcy proceedings. . . . Pierce subsequently filed a proof of claim for the defamation action, meaning that he sought to recover damages for it from Vickie's bankruptcy estate. See § 501(a). Vickie responded to Pierce's initial complaint by asserting truth as a defense to the alleged defamation and by filing a counterclaim for tortious interference with the gift she expected from J. Howard. As she had in state court, Vickie alleged that Pierce had wrongfully prevented J. Howard from taking the legal steps necessary to provide her with half his property. . . .

On November 5, 1999, the Bankruptcy Court issued an order granting Vickie summary judgment on Pierce's claim for defamation. On September 27, 2000, after a bench trial, the Bankruptcy Court issued a judgment on Vickie's counterclaim in her favor. The court later awarded Vickie over $400 million in compensatory damages and $25 million in punitive damages. . . .

In post-trial proceedings, Pierce argued that the Bankruptcy Court lacked jurisdiction over Vickie's counterclaim. In particular, Pierce renewed a claim he had made earlier in the litigation, asserting that the Bankruptcy Court's authority over the counterclaim was limited because Vickie's counterclaim was not a "core proceeding" under 28 U.S.C. § 157(b)(2)(C). . . . The Bankruptcy Court in this case concluded that Vickie's counterclaim was "a core proceeding" under § 157(b)(2)(C), and the court therefore had the "power to enter judgment" on the counterclaim under § 157(b)(1). . . .

The District Court disagreed. It recognized that "Vickie's counterclaim for tortious interference falls within the literal language" of the statute designating certain proceedings as "core," . . . [but] concluded that a "counterclaim should not be characterized as core" when it "is only somewhat related to the claim against which it is asserted, and when the unique characteristics and context of the counterclaim place it outside of the normal type of set-off or other counterclaims that customarily arise.". . .

* * *

The Court of Appeals reversed the District Court on a different ground, . . . , and we—in the first visit of the case to this Court—reversed the Court of Appeals on that issue. . . . On remand from this Court, the Court of Appeals held that § 157 mandated "a two-step approach" under which a bankruptcy judge may issue a final judgment in a proceeding only if the matter both "meets Congress' definition of a core proceeding *and* arises under or arises in title 11," the Bankruptcy Code. . . . The court also reasoned that allowing a bankruptcy judge to enter final judgments on all counterclaims raised in bankruptcy proceedings "would certainly run afoul" of this Court's decision in *Northern Pipeline*. . . . With those concerns in mind, the court concluded that "a counterclaim under § 157(b)(2)(C) is properly a 'core' proceeding 'arising in a case under' the [Bankruptcy] Code only if the counterclaim is so closely related to [a creditor's] proof of claim that the resolution of the counterclaim is necessary to resolve the allowance or disallowance of the claim itself.". . . The court ruled that Vickie's counterclaim did not meet that test. . . .

* * *

With certain exceptions not relevant here, the district courts of the United States have "original and exclusive jurisdiction of all cases under title 11." 28 U.S.C. § 1334(a). Congress has divided bankruptcy proceedings into three categories: those that "aris[e] under title 11"; those that "aris[e] in" a Title 11 case; and those that are "related to a case under title 11." § 157(a). District courts may refer any or all such proceedings to the bankruptcy judges of their district, *ibid.*, which is how the Bankruptcy Court in this case came to preside over Vickie's bankruptcy proceedings. . . .

The manner in which a bankruptcy judge may act on a referred matter depends on the type of proceeding involved. Bankruptcy judges may hear and enter final judgments in "all core proceedings arising under title 11, or arising in a case under title 11." § 157(b)(1). "Core proceedings include, but are not limited to" 16 different types of matters, including "counterclaims by [a debtor's] estate against persons filing claims against the estate." § 157(b)(2)(C). Parties may appeal final judgments of a bankruptcy court in core proceedings to the district court, which reviews them under traditional appellate standards. See § 158(a); Fed. Rule Bkrtcy. Proc. 8013.

When a bankruptcy judge determines that a referred "proceeding . . . is not a core proceeding but . . . is otherwise related to a case under title 11," the judge may only "submit proposed findings of fact and conclusions of law to the district court." § 157(c)(1). It is the district court that enters final judgment in such cases after reviewing *de novo* any matter to which a party objects. *Ibid.* . . .

Vickie's counterclaim against Pierce for tortious interference is a "core proceeding" under the plain text of § 157(b)(2)(C). That provision specifies that core proceedings include "counterclaims by the estate against persons filing claims against the estate." In past cases, we have suggested that a proceeding's "core" status alone authorizes a bankruptcy judge, as a statutory matter, to enter final judgment in the proceeding. . . . We have not directly addressed the question, however, and Pierce argues that a bankruptcy judge may enter final judgment on a core proceeding only if that proceeding also "aris[es] in" a Title 11 case or "aris[es] under" Title 11 itself. . . .

* * *

Although we conclude that § 157(b)(2)(C) permits the Bankruptcy Court to enter final judgment on Vickie's counterclaim, Article III of the Constitution does not.

* * *

As its text and our precedent confirm, Article III is "an inseparable element of the constitutional system of checks and balances" that "both defines the power and protects the independence of the Judicial Branch." *Northern Pipeline,* 458 U.S., at 58 (plurality opinion). Under "the basic concept of separation of powers . . . that flow[s] from the scheme of a tripartite government" adopted in the Constitution, "the 'judicial Power of the United States' . . . can no more be shared" with another branch than "the Chief Executive, for example, can share with the Judiciary the veto power, or the Congress share with the Judiciary the power to override a Presidential veto." *United States v. Nixon,* 418 U.S. 683, 704, 94 S.Ct. 3090, 41 L.Ed.2d 1039 (1974) (quoting U.S. Const., Art. III, § 1).

* * *

We have recognized that the three branches are not hermetically sealed from one another, . . . but it remains true that Article III imposes some basic limitations that the other branches may not transgress. Those limitations serve two related purposes. "Separation-of-powers principles are intended, in part, to protect each branch of government from incursion by the others. Yet the dynamic between and among the branches is not the only object of the Constitution's concern. The structural principles secured by the separation of powers protect the individual as well." . . .

Article III protects liberty not only through its role in implementing the separation of powers, but also by specifying the defining characteristics of Article III judges . . . . By appointing judges to serve without term limits, and restricting the ability of the other branches to remove judges or diminish their salaries, the Framers sought to ensure that each judicial decision would be rendered, not with an eye toward currying favor with Congress or the Executive, but rather with the "[c]lear heads . . . and honest hearts" deemed "essential to good judges." . . .

Article III could neither serve its purpose in the system of checks and balances nor preserve the integrity of judicial decisionmaking if the other branches of the Federal Government could confer the Government's "judicial Power" on entities outside Article III. That is why we have long recognized that, in general, Congress may not "withdraw from judicial cognizance any matter which, from its nature, is the subject of a suit at the common law, or in equity, or admiralty." . . . When a suit is made of "the stuff of the traditional actions at common law tried by the courts at Westminster in 1789," *Northern Pipeline,* 458 U.S., at 90 . . . (Rehnquist, J., concurring in judgment), and is brought within the bounds of federal jurisdiction, the responsibility for deciding that suit rests with Article III judges in Article III courts. . . .

* * *

After our decision in *Northern Pipeline,* Congress revised the statutes governing bankruptcy jurisdiction and bankruptcy judges. In the 1984 Act, Congress provided that the judges of the new bankruptcy courts would be appointed by the courts of appeals for the circuits in which their districts are located. 28 U.S.C. § 152(a). And, as we have explained, Congress permitted the newly constituted bankruptcy courts to enter final judgments only in "core" proceedings. . . .

. . . As in *Northern Pipeline,* the new courts in core proceedings "issue final judgments, which are binding and enforceable even in the absence of an appeal." . . . And, as in *Northern Pipeline,* the district courts review the judgments of the bankruptcy courts in core proceedings only under the usual limited appellate standards. That requires marked deference to, among other things, the bankruptcy judges' findings of fact. See § 158(a); Fed. Rule Bkrtcy. Proc. 8013 (findings of fact "shall not be set aside unless clearly erroneous"). . . .

Vickie and the dissent argue that the Bankruptcy Court's entry of final judgment on her state common law counterclaim was constitutional, despite the similarities between the bankruptcy courts under the 1978 Act and those exercising core jurisdiction under the 1984 Act. We disagree. It is clear that the Bankruptcy Court in this case exercised the "judicial Power of the United States" in purporting to resolve and enter final judgment on a state common law claim, just as the court did in *Northern Pipeline.* No "public right" exception excuses the failure to comply with Article III in doing so, any more than in *Northern Pipeline.* Vickie argues that this case is different because the defendant is a creditor in the bankruptcy. But the debtors' claims in the cases on which she relies were themselves federal claims under bankruptcy law, which would be completely resolved in the bankruptcy process of allowing or disallowing claims. Here Vickie's claim is a state law action independent of the federal bankruptcy law and not necessarily resolvable by a ruling on the creditor's proof of claim in bankruptcy. . . .

* * *

Vickie and the dissent next attempt to distinguish *Northern Pipeline* and *Granfinanciera* [Granfinanciera, S.A. v. Nordberg, 492 U.S. 33 (1989)] on the ground that Pierce, unlike the defendants in those cases, had filed a proof of claim in the bankruptcy proceedings. . . .

We do not agree. As an initial matter, it is hard to see why Pierce's decision to file a claim should make any difference with respect to the characterization of Vickie's counterclaim. "'[P]roperty interests are created and defined by state law,' and '[u]nless some federal interest requires a different result, there is no reason why such interests should be analyzed differently simply because an interested party is involved in a bankruptcy proceeding.'" . . . Pierce's claim for defamation in no way affects the nature of Vickie's counterclaim for tortious interference as one at common law that simply attempts to augment the bankruptcy estate—the very type of claim that we held in *Northern Pipeline* and *Granfinanciera* must be decided by an Article III court.

* * *

(Citations omitted.)

NOTES AND COMMENTS

1. The Court concludes by noting that the question it answers is a narrow one. What is the question that the Court answers? What questions does the Court *not* answer?

2. Following the *Stern* decision, a new phrase arose in bankruptcy parlance—a "*Stern*" claim. *Stern* claims include claims that a bankruptcy court lacks constitutional authority on which to render a final decision, even though deemed core under 28 U.S.C. § 157(b)(2).

3. In *Granfinanciera*, referenced in the *Stern* decision, the Supreme Court seemed to suggest that a creditor who voluntarily filed a proof of claim enjoys different status from one who does not so enter the bankruptcy: "Because petitioners . . . have not filed claims against the estate, respondent's fraudulent conveyance action does not arise 'as part of the process of allowance and disallowance of claims.' Nor is that action integral to the restructuring of debtor-creditor relations. Congress

therefore cannot divest petitioners of their Seventh Amendment right to a trial by jury." *Granfinanciera*, 492 U.S. 33, 58-59 (1989). The *Stern* court disagreed, noting that Pierce's filing of a proof of claim does not alter the bankruptcy court's jurisdiction. Should filing of a proof of claim subject the creditor to the jurisdiction of the bankruptcy court?

APPELLATE STANDARDS OF REVIEW

Part of the *Stern* decision and its progeny focuses on which standard the district court uses in reviewing the decisions of the bankruptcy court. The typical standard of review on appeal is generally deferential to the factual findings of the court from which an order is appealed—looking for "clear error"—while reviewing the conclusions of law on a "de novo" standard—meaning that the court renders its own determination without deference to the initial court. But when reviewing findings of fact from the bankruptcy court on a noncore matter, the district court reviews both the findings of fact *and* conclusions of law using the de novo standard. Fed. R. Bankr. Proc. 9033(d).

The *Stern* case left open several unanswered questions that the Supreme Court had an opportunity to hear shortly thereafter. Following *Stern*, courts recognized a "gap" in procedure. Title 28 and the Bankruptcy Rules provide procedures for handling core claims, but *Stern* claims cannot fall within those procedures. Title 28 and the Bankruptcy Rules also provide procedures for handling noncore claims, but because the Bankruptcy Code designates them as core proceedings, *Stern* claims ostensibly cannot fall within those procedures either.

In 2014, the Court decided Executive Benefits Ins. Agency v. Arkison, 134 S. Ct. 2165 (2014), a case involving allegedly fraudulent conveyances from the debtor to a sister company prior to the bankruptcy filing. The sister company was not a creditor in the bankruptcy case and was brought into the case solely as a party to the fraudulent conveyance action. The bankruptcy court found that a fraudulent conveyance had occurred; its decision was affirmed by the district court following de novo review of the case. The sister company argued that the fraudulent conveyance claim constituted a *Stern* claim, and because the Code did not provide a procedure for dealing with such claims, the district court's affirmation of the fraudulent conveyance finding was inappropriate. The Court specifically declined to decide whether fraudulent conveyance claims constitute *Stern* claims, but instead focused on the question of whether a gap exists as to how to treat *Stern* claims. It determined that no such gap existed:

> The statute permits *Stern* claims to proceed as non-core within the meaning of § 157(c). In particular, the statute contains a severability provision that accounts for decisions, like *Stern*, that invalidate certain applications of the statute:
>
> "If any provision of this Act or the application thereof to any person or circumstance is held invalid, the remainder of this Act, or the application of that provision to persons or circumstances other than those as to which it is held invalid, is not affected thereby." 98 Stat. 344, note following 28 U.S.C. § 151.

Id. at 2173. The plain text of this severability provision closes the so-called gap created by *Stern* claims. Thus, even if the claim was a *Stern* claim, the district court's de novo review of the bankruptcy court's decision sufficed.

In its next term, the Supreme Court visited the Article I jurisdiction issue yet again in Wellness Int'l Network, Ltd. v. Sharif, 135 S. Ct. 1932 (2015). *Sharif* involved the consent question hinted at in *Stern*—the question of whether a party could consent to allow the bankruptcy court to render *final* judgments on a noncore or *Stern* claim. Wellness held a judgment against Sharif at the time of Sharif's bankruptcy petition, and Wellness filed an adversary proceeding in the bankruptcy case seeking nondischargeability of its claim. Sharif responded, including a request for a finding that a trust that Wellness claimed had been used to conceal Sharif's assets did not belong to the bankruptcy estate. The bankruptcy court found in Wellness's favor on both issues. Between the time of the bankruptcy court's decision and the appeal to the District Court, the Supreme Court decided Stern v. Marshall; Sharif argued that *Stern* prohibited the bankruptcy court's final orders in favor of Wellness. The Supreme Court held that even if *Stern* claims were involved, the parties had consented to final disposition by the bankruptcy court, and such consent did not violate the Constitution. After considering prior decisions in two other cases, the Court determined that "The entitlement to an Article III adjudicator is 'a personal right' and thus ordinarily 'subject to waiver,' . . . allowing Article I adjudicators to decide claims submitted to them by consent does not offend the separation of powers so long as Article III courts retain supervisory authority over the process." *Id.* at 1944. Because Article III judges control the appointment and removal of Article I judges, the requisite control exists, and parties can consent to the jurisdiction of the bankruptcy court to render final orders of *Stern* claims. The Court also considered how a party should express such consent, finding that consent need not be "express" but must be "knowing and voluntary." *Id.* at 1948. It remanded the decision for a finding on whether Sharif's consent met those requirements, and it is likely that much litigation will ensue to flesh out what knowing and voluntary consent to a bankruptcy court's final resolution means.

2. Federalism

One of the primary issues considered when crafting the Constitution of the United States was the balance of power between the states and the federal government. The development of bankruptcy law was given to the federal government under Article I of the Constitution. This delegation of power to the federal government occurred because of problems that existed when each state created its own bankruptcy laws. Various laws meant that a debtor could be punished differently for the same type of debt in different states. And discharge of the debt granted by one state did not protect that debtor if he or she left the state and fell under the jurisdiction of a different state that had not discharged the debt. Debtors were not the only ones inconvenienced by different legal schemes; different states might award property to different creditors, creating conflicting judgments with no way to resolve the differences. Complicating matters further, Congress and the courts ultimately have had to wrestle with the bankruptcy issues raised by municipalities needing to file for bankruptcy, and what to do about U.S. territories that might pursue their own procedures for bankruptcy situations.

a. State Sovereign Immunity

One unified bankruptcy system ensured consistent treatment of debtors and creditors across the country. But creation of a federal bankruptcy system left open the question of how to treat the states *as creditors* in a bankruptcy case. The Eleventh Amendment protects states from lawsuits by their own citizens or citizens of another state. But whether the states would be immune from the authority of the bankruptcy courts is another question. The degree to which states ceded their own sovereignty to the federal government in order to achieve this national system of bankruptcy is considered in the cases below.

Tennessee Student Assistance Corp. v. Hood

541 U.S. 440 (2004)

REHNQUIST, Chief Justice

* * *

Petitioner, Tennessee Student Assistance Corporation (TSAC), is a governmental corporation created by the Tennessee Legislature to administer student assistance programs. . . . TSAC guarantees student loans made to residents of Tennessee and to nonresidents who are either enrolled in an eligible school in Tennessee or make loans through an approved Tennessee lender. . . .

Between July 1988 and February 1990, respondent, Pamela Hood, a resident of Tennessee, signed promissory notes for educational loans guaranteed by TSAC. In February 1999, Hood filed a "no asset" Chapter 7 bankruptcy petition in the United States Bankruptcy Court for the Western District of Tennessee; at the time of the filing, her student loans had an outstanding balance of $4,169.31. TSAC did not participate in the proceeding, but Sallie Mae Service, Inc. (Sallie Mae), submitted a proof of claim to the Bankruptcy Court, which it subsequently assigned to TSAC. The Bankruptcy Court granted Hood a general discharge in June 1999. See 11 U.S.C. § 727(a).

Hood did not list her student loans in the bankruptcy proceeding, and the general discharge did not cover them. . . . In September 1999, Hood reopened her bankruptcy petition for the limited purpose of seeking a determination by the Bankruptcy Court that her student loans were dischargeable as an "undue hardship" pursuant to § 523(a)(8). . . .

In response, TSAC filed a motion to dismiss the complaint for lack of jurisdiction, asserting Eleventh Amendment sovereign immunity. The Bankruptcy Court denied the motion, holding that 11 U.S.C. § 106(a) was a valid abrogation of TSAC's sovereign immunity . . . , and a unanimous Bankruptcy Appellate Panel of the Sixth Circuit affirmed. . . . TSAC appealed the panel's decision to the United States Court of Appeals for the Sixth Circuit. That court affirmed, holding that the States ceded their immunity from private suits in bankruptcy in the Constitutional Convention, and therefore, the Bankruptcy Clause, U.S. Const., Art. I, § 8, cl. 4, provided Congress with the necessary authority to abrogate state sovereign immunity in 11 U.S.C. § 106(a). . . . We granted certiorari, . . . and now affirm the judgment of the Court of Appeals. . . .

By its terms, the Eleventh Amendment precludes suits "in law or equity, commenced or prosecuted against one of the United States by Citizens of another State, or by Citizens or Subjects of any Foreign State." For over a century, however, we have recognized that the States' sovereign immunity is not limited to the literal terms of the Eleventh Amendment. . . . Although the text of the Amendment refers only to suits against a State by citizens of another State, we have repeatedly held that an unconsenting State also is immune from suits by its own citizens. . . .

States, nonetheless, may still be bound by some judicial actions without their consent. In *California v. Deep Sea Research, Inc.*, 523 U.S. 491 (1998), we held that the Eleventh Amendment does not bar federal jurisdiction over *in rem* admiralty actions when the State is not in possession of the property. . . .

The discharge of a debt by a bankruptcy court is similarly an *in rem* proceeding. . . . Bankruptcy courts have exclusive jurisdiction over a debtor's property, wherever located, and over the estate. See 28 U.S.C. § 1334(e). In a typical voluntary bankruptcy proceeding under Chapter 7, the debtor files a petition for bankruptcy in which he lists his debts or his creditors,. . . . The court clerk notifies the debtor's creditors . . . and if a creditor wishes to participate in the debtor's assets, he files a proof of claim,. . . . If a creditor chooses not to submit a proof of claim, once the debts are discharged, the creditor will be unable to collect on his unsecured loans. . . . The discharge order releases a debtor from personal liability with respect to any discharged debt by voiding any past or future judgments on the debt and by operating as an injunction to prohibit creditors from attempting to collect or to recover the debt. §§ 524(a)(1), (2) . . . .

A bankruptcy court is able to provide the debtor a fresh start in this manner, despite the lack of participation of all of his creditors, because the court's jurisdiction is premised on the debtor and his estate, and not on the creditors. . . . A bankruptcy court's *in rem* jurisdiction permits it to "determin[e] all claims that anyone, whether named in the action or not, has to the property or thing in question. The proceeding is 'one against the world.'" . . . Because the court's jurisdiction is premised on the res, however, a nonparticipating creditor cannot be subjected to personal liability. . . .

Under our longstanding precedent, States, whether or not they choose to participate in the proceeding, are bound by a bankruptcy court's discharge order no less than other creditors. In *New York v. Irving Trust Co.*, 288 U.S. 329 (1933), we sustained an order of the Bankruptcy Court which barred the State of New York's tax claim because it was not filed within the time fixed for the filing of claims. . . . And in *Van Huffel v. Harkelrode,* 284 U.S. 225 . . . (1931), we held that the Bankruptcy Court had the authority to sell a debtor's property "free and clear" of a State's tax lien. At least when the bankruptcy court's jurisdiction over the res is unquestioned, . . . our cases indicate that the exercise of its *in rem* jurisdiction to discharge a debt does not infringe state sovereignty. . . .

TSAC concedes that States are generally bound by a bankruptcy court's discharge order, . . . but argues that the particular process by which student loan debts are discharged unconstitutionally infringes its sovereignty. Student loans used to be presumptively discharged in a general discharge. But in 1976, Congress provided a significant benefit to the States by making it more difficult for debtors to discharge student loan debts guaranteed by States. . . . unless excepting the debt from the order would impose an "undue hardship" on the debtor. . . .

Section 523(a)(8) is "self-executing." . . . Unless the debtor affirmatively secures a hardship determination, the discharge order will not include a student loan debt. . . . Thus, the major difference between the discharge of a student loan debt and the discharge of most other debts is that governmental creditors, including States, that choose not to submit themselves to the court's jurisdiction might still receive some benefit: The debtor's personal liability on the loan may survive the discharge.

* * *

No matter how difficult Congress has decided to make the discharge of student loan debt, the bankruptcy court's jurisdiction is premised on the res, not on the persona; that States were granted the presumptive benefit of nondischargeability does not alter the court's underlying authority. A debtor does not seek monetary damages or any affirmative relief from a State by seeking to discharge a debt; nor does he subject an unwilling State to a coercive judicial process. He seeks only a discharge of his debts.

* * *

(Citations omitted.)

NOTES AND COMMENTS

1. The Court cites the well-accepted doctrine that the bankruptcy courts' jurisdiction is in rem jurisdiction based on its authority over the debtor's bankruptcy estate. But discharge of the debt releases claims not only against the debtor's property but also against the debtor personally. Does that take the court out of its in rem jurisdiction?

2. Section 528(a)(8)'s heightened standard for discharge of student debt protects states and other student loan lenders more than other creditors by ensuring that debtors will not discharge the debt without the court's consideration of the necessity of such discharge. It is the only debt that requires such a determination before discharge. As the Court notes,

even if the state does not object to discharge, such a determination must be made. Do you think that the protections offered to the state in this subsection affected the Court's analysis?

Hood involved a benefit to the state: nondischargeability of student loan debt. But states that are involved in the bankruptcy case are not always seeking payment from the debtor. In some cases, the trustee asks the state to pay money into the estate. In such cases, the state is essentially the defendant in a lawsuit.

Central Virginia Community College v. Katz

546 U.S. 356 (2006)

STEVENS, Justice

Article I, § 8, cl. 4, of the Constitution provides that Congress shall have the power to establish "uniform Laws on the subject of Bankruptcies throughout the United States." In *Tennessee Student Assistance Corporation v. Hood,* 541 U.S. 440 . . . (2004), we granted certiorari to determine whether this Clause gives Congress the authority to abrogate States' immunity from private suits. . . . Without reaching that question, we upheld the application of the Bankruptcy Code to proceedings initiated by a debtor against a state agency to determine the dischargeability of a student loan debt . . . . In this case we consider whether a proceeding initiated by a bankruptcy trustee to set aside preferential transfers by the debtor to state agencies is barred by sovereign immunity. Relying in part on our reasoning in *Hood,* we reject the sovereign immunity defense advanced by the state agencies. . . .

Petitioners are Virginia institutions of higher education that are considered "arm[s] of the State" entitled to sovereign immunity. . . . Wallace's Bookstores, Inc., did business with petitioners before it filed a petition for relief under chapter 11 of the Bankruptcy Code. . . . Respondent, Bernard Katz, is the court-appointed liquidating supervisor of the bankrupt estate. He has commenced proceedings in the Bankruptcy Court pursuant to §§ 547(b) and 550(a) to avoid and recover alleged preferential transfers to each of the petitioners made by the debtor when it was insolvent. Petitioners' motions to dismiss those proceedings on the basis of sovereign immunity were denied by the Bankruptcy Court.

The denial was affirmed by the District Court and the Court of Appeals for the Sixth Circuit . . . on the authority of the Sixth Circuit's prior determination that Congress has abrogated the States' sovereign immunity in bankruptcy proceedings. . . . We granted certiorari . . . to consider the question left open by our opinion in *Hood:* whether Congress' attempt to abrogate state sovereign immunity in 11 U.S.C. § 106(a) is valid. As we shall explain, however, we are persuaded that the enactment of that provision was not necessary to authorize the Bankruptcy Court's jurisdiction over these preference avoidance proceedings.

Bankruptcy jurisdiction, at its core, is *in rem.* . . . As we noted in *Hood,* it does not implicate States' sovereignty to nearly the same degree as other kinds of jurisdiction. . . .

It is appropriate to presume that the Framers of the Constitution were familiar with the contemporary legal context when they adopted the Bankruptcy Clause—a provision which, as we explain in Part IV, *infra,* reflects the States' acquiescence in a grant of congressional power to subordinate to the pressing goal of harmonizing bankruptcy law sovereign immunity defenses that might have been asserted in bankruptcy proceedings. The history of the Bankruptcy Clause, the reasons it was inserted in the Constitution, and the legislation both proposed and enacted under its auspices immediately following ratification of the Constitution demonstrate that it was intended not just as a grant of legislative authority to Congress, but also to authorize limited subordination of state sovereign immunity in the bankruptcy arena. . . . As discussed below, to remedy this problem, the very first Congresses considered, and the Sixth Congress enacted, bankruptcy legislation authorizing federal courts to, among other things, issue writs of habeas corpus directed at state officials ordering the release of debtors from state prisons.

* * *

Critical features of every bankruptcy proceeding are the exercise of exclusive jurisdiction over all of the debtor's property, the equitable distribution of that property among the debtor's creditors, and the ultimate discharge that gives the debtor a "fresh start" by releasing him, her, or it from further liability for old debts. . . . "Under our longstanding precedent, States, whether or not they choose to participate in the proceeding, are bound by a bankruptcy court's discharge order no less than other creditors." *Hood,* 541 U.S., at 448. . . .

* * *

Bankruptcy jurisdiction, as understood today and at the time of the framing, is principally *in rem* jurisdiction. . . . In bankruptcy, "the court's jurisdiction is premised on the debtor and his estate, and not on the creditors." *Hood,* 541 U.S., at 447 . . . . As such, its exercise does not, in the usual case, interfere with state sovereignty even when States' interests are affected. . . .

The text of Article I, § 8, cl. 4, of the Constitution, however, provides that Congress shall have the power to establish "uniform Laws on the subject of Bankruptcies throughout the United States." . . .

The Framers would have understood that laws "on the subject of Bankruptcies" included laws providing, in certain limited respects, for more than simple adjudications of rights in the res. The first bankruptcy statute, for example, gave bankruptcy commissioners appointed by the district court the power, *inter alia,* to imprison recalcitrant third parties in possession of the estate's assets. . . . More generally, courts adjudicating disputes concerning bankrupts' estates historically have had the power to issue ancillary orders enforcing their *in rem* adjudications. . . .

Our decision in *Hood* illustrates the point. As the dissenters in that case pointed out, it was at least arguable that the particular procedure that the debtor pursued to establish dischargeability of her student loan could have been characterized as a suit against the State rather than a purely *in rem* proceeding. . . . But because the proceeding was merely ancillary to the Bankruptcy Court's exercise of its *in rem* jurisdiction, we held that it did not implicate state sovereign immunity. . . .

The interplay between *in rem* adjudications and orders ancillary thereto is evident in the case before us. Respondent first seeks a determination under 11 U.S.C. § 547 that the various transfers made by the debtor to petitioners qualify as voidable preferences. The § 547 determination, standing alone, operates as a mere declaration of avoidance. That declaration may be all that the trustee wants; for example, if the State has a claim against the bankrupt estate, the avoidance determination operates to bar that claim until the preference is turned over. See § 502(d). In some cases, though, the trustee, in order to marshal the entirety of the debtor's estate, will need to recover the subject of the transfer pursuant to § 550(a). A court order mandating turnover of the property, although ancillary to and in furtherance of the court's *in rem* jurisdiction, might itself involve *in personam* process.

As we explain in Part IV, *infra,* it is not necessary to decide whether actions to recover preferential transfers pursuant to § 550(a) are themselves properly characterized as *in rem*. Whatever the appropriate appellation, those who crafted the Bankruptcy Clause would have understood it to give Congress the power to authorize courts to avoid preferential transfers and to recover the transferred property. Petitioners do not dispute that that authority has been a core aspect of the administration of bankrupt estates since at least the 18th century. . . . And it, like the authority to issue writs of habeas corpus releasing debtors from state prisons, see Part IV, *infra*, operates free and clear of the State's claim of sovereign immunity.

* * *

This history strongly supports the view that the Bankruptcy Clause of Article I, the source of Congress' authority to effect this intrusion upon state sovereignty, simply did not contravene the norms this Court has understood the Eleventh Amendment to exemplify. . . . Petitioners, ignoring this history, contend that nothing in the *words* of the Bankruptcy Clause evinces an intent on the part of the Framers to alter the "background principle" of state sovereign immunity. . . . Specifically, they deny that the word "uniform" in the Clause implies anything about pre-existing immunities or Congress' power to interfere with those immunities. . . . Whatever the merits of petitioners' argument, it misses the point; text aside, the Framers, in adopting the Bankruptcy Clause, plainly intended to give Congress the power to redress the rampant injustice resulting from States' refusal to respect one another's discharge orders. As demonstrated by the First Congress' immediate consideration and the Sixth Congress' enactment of a provision granting federal courts the authority to release debtors from state prisons, the power to enact bankruptcy legislation was understood to carry with it the power to subordinate state sovereignty, albeit within a limited sphere.

The ineluctable conclusion, then, is that States agreed in the plan of the Convention not to assert any sovereign immunity defense they might have had in proceedings brought pursuant to "Laws on the subject of Bankruptcies." . . . The scope of this consent was limited; the jurisdiction exercised in bankruptcy proceedings was chiefly *in rem*—a narrow jurisdiction that does not implicate state sovereignty to nearly the same degree as other kinds of jurisdiction. But while the principal focus of the bankruptcy proceedings is and was always the res, some exercises of bankruptcy courts' powers—issuance of writs of habeas corpus included—unquestionably involved more than mere adjudication of rights in a res. In ratifying the Bankruptcy Clause, the States acquiesced in a subordination of whatever sovereign immunity they might otherwise have asserted in proceedings necessary to effectuate the *in rem* jurisdiction of the bankruptcy courts.

* * *

Justice THOMAS, with whom THE CHIEF JUSTICE, Justice SCALIA, and Justice KENNEDY join, dissenting.

Under our Constitution, the States are not subject to suit by private parties for monetary relief absent their consent or a valid congressional abrogation, and it is "settled doctrine" that nothing in Article I of the Constitution establishes those preconditions. *Alden v. Maine,* 527 U.S. 706 . . . (1999). Yet the Court today casts aside these long-established principles to hold that the States are subject to suit by a rather unlikely class of individuals—bankruptcy trustees seeking recovery of preferential transfers for a bankrupt debtor's estate. This conclusion cannot be justified by the text, structure, or history of our Constitution. In addition, today's ruling is not only impossible to square with this Court's settled state sovereign immunity jurisprudence; it is also impossible to reach without overruling this Court's judgment in *Hoffman v. Connecticut Dept. of Income Maintenance,* 492 U.S. 96 . . . (1989).

* * *

The majority does not appear to question the established framework for examining the question of state sovereign immunity under our Constitution. The Framers understood, and this Court reiterated over a century ago in *Hans v. Louisiana,* 134 U.S. 1 . . . (1890):

> 'It is inherent in the nature of sovereignty not to be amenable to the suit of an individual without its consent. This is the general sense and the general practice of mankind; and the exemption, as one of the attributes of sovereignty, is now enjoyed by the government of every State in the Union. *Unless, therefore, there is a surrender of this immunity in the plan of the convention, it will remain with the States . . . .'*

Id., at 13 . . . (quoting The Federalist No. 81, pp. 548-549 (J. Cooke ed.1961) (hereinafter The Federalist No. 81); emphasis added and deleted).

* * *

These principles were further reinforced early in our Nation's history, when the people swiftly rejected this Court's decision in *Chisholm v. Georgia* . . . , by ratifying the Eleventh Amendment less than two years later. . . .

The majority finds a surrender of the States' immunity from suit in Article I of the Constitution, which authorizes Congress "[t]o establish . . . uniform Laws on the subject of Bankruptcies throughout the United States." § 8, cl. 4. But nothing in the text of the Bankruptcy

Clause suggests an abrogation or limitation of the States' sovereign immunity. Indeed, as this Court has noted on numerous occasions, "[t]he Eleventh Amendment restricts the judicial power under Article III, and Article I cannot be used to circumvent the constitutional limitations placed upon federal jurisdiction." *Seminole Tribe, supra,* at 72-73 . . . . "[I]t is settled doctrine that neither substantive federal law nor attempted congressional abrogation under Article I bars a State from raising a constitutional defense of sovereign immunity in federal court." *Alden, supra,* at 748 . . . . And we have specifically applied this "settled doctrine" to bar abrogation of state sovereign immunity under various clauses within § 8 of Article I. . . .

It is difficult to discern an intention to abrogate state sovereign immunity through the Bankruptcy Clause when no such intention has been found in any of the other clauses in Article I. Indeed, our cases are replete with acknowledgments that there is nothing special about the Bankruptcy Clause in this regard. See *Seminole Tribe,* 517 U.S., at 72-73, n. 16. . . .

The majority's departure from this Court's precedents is not limited to this general framework, however; the majority also overrules *sub silentio* this Court's holding in *Hoffman, supra.* The petitioner in *Hoffman* . . . —like respondent Katz here—sought to pursue a preference avoidance action against a state agency pursuant to 11 U.S.C. § 547(b). The plurality opinion, joined by four Members of this Court, held that Eleventh Amendment immunity barred suit because Congress had failed to enact legislation sufficient to abrogate that immunity, and expressed no view on whether Congress possessed the constitutional power to do so. . . .

After today's decision, however, *Hoffman* can no longer stand. For today's decision makes clear that *no action* of Congress is needed because the Bankruptcy Clause itself manifests the consent of the States to be sued. . . .

* * *

In contending that the States waived their immunity from suit by adopting the Bankruptcy Clause, the majority conflates two distinct attributes of sovereignty: the authority of a sovereign to enact legislation regulating its own citizens, and sovereign immunity against suit by private citizens. Nothing in the history of the Bankruptcy Clause suggests that, by including that clause in Article I, the founding generation intended to waive the latter aspect of sovereignty. These two attributes of sovereignty often do not run together-and for purposes of enacting a uniform law of bankruptcy, they need not run together.

* * *

Nor is the abrogation of state sovereign immunity from suit necessary to the enactment of nationally uniform bankruptcy laws. The sovereign immunity of the States against suit does not undermine the objective of a uniform national law of bankruptcy, any more than does any differential treatment between different categories of creditors. . . .

* * *

The availability of habeas relief in bankruptcy between 1800 and 1803 does not support respondent's effort to obtain monetary relief in bankruptcy against state agencies today. The habeas writ was well established by the time of the framing, and consistent with then-prevailing notions of sovereignty. In *Ex parte Young,* 209 U.S. 123 . . . (1908), this Court held that a petition for the writ is a suit against a state official, not a suit against a State, and thus does not offend the Eleventh Amendment . . .

* * *

Finally, the majority observes that the bankruptcy power is principally exercised through *in rem* jurisdiction. *Ante,* at 1000-1002. The fact that certain aspects of the bankruptcy power may be characterized as *in rem,* however, does not determine whether or not the States enjoy sovereign immunity against such *in rem* suits. And it certainly does not answer the question presented in this case: whether the Bankruptcy Clause subjects the States to transfer recovery proceedings—proceedings the majority describes as "ancillary to and in furtherance of the court's *in rem* jurisdiction," though not necessarily themselves *in rem, ante,* at 1001.

Two years ago, this Court held that a State is bound by a bankruptcy court's discharge order, notwithstanding the State's invocation of sovereign immunity, because such actions arise out of *in rem* jurisdiction. See *Tennessee Student Assistance Corporation v. Hood,* 541 U.S. 440, 448 . . . (2004). In doing so, however, the Court explicitly distinguished recovery of preferential transfers, noting that the debt discharge proceedings there were "unlike an adversary proceeding by the bankruptcy trustee seeking to recover property in the hands of the State on the grounds that the transfer was a voidable preference." *Id.,* at 454. . . .

* * *

(Citations omitted.)

NOTES AND COMMENTS

1. The Court expressly notes that it does not render judgment on whether a preferential transfer recovery action constitutes an in rem proceeding. Preferential transfers involve situations in which the trustee seeks to recover payments made to a creditor pre-bankruptcy and bring them back into the bankruptcy estate so that they can be distributed fairly and equitably among similarly situated creditors. Would that be an in rem action?

2. The Court noted that a prior case had—in dicta—suggested that the Constitution's mention of bankruptcy law did not inherently abrogate state sovereign immunity. Seminole Tribe of Fla. v. Fla., 517 U.S. 44 (1996), involved the Indian Gaming Regulatory Act, 25 U.S.C. § 2710(d)(1)(C), which limited tribes to engage in gaming activities only to the extent agreed upon with the state in which the gaming activities occurred. The Supreme Court held the Act to be an unconstitutional infringement on the sovereignty of the states by mandating good faith negotiations by the states with the tribes and by making the states subject to suit from the tribes. In his dissent, Justice Stevens noted the potential implications of the *Seminole Tribe* decision upon bankruptcy law:

   > The importance of the majority's decision to overrule the Court's holding in *Pennsylvania v. Union Gas Co.* cannot be overstated. The majority's opinion does not simply preclude Congress from establishing the rather curious statutory scheme under which Indian tribes may seek the aid of a federal court to secure a State's good-faith negotiations over gaming regulations. Rather, it prevents Congress from providing a federal forum for a broad range of actions against States, from those sounding in copyright and patent law, to those concerning bankruptcy, environmental law, and the regulation of our vast national economy.

   Id. at 77 (J. Stevens, dissenting).

3. Would the state abrogation of sovereign immunity extend to a tort action that a debtor wants to bring against the state? For example, if the debtor was injured in a car accident with a state trooper, would the trustee be able to bring a cause of action against the state in the bankruptcy court?

4. The dissent concludes that creation of a uniform bankruptcy system does not necessarily require abrogation of state sovereignty, and thus the history of that constitutional provision should not be read to include such an abrogation. Could a uniform system of bankruptcy laws still allow immunity for the states?

b. Municipalities and U.S. Territories

While the states reserved some rights in the Constitutional Convention, municipalities and U.S. territories do not enjoy the same constitutional protections. In fact, Congress enacted Chapter 9 of the Bankruptcy Code to govern the bankruptcy filings of municipalities, which are thereby subjected to the power and oversight of the states within which they are located. While filings under Chapter 9 are relatively rare, municipalities such as Detroit, Michigan, and Stockton, California, have filed Chapter 9 cases in recent years.

BANKRUPTCY CODE CHAPTER 9 AND PREEMPTION

Chapter 9 of the Bankruptcy Code governs filings by municipalities. It creates a plan of adjustment of the debts of the municipalities, somewhat similar to a reorganization plan under Chapter 11. In order for a municipality to file under Chapter 9, several requirements must be met (for example, the municipality must be insolvent), and the state in which the municipality is organized must approve of the filing. 11 U.S.C. § 109(c). Chapter 9 cannot be used by states or the United States; in fact, there is no federal law governing state insolvency and no international law that governs the insolvency of countries.

Chapter 9 also includes express preemption language, preempting states from enacting bankruptcy laws that differ from the mandates of Chapter 9. Recall that Article VI of the Constitution states that federal law "shall be the supreme law of the land . . . anything in the Constitution or laws of any State to the contrary notwithstanding." Thus, where preemption exists, state and local laws give way to the federal law.

Preemption can be express or implied. Preemption is express, as with Chapter 9, when the federal law expressly states that it preempts state and local laws on certain topics. Preemption is implied where the state or local law: (1) would conflict with the federal law, (2) would impair the goal of the federal law, or (3) would regulate the same field as the federal law.

Congress never specifically addressed whether or how the Bankruptcy Code would apply to U.S. territories. The interaction of these territories with federal law such as the Bankruptcy Code creates unique preemption issues—particularly when the laws coalesce to create a potential gap.

Puerto Rico v. Franklin California Tax-Free Trust

136 S. Ct. 1938 (2016)

THOMAS, Justice

* * *

Puerto Rico and its instrumentalities are in the midst of a fiscal crisis. More than $20 billion of Puerto Rico's climbing debt is shared by three government-owned public utilities companies: the Puerto Rico Electric Power Authority, the Puerto Rico Aqueduct and Sewer Authority, and the Puerto Rico Highways and Transportation Authority. For the fiscal year ending in 2013, the three public utilities operated with a combined deficit of $800 million. The Government Development Bank for Puerto Rico (Bank)—the Commonwealth's government-owned bank and fiscal agent—has previously provided financing to enable the utilities to continue operating without defaulting on their debt obligations. But the Bank now faces a fiscal crisis of its own. As of fiscal year 2013, it had loaned nearly half of its assets to Puerto Rico and its public utilities. . . .

Puerto Rico responded to the fiscal crisis by enacting the Puerto Rico Corporation Debt Enforcement and Recovery Act (Recovery Act) in 2014, which enables the Commonwealth's public utilities to implement a recovery or restructuring plan for their debt . . . . Chapter 2 of the Recovery Act creates a "consensual" debt modification procedure that permits the public utilities to propose changes to the terms of the outstanding debt instruments, for example, changing the interest rate or the maturity date of the debt . . . . Chapter 3 of the Recovery Act, on the other hand, mirrors Chapters 9 and 11 of the Federal Bankruptcy Code by creating a court-supervised restructuring process intended to offer the best solution for the broadest group of creditors. . . .

A group of investment funds, including the Franklin California Tax-Free Trust, and BlueMountain Capital Management, LLC, brought separate suits against Puerto Rico and various government officials, including agents of the Bank, to enjoin the enforcement of the Recovery Act. Collectively, the plaintiffs hold nearly $2 billion in bonds issued by the Electric Power Authority, one of the distressed utilities. The complaints alleged, among other claims, that the Federal Bankruptcy Code prohibited Puerto Rico from implementing its own municipal bankruptcy scheme.

The District Court [] concluded that the pre-emption provision in Chapter 9 of the Federal Bankruptcy Code, 11 U.S.C. § 903(1), precluded Puerto Rico from implementing the Recovery Act and enjoined its enforcement. . . .

The First Circuit [] concluded that the amendment did not remove Puerto Rico from the scope of the pre-emption provision and held that the pre-emption provision barred the Recovery Act. . . .

* * *

These cases require us to parse three provisions of the Bankruptcy Code: the "who may be a debtor" provision requiring States to authorize municipalities to seek Chapter 9 relief, § 109(c), the pre-emption provision barring States from enacting their own municipal bankruptcy schemes, § 903(1), and the definition of "State," § 101(52). We first explain the text and history of these provisions. We then conclude that Puerto Rico is still a "State" for purposes of the pre-emption provision and hold that this provision pre-empts the Recovery Act.

* * *

. . . the provision of the Bankruptcy Code defining who may be a debtor under Chapter 9, which we refer to here as the "gateway" provision, requires the States to authorize their municipalities to seek relief under Chapter 9 before the municipalities may file a Chapter 9 petition:

* * *

"(c) An entity may be a debtor under chapter 9 of this title if and only if such entity—
(1) is a municipality;
(2) is specifically authorized, in its capacity as a municipality or by name, to be a debtor under such chapter by State law, or by a governmental officer or organization empowered by State law to authorize such entity to be a debtor under such chapter. . . ."

The States' powers are not unlimited, however. The federal bankruptcy laws changed again in 1946 to bar the States from enacting their own municipal bankruptcy schemes. . . .

The express pre-emption provision, central to these cases, is now codified with some stylistic changes in § 903(1):

* * *

"This chapter does not limit or impair the power of a State to control, by legislation or otherwise, a municipality of or in such State in the exercise of the political or governmental powers of such municipality, including expenditures for such exercise, but—

(1) a State law prescribing a method of composition of indebtedness of such municipality may not bind any creditor that does not consent to such composition; and

(2) a judgment entered under such a law may not bind a creditor that does not consent to such composition."

The third provision of the Bankruptcy Code at issue is the definition of "State," which has included Puerto Rico since it became a Territory of the United States in 1898. The first Federal Bankruptcy Act, also enacted in 1898, defined "States" to include "the Territories, the Indian Territory, Alaska, and the District of Columbia." 30 Stat. 545. . . . The amended definition includes Puerto Rico as a State for purposes of the Code with one exception:

* * *

"(52) The term 'State' includes the District of Columbia and Puerto Rico, except for the purpose of defining who may be a debtor under chapter 9 of this title."

. . . It is our task to determine the effect of the amended definition of "State" on the Code's other provisions governing Chapter 9 proceedings. We must decide whether, in light of the amended definition, Puerto Rico is no longer a "State" only for purposes of the gateway provision, which requires States to authorize their municipalities to seek Chapter 9 relief, or whether Puerto Rico is also no longer a "State" for purposes of the pre-emption provision.

* * *

The parties part ways . . . in deciphering how the 1984 amendment to the definition of "State" affected the pre-emption provision. Petitioners interpret the amended definition of "State" to exclude Puerto Rico altogether from Chapter 9. If petitioners are correct, then the pre-emption provision does not apply to them. Puerto Rico, in other words, may enact its own municipal bankruptcy scheme without running afoul of the Code. Respondents, on the other hand, read the amended definition narrowly. They contend that the definition precludes Puerto Rico from "specifically authoriz[ing]" its municipalities to seek relief, as required by the gateway provision, § 109(c)(2), but that Puerto Rico is no less a "State" for purposes of the pre-emption provision than the other "State[s]," as that term is defined in the Code. If respondents are correct, then the pre-emption provision applies to Puerto Rico and bars it from enacting the Recovery Act.

Respondents have the better reading. We hold that Puerto Rico is still a "State" for purposes of the pre-emption provision. The 1984 amendment precludes Puerto Rico from authorizing its municipalities to seek relief under Chapter 9, but it does not remove Puerto Rico from the reach of Chapter 9's pre-emption provision.

* * *

The amended definition of "State" excludes Puerto Rico for the single "purpose of defining *who may be a debtor* under chapter 9 of this title." § 101(52) (emphasis added). That exception unmistakably refers to the gateway provision in § 109, titled "who may be a debtor." Section 109(c) begins, "An entity may be a debtor under chapter 9 of this title if and only if. . . ." § 109(c). We interpret Congress' use of the "who may be a debtor" language in the amended definition of "State" to mean that Congress intended to exclude Puerto Rico from this gateway provision delineating who may be a debtor under Chapter 9. . . . Puerto Rico, therefore, is not a "State" for purposes of the gateway provision, so it cannot perform the single function of the "State[s]" under that provision: to "specifically authoriz[e]" municipalities to seek Chapter 9 relief. § 109(c). As a result, Puerto Rico's municipalities cannot satisfy the requirements of Chapter 9's gateway provision until Congress intervenes.

* * *

The dissent concludes that "the government and people of Puerto Rico should not have to wait for possible congressional action to avert the consequences" of the Commonwealth's fiscal crisis. But our constitutional structure does not permit this Court to "rewrite the statute that Congress has enacted." . . . Federal law, therefore, pre-empts the Recovery Act. The judgment of the Court of Appeals for the First Circuit is affirmed.

(Citations omitted.)

NOTES AND COMMENTS

1. As the Court notes, a municipality cannot file for bankruptcy protection unless the state authorizes the municipality to do so. Why does the Code require state authorization of municipal filings, and why is that less of a concern for Puerto Rico's municipalities?

2. The dissent focused on the challenges facing Puerto Rico's municipalities in light of the Supreme Court's ruling. Following this opinion, what options remain for Puerto Rico's municipalities to deal with the financial crisis?

B. INDIVIDUAL RIGHTS (§§101(3), 101(12A), 526)

1. Freedom of Speech

The first ten Constitutional amendments, known as the Bill of Rights, were adopted in 1791, and provide protections for individuals and the states. The First Amendment includes several personal liberties—freedom of speech, freedom of the press, freedom of religion, and freedom of association. Some of the most interesting bankruptcy cases involve how to protect these rights in the context of a bankruptcy case.

While the First Amendment protects citizens from governmental intrusion on free speech, the right to speak freely is not unlimited. A common example of the limits on free speech is shouting "fire" in a crowded movie theater to induce panic when there is not actually a fire. That speech is not protected.[4] Before considering how restrictions on free speech are scrutinized, it is important to remember that the protection of free speech is against intrusion upon that speech by the government or a state actor.

Some restrictions on free speech are based on the time, place, or manner of the speech—known as "content-neutral" restrictions. Limitations on political speech within a certain distance of voting places provide an example of such restrictions—whether the speaker is in favor of one candidate or the other is irrelevant because all speech (albeit, politically motivated) is banned in that location at that time.

When the government places content-neutral restrictions on speech, that restriction is reviewed using "intermediate" scrutiny. Intermediate scrutiny requires that the regulation on speech be *narrowly tailored* to meet a *substantial governmental interest*. Of course, the restriction must actually be content-neutral, a determination that is not always evident.

For example, in Ward v. Rock Against Racism, 491 U.S. 781 (1989), the Supreme Court considered whether a regulation that mandated use of city employees to control the sound system at outdoor concerts violated the Free Speech clause. The city passed the regulation in order to prevent excessive noise in a residential area. The Supreme Court deemed the regulation content-neutral, despite the petitioner's argument that one of the goals of the regulation was to ensure "good" sound, and despite the fact that the regulation had been enacted following complaints about the petitioner's concert in a prior year. *Id.* at 791-792. The Court then considered the regulation under the intermediate scrutiny test, finding that the government

---

4. Schenck v. U.S., 39 U.S. 247, 249 (1919).

has a "substantial interest" in protecting the public from excessive noise, *id.* at 796-797, and that the regulation was "narrowly tailored" to meet that interest even if other feasible and less intrusive means of meeting that goal existed. *Id.* at 797-798.

When the government bases a restriction on speech on the content of that speech, the scrutiny typically given such a restriction changes to "strict scrutiny"—a requirement that the restriction be *narrowly tailored* to meet a *compelling state interest.* Reed v. Town of Gilbert, Arizona, 135 S. Ct. 2218 (2015) provides an example of such an analysis. *Reed* involved a town ordinance that provided different limitations on different types of signs posted. While all signs required a permit before posting, where and when signs could be posted and the size of the sign permitted depended upon what type of sign was posted (political message, ideological message, directions to an event). *Id.* at 2224. The Court held that the ordinance was content-based because the restrictions depended upon "the topic or the idea or message" of the sign. *Id.* at 2227. Meeting the strict scrutiny test can be almost impossible, and the Court held that the government had no compelling interest in adopting the sign restrictions. *Id.* at 2231-2232. Not all content-based restrictions on free speech face strict scrutiny analysis. Some restrictions that are content-based but receive no First Amendment protection include obscenity, fraud, and speech designed to incite.

Further, in limited areas courts have essentially applied variations on a rational basis review to government restrictions on free speech. That level of review is illustrated in the *Milavetz* case excerpted below. As discussed there, when the government prescribes commercial speech designed to protect the public, a standard that is less exacting than intermediate scrutiny is used. That standard is satisfied when the government action is rationally related to its purpose to protect the public.

Free Speech Scrutiny

As with substantive due process and equal protection claims, free speech claims are subject to different levels of scrutiny, depending on the regulation in question. Again, the jurisprudence in this area is complex, and many regulations affecting speech are subject to a very specific test to see if the regulation is constitutional. Nonetheless, it is possible and useful to summarize the basic levels of scrutiny that are applied to government intrusions on free speech. Remember that there are many variations on these frameworks for analysis, depending on exactly what the regulation is.

Unprotected speech—The government may regulate without First Amendment limitation some types of speech including obscenity, fraud or speech designed to incite violence unless the regulation discriminates on the basis of viewpoint.

Rational basis—Applied to government disclosure requirements designed to prevent misleading commercial speech; here the government action must be *rationally related* to its protective purpose.

Intermediate scrutiny—Applied to regulations that are content-neutral or restrict the time, place, and manner of speech rather than the speech itself; here the government action must be *narrowly tailored* to meet a *substantial government interest*.

Strict scrutiny—Applied to content-based speech regulations, including regulations that restrict religious and political speech; here the government action should be *narrowly tailored* to advance a *compelling interest*.

When Congress adopted the Bankruptcy Abuse Prevention and Consumer Protection Act (BAPCPA) in 2005, it included several provisions regarding "debt relief agencies." These provisions both required certain disclosures and prohibited other statements by debt collection agencies. Free speech implications for attorneys arose in this context.

Milavetz, Gallop & Milavetz, P.A. v. U.S.

559 U.S. 229 (2010)

SOTOMAYOR, Justice

Congress enacted the Bankruptcy Abuse Prevention and Consumer Protection Act of 2005 (BAPCPA or Act) to correct perceived abuses of the bankruptcy system. Among the reform measures the Act implemented are a number of provisions that regulate the conduct of "debt relief agenc[ies]"—*i.e.,* professionals who provide bankruptcy assistance to consumer debtors. See 11 U.S.C. §§ 101(3), (12A). These consolidated cases present the threshold question whether attorneys are debt relief agencies when they provide qualifying services. Because we agree with the Court of Appeals that they are, we must also consider whether the Act's provisions governing debt relief agencies' advice to clients, § 526(a)(4), and requiring them to make certain disclosures in their advertisements, §§ 528(a) and (b)(2), violate the First Amendment rights of attorneys. Concluding that the Court of Appeals construed § 526(a)(4) too expansively, we reverse its judgment that the provision is unconstitutionally overbroad. Like the Court of Appeals, we uphold § 528's disclosure requirements as applied in these consolidated cases.

I

In order to improve bankruptcy law and practice, Congress enacted through the BAPCPA a number of provisions directed at the conduct of bankruptcy professionals. Some of these measures apply to the broad class of bankruptcy professionals termed "debt relief agenc[ies]." That category includes, with limited exceptions, "any person who provides any bankruptcy assistance to an assisted person in return for . . . payment . . . , or who is a bankruptcy petition preparer." § 101(12A). "Bankruptcy assistance" refers to goods or services "provided to an assisted person with the express or implied purpose of providing information, advice, counsel, document preparation, or filing, or attendance at a creditors' meeting or appearing in a case or proceeding on behalf of another or providing legal representation with respect to a case or proceeding" in bankruptcy. § 101(4A). An "assisted person" is someone with limited nonexempt property whose debts consist primarily of consumer debts. § 101(3). The BAPCPA subjects debt relief agencies to a number of restrictions and requirements, as set forth in §§ 526, 527, and 528. As relevant here, § 526(a) establishes several rules of professional conduct for persons qualifying as debt relief agencies. Among them, § 526(a)(4) states that a debt relief agency shall not "advise an assisted person . . . to incur more debt in contemplation of such person filing a case under this title or to pay an attorney or bankruptcy petition preparer fee or charge for services performed as part of preparing for or representing a debtor in a case under this title."

Section 528 requires qualifying professionals to include certain disclosures in their advertisements. Subsection (a) provides that debt relief agencies must "clearly and conspicuously disclose in any advertisement of bankruptcy assistance services or of the benefits of bankruptcy directed to the general public . . . that the services or benefits are with respect to bankruptcy relief under this title." § 528(a)(3). It also requires them to include the following, "or a substantially similar statement": "We are a debt relief agency. We help people file for bankruptcy relief under the Bankruptcy Code." § 528(a)(4). Subsection (b) requires essentially the same disclosures in advertisements "indicating that the debt relief agency provides assistance with respect to credit defaults, mortgage foreclosures, eviction proceedings, excessive debt, debt collection pressure, or inability to pay any consumer debt." § 528(b)(2). Debt relief agencies advertising such services must disclose "that the assistance may involve bankruptcy relief," § 528(b)(2)(A), and must identify themselves as "debt relief agenc[ies]" as required by § 528(a)(4), see § 528(b)(2)(B).

II

The plaintiffs in this litigation . . . filed a preenforcement suit in Federal District Court seeking declaratory relief with respect to the Act's debt-relief-agency provisions. Milavetz asked the court to hold that it is not bound by these provisions and thus may freely advise clients to incur additional debt and need not identify itself as a debt relief agency in its advertisements.

Milavetz first argued that attorneys are not "debt relief agenc[ies]" as that term is used in the BAPCPA. In the alternative, Milavetz sought a judgment that §§ 526(a)(4) and 528(a)(4) and (b)(2) are unconstitutional as applied to attorneys. The District Court agreed with Milavetz that the term "debt relief agency" does not include attorneys, . . . but only after finding that §§ 526 and 528—provisions expressly applicable only to debt relief agencies—are unconstitutional as applied to this class of professionals.

The Court of Appeals for the Eighth Circuit affirmed in part and reversed in part. Relying on the Act's plain language, the court unanimously rejected the District Court's conclusion that attorneys are not "debt relief agenc[ies]" within the meaning of the Act. The Court of Appeals also parted ways with the District Court concerning the constitutionality of § 528. Concluding that the disclosures are intended to prevent consumer deception and are "reasonably related" to that interest, the court upheld the application of § 528's disclosure requirements to attorneys. . . .

A majority of the Eighth Circuit panel, however, agreed with the District Court that § 526(a)(4) is invalid. Determining that § 526(a)(4) "broadly prohibits a debt relief agency from advising an assisted person . . . to incur *any* additional debt when the assisted person is contemplating bankruptcy," even when that advice constitutes prudent prebankruptcy planning not intended to abuse the bankruptcy laws, 541 F.3d at 793, the majority held that § 526(a)(4) could not withstand either strict or intermediate scrutiny. . . .

* * *

We first consider whether the term "debt relief agency" includes attorneys. If it does not, we need not reach the other questions presented. . . .

As already noted, a debt relief agency is "any person who provides any bankruptcy assistance to an assisted person" in return for payment. § 101(12A). By definition, "bankruptcy assistance" includes several services commonly performed by attorneys. Indeed, some forms of bankruptcy assistance, including the "provi[sion of] legal representation with respect to a case or proceeding," § 101(4A), may be provided only by attorneys. See § 110(e)(2) (prohibiting bankruptcy petition preparers from providing legal advice). Moreover, in enumerating specific exceptions to the definition of debt relief agency, Congress gave no indication that it intended to exclude attorneys. See §§ 101(12A)(A)-(E). Thus, as the Government contends, the statutory text clearly indicates that attorneys are debt relief agencies when they provide qualifying services to assisted persons.

In advocating a narrower understanding of that term, Milavetz relies heavily on the fact that § 101(12A) does not expressly include attorneys. That omission stands in contrast, it argues, to the provision's explicit inclusion of "bankruptcy petition preparer[s]"—a category of professionals that excludes attorneys and their staff, ... But Milavetz does not contend, nor could it credibly, that only professionals expressly included in the definition are debt relief agencies. On that reading, no professional other than a bankruptcy petition preparer would qualify—an implausible reading given that the statute defines "debt relief agency" as "any person who provides any bankruptcy assistance to an assisted person . . . *or* who is a bankruptcy petition preparer." § 101(12A) (emphasis added). . . .

* * *

Having concluded that attorneys are debt relief agencies when they provide qualifying services, we next address the scope and validity of § 526(a)(4). . . .

Section 526(a)(4) prohibits a debt relief agency from "advis[ing] an assisted person" either "to incur more debt in contemplation of" filing for bankruptcy "or to pay an attorney or bankruptcy petition preparer fee or charge for services" performed in preparation for filing. Only the first of these prohibitions is at issue. In debating the correctness of the Court of Appeals' decision, the parties first dispute the provision's scope. The Court of Appeals concluded that "§ 526(a)(4) broadly prohibits a debt relief agency from advising an assisted person . . . to incur *any* additional debt when the assisted person is contemplating bankruptcy." *Id.*, at 793. Under that reading, an attorney is prohibited from providing all manner of "beneficial advice—even if the advice could help the assisted person avoid filing for bankruptcy altogether." *Ibid.*

Agreeing with the Court of Appeals, Milavetz contends that § 526(a)(4) prohibits a debt relief agency from advising a client to incur any new debt while considering whether to file for bankruptcy. Construing the provision more broadly still, Milavetz contends that § 526(a)(4) forbids not only affirmative advice but also any discussion of the advantages, disadvantages, or legality of incurring more debt. Like the panel majority's, Milavetz's reading rests primarily on its view that the ordinary meaning of the phrase "in contemplation of" bankruptcy encompasses any advice given to a debtor with the awareness that he might soon file for bankruptcy, even if the advice seeks to obviate the need to file. Milavetz also maintains that if § 526(a)(4) were construed more narrowly, as urged by the Government and the dissent below, it would be so vague as to inevitably chill some protected speech.

. . . The Government contends that § 526(a)(4)'s restriction on advice to incur more debt "in contemplation of" bankruptcy is most naturally read to forbid only advice to undertake actions to abuse the bankruptcy system. Focusing first on the provision's text, the Government points to sources indicating that the phrase "in contemplation of" bankruptcy has long been, and continues to be, associated with abusive conduct. . . . Use of the phrase by Members of Congress illustrates that traditional coupling. See, *e.g.,* S. Rep. No. 98–65, p. 9 (1983) (discussing the practice of "'loading up' [on debt] in contemplation of bankruptcy"); Report of the Commission on the Bankruptcy Laws of the United States, H.R. Doc. No. 93–137, pt. I, p. 11 (1973) ("[T]he most serious abuse of consumer bankruptcy is the number of instances in which individuals have purchased a sizable quantity of goods and services on credit on the eve of bankruptcy in contemplation of obtaining a discharge"). . . .

To bolster its textual claim, the Government relies on § 526(a)(4)'s immediate context. According to the Government, the other three subsections of § 526(a) are designed to protect debtors from abusive practices by debt relief agencies: § 526(a)(1) requires debt relief agencies to perform all promised services; § 526(a)(2) prohibits them from making or advising debtors to make false or misleading statements in bankruptcy; and § 526(a)(3) prohibits them from misleading debtors regarding the costs or benefits of bankruptcy. When § 526(a)(4) is read in context of these debtor-protective provisions, the Government argues, construing it to prevent debt relief agencies from giving advice that is beneficial to both debtors and their creditors seems particularly nonsensical.

Finally, the Government contends that the BAPCPA's remedies for violations of § 526(a)(4) similarly corroborate its narrow reading. Section 526(c) provides remedies for a debt relief agency's violation of § 526, § 527, or § 528. Among the actions authorized, a debtor may sue the attorney for remittal of fees, actual damages, and reasonable attorney's fees and costs; a state attorney general may sue for a resident's actual damages; and a court finding intentional abuse may impose an appropriate civil penalty. § 526(c). . . .

* * *

After reviewing these competing claims, we are persuaded that a narrower reading of § 526(a)(4) is sounder, although we do not adopt precisely the view the Government advocates. The Government's sources show that the phrase "in contemplation of" bankruptcy has so commonly been associated with abusive conduct that it may readily be understood to prefigure abuse. As used in § 526(a)(4), however, we think the phrase refers to a specific type of misconduct designed to manipulate the protections of the bankruptcy system. In light of our decision in [Conrad, Rubin & Lesser v. Pender, 289 U.S. 472 (1933)] and in context of other sections of the Code, we conclude that § 526(a)(4) prohibits a debt relief agency only from advising a debtor to incur more debt because the debtor is filing for bankruptcy, rather than for a valid purpose.

Pender addressed the meaning of former § 96(d), which authorized reexamination of a debtor's payment of attorney's fees "in contemplation of the filing of a petition." Recognizing " 'the temptation of a failing debtor to deal too liberally with his property in employing counsel to protect him,' " . . . we read "in contemplation of . . . filing" in that context to require that the portended bankruptcy have "induce[d]" the transfer at issue, . . . understanding inducement to engender suspicion of abuse. In so construing the statute, we identified the "controlling question" as "whether the thought of bankruptcy was the impelling cause of the transaction." *Ibid.* Given the substantial similarities between §§ 96(d) and 526(a)(4), we think the controlling question under the latter provision is likewise whether the impelling reason for "advis[ing] an assisted person . . . to incur more debt" was the prospect of filing for bankruptcy.

* * *

The statutory context supports the conclusion that § 526(a)(4)'s prohibition primarily targets this type of abuse. Code provisions predating the BAPCPA already sought to prevent the practice of loading up on debt prior to filing. Section 523(a)(2), for instance, addressed the attendant risk of manipulation by preventing the discharge of debts obtained by false pretenses and making debts for purchases of luxury goods or services presumptively nondischargeable. See §§ 523(a)(2)(A) and (C) (2000 ed.). The BAPCPA increased the risk of such abuse, however, by providing a new mechanism for determining a debtor's ability to repay. . . . The [means] test promotes debtor accountability but also enhances incentives to incur additional debt prior to filing, as payments on secured debts offset a debtor's monthly income under the formula. Other amendments effected by the BAPCPA reflect a concern with this practice. . . . In context, § 526(a)(4) is best understood to provide an additional safeguard against the practice of loading up on debt prior to filing.

The Government's contextual arguments provide additional support for the view that § 526(a)(4) was meant to prevent this type of conduct. The companion rules of professional conduct in §§ 526(a) (1)-(3) and the remedies for their violation in § 526(c) indicate that Congress was concerned with actions that threaten to harm debtors or creditors. Unlike the reasonable financial advice the Eighth Circuit's broad reading would proscribe, advice to incur more debt because of bankruptcy presents a substantial risk of injury to both debtors and creditors. . . . the prudent advice that the Eighth Circuit's view of the statute forbids would likely benefit both debtors and creditors and at the very least should cause no harm. . . . For all of these reasons, we conclude that § 526(a)(4) prohibits a debt relief agency only from advising an assisted person to incur more debt when the impelling reason for the advice is the anticipation of bankruptcy.

* * *

For the same reason, we reject Milavetz's suggestion that § 526(a)(4) broadly prohibits debt relief agencies from discussing covered subjects instead of merely proscribing affirmative advice to undertake a particular action. Section 526(a)(4) by its terms prevents debt relief agencies only from "advis[ing]" assisted persons "to incur" more debt. Covered professionals remain free to "tal[k] fully and candidly *about* the incurrence of debt in contemplation of filing a bankruptcy case." Section 526(a)(4) requires professionals only to avoid instructing or encouraging assisted persons to take on more debt in that circumstance. . . . Even if the statute were not clear in this regard, we would reach the same conclusion about its scope because the inhibition of frank discussion serves no conceivable purpose within the statutory scheme. . . .

Finally, we reject Milavetz's contention that, narrowly construed, § 526(a)(4) is impermissibly vague. Milavetz urges that the concept of abusive prefiling conduct is too indefinite to withstand constitutional scrutiny and that uncertainty regarding the scope of the prohibition will chill protected speech. We disagree.

Under our reading of the statute, of course, the prohibited advice is not defined in terms of abusive prefiling conduct but rather the incurrence of additional debt when the impelling reason is the anticipation of bankruptcy. Even if the test depended upon the notion of abuse, however, Milavetz's claim would be fatally undermined by other provisions of the Bankruptcy Code, to which that concept is no stranger. As discussed above, the Code authorizes a bankruptcy court to decline to discharge fraudulent debts, see § 523(a)(2), or to dismiss a case or convert it to a case under another chapter if it finds that granting relief would constitute abuse, see § 707(b)(1). Attorneys and other professionals who give debtors bankruptcy advice must know of these provisions and their consequences for a debtor who in bad faith incurs additional debt prior to filing. Indeed, § 707(b)(4)(C) states that an attorney's signature on bankruptcy filings "shall constitute a certification that the attorney has" determined that the filing "does not constitute an abuse under [§ 707(b)(1)]." Against this backdrop, it is hard to see how a rule that narrowly prohibits an attorney from affirmatively advising a client to commit this type of abusive prefiling conduct could chill attorney speech or inhibit the attorney-client relationship. . . .

* * *

We next consider the standard of scrutiny applicable to § 528's disclosure requirements. The parties agree, as do we, that the challenged provisions regulate only commercial speech. . . .

. . . Unjustified or unduly burdensome disclosure requirements offend the First Amendment by chilling protected speech, but "an advertiser's rights are adequately protected as long as disclosure requirements are reasonably related to the State's interest in preventing deception of consumers.". . . .

. . . § 528's required disclosures are intended to combat the problem of inherently misleading commercial advertisements—specifically, the promise of debt relief without any reference to the possibility of filing for bankruptcy, which has inherent costs. Additionally, the disclosures entail only an accurate statement identifying the advertiser's legal status and the character of the assistance provided, and they do not prevent debt relief agencies like Milavetz from conveying any additional information.

* * *

(Citations omitted.)

NOTES AND COMMENTS

1. What is the purpose served by the BAPCPA restriction on advising someone contemplating a bankruptcy filing to incur additional debt?

2. The circuit court found the BAPCPA restrictions to be unconstitutional as applied to attorneys because they might prohibit an attorney from advising a client to incur debt, even when incurring debt would be sound bankruptcy planning advice. Should an attorney ever be able to advise a client to incur additional debt, knowing that the client will be filing a bankruptcy case? Or should the attorney be limited—as the Supreme Court suggests—to advising clients to incur debt only when the incurrence of such debt is designed to *limit* the likelihood that the client will file for bankruptcy protection or to provide sound bankruptcy advice? Note the Supreme Court's mention of the Model Rules of Professional Conduct, Rule 1.2(d), which prohibits a lawyer from advising a client to engage in criminal conduct or fraud, but allows the lawyer to discuss the consequences of such actions with a client. How does this instruct your view on what is permissible?

3. While not included in the excerpt above, the Supreme Court noted that it took the case to resolve a circuit court split on the issue: "Compare 541 F.3d 785, 794 (C.A.8 2008) [*Milavetz*, a circuit court case, which decided that provision was unconstitutional because it prohibited any type of advice no matter how prudent] with *Hersh v. United States ex rel. Mukasey*, 553 F.3d 743, 761, 764 (C.A.5 2008) (holding that § 526(a)(4) can be narrowly construed to prohibit only advice to abuse or manipulate the bankruptcy system and that, so construed, it is constitutional)." One of the principles often used by the courts is to construe laws as narrowly as possible to avoid declaring them unconstitutional, Crowell v. Benson, 285 U.S. 22, 62 (1932), unless such a construction is contrary to the plain language of the statute or other principles of construction, Boumediene v. Bush, 553 U.S. 723, 787 (2008). Did the Supreme Court use such a principle here?

4. As the court noted, the parties agreed that the challenged speech qualified as commercial speech, which receives less protection under the First Amendment. While commercial speech is sometimes judged by the intermediate scrutiny standard, in this case the court applied the "rational basis" standard—the lowest standard of review. Such a standard merely requires that the restriction be rationally related to the government's interest. Not surprisingly, the government can almost always show such a relationship. Why did the court choose to apply this lenient review standard?

2. Freedom of Religion

Recall that the First Amendment's protection of freedom of religion actually includes two different protections. First, it includes a protection against the establishment or promotion of religion by the government (the "establishment" clause). Second, it ensures that citizens are free to practice their religions without encroachment by the government (the "free exercise" clause). Added to these constitutional provisions is the Religious Freedom Restoration Act (RFRA), passed in 1993 that makes it unlawful for the government to burden religious freedom, unless it has a compelling interest and the action is the least restrictive means available to achieve that interest.

An example of how religious freedom can clash with bankruptcy law arose in a case that ended up being decided by the Seventh Circuit in 2015. The Catholic Archdiocese of Milwaukee had filed for bankruptcy protection in 2011. In 2008, facing a case where victims of alleged abuse were suing the Archdiocese, the Archdiocese transferred $55 million to a trust established for the perpetual care of Catholic cemeteries in the Milwaukee area. Creditors of the Archdiocese in the bankruptcy case, including the victims of the abuse, claimed that the $55 million transfer was fraudulent and preferential under the Bankruptcy Code. The Archdiocese, by contrast, argued that its free exercise rights and rights under RFRA prevented the Bankruptcy Code from even being applied to the transfer. The Seventh Circuit rejected both of the Archdiocese's arguments.

Regarding RFRA, the Seventh Circuit held that, per the statute, a government entity must be involved in creating the burden on religion (and simply was not in this case). Regarding free exercise, it held the Bankruptcy Code to be of neutral application. When laws are neutral, generally speaking, strict scrutiny need not be met for the government regulation to be upheld. If, however, even a neutral law presents a burden on religious freedom, in the Seventh Circuit, the regulation still must meet the strict scrutiny test. The Seventh Circuit went on to find that, in this situation, the Bankruptcy Code did meet strict scrutiny review. It found that the protection of creditors is a compelling government interest, and that the Bankruptcy Code provisions are narrowly tailored to achieve that interest. *See* Listecki v. Official Committee of Unsecured Creditors, 780 F.3d 731 (7th Cir. 2015).

Religious freedom issues arise in a variety of contexts. For example, tithing by a debtor in bankruptcy presents a unique issue in the bankruptcy context. For many years, courts debated whether a debtor could tithe or otherwise donate to the church, even if that meant a lower distribution to creditors in bankruptcy. *See, e.g.,* In re Packham, 126 B.R. 603 (Bankr. D. Utah 1991) (a requirement that the debtor put all disposable income into a Chapter 13 plan, and in doing so not tithe to church, did not violate debtor's free exercise rights), In re Green, 73 B.R. 893 (Bankr. W.D. Mich. 1987) (failure to confirm plan solely due to inclusion of tithes in plan would unconstitutionally burden free exercise of religion of debtor). Congress has since enacted the Religious Liberty Charitable Donation Act, PL 105–183, 112 Stat. 517 (1998). The Religious Liberty Act modifies the Bankruptcy Code to ensure that qualifying contributions to religious and charitable organizations will not be recovered by the trustee, and can continue as part of the debtor's bankruptcy plan. For the time being, the constitutionality of these provisions has not been successfully challenged in the Supreme Court or any courts of appeals. Another issue that has received some attention from scholars, but has not yet been invoked in a case, involves whether appointment of a trustee to participate in a church's bankruptcy case would be construed as governmental imposition on the free exercise of religion. *See, e.g.*, David A. Skeel, Jr., *"Sovereignty" Issues and the Church Bankruptcy Cases*, 29 Seton Hall Legis. J. 345 (2005).

C. BANKRUPTCY IN PRACTICE

1. Recall that Diana has a number of claims pending. On which of the following claims can the bankruptcy court render a final decision following *Stern* and its progeny?

   a. Bryan's claims against Diana alleging that she is past due on child support payments.
   b. Diana's claims against her health insurance provider for failure to pay some of Catie's medical expenses.
   c. Diana's boss's claim against her for intentional infliction of emotional distress for destroying his car.
   d. The insurance companies' claims against Diana for the payment on the boss's car and medical expenses.

2. When Diana first came to see you, she mentioned that she leases her car, and the lease has almost concluded. You know that Diana will likely need a car going forward. Can you advise her to enter into a new car lease or to purchase a new car *before* she files for bankruptcy? Once she files for bankruptcy protection, it may be more difficult for her to obtain financing for a car—at least without paying more for that credit!

CHAPTER

3

Property Law: Property of the Estate, Exemptions, and Avoiding Powers

Home is a shelter from storms — all sorts of storms.[1]

Bankruptcy requires a delicate balance between the rights of creditors and the needs of debtors. Creditors want to be paid, but leaving debtors with nothing makes recovery (and preventing future bankruptcy cases) difficult. The Code seeks to provide debtors with some assets for a financial future, while maximizing the recovery for creditors.

RECALL DIANA DETTER

Throughout this chapter we will consider the distribution of property to our debtor, Diana Detter, and to the bankruptcy trustee for the payment of creditors. Before Diana entered bankruptcy, she had several assets. Some of the assets were owned outright (her clothes, for example). Others were leased, like her car. She owed money against some of the assets, such as the mortgage on her house. And while she is in the bankruptcy case, she will acquire even more assets, such as income she earns from her job. The creditors would like to see those assets used to pay their claims, but Diana needs some assets to survive and be a productive member of society. Consider the Code provisions and the policies inherent in determining how to use assets to meet these competing goals.

---

1. William J. Bennett

A. PROPERTY OF THE ESTATE (§ 541)

At the heart of a bankruptcy case lies the property of the estate—property that will be used to make money for the estate and/or to make distributions to creditors. Section 541 of the Bankruptcy Code provides that the "estate is comprised of all the following property, wherever located and by whomever held," listing seven categories of property including "all legal or equitable interests of the debtor in property as of the commencement of the case." Read through § 541. You will see that § 541(a) provides a list of property that belongs to the bankruptcy estate, while § 541(b) provides exclusions from property of the estate. Consider your own assets and what would be property of the bankruptcy estate if you were to file a bankruptcy case (though, as you will see in the next section, many of your assets would be "exempted" from the bankruptcy case!).

As the Supreme Court has noted, the definition of "property of the estate" is very broad. In U.S. v. Whiting Pools, 462 U.S. 198 (1983), the Court considered whether property seized pre-petition from the debtor by the Internal Revenue Service belonged to the bankruptcy estate. In determining that property of the estate included the seized property, the Court held that Congress intended a broad reading of "property of the estate" and that broad reading could include property no longer in the debtor's possession. *Id.* at 204-205.

The Bankruptcy Code does not define "all legal or equitable interests of the debtor in property[]." Rather, that typically comes from state law—everything you learned in a first-year property course.

One topic you may have considered in first-year property is that ownership comprises possession and control (although many old cases use slightly different words to convey the same meaning). Particularly with personal property ("chattel"), possession is equivalent to ownership for most purposes. For example, you do not generally have to show a receipt to prove that you purchased your clothing you are wearing and therefore possess. The next case considers possession without ownership.

REMEMBER PROPERTY?

Property Law is a foundational first-year course at most law schools, sometimes called Real Property. You may recall that Property was different than most of your other first-year courses, because Property is more of a survey course than one specific doctrine. For example, while you covered a great many topics in Contracts or Torts, they led to a coherent understanding of a single doctrine. Property, on the other hand, covers personal property (chattel) and real property (land); other than an amorphous concept of ownership, the two have little in common. In addition, your Property course likely covered gifts, estates in land, future interests, concurrent interests, real estate transactions, urban planning and zoning, easements and covenants, and takings under the Fifth and Fourteenth Amendments. The broad range of these topics is why some students enjoy Property less than other first-year classes (although it is also the same reason why so many students like Property).

One recurring theme in Property is the "bundle of sticks." It may bring back less-than-pleasant memories for a few, but a brief refresher is important. We can own something outright (in which case we would possess the entire bundle of sticks). But we can share ownership with one or more people, and we can decide that others may get some or all of our property in the future. Under these circumstances, we no longer hold every twig in the bundle of sticks, and the twigs held by others are legally recognized property rights. In bankruptcy, we must review not just property owned outright (the whole bundle of sticks, or fee simple absolute in real property). In bankruptcy all of a debtor's assets are taken into account, which includes ownership rights that may be just one twig in the bundle. In fact, if a debtor benefits from a twig held by someone else, that twig may be in the mix as well.

The range of different kinds of property is so broad that it is difficult to come up with a single definition of property. But consider this: Property is not the thing (chattel or real property) you own as much as legal recognition of your ownership. It can therefore be said that property is a package of legally recognized rights held by one or more people. For bankruptcy law, Congress intended the definition of property "to sweep broadly to include 'all kinds of property, including tangible or intangible property, causes of action . . . and all other forms of property'" in the Bankruptcy Code. Westmoreland Human Opportunities v. Walsh, 246 F.3d 233, 242 (3d Cir. 2001) (citing U.S. v. Whiting Pools, Inc., 462 U.S. 198 (1983)).

Consider the legal recognition part of ownership to be key. An older relative may tell you that she will leave you a valuable family heirloom when she passes away. You now have a future interest called an "expectancy." The law recognizes many future interests, some just as speculative as a potential inheritance. But an expectancy is not a legally recognized future interest, probably because we want last wishes to be put in writing in a will to avoid confusion after a person's death. So while in a layperson sense you have been promised something of value, the law recognizes no ownership.

You may have learned in your Property class that ownership of property is based on possession and control; you probably considered this formula in the context of wild animals, particularly the famous case involving the fox, Pierson v. Post, 3 Cai. R. 175, 1805 N.Y. You may rightfully believe that you possess and control your body, including your kidneys. But the law does not recognize your ownership of your body in a conventional sense because you cannot sell a kidney, although you can gift one. Surprisingly, you do not possess every twig in the bundle of sticks when it comes to ownership of your body. While this may seem unfair or even outrageous to some, it illustrates that property, or at least property under the law, is limited (or even expanded) by choices of the people and the government in a democratic system.

Owning a wild animal through possession and control still works today, provided you were hunting the animal on land you own or had permission to be on, and as long as you complied with relevant laws and permitting processes regulating the taking of wild animals. And while the lesson of possession and control works well in an early introduction to property law, it is certainly not the end of the story.

Consider a thief. At least in a layperson sense, if a thief steals your chattel, the thief has both possession and control. But the law does not promote trespass or recognize ownership of a stolen item, regardless of possession and control; we the people, through our democratically elected government, do not recognize the thief's ownership of the stolen chattel. So instead we adopt a legal fiction and are considered to have constructive possession (and sometimes constructive control) of all our chattel wherever it is, at least with regard to a trespasser taking our chattel without our permission. So regardless of where the thief has taken your property, the thief does not legally possess the item because you continue to have constructive possession of it, even if you don't know where it is.

Reviewing these concepts is helpful for understanding bankruptcy. The disposition of a debtor's property is one of the most important aspects of bankruptcy. Regardless of a lay definition of property that works for most people without question, lawyers understand that property and ownership of property is a legal construct that sometimes is the same as a lay definition, but sometimes is quite different than what nonlawyers might expect. Bankruptcy is a statutory regime created by Congress that balances rights of creditors and debtors, as well as the interests of the nation as a whole. Bankruptcy limits some lay concepts and definitions of property and expands others. It is critical when studying bankruptcy law to look to the Code, bankruptcy case law, and often state law; the Bankruptcy Code contains some definitions of property, but more frequently applies state law to define property in the context of the Bankruptcy Code requirements. Do not assume that what might be considered property in torts or criminal law (or even first-year Property) is property for the purposes of bankruptcy.

Kitchen v. Boyd (In re Newpower)

233 F.3d 922 (6th Cir. 2000)

KENNEDY, Circuit Judge

Robert Kitchen ("Kitchen") and New Properties, Inc., ("NPI") (collectively referred to as "movants") moved the bankruptcy court to lift the 11 U.S.C. § 362 automatic stay in bankruptcy with respect to money that debtor George D. Newpower, Jr., ("Newpower" or "debtor") embezzled. Movants argued that the embezzled funds were not property of Newpower's bankruptcy estate because: as a thief Newpower did not take title[2] to the funds he embezzled; Newpower was acting as an agent and thus never had title to money loaned to NPI; money was held by Newpower pursuant to an express trust. The bankruptcy court held that the $171,516.48 that Newpower transferred directly to third parties from NPI was not property of Newpower's estate, but declined to lift the stay on the remaining $582,463. The Kitchens and NPI appealed the bankruptcy court's ruling to the district court, which held that none of the embezzled funds were property of Newpower's bankruptcy estate, and thus, were not subject to the automatic stay in bankruptcy. For the reasons that follow, we shall affirm in part and reverse in part.

* * *

In January of 1996, Kitchen and Newpower, a licensed Michigan real estate broker, entered an agreement to form NPI. The corporation's purpose was to purchase and develop real estate in northern Michigan. Kitchen and Newpower were the sole shareholders and directors of the corporation. . . .

Kitchen and Newpower agreed that Newpower would identify properties in Michigan for purchase and development by the corporation. If both shareholders agreed to purchase the property, NPI would do so, with a loan in the amount of 50% of the purchase price to the corporation by each shareholder. . . .

The first property that the shareholders agreed to purchase was an eighty-acre parcel in Kalkaska County, Michigan. The price of the property was $400,000, and as agreed, Kitchen and his wife (the

---

2. The term "title" is often used to describe ownership of property, but in the United States the word has more than one legal meaning. Most states issue a paper or electronic "title" to signify ownership of a motor vehicle or a house. States do not generally issue paper or electronic title for personal property, but even the law often uses the word "title" when referencing ownership of chattel. No one in the United States has a paper or electronic title to currency. Another refresher from first-year Property: Money is a form of chattel.

"Kitchens") sent a check to Newpower for $200,000. . . . Instead of using the money to purchase the agreed upon property, Newpower deposited the check in his personal account and used the $200,000 for his own purposes.

Thereafter, for the remainder of 1996, Kitchen and Newpower conducted regular telephone discussions regarding the Kalkaska property, as well as four other parcels. Prior to each closing, Newpower would tell Kitchen how much money was needed to purchase the specified property. The Kitchens would then wire funds totaling one-half of the purchase price of the property to the corporate account, on which Newpower was the sole authorized signatory. Newpower continued his practice of misappropriating the funds for his own use with respect to these transfers as well . . . .

When the Kitchens traveled to Michigan in December 1996 to check on the status of the properties, they quickly discovered that no properties had actually been purchased by Newpower. By investigating Newpower's financial records, the Kitchens were able to determine what Newpower had done with their money. Among other things, Newpower: bought a Corvette, a four-wheel drive pickup truck, and a power boat; built a new house for his girlfriend; loaned $60,000 to a former fiance; invested $50,000 in the production of a music CD for another girlfriend; spent tens of thousands of dollars in "loan repayments" to customer trust accounts for Newpower's real estate business; and made thousands of dollars of cash distributions to himself for "walking around money."

The Kitchens also filed a complaint with the Michigan Attorney General's office and a Michigan State Police investigation was commenced. Newpower initially fled, but eventually turned himself in and pled guilty to embezzlement. He was sentenced to six-to-ten years in prison and ordered to pay $755,000 in restitution to the Kitchens. Shortly thereafter, Newpower filed for bankruptcy . . . .

. . . The bankruptcy court concluded that the funds which were transferred by Newpower directly from the NPI account to a third party, without passing through Newpower's personal account, were not property of the estate. Accordingly, the court concluded that the Kitchens were entitled to proceed on their actions to recover such funds from the recipients. However, as to money that passed through Newpower's hands in any way or that was used to purchase assets titled in Newpower's name, the court concluded that it was property of the estate . . . .

Kitchen and NPI appealed the bankruptcy court's ruling to the district court. The district court held that the bankruptcy court erred in concluding that property traceable to the Kitchens' embezzled funds were property of Newpower's estate. . . .

* * *

This appeal raises the question of whether the money misappropriated by debtor, money and property traceable to the misappropriated funds, and claims or causes of action to recover money and property traceable to the misappropriated funds are property of debtor's bankruptcy estate. If the $582,463 of assets traceable to the money the Kitchens lent NPI is estate property, then pursuant to 11 U.S.C § 541, the trustee must collect and distribute the money in proportional shares to all creditors of the bankruptcy estate.

Section 541 provides: "(a) The commencement of a case under section 301, 302, or 303 of this title creates an estate. Such estate is comprised of all the following property, wherever located and by whomever held: (1) Except as provided in subsections (b) and (c)(2) of this section, all legal or equitable interests of the debtor in property as of the commencement of the case." 11 U.S.C. § 541(a). What qualifies as a property interest is determined by reference to state law, unless some federal interest requires a different result.

* * *

. . . Such property may take the form of legal or equitable interest in property held by the debtor as of the commencement of the case. . . . If debtor's estate had a property interest in the funds at issue, then as a fundamental principle of bankruptcy law, the funds should be ratably distributed to the creditors of the bankrupt estate . . . .

Movants argued that debtor stole the funds embezzled from NPI and further assert that because a thief takes no title under Michigan law, embezzled funds or proceeds thereof are not property of debtor's bankruptcy estate. . . .

* * *

A thief does not ordinarily become the owner of property he steals; he has mere possession. If the stolen property is found in his hands, it is recoverable by the injured party in a possessory action at law. There is no basis for a constructive trust as to the stolen property in the hands of the thief because of his lack of a property interest.

Bogert, Trust & Trustees § 476 at 119 (2d ed. 1978 & Supp. 1999) (citing cases recognizing this principle).

Appellees argue, however, that under Michigan law when title to property is obtained by fraud, the title is voidable, not void. . . . Appellees argue that this is significant, because Newpower pled guilty to embezzlement, which includes intent to defraud as a necessary element. . . . As a consequence, appellees conclude that Newpower obtained voidable title to the money he embezzled. In support, by way of analogy, appellees point out that under Michigan's crime of false pretenses with intent to defraud—which also contains fraud as an element of the offense—title to the stolen property is viewed as passing to the debtor. Thus, appellees reason, by defrauding the Kitchens and NPI, debtor obtained at least voidable title to the funds he stole.

Appellees correctly observe that under Michigan law, the critical difference between larceny crimes and false pretense crimes is the passage of title. . . . However, appellees' attempt to analogize the offense of embezzlement to false pretenses fails. . . . [A]n individual commits the crime of false pretenses when he fraudulently convinces another to part with *both* possession of and title to property. In such a situation, the offender obtains voidable title to the property . . . .

In contrast, the offense of embezzlement involves the fraudulent appropriation of property of which the embezzler is rightfully in possession; the owner of the property retains title to the funds because he never intends for it to pass to the embezzler. . . .

Moreover, regardless of what crime debtor pled guilty to, it is clear that NPI never intended to pass title in the appropriated funds to debtor. As the district court observed, Newpower had only limited authority to move corporate funds for authorized corporate purposes, i.e., to purchase the agreed upon properties. Thus, the $382,463 that debtor embezzled directly from NPI was never property of debtor's estate. . . . However, the same cannot be said of property that debtor purchased for himself with the stolen money. The good faith seller from which the thief purchases property intends to pass both title and possession of the property sold to the thief, and obtains good title to the money the thief provides. . . . Accordingly, the thief obtains legal title to the goods purchased, which thereby become part of his estate. . . .

The original owner would normally not be without remedy in such a situation, as a constructive trust may be imposed on the proceeds held by the thief or embezzler. Bogert, Trust & Trustees § 476 at n. 74 (2d ed. 1978 & Supp. 1999) (collecting cases standing for this proposition). However, under *In re Omegas,* a constructive trust is an equitable interest that exempts property from the bankrupt's estate under § 541(d), *only* if the trust is declared by a court in a separate *prepetition* proceeding or a state statute provides that the property is to be held in trust for a particular purpose.

Thus, we hold that the bankruptcy court erred in concluding that money which debtor embezzled from NPI was part of debtor's bankruptcy estate. Consequently, we also hold that the debtor's bankruptcy estate has no property interest in such embezzled funds which are now in the hands of third parties. As discussed, debtor never had a legal interest in such funds and appellants should be allowed to pursue third party recipients to recover embezzled funds and property traceable to such funds to the extent that the law allows. Finally, with respect to items debtor obtained with the embezzled funds, while debtor did not obtain equitable title to these proceeds, he did obtain legal title; all that is necessary to include those assets in the bankruptcy estate. Consequently, we conclude such proceeds are part of debtor's bankruptcy estate and are thus subject to an automatic stay in bankruptcy under 11 U.S.C. § 362 . . . .

(Citations omitted.)

NOTES AND COMMENTS

1. The trustee argued that the debtor's title to the embezzled funds was "voidable" rather than "void." Why would that make a difference under 11 U.S.C. § 541(a)?

2. Keep in mind the importance of state property rights in determining whether the debtor has an interest in property such that it becomes part of the estate. The court in In re Berkman, 517 B.R. 288 (Bankr. M.D. Fla. 2014) distinguished the facts in the case from the situation in the *Newpower* case. Of particular importance was a state-law exception that allowed a thief to pass good title to an innocent purchaser. *Id.* at 307.

3. Intent is a relevant element in criminal law and torts. How does the intent of parties other than the debtor matter in determining whether property falls within the estate?

4. Consider the case of In re Mississippi Valley Livestock, Inc., 745 F.3d 299 (7th Cir. 2014). The debtor had contracted with J & R Farms to sell cattle on J & R's behalf. The debtor made a $900,000 payment to J & R Farms before filing, and the trustee sought to return those funds to the debtor's estate in an action that will be discussed later in this chapter entitled a "preferential transfer." To determine whether the money could be recovered required a determination of whether the payment

constituted property of the estate. The court held that the debtor held J & R Farms' cattle as a bailee, such that the property never actually *belonged* to the debtor. The money resulting from the sale of those items held in a bailment relationship was then held in a constructive trust for the benefit of J & R Farms. Funds held in trust are excluded from the estate under § 541(b)(1). Thus, J & R Farms always owned the cattle and the cash proceeds of that cattle outside of the bankruptcy case.

5. Though the property fell within the estate in this case, the Kitchens had a remedy that will be discussed later in the chapter to seek recovery outside of the bankruptcy system.

11 U.S.C. § 542

Recovery of Property of the Estate by Trustee
Section 542 of the Bankruptcy Code provides the mechanism for a trustee to recover property of the estate from parties in possession of that property. This includes any property that the trustee might be able to "use, sell, or lease" in the case, any property which the debtor may exempt, or any claims due and payable to the debtor that are property of the estate.

Of course, property of the estate has some limitations—not everything that the debtor has ever touched belongs in the bankruptcy estate. Some of those limitations are provided in 11 U.S.C. § 541(b); a few are more likely to arise in individual cases. For example, to the extent that the debtor has a legal right, but only for the benefit of another, the property is not included in the estate under § 541(b)(1). This would preclude the assets of a trust from being included in the trustee's bankruptcy estate. Certain educational accounts are also excluded from property of the estate under §§ 541(b)(5) and (b)(6). Finally, employee withholding for various benefit plans are also kept out of the estate under § 541(b)(7).

WHAT IS A TRUST?

A trust is a fiduciary relationship in three parts: the *settlor* transfers ownership of property (generally money) to a *trustee* (not to be confused with the bankruptcy trustee) to manage on behalf of the *beneficiary*. Some states permit one person to have all three roles, but the concept is best understood when three individuals or entities are involved. Trusts can be irrevocable or revocable. A revocable trust remains in the grantor's estate until death. Since the settlor in a revocable trust retains the power to revoke the trust, the trust property is subject to the claims of creditors.

In an irrevocable trust, once the settlor creates the trust and transfers the property, the settlor forfeits all property rights. The trustee has legal ownership of the property but has a fiduciary duty to manage the property for the beneficiary. The beneficiary has equitable ownership of the property and receives whatever benefits are afforded under the terms of the trust as established by the settlor.

Trusts are used in a myriad of ways, including allowing children to benefit from money without controlling it. Trusts have many positive attributes that can be used in estate planning and to minimize taxation. Most pensions are set up as a trust, where the employer is the settlor and the employees are the beneficiaries.

The Bankruptcy Code and case law frequently refer to a debtor's "legal or equitable interest in property." A legal interest is simple ownership, or at least ownership recognized by the Bankruptcy Code through the lens of relevant state law.

Equitable interest is more complicated, but a trust is an excellent example. The beneficiary of a trust does not own the trust's assets but benefits by owning an equitable interest in disbursements from the trust. The beneficiary does not own the trust, but is the only party permitted to receive any financial gain from the trust, and thus has an equitable interest. Similarly, the trustee controls the instrument that has legal ownership of the trust and its assets but is not permitted to financially benefit from the trust.

Whether the debtor holds an interest in property must be determined as of commencement of the case. But determination of the date on which a person or entity obtains a right to the property is not always clear. For example, an employee who works an eight-hour day has a right to be paid for that work as soon as the work is performed, even if the employee won't actually receive the paycheck for a few weeks. On the other hand, it is less clear when an employee who received an annual bonus at the end of the year earned that bonus. Is it earned at the end of the year, or by working throughout the year? The next case considers the timing of an income tax refund from the IRS and whether it becomes a part of the bankruptcy estate.

In re Meyers

616 F.3d 626 (7th Cir. 2010)

WOOD, Circuit Judge

This case involves a recurring question under the bankruptcy laws: what belongs in the bankruptcy estate? In general, assets that were acquired before the time when the bankruptcy petition is filed—so-called pre-petition assets—are available to satisfy pre-petition debts. Overgeneralizing, one can say that post-petition assets belong to the debtor and are not encumbered by any liabilities that were discharged in bankruptcy. By the same token, any liabilities incurred by the debtor post-petition may not be discharged in the bankruptcy proceeding, nor should the bankruptcy process compel the pre-petition creditors to bear any burden as a result of these post-petition obligations.

Allocating assets and liabilities to the correct side of the pre- and post-petition line is usually a straightforward task, but occasionally the job becomes challenging. Debtor Andrea Meyers's case falls in the latter category. The question we must resolve in her appeal is how best to allocate post-petition tax refunds when the debtor filed her bankruptcy petition in the middle of the tax year. The bankruptcy court used a mechanical system known as the *"pro rata* by days" method to calculate the proportion of the refunds that belonged to the pre-petition asset pool. Meyers filed her petition approximately 73% of the way through the tax year, and accordingly, using that method, 73% of her tax refund qualified as a pre-petition asset. In taking that approach, the bankruptcy court followed a well-trodden path. Meyers, however, thought that it was the wrong path and took an appeal to the district court. That court affirmed the bankruptcy court. . . . While we recognize that the *pro rata* method may not be appropriate for all cases, we find that the bankruptcy court properly applied it here, and so we affirm.

. . . The facts of this case are undisputed. Meyers filed a petition for relief under Chapter 7 of the Bankruptcy Code on September 25, 2007. September 25 was the 268th day of 2007, meaning that approximately 73.42% of the year had passed by then. At that point, Meyers's pay stub indicates that she had earned $37,133.43 in 2007, with gross taxable income of $33,855.26. Meyers's total 2007 income turned out to be $47,256.42 and total 2007 gross taxable income was $44,136; the September 25 figures therefore represent about 78.6% and 76.7% of the annual totals, respectively. Meyers's federal and state withholding tracked her income; her September

25 pay stub reflects that about 77% of her total 2007 withholding accrued prior to that date. For ease of reference, we have presented this information about Meyers's 2007 income and withholding in the table below:

MEYERS'S 2007 INCOME AND WITHHOLDING			
Category	2007 Totals	2007 Pre-Petition	2007 Pre-Petition Ratio
Gross Income	$47,256.42	$37,133.43	78.6%
Gross Taxable Income	$44,136.00	$33,855.26	76.7%
Federal Withholding	$ 5,983.00	$ 4,634.91	77.5%
State Withholding	$ 1,727.00	$ 1,330.00	77.0%

The next important step for our purposes occurred when Meyers filed her 2007 federal and state income tax returns. Meyers's federal tax return reported that she owed $2,661 and had withheld $5,983. On that basis, she requested a refund of $3,322. Her Missouri tax return reported an overpayment of $216 for which she also requested a refund. (Meyers works in Missouri, but she is a resident of Illinois and filed her bankruptcy petition in Illinois, which explains why this case ended up here rather than the Eighth Circuit.) In 2008, months after filing her bankruptcy petition, Meyers received federal and state tax refunds for 2007 totaling $3,538.

This $3,538 is the subject of Meyers's appeal. In August 2008, Trustee Laura K. Grandy (the "Trustee") filed a motion for turnover of the bankruptcy estate's share of Meyers's 2007 federal and state tax refunds. See 11 U.S.C. § 542. Conceptually, the Trustee regarded the amounts withheld in excess of the taxes due as a form of enforced savings; if Meyers's withholding had been exactly equal to the taxes she owed, and she had put the remainder in a savings account during the pre-petition period, it would be plain that the amount saved would belong in the bankruptcy estate. Relying on this theory, the Trustee asserted that the bankruptcy estate was entitled to the pre-petition portion of each refund, calculated based on the *pro rata* by days method. Since Meyers filed for bankruptcy 73.42% of the way through the tax year, this method yielded $2,597.60 as the portion of the refunds that belonged to the estate. . . .

* * *

Before analyzing Meyers's specific situation, we step back to discuss why tax refunds pose a particular problem. Under the Bankruptcy Code, a trustee is assigned to administer the bankruptcy estate; to that end, the property of the estate must be turned over to the trustee. 11 U.S.C. § 542. Property of the bankruptcy estate is defined to include "all legal and equitable interests of the debtor in property as of the commencement of the case." *Id.* § 541(a)(1). As noted earlier, the time of the petition (the "commencement of the case," *id.* § 301(a)) is the key point for identifying the assets of the estate.

Courts have recognized that tax refunds received after the petition may, in some cases, represent pre-petition assets and thus are part of the bankruptcy estate. . . . The background rule under the old Bankruptcy Act, to which courts still refer in the era of the Bankruptcy Code, defines the bankruptcy estate to include property that is "sufficiently rooted in the pre-bankruptcy past and so little entangled with the bankrupts' ability to make an unencumbered fresh start." . . .

These general rules provide the background for resolving disputes over tax refunds, but they are only a starting point. The fact that reasonable people can identify competing methods for calculating the pre-petition share of the refunds betrays the incompleteness of a rule that simply calls for identifying at what time an asset became "rooted." In this case, the parties proffer two competing calculations. As described above, the Trustee argues that the best method for this case is the *pro rata* by days calculation. The Trustee recognizes that this method is not appropriate in all cases—for example, for debtors whose income fluctuates widely from month to month throughout the year—but given the steady rate with which Meyers's income, withholding, and anticipated refunds grew, it works here. . . .

Meyers urges us to select a different methodology, one articulated by the U.S. Bankruptcy Court for the Western District of Texas in *In re Donnell,* 357 B.R. 386 (Bankr. W.D. Tx. 2006). . . . The bankruptcy court . . . noted that the *pro rata* method assumed that "the debtor had a steady income during the tax year, had regular withholding of income taxes throughout the tax year, and had an interest in any refundable tax credits that grew regularly over the tax year." The Donnells did not. Therefore, the court concluded that it had to "examine each of the *components* of the tax refund to determine whether, on the petition date, the debtor possessed a legal or equitable interest in that component." Most importantly for Meyers's case, the court in *Donnell* held that the bankruptcy estate was entitled to the debtor's tax refund only to the extent that the pre-petition withholding amount exceeded the tax liability for the entire year. It is this formula that Meyers asks us to apply to her case.

* * *

Under the defunct Bankruptcy Act, we laid out the burdens of persuasion in turnover actions as follows. The trustee must bring the action to claim property for the bankruptcy estate, and she bears the burden of establishing a *prima facie* case for turnover . . . .

* * *

With this background established, we are ready to look at the Trustee's *prima facie* case. . . . The Trustee identified the value of the 2007 tax refunds, properly calculated the *pro rata* by days share, and asked the district court to accept this calculation. This evidence alone may be enough for a *prima facie* case, but the Trustee went further here. She noted, as described above, that the debtor's income and withholding advanced at a fairly steady rate throughout the tax year, and there were no income or withholding spikes after she filed her bankruptcy petition that would be swept in unfairly by the *pro rata* method. The district court noted, for example, that Meyers's pre-petition and post-petition withholding represented similar percentages of her taxable earnings (17.6% versus 16.9%). . . . In fact, as our table above indicates, the *pro rata* by days method represents a smaller request (73.42% of the refunds) than a calculation based on the pre-petition proportion of Meyers's total income, gross taxable income, or federal and state withholding (ranging from 76% to 78%). These data were good enough for the bankruptcy court and the district court, and they are good enough for us.

Having established the *prima facie* case for turnover, we look to the debtor for reason to go forward. Meyers did not meet this obligation. One would have expected a debtor in her position to present specific facts showing where and how the progression of her income, liabilities, and withholding deviated from a perfectly linear function, thus making the *pro rata* by days method a poor fit. Meyers took a different tack, arguing vociferously for an alternative calculation of the estate's share, without much attention paid to the specifics of her case. Meyers wants us to apply *Donnell,* and that is nearly all she has to say on the matter . . . .

* * *

(Citations omitted.)

NOTES AND COMMENTS

1. The issue of allocation between pre- and post-petition assets arises in a variety of contexts other than tax refunds. Consider each of the following cases:

   a. In re Powell, 511 B.R. 107 (Bankr. C.D. Ill. 2014) — Consolidated cases involving debtors who were entitled to profit sharing at their company; profit-sharing year began in November and ended the following November; share of profits was determined based on hours worked and hourly wages; each debtor filed bankruptcy petition during the summer; to qualify, the employee must have been employed for at least a year at the beginning of the profit-sharing period and must be employed at the end of the profit-sharing period.

   b. In re Jokiel, 447 B.R. 868 (Bankr. N.D. Ill. 2011) — The severance payment was received post-petition; the employment contract entered into pre-petition provided for payment based on date of future dismissal; the amount the debtor received upon severance was same amount that the debtor would have received had the debtor been let go pre-petition — the only reason the debtor received it post-petition is that is when he was let go from company.

   c. In re Prochnow, 467 B.R. 656 (Bankr. C.D. Ill. 2012) — The real estate commission was based on pre-petition sale but not received until post-petition when closing occurred; the commission contract provided that commissions were not "earned or payable" until closing.

2. Who has the burden of proof in determining whether property belongs to the estate, and how does that burden change as evidence is presented?

EXPANSION OF PROPERTY OF THE ESTATE: INHERITANCE, SETTLEMENT, LIFE INSURANCE, AND OTHER "WINDFALLS" (11 U.S.C. § 541(A)(5))

While property that the debtor acquires post-petition is ordinarily excluded from the estate in a Chapter 7 case, there are some instances in which the debtor receives property post-petition that must be turned over to the estate if the debtor becomes entitled to them within 180 days post-petition. These include any interest as a result of inheritance, divorce property settlement, life insurance beneficiary benefits, or death benefit plans.

Lottery winnings are generally considered to be part of the bankruptcy estate only if the lottery ticket was purchased pre-petition.

Chapter 13 expands upon § 541's definition of property of the estate, including "all property . . . that the debtor acquires" and "earnings from services performed by the debtor" between commencement and termination (whether "closed, dismissed, or converted") of the Chapter 13 case.

11 U.S.C. § 1306. Thus, while Chapter 7 provides a relatively clear delineation between pre-petition and post-petition property in determining whether property belongs to the estate, Chapter 13 continues to add property to the estate as long as the case continues.

In the next case the court considers whether an inheritance can be considered part of a bankruptcy estate when the money was gifted after the Chapter 13 proceedings began.

Carroll v. Logan

735 F.3d 147 (4th Cir. 2013)

WYNN, Circuit Judge

This appeal concerns whether Bankruptcy Code Section 1306(a) extends the 180–day time limit under Bankruptcy Code Section 541 for identifying property that may be included in a bankruptcy estate. Appellants Rickey Dean Carroll and Cheri Carroll argue that the bankruptcy court erred by including an inheritance that postdated their Chapter 13 bankruptcy petition by more than 180 days as part of their bankruptcy estate. Because Section 1306(a) plainly extends the timeline for including "the kind" of property "specified in" Section 541 in Chapter 13 bankruptcy estates, we affirm the bankruptcy court's inclusion of the inheritance in the Carrolls' Chapter 13 bankruptcy estate.

. . . In February 2009, the Carrolls filed a joint petition for relief under Chapter 13 of the Bankruptcy Code. Under that reorganization chapter, debtors with regular income pay back a portion of their debts through a repayment plan. The Carrolls' repayment plan, approved in August 2009, required them to pay $2,416 for 6 months followed by $2,480 for 54 months.

In August 2012, over three years after filing their Chapter 13 petition, the Carrolls notified the bankruptcy court that Mr. Carroll's mother had died in December 2011 and that, as a consequence, Mr. Carroll anticipated an inheritance of approximately $100,000. Because Mr. Carroll acquired the inherited interest before their bankruptcy case was closed, dismissed, or converted to a proceeding under another bankruptcy code chapter, the Chapter 13 trustee moved to modify the Carrolls' repayment plan to include "an amount of the Inheritance, if and when received, sufficient to pay in full all of the allowed general unsecured claims. . . ." . . . .

Over the Carrolls' objection, the bankruptcy court held that Mr. Carroll's inheritance was property of the bankruptcy estate. . . . The Carrolls noticed their appeal, and the bankruptcy court stayed its order and certified a direct appeal to this Court.

* * *

The interplay of Bankruptcy Code Sections 541 and 1306 is at the heart of this dispute. We begin our analysis with the statutes' plain language . . . .

Bankruptcy Code Section 541 identifies the property included in bankruptcy estates generally. 11 U.S.C. § 541. The statute, which is not specific to any particular type of bankruptcy proceeding, includes in estates:

> (5) Any interest in property that would have been property of the estate if such interest had been an interest of the debtor on the date of the filing of the petition, and that the debtor acquires or becomes entitled to acquire within 180 days after such date—
> (A) by bequest, devise, or *inheritance.* . . .

11 U.S.C. § 541(a)(5) (emphasis added).

Section 1306(a) then expands the definition of estate property for Chapter 13 cases specifically, stating:

> (a) Property of the estate includes, *in addition to the property specified in section 541* of [the Code]—
> (1) all property *of the kind specified in such section* that the debtor acquires after the commencement of the case but *before the case is closed, dismissed, or converted* to a case under chapter 7, 11, or 12 of [the Code], whichever occurs first; . . . .

11 U.S.C. § 1306(a) (emphasis added).

Congress has harmonized these two statutes for us. With Section 541, Congress established a general definition for bankruptcy estates. With Section 1306, it then expanded on that definition specifically for purposes of Chapter 13 cases. Thus, "Section 1306 broadens the definition of property of the estate for chapter 13 purposes to include all property acquired and all earnings from services performed by the debtor after the commencement of the case." S.Rep. No. 95–989, at 140–41 (1978).

The statutes' plain language manifests Congress's intent to expand the estate for Chapter 13 purposes by capturing the types, or "kind," of property described in Section 541 (such as bequests, devises, and inheritances), but not the 180–day temporal restriction. 11 U.S.C. § 1306(a). This is because "[t]he kind of property is a distinct concept from the time at which the debtor's interest in the property was acquired." . . . And on its face, Section 1306(a) incorporates only the kind of property described in Section 541 into its expanded temporal framework.

In essence, Section 1306 is a straightforward formula for calculating Chapter 13 estates:

A Chapter 13 Bankruptcy Estate	=	Property described in Section 541	+	The kind of property (e.g., inheritances) described in Section 541 and acquired before the Chapter 13 case is closed, dismissed, or converted

See 11 U.S.C. 1306(a).

. . . Chapter 13 proceedings provide debtors with significant benefits: For example, debtors may retain encumbered assets and have their defaults cured, while secured creditors have long-term payment plans imposed upon them and unsecured creditors may receive payment on only a fraction of their claims. See 11 U.S.C. §§ 1322, 1325.

In exchange for those benefits, a Chapter 13 debtor makes a multi-year commitment to repay obligations under a court-confirmed plan. *Id.* The repayment plan remains subject to modification for reasons including a debtor's decreased ability to pay according to plan, as well as the debtor's increased ability to pay. See 11 U.S.C. § 1329. As we have stated before, "[w]hen a [Chapter 13] debtor's financial fortunes improve, the creditors should share some of the wealth."

* * *

The Carrolls nevertheless contend that Mr. Carroll's inheritance should be excluded from their Chapter 13 bankruptcy estate under two principles of statutory interpretation: the principle that courts "must give effect to every word of a statute," and the principle that "specific language in a statute governs general language." . . .

Unquestionably, we agree that courts should give effect to every word of a statute whenever possible. . . . And doing so here requires us to reject the Carrolls' argument. For if Section 541's 180–day rule restricts what is included in a Chapter 13 estate, then Section 1306(a), which expands the temporal restriction for Chapter 13 purposes, loses all meaning. By contrast, neither statute is rendered superfluous, and both are given effect, if Section 1306(a)'s extended timing applies to Chapter 13 estates and supplements Section 541 with property acquired before the Chapter 13 case is closed, dismissed, or converted.

Further, while we know well the "canon of construction that 'the specific governs the general,'" . . . applying that canon here does not further the Carrolls' cause. In particular, we reject the Carrolls' contention that Section 541(a)(5) is "specific" while Section 1306(a) is "general." On the contrary, Section 1306(a) is specific to Chapter 13 bankruptcies and defines estates solely for purposes of that reorganization chapter. Section 541, by contrast, is a general provision that provides generic contours for bankruptcy estates. Thus, even under the two statutory interpretation principles the Carrolls press, the bankruptcy court properly included the inherited property in the Carrolls' bankruptcy estate.

* * *

(Citations omitted.)

NOTES AND COMMENTS

1. Consider the various policies at work here. Why does § 541 include property that a debtor obtains as a result of inheritance, property settlement, or life insurance within six months post-petition? And what are the policies behind expansion of property of the estate in Chapter 13? When combined, do the policies suggest whether § 541's temporal limitation should apply in Chapter 13 cases?

2. The court also noted that the majority of other courts considering the issue have held that the 180-day limitation of § 541(a)(5) does not apply in Chapter 13 cases. *Carroll*, 735 F.3d at 151, citing In re Vannordstrand, 356 B.R. 788 (B.A.P. 10th Cir. 2007). While the majority view, other courts have held that the time limitation in § 541(a)(5) applies even in the Chapter 13 context. *See, for example*, Le v. Walsh (In re Walsh), 2011 WL 2621018 at *2 (Bankr. S.D. Ga. June 15, 2011), which analyzed the same provision, finding that:

> a proper construction of the provisions incorporates the time limitation of § 541(a)(5) into § 1306(a)(1). In this way, "of the kind specified" draws in all of the specifications set forth in § 541(a)(5) rather than discarding a time limitation—a defining clause—absent evidence that Congress had intended that result. Such a reading does not render the seemingly conflicting time limitations set forth in 1306(a)(1) superfluous. Indeed, any interest in an inheritance acquired by a debtor in a chapter 13 case postconfirmation but within 180 days of the filing of a petition is undoubtedly property of the estate.

In addition, principles of statutory construction advise that general provisions within a statute should not, as a rule, be read to supersede specific substantive provisions. . . . Here, the more specific date restriction that helps define the kind of property included in the estate pursuant to § 541(a)(5) controls and is not superseded by conflicting temporal elements of § 1306(a)(1).

B. THE AUTOMATIC STAY (§ 362)

Once property is part of the bankruptcy estate, the Code protects it from the advances of creditors. This not only promotes the fresh start of the debtor, but also ensures a fair distribution to creditors. But the automatic stay covers much more than just the property of the estate. Read § 362 and consider which of the following actions would be permitted after a bankruptcy filing:

- A creditor's action to create a security interest (known as a "lien") against the debtor's car obtained post-petition in order to satisfy a pre-petition claim
- Criminal prosecution of the debtor for shoplifting
- A creditor's attempt to bring a lawsuit against the debtor on the basis of a pre-petition breach of contract
- A creditor's attempt to repossess property of the estate on the basis of a judgment obtained against the debtor pre-petition
- An ex-wife's attempt to collect child support owed pre-petition from the debtor's post-petition earnings

Generally, any action against the debtor on a pre-petition claim or against property of the estate is stayed in order to allow pre-petition assets to be fairly distributed to pre-petition creditors in the bankruptcy case. For that reason, the creditor cannot attempt to create a lien (§ 362(a)(5)), bring (or continue) a lawsuit on a pre-petition claim (§ 362(a)(1)), or attempt to repossess property from the estate (§ 362(a)(3)). Nor can the debtor enforce pre-petition judgments (§ 362(a)(2)), place liens on property of the estate (§ 362(a)(4)), or set off debts owed to the debtor (§ 362(a)(7)). But there are situations in which pre-petition claims against the debtor or claims against property of the estate are permitted. For example, a pre-petition domestic support obligation can be collected against property of the *debtor* (§ 362(b)(2)(B)) and even against property of the *estate* if pursuant to a statute or an order (§ 362(b)(2)(C)). Criminal actions against the debtor are not stayed (§ 362(b)(1)), and the government can audit debtors and assess tax liabilities (§ 362(b)(9)). Section 362(b) provides many other non-stayed actions which come up in more specialized situations. An interesting question is whether a university's refusal to provide a transcript violates the automatic stay. See if you agree with the court's decision.

In re Kuehn

563 F.3d 289 (7th Cir. 2009)

EASTERBROOK, Chief Judge

This case presents a single question: Does a university violate the Bankruptcy Code's automatic stay or discharge injunction by refusing to provide a transcript because pre-petition debt remains unpaid?

Stefanie Kim Kuehn, an art teacher, enrolled in a two-year master's degree program at Cardinal Stritch University. She took advantage of the University's pay-as-you-go plan but stopped paying midway through the first year. The University nonetheless allowed her to take exams, receive grades, and sign up for new classes. She completed all of the work required for a master's degree, which the University awarded. But when Kuehn asked for a transcript—the proof necessary to receive an increase in salary from her school district—the University refused because she owed more than $6,000 in tuition.

Unwilling to pay her debt to the University—even though the increase in her salary would cover the whole tuition in less than two years, and she could have borrowed against that increase—and unable to obtain a transcript without payment, Kuehn filed a bankruptcy petition listing the University as a creditor. (Kuehn's lawyer had advised her that the University would have to provide her a transcript if she filed for bankruptcy.) While the case was pending Kuehn again requested a transcript, and the University again refused to provide one. After the bankruptcy court issued an order discharging her debt to the University, 11 U.S.C. § 727, Kuehn yet again asked for a transcript and as before agreed to pay the transcript fee, but not the tuition. Again the University refused. Kuehn contends that the pre-discharge refusal violated the Bankruptcy Code's automatic stay, 11 U.S.C. § 362(a), and the later one the discharge injunction, 11 U.S.C. § 524(a), because the refusals were acts to collect her unpaid debt. Bankruptcy Judge Martin ordered the University to provide a transcript and pay damages and attorneys' fees. The district court affirmed . . . .

Section 362(a)(6) prohibits pre-petition creditors from taking "any act to collect, assess, or recover a claim against the debtor that arose before [the filing of a bankruptcy petition]" until the bankruptcy proceeding is closed or dismissed. Section 524(a)(2) "operates as an injunction against . . . an act, to collect . . . [discharged debt] as a personal liability of the debtor". Other subsections prohibit using legal process to collect, enforcing a pre-petition judgment, or exercising control over the property of the debtor. See §§ 362(a)(1)-(3), 524(a)(1)-(3). Kuehn argues that the University violated these sections when it refused to produce her transcript. According to her, because a transcript has no intrinsic value to the University, a refusal to provide one must be an act to collect. The University concedes that its policy is designed to induce students to pay their tuition, but it maintains that an "act to collect" for the purpose of the Bankruptcy Code is limited to a positive step, such as repossessing a car. A passive failure to do what the debtor desires is not an "act," the University submits. The University treats the transcript as a product that it is not obliged to sell to someone with whom it no longer wants to do business.

* * *

But Kuehn is willing to pay in advance for a transcript of her grades, and the University's only reason for balking is to induce her to pay for the education—yet that debt has been discharged. The University contends that it does not have a contractual obligation to provide a transcript and that, without an obligation, a passive refusal to deal cannot be an act to collect. It relies on *Citizens Bank of Maryland v. Strumpf*, 516 U.S. 16 . . . (1995). . . . *Strumpf* held that a bank did not violate the automatic stay by placing a hold on a checking account while asking the bankruptcy court to lift the stay, so that the bank could set off the account's balance against an obligation the debtor owed to the bank. The Court concluded that a hold designed to maintain the status quo while the bankruptcy court considers the request does not violate § 362. . . . This does not imply that the bank could keep the account blocked no matter what happened in the bankruptcy, or even after a discharge. The Court concluded that the bank's delay was not an act to collect because it had a right under state law, a right preserved by the Bankruptcy Code, to set off the checking-account balance against the debt to the bank. That right would be undercut if the automatic stay permitted the debtor to drain the checking account while the bank's hands were tied. But money owed to a university cannot be set off against a transcript of grades—the two items are not of similar character, . . . and the University's refusal is not designed to afford time for judicial decision.

* * *

At oral argument we asked the University if it could charge Kuehn a large sum (say, 25% of the salary increase she stands to receive from her employer) for a transcript. It replied that it could not. That answer undermines its position that it has no obligation to provide a transcript to Kuehn. . . . [P]roviding a transcript is an implicit part of the educational contract, covered by the fee for the course hours, and . . . Kuehn therefore has a contract or property right for which she has already paid. (Well, she hasn't paid, but her obligation to do so has been discharged, so it comes to the same thing.) The University cannot charge Kuehn extra if the fee for instruction covers transcripts too. Then the University's refusal to certify a transcript of Kuehn's grades would be an act to collect the discharged debt and would violate both the automatic stay and the discharge injunction. . . .

Well, then, does Kuehn have a property interest because a certified transcript is part of the package of goods and services that a college offers in exchange for tuition? Property interests are created and defined by state law unless a federal law requires a different result. . . .

Wisconsin courts have not considered whether a student has a contract or property right to receive a transcript. No Wisconsin statute is on point. Under Wisconsin common law, property rights may arise from custom and usage. . . . Universities have consistently provided transcripts at or around cost. . . . We could not find any case in any court where a university had asserted that it could charge a student more than cost for a transcript, and, as far as we can tell, no university has ever tried to profit by charging a fee based on the transcript's effect on a student's future income. . . .

That Wisconsin has not previously recognized a right to receive a transcript does not affect our analysis. Since colleges don't treat registrars' offices as profit centers, the question has not arisen. What we need to know is how the Supreme Court of Wisconsin would handle it if it were to come up. And we think it likely—it is impossible to say more—that the state judiciary would deem the students and colleges to be joint owners of the data reflecting grades, because that is how the educational contract is routinely understood.

* * *

Kuehn's property right might be limited to her grades, an intangible right similar to the right in a name or likeness, . . . and not include a right to receive a transcript from the University certifying those grades. But the custom of universities has been to provide certified transcripts, and for good reason. Intangible grades are worthless without proof. Kuehn's school district increases compensation only after it receives a certified transcript. . . . A right to receive a certified copy of a transcript is essential to a meaningful property right in grades.

That a student has a right to a copy of the transcript does not leave educational institutions without the means to collect tuition. The University is unable to collect Kuehn's tuition only because it was careless. When Kuehn failed to pay her mounting bills the University could have refused to let her enroll in new classes. It could have refused to let her take exams. It could have refused to award a degree. Or the University could have required Kuehn to borrow from a third party to pay for her education. . . . Presumably the University will protect itself in one or more of these ways in the future.

Giving weight to custom that amounts to an implicit term of the educational contract, and following the reasoning in *Hirsch,* we conclude that Kuehn has a state-law right to receive a certified copy of her transcript. The University's refusal to honor that right until Kuehn paid her back tuition was an act to collect a debt and thereby violated the automatic stay and discharge injunction. . . .

(Citations omitted.)

NOTES AND COMMENTS

1. Why does Kuehn's property right in the transcript matter to the court's analysis? If the court had determined that Kuehn had no right to the transcript, could it still have determined that a violation of the stay (and ultimately, the discharge order) occurred?

2. The court refers to the U.S. Supreme Court case of Citizens Bank of Md. v. Strumpf, 516 U.S. 16 (1995). *Strumpf* involved a bank freezing the debtor's bank account in order to prevent the debtor from draining the account while the bank pursued a motion for relief from the automatic stay. The Supreme Court held that freezing the account did not violate the stay. Under what provision would the debtor have argued that freezing the account is a violation of the stay?

3. Consider whether the case would have been decided differently if the university had the following policy in place: "Transcript Fee: Students and alumni in good standing may purchase transcripts for $10. Students and alumni with unpaid fees due to the university will be charged the amount of the unpaid fees plus $10 in order to receive a transcript."

Creditors may enter the bankruptcy case as secured creditors—creditors who have a lien on specific assets that now belong in the bankruptcy estate. For those creditors, the automatic stay creates a barrier to recovery that does not exist outside of the bankruptcy system. But § 362(d) provides some ability to take property out of the estate—known as "relief from stay." Two of the bases for relief from stay arise most frequently: (1) the debtor has no equity in the property and it "is not necessary to an effective reorganization," or (2) relief for cause. In a case discussed in the last section, the court went on to consider how bringing property into the estate invokes the automatic stay. Recall that in *Kitchen*, the court determined that property that a debtor purchased with stolen funds became part of the bankruptcy estate because the debtor held a legal right resulting from the seller's intent to transfer legal title to the debtor. The Kitchens then sought relief from the stay in order to pursue a state-law constructive trust action against the purchased property. The court granted the Kitchens' motion for relief from the stay in order to pursue a state-law constructive trust action against the purchased items. Thus, the court utilized a two-step process: first determining that the property purchased qualified as property of the estate (which, in turn, meant that the property was protected by the stay) and, second, granting relief to the creditor to go after the property once in the bankruptcy estate. The following case discusses relief from the automatic stay in the context of collecting on a pre-petition arbitration award.

Chizzali v. Gindi (In re Gindi)

642 F.3d 865 (10th Cir. 2011)

HARTZ, Circuit Judge

Jack Gindi filed a voluntary petition for relief under Chapter 11 of the Bankruptcy Code while the Colorado Court of Appeals was considering two appeals arising out of a lawsuit brought against him by Andreas Chizzali, his former partner in two companies. The bankruptcy court refused to lift the automatic stay to permit further proceedings regarding the two issues raised by Chizzali in his appeal; but it ruled that the automatic stay did not apply to Gindi's separate appeal. The Tenth Circuit Bankruptcy Appellate Panel (BAP) affirmed and Chizzali timely appealed to this court. We affirm except that we hold that Chizzali was entitled to relief from the stay on one of his issues before the Colorado appellate court.

I. Background

Chizzali sued Gindi in Colorado state court to resolve their respective liabilities incurred in their business ventures. In September

2007 they reached a settlement on several issues and agreed to submit the remaining disputes to binding arbitration. But matters did not proceed smoothly. The following January Chizzali filed a motion with the court complaining that Gindi had not performed as promised, and the court issued an order requiring Gindi to pay Chizzali $328,070.30 within 30 days. Gindi did not comply with the order. . . .

Meanwhile, in May 2008 Chizzali had sought to collect on his judgment by serving a writ of garnishment on Bank of the West, where Gindi had an account with a balance of $263,856.75. When the bank did not serve a timely answer to the writ, the court clerk entered a default. But on the bank's motion the state court set aside the entry of default in August 2008, ruling that the bank's failure to file a timely response was excusable neglect and that it had raised a meritorious defense. . . . Chizzali's challenge to the state court's setting aside the entry of default is the second issue in his appeal to the Colorado Court of Appeals.

Chizzali had greater success in the arbitration. The arbitrator awarded him $2.16 million; and the state court affirmed the award and entered judgment against Gindi in July 2008. Chizzali's effort to stay Gindi's appeal of that judgment presents the final issue before us.

On July 20, 2009, while the appeals by Chizzali and Gindi were still pending, Gindi filed in the United States Bankruptcy Court for the District of Colorado a voluntary petition under Chapter 11 of the Bankruptcy Code. Chizzali sought relief from the automatic stay to pursue his appeal in the Colorado Court of Appeals. . . . He also argued two grounds why the bankruptcy court should lift the stay of his appeal of the state court's setting aside the entry of default against Bank of the West: first, under 11 U.S.C. § 362(d)(1) he had shown cause to lift the stay, and second, under § 362(d)(2) he had shown that Gindi had no equity in the bank account. The bankruptcy court rejected Chizzali's arguments and refused to lift the stay. Gindi, however, successfully argued that the stay did not apply to his appeal of the judgment against him.

Chizzali appealed to the BAP the adverse decisions regarding the automatic stay. The BAP affirmed the bankruptcy court, and Chizzali filed a timely appeal in this court. We affirm in part and reverse and remand in part. . . . We hold that Chizzali did not show cause under § 362(d)(1) to lift the stay of his state-court appeal of the entry-of-default issue because he failed to show a likelihood of succeeding on that appeal. But . . . Chizzali established the right to have the stay on that issue lifted under § 362(d)(2) because he showed that Gindi had no equity in his Bank of the West account, and Gindi failed to show that the money in the account was necessary to an effective reorganization under Chapter 11. . . .

. . . The automatic stay is created by 11 U.S.C. § 362. As we have stated, it:

"is the central provision of the Bankruptcy Code. When a debtor files for bankruptcy, section 362 prevents creditors from taking further action against him except through the bankruptcy court. The stay protects debtors from harassment and also ensures that the debtor's assets can be distributed in an orderly fashion, thus preserving the interests of the creditors as a group."

. . . . The scope of the stay is broad, encompassing "almost any type of formal or informal action taken against the debtor or the property of the [bankruptcy] estate." . . . But the reach of the stay is not unlimited. . . . And even when the stay applies, 11 U.S.C. § 362(d) sets forth various circumstances in which a party may seek relief from the stay. The provisions relevant here are § 362(d)(1), under which "[r]elief from the stay must be granted upon a showing of cause," . . . and § 362(d)(2), under which a stay of an act against property may be lifted "when the debtor has no equity in the property and the property is not necessary for an effective reorganization." . . .

* * *

Chizzali contends that under both 11 U.S.C. § 362(d)(1) and (2) he should have been granted relief from the automatic stay so that he could pursue his state appeal of the state trial court's decision to set aside the entry of default against Bank of the West. Section 362(d) states in relevant part:

On request of a party in interest and after notice and a hearing, the court shall grant relief from the stay provided under subsection (a) of this section, such as by terminating, annulling, modifying, or conditioning such stay—

(1) for cause, including the lack of adequate protection of an interest in property of such party in interest;

(2) with respect to a stay of an act against property under subsection (a) of this section, if—

(A) the debtor does not have an equity in such property; and

(B) such property is not necessary to an effective reorganization[.]

* * *

Chizzali . . . argues that the bankruptcy court should have lifted the automatic stay under § 362(d)(2), because he proved that Gindi has no equity in the Bank of the West account and no one has shown that the account is "necessary to an effective reorganization" under Chapter 11. 11 U.S.C. § 362(d)(2)(B); *see id.* § 362(g) (party moving to lift stay has burden of proving that debtor has no equity in the property, while opposing party has burden on all other issues).

A debtor "has no equity in property . . . when the debts secured by liens on the property exceed the value of the property." Chizzali has satisfied his burden of showing that Gindi has no equity in the funds at Bank of the West. As noted above, the writ of garnishment sought to collect upon a judgment for $328,070.30. Chizzali correctly points out that under Colorado law the service of the writ created a lien in that amount on the funds. . . . This lien alone exceeded the value of the account. . . .

Accordingly, the stay should have been lifted under § 362(d)(2) unless Gindi or Bank of the West established that the money in the bank account was necessary to an effective reorganization. *See* 11 U.S.C. § 362(g)(2). They had the burden of "not merely showing that if there is conceivably to be an effective reorganization, this property will be needed for it; but that the property is essential for an effective reorganization *that is in prospect.* This means . . . that there must be a reasonable possibility of a successful reorganization within a reasonable time." . . . This they failed to do, or even attempt to do, in the bankruptcy court. Consequently, we must reverse and remand with instructions to order relief from the automatic stay under § 362(d)(2).

* * *

(Citations omitted.)

NOTES AND COMMENTS

1. How might the court's analysis have changed if Gindi had filed under Chapter 7 of the Bankruptcy Code instead of Chapter 11 on the grounds for relief from stay that debtor lacks equity in the property and the property is not necessary for an effective reorganization? Why should a creditor be entitled to relief from stay when those two factors are met, and do they apply in the context of a Chapter 7?

2. In the introductory paragraph of the case, the court notes that the debtor, Mr. Gindi, successfully argued that the automatic stay did not

apply to *his* appeal of the bankruptcy court's decision. At the time, the Tenth Circuit was in the minority of circuit courts, holding that the automatic stay prohibited actions by creditors but not actions by debtors on pre-petition claims. The Tenth Circuit changed its position, siding with the majority of circuit courts in holding that a debtor is stayed from appealing a pre-petition judgment less than a year after the *Gindi* decision. TW Telecom Holdings Inc. v. Carolina Internet Ltd., 661 F.3d 495, 497 (10th Cir. 2011) (holding that stay applies to "all appeals in proceedings that were *originally brought* against the debtor, regardless of whether the debtor is the appellant or appellee") (quoting Assn. of St. Croix Condo. Owners v. St. Croix Hotel Corp., 682 F.2d 446, 449 (3d Cir. 1982)).

C. EXEMPTIONS (§ 522)

Once property is deemed to belong to the estate, it no longer belongs to the debtor. However, debtors have the ability to take property out of the estate through bankruptcy exemptions. The policy behind exemptions is relatively straightforward—ensuring that the debtor has some property for financial viability post-bankruptcy:

> Protecting property so each person can be a productive member of society has been the foundation of exemption laws. . . . The policy reasons are basic. Debtors cannot go to the workplace without clothes, nor can they perform their jobs without tools of their trades. Exemptions preserve citizens' ability and incentive to earn and pay taxes. Protecting future wages ensures that individuals retain their incentives to continue working, to work longer hours or under more adverse conditions, and to be productive, tax-paying members of society. Similarly, exemptions are intended to promote savings. Laws exempt some retirement funds to encourage all citizens to make adequate provisions rather than becoming public charges in their post-employment years. Laws also shield disability payments so the government need not increase its grants to provide a basic standard of living for its disabled citizens. Finally, property exemptions protect items of nominal value that may not be necessary to earn a living, but would do little to satisfy obligations to creditors. For example, used clothes or household goods have little resale value for creditors that seized and sold them. Additionally, wedding bands, family heirlooms and photographs may be highly valued by their owners, but have no resale value at all. However, a creditor's threat to seize this property can lead a family to liquidate other assets, borrow from other people, or use any other means to find to protect these items from creditors. To curb this leverage, exemptions often protect this personal property.

National Bankruptcy Review Commission Report, Chapter 1 at *1 1997 WL 985124 (1997). Determining what property a debtor needs to be financially viable presents a challenge. Review the list of federal bankruptcy exemptions in § 522(d); they provide an idea of the types of property that exemptions often cover. These often include residences, cars, household goods, certain types of savings, tools of the trade, or a wildcard exemption that allows the debtor to select items of particular importance to that debtor.

Debtors are often foreclosed from using the list of exemptions in § 522(d). Section 522(b)(1) provides for two alternative sets of exemptions—referred to in paragraphs 2 and 3 of that section. Paragraph 3 allows use of exemptions under "applicable" nonbankruptcy laws—state law and retirement funds exempt under the Internal Revenue Code. Paragraph 2 gives the alternative of the federal exemptions listed in § 522(d), "unless the State law that is applicable to the debtor under paragraph (3)(A) specifically does not so authorize." A state that does not authorize its debtors to use federal exemptions is known as an "opt-out" state. Roughly two-thirds of the states are opt-out states, making the federal exemptions a nonoption for most debtors. Regardless of the exemptions used, courts face the competing policy concerns of promoting the debtor's fresh start and maximizing payment to creditors. In balancing those concerns, the courts are faced with interpretation of the limitations created by those exemptions. The following case considers the limits of an exemption for personal copy of a religious text.

In re Robinson

811 F.3d 267 (7th Cir. 2016)

RIPPLE, Circuit Judge

* * *

On February 25, 2013, Ms. Robinson filed a Chapter 7 bankruptcy petition in the Southern District of Illinois seeking to discharge unsecured debt in the amount of $23,834.00. Among her scheduled personal property, Ms. Robinson listed an "old Morm[o]n bible" of unknown value. Ms. Robinson noted that she "ha[d] been told that there is a 100% exemption for bibles but valuable bibles may or may not be covered under such exemption."

A trustee was appointed and, at the meeting of creditors, inquired about the Book of Mormon. Ms. Robinson confirmed that it was a rare, 1830 first edition Book of Mormon and that she possessed several additional copies of the Book of Mormon in print or digital form. On the basis of this information, the trustee filed an objection to the claimed exemption. The trustee acknowledged that 735 ILCS 5/12–1001(a) provides an exemption for a "bible"; nevertheless, the trustee asserted that, given that Ms. Robinson owned many other copies of the Book of Mormon, the valuable first edition should be used for the benefit of the creditors.

During a hearing on the trustee's objection, Ms. Robinson testified that, in 2003, while employed at the local public library, she made an agreement with the library director that, if she cleaned out a storage area, she could use the area as an office and keep any books she found. While cleaning, Ms. Robinson found the Book of Mormon and later had it authenticated as an 1830 first edition Book of Mormon, one of only 5,000 copies printed by Joseph Smith. At the time, it was valued at $10,000.00. Ms. Robinson explained that she stores the Book of Mormon in a Ziploc bag to preserve it. She does not use it regularly, but does take it out occasionally to show her children and fellow church members.

On August 20, 2013, the bankruptcy court entered an order sustaining the trustee's objection. The bankruptcy court believed that "allowing the debtor's exemption w[ould] violate the intent and purpose of the statute," namely "to protect a bible of ordinary value so as not to deprive a debtor of a worship aid."

* * *

Ms. Robinson appealed. . . . The district court determined that, because the legislature did not place a monetary limitation on the items exempted in 735 ILCS 5/12–1001(a), a bible is exempt without regard to its value. The district court therefore vacated the bankruptcy court's order denying the exemption; it also vacated the bankruptcy court's order denying the motion to reconsider. . . .

* * *

When interpreting a statute, . . . "the primary rule of statutory construction is to ascertain and effectuate the legislature's intent. In doing so a court looks first to the statutory language itself. If the language is clear, the court must give it effect and should not look to extrinsic aids for construction." . . .

Our analysis, therefore, begins with the language of the statute, which provides in relevant part:

The following personal property, owned by the debtor, is exempt from judgment, attachment, or distress for rent:

> (a) *The necessary wearing apparel, bible, school books, and family pictures of the debtor and the debtor's dependents;*

* * *

The trustee acknowledges that "the term 'bible' has a well settled meaning when standing alone"—"a religious text." Moreover, it is not disputed that the Book of Mormon falls within this meaning. Finally, there is nothing in the wording of subsection (a) that imposes a dollar limit on the items listed therein. The trustee nevertheless maintains that the meaning of subsection (a), as applied to Ms. Robinson's Book of Mormon, "is not so clear" when it is "considered in the context of Section 1001."

The trustee, however, does not point to anything in the language or structure of 735 ILCS 5/12–1001 that modifies or narrows the term as it is generally understood. As already noted, nothing suggests that the legislature meant to impose a dollar-value limitation on the items set forth in subsection (a). Indeed, given that other subsections of 735 ILCS 5/12–1001 include dollar-value limitations, it seems clear that the legislature *did not* intend to limit subsection (a) to items under a certain value.

The plain wording of the statute does support the trustee's argument that the exemption applies to *one* "bible." However, the trustee does not seek simply to limit Ms. Robinson to one Book of Mormon; the trustee seeks to limit Ms. Robinson to one Book of Mormon *of negligible monetary value.* Given that the legislature did not place a dollar limit on the subsection (a) exemptions as it did with exemptions in other subsections, this argument appears at odds with the wording and structure of the personal property exemption statute.

Moreover, the "of negligible value" construction adopted by the bankruptcy court, and urged by the trustee, does not find support in case law. In *In re Deacon,* 27 F.Supp. 296 (S.D.Ill.1939), the court determined that "one watch, one consistory ring, [and] one diamond shirt stud" fell within the category of "necessary wearing apparel." If the statute were to be strictly construed to provide the debtor with the "bare necessities," none of these items should have been exempted. Moreover, in *In re Barker,* 768 F.2d 191 (7th Cir.1985), we noted that, in a case "where an exemption statute might be interpreted either favorably or unfavorably vis-á-vis a debtor, we should interpret the statute in a manner that favors the debtor." . . .

* * *

The trustee argues that the subsection (a) exemption . . . is susceptible to more than one interpretation. The trustee maintains that Ms. Robinson acknowledged as much when she wrote in her schedule "debtor has been told that there is a 100% exemption for bibles but valuable bibles may or may not be covered under such exemption." The trustee also argues that the "interpretive conflict" between the parties here establishes that . . . subsection (a) is ambiguous and therefore "is appropriately resolved by examining the legislative history of Section 1001(a) in order to determine the legislature's intent."

We do not believe that the statement in Ms. Robinson's filing constitutes an admission that the statute is ambiguous. Instead, it simply acknowledges the absence of controlling case law interpreting the "bible" exemption to include a valuable religious text.

Moreover, we cannot conclude that the "interpretive conflict" alone leads to the conclusion that the plain wording of the statute is ambiguous. The trustee and the bankruptcy court rely heavily on "the intent and purpose of the statute" to inform their understanding of the "bible" exemption. In "ascertain[ing] and effectuat[ing] the legislature's intent," "a court looks first to the statutory language itself." . . . It is only when "the meaning of an enactment is unclear from the statutory language itself" that "the court may look beyond the language employed and consider the purpose behind the law and the evils the law was designed to remedy, as well as other sources such as legislative history." . . .

* * *

(Citations omitted.)

NOTES AND COMMENTS

1. Would Ms. Robinson be allowed to keep her copy of the Bible if she were an atheist rather than Mormon? The *American Heritage Dictionary* defines a "bible" as "a. The sacred book of Christianity, a collection of ancient writings including the books of both the Old Testament and the New Testament. b. The Hebrew Scriptures, the sacred book of Judaism. c. A particular copy of a Bible: *the old family Bible.* A book or collection of writings constituting the sacred text of a religion." Does this definition help in any way?

Some of the most widely debated exemptions fall within the homestead exemption, which exists in all states, although it is very limited in a small number of states. The homestead exemption exists to protect residents' primary home from creditors and increases in property taxes. Homestead exemptions support the public policy of encouraging home ownership and allowing even those in bankruptcy to remain in their homes.

For most homeowners, the home is the most valuable asset that a debtor owns. In bankruptcy the homestead exemption removes from the bankruptcy estate some portion of the value of the debtor's principal residence. Homestead exemptions differ widely, with some states offering only a few thousand dollars in protection for the homestead and others protecting the entire value of the homestead regardless of the value of the homestead. While this may create an incentive to live in and file bankruptcy protection in a state with a generous homestead exemption, the 2005 BAPCPA amendments sought to curb such potential abuse through two provisions. The first requires debtors to reside in a state for two years before claiming any of that state's exemptions. 11 U.S.C. § 522(a)(3)(A). The second applies specifically to the homestead exemption and limits the value of any interest in the exemption acquired during the 1,215 days pre-petition. 11 U.S.C. § 522(p).

Although a homestead exemption is critical for bankruptcy law, most homeowners become familiar with it because it generally reduces property taxes on a principal residence. Most states will exempt from taxation some fixed-dollar amount from a home's value, or an overall percentage of the home's value. For example, a state may assess the value of a home at current market rates, but then reduce the assessed value by $75,000 in calculating property taxes owed if the home is the owner's principal residence. Even though they are both called homestead exemptions, the specific dollar homestead exemption for bankruptcy may be entirely different than the dollar amount (or percent of value) exempted to reduce property taxes.

Florida, with its unlimited-value homestead exemption, has been the epicenter of cases regarding the ability to use the homestead exemption. In the following case, the debtors did not use Florida's homestead exemption; under Florida law, a debtor who does not use the generous homestead exemption may instead utilize a larger "wildcard" exemption that allows the debtor to exempt property of the debtor's choice. The case turns on what it means to use a homestead exemption under Florida law.

In re Valone

784 F.3d 1398 (11th Cir. 2015)

WILSON, Circuit Judge

This is an appeal from a district court order affirming a bankruptcy court's disallowance of an exemption claimed by Michael and Kristie

Valone in their Chapter 13 bankruptcy petition. The Chapter 13 trustee, Jon Waage, objected to their personal property exemption, arguing that, as homeowners filing under Chapter 13 of the Bankruptcy Code, the Valones were ineligible for the exemption. The bankruptcy and district courts agreed. We reverse the district court and remand with instructions to remand to the bankruptcy court for proceedings consistent with this opinion.

I.

The Valones are Florida residents who filed jointly for bankruptcy under Chapter 13 of the Bankruptcy Code. In their petition, they claimed exemptions for personal property under section 222.25(4) of the Florida Statutes, known as the "wildcard" exemption. The wildcard exemption permits a debtor to exempt from legal process "[a] debtor's interest in personal property, not to exceed $4,000, if the debtor does not claim or receive the benefits of a homestead exemption under s. 4, Art. X of the State Constitution." Fla. Stat. § 222.25(4). At the date of their petition, the Valones owned a home, but they did not claim the homestead exemption in their petition, presumably because they had no equity in the home.

Waage objected to the Valones' wildcard exemption claim, arguing that because Chapter 13, like the homestead exemption, protects debtors' homes, debtors who file under Chapter 13 receive the benefits of the homestead exemption. The bankruptcy court sustained the objection. In the bankruptcy court's memorandum opinion sustaining the objection, it cited [a case in which] the Florida Supreme Court answered a question certified to it by this court and held that a debtor may still receive the benefits of the homestead exemption without claiming it on the bankruptcy petition, rendering the debtor ineligible for the wildcard exemption. . . .

* * *

We hold, in accordance with the Florida Supreme Court's holding in *Osborne,* that the filing of a petition under Chapter 13 of the Bankruptcy Code by a Florida debtor who owns, or debtors who own, homestead property does not foreclose the availability of Florida's wildcard exemption to that debtor or those debtors. Courts should consider the facts of each case to determine whether it is the Florida homestead exemption or some other source that protects the residence from forced sale. Under the facts presented in this appeal, the Valones' residence was protected from creditors by the

Bankruptcy Code's automatic stay, not by the homestead exemption, and they are accordingly eligible to claim the wildcard exemption.

* * *

When construing the language of a statute, we "begin [] where all such inquiries must begin: with the language of the statute itself," and we give effect to the plain terms of the statute. . . . The wildcard exemption exempts "[a] debtor's interest in personal property, not to exceed $4,000, if the debtor does not claim or receive the benefits of a homestead exemption under s. 4, Art. X of the State Constitution." Fla. Stat. § 222.25(4). The parties' dispute centers on the meaning of the phrase "receive the benefits of a homestead exemption under s. 4, Art. X of the State Constitution." It is exceedingly clear that this phrase is triggered only if the homestead exemption—and the homestead exemption alone—protects the debtor's home from creditors. Because the homestead exemption does not reference Chapter 13, the Bankruptcy Code, federal law, or any other source that might implicate Chapter 13, receiving the protection of the automatic stay and discharge simply cannot trigger the limiting phrase.

The bankruptcy court's holding to the contrary is likely rooted in the language in *Osborne* noting the possibility that a debtor who does not claim the homestead exemption may yet receive its benefits. . . . Nothing in that opinion, however, would extend the potential for receiving benefits to situations—like this one—where the protection of the home emanates from a source other than the homestead exemption. In fact, the Court clearly ruled out disallowance under § 222.25(4) when the protection comes from any source besides the homestead exemption: "[I]f under the facts of the case *the article X homestead exemption* does not otherwise present an obstacle to the bankruptcy trustee's administration of the estate, then the debtor in bankruptcy is not receiving the benefits of the homestead exemption and is eligible to claim the [wildcard exemption]." . . .

Moreover, the example cited by the Florida Supreme Court drives the point home. That example involved a debtor who indirectly received the benefits of the homestead exemption through his nondebtor spouse's retention of the right to exercise the homestead exemption. . . . This example reinforces the straightforward command of § 222.25(4) that requires protection from the homestead exemption for a debtor to be ineligible for the wildcard exemption.

Alternatively, Waage argues, because the homestead exemption is "self-executing," . . . the very act of owning a home that constitutes homestead property under the Florida Constitution may make a debtor ineligible for the wildcard exemption . . . .

When a debtor files for bankruptcy, all of the debtor's property becomes property of the bankruptcy estate. 11 U.S.C. § 541. The debtor may affirmatively exempt certain property from the estate, including property that is exempt under the law of the debtor's domicile. *Id.* § 522(b)(1), (b)(3)(A). In other words, if the debtor fails to claim an exemption, the property remains in the estate and is subject to administration by the trustee . . . . These considerations led the Florida Supreme Court to conclude that the additional step of actual abandonment of the real property or an expression of intent to abandon the homestead is not required to bring the debtor within the category of those debtors who do not claim or receive the benefits of . . . [the] homestead exemption. . . . [W]hen the real property which has been occupied by a debtor as his homestead becomes subject to administration by the bankruptcy trustee, the debtor has lost the benefits of the homestead exemption.

. . . Because the debtor loses the benefits of the homestead exemption by subjecting his home to the trustee's administration, he is eligible for the wildcard exemption. It makes no difference whether the debtor elects Chapter 7 or Chapter 13. In either situation, the debtor may decline to claim the homestead exemption.

Implicit in Waage's argument, however, is the assertion that, because Chapter 13 protects a debtor's home until conclusion of the case, the homestead exemption survives and is present throughout bankruptcy, even if the automatic stay is what is protecting the home when the debtor files. This, however, does not distinguish Chapter 13 from Chapter 7 in any meaningful way. Under Florida law, the relevant period for determining whether a debtor receives the benefits of the homestead exemption is "the period when the debtor asserts the personal property exemption." . . . [T]he fact that the homestead exemption becomes effective after the bankruptcy case closes is irrelevant.

Moreover, even if the relevant period were extended beyond case closure, any distinction between Chapters 7 and 13 remains immaterial. In either case, if the debtor retains ownership of the homestead after the close of the bankruptcy case, the homestead exemption continues to protect the home from creditors after the case is closed. Said differently, whether the debtor files under Chapter 7 or 13, the homestead exemption lies dormant during the bankruptcy case, and its protections reactivate after the case closes should the debtor retain ownership of the residence . . . .

* * *

Section 222.25(4) is clear. The wildcard exemption is available to debtors as long as they do not claim or receive the benefits of the homestead exemption. It is irrelevant that a debtor receives protection from other sources, including Chapter 13. Therefore, the Valones did not claim or receive the benefits of the homestead exemption, and we reverse and remand to the district court with instructions to remand to the bankruptcy court for proceedings consistent with this opinion.

(Citations omitted.)

NOTES AND COMMENTS

1. Early in its decision, the court references the debtors' lack of equity in the property. What is the role of equity in the determination of whether the debtor receives an exemption? *See* 11 U.S.C. § 522(d); Fla. Const. Art. X § 4 ("There shall be exempt from forced sale under process of any court, and no judgment, decree or execution shall be a lien thereon . . . a homestead . . . "; Fla. Stat. 222.25(4) ("The following property is exempt from attachment, garnishment, or other legal process: . . . A debtor's interest in personal property, not to exceed $4,000, if the debtor does not claim or receive the benefits of a homestead exemption under s. 4, Art. X of the State Constitution.")

2. The court relies extensively on the Florida Supreme Court decision of Osborne v. Dumoulin, 55 So. 3d. 577 (Fla. 2011). The debtor claimed the homestead exemption on her schedules, but then amended the schedules to remove the homestead exemption and use Florida's personal property wildcard exemption instead. Florida law does not require a debtor to claim homestead to be entitled to its protections. *Id.* at 584. The benefit of the exemption for debtors is the inability of creditors to use the homestead to satisfy claims. By not selecting the homestead exemption, a debtor leaves the property in the bankruptcy estate, thereby subjecting it to administration by the bankruptcy trustee. As a result, the debtor loses the benefit of absolutely protecting the homestead from creditors, even if the homestead would otherwise be protected under Florida law. *Id.* at 587-588. Thus, the court concluded that a debtor not electing the homestead exemption does not enjoy the benefits of the exemption and

can instead elect the wildcard exemption. Why does the *Valone* court rely so heavily on the *Osborne* decision?

MODIFYING DOLLAR AMOUNTS WITHIN THE BANKRUPTCY CODE

When originally drafted, 11 U.S.C. § 522(p) limited the state homestead exemption to a $125,000 interest acquired within the 1215 days pre-petition. That dollar amount changes every three years (2010, 2013, 2016, etc.) and is tied to changes in the Consumer Price Index. The Judicial Conference of the United States publishes the new figures each year in the Federal Register, and those new dollar figures become effective as of April 1. 11 U.S.C. § 104.

The debtor claims exemptions in Schedule C, filed with or shortly after the bankruptcy petition. For each piece of property claimed as exempt, the debtor must include a description of the property, its value, the amount of the exemption claimed, and the law that allows the exemption. Schedule C now includes an option for the value of the exemption of "100% of fair market value, up to any applicable statutory limit"; that language was added in response to the following case. Look at Schedules B and C before you read the case; the schedules may be found at https://www.uscourts.gov/forms/bankruptcy-forms. In the following case the Supreme Court considers the debtor's estimation of the value of exempted property.

Schwab v. Reilly

560 U.S. 770 (2010)

THOMAS, Justice

* * *

Respondent Nadejda Reilly filed for Chapter 7 bankruptcy when her catering business failed. She supported her petition with various schedules and statements, two of which are relevant here: Schedule B, on which the Bankruptcy Rules require debtors to list their assets (most of which become property of the estate), and Schedule C, on which the Rules require debtors to list the property they wish to reclaim as exempt. The assets Reilly listed on Schedule B included an itemized list of cooking and other kitchen equipment that she described as "business equipment," and to which she assigned an estimated market value of $10,718. . . .

On Schedule C, Reilly claimed two exempt interests in this equipment pursuant to different sections of the Code. Reilly claimed a "tool[s] of the trade" exemption of $1,850 in the equipment under § 522(d)(6), which permits a debtor to exempt his "aggregate interest, not to exceed $1,850 in value, in any implements, professional books, or tools, of [his] trade." . . . And she claimed a miscellaneous exemption of $8,868 in the equipment under § 522(d)(5), which, at the time she filed for bankruptcy, permitted a debtor to take a "wildcard" exemption equal to the "debtor's aggregate interest in any property, not to exceed" $10,225 "in value." . . . The total value of these claimed exemptions ($10,718) equaled the value Reilly separately listed on Schedules B and C as the equipment's estimated market value . . . .

Subject to exceptions not relevant here, the Federal Rules of Bankruptcy Procedure require interested parties to object to a debtor's claimed exemptions within 30 days after the conclusion of the creditors' meeting held pursuant to Rule 2003(a). See Fed. Rule Bkrtcy. Proc. 4003(b). If an interested party fails to object within the time allowed, a claimed exemption will exclude the subject property from the estate even if the exemption's value exceeds what the Code permits . . . .

Petitioner William G. Schwab, the trustee of Reilly's bankruptcy estate, did not object to Reilly's claimed exemptions in her business equipment because the dollar value Reilly assigned each exemption fell within the limits that §§ 522(d)(5) and (6) prescribe . . . . But because an appraisal revealed that the total market value of Reilly's business equipment could be as much as $17,200, Schwab moved the Bankruptcy Court for permission to auction the equipment so Reilly could receive the $10,718 she claimed as exempt, and the estate could distribute the equipment's remaining value (approximately $6,500) to Reilly's creditors . . . .

Reilly opposed Schwab's motion. She argued that by equating on Schedule C the total value of the exemptions she claimed in the equipment with the equipment's estimated market value, she had put Schwab and her creditors on notice that she intended to exempt the equipment's full value, even if that amount turned out to be more than the dollar amount she declared, and more than the Code allowed . . . .

The Bankruptcy Court denied both Schwab's motion to auction the equipment and Reilly's conditional motion to dismiss her case. . . .

Schwab sought relief from the District Court, arguing that neither the Code nor Rule 4003(b) requires a trustee to object to a claimed exemption where the amount the debtor declares as the "value of [the debtor's] claimed exemption" in certain property is an amount within the limits the Code prescribes. The District Court rejected Schwab's argument, and the Court of Appeals affirmed . . . .

* * *

The parties agree that this case is governed by § 522(l), which states that a Chapter 7 debtor must "file a list of property that the debtor claims as exempt under subsection (b) of this section," and further states that "[u]nless a party in interest objects, the property claimed as exempt on such list is exempt." The parties further agree that the "list" to which § 522(l) refers is the "list of property . . . claim[ed] as exempt" currently known as "Schedule C." . . . . The parties, like the Courts of Appeals, disagree about what information on Schedule C defines the "property claimed as exempt" for purposes of evaluating an exemption's propriety under § 522(l) . . . .

According to Reilly, Schwab was required to treat the estimate of market value she entered in column four as part of her claimed exemption in identifying the "property claimed as exempt" under § 522(l). . . .

Schwab does not dispute that columns three and four apprised him that Reilly equated the total value of her claimed exemptions in the equipment ($1,850 plus $8,868) with the equipment's market value ($10,718). He simply disagrees with Reilly that this "identical listing put [him] on notice that Reilly intended to exempt the property fully," regardless whether its value exceeded the exemption limits the Code prescribes . . . . Schwab and *amicus* United States instead contend that the Code defines the "property" Reilly claimed as exempt under § 522(l) as an "interest" whose value cannot exceed a certain dollar amount . . . .

We agree. The portion of § 522(l) that resolves this case is not, as Reilly asserts, the provision stating that the "property claimed as exempt on [Schedule C] is exempt" unless an interested party objects. Rather, it is the portion of § 522(l) that defines the target of the objection, namely, the portion that says Schwab has a duty to object to the "list of property that the debtor claims as exempt *under subsection (b)*." (Emphasis added.) That subsection, § 522(b), does *not* define the "property claimed as exempt" by reference to the estimated market value on which Reilly and the Court of Appeals rely . . . . Section 522(b) refers only to property defined in § 522(d), which in turn lists 12 categories of property that a debtor may claim as exempt. As we have recognized, most of these categories (and all of the categories applicable to Reilly's exemptions) define the "property" a debtor may "clai[m] as exempt" as the debtor's "interest"—up to a specified dollar amount—in the assets described in the category, *not* as the assets themselves. §§ 522(d)(5)-(6); . . . . Viewing Reilly's form entries in light of this definition, we agree with Schwab and the United States that Schwab had no duty to object to the property Reilly claimed as exempt (two interests in her business equipment worth $1,850 and $8,868) because the stated value of each interest, and thus of the "property claimed as exempt," was within the limits the Code allows.

* * *

For all of these reasons, we conclude that Schwab was entitled to evaluate the propriety of the claimed exemptions based on three, and only three, entries on Reilly's Schedule C: the description of the business equipment in which Reilly claimed the exempt interests; the Code provisions governing the claimed exemptions; and the amounts Reilly listed in the column titled "value of claimed exemption." In reaching this conclusion, we do not render the market value estimate on Reilly's Schedule C superfluous. We simply confine the estimate to its proper role: aiding the trustee in administering the estate by helping him identify assets that may have value beyond the dollar amount the debtor claims as exempt, or whose full value may not be available for exemption because a portion of the interest is, for example, encumbered by an unavoidable lien. . . . [I]t is at least useful for a trustee to be able to compare the value of the claimed exemption (which typically represents the debtor's interest in a particular asset) with the asset's estimated market value (which belongs to the estate subject to any valid exemption) without having to consult separate schedules.

* * *

The Court of Appeals erred in holding that our decision in *Taylor* dictates a contrary conclusion. . . . *Taylor* does not rest on what the debtor "meant" to exempt. . . . Rather, *Taylor* applies to the face of a debtor's claimed exemption the Code provisions that compel reversal here.

The debtor in *Taylor*, like the debtor here, filed a schedule of exemptions with the Bankruptcy Court on which the debtor described the property subject to the claimed exemption, identified the Code provision supporting the exemption, and listed the dollar value of the exemption. Critically, however, the debtor in *Taylor* did *not,* like the debtor here, state the value of the claimed exemption as a specific dollar amount at or below the limits the Code allows. Instead, the debtor in *Taylor* listed the value of the exemption itself as "$ *unknown*". . . .

. . . although this case and *Taylor* both concern the consequences of a trustee's failure to object to a claimed exemption within the time specified by Rule 4003, the question arose in *Taylor* on starkly different facts. In *Taylor,* the question concerned a trustee's obligation to object to the debtor's entry of a "value claimed exempt" that was *not* plainly within the limits the Code allows. In this case, the opposite is true. The amounts Reilly listed in the Schedule C column titled "Value of Claimed Exemption" *are* facially within the limits the Code prescribes and raise no warning flags that warranted an objection . . . .

Taylor supports this conclusion. . . . It establishes and applies the straightforward proposition that an interested party must object to a claimed exemption if the amount the debtor lists as the "value claimed exempt" is not within statutory limits, a test the value ($ *unknown*) in *Taylor* failed, and the values ($8,868 and $1,850) in this case pass.

* * *

In a final effort to defend the Court of Appeals' judgment, Reilly asserts that her approach to § 522(l) is necessary to vindicate the Code's goal of giving debtors a fresh start, and to further its policy of discouraging trustees and creditors from sleeping on their rights. . . . This approach threatens to convert a fresh start into a free pass.

As we emphasized in *Rousey,* "[t]o help the debtor obtain a fresh start, the Bankruptcy Code permits him to *withdraw from the estate* certain *interests in* property, such as his car or home, *up to certain values.*" . . . The Code limits exemptions in this fashion because every asset the Code permits a debtor to withdraw from the estate is an asset that is not available to his creditors. See § 522(b)(1). Congress balanced the difficult choices that exemption limits impose on debtors with the economic harm that exemptions visit on creditors, and it is not for us to alter this balance by requiring trustees to object to claimed exemptions based on form entries beyond those that govern an exemption's validity under the Code . . . .

* * *

Where, as here, it is important to the debtor to exempt the full market value of the asset or the asset itself, our decision will encourage the debtor to declare the value of her claimed exemption in a manner that makes the scope of the exemption clear, for example, by listing the exempt value as "full fair market value (FMV)" or "100% of FMV." Such a declaration will encourage the trustee to object promptly to the exemption if he wishes to challenge it and preserve for the estate any value in the asset beyond relevant statutory limits. If the trustee fails to object, or if the trustee objects and the objection is overruled, the debtor will be entitled to exclude the full value of the asset. If the trustee objects and the objection is sustained, the debtor will be required either to forfeit the portion of the exemption that exceeds the statutory allowance, or to revise other exemptions or arrangements with her creditors to permit the exemption . . . . Either result will facilitate the expeditious and final disposition of assets, and thus enable the debtor (and the debtor's creditors) to achieve a fresh start free of the finality and clouded-title concerns Reilly describes. . . .

* * *

Justice GINSBURG, with whom THE CHIEF JUSTICE [ROBERTS] and Justice BREYER join, dissenting.

* * *

. . . The Court's decision drastically reduces Rule 4003's governance, for challenges to valuation have been, until today, the most common type of objection leveled against exemption claims. . . . In addition to departing from the prevailing understanding and practice, the Court's decision exposes debtors to protracted uncertainty concerning their right to retain exempt property, thereby impeding the "fresh start" exemptions are designed to foster. . . .

* * *

The District Court and Court of Appeals similarly concluded that, by listing the identical amount, $10,718, as the property's market value and the value of the claimed exemptions, Reilly had signaled her intention to safeguard all of her kitchen equipment from inclusion in the bankruptcy estate . . . . Both courts looked to § 522(l) and Federal Rule of Bankruptcy Procedure 4003(b), which state, respectively:

"The debtor shall file a list of property that the debtor claims as exempt . . . . Unless a party in interest objects, the property claimed as exempt on such list is exempt." § 522(l).

"A party in interest may file an objection to the list of property claimed as exempt only within 30 days after the meeting of creditors held under § 341(a) is concluded . . . . The court may, for cause, extend the time for filing objections if, before the time to object

expires, a party in interest files a request for an extension."
Rule 4003(b).

* * *

Pursuant to § 522(l), Reilly filed a list of property she claimed as
exempt from the estate-in-bankruptcy. Her filing left no doubt that
her exemption claim encompassed her entire inventory of kitchen
equipment. Schwab, in fact, was fully aware of the nature of the claim
Reilly asserted. At the meeting of creditors, Reilly reiterated that she
sought to keep the equipment in her possession; she would rather
discontinue the bankruptcy proceeding, she made plain, than lose
her equipment . . . .

* * *

To support the conclusion that Rule 4003's timely objection
requirement does not encompass the debtor's estimation of her
property's market value, the Court hones in on the language of
exemption prescriptions that are subject to a monetary cap . . . .

The Court's account, however, shuts from sight the vital part played
by the fourth entry on Schedule C—current market value—when
a capped exemption is claimed. A debtor who estimates a market
value *below* the cap, and lists an identical amount as the value of
her claimed exemption, thereby signals that her aim is to keep the
listed property in her possession, outside the estate-in-bankruptcy. In
contrast, a debtor who estimates a market value *above* the cap, and
above the value of her claimed exemption, thereby recognizes that
she cannot shelter the property itself and that the trustee may seek
to sell it for whatever it is worth. Schedule C's final column, in other
words, alerts the trustee whether the debtor is claiming a right to
retain the listed property itself as her own, a right secured to her if
the trustee files no timely objection.

Because an asset's market value is key to determining the character
of the interest the debtor is asserting in that asset, Rule 4003(b) is
properly read to require objections to valuation within 30 days, just
as the Rule requires timely objections to the debtor's description of
the property, the asserted legal basis for the exemption, and the
claimed value of the exemption . . . .

* * *

With the benefit of closure, and the certainty it brings, the debtor
may, at the end of the 30 days, plan for her future secure in the
knowledge that the possessions she has exempted in their entirety
are hers to keep . . . .

By permitting trustees to challenge a debtor's valuation of exempted property anytime before the administrative closing of the bankruptcy estate, the Court casts a cloud of uncertainty over the debtor's use of assets reclaimed in full. If the trustee gains a different opinion of an item's value months, even years, after the debtor has filed her bankruptcy petition, he may seek to repossess the asset, auction it off, and hand the debtor a check for the dollar amount of her claimed exemption . . . .

* * *

The Court suggests that requiring timely objections to a debtor's valuation of exempt property would saddle trustees with an unmanageable load. . . . But trustees, sooner or later, must attempt to ascertain the market value of exempted assets . . . .

The 30–day objection period, I note, does not impose on trustees any *additional* duty, but rather guides the exercise of *existing* responsibilities; under Rule 4003(b), a trustee must rank evaluation of the debtor's exemptions as a priority item in his superintendence of the estate. And if the trustee entertains any doubt about the accuracy of a debtor's estimation of market value, the procedure for interposing objections is hardly arduous. The trustee need only file with the court a simple declaration stating that an item's value exceeds the amount listed by the debtor.

If the trustee needs more than 30 days to assess market value, moreover, the time period is eminently extendable. Rule 4003(b) prescribes that a trustee may, for cause, ask the court for an extension of the objection period. Alternatively, the trustee can postpone the conclusion of the meeting of creditors, from which the 30–day clock runs, simply by adjourning the meeting to a future date. Rule 2003(e). A trustee also may examine the debtor under oath at the creditors' meeting, Rule 2003(b)(1); if he gathers information impugning her exemption claims, he may ask the bankruptcy court to hold a hearing to determine valuation issues, Rule 4003(c). . . . Trustees, in sum, have ample mechanisms at their disposal to gain the time and information they need to lodge objections to valuation.

* * *

Training its attention on trustees' needs, moreover, the Court overlooks the debtor's plight. As just noted, the Court counsels debtors wishing to exempt an asset in full to write "100% of FMV" or "full FMV" in the value-of-claimed-exemption column. But a debtor following the instructions that accompany Schedule C would consider such a response nonsensical, for those instructions direct her to "state the *dollar value* of the claimed exemption in the space provided." . . . Chapter 7 debtors are often unrepresented. How are they to know they must ignore Schedule C's instructions and employ the "warning flag" described today by the Court, if they wish to trigger the trustee's obligation to object to their market valuation in a timely fashion? . . .

Schwab finally urges that requiring timely objections to a debtor's market-value estimations "would give debtors a perverse incentive to game the system by undervaluing their assets." . . . Multiple measures, *Taylor* explained, discourage undervaluation of property claimed as exempt . . . . Among those measures: The debtor files her exemption claim under penalty of perjury. See Rule 1008. She risks judicial sanction for signing documents not well grounded in fact. Rule 9011. And proof of fraud subjects her to criminal prosecution, 18 U.S.C. § 152; extends the limitations period for filing objections to Schedule C, Rule 4003(b); and authorizes denial of discharge, 11 U.S.C. § 727(a)(4)(B) . . . .

* * *

(Citations omitted.)

NOTES AND COMMENTS

1. The Court's opinion holds that the trustee has no duty to object if the debtor's claimed value and exemption fall within the limits allowed by the Code. Would that still apply if the debtor listed the value of the property at an amount that is *clearly* too low and for which no appraisal is needed to determine its inaccuracy? What if the debtor had listed the value of the kitchen equipment as $5?

2. In its opinion, the Court states that the trustee need only look at three things to determine whether to object the debtor's proposed exemptions during the 30-day objection period: "the description of the business equipment in which Reilly claimed the exempt interests; the Code provisions governing the claimed exemptions; and the amounts Reilly listed in the column titled 'value of claimed exemption.'" *Schwab*, 560 U.S. at 785. How does the Court's suggestion of writing "100% of FMV" for the value of the exemption change the trustee's analysis of these three items, such that the trustee will then need to object within the requisite time period?

3. The dissent expresses concern regarding the trustee's ability to value property later in the administration of a case: "If the trustee gains a

different opinion of an item's value months, even years, after the debtor has filed her bankruptcy petition, he may seek to repossess the asset, auction it off, and hand the debtor a check for the dollar amount of her claimed exemption. . . ." *Schwab*, 560 U.S. 804. If the trustee is appraising the property value later in the case, should the appraisal be as of the date of the appraisal, or is there a different measuring point for the value of exempt property? *See* 11 U.S.C. § 522(a)(2).

The 341 Meeting of Creditors

The *Schwab* case referenced a meeting under § 341 of the Code, also known as the meeting of creditors. This is a meeting at which the trustee questions the debtor under oath, primarily about information contained in the schedules. The trustee's goal is to ensure that all eligible property is located and brought back into the estate; the trustee also needs to determine whether the debtor has committed fraud or is otherwise hiding assets. Creditors, as the name implies, may also attend the meeting (though few actually do so) and may even ask questions of the debtor. The 341 meeting is not held at the courthouse, and the judge is not present. However, information or debtor's statements from the 341 meeting may be brought into court in later proceedings.

Generally, a debtor may only exempt the debtor's equity in property. In other words, a lien against the property takes precedence over the debtor's right to exempt the property. However, § 522(f) provides two exceptions (with limitations) to this rule, discussed below. When those liens "impair" the debtor's exemptions, the liens may be avoided to the extent of impairment.

Impairment simply means that the value of the collateral is not sufficient to satisfy the lien and provide the debtor with the full benefit of the exemption. For example, if state law allows a $1,000 automobile exemption, the debtor's automobile is worth $7,000, and a judicial lien exists against that automobile on a $10,000 debt, the exemption is impaired because the value of the automobile ($7,000) is not enough to pay the exemption and the debt ($11,000 cumulatively). If the automobile is worth $12,000, there is no impairment because the automobile can be sold and the proceeds distributed in a manner that pays the lien in full and gives the debtor the full exemption.

Not all liens may be avoided under § 522(f). Rather, for a debtor to be allowed to limit the lien, it must fall into one of two categories: a judicial lien or a lien on household, work, or health items. And there are limitations even within these categories to a debtor's ability to impair the lien by taking the exemption. For a debtor to avoid a judicial lien with the exemption, the judicial lien must secure a debt other than a domestic support obligation. For a debtor to avoid a nonjudicial lien, the lien must be on household, work, or health items used by the debtor or the debtor's dependents *and* the creditor must not have either possession of the collateral or a purchase-money security interest[3] in the collateral.

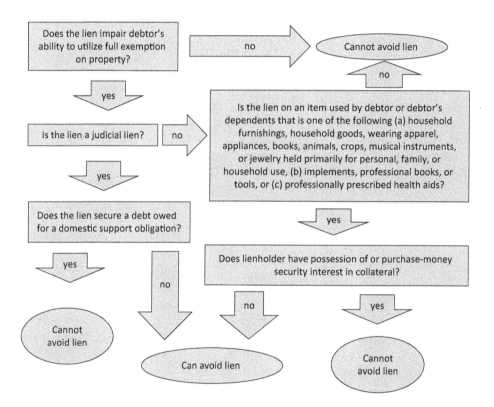

The following case considers the relationship between the debtor's exemption and the ability to avoid a lien.

_____

3. A purchase-money security interest occurs when the creditor loans the debtor value used to purchase the collateral securing that debt. Common examples include a home mortgage, a car loan, or a credit purchase from a furniture store that takes the furniture purchased as collateral for the loan.

Botkin v. DuPont Community Credit Union

650 F.3d 396 (4th Cir. 2011)

TRAXLER, Chief Judge

* * *

Annie Botkin owns certain residential property in Highland County, Virginia, with a current market value of $22,500. A purchase money deed of trust in favor of First and Citizens Bank encumbers the property and secures an outstanding loan balance of approximately $24,124. The property is also encumbered by a $9,800 judicial lien held by DuPont Community Credit Union.

Botkin filed a voluntary petition for Chapter 7 bankruptcy relief on August 13, 2009. In conjunction with her filing, she recorded a homestead deed in the Circuit Court of Highland County. . . . Botkin . . . was entitled to an exemption of up to $5,500. . . . Botkin . . . did not claim an exemption for any portion of her residential property, as she had no equity in the property. . . .

On September 22, 2009, the bankruptcy trustee conducted a meeting of Botkin's creditors, . . . and subsequently reported, as is relevant here, that the estate had been fully administered and "that there [was] no property available for distribution from the estate over and above that exempted by law." . . . In October 2009, Botkin filed a motion to avoid DuPont's judicial lien under 11 U.S.C.A. § 522(f) . . . which provides, in relevant part, that a debtor "may avoid the fixing of a lien on an interest of the debtor in property to the extent that such lien impairs an exemption to which the debtor would have been entitled under subsection (b) of this section, if such lien is . . . a judicial lien." . . .

* * *

A bankruptcy estate comprises all the legal and equitable interests in property that a debtor possesses at the time of filing, as well as the interests that are recovered or recoverable via transfer and lien-avoidance provisions. . . . However, to help the debtor achieve a "fresh start," . . . the Code exempts certain property from the bankruptcy estate. . . .

The Code requires a debtor to file a list of the property claimed to be exempt from the bankruptcy estate . . . . That list (Schedule C) generally must be filed with the petition in a voluntary case or within 14 days after the entry of an order for relief in an involuntary proceeding unless the court extends the deadline . . . . A debtor may amend her list as a matter of course at any time before a case is closed. . . . Following an amendment to a Schedule C, a creditor generally has 30 days to object to any new exemption . . . .

In addition to the rights to exempt certain property from the bankruptcy estate, debtors also, under 11 U.S.C.A. § 522(f), can move to avoid, or wipe out, a lien or interest that a creditor has in particular property. It is this right that is the subject of the current appeal. 11 U.S.C.A. § 522(f)(1) provides, as is relevant here, that a debtor "may avoid the fixing of a lien on an interest of the debtor in property to the extent that such lien impairs an exemption to which the debtor would have been entitled under subsection (b) of this section, if such lien is . . . a judicial lien." 11 U.S.C.A. § 522(f)(2) defines when a lien "shall be considered to impair an exemption": It is considered to do so

> to the extent that the sum of
> (i) the lien;
> (ii) all other liens on the property; and
> (iii) the amount of the exemption that the debtor could claim if there were no liens on the property;
> exceeds the value that the debtor's interest in the property would have in the absence of any liens.

11 U.S.C.A. § 522(f)(2). DuPont concedes that this mathematical test is satisfied here.

DuPont nevertheless argues that the district court erred by concluding that a debtor can avoid a judicial lien under § 522(f) without having already claimed an exemption in the property subject to the lien. On this issue, the Supreme Court's decision in *Owen v. Owen,* 500 U.S. 305 . . . (1991), is instructive. In *Owen,* the respondent obtained a judgment against her ex-husband ("the debtor") for approximately $160,000, which was recorded in Sarasota County, Florida. . . . In 1984, the debtor purchased a condominium in Sarasota County that became subject to his ex-wife's judgment lien. . . . Florida subsequently amended its homestead law such that the condominium, which had not previously qualified as a homestead, qualified as one . . . . However, while Florida's constitution generally provides that homestead property is exempt from creditor process, the exemption does not apply to liens that pre-existed the homestead amendment . . . . Nevertheless, in 1986, the debtor filed for Chapter 7 bankruptcy and claimed a homestead exemption in his condominium . . . . The bankruptcy court sustained his claimed exemption and discharged his personal liability for his debts, but the condominium remained subject to his former wife's pre-existing lien . . . . When the debtor later moved to reopen his case to avoid the lien under § 522(f)(1), the bankruptcy court denied his request . . . .

Before the Supreme Court, the respondent argued that her judicial lien did not impair the exemption in question because, as a matter of state law, the existence of the lien prevented the debtor from being entitled to the exemption . . . .

The Supreme Court concluded that her argument was at odds with § 522(f)'s language, explaining:

> To determine the application of § 522(f) [courts] ask not whether the lien impairs an exemption to which the debtor is in fact entitled, but whether it impairs an exemption to which he *would have been* entitled but for the lien itself.
> As the preceding [underlined] words suggest, this reading is more consonant with the text of § 522(f) — which establishes as the baseline, against which impairment is to be measured, not an exemption to which the debtor "*is* entitled," but one to which he "*would have been* entitled."

Id. at 310–11 . . . (emphasis in original and footnote omitted).

It was after *Owen,* in 1994, that Congress amended § 522, to add subsection f(2), providing the aforementioned mathematical formula under which courts can determine whether the judicial lien at issue actually impairs the relevant exemption . . . . Importantly, one of the components is "the amount of the exemption that the debtor *could claim* if there were no liens on the property." 11 U.S.C.A. § 522(f)(2) (emphasis added). As was the case with the statutory language on which *Owen* relied, this language reflects § 522's focus not on any actual claim of exemption, but rather on the hypothetical exemption that the debtor would have been entitled to in the absence of the lien.

Furthermore, the Code's plain language does not even appear to allow a debtor to claim an exemption at a time when the existence of a lien is preventing the property from being exempt. *See* 11 U.S.C.A. § 522(b)(2)(A) (allowing a debtor to exempt "any property that *is* exempt under . . . State or local law that is applicable on the date of the filing of the petition" (emphasis added)); *see also Owen,* 500 U.S. at 308, 111 S.Ct. 1833 ("No property can be exempted . . . unless it first falls *within* the bankruptcy estate."). Only if the lien is in fact avoided does the debtor become entitled to claim the exemption under that scenario, and a debtor can amend her Schedule C at that time to do so, *see* Fed. R. Bankr. P. 1009(a). For all of these reasons, we conclude that the Code plainly provides that debtors need not claim an exemption as a precondition of avoiding a lien that the debtor contends impairs that exemption.

DuPont argues that allowing avoidance of a lien under § 522(f) before an exemption has actually been claimed would deny creditors the right to object. But that is simply not true.

Creditors are free to raise exemption issues during litigation of a § 522(f) lien-avoidance issue. *See* Fed. Bankr.R. 4003(d) ("[A] creditor may object to a motion filed under § 522(f) by challenging the validity of the exemption asserted to be impaired by the lien."). Additionally, when a debtor amends her Schedule C to add an exemption that a lien had previously prevented, her creditors have 30 days from the amendment to object to the exemption. *See* Fed. Bankr.R. 4003(b).

* * *

DuPont further maintains that allowing Botkin to avoid DuPont's lien without ever having claimed an exemption "permit[s] her to gain all the benefits of § 522(f) without having to bear the consequences of having to use her limited exemptions." . . . However, for the reasons we have explained, the language of the Code plainly does not require a debtor to claim an exemption in order to avoid a judicial lien on the basis that it impairs the exemption. Whether such a requirement could have carried with it certain policy advantages is a question we need not address . . . .

* * *

(Citations omitted.)

NOTES AND COMMENTS

1. Calculate the lien impairment on Botkin's home exemption. Remember that First and Citizens Bank hold a lien of $24,124, DuPont holds a lien of $9,800, and Botkin was entitled to a $5,500 property exemption. The property was worth $22,500. Which of the liens does Botkin hope to avoid? If she did not seek to avoid all of the liens, why not?

2. Can Botkin now claim the benefit of her homestead exemption following the court's decision? Why did she not claim the exemption in the first place?

3. DuPont argued that the court's decision allowed Botkin to enjoy the benefits of lien avoidance under § 522(f) without the burden of limited exemptions. Is that true and, if so, why does the court reject that argument?

4. For a contrary opinion, *see* In re Schneider, 2013 WL 5979756 (Bankr. E.D.N.Y. 2013). *Schneider* involved two consolidated cases with facts that were relatively similar to the *Botkin* facts. The court held that the debtors' failure to claim a homestead exemption barred them from avoiding the creditors' judicial liens under § 522(f). *Id.* at *7-10 (holding that statute is ambiguous and legislative history and policy support conclusion that debtor must claim exemption to avoid lien).

D. SURRENDER OF PROPERTY (§ 521)

When a debtor files for bankruptcy protection, the debtor takes on several duties. As noted, those duties include filing the schedules that accompany the bankruptcy petition. Section 521(a)(2)(A) requires that the debtor file a statement of intention regarding property of the estate encumbered by a lien. That statement of intention can indicate a debtor's desire to do one of several things with the property:

- Retain the property
- Surrender the property
- Claim the property as exempt
- Redeem[4] the property
- Reaffirm the debt[5] secured by the property

If the debtor chooses to retain property, the choice frequently involves a "ride-through," where a particular debt attached to that property rides through the bankruptcy case unaffected. For example, if a debtor is currently making timely payments on a loan secured by property, the debtor

---

4. *See* 11 U.S.C. § 722: "An individual debtor may . . . redeem tangible personal property . . . by paying the holder of such lien the amount of the allowed secured claim of such holder that is secured by such lien in full at the time of redemption." Redemption of a debt occurs when the debtor pays the creditor the entire debt in one lump sum in order to keep the collateral. *Black's Law Dictionary* (11th ed. 2019) (Defining redemption as "1. The act or an instance of reclaiming or regaining possession by paying a specific price.")

5. Reaffirmation occurs when the debtor agrees to pay debt after the conclusion of the bankruptcy case that would otherwise be discharged in the case. *Black's Law Dictionary* (11th ed. 2019) (Defining reaffirmation as "An agreement between the debtor and a creditor by which the debtor promises to repay a prepetition debt that would otherwise be discharged at the conclusion of the bankruptcy."). Reaffirmation agreements are discussed in more detail in Chapter 5.

may elect to keep the property but also must keep the associated debt and payment schedule. BAPCPA ended ride-throughs for personal property (such as a car) but allows for ride-throughs on real property (land and fixtures attached to the land, such as a house).

Alternatively, the debtor may choose to surrender property because the debtor does not want to be saddled with the debts associated with the property. Unfortunately, in some cases the property has so little value that no party wants it.

Beneficial Maine, Inc. v. Canning (In re Canning)

706 F.3d 64 (1st Cir. 2013)

Torruella, Circuit Judge

. . . Ralph G. Canning III and Megan L. Canning . . . filed a Chapter 7 bankruptcy petition and sought to surrender their residence. When their mortgage lenders . . . (collectively "Beneficial"), refused to foreclose or otherwise take title to the residence, the Cannings demanded that the mortgage lien be released. Beneficial also refused to do so, and the Cannings began an adversary proceeding claiming a discharge injunction violation. . . .

After an unsuccessful attempt to refinance the two-year old mortgage loan encumbering their residence, defaulting on the terms of said loan, and with foreclosure proceedings already underway in state court, the Cannings filed a Chapter 7 bankruptcy petition on March 5, 2009. According to their bankruptcy schedules, the mortgage loan had an outstanding balance of $186,521, while the residence had a market value of $130,000. The schedules also indicated that the Cannings intended to surrender the residence.

Early in the bankruptcy case, Beneficial voluntarily dismissed the state court foreclosure proceedings without prejudice "due to the [Cannings'] filing Chapter 7 bankruptcy." The Cannings received their bankruptcy discharge on June 3, 2009, and thus were released from their outstanding personal obligations on the mortgage loan. The exchange of correspondence underlying this appeal ensued two months thereafter.

Beneficial began the exchange with a letter informing the Cannings that it would "not initiate and/or complete foreclosure proceedings on [your residence]. You will retain ownership of the property" and "we will no longer advance any payments for taxes and insurances. You will be solely responsible for the payment of taxes, insurance, and maintenance of this property."

In response, the Cannings reminded Beneficial of the bankruptcy discharge injunction and demanded that it either "(1) immediately commence foreclosure proceedings or (2) immediately discharge the mortgage on the property." With no answer from Beneficial, on October 1, 2009, the Cannings sent it another letter to follow up on their demand.

Beneficial responded by letter dated October 19, 2009. As relevant here, Beneficial's letter stated: "we are unable to honor your request to release the lien until the lien balance is satisfied in the amount of $186,324.15. However, we could consider a settlement option or a short sale." Beneficial also explained that the Cannings' account had been charged off, that they had no personal obligation to pay the lien balance, and that its letter was not an attempt to collect from them personally.

Despite this disclaimer from Beneficial, the Cannings interpreted the letter as a further violation of the discharge injunction. The next letter they sent to Beneficial emphatically indicated so and warned that a bankruptcy adversary proceeding would be filed if Beneficial failed to either foreclose or release its lien. But Beneficial did not budge, reiterating, instead, its prior response. The Cannings subsequently informed Beneficial that: (1) the residence had been vacated; (2) the utilities had been turned off; and (3) the municipal authorities, as well as the sewerage company, had been notified that Beneficial was the responsible party for any obligations pertaining to the residence.

True to their word, on December 21, 2009, the Cannings reopened their bankruptcy case and initiated an adversary proceeding against Beneficial. Among other things, they claimed actual and punitive damages in connection with Beneficial's "failure or refusal to commence foreclosure or otherwise recover possession of the [residence]." The Cannings also sought a declaratory judgment "ordering [Beneficial] to either recover possession of the Property or deliver unencumbered title to . . . the[m]." In its responsive pleading, Beneficial denied all material allegations and raised nine affirmative defenses, including lack of intent to violate the discharge injunction. At that time, Beneficial estimated the market value of the residence to be $75,000.

* * *

The Cannings' complaint is premised on 11 U.S.C. § 524(a), which sets forth an automatic injunction against efforts intended to collect an already discharged debt. The injunction affords honest but unfortunate debtors with a "fresh start" from the burdens of personal liability for unsecured prepetition debts and thus advances the overarching purpose of the Bankruptcy Code . . . .

Despite its broad scope, the discharge injunction does not enjoin a secured creditor from recovering on valid prepetition liens, which, unless modified or avoided, ride through bankruptcy unaffected and are enforceable in accordance with state law. . . . One of the ways through which debtors might free themselves from a prepetition lien is by surrendering the encumbered collateral to the secured creditor under 11 U.S.C. § 521(a)(2). . . . "Surrendering" in this context means "that the debtor agree[s] to make the collateral available to the secured creditor-*viz.*, to cede his possessory rights in the collateral. . . ." . . . The secured creditor, however, has the prerogative to decide whether to accept or reject the surrendered collateral, since "nothing in subsection 521(a)(2) remotely suggests that the secured creditor is required to accept possession of the [collateral]." . . . But the creditor's decision in this respect must not constitute a subterfuge intended to coerce payment of a discharged debt. . . .

We set forth and applied the foregoing requirements in *Pratt* [Pratt v. General Motors Acceptance Corp. (In re Pratt), 462 F.3d 14 (1st Cir. 2006)], hence the Cannings' steadfast reliance on that case. As previewed above, *Pratt* revolved around a secured creditor's refusal to either repossess or release a lien on an inoperable, worthless car that Chapter 7 debtors moved to surrender in bankruptcy. Finding the value of the car insufficient to satisfy foreclosure expenses, the secured creditor wrote off the balance of its loan, and left the debtors in possession of the encumbered collateral. Upon receiving their bankruptcy discharge, the debtors promptly sought to dispose of the car at a salvage dealer. But because under applicable state law a dealer could receive a junk car only if free from all liens, the debtors were unsuccessful in their attempt to transfer possession of the car. And when the debtors asked the secured creditor to either repossess the car or release its lien, it repeatedly refused, informing the debtors that the lien would be released only upon full satisfaction of the unpaid loan amount.

After reopening their bankruptcy case, the debtors filed an adversary complaint, alleging that the secured creditor's posture was intended to coerce payment on a discharged debt, in violation of the discharge injunction. In reversing the bankruptcy court's judgment for the secured creditor, we zeroed in on the following facts: (1) the secured creditor refused to repossess the car, but conditioned release of its lien upon full payment of the loan balance; (2) the debtors could not dispose of the car while encumbered and thus would have to keep it indefinitely (together with the accompanying costs) unless they "paid in full"; and (3) there were no reasonable prospects that the car would generate sale proceeds for the secured creditor to attach, as it was essentially worthless with limited possibilities of appreciation over time.

Based on those facts, we held that the secured creditor's posture in exclusively conditioning release of its lien on full payment of the loan balance amounted to a reaffirmation of debt demand that contravened "the stringent 'anti-coercion' requirements of [the] Bankruptcy Code. . . ." Similarly, we noted that the secured creditor's refusal to release its lien "had the practical effect of eliminating the [debtors'] 'surrender' option under § 521(a)(2)." *Id.*

But given the secured creditor's prerogative to insist on its state-law *in rem* rights, we did not stop our analysis there. Rather, we set out to determine whether the secured creditor had articulated any reasons to explain away its posture. Since the secured creditor only proffered its state-law rights as a defense, we analyzed the creditor's underlying conduct to see whether it could be legitimized as a valid pursuit of those rights. We found that it could not, underscoring both the minimal value of the collateral and the lack of reasonable prospects that the collateral would ever be converted to attachable sale proceeds . . . .

In this case, contrary to the Cannings' contentions, the factual scenario is much different than that in *Pratt*. Absent from this case is the exclusive "pay in full" conditional release presented in *Pratt*. Rather, in this case, Beneficial offered to release its lien through either a settlement offer or a short sale. This not only indicates the intent to collect no more than the value secured by the underlying lien, as the bankruptcy court observed, but also denotes a willingness to negotiate a palatable solution for all involved.

By like token, this case is missing the quandary the debtors in *Pratt* faced, where they were required to either yield to the secured creditor's "pay in full" demand or indefinitely remain in possession of inoperable, worthless and burdensome collateral. The BAP's opinion was right on point in this respect: "there is nothing in the record . . . to evidence any expenses related to [the Cannings' continued] equitable ownership other than the . . . reference in their brief to being exposed to liability." 462 B.R. at 267. And to that we add that the appellate record also lacks evidence to show that the Cannings' residence was "inoperable" or unlivable when it was abandoned.

Furthermore, the record here does not paint a picture in which a secured creditor cornered the debtors between a rock and hard place. The record before us contains no evidence showing that the alternatives Beneficial proposed were unfeasible—that is, the Cannings never explained to the court exactly why a short sale or a settlement was out of the question for them. The record is also devoid of any other indicia of coercion, such as, for example, Beneficial's refusal to negotiate with the Cannings a compromise different to the one originally proposed. In fact, from the record available to us, it seems that the Cannings employed a "take it or leave it" approach in negotiating with their mortgage lender, who, given its state-law rights over the collateral, did not have to accept the two choices presented. Bankruptcy law, we must emphasize, cannot alter a secured creditor's state-law rights, unless it is shown that those rights are relied upon to coerce payment of a discharged debt. The record before us simply lacks that evidence.

Last but not least, unlike the collateral in *Pratt*, the collateral involved here is far from worthless, and its value may increase over time. A reasonable possibility that the collateral could be converted to attachable sale proceeds therefore exists, and, unlike *Pratt's* secured creditor, Beneficial can point to its state-law rights as one of the factors supporting its posture.

The Cannings downplay the foregoing differences and instead invite us to focus on the fact that their residence plummeted in value to little more than 38% of its original market price. According to the Cannings, that fact invites the inference that "Beneficial decided not to foreclose on the property [because] it would not be cost effective." Such a business decision, the Cannings continue, "clearly put into question [their] fresh start, which is what the First Circuit in *Pratt* specifically prohibited a creditor from doing." There are several problems with the Cannings' contentions.

. . . Under the Cannings' reading, we would have to find a discharge injunction violation every time a secured creditor opposes a debtor's "foreclose or release" demand based on the business determination that repossession is not cost effective. . . . *Pratt* sought to strike a balance between the competing state-law rights of secured creditors and the bankruptcy rights of debtors, and the reading the Cannings advance improperly skews that balance against secured creditors.

. . . The debtors in *Pratt* sought to disentangle themselves from an unduly burdensome situation by following a legally feasible alternative, without improperly burdening others. The Cannings, in contrast, invoke the "fresh start" to indirectly validate the decision to abandon their residence. They do so without providing any evidence showing that the residence posed an undue burden upon them after their bankruptcy discharge. The Cannings also fail to advance any legal authority, and we are not aware of any, to support the proposition that a homeowner may walk away, with no strings attached, from their legally owned residence. But even worse, in vacating their residence, the Cannings placed many of the burdens of dealing with an abandoned property on their neighbors, their town, and their city—in other words, on everyone but them. The "fresh start" does not countenance that result . . . .

A coda is necessary before we conclude. Today, where both lenders and homeowners strive to recuperate from hard economic times, this opinion should not be relied upon to leverage a way out of the bargaining table. It is one thing to insist upon state-law rights in refusing a recalcitrant "foreclose or release" demand by a debtor, and completely another to refuse negotiating with a debtor willing to compromise. Put differently, while this case may provide some guidance on the dos and don'ts applicable to the bargaining dynamics between secured creditors and bankruptcy debtors, our remarks in *Pratt* still control: "the line between forceful negotiation and improper coercion is not always easy to delineate, and each case must therefore be assessed in the context of its particular facts." . . .

* * *

(Citations omitted.)

NOTES AND COMMENTS

1. Why would a debtor surrender property in the bankruptcy case? And why would the bank refuse to take possession of the surrendered property? What options existed for the parties?

2. The court references a prior decision, Pratt v. General Motors Acceptance Corp. (In re Pratt), 462 F.3d 14 (1st Cir. 2006). How did the *Pratt* facts differ from the *Canning* facts, and why did that matter to the court?

E. TRUSTEE AVOIDING POWERS (§§ 544, 547, 548)

Normally, if a debtor lacks a legal or equitable interest in property on the day that the bankruptcy petition is filed, that property is excluded from the bankruptcy estate. However, the Code gives the bankruptcy trustee several "avoiding" powers that allow the trustee to avoid pre-petition actions in which the debtor granted a property interest to another. In avoiding these actions, the trustee regains the property for the estate despite the debtor's pre-petition actions. These powers include:

- 11 U.S.C. § 544 ("strong-arm" powers): the trustee's ability to void transfers by stepping in the shoes of another party who could avoid the transfer
- 11 U.S.C. § 547 ("preferential transfers"): the trustee's ability to void transfers that allow a pre-petition creditor to receive more than its fair share of property from the debtor
- 11 U.S.C. § 544 ("fraudulent transfers"): the trustee's ability to void transfers that either occur in order to defraud creditors or in which the recipient receives a benefit without due consideration in return

Section 550 of the Code provides the working mechanism for recovery of the voided transfers, providing that once a transfer is avoided under these (and other) sections of the Code, the trustee may recover the property or the value of the property from the entity receiving the voided transfer or from a subsequent transferee. This power to recover from subsequent transferees is limited; the chain of recovery breaks once a subsequent transferee takes the property for value and in good faith. 11 U.S.C. § 550(b).

1. Strong-Arm Powers

Section 544 of the Bankruptcy Code grants to the trustee the ability to step in the shoes of three types of competing parties: (1) a creditor with a judicial lien on all of the property of the estate, (2) a creditor with an unsatisfied execution claim against the debtor, and (3) a bona fide purchaser of all real property of the estate. But to fully understand what this status means in a particular bankruptcy case, one must know who the other claimants to the property of the estate are, what they have done to perfect an interest in that property, and what priority the relevant state's laws give to those parties. In other words, the trustee steps in the shoes of a competing party, but the state law dictates which of the competing parties wins the property.

For example, the UCC provides that if you have a secured creditor with an interest in the debtor's equipment (a creditor whose interest was voluntarily given by the debtor in exchange for a loan) and a judicial lien creditor with an interest in the same equipment (a creditor whose interest was given by a court due to unpaid debt), the secured creditor has priority over the judicial lien creditor *if* the secured creditor "perfected"[6] its interest in the equipment before the judicial lien creditor was given its lien. When was the trustee "given" the judicial lien? Under 11 U.S.C. § 544(a)(1), on the date that the bankruptcy case was filed. At that moment, the trustee is known as a "hypothetical lien creditor." If the secured creditor perfected before the bankruptcy petition was filed, state law dictates that the secured creditor takes priority in the equipment. If the secured creditor failed to perfect before the bankruptcy petition was filed, state law dictates that the trustee takes priority in the equipment. In that case, the secured creditor loses its interest in the property—becoming unsecured—and the trustee can use that property to satisfy the claims of all unsecured creditors. The following case considers a different strong-arm power given to the trustee—the status of a hypothetical bona fide purchaser of real property on the date of the bankruptcy filing. At issue was an Illinois law proscribing the information that needed to be included in a notice of a lien on the real property, and whether the failure to include some of that information would negate the lien as to a bona fide purchaser of property.

In re Crane

742 F.3d 702 (7th Cir. 2013)

HAMILTON, Circuit Judge

Under 11 U.S.C. § 544(a)(3), a trustee in bankruptcy has the so-called "strong-arm" power to "avoid . . . any obligation incurred by the debtor that is voidable by—a bona fide purchaser of real property . . . from the debtor. . . ." In these two appeals, we address a question that has divided bankruptcy courts in Illinois and pitted mortgage lenders against unsecured creditors. The question is whether, before a 2013 amendment to the Illinois mortgage recording statute, a bankruptcy trustee could use the strong-arm power to avoid a mortgage recorded in Illinois on the ground that the mortgage did not state on its face either a maturity date or an interest rate. Our answer is no. The Illinois statute on the form for recorded mortgages upon which the trustees base their strong-arm efforts, 765 Ill. Comp. Stat. 5/11 (2012), was written in permissive rather than mandatory terms. The absence of a maturity date and/or an interest rate did not allow a bankruptcy trustee to avoid a mortgage under the pre-amendment version of 765 ILCS 5/11. Accordingly, we affirm the judgment of the

---

6. The secured creditor can also take priority if it meets one of the evidentiary requirements for attachment and files its UCC-1 financing statement, even if full perfection is not met. This concept is more appropriate for a course in Secured Transactions.

district court in the *Crane* case, No. 13–1518, and the judgment of the bankruptcy court in the *Klasi Properties* case, No. 13–1277.

I. Factual and Procedural Background

The debtors in both appeals, Gary and Marsa Crane and Klasi Properties, LLC, borrowed money secured by mortgages on real estate. In both cases, the mortgages were recorded by the lenders to ensure the priority of their mortgage liens. In both cases, the recorded mortgages did not state the maturity date of the secured debt or the applicable interest rate. Those terms were included in the promissory notes, of course, which were fully incorporated by reference in the mortgages.

The Cranes sought bankruptcy protection in the Central District of Illinois, and Klasi Properties sought bankruptcy protection in the Southern District of Illinois. In both cases, the trustees filed adversary complaints under 11 U.S.C. § 544(a)(3) seeking to avoid the mortgages because they did not state the maturity dates or interest rates for the secured debts . . . .

II. Analysis

Our analysis begins with a bankruptcy trustee's "strong-arm" powers under 11 U.S.C. § 544(a)(3), which provides:

> The trustee shall have, as of the commencement of the case, and without regard to any knowledge of the trustee or of any creditor, the rights and powers of, or may avoid any transfer of property of the debtor or any obligation incurred by the debtor that is voidable by . . . a bona fide purchaser of real property, other than fixtures, from the debtor, against whom applicable law permits such transfer to be perfected, that obtains the status of a bona fide purchaser and has perfected such transfer at the time of the commencement of the case, whether or not such a purchaser exists.

For present purposes, the key is that a bankruptcy trustee may avoid any obligation or transfer of the debtor's property that a hypothetical bona fide purchaser could avoid, "without regard to any knowledge of the trustee or of any creditor." State law governs who would count as a bona fide purchaser and what constitutes constructive notice sufficient to defeat a bankruptcy trustee's section 544(a)(3) power . . . .

* * *

A bona fide purchaser in Illinois is one who acquires an "interest in [the] property for valuable consideration without actual or constructive notice of another's adverse interest in the property." . . . Actual notice is knowledge the purchaser had at the time of the conveyance, . . . but the terms of section 544(a)(3) provide that a bankruptcy trustee cannot be charged with actual notice. A trustee can be charged with constructive notice, however . . . .

Illinois defines constructive notice as knowledge that the law imputes to a purchaser, whether or not the purchaser had actual knowledge at the time of the conveyance . . . . There are two kinds of constructive notice: record notice and inquiry notice . . . . Record notice "imputes to a purchaser knowledge that could be gained from an examination of the grantor-grantee index in the office of the Recorder of Deeds, as well as the probate, circuit, and county court records for the county in which the land is situated." . . .

The trustees argue here that the mortgages were legally insufficient to give constructive notice to hypothetical bona fide purchasers because they failed to satisfy what the trustees call the formal "requirements" in the mortgage recording statute as it existed when these debtors filed their bankruptcy petitions, 765 ILCS 5/11 (2012).

* * *

The recorded mortgages at issue in these appeals accurately disclosed the mortgagors, the mortgagees, the amounts of indebtedness, the descriptions of the properties subject to the mortgages, and the dates of the mortgages. The mortgages also stated that the underlying debts were secured by separate but contemporaneously-signed promissory notes. The recorded mortgages did not set forth the maturity dates or the interest rates of the underlying loans.

If all the elements set forth by in the pre-amendment form of 765 ILCS 5/11, including the interest rate and maturity date, were mandatory, the trustees would have a stronger argument that each element listed in the mortgage "form" set forth in that section, including the interest rate and maturity date of the underlying debt, would need to appear on the face of the recorded mortgage for that document to serve as effective notice of the mortgage to a potential buyer of the property. If the elements listed in section 5/11's "form" were permissive, a recording may be deemed sufficient if it contains the indispensable elements of a mortgage even if the recorded document does not include every element listed in the recording statute.

Statutory interpretation here is a question of state law, and our role is to predict how the Illinois Supreme Court would decide the question . . . .

* * *

We believe the better view, and the one most likely to be adopted by the Illinois Supreme Court, is that the form set forth in section 5/11 has always been a permissive safe harbor, that the mortgages recorded in these cases supplied the indispensable elements of a mortgage under Illinois common law, and that the recorded mortgages were effective to give constructive record notice of the mortgages to potential buyers.

Thus, the trustees' section 544 strong-arm powers cannot avoid the banks' recorded mortgage liens.

. . . Here the statute's operative language is plainly permissive, not mandatory: "Mortgages of lands *may* be *substantially* in the following form." 765 ILCS 5/11 (emphasis added). The statute simply does not say that a recorded mortgage must set forth every element listed for the recording to be effective against third parties. Strict compliance with the *suggested* form is not required to ensure a valid mortgage enforceable against subsequent lenders and purchasers.

* * *

(Citations omitted.)

NOTES AND COMMENTS

1. The Illinois statute at issue in *Crane* now provides that "(b) The provisions of subsection (a) regarding the form of a mortgage are, and have always been, permissive and not mandatory. Accordingly, the failure of an otherwise lawfully executed and recorded mortgage to be in the form described in subsection (a) in one or more respects, including the failure to state the interest rate or the maturity date, or both, shall not affect the validity or priority of the mortgage, nor shall its recordation be ineffective for notice purposes regardless of when the mortgage was recorded." 765 ILCS 5/11 (2013).

2. If the mortgage had not been recorded, a bona fide purchaser could clearly take without being subject to the mortgage. Had that been the case and the trustee, stepping in the shoes of that hypothetical bona fide purchaser, could "take" the property not subject to the mortgage, how would that benefit the trustee?

3. The grantor-grantee index referenced by the court is the document and filing system used to record property ownership in most of the United States. It is notoriously difficult to use, and it is one of the reasons that most purchasers of real property in the United States (including houses) also buy title insurance, because mistakes are made not infrequently in determining who actually owns property. The court imputed to the creditor whatever knowledge could be discerned from the grantor-grantee index, including some information that was not specifically listed. Here the creditor was a sophisticated mortgage lender. Should a court impute such knowledge if the creditor is far less sophisticated than a bank?

2. Preferential Transfers

Section 547 of the Bankruptcy Code allows the trustee to recover preferential transfers. To qualify, the transaction must meet all of the elements listed in § 547(b):

- A transfer
- Of the debtor's property interest
- To or for the benefit of a creditor
- Made on account of existing debt
- Made while the debtor was insolvent (which is rebuttably presumed during the 90 days pre-petition pursuant to § 547(f))
- Made during the reachback period (90 days, or one year if the transferee is an insider)
- That allows the creditor to receive more than the creditor would have received had the creditor *not* received the transfer and the debtor had filed a liquidation proceeding

In some cases, a debtor truly "prefers" one creditor over another. For example, if a debtor is about to file for Chapter 7 and chooses to repay unsecured debt owed to his sister over debt owed to a credit card company just before filing, the debtor has preferred his sister, and the payments made to her may be recovered by the trustee. Read § 547(b) and consider how each element is met in that scenario. The debtor's sister has received property of the debtor by being paid. She is a creditor and is paid on a debt. Assuming that the payment was made during the 90 days before the debtor filed for bankruptcy protection, the debtor is presumed insolvent and the payment fell within the appropriate reachback period. Does the sister receive more with the transfer than without it? Without the transfer, she would have entered bankruptcy with an unsecured claim, to be paid pennies on the dollar. With the transfer, she was paid in full (at least as to the portion of the debt that was paid). All of the elements are met, and she received a preferential transfer.

What if the debtor paid an unsecured creditor prepetition not out of familial affection, but simply because the payment was past due? You will see that the elements still cause the payment to qualify as preferential because the creditor is really no different than the sister above. Note that the elements do not require intent of the debtor to prefer one creditor over the other, nor do they look at the knowledge or intent of the recipient. Instead, preferential transfer law seeks only to ensure a fair distribution among creditors by ensuring that payments made during the debtor's slide into bankruptcy are redistributed according to the Bankruptcy Code's scheme. The following case considers what constitutes a transfer of an *interest* in the debtor's property. Since a preferential transfer only exists if *all* of the § 547(b) elements are met, if the debtor does not transfer an interest in its property, no preference has occurred.

Ute Mesa Lot 1, LLC v. First-Citizens Bank & Trust Co. (In re Ute Mesa Lot 1, LLC)

736 F.3d 947 (10th Cir. 2013)

KELLY, Circuit Judge

Plaintiff–Appellant Ute Mesa Lot 1, LLC, ("Ute Mesa") appeals from a bankruptcy court order denying it relief under 11 U.S.C. § 547(b). The narrow issue is whether a notice of lis pendens filed in Colorado can constitute a preferential transfer under 11 U.S.C. § 547(b). Both the bankruptcy and district courts held that a lis pendens is not a transfer because it merely serves as notice of pending litigation. Exercising jurisdiction under 28 U.S.C. § 158(d)(1), we affirm.

. . . Ute Mesa is a real estate developer in Colorado. In October 2007, it received a $12 million loan from Defendant–Appellee United Western Bank ("Bank") to finance the construction of a single family home on property it owned in Aspen ("property"). To secure the loan, the Bank prepared a deed of trust incorrectly identifying Ute Mesa's sole member (Leathem Stern) as the owner rather than Ute Mesa. Because the grantor under the deed of trust was not the owner of the property, the deed of trust was ineffective in giving the Bank a lien on the property.

On May 19, 2010, the Bank filed suit in Colorado state court seeking reformation of the deed of trust and a declaration that it had a first priority lien on the property. Two days later, the Bank filed a notice of lis pendens in the Pitkin County real property records.

On August 13, 2010, Ute Mesa petitioned for Chapter 11 bankruptcy relief. Ute Mesa continues as debtor in possession of the property. In April 2011, Ute Mesa filed an adversary proceeding against the Bank seeking to avoid the lis pendens as a preferential transfer. The bankruptcy court granted the Bank's motion to dismiss, and the federal district court affirmed.

. . . the district court . . . agreed with the bankruptcy court that, "since a lis pendens only serves the limited purpose of *notice,* the filing of a lis pendens is not a transfer disposing of or parting with an *interest in the property* within the meaning of § 101(54)(D)(ii)." . . . Thus, no preferential transfer occurred, and Ute Mesa could not avoid the lis pendens.

* * *

Under § 547 of the Bankruptcy Code, a debtor in possession "may avoid any transfer of an interest of the debtor in property, to or for the benefit of a creditor," if that transfer occurs within 90 days prior to the filing of the bankruptcy petition. 11 U.S.C. § 547(b)(1), (4). . . . Fundamentally, however, the "keystone of a preference is a transfer of the debtor's property." . . . In pertinent part, the Bankruptcy Code defines a "transfer" as:

> each mode, direct or indirect, absolute or conditional, voluntary or involuntary, of disposing of or parting with—
> (i) property; or
> (ii) an interest in property.

11 U.S.C. § 101(54)(D). The Bankruptcy Code, however, does not define "property" or "interest in property." . . . Thus we must look to the property rights attendant to the filing of a lis pendens under Colorado law.

. . . In Colorado, a party may record a notice of lis pendens against real property after initiating an action "wherein relief is claimed affecting the title to real property." Colo. Rev. Stat. § 38–35–110(1). Recording a lis pendens provides "notice to any person thereafter acquiring, by, through, or under any party named in such notice, an interest in the real property . . . that the interest so acquired may be affected by the action described in the notice." *Id.*

Colorado cases applying the doctrine of lis pendens make clear that a "lis pendens does not constitute a lien against real property." . . . A judgment lien does not arise against real property until a "transcript of the judgment" is recorded. Colo. Rev. Stat. § 13–52–102(1) . . . .

Nonetheless, the recordation of a lis pendens does have a very real legal effect: "Once a lis pendens is filed, it renders title unmarketable and therefor effectively prevents the property's transfer until the litigation is resolved or the lis pendens is expunged." . . . This protects "the judgment of the court [so that it] cannot be frustrated by alienation of the property to a third party not bound by the outcome of the litigation." . . . Despite a lis pendens's attendant consequences, "[h]owever, it is still only a notice." . . .

* * *

Ute Mesa argues that, although the lis pendens did not transfer its property per se, the lis pendens did transfer one of its discrete interests in the property—its right to convey fee simple title free of the interests of the Bank . . . . Because the lis pendens rendered the property unmarketable and subject to the Bank's claims, Ute Mesa contends that its rights were diminished upon the recording of the lis pendens, thus reducing the value of the property to the detriment of its creditors . . . .

Not only is a disposition of the debtor's "property" a transfer, a disposition of any of the debtor's separate "interests in property" is likewise a transfer under the Bankruptcy Code. 11 U.S.C. § 101(54) (D)(i)-(ii). We recognize that a lis pendens in Colorado clouds an owner's title thereby impairing its marketability . . . . However, we do not see how clouding title constitutes "disposing of or parting with" an interest of the debtor in property within the Bankruptcy Code's definition of a "transfer." 11 U.S.C. § 101(54)(D). Certainly, fee simple ownership is the most comprehensive bundle of rights and includes the right to convey property. That right, however, is not destroyed by a notice of lis pendens. Although a lis pendens might render title "unmarketable" under Colorado law, the owner still retains the right to convey that property, assuming he finds a willing buyer . . . .

In fact, the Colorado Supreme Court has addressed this very argument. . . . The Colorado Supreme Court flatly rejected that assertion by stating that a lis pendens "harm[s] no legitimate interest of the owner." . . .

Here, Ute Mesa may find it difficult to locate a purchaser willing to buy the property at full price, pending the resolution of the Bank's claims. However, this does not detract from the fact that the lis pendens itself "harm[s] no legitimate interest of the owner," . . . . Though the right to convey property may have been devalued, it has not been "disposed of" or "parted with" so to qualify as a "transfer" under the Bankruptcy Code. Contrary to Ute Mesa's argument, a "diminished" interest does not equate to a "transferred" interest.

Ute Mesa has been deprived of no more than its ability to convey the property without first informing the prospective purchaser of the existence of the Bank's claim. Accordingly, under Colorado law, the effect of a lis pendens rendering title unmarketable is, on its own, not a transfer of an interest of the debtor in property.

(Citations omitted.)

NOTES AND COMMENTS

1. The Tenth Circuit's *Ute Mesa* decision created a circuit split. In Hurst Concrete Prods., Inc. v. Lane (In re Lane), the Ninth Circuit BAP determined that a lis pendens against real property did transfer an interest in the debtor's property. The Ninth Circuit BAP likened a lis pendens to perfection of a lien on the property because of its impact on future creditors:

   > Due to the constructive notice supplied by a lis pendens, a conveyance of the real property to a subsequent bona fide purchaser "is void as against . . . any judgment affecting the title, unless such conveyance shall have been duly recorded prior to the record of notice of action." Cal. Civ. Code § 1214. Once Hurst recorded the lis pendens, its interest was perfected, because no subsequent purchaser of the Lanes' property could acquire an interest superior to its interest . . . .

   Hurst Concrete Prods., Inc. v. Lane (In re Lane), 980 F.2d 601, 605 (9th Cir. BAP 1992). The Code defines a transfer as "the creation of a lien; . . . the retention of title as a security interest; . . . the foreclosure of a debtor's equity of redemption; or . . . each mode, direct or indirect, absolute or conditional, voluntary or involuntary, of disposing of or parting with—(i) property; or (ii) an interest in property." 11 U.S.C. § 101(54). Does this definition aid in determining whether the *Lane* or *Ute Mesa* decision is correct? Does the policy of preferential transfers—ensuring fair distribution among creditors—provide any guidance?

2. Consider whether each of the following constitutes a transfer of an interest in debtor's property: (1) the grant of a security interest in the debtor's automobile; (2) the appointment of a receiver permitted to take funds from debtor's bank account; or (3) the debtor relinquishing leases on its stores back to the landlord. Each has been deemed a transfer, though the timing of the transfer differed slightly. *See* Russell v. Quality Auto City, Inc. (In re Hermann), 271 B.R. 892, 894 (Bankr. D. Wyo.

2001), *citing* Fidelity Financial Services, Inc. v. Fink, 522 U.S. 211 (1998) (perfection of security interest in car deemed a transfer that occurred when last act for perfection done); Flooring Sys., Inc. v. Chow (In re Poston), 765 F.3d 518 (5th Cir. 2014) (transfer of interest in debtor's property occurred when bank at which funds were located received receivership order, not when receiver was appointed, even though bank actually relinquished funds to receiver some time after receiving order); Official Comm. of Unsec. Creditors v. T.D. Invs. I, LLP (In re Great Lakes Quick Lube LP), 816 F.3d 482 (7th Cir. 2016) (transfer occurred when debtor gave up leases back to landlord).

The final requirement of a preferential transfer requires that the creditor receive more via the transfer than would be received in bankruptcy had the transfer not occurred. Normally, that means that if a creditor would have been paid in full either way, the creditor cannot receive a preferential transfer. The following case provides an unusual exception to that principle because the payment to the creditor without the preference would have come from a different source.

Committee of Creditors Holding Unsecured Claims v. Koch Oil Co. (In re Powerine Oil Co.)

59 F.3d 969 (9th Cir. 1995)

KOZINSKI, Circuit Judge

Can an unsecured creditor be better off when the debtor defaults rather than paying off the debt? Yes: Law can be stranger than fiction in the Preference Zone.

. . . Powerine Oil Company (the debtor here) obtained a $250.6 million line of credit from a syndicate consisting of several banks and insurance companies; the loan was secured by most of Powerine's personal property. The security agreement provided that the collateral would serve as security for all letters of credit that "have been, or are in the future, issued on the account of Debtor." . . .

Koch Oil Company thereafter agreed to sell crude oil to Powerine. To secure Powerine's obligation, it designated Koch as beneficiary of two irrevocable standby letters of credit issued by First National Bank of Chicago, one of the lenders covered by the security agreement. The letters, which were to expire in April 1984, totaled approximately $8.7 million, an amount at all times sufficient to cover the cost of the oil Koch sold to Powerine.

In January and February 1984, Koch billed Powerine $3.2 million for oil it had delivered in December and January. Powerine eventually paid this amount but, unfortunately for Koch, it also filed a chapter 11 bankruptcy petition less than 90 days later. The Committee of Creditors Holding Unsecured Claims (the Committee) eventually brought an action to recover the payment, claiming it was a preference under 11 U.S.C. § 547(b).

The bankruptcy court held that the transfer was protected by the "contemporaneous exchange for new value" exception of 11 U.S.C. § 547(c)(1) and granted Koch's motion for summary judgment. The Bankruptcy Appellate Panel (BAP) affirmed on a different ground: It held that the payment wasn't a preference because it didn't enable Koch to recover more than it would in a chapter 7 liquidation. Even if Powerine hadn't made the $3.2 million transfer, the BAP reasoned, Koch would have been paid in full because it would have drawn on First National's letters of credit.

. . . Bankruptcy Code section 547(b) sets forth the five elements of a preferential transfer. The parties dispute only whether the last element—section 547(b)(5)—was satisfied here. Under this provision, the Committee must prove that Koch "received more than it would [have] if the case were a chapter 7 liquidation case, the transfer had not been made, and [Koch] received payment of the debt to the extent provided by the provisions of the Code." . . .

Whether section 547(b)(5)'s requirements have been met turns in part on the status of the creditor to whom the transfer was made. Pre-petition payments to a fully secured creditor generally "will not be considered preferential because the creditor would not receive more than in a chapter 7 liquidation.". . . With respect to unsecured creditors, however, the rule is quite different: "[A]s long as the distribution in bankruptcy is less than one-hundred percent, *any* payment 'on account' to an unsecured creditor during the preference period will enable that creditor to receive more than he would have received in liquidation had the payment not been made." . . .

Vis-a-vis Powerine, Koch was an unsecured creditor as it didn't hold any security interest in Powerine's property. *See* 11 U.S.C. § 506(a). Because most of Powerine's assets on the date it filed for bankruptcy were subject to the lien held by the secured creditors, Powerine's unsecured creditors could expect to receive much less than one-hundred cents on the dollar in a chapter 7 liquidation. Consequently, Powerine's $3.2 million pre-petition payment enabled Koch to recover more than it would have in a chapter 7 liquidation, and it was therefore a preference.

The BAP came to the contrary conclusion by focusing on the fact that Koch could have drawn down the letters of credit, had Powerine not paid it directly. Since Koch would have recovered the full amount owed to it (albeit from First National) had Powerine defaulted, the BAP reasoned that the $3.2 million payment wasn't a preference.

Courts have long held, however, that the key factor in determining whether a payment is a preference is the "percentage [] . . . [creditors'] claims are entitled to draw out of the *estate of the bankrupt*." . . . Thus, the relevant inquiry focuses "not on whether a creditor may have recovered all of the monies owed by the debtor *from any source whatsoever*, but instead upon whether the creditor would have received less than a 100% payout" from the debtor's estate . . . . That Koch had recourse against a third party in case the debtor defaulted thus has no bearing on this issue.

The BAP nonetheless invoked a "rule of reason" to avoid what it viewed as an inequitable result . . . . Koch's right to collect under the letters could be taken into account, the BAP held, because the letters of credit had expired by the time the Committee initiated its preference action. Koch was thus left far worse off because Powerine paid its bill rather than defaulting. The BAP recognized that a creditor's "rights against a surety are not relevant to whether a transfer is preferential so long as those rights are still in place after the preference action is commenced." It concluded, however, that "when that right of action against the surety no longer exists, it is incumbent upon the court to measure the net recovery that the transferee would have obtained from the surety had the transfer not been made.". . . The BAP cited no authority for this proposition and we construe it to have been an exercise of its equitable powers.

Although bankruptcy courts are sometimes referred to as courts of equity, the Supreme Court has reminded us that "whatever equitable powers remain in the bankruptcy courts must and can only be exercised within the confines of the Bankruptcy Code.". . . Equity may not be invoked to defeat clear statutory language, nor to reach results inconsistent with the statutory scheme established by the Code . . . . Because the statutory language here provides no basis for the BAP's "rule of reason," we conclude that it was error to consider the right to draw on third-party letters of credit in deciding whether Koch had received a preference.

(Citations omitted.)

NOTES AND COMMENTS

1. Notice that the party bringing the preference action in this case was not the debtor-in-possession (which enjoys the powers of a trustee in a Chapter 11 case), but instead the creditors' committee. Debtors-in-possession may be reluctant to bring preference actions against creditors, particularly creditors that they hope to continue to do business with post-petition. Courts have used various Code provisions and policies to provide standing to creditors' committees, known as "derivative standing," and sometimes to individual creditors, to pursue avoidance actions when the trustee of debtor-in-possession "unjustifiably refuses" to bring an action. Hyundai Translead, Inc. v. Jackson Truck & Trailer Repair, Inc. (In re Trailer Source, Inc.), 555 F.3d 231, 242-243 (6th Cir. 2009); *see also* 11 U.S.C. §§ 503, 1103.

2. There are many ways in which a creditor that is not paid in full in bankruptcy might be able to recover. A letter of credit operates as a bank's guaranty of a debt. Debts might also be guaranteed by other parties—executives of a company, parent or sibling companies, family members, and so on. Why is the fact that the creditor could receive full payment of the debt outside of bankruptcy through one of these guaranties *not* a defense to the preference action? In other words, why make the creditor return the preference to the estate and seek the payment from another source?

Even when the bankruptcy trustee proves that a preferential transfer occurred, that transfer cannot be recovered if it meets one of several exceptions listed in § 547(c). As each exception below is discussed, review §547(b) to see why the elements of a preferential transfer are met, and then review §547(c) to see why the exception applies. The primary exceptions include:

- Substantially contemporaneous exchange (§ 547(c)(1)): A preferential transfer cannot be avoided if it was both intended by the parties to be in exchange for new value received by the debtor *and* was actually substantially contemporaneous

---

Example

Debtor purchases a boat from Creditor. Debtor takes possession of the boat on March 1, creating an obligation to pay Creditor. Debtor actually makes payment 15 days later because the parties agreed to allow the debtor some time to test the boat before making payment. Technically, the elements of a preferential transfer are met, but the parties likely intended that the exchange be contemporaneous, and the transfer is likely close enough in time to qualify such that the trustee cannot avoid the preferential transfer.

- Ordinary course of business (§ 547(c)(2)): A preferential transfer cannot be avoided if the debt paid was incurred in the ordinary course of business of the parties *and* the payment itself was made in the ordinary course of business of either the parties or the industry

---

Example

Debtor purchases a boat on credit from Creditor. Under the terms of the agreement, which are standard in the industry, Debtor will pay for the boat in equal monthly installments over the next two years at a typical interest rate. Debtor takes possession of the boat on March 1, making payments each month on schedule. When Debtor files for bankruptcy on December 1 of the same year, the payments made in September, October, and November meet the elements of a preferential transfer, but because the debt was incurred in the ordinary course of business and the payments were made in the ordinary course of business, the trustee cannot avoid the preferential transfer.

- Purchase-money security interest (the enabling loan exception) (§ 547(c)(3)): A preferential transfer that involves the creation of a security interest in debtor's property cannot be avoided if it secured value given in order to purchase the collateral that is the subject of the transfer as long as the security interest was perfected within 30 days of debtor taking possession of it.

Example

Debtor purchases a boat on credit from Creditor, granting to Creditor a security interest in the boat as collateral for the loan. This is known as a "purchase-money security interest" because the loan was used to buy the collateral. Debtor takes possession of the boat on March 1, and Creditor "perfects" its interest in the boat by following state-law perfection methods on March 29. Debtor files for bankruptcy protection on June 15. The March 29 perfection of the interest in the boat would qualify as a preferential transfer, but because Creditor's interest in the boat was a purchase-money security interest and Creditor perfected within 30 days of Debtor's receipt of the boat, the trustee cannot avoid the preferential transfer.

- New value (§ 547(c)(4)): A preferential transfer can be offset against new value extended to the debtor by the creditor receiving the preferential transfer *after* the preferential transfer was made.

Example

Debtor purchases a boat on credit from Creditor. Under the terms of the agreement, Debtor will pay for the boat in equal monthly installments over the next two years, at a typical interest rate. Debtor misses several payments during the summer after losing his job. On October 15, Debtor, having secured a new job, makes a lump-sum payment (of $7,000) to make up for the missed payments. Debtor then buys a boat cover on credit from Creditor on November 15; the boat cover costs $5,000, of which Debtor pays nothing at the time of sale. When Debtor files for bankruptcy on December 1 of the same year, the payments made on October 15 meet the elements of a preferential transfer and do not qualify as ordinary course payments. But because Creditor then extended $5,000 of additional credit to Debtor, the amount that the trustee can recover from Creditor is reduced from $7,000 to $2,000. Note that Creditor enters bankruptcy with a $7,000 claim anyway, but now it is a $2,000 claim on the initial loan and a $5,000 claim on the new loan.

- Floating lien (§ 547(c)(5)): If the creditor receiving a preferential transfer has a security interest in either inventory or accounts receivable, the preferential transfer exists only to the extent that payments made to the creditor and interests given in new accounts or inventory allowed the creditor to become *more* secure comparing the point in time that is 90 days prior to the petition date.

Example

The boat seller has a $1 million line of credit with Bank, secured by all of the seller's inventory (boats, of course). On January 1, Bank is owed $800,000 and the seller has $600,000 of inventory, and is thus $200,000 undersecured. On January 15, the seller paid Bank $100,000. On February 5, the seller obtained $200,000 in additional boats. On February 15, the seller borrowed an additional $300,000 on the line of *credit. On March 1, the seller sold $100,000 of boats. Finally, on March 15, the seller paid Bank $100,000. When the seller files for bankruptcy on April 1—90 days after January 1—Bank is owed $900,000 ($800,000 − $100,000 + $300,000 − $100,000). The collateral is worth $700,000 ($600,000 + $200,000 − $100,000). On the petition date, Bank is $200,000 unsecured. Every time that Bank was paid during the preference period (two $100,000 payments) and every time that Bank attached to new collateral ($200,000 of new boats), a preferential transfer occurred. But some exceptions (ordinary course and new value) might apply. Rather than trying to match up all of the transactions that might occur during this 90-day period, the Code allows comparing the status of the creditor at the beginning of the preference period to the end of the preference period. Here, the creditor's position in unchanged because the creditor started and ended $200,000 undersecured. Thus, the trustee cannot avoid the preferential transfer.*

The next case considers whether some transactions are structured to fall outside preferential transfer, and, if so, what the consequences are.

Dietz v. Calandrillo (In re Genmar Holdings, Inc.)

776 F.3d 961 (8th Cir. 2015)

LOKEN, Circuit Judge

The bankruptcy trustee for Chapter 7 debtor Genmar Holdings, Inc. commenced this adversary proceeding seeking to avoid as preferential a $65,000 payment made to Michael Calandrillo within ninety days of bankruptcy. *See* 11 U.S.C. § 547(b) . . . .

The relevant facts are undisputed. In April 2007, Calandrillo purchased a boat manufactured by Hydra–Sports, a subsidiary of Genmar Tennessee, a subsidiary of Genmar Holdings. Calandrillo claimed the boat was defective and commenced an arbitration proceeding. On February 19, 2009, Calandrillo entered into a settlement agreement with "Genmar Tennessee, Inc. . . . together with its . . . parents [and] subsidiaries." Calandrillo agreed to convey title to the boat to Genmar Tennessee, free of liens and encumbrances; Hydra–Sports agreed to pay Calandrillo $205,000 in the following manner:

A. Hydra–Sports shall pay to the Bank (which currently holds a lien on the Boat) such amounts as necessary to obtain a discharge of the Bank's lien on the Boat, and it is an express condition of this agreement that Hydra–Sports is to receive a lien waiver from the Bank immediately upon payment to the Bank . . .

B. The remainder of the Settlement Payment shall be paid to the trust account of [Calandrillo's attorneys], in trust for and on behalf of [Calandrillo], no sooner tha[n] 15 days after Genmar Tennessee receives the lien waiver confirming the Bank's discharge of the lien and all title assignment documents . . . for the Boat.

The next day, the bank received $140,000 from a Genmar entity and issued a lien waiver. On February 25, Calandrillo executed a bill of sale conveying the boat to Genmar Tennessee. On March 4, he sent documents assigning title to Genmar Tennessee. On March 23, Genmar Holdings sent Calandrillo a check for the $65,000 settlement balance. On June 1, 2009, Genmar Holdings and twenty-one subsidiaries, including Genmar Tennessee, filed for bankruptcy. The trustee brought this suit seeking recovery of the $65,000 payment from Calandrillo as a preferential transfer. The $140,000 payment to the bank a month earlier was outside the ninety-day preference period in § 547(b).

The avoidance of preferential transfers under § 547 "is intended to discourage creditors from racing to dismember a debtor sliding into bankruptcy and to promote equality of distribution to creditors in bankruptcy." . . . Contemporaneous new value exchanges are excepted from avoidance because they "encourage creditors to continue doing business with troubled debtors who may then be able to avoid bankruptcy altogether," and "because other creditors are not adversely affected if the debtor's estate receives new value." . . .

Calandrillo claims that the § 547(c)(1) exception applies to the $65,000 payment because he provided new value to the debtor when he conveyed the boat in a contemporaneous exchange. "The critical inquiry in determining whether there has been a contemporaneous exchange for new value is whether the parties intended such an exchange." . . . Calandrillo bears the burden of proving this fact. § 547(g) . . . . Here, the BAP affirmed the bankruptcy court's conclusion that Calandrillo presented no evidence permitting a reasonable fact-finder to find that the parties to the settlement agreement intended a contemporaneous exchange for new value. We agree.

Calandrillo's conveyance of the boat was completed on March 4, when he sent executed title documents to Genmar Tennessee. He received payment of the $65,000 settlement balance on March 23. This time lag, by itself, does not resolve whether the transaction was intended to be a "contemporaneous exchange." . . . Many exchanges the parties intend to be contemporaneous cannot be completed instantly, or even within a few days. For example, in *In re Lewellyn & Co., Inc.,* we upheld the bankruptcy court's finding that the parties intended stock purchases settled seven business days later to be contemporaneous exchanges . . . . "[C]ontemporaneity is a flexible concept which requires a case-by-case inquiry into all relevant circumstances." . . .

In this case, the essential question of the parties' intent is not conceded or obvious. Calandrillo argues the requisite intent can be found in the settlement agreement. The settlement agreement provided that Genmar Tennessee would make two payments to re-acquire clear title to the allegedly defective boat. First, the bank holding a substantial lien would be paid and provide a lien waiver. Initially satisfying an existing lien creditor is not inconsistent with the parties intending a contemporaneous exchange. Second, after Calandrillo transferred the necessary title documents to Genmar Tennessee, he would be paid the $65,000 balance of the "purchase" price. Again, providing a reasonable time for the buyer to review title documents is a type of delay that, if reasonable, would not be inconsistent with the parties intending a contemporaneous exchange. But here, the settlement agreement provided that the final $65,000 payment would be made to Calandrillo *no sooner than* fifteen days after Genmar Tennessee received the lien waiver and title documents. Thus, on its face, the settlement agreement reflected that what might have been a contemporaneous exchange of a boat for $205,000 was instead a short-term loan of $65,000 to the debtor. A debtor's repayment of a loan within ninety days of bankruptcy is an avoidable preference.

Calandrillo produced no evidence explaining the reason for this open-ended payment delay in the settlement agreement. . . . a reasonable fact-finder could only conclude that the settlement agreement's unexplained fifteen-day holding period evidenced the intent to provide the debtor a short-term loan.

* * *

(Citations omitted.)

NOTES AND COMMENTS

1. Why might the parties have agreed to a 15-day waiting period before payment on the boat? Parties often consider how to avoid preferential

transfers when entering into transactions. What could the parties have done to avoid the potential for a preference, and whose responsibility is it in the negotiations?

2. The court notes that the purpose of the contemporaneous exchange exception is to encourage creditors to continue to work with defaulting debtors. What are the purposes behind the other exceptions?

3. Fraudulent Transfers (§ 548)

Section 548 allows a trustee to recover fraudulent transfers from the debtor's estate. Fraudulent transfers fall under one of two categories: actual fraud or constructive fraud. Actual fraud, as the name implies, occurs when the debtor transfers the property with fraudulent intent toward the creditors. The bankruptcy code does not provide any elements for determining the existence of actual fraud or intent. Determining a debtor's intent provides a unique challenge, particularly when the debtor is not a party to the litigation. Consider the following case and how it determines the existence of actual fraud.

Ponzi Schemes

A pyramid scheme is a fraudulent business model that recruits victims with a promise of payments for recruiting even more victims to the scheme. A Ponzi scheme is a particular type of pyramid scheme generally involving some esoteric investment strategy "in which returns to investors are not financed through the success of the underlying business venture, but are taken directly from money invested by new participants. Typically, investors are promised large returns for their investments. Initial investors are actually paid the promised returns, which attract additional investors." Sender v. Heggland Family Trust (In re Hedged-Invs. Assocs., Inc.), 48 F.3d 470 (10th Cir. 1995), citing *In re Independent Clearing House Co.,* 41 B.R. 985, 994 n. 12 (Bankr. D. Utah 1984). It is named for Charles Ponzi, who convinced numerous people to invest in international "postal reply coupons"—a bond used for handling international postage—following World War I, and paid returns to earlier investors with the money given to him by later investors. http://postalmuseum.si.edu/behindthebadge/ponzi-scheme.html. More recently, former NASDAQ chairman Bernard Madoff used a Ponzi scheme to defraud investors of $65 billion.

Ritchie Capital Management, LLC v. Stoebner

779 F.3d 857 (8th Cir. 2015)

RILEY, Chief Judge

This case marks yet another dispute stemming from Tom Petters's multi-billion dollar fraud. The bankruptcy trustee for Polaroid Corporation (Polaroid)—a Petters company—succeeded in the bankruptcy court in avoiding as fraudulent the transfer of several Polaroid trademarks to [Ritchie Capital Management, LLC] . . . . On appeal, the district court affirmed the bankruptcy court's decision . . . .

I. Background

. . . Petters, through his company Petters Company, Inc. (PCI), purported to run a "diverting" business that purchased electronics in bulk and resold them at high profits to major retailers. The business was a sham, and the only influx of money came from loans or investments. Petters was convicted of multiple counts of mail fraud, wire fraud, and money laundering perpetrated through PCI and PGW [Peters Group Worldwide] and was sentenced to fifty years in prison.

In 2005, Petters, as PGW's sole board member, directed PGW to purchase Polaroid, becoming the 100% beneficial owner of Polaroid stock, and Petters became the sole member and "Chairman" of Polaroid's board of directors. Although a subsidiary of PGW, Polaroid operated as an independent, stand-alone corporation and engaged in legitimate business operations. On at least two occasions, Petters took several million dollars from Polaroid to satisfy PCI debts.

In late 2007 and early 2008, Petters's companies—including Polaroid—began to experience "major" financial difficulty. On January 31, 2008, a broker for PGW approached Ritchie about obtaining a loan. The next day, Ritchie loaned PGW $31 million to pay off Polaroid and PGW debts. The loan bore an 80% annual interest rate and was to be repaid within ninety days. Petters personally guaranteed the loan, but Ritchie was told the loan would also be "backed by the entire Polaroid corporation." . . . Throughout February, Ritchie extended a number of additional loans, totaling $115 million, under the same terms. On May 9, 2008, Ritchie lent PGW and PCI an additional $12 million to be repaid in three weeks and bearing 362.1% annual interest. Polaroid was not a signatory on any of the loans, and although the initial loan was used to repay a Polaroid debt, the proceeds of the loans did not go to Polaroid.

By September 1, 2008, all of the loans were past due, and Ritchie began demanding collateral to secure the overdue loans. On September 19, five days before Petters was raided by the Federal Bureau of Investigation (FBI), Petters executed a Trademark Security Agreement (TSA) giving Ritchie liens on several Polaroid trademarks as consideration for Ritchie's extensions of the loans' repayment dates.

Polaroid's CEO, Mary Jeffries, objected to the TSA because she feared it would impede Polaroid's ability to raise new capital for the company. Although Polaroid had valuable assets such as trademarks, it had a cash shortage and was having trouble paying its creditors . . . .

On September 24, 2008, the FBI, suspecting Petters's fraud, raided Petters's offices and home—a raid that would lead to his eventual conviction. Shortly thereafter, Ritchie sent notice that Petters was in default and accelerated the amounts due on all of the loans. Polaroid filed for Chapter 11 reorganization on December 18, 2008.

Polaroid sued Ritchie arguing, among other things, the TSA was unenforceable because it resulted from an actual fraudulent transfer under both federal and Minnesota bankruptcy law. Polaroid's proceeding was thereafter converted to a Chapter 7 bankruptcy, and John R. Stoebner was appointed trustee (trustee) and substituted as a party . . . .

* * *

"[O]ur cases have used the inferential 'badges of fraud' approach to determine whether a debtor acted with 'intent to hinder, delay, or defraud []' a creditor regardless of whether the intent language came from a state fraudulent transfer statute or applicable bankruptcy law." . . . "Once a trustee establishes a confluence of several badges of fraud, the trustee is entitled to a presumption of fraudulent intent. In such cases, 'the burden shifts to the transferee to prove some legitimate supervening purpose for the transfers at issue,'" . . . .

Several courts have decided "[w]ith respect to Ponzi schemes, transfers made in furtherance of the scheme are presumed to have been made with the intent to defraud for purposes of recovering the payments under [11 U.S.C.] § 548(a)." . . . The trustee and various amici urge us to either adopt or reject this presumption. We need not do so because we affirm the bankruptcy court's finding of actual fraudulent intent under the badges of fraud approach. We thus draw no conclusions as to the validity or future applicability of the Ponzi scheme presumption in the Eighth Circuit.

. . . Fraudulent transfer law focuses on the intent of the debtor. If the debtor transfers its assets with the intent to defraud its creditors, the transfer can be avoided as fraudulent. *See* 11 U.S.C. § 548(a); Minn. Stat. § 513.44(a). In a case that involves numerous entities, it is important to identify precisely *whose* intent is relevant to the consideration of fraudulent intent. Polaroid is the debtor. Polaroid granted the liens which the trustee seeks to avoid as fraudulent, so the relevant intent is Polaroid's. Because Petters unilaterally granted these liens on Polaroid's behalf, his intent in transferring the liens *was* that of Polaroid . . . .

In conducting its badges of fraud analysis, the bankruptcy court found five of the badges listed in Minn. Stat. § 513.44(b), but observed that the badges "do not lie perfectly on their wording, for this case." We disagree with Ritchie's contention that this observation is an acknowledgment by the bankruptcy court that the badges of fraud "do not apply." Courts may consider any factors they deem relevant to the issue of fraudulent intent:

> Badges of fraud represent nothing more than a list of circumstantial factors that a court may use to infer fraudulent intent. Given the fact that direct evidence of fraud is rare, a court in most instances can only infer fraud by considering circumstantial evidence. Furthermore, we note that . . . a court is not limited to only those factors or "badges" enumerated, but is free to consider any other factors bearing upon the issue of fraudulent intent.

. . . While we may not totally agree with the bankruptcy court's analysis and application of all the badges, the bankruptcy court did not err in concluding the trustee was entitled to a presumption of actual fraudulent intent. Assessing the relevant factors, we conclude the circumstances surrounding the TSA "are so unfair [they amount to] evidence of [Petters's] fraudulent intent." . . .

* * *

Polaroid was not a party to the Ritchie loans and received no money from the loans, and Petters executed the TSA to prevent a PGW default. The TSA encumbered Polaroid's valuable trademarks without bestowing any real benefit on Polaroid. Ritchie argues Polaroid received value in the form of its parent company—PGW—staying viable after PGW was delinquent on the loans. However, the viability of a parent company is not the type of value contemplated by the fraudulent transfer laws. *See* Minn. Stat. § 513.43(a) ("Value is given for a transfer . . . if, in exchange for the transfer . . . . property is transferred or an antecedent debt is secured or satisfied, but value does not include an unperformed promise made otherwise than in the ordinary course of the promisor's business to furnish support to the debtor or another person.") . . . .

Another significant badge of fraud is whether "the transfer . . . was to an insider." Minn. Stat. § 513.44(b)(1). This badge typically is implicated when the debtor, faced with impending insolvency, transfers property to a business partner or relative to place it beyond the reach of his creditors. . . .

Polaroid executed the TSA for the sole benefit of Petters—an insider. At the time the lien was executed, Petters's Ponzi scheme was in a precarious financial position. The pool of willing investors had run dry and his companies were running out of money. One investor had already filed suit against Petters, and Ritchie—holding numerous overdue notes with no payment in sight—was "intense[ly]" demanding collateral. Petters became increasingly anxious during this period as he confronted the reality he would not be able to raise the capital needed to sustain his corporations.

The TSA tempered Ritchie and kept the loans—which Petters had personally guaranteed—out of default, at least temporarily. Yet the TSA merely postponed an inevitable default, because PGW had no foreseeable way to repay the Ritchie loans. Petters knew of Polaroid's money troubles, and the recent transfer of cash to PCI left Polaroid unable to make payments to its vendors. These dire circumstances indicate the transfer of the liens was nothing more than a desperate attempt to maintain a crumbling Ponzi scheme at the expense of Polaroid's creditors.

While the statutory badge of fraud—a "transfer . . . to an insider," Minn. Stat. § 513.44(b)(1)—does not apply directly, the factual context surrounding the transfer supports an inference of fraudulent intent. Polaroid did not execute the liens *to* an insider, as the statute suggests, but the liens were executed *for the benefit of* an insider . . . .

. . . There is nothing per se fraudulent about an individual owning multiple entities and using the assets of one entity for the benefit of another . . . . When considered in conjunction with the other indicia of fraud present in this case, Petters's execution of the liens for his personal benefit supports the bankruptcy court's presumption of actual fraudulent intent.

* * *

Also relevant to our inquiry, although not an enumerated statutory badge, is Polaroid CEO Mary Jeffries's objections to the TSA . . . . After first receiving a copy of the TSA on September 11, 2008—eight days before the document was signed—Jeffries informed Petters and another PGW official that she opposed the TSA. Jeffries feared the TSA would "ma[k]e it difficult to raise new financing for Polaroid . . . [b]ecause it was taking assets that would otherwise be used as collateral or value in Polaroid in raising capital."

Polaroid's issuance of a lien on its valuable trademarks over the objection of its own CEO is relevant in attempting to discern Petters's intent . . . . Jeffries's objection gives insight into Petters's intent in executing the liens because it suggests Petters chose to issue the liens even knowing Polaroid's CEO feared the liens would thwart Polaroid's efforts to raise much-needed capital. Jeffries's lack of knowledge of the carve-out does not change this contention. Polaroid was seeking funding from multiple sources and, at the time the liens were executed, was negotiating with both a potential lender and a potential purchaser of Polaroid stock. The liens, even with the carve-out, reduced the collateral Polaroid had available to secure loans and had the potential to decrease Polaroid's value to an interested purchaser. Our focus is on Petters's intent, and Ritchie has presented no evidence suggesting Petters was aware of Jeffries's lack of knowledge of the carve-out. Petters executed the liens over the objection of Polaroid's CEO and complicated Polaroid's efforts to secure capital to repay its creditors.

* * *

(Citations omitted.)

NOTES AND COMMENTS

1. The court declines to adopt or use the Ponzi presumption to find a fraudulent transfer. The Ponzi presumption provides that "[a]ll transfers made *in furtherance of that Ponzi scheme* are presumed to have been made with fraudulent intent." In re Palladino, — B.R. —, 2016 WL 4259787 (Bankr. D. Mass. 2016), quoting Inv'r Prot. Corp. v. Bernard L. Madoff Inv. Sec. LLC, 531 B.R. 439, 471 (Bankr. S.D.N.Y.2015). Why did the court decline to use this presumption?

2. The Bankruptcy Code does not have a specific list of the badges of fraud. Instead, the courts look to state statutes and common law badges of fraud. Different circuits vary in the list of the badges of fraud, but they are often similar to this list: "1. The transfer was to an insider; 2. The debtor retained possession or control of the property transferred after the transfer; 3. The transfer was disclosed or concealed; 4. Before the

transfer was made the debtor had been sued or threatened with suit; 5. The transfer was of substantially all the debtor's assets; 6. The debtor absconded; 7. The debtor removed or concealed assets; 8. The value of the consideration received by the debtor was reasonably equivalent to the value of the asset transferred; 9. The debtor was insolvent or became insolvent shortly after the transfer was made; 10. The transfer occurred shortly before or shortly after a substantial debt was incurred; and 11. The debtor transferred the essential assets of the business to a lienor who transferred the assets to an insider of the debtor." Andrews v. RBL, LLC (In re Vista Bella, Inc.), 511 B.R. 163 (Bankr. S.D. Ala. 2014) citing In re XYZ Options, Inc., 154 F.3d 1262 (11th Cir.1998). Which badges of fraud were met in the *Ritchie* case? How many should be met to determine the existence of actual fraud?

Constructive fraud may not involve any fraud at all. It occurs when the debtor transfers property during the reachback period, which under § 548 is typically two years for fraudulent transfers, *and* two conditions are met: (1) the debtor meets one of many definitions of insolvency, *and* (2) the debtor received "less than reasonably equivalent value" as consideration for the transfer. These requirements reflect the debtor's responsibility to its creditors when it is insolvent. A debtor may be entitled to give gifts or transfer its property for a bargain when it has means to pay creditors. But a debtor that is struggling to make ends meet should only be giving away property if the debtor receives the same amount of value in return. The following case considers a situation in which the question of value is harder to determine.

Zeddun v. Griswold (In re Wierzbicki)

830 F.3d 683 (7th Cir. 2016)

* * *

Per Curiam

Debtor Laura Wierzbicki owned a 40-acre farm in Cross Plains, Wisconsin, where she lived for a time with her three minor children and their father, appellant Greg Griswold. In March 2012 Wierzbicki gave Griswold a quitclaim[7] deed to the farm. Fourteen months later she filed for Chapter 7 bankruptcy. The bankruptcy trustee brought an adversary proceeding in bankruptcy court against Griswold to

---

7. A quitclaim deed transfers an interest in property from the grantor to the grantee. Like any deed, grantors can only convey the interest they own, but in a quitclaim deed no warranties are made. In other words, a grantor transferring property with a quitclaim deed transfers what is owned—which may be everything or nothing at all; no further representations are made. Quitclaim deeds are used most frequently to transfer property between family members as a gift or to transfer property in a divorce settlement.

avoid the transfer as fraudulent. The trustee alleged that Wierzbicki was insolvent at the time of the transfer and that she had not received reasonably equivalent value in exchange for the property. See 11 U.S.C. § 548(a)(1)(B).

After a trial Bankruptcy Judge Martin avoided the transfer, concluding that Griswold had exchanged nothing of value for the farm. Whether a debtor has received reasonably equivalent value in an exchange of property is a question of fact, and appellate review of such a finding is deferential, asking whether the finding of fact is clearly erroneous . . . .

Wierzbicki and Griswold lived and worked together on the farm, where they also operated a business salvaging boats. Sometime before 2009 their personal and business relationships soured. Griswold sued Wierzbicki in state court for unjust enrichment and collateral estoppel. Wierzbicki counterclaimed for slander of title. In 2011 a state trial court sided with Wierzbicki, finding that Griswold "does not have, and has never had, any interest in or title to" the farm. Griswold appealed that decision . . . . Wierzbicki apparently wanted an end to the litigation, and she accepted Griswold's promise to drop the rest of the litigation if she gave up the farm. Griswold set out the deal in a document providing that Wierzbicki would give him one dollar and the quitclaim deed. In exchange, Wierzbicki would receive Griswold's promise to abandon the litigation . . . and to assume about $149,000 in liabilities secured by the property. The document also said that the deal would "bring closure" to Wierzbicki's potential liability arising from a zoning dispute with the county that "continues to be directly adversely affecting their children's security and welfare." Both Wierzbicki and Griswold signed the document. Wierzbicki then executed the quitclaim deed, which Griswold recorded with the register of deeds.

The trustee alleged in her adversary complaint that the transfer of the farm was constructively fraudulent and thus avoidable because (a) it had occurred within two years of the bankruptcy filing, (b) Wierzbicki was insolvent at the time of the transfer, and (c) she did not receive "a reasonably equivalent value in exchange for" the property. 11 U.S.C. § 548(a)(1)(B). The parties agree that the transfer fell within the two-year window and that Wierzbicki was insolvent at the time. The dispute here is about reasonably equivalent value. Griswold has argued that his promises to Wierzbicki provided reasonably equivalent value and that the farm's value to Wierzbicki at the time of the transfer was essentially nothing because of various encumbrances.

After a trial at which both Griswold and Wierzbicki testified, the bankruptcy court concluded that the transfer was fraudulent. The court found that, at the time of the transfer, the fair market value of the farm was $300,000. The property was encumbered by three mortgages, two judgment liens, and outstanding real estate taxes, but the court found that Wierzbicki still had equity of approximately $151,000 at the time of the transfer to Griswold. The bankruptcy court further found that Griswold's promise to cease his "meritless appeals" in exchange for that interest had no material value. The bankruptcy court thus avoided the transfer.

* * *

In determining whether a debtor received "reasonably equivalent value," courts consider all the circumstances of the transfer, including "the fair market value of what was transferred and received, whether the transaction took place at arm's length, and the good faith of the transferee.". . . The transaction between Wierzbicki and Griswold was not at arm's length, and Wierzbicki's testimony that "the main reason" she agreed to give Griswold the farm was to "stop the litigation"—which was frivolous—suggests that Griswold was not negotiating in good faith. In light of these standards, we consider Griswold's specific arguments.

Griswold first argues that the bankruptcy court overvalued Wierzbicki's interest in the property at the time of the transfer by not taking into account a *lis pendens* that he had filed in relation to the property. Griswold misunderstands the significance of a *lis pendens*. Under Wisconsin law a *lis pendens* simply alerts third parties to judicial proceedings involving real estate. It does not create an encumbrance on the property. See Wis. Stat. § 840.10. . . .

Griswold argues next that two separate $75,000 homestead exemptions that he says would have been available to him and Wierzbicki should have brought her equity in the property to zero. This argument has no merit at all. State-created homestead exemptions, which are incorporated into the Bankruptcy Code by 11 U.S.C. § 522(b), facilitate fresh starts for debtors by allowing them to shield from creditors specific assets or amounts that otherwise would be part of the bankruptcy estate . . . . Griswold, however, is not the debtor in this bankruptcy action, so he is not entitled to a homestead exemption from Wierzbicki's creditors . . . . And the availability of a homestead exemption to Wierzbicki has nothing to do with the fair market value of the farm when she transferred it.

Griswold next argues that the bankruptcy court erred by undervaluing his promise to drop his appeals in state court; that his promises to assume liability for the mortgages and other liens on the farm provided value; and that the court also failed to consider the additional benefit to Wierzbicki in limiting her exposure to liability in a county zoning dispute and ensuring that their children could remain in their home. All of these arguments fail, as well.

What Wierzbicki received for the farm was not worth anywhere close to her $151,000 interest. Griswold's promise to assume liability for the mortgages and other liens on the property was worth no more than the amount of those encumbrances—roughly $149,000 or half the property's value. Those amounts were already taken into account when the court estimated that Wierzbicki's equity was about $151,000.

* * *

The bankruptcy court did not err as a matter of fact that Griswold's appeals had only nuisance value, obviously far below the value of Wierzbicki's equity in the farm. Putting aside the slim chance that Griswold would prevail in those matters, there was an even more fundamental problem with Griswold's theory of value. The stakes of the state-court litigation had been ownership of the farm. The deal was to end the litigation. According to Griswold's theory of the value he supposedly provided, Wierzbicki *gave up the farm* to eliminate the risk of *losing the farm*. The only real value to Wierzbicki was saving the cost of defending against the frivolous remains of Griswold's litigation, but as the bankruptcy court found, that cost would have been minimal compared to her $151,000 interest in the farm.

As noted, the bankruptcy court's judgment about reasonably equivalent value is a question of fact. Valuing real estate and settlements of nuisance litigation is not an exact science. We have no trouble affirming the bankruptcy court's judgment in this case since Wierzbicki gave up a $300,000 farm in which she had $151,000 equity in exchange for very little value . . . . Considering the totality of the circumstances, the bankruptcy court's finding that Wierzbicki did not receive reasonably equivalent value was exactly right. It certainly was not clearly erroneous.

The bankruptcy court did not consider as part of the value received from Griswold two purported benefits to Wierzbicki listed in the opening recitals of the document they signed: "bringing closure" to her zoning dispute with the county and assurance that the couple's children would "continue to enjoy the security provided them from residing at their farm homestead." The district court addressed these purported benefits and found they were not reasonably equivalent to the value of the farm. As for the zoning litigation, Griswold did not promise to assume liability for the cost or consequences of the zoning litigation. In fact, the district court found, Wierzbicki had been fined $500 for a zoning violation even after she transferred the property to Griswold. Griswold testified that he had paid $32,000 to remove boats from the farm to comply with zoning regulations, but the district court correctly recognized that this amount was not reasonably equivalent to the value of the farm itself.

The district court also found that the benefit of avoiding further family conflict was too "nebulous" to "support a finding of reasonable equivalence" in the bankruptcy context, where a transfer would put an insolvent debtor's valuable property beyond the reach of creditors . . . . As cold and unsentimental as that rule might seem, it is easier to understand from the perspective of creditors, most of whom would probably be unwilling to volunteer to provide a financial subsidy to enhance the insolvent debtor's family relationships by allowing the debtor to put valuable property beyond their reach . . . .

(Citations omitted.)

NOTES AND COMMENTS

1. The named parties in the adversary proceeding included Griswold, the transferee, and Zeddun, the bankruptcy trustee. Why isn't the debtor, Wierzbicki, a named party?

2. Could the *Ritchie* court have used a constructive fraud analysis instead of an actual fraud analysis in determining that Petters committed an avoidable fraudulent transfer? If so, why did the court focus on actual fraud?

3. Transfers to family members often present a valuation challenge because services performed by family members may be hard to value. Take the facts of Doeling v. Grueneich (In re Grueneich), 400 B.R. 688 (8th Cir. B.A.P. 2009). In *Grueneich*, the debtor transferred property worth $119,000 to his parents, who paid $65,000 on the mortgage debt. However, the parents argued that they also gave value in the form of repairs on the property. The bankruptcy court, affirmed by the Bankruptcy Appellate Panel, refused to consider the additional services, looking only to the value listed in the quitclaim deed.

4. What if the debtor does not voluntarily transfer real property, but it is foreclosed upon by a creditor within the two years pre-petition? In that case, the creditor takes the value of the real property in exchange for some or all of the debt owed. But the value of the property may actually exceed the debt owed, leaving a possibility that what the debtor received (forgiveness of part or all of the debt) did not equate to what was transferred away from the debtor (the real property). In 1994, the Supreme Court determined that whatever value the real property was sold for in a properly conducted foreclosure sale is the value of the property. As long as the creditor sold the property at a proper foreclosure sale and, if the property generated more revenue than the creditor was owed (including costs of sale), the creditor turned over that value to the next creditor in line or to the debtor, the creditor could not possibly have received more than the creditor gave in return. BFP v. Resolution Trust Corp., 511 U.S. 531 (1994). However, in some cases, collateral is not sold quickly—and maybe not at all—leaving the *BFP* decision unable to resolve the issue of reasonably equivalent value. *See* Federal National Mortgage Assn. v. Fitzgerald (In re Fitzgerald), 237 B.R. 252 (Bankr. D. Conn. 1999) (*BFP* does not stand for proposition that following state foreclosure rules automatically equates with reasonably equivalent value when the state allows "strict" foreclosure without sale of real property); *cf.* Talbot v. Federal Home Loan Mortgage Corp. (In re Talbot), 254 B.R. 63 (Bankr. D. Conn. 2000) (a creditor that follows state foreclosure rules automatically gave reasonably equivalent value, even if real estate is not actually sold).

Congress added 11 U.S.C. § 548(a)(2) as part of the Religious Liberty and Charitable Donation Act of 1998, 112 Stat. 517 (1998). Under that subsection, a debtor may tithe or donate to qualified charities up to 15 percent of gross income, and may exceed 15 percent of gross income if the debtor established a pattern of giving in that amount pre-petition. The section was enacted in the wake of concerns about trustees suing churches under fraudulent transfer laws to recover tithes paid by a debtor before filing for bankruptcy protection.

F. BANKRUPTCY IN PRACTICE

1. Which of Diana's assets are property of the estate under § 541? On the leased car, what—if anything—transfers to the estate? What if Diana is the named trustee of funds left to her minor children by their grandparents? If Diana has a retirement account through her former

employer, will it become property of the estate, or do you need more information to make that determination?

2. Of the assets that are property of the estate, what will Diana be able to exempt (using your state's exemptions or, if applicable in your state, federal exemptions under § 522(d))?

3. If Diana files for bankruptcy protection, what happens to her home?

   a. If she missed several mortgage payments shortly before the bankruptcy filing, can the bank foreclose on the home after the bankruptcy filing, either with or without petitioning the bankruptcy court to do so?
   b. Can she use an exemption to protect the house (use the exemption laws of the state you live in or, if applicable in your state, the federal exemptions under § 522(d))?
   c. If her ex-husband had obtained a judicial lien against the home to secure payment of $30,000 of overdue domestic support obligations and property settlements, could she avoid that lien?

4. Diana has been making the minimum monthly payments on her credit cards and student loans on a regular basis. If she files for bankruptcy, can the trustee recover any of those payments as a § 547 preferential transfer to augment the bankruptcy estate?

5. Assume that Diana gave $15,000 to her cousin one-and-a-half years ago, telling her cousin that she wanted to reduce her assets to better her position in the divorce proceedings. Can the trustee recover the $15,000 from the cousin to augment the bankruptcy estate under § 548? Would your answer change if the cousin did not know why Diana gave him the money?

4

Contracts and Bankruptcy: Claim Allowance and Executory Contracts

Capitalism without bankruptcy is like Christianity without hell.[1]

When a debtor enters bankruptcy, it affects every party with which the debtor has a contract. For individuals, contracts include everything from home mortgages to employment contracts to purchase agreements. Businesses may have leases, employee agreements, purchase and sale agreements, and much more. How each of these contracts is handled in the bankruptcy case depends largely on the status of the contract. A contract that is substantially completed, at least by one of the parties, may generate a claim against the debtor's estate in the bankruptcy case. But if both parties to the contract have continuing material obligations to the contract—what is known as an "executory" contract—the Code deals with them differently under 11 U.S.C. § 365. This chapter will consider both treatments of contract obligations in bankruptcy.

RECALL DIANA DETTER

Remember that several potential creditors have claims against Diana. Some of these claimants hold an interest in particular assets, such as Diana's car, as collateral for their claim, while others have a right to

---

1. Frank Borman, *The Growing Bankruptcy Brigade*, Time Magazine (Oct. 18, 1982). Mr. Borman was a famous astronaut and later Chairman of Eastern Air Lines, which was one of the largest airlines in the United States, beginning operations in 1926 and continuing on until its ultimate dissolution in 1991.

payment but not a right to a specific asset. The claims arise from tort, family law, contract, and other laws. As you work through this chapter, consider how these creditors bring their claims and interests to the bankruptcy court's attention, and how they will be paid from the assets of the bankruptcy estate. Keep in mind that bankruptcy distributions come from a limited pot of money, meaning that payment made to one creditor likely lessens the payment made to another creditor. This creates often conflicting interests between the creditors.

A. REVIEW OF CORE DOCTRINE: CONTRACTS

In evaluating the claims of creditors, it is crucial to understand the fundamentals of contract law. Remember, however, that claims come from other areas of law as well, such as tort law. This section will review the core doctrine of contracts by examining the elements of a contract and the canons of contractual interpretation before turning to the treatment of those contracts in bankruptcy cases.

1. The Elements of a Contract

The Restatement (Second) of Contracts § 1 defines a contract as "a promise or a set of promises for the breach of which the law gives a remedy, or the performance of which the law in some way recognizes as a duty." This definition does not provide much guidance to students of contract law, as it is somewhat of a tautology. The definition might be reframed to say that a contract is a promise that the law recognizes as a contract. So we need to know more. Thankfully, case law and the Restatement (Second) of Contracts[2] give us further guidance.

In the United States, in order to find a legally binding and enforceable contract, there must be an **offer**, an **acceptance** of that offer, and **consideration** given by each of the parties to the contract that forms the basis of their bargain.[3]

---

2. The Restatement (Second) of Contracts will be referred to throughout this chapter. Please bear in mind that it is only a secondary source, and, while it is a convenient reference point for the law of contracts, it is not a primary source of law.

3. See the Sections of the Restatement (Second) of Contracts that are relevant: § 17 (requirements of a bargain), § 22 (mode of assent), § 24 (offer defined), § 50 (acceptance defined), and § 71 (consideration defined).

Ultimately, these elements of a contract can handily be understood through a fundamental contract equation: $K = O + A + C$, where K is contract, O is offer, A is acceptance, and C is consideration. Each of these basic elements must be present in order to find that a binding contract exists.

The Elements of a Contract
$$K = O + A + C$$

Offer—any indication of an invitation to enter into and be bound by the bargain described.

Acceptance—any indication of assent to the terms of the offer.

Consideration—that which is exchanged in the bargain.

An **offer** is "the manifestation of willingness to enter into a bargain, so made as to justify another person in understanding that his assent to that bargain is invited and will conclude it."[4] Again, this may at first appear confusing but can be described with reference to a rule of reason. An offer is just about anything that would clearly appear to be an offer, meaning that the listener (the "offeree") must understand that the offer is capable of being accepted in accordance with its terms in a way that would create a binding contract.

Similarly, an **acceptance** of an offer is "a manifestation of assent to the terms thereof made by the offeree in a manner invited or required by the offer."[5] Put more simply, an acceptance is anything that indicates an agreement with the terms of the offer. Assuming there is consideration as part of the bargain (discussed in more detail shortly), an acceptance is the act that finalizes the contract. It is the act of the counterparty agreeing to the terms of the deal. Once you have acceptance (again, assuming you have consideration), you have a contract.

It is often said that an offeror (the person making the offer) is the master of the offer. That is true and is helpful in understanding that the offeror can set the terms for acceptance. The offeror can set a particular period of time during which an offer can be accepted. The offeror can describe a particular manner in which the offer can be accepted (for example, by written reply only). The offeror can describe exactly what is being offered with clarity and particularity. If the counterparty (the offeree) attempts to change the terms of the deal in any way, then the response is typically deemed to be a counteroffer and not an acceptance. A counteroffer then

---

4. Restatement (Second) of Contracts § 24.
5. Restatement (Second) of Contracts § 50.

starts the bargaining all over again and needs its own acceptance in order for a contract to exist.[6]

Consideration is essentially that which is exchanged in the bargain. The requirement of consideration ensures that every contract involves a bargain for some exchange of goods, services, promises, or performance of some sort. The consideration is that which is being exchanged by each of the parties to the contract.

Consideration can be tangible. For example, you can exchange money for goods. However, consideration is often intangible in that you can exchange a promise or set of promises for another promise or set of promises. You can also exchange something tangible for something intangible: "I will gladly pay you next Tuesday for a hamburger today."[7] The prior statement represents an exchange of something tangible, a hamburger now, for something intangible, a promise to pay next Tuesday. The Restatement (Second) of Contracts states that in order to constitute consideration "a performance or a return promise must be bargained for."[8]

The requirement of consideration is meant to distinguish binding contracts from gratuitous promises and gifts. One infamous contract law case involved an elder uncle who promised his nephew $5,000 if the nephew refrained from smoking, drinking alcohol, using tobacco, or gambling for a particular period of time. When the nephew complied and sought to collect, the court found that there was consideration because the boy had exchanged his performance (refraining from engaging in those toxic actions) for the money in accord with the bargain.[9] So the essence of a contract in the United States is a bargain where both sides agree to the terms of some exchange of goods, services, promises, or performance of some sort.

2. Interpretation

Once you have a contract, one of the central points of contention is often how to interpret a particular word, phrase, or clause. As with statutory interpretation, contract interpretation has a set of interpretation methods

---

6. Please note that the Uniform Commercial Code (the UCC) nuances this rule for sales of goods transactions. UCC § 2-207 essentially provides that if a purported acceptance contains differences from the offer but those differences are immaterial, then there is a contract and the terms include those immaterial differences in the acceptance. In accord with § 2-207, however, as between merchants, if the differences are material and there is a clear indication of acceptance (for example, the parties have performed) then the contract is formed and consists of only the terms upon which the parties agreed.

7. In the classic comic strip and cartoon *Popeye*, this is the standard refrain of Popeye's friend, J. Wellington Wimpy, a corpulent soul who was generally short on cash and long on appetite, particularly for a good burger.

8. Restatement (Second) of Contracts § 71.

9. Hamer v. Sidway, 124 N.Y. 538, 27 N.E. 256 (N.Y. 1891).

known as "canons." Those canons really become weapons in an advocate's arsenal that can be wielded to argue that their party's interpretation should prevail.

The starting point for understanding contract interpretation is to understand whether contract interpretation in the United States is **subjective** or **objective**. As is so often the case in law, the answer is mixed. The first thing to do in interpreting any particular part of a contract is to determine what was the subjective intent of the parties. If the subjective intent of the parties matches, then that subjective intent will indeed govern the contract.[10]

However, if there is a dispute, it likely means that the parties do not have the same subjective understanding of the contract language at issue. In that case, the subjective intent of one of the parties should prevail where that subjective intent should have been clear to the other party (even if the other party denies that at the time of the dispute).[11] In other words, the party asserting the meaning must prove that the other party did in fact know of the meaning that party is asserting at the time the parties entered into the contract.

If, however, both parties in fact have a different subjective understanding of the clause in question and neither party had reason to know of the other party's intent, then the objectively reasonable interpretation of the language will prevail. To determine that objective meaning, a variety of other canons come into play.

The most important canon of interpretation at this stage is generally **the plain meaning rule**. This rule imposes the ordinary, commonsense, plain meaning understanding of the contract language on the parties.

One of the most famous cases about contract interpretation, Frigaliment Importing Company v. B.N.S. International Sales Corp., involved an international sale of goods: chicken.[12] The Swiss buyer thought it was ordering young chicken suitable for broiling or frying, while the American party argued that since the contract language used simply the word "chicken," that any chicken would do, including any old stewing chicken. In the *Frigaliment* case, Judge Friendly quotes a famous passage from Judge Holmes "that the making of a contract depends not on the agreement of two minds in one intention, but on the agreement of two sets of external signs—not on the parties' having meant the same thing, but on their having said the same thing."[13] Ultimately, the court used the plain meaning rule to find that the

---

10. Restatement (Second) of Contracts § 201.
11. *Id.*
12. 190 F. Supp. 116 (S.D.N.Y. 1960).
13. *Id.* at 117.

objective plain meaning of the term "chicken" as any old (or young) chicken was justified.

But the *Frigaliment* case became so famous as a teaching case because the decision also used a wide array of other canons of contractual interpretation. The court looked to the contract and its purpose as a whole to see if that aided in finding the true intent of the parties. Finding little help from that tool in this case, the court then looked at the course of negotiations before the contract was executed to see if that helped provide evidence of what the parties meant. It looked to the pricing set for the chicken to see if that pricing coincided with typical pricing for young broilers or a wider array of chickens, including old stewing chickens. It looked at trade norms to see what parties ordinarily say if they mean "young chickens suitable for broiling." It also looked at the course of performance after the contract was concluded to see if that shed light on the parties' intent.

After assessing each of these indicia of intent, the court was convinced that the Swiss party's professed subjective intent did not coincide with the objective understanding of the language in the contact. Further, the court found that the American party neither knew nor should have known of the Swiss party's more narrow intent. Thus, the more typical, objective plain meaning of the word "chicken," meaning any kind of chicken, was held to be the meaning of that contract term.

A list of these and other important canons of contract interpretation is set forth in the breakout box below. Remember, these canons are tools in your arsenal for arguing about contractual interpretation. However, beware, as these canons can also be used against you.

Canons of Contract Interpretation[14]

1. If the parties' subjective intent matches, it prevails.
2. If one party knew or should have known of the other party's subjective intent, that intent prevails.
3. If the parties' subjective intent does not match and neither party knew or should have known of the other party's subjective intent, then the objective meaning of the word or phrase should prevail.
4. Use a reasonable, commonsense, plain meaning approach to interpretation.
5. Consider the context and purpose of the contract.

---

14. For a description of a wide array of these and other canons, *see* the Restatement (Second) of Contracts §§ 201–207.

6. Specific terms trump general terms.
7. Negotiated terms trump boilerplate.
8. All intentions should be construed consistently.
9. All intentions should also be consistent with course of performance on the contract, course of dealing between the parties more generally, and general usage of the term in the relevant trade.
10. Where there are inconsistencies, course of performance trumps the more general course of dealing, which trumps the more general trade usage.
11. Any ambiguities should be construed against the drafter (known as *contra proferentum*).
12. Every contract is presumed to include an obligation of good faith.

While most of this chapter will focus on the debtor's obligations to non-debtor parties to a contract, bankruptcy can impact contracts that do not directly involve the debtor. Consider how the court used contract interpretation in the following case—one which involved a contract between two non-debtors impacted by another entity's bankruptcy filing. It serves as a cautionary tale when drafting contracts, and a reminder to consider the impact of a bankruptcy filing.

Edwards Family P'ship, L.P. v. Dickson

821 F.3d 614 (5th Cir. 2016)

Smith, Circuit Judge

* * *

In 2010, Edwards Family Partnership, L.P. (the "Partnership"), and Beher Holdings Trust, Ltd. ("Beher") (sometimes referred to jointly as the "Lenders"), loaned Community Home Financial Services ("Community") $16 million . . . Dickson—Community's founder, president, and CEO—signed the identical loan agreements on behalf of Community and as a personal guarantor. Community also executed notes to secure its obligations to the Partnership and Beher, respectively, set to mature on August 1, 2013, and Dickson signed them on behalf of Community and as a personal guarantor.

Dickson executed contemporaneous, independent, respective guaranties in favor of the Lenders; by each guaranty, Dickson "unconditionally and absolutely guarantee[d] [] the due and punctual payment and performance when due of the principal of the Note and the interest thereon. . . ." He accepted liability that would be "primary and direct and not conditional or contingent upon the enforceability of any obligation, the solvency of [Community] . . . , [or] any obligation or circumstance which might otherwise constitute a legal or equitable discharge or defense of a surety or guaranty. . . ." He also assured the Lenders that they would not need to "make any demand" upon or "exhaust [their] remedies against" Community, any collateral, or other guarantor before recovering from him. The guaranty contracts included other language worthy of reproduction here:

> The obligations of [Dickson] hereunder shall not in any way be affected by any action taken or not taken by [the Lenders], which action or inaction is hereby consented and agreed to by [Dickson], *or by the partial or complete unenforceability or invalidity of* . . . the value, genuineness, validity or enforceability of the Collateral or any of the Guaranteed Obligations.

* * *

> [Dickson] hereby waives . . . *all defenses* with respect to . . . any other action taken by Lender in reliance hereon . . . it being the intention hereof that [Dickson] shall remain liable as a principal until the full amount of all Guaranteed Obligations shall have been indefeasibly paid in full in cash and performed and satisfied . . . in full . . . and the Loan Agreement terminated, notwithstanding any act, omission or anything else which might otherwise operate as a legal or equitable discharge of [Dickson].

> [Dickson] acknowledges and agrees that his obligations as Guarantor shall not be impaired, modified, changed, *released or limited in any manner whatsoever* by any impairment, modification, change, release or limitation of the liability of [Community] or any other guarantor of the Guaranteed Obligations or any other Person or his or their respective estates in bankruptcy resulting from the operation of any present or future provision of the bankruptcy laws or other similar statute, *or from the decision of any court.*

* * *

> [Dickson] agrees that his obligations hereunder are irrevocable, joint and several, and *independent of the obligation of* [Community] or any other guarantor of the Guaranteed Obligations. . . .

(Emphasis added.)

Dickson testified that Community had made payments until October 2011 but defaulted by failing to pay thereafter. The Lenders demanded that Community cure the defaults; neither Community nor Dickson cured but instead sued the Lenders under theories ranging from breach of contract to conversion; the Lenders counterclaimed against Community for judgment on the loan transactions and notes and against Dickson personally for judgment on the guaranty contracts. Shortly after the Lenders counterclaimed, Community filed for bankruptcy, which automatically stayed all other proceedings against it.

The Lenders moved to sever their claims against Dickson under the guaranties. Shortly thereafter, Community and Dickson filed an adversary complaint in the bankruptcy proceeding, contesting the "extent and validity" of Community's obligations to the Lenders. The court granted the Lenders' motion to sever, allowing their claims against Dickson to proceed because Dickson personally was not in bankruptcy and thus was not protected by the stay.

The notes matured and remained unpaid, so on October 11, 2013, the Lenders moved for partial summary judgment as to Dickson's liability as guarantor. The court granted summary judgment and ordered the parties to file affidavits establishing the extent of Dickson's liability, ...

* * *

Under Mississippi law, guaranty contracts are subject to the same rules of construction that apply to other contracts. Dickson's theory carries some intuitive force because Mississippi defines a "guaranty" as "a *collateral* undertaking by one person to answer for the payment of a debt or the performance of some contract or duty in case of the default of another person who is liable for such payment or performance in the first instance." Also, "[i]f the principal underlying obligation is extinguished, generally the guarantor's obligation is also extinguished." From this, Dickson reasons persuasively that his guarantor liability is entirely derivative of Community's obligation, which could be discharged in the bankruptcy proceeding. Dickson posits that if Community's obligation falls away, so must his.

Though colorable, Dickson's argument ignores the unambiguous language of the guaranty contracts, under which Dickson's liability is "independent of the obligations of [Community]" and "primary and direct and not conditional or contingent upon the enforceability of any obligation." Dickson agreed that the Lenders need not exhaust their remedies against Community or any other entity. He expressly waived any and all defenses to enforcement. Finally, his personal guarantees are not affected by the "unenforceability or invalidity" of the notes or loans, any bankruptcy proceedings, any limitation on Community's obligations, or "the decision of any court."

In sum, Dickson personally guaranteed the Lenders that he would satisfy the obligations represented by the promissory notes no matter what. He does not allege that the guaranty contracts are ambiguous, unenforceable, or invalid but only that he cannot be liable as a guarantor until the Lenders show that Community is liable.

That might be a sensible provision to include in a guaranty, but it was not included here, and under Mississippi law, "[t]he most basic principle of contract law is that contracts must be interpreted by objective, not subjective standards. A court must effect a determination of the language used, not the ascertainment of some possible but unexpressed intent of the parties." We enforce the unambiguous language of the guaranty contracts, which requires that Dickson fulfill the obligations under the notes regardless of any outcome of the bankruptcy proceedings or challenges to the underlying obligation.

That conclusion does not end the matter, because the Lenders have the burden to show Dickson is liable under the guaranty contracts. They must show that (1) Dickson signed the guaranty contracts; (2) those contracts encompass Community's obligations under the promissory notes and loan agreements; (3) they are the current holders and owners of the notes; (4) the notes are in default; and (5) the conditions (if any) of Dickson's liability—as laid out in the guaranty contracts—have been met.

The Lenders presented evidence sufficient to establish Dickson's liability as guarantor. They attached copies of the loan agreements, the notes, and the guaranty contracts, each of which Dickson signed on behalf of Community and as guarantor. The guaranties specifically make reference to the notes and loan agreements. The record revealed that the Lenders are the current holders and owners of the notes. Dickson testified that Community defaulted on the notes by failing to pay after October 2011, and the evidence showed that the notes remained unpaid when they matured on August 1, 2013. Finally, the guaranty contracts reveal no conditions on Dickson's liability save Community's default on the notes, which the Lenders proved. Dickson offers no evidence whatsoever in response, claiming only that the bankruptcy proceeding may result in the invalidity of the underlying obligation. Thus, the Lenders met their burden to recover on the guaranties.

* * *

(Citations omitted.)

NOTES AND COMMENTS

1. Mr. Dickson specifically disavowed any claim based on the liability or lack of liability for the debt by Community. How might Community's bankruptcy case have impacted its obligations owed to the lenders, and how might Mr. Dickson have used that as a defense absent the contractual provision he agreed to?

2. The court notes that Mississippi law provides that a guaranty is in effect in case of nonpayment by the primary debtor. How does the court use the language of the contract to demonstrate that the parties mutually agreed to veer from the typical definition of a guaranty?

CLAIMS OF DEBTOR AGAINST NON-DEBTOR PARTIES

When the debtor has a claim against a party not in bankruptcy, that claim may have value for the bankruptcy estate. As a result, the claim itself becomes property of the bankruptcy estate, and the trustee has the right to pursue that claim on the debtor's behalf for the benefit of the estate. *See* Smith v. Arthur Anderson LLP, 421 F.3d 989 (9th Cir. 2005) (noting that the trustee has right to sue to the extent that the pre-petition debtor had such a right, and that the debtor's claim becomes property of the estate); 11 U.S.C. § 323 (giving the trustee the right to sue).

In some cases, the debtor's pre-petition claim is against a third party who will be a creditor with its own claim against the debtor in the bankruptcy case. In those cases, the creditor may invoke any right it has under state law to set off the debts. Set-off can be a great benefit to an unsecured creditor who would have to pay 100 percent of the debt it owes to the debtor to the bankruptcy estate while receiving only pennies on the dollar on its claim in the bankruptcy distribution. Set-off ensures that the creditor receives a dollar-for-dollar exchange on the money it owes to the estate and, in return, is owed from the estate. *See* 11 U.S.C. § 553.

B. CLAIM ALLOWANCE (§§ 501-502, RULES 3001-3008)

1. Filing a Proof of Claim

Assuming that a valid contract exists, it can serve as the basis for a claim in the bankruptcy case. The claims allowance process serves to bring all claims against the debtor—including those resounding in contract law, torts, or other basis—into the bankruptcy forum for fair and equitable payment from the bankruptcy estate. Bankruptcy law does not determine the existence of a claim. Rather, the existence of the claim falls under state or federal law establishing a right against the debtor. In the context of contracts, that will likely involve state law—determining whether a contract has been formed and whether the non-debtor party has a cause of action against the debtor under that contract. Once a claim exists, however, the non-debtor party must comply with the Bankruptcy Code to have the claim "allowed" and paid to the extent feasible in the case and pursuant to the Code.

The Bankruptcy Code requires that any creditor seeking to assert a claim in a bankruptcy case file a proof of claim in order to have its claim "allowed" in the case, except that creditors in a Chapter 9 or Chapter 11 case do *not* need to file a proof of claim if they agree with how the debtor's schedules list the claim and the claim is not listed as disputed, contingent, or unliquidated. *See* 11 U.S.C. § 502(b)(9); Bankruptcy Rules 3002(a), 3003(b)(1).

How does a creditor know to file a proof of claim? Bankruptcy Schedules D, E, and F provide the lists of debts owed by the debtor. Look at those schedules, which are available at https://www.uscourts.gov/forms/bankruptcy-forms. Each creditor listed on those schedules will receive a notice from the bankruptcy court alerting it to the bankruptcy filing and of the need to file a proof of claim.

FILING OF PROOF OF CLAIM BY PARTY OTHER THAN DEBTOR

Section 501(b) and (c) of the Bankruptcy Code allow several parties to file a proof of claim if the creditor fails to do so. Subsection (b) gives that option to parties that are jointly liable with the debtor. In so doing, the co-debtor may lower its own liability by providing for some payment to the creditor in the bankruptcy case. Subsection (c) allows the debtor or trustee to file a proof of claim on the creditor's behalf, thereby ensuring that the claim will be handled in the bankruptcy case.

NOTES AND COMMENTS

1. Notice that the proof of claim form asks questions that are redundant of the information included in the debtor's schedules, such as the amount of the claim and whether the creditor is secured or unsecured. Why

does the proof of claim ask these questions when that information is already included by the debtor in the schedules?

2. The proof of claim form does not require that the creditor attach proof of the existence of its claim. Review 11 U.S.C. § 502(a); Bankruptcy Rule 3001(c)(1), (d), (f). How does the lack of evidence required fit with the burdens of proof in the claims allowance process? Consider this question in conjunction with the next case.

As you read the next case, take note of the shifting burdens of proof. The claimant enjoys an initial presumption of claim validity but then bears the burden of proof if the claim is disputed. Further, the court uses relevant state and federal law standards for evaluating the merits of any claim, even in bankruptcy.

In re Hall

403 B.R. 224 (Bankr. D. Conn. 2009)

DABROWSKI, Chief Judge

Before the Court is the above-captioned Debtor's objection to the referenced proof of claim of Unifund CCR Partners. . . . Based upon the entire record of this case and contested matter, including the documentary and testimonial evidence adduced at the Hearing, the Court FINDS as follows:

1. On or about April 15, 2005, the Connecticut Superior Court (hereafter, "Superior Court") entered a default monetary judgment (hereafter, the "Judgment") in favor of Unifund CCR Partners (hereafter, the "Claimant") against Dolores J. Hall (hereafter, the "Debtor") in a civil action . . . (hereafter, the "Civil Action").

2. The basis for the Judgment was an alleged credit card agreement between the Debtor and the Claimant's predecessor-in-interest, Wachovia Bank (hereafter, "Wachovia").

3. In fact, no credit agreement ever existed between the Debtor and Wachovia and/or the Claimant.

4. According to a Connecticut Marshal's Return of Service, service of process upon the Debtor in the Civil Action was accomplished by so-called "abode service," specifically, by leaving the relevant process (hereafter, the "Process") "at the usual place and abode of said defendant, at 23 Princess Dr., Madison, CT." The Princess Drive location referenced by the Marshal shall hereafter be referred to as the "Madison Property".

5. At no time relevant to the Civil Action or this contested matter did the Debtor reside at the Madison Property.

6. At no time relevant to the Civil Action or this contested matter did anyone residing at the Madison Property provide the Process to the Debtor, or otherwise notify her of the pendency of the Civil Action.

7. On December 13, 2006, the Debtor commenced the instant Chapter 13 bankruptcy case through the filing of a voluntary petition.

8. On April 16, 2007, the Claimant filed the proof of claim that is the subject of the instant matter (Claim No. 9) (hereafter, the "Proof of Claim") based upon the Judgment.

9. On April 25, 2007, the Debtor filed the pending objection to the Claimant's Proof of Claim.

Based upon the entire record of this case and contested matter, and the governing legal authorities, the Court FINDS AND CONCLUDES as follows:

This matter is governed, in the first instance, by the claim allowance standards and procedures of Bankruptcy Code Section 502. Section 502 instructs that if an objection to a proof of claim is made, the Court shall "determine the amount of such claim . . . as of the date of the filing of the petition". Although a claimant enjoys an initial presumption of claim validity based upon a filed proof of claim, see 11 U.S.C. § 502(a), it bears the ultimate burden of persuasion as to the allowance of its claim. When an objector articulates a reasonable basis for the disallowance of all or part of a claim, the initial presumption is overcome, and the production burden shifts to the Claimant to prove its entitlement by a preponderance of the evidence.

Under the terms of Section 502(b)(1), this Court must *disallow* any claim that is "*unenforceable* against the debtor and property of the debtor, under . . . *applicable law*. . . . " (emphasis supplied). In essence, the Debtor here is arguing, consistent with Section 502(b)(1), that the Judgment is "unenforceable" against her under "applicable law" because the Superior Court never acquired personal jurisdiction over her.

* * *

With respect to applicable *federal* law, while federal courts are generally required to grant full faith and credit to a state court judgment pursuant to, *inter alia,* 28 U.S.C. § 1738, bankruptcy courts are nonetheless permitted to re-examine a state court default judgment that was allegedly obtained without the rendering court having obtained personal jurisdiction over the defendant.

The analysis and result are similar under applicable *state* law—which is the relevant standard if this Court is limited by the full faith and credit rules of 28 U.S.C. § 1738. . . . On jurisdictional grounds, a Connecticut court possesses the inherent authority to open and modify a judgment at *any* time. Unless process is served as prescribed by state statute, the Superior Court does not acquire jurisdiction over a defendant. And while Connecticut law provides for "abode service", C.G.S. §§ 52–54, 52–57(a), the location of the server's deposit of process must indeed be the "usual place of abode" of the defendant.

This Court determines that the Superior Court lacked sufficient personal jurisdiction over the Debtor to render the Judgment against her. The Madison Property was not, in the relevant time-frame, the "usual place of abode" of the Debtor. Thus, the delivery of any process at that property, could not alone have constituted appropriate notice to the Debtor of the pendency of the Civil Action so as to establish the Superior Court's *in personam* jurisdiction over her.

Finally, this Court determines that the claim underlying the Judgment is unenforceable against the Debtor on its merits. The evidence before this Court conclusively establishes that there was never any actual relationship—and thus, no meeting of minds—between the Debtor and Wachovia; nor was the Claimant able to establish any basis for a determination that the Debtor might have become obligated to Wachovia through the actions of an agent. Simply put, there has never been any privity of contract between the Debtor and Wachovia and/or the Claimant. Accordingly, it is hereby

ORDERED that the objection of the Debtor (Doc. I.D. No. 36) to the proof of claim of Unifund CCR Partners (Claim No. 9) is SUSTAINED. Claim No. 9 is DISALLOWED in its entirety.

(Citations omitted.)

NOTES AND COMMENTS

1. Is the *Hall* case a civil procedure case or a contracts case? Consider whether the outcome would have been different if the court rendered a

default judgment with proper jurisdiction over Ms. Hall. Then consider whether the outcome would have been different if, despite lack of jurisdiction, Wachovia (through its successor Unifund) and Ms. Hall had an enforceable contract agreement.

2. The case discusses the shifting burdens of proof between the debtor and claim holder in the claims allowance process. What type of evidence would Unifund have needed to establish its claim, and why isn't that evidence required in the initial proof of claim?

2. Objections to the Proof of Claim

Once a proof of claim is filed, the debtor or trustee may object to the proof of claim. Often, the objection is to the value of the claim, leaving the court to determine the actual amount owed by the debtor to the creditor. To do so, the court will often return to principles of contract law.

Hess Management Firm v. Bankston (In re Bankston)

749 F.3d 399 (5th Cir. 2014)

LEMELLE, District Judge

In this adversary proceeding connected to the bankruptcy of Denise M. Bankston (Bankston), Hess Management Firm, L.L.C. (Hess) sought to enforce Bankston's guaranty on a contract between Hess and Premier Aggregates, L.L.C (Premier). The bankruptcy court held that Premier breached the contract in bad faith, but the court limited the damages award to $375,000. Hess appealed to the district court, which overruled the bankruptcy court and awarded Hess the full value of the contract—$1.5 million. Bankston appealed to this Court. For the reasons enumerated below, we reverse.

Facts and Procedural History

The contract (Management Agreement or Agreement) had been entered into by Hess and Premier; Bankston was a member in Premier and served as a guarantor of the agreement. Hess sought to enforce the guaranty against Bankston following Premier's breach of the contract and subsequent insolvency.

The Agreement stated that Hess would provide certain management services related to the operation of the Fluker Pit, a gravel pit owned by Premier. In return for providing these services, Premier promised to pay Hess the greater of (1) $25,000 per month or (2) $0.50 per ton on all gravel produced by the Fluker Pit during a particular month. The Agreement provided for an initial term of five years and for the option of one-year renewals that could extend the term for another five years. The Agreement also provided that it could be terminated on certain conditions, as follows:

> [A]t any time, either party may terminate this Agreement as to that Managed Pit on 180 days notice provided that Owner [(Premier)] may only terminate this Agreement as to that Managed Pit if Manager [(Hess)] is then in default of any of its material obligations under this Agreement, which Manager has not cured within 5 days notice thereof, or if Owner permanently shuts down the use of that Managed Pit . . . Notwithstanding the foregoing, in the event that the operation of a Managed Pit(s) is unprofitable, then Owner may terminate this Agreement with respect to that Managed Pit(s) on a one month advanced notice to Manager.

In addition, the Agreement separately provided that it could be terminated by Premier if Hess did not remedy any deficient performance within three business days of receiving notice. The parties executed the Agreement on November 6, 2007, but provided that the Agreement was retroactively effective as of August 21, 2007.

On November 30, 2007, Premier, through its attorneys, sent Hess a notice stating that it was "completely dissatisfied with Hess's performance as Manager" and warning Hess that if it did not begin performing fully within three days, Premier would terminate the Agreement. Hess responded through its attorneys, contending that Premier had made it difficult for it to perform its duties and observing that Premier had not paid Hess since the inception of the Agreement. On December 18, 2007, representatives of Premier met with Hess stating that Hess's services were no longer needed and asked it to vacate the premises. Premier's attorneys sent Hess a notice that the Agreement was terminated as of that date. Hess was thereafter excluded from carrying out any activities at the Fluker Pit.

After Premier's repudiation of the Agreement, on May 16, 2008, the Fluker Pit shut down. The Fluker Pit had operated at a loss from the inception of the pit's operations in August 2007. Although Hess never received notice of the shutdown under the procedures set out in the Agreement, on or about May 18, 2008, Hess's owner went to the pit to recover its remaining equipment. By observation, Hess was aware that the pit was shut down.

Hess filed suit in state court. Before a state court could rule on the matter, however, Premier and Bankston filed for bankruptcy. Hess then filed the instant adversary proceeding. After trial, the bankruptcy court ruled in favor of Hess. It determined that Premier had breached the Agreement on two occasions: first, by failing to pay Hess at all for the months leading up to its repudiation of the Agreement, and second, by terminating the Agreement in December of 2007. Furthermore, it determined that the termination was in bad faith. Noting that Premier could have invoked the provision in the Agreement providing for termination on 30 days notice if the Fluker Pit was unprofitable, the court concluded that Premier's failure to do so signified their bad faith. No party contests this bad faith finding.

The bankruptcy court concluded that Hess was owed $375,000 in damages. To arrive at this figure, the court held that the ultimate shutdown of the Fluker Pit subsequent to Premier's breach limited damages to 180 days after the pit closed—the contractual period for adequate notice of closure. The court held that Hess was entitled to damages for the period from August 21, 2007, to approximately November 12, 2008, 180 days after the Fluker Pit's permanent shutdown in mid-May. Since the Fluker Pit never produced a sufficient tonnage to trigger the per-ton fee provision for compensation in the Agreement, the court concluded that Hess was entitled to $25,000 per month for that 15–month period, or $375,000.

On appeal, the district court reversed the bankruptcy court's damages determination. Accepting the facts found by the bankruptcy court, the district court held that under Louisiana law the amount of damages owed accrues solely at the time of breach and is unaffected by post-breach events. In this case, as of the time of breach, Hess's damages consisted of the $25,000 monthly minimum payment for the sixty-month term of the Agreement, or $1.5 million. The court concluded that the subsequent closure of the Fluker Pit was irrelevant to the determination of accrued damages. The court therefore entered a damages award of $1,427,216.87 plus interest to Hess, which the parties agreed was the present value of the $1.5 million due Hess under the Agreement. This appeal followed.

* * *

Calculation of Damages

Louisiana has embraced the contract damages principle of "expectation" damages. Under this principle, the general purpose of contract damages is not to punish breaching parties or enrich non-breaching parties, but rather to produce the same result as would have occurred if there was no breach. As stated by the Louisiana Supreme Court, the calculation of damages should place the non-breaching party "in the same position he would have been in" had the contract been fulfilled. A court must take "great care . . . to ensure that the plaintiff is not actually placed in a *better* position than he would have attained had the contract been performed."

With this general principle in mind, we move to more specific provisions of Louisiana law to determine at what point damages are properly calculated in the instant case: At the time of breach? Or at the time of trial, taking into account post-breach events? As this case demonstrates, the time when damages are calculated is critical, and can change the damage award amount. Premier breached the contract on December 18, 2007. If damages are calculated from that date, Hess would be entitled to damages amounting to the full term of the contract—as the district court concluded. However, this analysis should also consider what the parties contemplated and the eventual result—that the Fluker Sand Pit closed on May 16, 2008. Parties do not dispute that, had the sand pit closed in the normal course without bad faith breach, Hess would not be entitled to the full value of the contract. Indeed, the contract between the parties states "at any time, either party may terminate this Agreement as to that Managed Pit on 180 days notice provided that Owner [(Premier)] may only terminate this Agreement . . . if Owner permanently shuts down the use of that Managed Pit." Therefore, if the post-breach closure of the pit is taken into account, Hess would only be entitled to damages up to 180 days after the closure of the pit—as the bankruptcy court found.

Louisiana law does not speak to the effect that post-breach events—like the post-breach closure of the sand pit—have on contract damage calculations. . . .

* * *

Finding no clear indication on the effect of post-breach events on damage calculations in Louisiana law, we look to secondary sources for guidance. The Louisiana Civil Law Treatise states "[i]n Louisiana, where breach of contract is concerned, the civil code supports the conclusion that compensatory damages are *assessed* as of the time of breach. . . ." 6 La. Civ. L. Treatise, Law Of Obligations § 4.17 (2d ed.) (emphasis added). This passage seems to bolster the position that damages are calculated solely at the time of breach without regard to post-breach events—since the term "assessed" more clearly demands calculation than the statutory phrase "owed," and the time period is firmly defined as "the time of breach." However, upon closer inspection, the only case law cited by the treatise in support of this proposition is the district court's opinion *in this case*. The Court, reviewing this matter de novo, is not bound by the lower court's legal determinations, nor secondary sources relying solely on that interpretation.

No Louisiana Supreme Court opinion clearly resolves when damages are to be calculated. We are only able to find corollary cases that do not fully resolve the issue at hand. . . .

* * *

Louisiana law being unclear, the Court is obligated to consider other provisions of Louisiana law and decide what the Louisiana Supreme Court would decide were it to hear the instant case.

Hess argues, and the district court found, that Hess is entitled to receive the full value of the contract—60 payments of $25,000 each, for a total of $1.5 million. We disagree with the analysis by the learned jurist below.

By awarding Hess the full $1.5 million, Hess would be placed in a *better* position than it would have been had the contract been fulfilled. This would violate Louisiana's general principle of expectation damages. Had the contract been in effect at the time the pit closed, Hess would not have been entitled to receive profits past 180 days from the pit's closure. Thus, consistent with the concept of expectation damages, the Court finds that the proper measure of damages was that found by the bankruptcy court—Hess is entitled to $375,000, based on damages sustained for the period from August 21, 2007 to November 12, 2008, 180 days after the Fluker Pit's permanent shutdown in mid-May. A contrary result would defeat the maxim of placing a non-breaching party in the same position they would have been had breach not occurred, and award Hess more than their expectation interest.

It should also be noted that the parties specifically contracted for the closure of the pit. The contract language allows the closure, if notice is provided. This evidences the parties understanding and foresight that the pit's closing was anticipated, and not an event that should result in a windfall of damages to Hess. It additionally makes this situation different than one where a fortuitous event prevents performance. Far from being unforeseen, the closure of the pit was understood as a possibility by the parties, as evidenced by the contract terms allowing for closure of the pit.

* * *

In a different context, we find analogous support for our analysis in another provision of Louisiana law regarding damages. Specifically, Louisiana's rule on mitigation makes clear that a non-breaching party must take "reasonable efforts to mitigate the damage caused by the obligor's failure to perform." La. Civ. Code art. 2002. If a non-breaching party fails to mitigate damages, the breaching party "may demand that the damages be accordingly reduced." *Id.* Thus, in a mitigation case, despite damages being "owed" at the time of breach, the amount of damages may be reduced after an analysis of the non-breaching party's post-breach conduct and related events. This demonstrates that damages are not set in stone, and strengthens our conclusion that post-breach events may effect the amount of damages awarded.

* * *

(Citations omitted.)

NOTES AND COMMENTS

1. Reread the provision on termination of the contract. Is the provision clear as to when either party may terminate the agreement? Could you redraft the provision to be more clear?

2. Why would the contract require 180-day notice of termination *and* a default by Hess? Could this create a challenge for Premier in the event of an immediate failure to perform by Hess and, if so, could the contract be unconscionable?

3. In the end, Hess received a judgment of $375,000. However, that judgment will be paid through the bankruptcy case and, absent a basis for nondischargeability or priority, will likely be paid pennies on the dollar. Can or should the courts consider this in determining damages? After all, will Hess actually be made whole by this judgment?

3. Ipso Facto Clauses

Contracts often include provisions that allow the creditor to declare default if the debtor becomes insolvent or declares bankruptcy. Such provisions are known as ipso facto clauses. These clauses can disadvantage a debtor, who may be reticent to take advantage of bankruptcy protections due to the possibility of default. Contracts or clauses within contracts that are against public policy may be unenforceable.

PUBLIC POLICY

"A promise or other term of an agreement is unenforceable on grounds of public policy if legislation provides that it is unenforceable or the interest in its enforcement is clearly outweighed in the circumstances by a public policy against the enforcement of such terms."

—Restatement (Second) of Contracts, Section 178

In re Jones

591 F.3d 308 (4th Cir. 2010)

SHEDD, Circuit Judge

* * *

The Joneses purchased a vehicle under a Retail Installment Contract with DaimlerChrysler that granted DaimlerChrysler a security interest in the vehicle to secure payment; the security interest was later perfected. The contract contains a clause which provides that the Joneses will be in default if they file a bankruptcy petition or if one is filed against them. Subsequently, David Jones filed a petition for relief under Chapter 7 of the Bankruptcy Code. Kirsten M. Jones did not file for bankruptcy but brought this adversary proceeding as the co-owner of the vehicle.

In filing for bankruptcy, Mr. Jones filed a statement of intention with respect to the contract for purchase of the Joneses' vehicle that indicated that he would "Continue Payments" on the vehicle but did not state whether he intended to redeem the vehicle or reaffirm the debt as required by 11 U.S.C. §§ 362(h) and 521(a)(2). He also failed to redeem the vehicle or enter into a reaffirmation agreement with DaimlerChrysler within 45 days of the first meeting of creditors held on June 16, 2006. *See* 11 U.S.C. § 521(a)(6). Mr. Jones made a payment on August 28, 2006, through DaimlerChrysler's automated telephone payment system. This was the only payment made after the § 521(a)(6) 45–day period to either redeem or reaffirm expired on July 31, 2006.

DaimlerChrysler thereafter moved to confirm termination of the automatic stay so that it could enforce its security interest by repossessing the vehicle pursuant to the default-upon-bankruptcy clause, also called an "*ipso facto*" clause. After a hearing, the bankruptcy court entered an agreed order confirming that the automatic stay was terminated. Thereafter, without providing written notice of default and right to cure, DaimlerChrysler repossessed the vehicle pursuant to the *ipso facto* clause. The Joneses then commenced this adversary proceeding.

As part of the adversary proceeding, the bankruptcy court enjoined the sale of the vehicle and required its return. The bankruptcy court held that DaimlerChrysler did not have the right under the Bankruptcy Code to repossess the Joneses' vehicle even though Mr. Jones failed to indicate either his intent to redeem the vehicle or reaffirm the debt on his statement of intention. The bankruptcy court relied on the "ride-through" option [which] permitted Chapter 7 debtors who were current on their installment payments to continue making payments and retain collateral after discharge without redeeming the collateral or reaffirming the debt. The bankruptcy court also held that West Virginia Code § 46A–2–106 required DaimlerChrysler to first give the Joneses notice of the right to cure default before repossessing the vehicle.

On appeal, the district court reversed both rulings and held that DaimlerChrysler had the right to repossess the vehicle. Specifically, the court held that the Bankruptcy Abuse Prevention and Consumer Protection Act of 2005 (BAPCPA) eliminated the ride-through option. . . . The district court also held that § 46A–2–106 is inapplicable here. The Joneses now appeal the order of the district court, challenging both of these rulings. For the following reasons, we reject their contentions and affirm.

* * *

We next turn to the question of whether DaimlerChrysler had authority to repossess the vehicle pursuant to the contract's *ipso facto* clause without giving the Joneses prior notice of a right to cure the default under state law.

The general rule is that an *ipso facto* clause in an installment loan contract is unenforceable as a matter of law. However, BAPCPA created an exception to this general prohibition by adding § 521(d), which permits creditors to enforce *ipso facto* clauses in consumer loan agreements secured by personal property if the debtor fails to comply with the provisions of §§ 521(a)(6) or 362(h). Specifically, § 521(d) provides that upon the debtor's failure to comply with these provisions,

> nothing in this title shall prevent or limit the operation of a provision in the underlying lease or agreement that has the effect of placing the debtor in default under such lease or agreement by reason

of the occurrence, pendency, or existence of a proceeding under this title or the insolvency of the debtor. Nothing in this subsection shall be deemed to justify limiting such a provision in any other circumstance.

Therefore, the filing of the bankruptcy petition constituted default, and Mr. Jones's failure to redeem the vehicle or reaffirm the debt permitted DaimlerChrysler to take action under its contract and § 521(d) as permitted by West Virginia law. § 521(a)(6).

The Joneses argue that DaimlerChrysler waived any default under the *ipso facto* clause based on the single payment made through DaimlerChrysler's automated telephone payment system after the § 521(a)(6) 45–day period expired. However, at the time that this payment was made, the bankruptcy court had not yet issued its order confirming the termination of the automatic stay.

We find that the acceptance of a single automated payment made prior to the bankruptcy court's order did not clearly waive default and did not estop DaimlerChrysler from repossessing the vehicle.

* * *

(Citations omitted.)

NOTES AND COMMENTS

1. Given that the prohibition on ipso facto clauses is located in § 365, does the prohibition apply only if the contract is executory? Consider whether the policy concerns apply to nonexecutory contracts in the same way that they apply to executory contracts. *See* In re Gen. Growth Properties, Inc., 451 B.R. 323, 329–31 (Bankr. S.D.N.Y. 2011) (holding that ipso facto provision only applies in executory contract context, but noting courts that have invalidated ipso facto clauses outside of executory contracts when clauses impaired debtor's fresh start).

2. As the court noted, § 521 provides an exception to the invalidity of ipso facto clauses. Other exceptions exist throughout the Code. *See, e.g.,* § 365(e)(2)(B) (ipso facto clauses in contracts to make loans remain enforceable); § 555 (ipso facto clauses not voided as to stockbroker and other financial institutions under securities contract). Why would the Code specifically provide these exceptions, thus allowing ipso facto clauses to be enforced?

4. Priority Claims (§ 507)

Recall that creditors may be secured or unsecured; secured creditors are promised specific collateral in the event that the debtor fails to meet its payment obligation. Unsecured creditors have no such promise of collateral, and under state law need to seek a judgment and judgment lien to execute upon specific assets of the debtor. Of course, the automatic stay in bankruptcy prevents an unsecured creditor from bringing such actions, leaving unsecured creditors to wait for the collection and distribution of assets by the bankruptcy trustee. And, in most cases, little remains for the unsecured creditors after the debtor exempts property and the secured creditors receive their collateral. However, some protection exists for certain unsecured claims. These claimants receive special treatment in bankruptcy, being granted priority in payment over other "general" unsecured claims. The ten types of claims listed in § 507 (and paid *in this order* per § 507(a)) include:

1. domestic support obligations

2. administrative expenses allowed under § 503(b)

3. "gap" claims allowed under § 502(f)

4. wages and similar employee claims, earned within the 180 days prepetition and subject to a monetary cap

5. claims for contributions of employees to an employee benefit plan, made within the 180 days pre-petition and subject to a monetary cap

6. certain claims of farmers and fisherman

7. claims for deposits given to debtor, subject to a monetary cap

8. certain taxes and customs duties owed to the government

9. claims based on obligations to maintain capital with an FDIC commitment

10. claims for death or personal injury resulting from operating a vehicle or vessel while under the influence

Each of these categories has requirements that must be met to qualify for priority, and those requirements are generally outlined within the provision granting priority. A debtor in a Chapter 7 case must pay each category of priority claim in full before moving on to the next category and before paying general (or subordinated) unsecured creditors.[15] Debtors in Chapter 13

---

15. 11 U.S.C. § 726(a)(1).

and Chapter 11 must pay priority creditors the minimum required under those chapters, but may pay other unsecured creditors simultaneously under the plan.[16]

Read § 507 and § 101's definitions. You will see that top priority goes to "domestic support obligations." What are domestic support obligations? Does Diana owe any of these? Go through each of the ten categories of priority claims and determine which are most likely to apply in a consumer bankruptcy case such as Diana's, and which are most likely to apply in a business bankruptcy case. One of the most common priority claims involves second-priority administrative expenses—expenses incurred in order to administer the bankruptcy case. While some of the administrative expenses (such as the cost of the trustee) are obvious, in other cases, creditors may seek to have their claims deemed to be administrative in an effort to enhance their priority and their chance of being paid in the bankruptcy case.

As the next case illustrates, § 503 of the Bankruptcy Code requires that expenses be "actual" and of "benefit" to the estate in order to qualify as administrative expenses. The case involves post-petition insurance reimbursement expenses and a request for administrative expense priority before the payments are actually made.

National Union Fire Ins. Co. v. VP Bldgs., Inc.

606 F.3d 835 (6th Cir. 2010)

KENNEDY, Circuit Judge

National Union Fire Insurance Company ("National Union") appeals the district court's affirmance of the bankruptcy court's decision disallowing National Union's petition for administrative expenses. National Union provided the estate with workers' compensation insurance, and asks that the estate's contractual obligation to reimburse it for certain anticipated payments be granted administrative expense priority. Both the bankruptcy court and the district court rejected this argument, finding that the claim was not "actual" and did not benefit the estate. . . . we AFFIRM.

. . . LTV Steel Company, Inc. and its subsidiaries filed voluntary petitions for Chapter 11 bankruptcy on December 29, 2000. LTV's subsidiaries include . . . the "VP debtors."

---

16. For Chapter 11, § 1129(a)(9) requires that, absent consent of the claimant, most priority claims must be paid in full. Chapter 13 requires the same under § 1322(a)(2).

The parties agree that National Union provided the LTV entities, including VP debtors, with workers' compensation insurance during calendar year 2001. This insurance, mandated by state law, guarantees that injured workers will be compensated in a timely manner regardless of the financial health of the employer. When an injury occurs in a covered year (such as 2001), National Union's insurance coverage is implicated. However, the actual payments to an injured employee are often required for years, or even decades, after the covered year.

The parties agree that under the terms of this agreement, which was entered into post-petition for post-petition activities and incorporates an earlier agreement, LTV and the VP Debtors are ultimately responsible for any workers' compensation claim that is incurred in 2001, regardless of when the benefits are actually paid (subject to certain limits not at issue). When a workers' compensation claim matures for an injury that occurred in 2001, the parties' contract requires National Union to pay the entirety of the claim and seek reimbursement from the VP Debtors.

. . . In return for National Union advancing this money, National Union charged LTV a premium (which was paid) and obtained collateral.

Employees were injured in 2001, imposing an obligation on National Union to pay out future benefits. National Union asked that the reimbursement of this obligation for payments that are not due until after the closure of the bankruptcy estate be given administrative priority status. Because the injured employees' claims are ongoing in nature, there is uncertainty as to the amount that National Union will ultimately pay. The parties agreed to arbitrate the amount of National Union's claim. The arbitration panel concluded that National Union's reimbursement claim for all LTV entities is valued at $2,494,498 for 2001. . . .

The bankruptcy plan to liquidate the VP Debtors' assets and dissolve the estates was confirmed by order of the bankruptcy court on December 17, 2003. The bankruptcy court denied National Union's claim for administrative expense priority on December 21, 2007. The court concluded that the expense was not "actual" because National Union had not yet paid the benefits for the years after the closure of the bankruptcy estate. Moreover, the bankruptcy court found that reimbursement of the payments would not benefit the estate. . . .

* * *

The bankruptcy code provides that administrative expenses, "the actual, necessary costs and expenses of preserving the estate," 11 U.S.C. § 503(b)(1)(A), "are, as a rule, entitled to priority over prepetition unsecured claims[.]" "The purpose of [this priority] is to facilitate the rehabilitation of insolvent businesses by encouraging third parties to provide those businesses with necessary goods and services." However, "[c]laims for administrative expenses under § 503(b) are strictly construed because priority claims reduce the funds available for creditors and other claimants." "'[A] debt qualifies as an 'actual, necessary' administrative expense only if (1) it arose from a transaction with the bankruptcy estate and (2) directly and substantially benefitted the estate.'" . . .

The parties agree that the provision of insurance benefitted the estate, and that the transaction was entered into post-petition. However, the parties dispute whether the claim is "actual" under the meaning of the Bankruptcy Code and whether National Union's claim for reimbursement benefitted the estate.

We do not decide this case without precedent. In a published opinion, we recently adopted the reasoning of a district court that rejected the claimant's arguments:

> To that effect, the narrow application of § 503(b)(1)(A) is rather unambiguous on its face: the claimed expense must have been an "actual" cost that is "necessary" to the "preservation" of the estate. . . . the claimed expenses are not "actual" (i.e., not yet realized) and the payment thereof, when the obligations are realized, cannot act to preserve an estate that no longer exists. . . .

* * *

In re HNRC Dissolution Co., 371 B.R. 210, 225-226 (E.D. Ky. 2007) (footnotes omitted), *aff'd,* 536 F.3d 683 (6th Cir. 2008) (per curiam), *cert. denied,* 129 S. Ct. 2866 (2009). Following this logic, National Union's claim will not be "actual" until it has made a payment and seeks reimbursement from the insured, which will typically occur years post-confirmation.

National Union argues that *HNRC* is distinguishable on several factual grounds, but none of the offered differences are material. First, National Union observes that the claimant in *HNRC* had only estimated the future indebtedness through a "report prepared by actuaries." In contrast, National Union has, through arbitration, reduced its future indebtedness to all LTV entities to a specific figure by which all parties are bound. With some of the uncertainty of naked actuarial estimation reduced by reason of arbitration to which each side is bound, National Union posits, the claim is more "actual" here than in *HNRC*. The arbitration process may have tested the parties' actuarial estimates, but it did not change the nature of the claim to an "actual" total due by the debtors during the pendency of the bankruptcy estate. Under the terms of National Union's contract, the need for reimbursement only arises when payments are made. Until the payments are due, they are "not yet realized." And under the reasoning of *HNRC*, it is only then that the claim becomes "actual."

Next, National Union argues that its claim can be paid under the provisions of the debtor's plan here because the plan creates a priority claims trust account from which administrative claims that are "not allowed as of the Effective Date" of the plan may be paid. However, it does not argue or point to any evidence that this was not the case in *HNRC* or how this transforms the claim to actual.

National Union further contends that the contractual language requiring reimbursement is different. In this case, the language of VP's contract provides that the payment obligation includes future deductible loss reimbursements that are not yet due. In *HNRC*, the insurance contract also required reimbursement of certain deductible amounts as they were incurred. We can discern no meaningful distinction between the language of the two contracts.

* * *

COOK, Circuit Judge.

Constrained by the rule announced in *HNRC*, I concur in the majority opinion. I write separately to question *HNRC*'s holding and to urge en banc review of the application of that rule to the present case.

HNRC holds that post-confirmation claims for deductible reimbursements by an insurance company fail to qualify as actual and necessary expenses that benefit the estate, and thus cannot attain administrative expense priority as a matter of law. The HNRC panel focused on whether the claim itself—a cost—provided an actual and necessary benefit to the estate. But framed this way, there can be just one answer—a cost incurred by a business (let alone a bankrupt one) by definition provides no benefits and, arguably, does not become actual or necessary until the debtor receives the bill, which may not occur until after plan confirmation. Only by analyzing the cost's purpose—assessing the services provided in exchange—can courts determine whether the expense meets § 503(b)'s requirements.

In our case, no party disputes that the debtor's survival as an operating entity required the insurance National Union provided. But under *HNRC*'s holding, by scheduling prospective payments (some of which arise after plan confirmation), the debtor receives a windfall, avoiding the entire post-confirmation portion of the obligation. The *HNRC* court accepted this result on grounds that such post-confirmation payments (unlike the pre-confirmation payments made on the same contract covering the same service) cannot qualify as actual, necessary, or a benefit to the estate by virtue of their post-confirmation nature. But the timing of the payments should not affect the analysis of whether the cost of the service can satisfy the criteria necessary to qualify for administrative priority.

Although *HNRC* noted a lack of authority "support[ing] the contention that expenses necessarily realized post-confirmation can legally be characterized as 'actual' under the Code," this statement ignores the two existing analytical frameworks—one developed by our circuit and the other by our sister circuits—both of which counsel in favor of treating the deductible reimbursements at issue as an administrative expense. Notably, the reasoning of these courts focused not on when a creditor bills the debtor for its services, but on either: 1) when the debtor obligates itself to pay or 2) when the service is rendered. This court, in particular, looks to when "the acts giving rise to a liability took place, not when they accrued" to determine administrative priority. Confirming that payment timing lacks legal significance in this circuit's bankruptcy law, we held that when a debtor enters a pre-petition agreement to pay for services, making post-petition payments (even if the services were actually rendered post-petition) does not transform the obligation into an administrative expense. Other courts contrast an actual benefit with a potential one, holding that "the mere potential of benefit to the estate is insufficient for the claim to acquire status as an administrative expense." Under either framework, National Union's claimed administrative expense qualifies—VP Debtors signed the insurance contract post-petition, incurring liability then, and acquired actual, not potential, insurance coverage.

The *HNRC* court likewise erred in rejecting the insurer's claim as neither "necessary to preserve the estate," nor for the "benefit of the estate." The panel held that "[t]he bottom line remains that [the insured] is not contractually obligated to pay any of the deductible obligations in question until claims are filed, which will necessarily occur post-confirmation." A cost incurred post-confirmation, so *HNRC* tells us, cannot be necessary to preserve or benefit an estate that no longer exists. But given that a *cost* cannot be necessary to or benefit anyone, let alone a bankrupt estate, the better approach asks whether a creditor provided a necessary service for the estate's benefit and preservation during the debtor's bankruptcy proceedings, not whether the creditor billed the debtor for those services during that time.

The Supreme Court held in *Reading Co. v. Brown*, 391 U.S. 471 . . . (1968), that "the cost of insurance against tort claims arising during [bankruptcy] is an administrative expense payable in full . . . before dividends to general creditors." The *HNRC* decision fails to adequately account for this clear and controlling statement of law. Though VP Debtors argue that *Reading Co.* applies to insurance premium payments only (and that this case implicates only loss-sensitive deductible reimbursement payments), they posit a distinction without difference. All agree that the post-confirmation insurance payments at issue represent part of the price of the insurance. If instead of insurance this case involved the purchase of raw materials for steel that the debtor, a steel producer, needed to fulfill an order, and managed to purchase on similar terms, no one would seriously contend that because the payments were slated to occur post-confirmation the steel was not necessary to preserve the estate.

This court consistently holds that when an estate derives a benefit from goods, services, or its own actions (breaching a contract, for example), the associated cost qualifies as an administrative expense, even when the cost remains unknown at plan confirmation. Neither the contingent or unliquidated nature of a claim nor the timing of the payments should affect whether the service in question qualifies as an actual expense necessary to preserve the estate.

* * *

(Citations omitted.)

NOTES AND COMMENTS

1. The debtor entities ultimately liquidated and went out of business. What impact did that have on the court's decision?

2. The concurring opinion focused on the purpose of administrative expense priority. What is that purpose, and how does the court's decision undermine that purpose?

5. Secured Claims (§ 506)

Priority claimants hold unsecured claims and receive special treatment in bankruptcy among unsecured creditors. But that priority does not impact secured creditors—creditors who have been given collateral (usually by a contract called a "security agreement" or "collateralization agreement") securing the debtor's obligation to pay the claim owed to the creditor. In consumer bankruptcy cases, common secured creditors include mortgage lenders and automobile lenders. Security interests abound in business bankruptcies; for example, sellers may have an interest in goods sold to the debtor, lenders may have an interest in the equipment or inventory of the business, and mortgages may exist on the business property. These creditors generally have a superior right to the collateral, or the value of that collateral, even over the rights of priority unsecured claimants.

a. Undersecured Creditors — Bifurcation of Claims

Secured creditors may be fully secured, meaning that the value of their collateral equals or exceeds the claim owed to them. However, secured creditors may also be undersecured when the value of their collateral is insufficient to pay the debt owed to them. For example, a homeowner-debtor may owe $20,000 on a boat worth just $15,000. In such situations, the claim may be separated into an unsecured portion (in the example, $5,000) and a secured portion ($15,000). But valuing the assets can be tricky, particularly when the asset is not being sold, as the following case demonstrates.

Santander Consumer USA, Inc. v. Brown (In re Brown)

746 F.3d 1236 (11th Cir. 2014)

BUCKLEW, District Judge

* * *

In July 2007, Brown purchased a 37-foot 2006 Keystone Challenger recreational vehicle. Brown entered into a loan agreement secured by the recreational vehicle. In July 2012, Brown filed for Chapter 13 bankruptcy. Santander, the owner of the loan agreement, filed a proof of secured claim in the bankruptcy court for $36,587.53, the outstanding payoff balance due at the petition date. Brown's modified Chapter 13 plan proposed surrendering the vehicle in full satisfaction of Santander's claim. Santander objected to the confirmation of the plan.

At the confirmation hearing on September 27, 2012, the parties disagreed on the method for valuing Brown's vehicle. Brown argued that § 506(a)(2)'s replacement value standard governed his vehicle's valuation, which in turn determined the amount of Santander's secured claim. Brown contended that if his vehicle's replacement value exceeded his debt, surrendering his vehicle would satisfy Santander's entire claim (and his debt) under § 1325(a)(5)(C). Santander argued that a surrendered vehicle's value should be based on its foreclosure value, not replacement value.

On December 3, 2012, the bankruptcy court overruled Santander's objection, holding that § 506(a)(2) required valuing Brown's vehicle based on its replacement value. The bankruptcy court found that while the Supreme Court's 1997 decision in *Associates Commercial Corp. v. Rash* supported applying a foreclosure value standard to Brown's surrendered vehicle, *Rash* preceded the Bankruptcy Abuse Prevention and Consumer Protection Act of 2005's ("BAPCPA") addition of § 506(a)(2), which required the replacement value standard. The court concluded Santander would have a secured claim to the extent of the vehicle's replacement value, and that Brown's surrender of the vehicle would satisfy that claim under § 1325(a)(5)(C).

Following a valuation and confirmation hearing, the bankruptcy court determined that the vehicle's replacement value at least equaled the debt and confirmed Brown's Chapter 13 plan. Santander appealed the bankruptcy court's decision to apply the replacement value standard to the district court, which rejected Santander's arguments and affirmed the bankruptcy court's decision.

* * *

Under § 1325(a)(5), a plan's treatment of an "allowed secured claim" can be confirmed if: the secured creditor accepts the plan, the debtor retains the collateral and makes payments to the creditor, or the debtor surrenders the collateral. 11 U.S.C. § 1325(a)(5)(A)-(C). In this case, Brown exercised the surrender option under § 1325(a)(5)(C).

The term "allowed secured claim" refers to § 506(a). Section 506(a)(1) bifurcates a secured creditor's allowed claim into secured and unsecured portions based on the underlying collateral's value and addresses how to determine such value:

> An allowed claim of a creditor secured by a lien on property in which the estate has an interest . . . *is a secured claim to the extent of the value* of such creditor's interest in the estate's interest in such

property . . . *and is an unsecured claim* to the extent that the value of such creditor's interest . . . is less than the amount of such allowed claim. *Such value shall be determined* in light of the purpose of the valuation and of the proposed *disposition or use* of such property. . . .

11 U.S.C. § 506(a)(1) (2006) (emphasis added).

In *Rash,* the debtor proposed to retain the collateral under § 1325(a)(5)(B), while valuing the collateral based on its foreclosure value. However, the Supreme Court interpreted "disposition or use" as requiring different valuation standards depending on whether the collateral was surrendered or retained. *Rash* held that the proper standard was replacement value, not foreclosure value, in the retention context. *Id.*

After *Rash,* BAPCPA added § 506(a)(2). Like § 506(a)(1)'s last sentence, § 506(a)(2) refers to § 506(a)(1)'s bifurcation provision and addresses how to determine value. Unlike § 506(a)(1), § 506(a)(2)'s scope is limited to certain cases and expressly mandates a replacement value standard:

> If the debtor is an individual in a case under chapter 7 or 13, *such value* with respect to personal property securing an allowed claim *shall be determined based on the replacement value* of such property as of the date of the filing of the petition without deduction for costs of sale or marketing. With respect to property acquired for personal, family, or household purposes, replacement value shall mean the price a retail merchant would charge for property of that kind considering the age and condition of the property at the time value is determined.

11 U.S.C. § 506(a)(2) (2006) (emphasis added). Thus, when § 506(a)(1) and (a)(2) both apply, a creditor holding an undersecured claim would have a secured claim equal to the collateral's judicially-determined replacement value and an unsecured claim to the extent the debt exceeds the collateral's replacement value.

* * *

. . . Section 506(a)(2)'s text—"[i]f the debtor is an individual in a case under chapter 7 or 13, such value . . . shall be determined based on the replacement value"—expressly requires applying a replacement value standard in cases falling within its ambit. And the cases that fall within the scope of § 506(a)(2)'s ambit include those involving a Chapter 13 debtor's personal property or property for personal, family, or household use—precisely the kind at issue here. Section 506(a)(2), by its plain terms, applies to this case.

We disagree with Santander's textual arguments. Santander argues that applying § 506(a)(2)'s replacement value standard when a debtor surrenders property under § 1325(a)(5)(C) would misapply *Rash* and violate § 506(a)(1)'s "disposition and use" language. . . .

But Santander fails to acknowledge that *Rash* preceded BAPCPA's addition of § 506(a)(2), which expressly requires applying the replacement value standard in this case. And while § 506(a)(2)'s replacement value standard mandate seemingly contradicts § 506(a)(1)'s broader "disposition and use" valuation language, a well-established canon "of statutory construction [is] that the specific governs the general." Here, § 506(a)(2) specifies how to value certain property in Chapter 7 and 13 cases, while § 506(a)(1) is more broadly worded and says nothing about Chapter 7 and 13 cases. . . .

* * *

Santander also asserts that § 506(a)(2) only applies to retained property under § 1325(a)(5)(B), because BAPCPA only added § 506(a)(2) to codify *Rash*'s holding that replacement value should govern in the retention context. We acknowledge that cases have described § 506(a)(2) as a codification of *Rash*, but they do not hold that § 506(a)(2) is limited to the facts of *Rash*. Nor does the text of § 506(a)(2) support that conclusion.

* * *

Nor are we persuaded by Santander's arguments that applying § 506(a)(2) in the surrender context would be absurd. Santander argues that it would be absurd because it allows debtors to surrender collateral in full satisfaction of the debt. This overstates the effect of § 506(a)(2). Surrender would satisfy the creditor's secured claim, not the entire debt. If a creditor holds an undersecured claim, the creditor would still have an unsecured claim to the extent the debt exceeds the collateral's judicially-determined replacement value.

Santander also argues that applying § 506(a)(2) would be absurd because it eliminates creditors' contract and state law rights to liquidate and pursue an unsecured claim for any deficiency. But state law does not govern if the Bankruptcy Code requires a different result. Here, the Bankruptcy Code is contrary to state law, as an unsecured claim under § 506(a)(1) and (a)(2) equals the amount that the debt exceeds the property's replacement value—not the amount of post-sale deficiency. Thus, state law cannot apply.

* * *

The district court's order affirming the bankruptcy court is AFFIRMED.

(Citations omitted.)

NOTES AND COMMENTS

1. As the court notes, valuation is critical to bifurcation of a claim. How does each party use its proposed method of valuation to maximize its interests in the bankruptcy case?

2. State contract law will govern whether the creditor has a security interest in the collateral, but, as the court notes, the Bankruptcy Code dictates how to value the collateral for the purpose of bifurcating the claim. What was the creditor's argument that this undermines the goals of state contract law?

THE PROBLEM OF "WHOLLY UNDERWATER" LIENS

Once a claim has been bifurcated, a court must determine how to treat each portion of the claim. The Supreme Court has tackled the issue of "wholly underwater" liens—situations in which a junior creditor has a security interest in the collateral but the collateral is not worth enough to pay anything to the junior creditor—in the context of Chapter 7 bankruptcy cases. *See* Bank of Am., N.A. v. Caulkett, 135 S. Ct. 1995 (2015). The Court disallowed "strip-off" of a wholly underwater mortgage lien, a practice that had previously turned a secured creditor into a completely unsecured creditor for bankruptcy purposes.

---

b. Oversecured Creditors — Entitlement to Fees and Interest

While an undersecured creditor is subject to bifurcation of its claim, a secured creditor who is "oversecured," meaning that the value of the collateral securing its claim exceeds the amount of the claim itself, may increase the amount of its claim to the extent of such oversecurity (also known as an "equity cushion"). The claim increase may be attributable to additional interest that accrues post-petition or to contractually permitted costs and fees. Read § 506 and its language allowing fees and interest before reading the next case. Note that the focus of this case is on *when* a court can value collateral, whether at a fixed date such as the petition date or whether courts can employ a more flexible approach. The court also delves into the question of *how* to compute post-petition interest and the degree of discretion given to courts in that determination in light of contract terms agreed to by the parties.

The Prudential Ins. Co. of America v. SW Boston Hotel Venture, LLC (In re SW Boston Hotel Venture, LLC)

748 F.3d 393 (1st Cir. 2014)

STAHL, Circuit Judge

This appeal presents multiple issues arising from a heavily contested Chapter 11 bankruptcy proceeding. Stated simply, a secured creditor appealed to the Bankruptcy Appellate Panel for the First Circuit ("the BAP") from the bankruptcy court's orders determining its entitlement to postpetition interest (and thus the total amount of its claim) and confirming the debtors' Chapter 11 plan. The BAP reversed in part, significantly increasing the secured creditor's entitlement to postpetition interest, and vacated and remanded the confirmation order. The debtors and the City of Boston ("City"), as a junior creditor, appealed to this court. After careful consideration, we conclude that the BAP erred in reversing the bankruptcy court's post-petition interest determination. And, because the BAP's confirmation order was based solely on its erroneous interest determination, we vacate that order as well.

. . . In 2007, Debtor-Appellant SW Boston Hotel Venture, LLC, ("SW Boston") sought financing to develop a mixed-used property that would become the W Hotel and Residences ("the W") in Boston's theater district. In January of 2008, after a previous lender withdrew its financing commitment, the Prudential Insurance Company of America ("Prudential") agreed to provide up to $192.2 million in financing ("the Prudential Loan") pursuant to a construction loan agreement ("the CLA"). Prudential took a mortgage and first priority security interest in SW Boston's real and personal property and any proceeds thereof. . . .

The W project consists of a 235-room hotel, 123 luxury condominium units, an underground parking garage, a restaurant, a spa and related retail space, and a bar. The hotel was to operate under the W Hotels brand of Starwood Hotels and Resorts Worldwide, Inc. ("Starwood"), with Starwood managing the operations.

The W opened on schedule in October of 2009, but, due in large part to the ongoing recession, obtained substantially fewer commitments to purchase condominiums than the CLA required. In addition, the restaurant, spa, and bar—all required to operate under the W Hotel flag—had not been completed, and the Debtors lacked sufficient funding to complete them. In December 2009, after Prudential declined to provide additional funds, SW Boston and the City entered into a loan agreement ("the City Loan"), with the City agreeing to provide $10.5 million in additional funding. The City Loan was secured by a junior lien on most of the collateral that secured the Prudential Loan. . . .

On April 28, 2010, after SW Boston failed to make a mandatory quarterly payment to Prudential and loan-restructuring negotiations failed, SW Boston . . . filed voluntary Chapter 11 bankruptcy petitions. . . . Prudential filed a proof of claim asserting secured claims of not less than $180,803,186, plus fees, costs, and pre- and post-petition interest. Shortly after the petition date, Prudential drew down the letter of credit, reducing its pre-petition claim to $165,592,659.

* * *

On March 28, 2011, SW Boston filed a motion for court approval of a purchase and sale agreement ("the P & S") for the sale of the hotel and garage to an unrelated third party for $89.5 million. The bankruptcy court granted the motion on May 24. But, before the sale could close, SW Boston was required to resolve several outstanding issues on which the P & S was contingent. . . . After SW Boston managed to resolve these contingencies, the sale closed on June 8, 2011, and the net proceeds of $88,322,017 were paid over to Prudential.

On March 31, 2011, three days after filing the hotel sale motion the Debtors filed their reorganization plan. The plan need not be described in great detail, but, in broad strokes, it called for Prudential to be paid in full by March of 2014 if the hotel sale closed, or after a more extended period if it did not. The plan contemplated that Prudential would receive post-effective-date interest of 4.25% per annum, but it made no provision for postpetition, pre-effective-date interest. Prudential objected to confirmation of the plan on multiple grounds.

Throughout the pendency of the bankruptcy case, SW Boston continued construction. After SW Boston resolved various issues with contractors who had suspended their work because of the bankruptcy filings, the spa was completed and opened on August 18, 2010. That September, after two work interruptions caused by a change in the building code and the state's appeal of a variance granted to SW Boston, SW Boston received all necessary approvals to recommence construction of the bar. Multiple open construction items on the W were completed. SW Boston continued to sell condominiums, paying over the proceeds (less certain deductions) to Prudential.

On April 15, 2011, Prudential moved for a determination that it was oversecured and therefore entitled to post-petition interest under 11 U.S.C. § 506(b). In general terms, a claim is oversecured if the value of the creditor's interest in its collateral exceeds the amount of its claim. Under § 506(b), an oversecured creditor is entitled to post-petition interest, as well as reasonable fees, costs, or charges provided for in the parties' contracts or by state law, up to the extent of its oversecurity. Prudential argued that it should receive post-petition interest at the contractual default rate of 14.5% per annum, 5% higher than the contractual base rate, accruing from the petition date. The Debtors argued that Prudential only became oversecured upon the closing of the hotel sale, and therefore could only receive postpetition interest from that point forward. They also claimed that the default rate was unenforceable and inequitable, and requested that, to the extent Prudential was entitled to any post-petition interest, it should accrue at the base rate of 9.5% per annum.

The bankruptcy court held a three-day combined trial addressing Prudential's § 506(b) motion and the Debtors' proposed plan. On October 4, 2011, it issued an order granting Prudential post-petition interest at 14.5% per annum, commencing on the hotel sale date. The court ruled that the hotel sale price, rather than its earlier valuation at the lift-stay hearing, was the best indicator of the hotel's value. However, it also noted that, in light of the ongoing improvements and the resolution of various contingencies, the sale price did not reflect its value on any earlier date. Therefore, it found that Prudential only became oversecured once the hotel sale closed. After receiving the parties' interest calculations (which differed only as to whether the interest should be compounding), the bankruptcy court entered an order fixing Prudential's claims, inclusive of non-compounding post-petition interest. Prudential appealed and the Debtors cross-appealed the § 506(b) decision and the resultant claim order to the BAP.

* * *

B. § 506(b) Order

As a general matter, unmatured interest is not allowed after the filing of a bankruptcy petition. 11 U.S.C. § 502(b)(2). However, Congress has created an exception to this rule in the case of "oversecured" creditors. Two provisions of § 506 of the Bankruptcy Code govern the award of post-petition interest to an oversecured creditor. First, § 506(a) sets the amount of a creditor's allowed secured claim. . . .

Next, § 506(b) defines an oversecured creditor's entitlement to post-petition interest:

> To the extent that an allowed secured claim is secured by property the value of which, after any recovery under subsection (c) of this section, is greater than the amount of such claim, there shall be allowed to the holder of such claim, interest on such claim, and any reasonable fees, costs, or charges provided for under the agreement or State statute under which such claim arose.

Id. § 506(b).

Thus, if the collateral is worth more than the amount of the secured claim, the creditor is entitled to post-petition interest on its claim up to the amount of the difference in values (this difference is referred to as an "equity cushion" or "security cushion"). Post-petition interest accrues until the secured claim is paid or until the effective date of the plan.

The parties agree that Prudential was oversecured during at least part of the bankruptcy proceeding and therefore is entitled to some amount of post-petition interest, but they differ as to how to determine oversecured status, when Prudential became oversecured, and the applicable interest rate and type.

* * *

Although § 506(a) dictates how courts should determine secured status and collateral value, it does not specify the time as of which these determinations should be made. Where these figures remain relatively constant, the choice of measuring date may not matter. But where, as here, the amount of the claim has decreased significantly and the value of the collateral has increased during the course of the bankruptcy, the choice can make the difference between a finding of oversecurity or undersecurity.

Courts have split on the timing issue. Several have adopted a "single-valuation" approach, where the determination of oversecurity for § 506(b) purposes always occurs at a fixed point in time (generally either the petition date or the confirmation date). Others have adopted a "flexible" approach, giving the bankruptcy court discretion to determine the appropriate measuring date based on the circumstances of the case. . . .

The bankruptcy court and the BAP both adopted the flexible approach, although their applications of it differed. The bankruptcy court found that the hotel sale price provided the best evidence of the hotel's value as of the sale date, but concluded that the sale price was not reflective of its value at any earlier point in time due to the previously outstanding contingencies. The BAP agreed that the sale price was the best evidence of value, but concluded that the sale price established that Prudential was oversecured throughout the pendency of the bankruptcy proceedings.

* * *

We agree with the bankruptcy court and the BAP that, at least in the circumstances presented here, a bankruptcy court may, in its discretion, adopt a flexible approach.

* * *

First, neither § 506(b)'s language, nor its legislative history, nor the bankruptcy rules define the measuring date for purposes of post-petition interest, suggesting flexibility. The language of § 506(a) also suggests that Congress intended bankruptcy courts to have flexibility. While § 506(a)(1) sets out a general rule that collateral value "shall be determined in light of the purpose of the valuation and of the proposed disposition or use of such property," § 506(a)(2) creates an exception to the general rule. . . .

The fact that Congress mandated particular measuring dates in the exception without mandating a particular measuring date in the general rule suggests that it intended flexibility under § 506(a)(1).

* * *

Third, rather than yielding the fairest result, a rigid single-valuation approach guarantees an all-or-nothing result that hinges more on fortuity than reality. For example, if the petition date were the required measuring date, a creditor that first became oversecured even one day later would be allowed no post-petition interest, even though it was oversecured throughout almost the entire bankruptcy and even though it could receive substantial post-petition interest under a flexible approach. Conversely, if the confirmation date were the required measuring date, a creditor that first became oversecured just one day earlier would be allowed post-petition interest for the entirety of the bankruptcy proceeding (up to the amount of the equity cushion). We do not believe that Congress intended entitlement to post-petition interest to depend so heavily on chance. Nor do we believe that Congress intended to restrict the bankruptcy courts' equitable discretion without explicitly saying so. The availability of a flexible approach strikes us as more likely to produce fair outcomes than allowing post-petition interest for the entire bankruptcy, or not at all, based on a rigidly defined one-shot vantage point.

* * *

For these reasons, we hold that, under the particular facts presented in this case, the bankruptcy court did not err in adopting a flexible approach for determining oversecured status.

* * *

The bankruptcy court considered several possible measuring dates (the petition date, the date of the lift-stay decision, the date SW Boston signed the hotel P & S and filed its motion for approval of the sale, the date the court approved the sale motion, the hotel sale date, and the date of the confirmation hearing), and determined that the sale closing date was the earliest that Prudential had established oversecured status.

As for the petition date, the court noted that Prudential had submitted no evidence that it was oversecured at that time, and that it instead relied on the Debtors' schedules of assets, which indicated that the value of Prudential's collateral, in the aggregate, was substantially more than its total pre-petition claim. As Prudential points out, these schedules were completed under penalty of perjury. But, as the Debtors point out, the schedules also specifically indicated that the listed values were book values that may not reflect the fair market value of the Debtors' interest in the relevant property. The bankruptcy court did not rely on these values because they were not substantiated by any evidence. We perceive no error, clear or otherwise.

* * *

Prudential next argues that the sale price is the best evidence of the hotel's value, and that that price necessarily established that it was oversecured throughout the bankruptcy proceedings. Courts have routinely held that "so long as the sale price is fair and is the result of an arm's-length transaction, courts should use the sale price, not some earlier hypothetical valuation, to determine whether a creditor is oversecured and thus entitled to postpetition interest under § 506(b)." We have no quibble with the proposition that an arm's-length sale generally provides better evidence of value at a given time than does an appraisal of its value at that same time. But that does not mean that a sale price at one time necessarily establishes the collateral's value at some other time. Where the value of collateral is changing, a one-size-fits-all valuation poorly reflects that reality.

Here, the bankruptcy court did note that the price obtained at the arm's-length sale provided the best indicator of the hotel's value, and it acknowledged that the price ($89.5 million) strongly suggested that the appraised values relied upon at the lift-stay hearing ($55 million and $65.6 million) were conservative, supporting Prudential's argument that it was oversecured at least as of the appraisal dates. However, the bankruptcy court went on to note that several contingencies "could have derailed the sale," even after it granted the hotel sale motion (about two weeks before the actual sale). It held that it was only when the last improvements were completed, all outstanding contingencies were resolved (including resolving issues with the Starwood contract, a contingency that Prudential itself described as "an essential element to the success of the [W]"), and the sale actually closed that the sale price accurately reflected its value. The court thus found that Prudential had not shown that it was oversecured as of the date SW Boston signed the hotel P & S or the date the court approved the sale motion. It seems plausible that Prudential's declining claim and the hotel's increasing value may have crossed paths at some point before the hotel closing date, but Prudential did not meet its burden to establish when that crossover may have occurred. On this record, we cannot say that the bankruptcy court clearly erred in determining when Prudential became oversecured.

* * *

Having established that the bankruptcy court did not clearly err in determining *when* Prudential's post-petition interest began to accrue, we now turn to two questions regarding how that interest accrued. . . .

Section 506(b) does not specify how to compute postpetition interest. The Supreme Court, construing § 506(b), has held that the phrase "provided for under the agreement or State statute under which such claim arose" modifies only "reasonable fees, costs, or charges," and not "interest on such claim." Thus, the statutory language does not dictate that bankruptcy courts look to the applicable contract provisions, if any, when computing postpetition interest. However, courts are largely in agreement that, although the "appropriate rate of pendency interest is . . . within the limited discretion of the court," where the parties have contractually agreed to interest terms, those terms should presumptively apply so long as they are enforceable under state law and equitable considerations do not dictate otherwise. . . .

The bankruptcy court and the BAP both held that Prudential was entitled to interest at 14.5%, the default rate specified in the CLA. There is no dispute that SW Boston defaulted under the terms of the CLA. However, the Debtors argue that the bankruptcy court erred by considering the enforceability of the default rate only under federal law, when what was required was a two-step analysis, first focusing on its enforceability under Massachusetts law before turning to federal law. While the above analysis suggests that, in all cases, the presumption in favor of applying a contractual interest provision can be rebutted by showing that is unenforceable under state law, we need not reach that issue today. Here, the CLA's default interest provision directs the court's inquiry to Massachusetts law, as the rate is limited to the lesser of the default rate or the "maximum rate permitted by applicable law." However, we do not believe that the Debtors have shown that the default rate exceeds that threshold.

* * *

We also find no error in the bankruptcy court's analysis under federal equitable principles. After discussing and applying factors that bankruptcy courts have used in balancing the equities, the court determined that application of the default rate would not be inequitable. Specifically, the court noted that: (1) other creditors would not be harmed because the plan contemplated payment of all creditors in full; (2) although Prudential was quite litigious, "raising multiple objections to virtually every motion made by the Debtors," its conduct did not rise to the level of obstruction of the bankruptcy process or other misconduct; (3) the Debtors did not rebut Prudential's evidence that the CLA's default rate was consistent with default rates of similar loans in the market, including where Prudential was either the lender or the borrower; and (4) courts have approved larger spreads between base and default interest rates. We find no error in the bankruptcy court's conclusion that the Debtors had failed to rebut the presumption in favor of enforcing the contractual provision.

* * *

For the foregoing reasons, we *vacate* the BAP's § 506(b) and confirmation orders and remand to that tribunal with instructions that it affirm the bankruptcy court's § 506(b) and confirmation orders and remand the case there for further proceedings consistent with this opinion. . . .

   (Citations omitted.)

NOTES AND COMMENTS

1. Read § 506(b). It allows oversecured creditors to receive interest and "reasonable fees, costs, or charges," so long as they are provided for in the contract or by law. The court noted that reasonableness does not modify interest. Did the court consider the reasonableness of the post-default interest rate in any way?

2. Can an unsecured creditor also receive post-petition interest and fees or costs? Courts have divided on the issue. Some have determined that, because § 506 grants them to oversecured creditors, Congress intentionally denied them to unsecured (and undersecured) creditors. *See, e.g.,* In re Electric Machinery Enterprises, Inc., 371 B.R. 549 (Bankr. M.D. Fla. 2007). Other courts have held that because § 506 applies specifically to secured creditors, no rule exists regarding unsecured creditors. *See, e.g.,* In re STNL Corp., 571 F.3d 826 (9th Cir. 2009) (allowing unsecured creditor to claim post-petition attorney's fees based in pre-petition contract, determining that it was a contingent claim). The Supreme Court expressly declined to resolve the issue. Travelers Cas. & Sur. Co. of America v. Pacific Gas & Elec. Co., 549 U.S. 443, 456 (2007).

C. EXECUTORY CONTRACTS

Section 365 of the Bankruptcy Code dictates the treatment of executory contracts in bankruptcy cases. In short, it allows the trustee[17] to assume the obligations of the executory contract or to reject (effectively breach) the executory contract. Before exploring these remedies further, however, it is important to determine whether a contract qualifies as executory. Contracts that are not executory cannot be assumed or rejected in bankruptcy. Instead non-executory contracts suffice as the basis for potential claims by the parties if there has been a breach of the contract.

---

17. Pursuant to § 1107, the debtor-in-possession takes over this function in a Chapter 11 case. Debtors-in-possession are discussed further in Chapter 10 of this book.

1. Definition of Executory Contract

While the Code fails to define an executory contract, the most cited definition of an executory contract comes from the late professor Vern Countryman. A recent report summarized and endorsed Professor Countryman's definition in the context of Chapter 11 cases while discussing more recent definitions of executory contracts.

American Bankruptcy Institute Commission to Study the Reform of Chapter 11: 2012-2014 Final Report and Recommendations

23 Am. Bankr. Inst. L. Rev. 1 (2015)

* * *

Section 365 of the Bankruptcy Code generally allows a debtor in possession to assume, assign, or reject executory contracts and unexpired leases in the chapter 11 case.[18] The debtor in possession typically makes this determination based on a variety of factors, including whether the contract or lease is above or below market, necessary to its ongoing business operations, and subject to assumption under the Bankruptcy Code. It also may consult with the unsecured creditors' committee on these issues or attempt to renegotiate the contract or lease with the nondebtor party. A debtor in possession's decision to assume, assign, or reject an executory contract or unexpired lease is subject to court approval, certain deadlines, and several other requirements detailed in section 365.[19]

* * *

Recommended Principles

The Bankruptcy Code should define the term "executory contract" for purposes of section 365 as "a contract under which the obligation of both the bankrupt and the other party to the contract are so far unperformed that the failure of either to complete performance would constitute a material breach excusing the performance of the other," provided that forbearance should not constitute performance.

---

18. 11 U.S.C. § 365.

19. *See, e.g., id.* § 365(b) (requirements for assumption); *id.* § 365(c) (contracts not subject to assumption or assignment); *id.* § 365(f) (requirements for assignments).

Vern Countryman, *Executory Contracts in Bankruptcy: Part I,* 57 Minn. L. Rev. 439, 460 (1973). The contours of this definition are well developed under the case law and reflect an appropriate balance between the rights of a trustee to assume or reject contracts unilaterally under the Bankruptcy Code and the nondebtor's obligations and rights in those circumstances.

a. Definition of Executory Contract: Background

Section 365(a) provides that a debtor in possession,[20] "subject to the court's approval, may assume or reject any executory contract or unexpired lease of the debtor."[21] The Bankruptcy Code does not define "executory contract," and the legislative history of section 365 provides little guidance.[22] Accordingly, the court on a case-by-case basis determines whether a particular contract is executory.

Courts traditionally have used what is commonly referred to as the "Countryman" definition of executory contracts.[23] This test was developed by Professor Vern Countryman and defines an executory contract for bankruptcy purposes as "a contract under which the obligation of both the bankrupt and the other party to the contract are so far unperformed that the failure of either to complete performance would constitute a material breach excusing the performance of the other."[24] Although widely used, courts have recognized limitations and potential inconsistencies in the application of the Countryman test.[25] In addition, the test may not be a good fit for certain kinds of contracts.[26]

---

20. As previously noted, references to the trustee are intended to include the debtor in possession as applicable under section 1107 of the Bankruptcy Code, and implications for debtors in possession also apply to any chapter 11 trustee appointed in the case. *See supra* note 76 and accompanying text. *See generally* Section IV.A.1, *The Debtor in Possession Model.*

21. 11 U.S.C. § 365(a).

22. H.R. Rep. No. 95-595, at 347 (1977) ("Though there is no precise definition of what contracts are executory, it generally includes contracts on which performance remains due to some extent on both sides.").

23. *See In re* Baird, 567 F.3d 1207, 1211 (10th Cir. 2009); *In re* Columbia Gas Sys., Inc., 50 F.3d 233, 239 (3d Cir. 1995); *In re* Streets & Beard Farm P'ship, 882 F.2d 233, 235 (7th Cir. 1989); Lubrizol Enters., Inc. v. Richmond Metal Finishers, Inc., 756 F.2d 1043, 1045 (4th Cir. 1985); *In re* Select-A-Seat Corp., 625 F.2d 290, 292 (9th Cir. 1980).

24. Vern Countryman, *Executory Contracts in Bankruptcy: Part I,* 57 Minn. L. Rev. 439, 460 (1973).

25. *See, e.g., In re* Gen. Dev. Corp., 84 F.3d 1364, 1374 (11th Cir. 1996); *In re* RoomStore Inc., 473 B.R. 107, 111-12 (Bankr. E.D. Va. 2012).

26. Some courts have struggled with the application of the Countryman definition in the context of the following kinds of agreements: options and rights of first refusal; restrictive covenants (covenants not to compete; restrictive covenants on land); oil and gas agreements (*e.g.*, the oil and gas leases themselves and variations thereof, like farmout agreements, and related agreements, like surface use agreements and joint operating agreements); licenses, distributor agreements, and trademark agreements; warranties; rights of first refusal; employment contracts; and severance agreements; arbitration clauses; forum

Given the noted flaws in the Countryman test, courts have developed alternative approaches to assess executoriness. For example, some courts use the "functional approach" to evaluate a debtor in possession's request to assume or reject an executory contract. Under this approach, developed by Professor Jay Westbrook, there is no threshold standard of "executoriness" that the debtor in possession must meet to assume or reject the contract.[27] Rather, the functional approach focuses on whether assumption or rejection would create a benefit for the bankruptcy estate and its creditors. The functional approach recognizes that courts often manipulate the threshold requirement of executoriness in order to produce the desired outcome.[28] Several courts have adopted the functional approach or used it in connection with the Countryman test.[29]

Another alternative approach is commonly referred to as the "exclusionary approach." This approach is a deviation from the Countryman test and was developed by Michael Andrew.[30] The following are the primary differences between the Countryman test and the exclusionary approach: (i) the concept of executoriness

---

selection clauses; distributor agreements; trademark agreements; and indemnity clauses; and settlement agreements. *See, e.g.,* Water Ski Mania Estates Homeowners Ass'n v. Hayes (*In re* Hayes), 2008 Bankr. LEXIS 4668, at *31-32 (B.A.P. 9th Cir. Mar. 31, 2008) ("[A]lthough restrictive covenants contain the characteristics of both a contract and an interest in land, the primary nature of such covenants is preservation of a land interest, not future duties in contract. Although there will almost always be some incidental continuing obligations under a restrictive covenant, those duties were not the kind of obligations Congress intended to impact in enacting § 365."); Frontier Energy, LLC v. Aurora Energy, Ltd. (*In re* Aurora Oil & Gas Corp.), 439 B.R. 674, 680 (Bankr. W.D. Mich. 2010) ("The court's conclusion that the [oil and gas leases] qualify as 'leases' within the meaning of Section 365 makes it unnecessary to consider whether the [oil and gas leases] meet either the functional test or Countryman definition for executory contracts. Given the confusion in the case law, it is also improvident to opine on the question."); *In re* Bergt, 241 B.R. 17, 29-31 (Bankr. D. Alaska 1999) (discussing the application of the Countryman test in recent case law to options); Bronner v. Chenoweth-Massie, P'ship (*In re* Nat'l Fin. Realty Trust), 226 B.R. 586, 589 (Bankr. W.D. Ky. 1998) ("The contingent nature of the obligations arising from an option agreement make them quite distinguishable from the typical contract. This distinction has puzzled many courts, resulting in two distinct lines of cases. The first line of cases, while recognizing the contingent nature of the obligations arising under option agreements, and while also expressly acknowledging that they are unilateral contracts until exercised, have nevertheless engaged in what could be described as analytical gymnasts to arrive at a finding that they are nonetheless executory contracts."); Cohen v. Drexel Burnham Lambert Grp., Inc. (*In re* Drexel Burnham Lambert Grp., Inc.), 138 B.R. 687, 699 (Bankr. S.D.N.Y. 1992) ("Our readings persuade us that in each case, use of the Countryman test was neither necessary nor determinative. It was, rather, merely window dressing for results determined in the first instance by resort to another, sometimes unspecified criterion.") (analyzing case law regarding application of Countryman test to employment agreements). *See also infra* note 424.

27. Jay L. Westbrook, *A Functional Analysis of Executory Contracts*, 74 Minn. L. Rev. 227, 282-85 (1989).

28. *Id.* at 287.

29. *See, e.g.,* Route 21 Assoc. of Belleville, Inc., v. MHC, Inc., 486 B.R. 75 (S.D.N.Y. 2012); *In re* Majestic Capital, Ltd., 463 B.R. 289, 300 (Bankr. S.D.N.Y. 2012).

30. Michael T. Andrew, *Executory Contracts in Bankruptcy: Understanding "Rejection,"* 59 U. Colo. L. Rev. 845 (1988); Michael T. Andrew, *Executory Contracts Revisited: A Reply to Professor Westbrook,* 62 U. Colo. L. Rev. 1 (1991).

is irrelevant in the rejection context;[31] and (ii) a contract is executory if each party has unperformed obligations, and if the debtor's nonperformance eliminates its right to the other party's performance.[32] Although courts have not adopted this approach, they have considered its factors in applying other tests.[33]

b. Definition of Executory Contract: Recommendations and Findings

The Commission conducted an in-depth review of the literature and case law on executoriness under the Bankruptcy Code. Some of the Commissioners noted their experience with litigation concerning the executoriness issue and the attendant uncertainty and expense. The focus of the executoriness inquiry is whether each party has significant unperformed obligations under the contract.[34] The Commissioners discussed examples of contracts when this issue may be of particular concern, such as options, covenants not to compete, and oil and gas leases.[35] Although executoriness is not necessarily a bright-line determination, the Commissioners generally agreed that courts resolve this issue fairly or parties are able to negotiate a resolution.

---

31. Andrew, *Executory Contracts in Bankruptcy, supra* note [30], at 894.

32. *Id.* at 893.

33. *See, e.g., In re* Family Snacks, Inc., 257 B.R. 884, 905 (B.A.P. 8th Cir. 2001).

34. The Seventh Circuit Court of Appeals explained: "The Bankruptcy Code's legislative history states that the term "executory contract" "generally includes contracts on which performance is due to some extent on both sides.' A common definition, which this court has cited with approval, states that a contract is executory for bankruptcy purposes where "the obligation of both the bankrupt and the other party to the contract are so far unperformed that the failure to complete performance would be a material breach excusing the performance of the other." *In re* Crippin, 877 F.2d 594, 596 (7th Cir. 1989). *See also* Counties Contracting & Constr. Co. v. Constitution Life Ins. Co., 855 F.2d 1054, 1060 (3d Cir. 1988) ("The [Bankruptcy] Code does not define the term executory contract, however, courts have generally employed what has become known as the 'Countryman' definition of an executory contract, *i.e.,* a contract under which the obligations of both the bankrupt and the other party remain so far unperformed that failure of either to complete performance would constitute a material breach excusing performance of the other.").

35. *See, e.g.,* COR Route 5 Co., LLC v. Penn Traffic Co. (*In re* Penn Traffic Co.), 524 F.3d 373, 380 (2d Cir. 2008) ("While some courts have held that options contracts under which the optionee fully paid its price for the option to buy property before the debtor filed for bankruptcy are not executory (because no performance is due from the optionor unless the option is exercised), . . . others treat such contracts as executory.") (citing conflicting case law) ; Powell v. Anadarko E&P Co., L.P. (*In re* Powell), 482 B.R. 873, 877-78 (Bankr. M.D. Pa. 2012) ("Some courts have assumed that an oil and gas lease is an executory contract. Other courts have considered an oil and gas lease a transfer of an interest in real property and therefore not an executory contract.") (citing conflicting case law); *In re* Teligent, Inc., 268 B.R. 723, 730-31 (Bankr. S.D.N.Y. 2001) ("As a rule, Delaware law treats the covenant not to compete and the reciprocal promise to pay as material. As a result, the failure to make payment will discharge the obligation not to compete. . . . Where the covenant is given in connection with the sale of a business, it is even more likely to be deemed material. A covenant not to compete is often included in a contract to sell a business to protect the purchaser and allow him to enjoy the built-up good will.").

The Commission also considered the possibility of eliminating the concept of executoriness from the Bankruptcy Code. Both the advisory committee and the 1997 NBRC endorsed this position.[36] The Commissioners debated at length the potential utility to this approach. They discussed the meaningful benefits to refocusing contract disputes on the merits of the proposed assumption or rejection rather than extensive litigation on executoriness. The Commissioners supporting this approach emphasized the value to such a clean solution: with the distraction of executoriness off the table, parties could devote more attention on their rights, obligations, and remedies under the contract. Many Commissioners found the simplicity of this approach attractive.

Further deliberations about the elimination proposal revealed, however, the potential of unintended consequences of such a dramatic shift in a fundamental bankruptcy principle. The Commissioners noted the common law origins of the executoriness requirement of section 365,[37] and they also perceived value in maintaining some type of gating feature to vet those contracts that a debtor in possession could assume, assign, or reject in the chapter 11 case. Thus, the elimination of the executoriness concept could simply shift, rather than reduce, the amount of litigation or uncertainty in the first instance under section 365. Moreover, many Commissioners believed that the assumption or rejection decision was largely irrelevant to contracts that have already been fully performed by at least one of the parties.

The Commissioners also discussed the functional approach to determining executoriness, but most perceived the test to be unfair toward counterparties and too heavily weighted in favor of the interests of the debtor and the estate. The Commissioners acknowledged the potential value of allowing a debtor in possession to assume or reject any contract that would provide a benefit to the estate. As with the elimination proposal, however, the Commissioners were concerned about diminishing the rights of the nondebtor counterparties under the contracts. Subjecting any contract to section 365 primarily, if not solely, for the benefit of the estate imposed a greater burden

---

36. *See* NBRC Report, *supra* note 37, at 21 ("Title 11 should be amended to delete all references to 'executory' in section 365 and related provisions, and 'executoriness' should be eliminated as a prerequisite to the trustee's election to assume or breach a contract.").

37. *See In re* Austin Dev. Co., 19 F.3d 1077, 1081 (5th Cir. 1994) ("Section 365 derives from § 70(b) of the former Bankruptcy Act, a provision that broadly codified the common law doctrine that allowed the trustee either to assume and perform the debtor's leases or executory contracts or to 'reject' them if they were economically burdensome to the estate.").

on nondebtor parties than necessary to achieve a fair result for the estate in a chapter 11 case.

On balance, the Commission voted to adopt the Countryman test and to recommend its express incorporation into the Bankruptcy Code. The Commission found that, although imperfect, the Countryman test strikes an appropriate balance between the rights of debtors in possession and nondebtor counterparties to a contract. If the parties have material unperformed obligations, it is fair and reasonable to allow a debtor to choose to assume, assign, or reject such an agreement under section 365. The Commission also determined that many of the potentially challenging issues under the Countryman test have been resolved by the courts and that this case law is a valuable resource that would guide the implementation of the codified standard.

NOTES AND COMMENTS

Consider whether each of the following is an executory contract, using the Countryman "material breach" standard:

1. A medical malpractice insurance contract in which the doctor prepaid the premiums (In re Baird, 567 F.3d 1207 (10th Cir. 2009)).

2. A settlement agreement between a developer and the homeowner's association, in which they agreed to division of property taxes between the parties, mutual release of claims, and the developer would convey certain parts of real property to the association. The developer conveyed some, but not all, real property required. The homeowners association paid its portion of taxes but did not finalize release of claims. (In re Spoverlook, 551 B.R. 481 (Bankr. D. N.M. 2016)).

3. Software licensing agreement in which the non-debtor party licensed software to the debtor, which prepaid the entire cost of the contract. At the time of bankruptcy filing, both parties owed a duty of confidentiality regarding source code developed by the other. (In re Sunterra Corp., 361 F.3d 257 (4th Cir. 2004)).

2. Assumption and Assignment of Executory Contract

Once deemed executory, the contract may be assumed or rejected and, if assumed, may be retained by the debtor or assigned to a third party unless the law or contract prohibits such assignment. The following case discusses a split in authority regarding the ability to assume a non-assignable contract, and provides a useful exercise in statutory interpretation.

Perlman v. Catapult Entm't, Inc. (In re Catapult Entm't, Inc.)

165 F.3d 747 (9th Cir. 1999)

Fletcher, Circuit Judge

Appellant Stephen Perlman ("Perlman") licensed certain patents to appellee Catapult Entertainment, Inc. ("Catapult"). He now seeks to bar Catapult, which has since become a Chapter 11 debtor in possession, from assuming the patent licenses as part of its reorganization plan. Notwithstanding Perlman's objections, the bankruptcy court approved the assumption of the licenses and confirmed the reorganization plan. The district court affirmed the bankruptcy court on intermediate appeal. Perlman appeals that decision. We are called upon to determine whether, in light of § 365(c)(1) of the Bankruptcy Code, a Chapter 11 debtor in possession may assume certain nonexclusive patent licenses over a licensor's objection. We conclude that the bankruptcy court erred in permitting the debtor in possession to assume the patent licenses in question.

I.

Catapult, a California corporation, was formed in 1994 to create an online gaming network for 16-bit console videogames. That same year, Catapult entered into two license agreements with Perlman, wherein Perlman granted to Catapult the right to exploit certain relevant technologies, including patents and patent applications.

In October 1996, Catapult filed for reorganization under Chapter 11 of the Bankruptcy Code. . . .

On October 24, 1996, as part of the reorganization plan, Catapult filed a motion with the bankruptcy court seeking to assume some 140 executory contracts and leases, including the Perlman licenses. Over Perlman's objection, the bankruptcy court granted Catapult's motion and approved the reorganization plan. The district court subsequently affirmed the bankruptcy court. This appeal followed. . . .

Section 365 of the Bankruptcy Code gives a trustee in bankruptcy (or, in a Chapter 11 case, the debtor in possession) the authority to assume, assign, or reject the executory contracts and unexpired leases of the debtor, notwithstanding any contrary provisions appearing in such contracts or leases. *See* 11 U.S.C. § 365(a) & (f). This extraordinary authority, however, is not absolute. Section 365(c)(1) provides that, notwithstanding the general policy set out in § 365(a):

(c) The trustee may not assume or assign any executory contract or unexpired lease of the debtor, whether or not such contract or lease prohibits or restricts assignment of rights or delegation of duties, if

(1)(A) applicable law excuses a party, other than the debtor, to such contract or lease from accepting performance from or rendering performance to an entity other than the debtor or the debtor in possession, whether or not such contract or lease prohibits or restricts assignment of rights or delegation of duties; and

(B) such party does not consent to such assumption or assignment. . . .

11 U.S.C. § 365(c). Our task, simply put, is to apply this statutory language to the facts at hand and determine whether it prohibits Catapult, as the debtor in possession, from assuming the Perlman licenses without Perlman's consent.

While simply put, our task is not so easily resolved; the proper interpretation of § 365(c)(1) has been the subject of considerable disagreement among courts and commentators. On one side are those who adhere to the plain statutory language, which establishes a so-called "hypothetical test" to govern the assumption of executory contracts. [citing cases from 11th, 3rd, and 4th Circuits.] On the other side are those that forsake the statutory language in favor of an "actual test" that, in their view, better accomplishes the intent of Congress. [citing case from 1st Circuit.] Although we have on two occasions declined to choose between these competing visions, today we hold that we are bound by the plain terms of the statute and join the Third and Eleventh Circuits in adopting the "hypothetical test."

. . . We begin, as we must, with the statutory language. The plain language of § 365(c)(1) "link[s] nonassignability under 'applicable law' together with a prohibition on assumption in bankruptcy." In other words, the statute by its terms bars a debtor in possession from *assuming* an executory contract without the nondebtor's consent where applicable law precludes *assignment* of the contract to a third party. The literal language of § 365(c)(1) is thus said to establish a "hypothetical test": a debtor in possession may not assume an executory contract over the nondebtor's objection if applicable law would bar assignment to a hypothetical third party, even where the debtor in possession has no intention of assigning the contract in question to any such third party.

* * *

. . . application of the statute to the facts of this case becomes relatively straightforward:

(c) *Catapult* may not assume . . . *the Perlman licenses,* . . . if

(1)(A) *federal patent law* excuses *Perlman* from accepting performance from or rendering performance to an entity other than *Catapult* . . .; and

(B) *Perlman* does not consent to such assumption. . . .

11 U.S.C. § 365(c) (substitutions in italics). Since federal patent law makes nonexclusive patent licenses personal and nondelegable, § 365(c)(1)(A) is satisfied. Perlman has withheld his consent, thus satisfying § 365(c)(1)(B). Accordingly, the plain language of § 365(c)(1) bars Catapult from assuming the Perlman licenses.

. . . Catapult urges us to abandon the literal language of § 365(c)(1) in favor of an alternative approach, reasoning that Congress did not intend to bar debtors in possession from assuming their own contracts where no assignment is contemplated. In Catapult's view, § 365(c)(1) should be interpreted as embodying an "actual test": the statute bars assumption by the debtor in possession only where the reorganization in question results in the nondebtor *actually* having to accept performance from a third party. Under this reading of § 365(c), the debtor in possession would be permitted to assume any executory contract, so long as no assignment was contemplated. Put another way, Catapult suggests that, as to a debtor in possession, § 365(c)(1) should be read to prohibit assumption *and* assignment, rather than assumption *or* assignment.

Catapult has marshalled considerable authority to support this reading. The arguments supporting Catapult's position can be divided into three categories: (1) the literal reading creates inconsistencies within § 365; (2) the literal reading is incompatible with the legislative history; and (3) the literal reading flies in the face of sound bankruptcy policy. Nonetheless, we find that none of these considerations justifies departing from the plain language of § 365(c)(1).

. . . Catapult first argues that a literal reading of § 365(c)(1) sets the statute at war with itself and its neighboring provisions. Deviation from the plain language, contends Catapult, is necessary if internal consistency is to be achieved. We agree with Catapult that a court should interpret a statute, if possible, so as to minimize discord among related provisions. However, the dire inconsistencies cited by Catapult turn out, on closer analysis, to be no such thing.

Catapult, for example, singles out the interaction between § 365(c)(1) and § 365(f)(1) as a statutory trouble spot. Subsection (f)(1) provides that executory contracts, once assumed, may be assigned notwithstanding any contrary provisions contained in the contract *or applicable law. . . .*

The potential conflict between subsections (c)(1) and (f)(1) arises from their respective treatments of "applicable law." The plain language of subsection (c)(1) bars assumption (absent consent) whenever "applicable law" would bar assignment. Subsection (f)(1) states that, *contrary provisions in applicable law notwithstanding,* executory contracts may be assigned. Since assumption is a necessary prerequisite to assignment under § 365, *see* 11 U.S.C. § 365(f)(2)(A), a literal reading of subsection (c)(1) appears to render subsection (f)(1) superfluous. In the words of the Sixth Circuit, "[S]ection 365(c), the recognized exception to 365(f), appears at first to resuscitate in full the very anti-assignment 'applicable law' which 365(f) nullifies." Faced with this dilemma, one district court reluctantly concluded that the "[c]onflict between subsections (c) and (f) of § 365 is inescapable."

Subsequent authority, however, suggests that this conclusion may have been unduly pessimistic. The Sixth Circuit has credibly reconciled the warring provisions by noting that "each subsection recognizes an 'applicable law' of markedly different scope." Subsection (f)(1) states the broad rule—a law that, as a general matter, "prohibits, restricts, or conditions the assignment" of executory contracts is trumped by the provisions of subsection (f)(1). Subsection (c)(1), however, states a carefully crafted exception to the broad rule—where applicable law does not merely recite a general ban on assignment, but instead more specifically "excuses a party . . . from accepting performance from or rendering performance to an entity" different from the one with which the party originally contracted, the applicable law prevails over subsection (f)(1). In other words, in determining whether an "applicable law" stands or falls under § 365(f)(1), a court must ask *why* the "applicable law" prohibits assignment. Only if the law prohibits assignment on the rationale that the identity of the contracting party is material to the agreement will subsection (c)(1) rescue it. We agree with the Sixth and Eleventh Circuits that a literal reading of subsection (c)(1) does not inevitably set it at odds with subsection (f)(1).

* * *

A third potential inconsistency identified by Catapult relates to § 365(c)(2). According to Catapult, a literal reading of subsection (c)(1) renders subsection (c)(2) a dead letter. Subsection (c)(2) provides:

> (c) The trustee may not assume or assign any executory contract or unexpired lease of the debtor, whether or not such contract or lease prohibits or restricts assignment of rights or delegation of duties, if
>> (2) such contract is a contract to make a loan, or extend other debt financing or financial accommodations, to or for the benefit of the debtor, or to issue a security of the debtor. . . .

11 U.S.C. § 365(c)(2). According to Catapult, the contracts encompassed by subsection (c)(2) are all nonassignable as a matter of applicable state law. As a result, a literal reading of subsection (c)(1) would seem to snare and dispose of every executory contract within subsection (c)(2)'s scope. Perlman, however, persuasively rebuts this argument, noting that even if the state law governing the assignability of loan agreements and financing contracts is relatively uniform today, Congress by enacting subsection (c)(2) cemented nationwide uniformity in the bankruptcy context, effectively ensuring creditors that these particular contracts would not be assumable in bankruptcy. Put another way, it is the national uniformity of applicable state law that has rendered subsection (c)(2) superfluous, not the terms of subsection (c)(1).

In any event, subsection (c)(1) does not completely swallow up subsection (c)(2). Subsection (c)(1) by its terms permits assumption and assignment of executory loan agreements *so long as the nondebtor consents. See* 11 U.S.C. § 365(c)(1)(B). Subsection (c)(2), in contrast, bans assumption and assignment of such agreements, *consent of the nondebtor notwithstanding.* Accordingly, contrary to Catapult's assertion, subsection (c)(1) does not necessarily catch upriver all the fish that would otherwise be netted by subsection (c)(2). Once again, the "inconsistency" identified by Catapult proves evanescent under close scrutiny. We see no reason why these two provisions cannot happily coexist.

We conclude that the claimed inconsistencies are not actual and that the plain language of § 365(c)(1) compels the result Perlman urges: Catapult may not assume the Perlman licenses over Perlman's objection. Catapult has not demonstrated that, in according the words of subsection (c)(1) their plain meaning, we do violence to subsection (c)(1) or the provisions that accompany it.

. . . Catapult next urges that legislative history requires disregard of the plain language of § 365(c)(1). First off, because we discern no ambiguity in the plain statutory language, we need not resort to legislative history.

We will depart from this rule, if at all, only where the legislative history clearly indicates that Congress meant something other than what it said. Here, the legislative history unearthed by Catapult falls far short of this mark. The legislative history behind § 365(c) was exhaustively analyzed by the bankruptcy court in *In re Cardinal Industries,* 116 B.R. at 978–80. Its discussion makes it clear that there exists no contemporaneous legislative history regarding the current formulation of subsection (c)(1). Catapult, however, argues that the language as ultimately enacted in 1984 had its genesis in a 1980 House amendment to an earlier Senate technical corrections bill. The amendment was accompanied by "a relatively obscure committee report." . . . However, since the report relates to a different proposed bill, predates enactment of § 365(c)(1) by several years, and expresses at most the thoughts of only one committee in the House, we are not inclined to view it as the sort of clear indication of contrary intent that would overcome the unambiguous language of subsection (c)(1).

. . . Catapult makes the appealing argument that, as a leading bankruptcy commentator has pointed out, there are policy reasons to prefer the "actual test." That may be so, but Congress is the policy maker, not the courts.

Policy arguments cannot displace the plain language of the statute; that the plain language of § 365(c)(1) may be bad policy does not justify a judicial rewrite. And a rewrite is precisely what the actual test requires. The statute expressly provides that a debtor in possession "may not assume *or* assign" an executory contract where applicable law bars assignment and the nondebtor objects. 11 U.S.C. § 365(c)(1) (emphasis added). The actual test effectively engrafts a narrow exception onto § 365(c)(1) for debtors in possession, providing that, as to them, the statute only prohibits assumption *and* assignment, as opposed to assumption *or* assignment.

* * *

(Citations omitted.)

NOTES AND COMMENTS

1. The *Catapult* court notes that the issue of nonassignability of a contract leading to inability to assume the contract arises primarily in the context of Chapter 11 debtors in possession. Why does the issue not arise as often when the trustee seeks to assume the contract?

2. The *Catapult* court seems most convinced by the debtor's policy argument for adopting the actual test, but determines that policy alone cannot trump the statutory language. What policies are advanced by the actual test, and how would the hypothetical test frustrate those policies?

3. While the debtor often seeks to call a contract "executory," in some cases the non-debtor party is the one seeking a determination that the contract is executory. Consider the situation in In re Sunterra Corp., 361 F.3d 257 (4th Cir. 2004). That case involved a software license. The non-debtor party, the licensor, sought a determination that the contract was executory and that, because the contract could not be assigned, it could not be assumed and thus must be deemed rejected. The non-debtor party won on both issues.

4. Though the circuit split on this issue has existed for decades, the Supreme Court has yet to step in to resolve the split. In denying certiorari on a case involving the issue of whether non-assignability of a contract prohibits assumption of that contract by a debtor-in-possession, some of the Justices noted the importance of the issue:

> . . . One arguable criticism of the hypothetical approach is that it pur-chases fidelity to the Bankruptcy Code's text by sacrificing sound bank-ruptcy policy. For one thing, the hypothetical test may prevent debtors-in-possession from continuing to exercise their rights under nonassignable contracts, such as patent and copyright licenses. Without these con-tracts, some debtors-in-possession may be unable to effect the successful reorganization that Chapter 11 was designed to promote. For another thing, the hypothetical test provides a windfall to nondebtor parties to valuable executory contracts: If the debtor is outside of bankruptcy, then the nondebtor does not have the option to renege on its agreement; but if the debtor seeks bankruptcy protection, then the nondebtor obtains the power to reclaim—and resell at the prevailing, potentially higher market rate—the rights it sold to the debtor.

> * * *

> The division in the courts over the meaning of § 365(c)(1) is an import-ant one to resolve for bankruptcy courts and for businesses that seek reorganization. This petition for certiorari, however, is not the most suit-able case for our resolution of the conflict. . . . In a different case the Court should consider granting certiorari on this significant question.

N.C.P. Mktg. Grp., Inc. v. BG Star Prods., Inc., 556 U.S. 1145 (Mem) (2009) (J. Kennedy and Breyer).

The N.C.P. Marketing Group case on which the Supreme Court denied certiorari involved an agreement granting NCP the right to sell products with the trademark Tae Bo®, and a subsequent licensing agreement providing details on use of the trademark. When NCP filed for Chapter 11 bankruptcy protection, the nondebtor party to the agreements argued that NCP could not assume the agreements because federal law prohibited assignment of those contracts. However, the district court rendered its decision based on the expiration date of the agreements, not a determination of the applicable test for assumability of nonassignable contracts. In re N.C.P. Mktg. Grp., Inc., 337 B.R. 230, 232–38 (D. Nev. 2005), *aff'd*, 279 F. App'x 561 (9th Cir. 2008). Why might Justices Kennedy and Breyer have written separately to encourage the Court to take a future case?

3. Rejection of an Executory Contract

The non-debtor party to a contract has no choice as to acceptance or rejection of the contract. Read §365(g); what is the consequence of rejection of a contract? You will quickly see that rejection of a contract is treated as a pre-petition breach of the contract, allowing the non-debtor party to make a claim for any damages caused by the rejection. But what if the non-debtor party wants to continue under the contract despite rejection of the contract? The Supreme Court recently considered the consequences of rejection in such a situation, settling a circuit split on the issue.

Mission Product Holdings, Inc. v. Tempnology, LLC

139 S. Ct. 1652 (2019)

KAGAN, Justice

Section 365 of the Bankruptcy Code enables a debtor to "reject any executory contract"—meaning a contract that neither party has finished performing. 11 U.S.C. § 365(a). The section further provides that a debtor's rejection of a contract under that authority "constitutes a breach of such contract." § 365(g).

Today we consider the meaning of those provisions in the context of a trademark licensing agreement. The question is whether the debtor-licensor's rejection of that contract deprives the licensee of its rights to use the trademark. We hold it does not. A rejection breaches a contract but does not rescind it. And that means all the rights that would ordinarily survive a contract breach, including those conveyed here, remain in place.

. . . This case arises from a licensing agreement gone wrong. Respondent Tempnology, LLC, manufactured clothing and accessories designed to stay cool when used in exercise. It marketed those products under the brand name "Coolcore," using trademarks (*e.g.*, logos and labels) to distinguish the gear from other athletic apparel. In 2012, Tempnology entered into a contract with petitioner Mission Product Holdings, Inc. The agreement gave Mission an exclusive license to distribute certain Coolcore products in the United States. And more important here, it granted Mission a non-exclusive license to use the Coolcore trademarks, both in the United States and around the world. The agreement was set to expire in July 2016. But in September 2015, Tempnology filed a petition for Chapter 11 bankruptcy. And it soon afterward asked the Bankruptcy Court to allow it to "reject" the licensing agreement. § 365(a).

Chapter 11 of the Bankruptcy Code sets out a framework for reorganizing a bankrupt business. See §§ 1101–1174. The filing of a petition creates a bankruptcy estate consisting of all the debtor's assets and rights. See § 541. The estate is the pot out of which creditors' claims are paid. It is administered by either a trustee or, as in this case, the debtor itself. See §§ 1101, 1107.

Section 365(a) of the Code provides that a "trustee [or debtor], subject to the court's approval, may assume or reject any executory contract." § 365(a). A contract is executory if "performance remains due to some extent on both sides." Such an agreement represents both an asset (the debtor's right to the counterparty's future performance) and a liability (the debtor's own obligations to perform). Section 365(a) enables the debtor (or its trustee), upon entering bankruptcy, to decide whether the contract is a good deal for the estate going forward. If so, the debtor will want to assume the contract, fulfilling its obligations while benefiting from the counterparty's performance. But if not, the debtor will want to reject the contract, repudiating any further performance of its duties. The bankruptcy court will generally approve that choice, under the deferential "business judgment" rule.

According to Section 365(g), "the rejection of an executory contract[] constitutes a breach of such contract." As both parties here agree, the counterparty thus has a claim against the estate for damages resulting from the debtor's nonperformance. But such a claim is unlikely to ever be paid in full. That is because the debtor's breach is deemed to occur "immediately before the date of the filing of the [bankruptcy] petition," rather than on the actual post-petition rejection date. § 365(g)(1). By thus giving the counterparty a pre-petition claim, Section 365(g) places that party in the same boat as the debtor's unsecured creditors, who in a typical bankruptcy may receive only cents on the dollar.

In this case, the Bankruptcy Court (per usual) approved Tempnology's proposed rejection of its executory licensing agreement with Mission. That meant, as laid out above, two things on which the parties agree. First, Tempnology could stop performing under the contract. And second, Mission could assert (for whatever it might be worth) a pre-petition claim in the bankruptcy proceeding for damages resulting from Tempnology's nonperformance.

But Tempnology thought still another consequence ensued, and it returned to the Bankruptcy Court for a declaratory judgment confirming its view. According to Tempnology, its rejection of the contract also terminated the rights it had granted Mission to use the Coolcore trademarks. Tempnology based its argument on a negative inference. Several provisions in Section 365 state that a counterparty to specific kinds of agreements may keep exercising contractual rights after a debtor's rejection. For example, Section 365(h) provides that if a bankrupt landlord rejects a lease, the tenant need not move out; instead, she may stay and pay rent (just as she did before) until the lease term expires. And still closer to home, Section 365(n) sets out a similar rule for some types of intellectual property licenses: If the debtor-licensor rejects the agreement, the licensee can continue to use the property (typically, a patent), so long as it makes whatever payments the contract demands. But Tempnology pointed out that neither Section 365(n) nor any similar provision covers trademark licenses. So, it reasoned, in that sort of contract a different rule must apply: The debtor's rejection must extinguish the rights that the agreement had conferred on the trademark licensee. The Bankruptcy Court agreed. . . .

The Bankruptcy Appellate Panel reversed, relying heavily on a decision of the Court of Appeals for the Seventh Circuit about the effects of rejection on trademark licensing agreements. Rather than reason backward from Section 365(n) or similar provisions, the Panel focused on Section 365(g)'s statement that rejection of a contract "constitutes a breach." Outside bankruptcy, the court explained, the breach of an agreement does not eliminate rights the contract had already conferred on the non-breaching party. . . . Mission could thus continue to use the Coolcore trademarks.

But the Court of Appeals for the First Circuit rejected the Panel's and Seventh Circuit's view, and reinstated the Bankruptcy Court decision terminating Mission's license. . . . It next reasoned that special features of trademark law counsel against allowing a licensee to retain rights to a mark after the licensing agreement's rejection. Under that body of law, the majority stated, the trademark owner's "[f]ailure to monitor and exercise [quality] control" over goods associated with a trademark "jeopardiz[es] the continued validity of [its] own trademark rights." So if (the majority continued) a licensee can keep using a mark after an agreement's rejection, the licensor will need to carry on its monitoring activities. And according to the majority, that would frustrate "Congress's principal aim in providing for rejection": to "release the debtor's estate from burdensome obligations.". . .

We granted certiorari to resolve the division between the First and Seventh Circuits. We now affirm the Seventh's reasoning and reverse the decision below.

* * *

What is the effect of a debtor's (or trustee's) rejection of a contract under Section 365 of the Bankruptcy Code? The parties and courts of appeals have offered us two starkly different answers. According to one view, a rejection has the same consequence as a contract breach outside bankruptcy: It gives the counterparty a claim for damages, while leaving intact the rights the counterparty has received under the contract. According to the other view, a rejection (except in a few spheres) has more the effect of a contract rescission in the non-bankruptcy world: Though also allowing a damages claim, the rejection terminates the whole agreement along with all rights it conferred. Today, we hold that both Section 365's text and fundamental principles of bankruptcy law command the first, rejection-as-breach approach. We reject the competing claim that by specifically enabling the counterparties in some contracts to retain rights after rejection, Congress showed that it wanted the counterparties in all other contracts to lose their rights. And we reject an argument for the rescission approach turning on the distinctive features of trademark licenses. Rejection of a contract—any contract—in bankruptcy operates not as a rescission but as a breach.

. . . We start with the text of the Code's principal provisions on rejection—and find that it does much of the work. . . . Section 365(g) describes what rejection means. Rejection "constitutes a breach of [an executory] contract," deemed to occur "immediately before the date of the filing of the petition." Or said more pithily for current purposes, a rejection is a breach. And "breach" is neither a defined nor a specialized bankruptcy term. It means in the Code what it means in contract law outside bankruptcy. . . .

Consider a made-up executory contract to see how the law of breach works outside bankruptcy. A dealer leases a photocopier to a law firm, while agreeing to service it every month; in exchange, the firm commits to pay a monthly fee. During the lease term, the dealer decides to stop servicing the machine, thus breaching the agreement in a material way. The law firm now has a choice (assuming no special contract term or state law). The firm can keep up its side of the bargain, continuing to pay for use of the copier, while suing the dealer for damages from the service breach. Or the firm can call the whole deal off, halting its own payments and returning the copier, while suing for any damages incurred. But to repeat: The choice to terminate the agreement and send back the copier is for the *law firm*. By contrast, the *dealer* has no ability, based on its own breach, to terminate the agreement. Or otherwise said, the dealer cannot get back the copier just by refusing to show up for a service appointment. The contract gave the law firm continuing rights in the copier, which the dealer cannot unilaterally revoke.

And now to return to bankruptcy: If the rejection of the photocopier contract "constitutes a breach," as the Code says, then the same results should follow (save for one twist as to timing). Assume here that the dealer files a Chapter 11 petition and decides to reject its agreement with the law firm. That means, as above, that the dealer will stop servicing the copier. It means, too, that the law firm has an option about how to respond—continue the contract or walk away, while suing for whatever damages go with its choice. (Here is where the twist comes in: Because the rejection is deemed to occur "immediately before" bankruptcy, the firm's damages suit is treated as a pre-petition claim on the estate, which will likely receive only cents on the dollar.) And most important, it means that assuming the law firm wants to keep using the copier, the dealer cannot take it back. A rejection does not terminate the contract. When it occurs, the debtor and counterparty do not go back to their pre-contract positions. Instead, the counterparty retains the rights it has received under the agreement. As after a breach, so too after a rejection, those rights survive.

All of this, it will hardly surprise you to learn, is not just about photocopier leases. Sections 365(a) and (g) speak broadly, to "any executory contract[s]." Many licensing agreements involving trademarks or other property are of that kind (including, all agree, the Tempnology-Mission contract). The licensor not only grants a license, but provides associated goods or services during its term; the licensee pays continuing royalties or fees. If the licensor breaches the agreement outside bankruptcy (again, barring any special contract term or state law), everything said above goes. In particular, the breach does not revoke the license or stop the licensee from doing what it allows. And because rejection "constitutes a breach," § 365(g), the same consequences follow in bankruptcy. The debtor can stop performing its remaining obligations under the agreement. But the debtor cannot rescind the license already conveyed. So the licensee can continue to do whatever the license authorizes.

In preserving those rights, Section 365 reflects a general bankruptcy rule: The estate cannot possess anything more than the debtor itself did outside bankruptcy. . . . So if the not-yet debtor was subject to a counterparty's contractual right (say, to retain a copier or use a trademark), so too is the trustee or debtor once the bankruptcy petition has been filed. The rejection-as-breach rule (but *not* the rejection-as-rescission rule) ensures that result. By insisting that the same counterparty rights survive rejection as survive breach, the rule prevents a debtor in bankruptcy from recapturing interests it had given up.

* * *

Tempnology's main argument to the contrary, here as in the courts below, rests on a negative inference. Several provisions of Section 365, Tempnology notes, "identif[y] categories of contracts under which a counterparty" may retain specified contract rights "notwithstanding rejection." Sections 365(h) and (i) make clear that certain purchasers and lessees of real property and timeshare interests can continue to exercise rights after a debtor has rejected the lease or sales contract. . . . Tempnology argues from those provisions that the ordinary consequence of rejection must be something different—*i.e.,* the termination, rather than survival, of contractual rights previously granted. Otherwise, Tempnology concludes, the statute's "general rule" would "swallow the exceptions."

But that argument pays too little heed to the main provisions governing rejection and too much to subsidiary ones. On the one hand, it offers no account of how to read Section 365(g) (recall, rejection "constitutes a breach") to say essentially its opposite (*i.e.,* that rejection and breach have divergent consequences). On the other hand, it treats as a neat, reticulated scheme of "narrowly tailored exception[s]," what history reveals to be anything but. Each of the provisions Tempnology highlights emerged at a different time, over a span of half a century. . . . And each responded to a discrete problem—as often as not, correcting a judicial ruling of just the kind Tempnology urges. Read as generously as possible to Tempnology, this mash-up of legislative interventions says nothing much of anything about the content of Section 365(g)'s general rule. Read less generously, it affirmatively refutes Tempnology's rendition. . . . On that account, Congress enacted the provisions, as and when needed, to reinforce or clarify the general rule that contractual rights survive rejection.

* * *

For the reasons stated above, we hold that under Section 365, a debtor's rejection of an executory contract in bankruptcy has the same effect as a breach outside bankruptcy. Such an act cannot rescind rights that the contract previously granted. Here, that construction of Section 365 means that the debtor-licensor's rejection cannot revoke the trademark license.

* * *

(Citations omitted.)

NOTES AND COMMENTS

1. Why would the trustee (or debtor-in-possession in a Chapter 11 case) want to reject the contract knowing that it will not rescind the contract?

D. BANKRUPTCY IN PRACTICE

Several potential creditors have claims against Diana. For each of these claims, determine whether the claimant is secured or unsecured. For secured creditors, determine whether the creditor is entitled to claim post-petition attorney's fees and interest. For unsecured creditors, determine whether the creditor is entitled to priority for his or her claim.

1. Bryan, Diana's ex-husband, who is owed past-due child support.

2. Diana's boss, who has sued Diana for intentional infliction of emotional distress based on the incident in which Diana destroyed his car.

3. The boss's insurance companies, which intend to sue Diana for reimbursement of the money paid to repair the boss's car and for the boss's medical expenses as a result of the incident.

4. Bank, which has a security interest in Diana's car. Diana owes the Bank $14,000 in principal and $2,000 in pre-petition interest. Since the filing of the petition, an additional $500 of interest has accrued. The contract provides for attorney's fees in the event that the Bank has to take action in order to repossess the car. The Bank has filed for relief from the automatic stay in order to repossess the car. It would cost Diana $15,000 to purchase a similar car, but the Bank would only be able to sell it after repossession for $10,000.

Does Diana have any executory contracts in her bankruptcy case? Remember, for example, that she has a current car lease. What considerations are important in determining whether to assume or reject any executory contract?

5

Torts, Other Consumer Debt, and Bankruptcy: Discharge of Debt

> Bankruptcy is about financial death and financial rebirth. Bankruptcy
> is the great American story rewritten. We're a nation of debtors.[1]

Most bankruptcy debtors seek a discharge of the debts that they cannot pay. While discharging debts allows those debtors a "fresh start" and the possibility of a financially stable future, it burdens creditors who will not be paid what is due under contract or law. The balance between a debtor's fresh start and a creditor's maximum recovery is a recurring theme in bankruptcy and may best be exemplified by the determination of which of a debtor's debts can be discharged. Debts that cannot be discharged often occur because a debtor engaged in egregious behavior—such as intentional torts—tipping the balance toward maximizing recovery for the injured creditor. Review § 523 to see the types of debts that cannot be discharged in a bankruptcy case. While this chapter focuses largely on the tort claims that cannot be discharged, you will see that other types of claims are also nondischargeable, such as certain tax claims and even some contract-based claims.

---

1. Elizabeth Warren, *Frontline: Secret History of the Credit Card* (PBS television broadcast Nov. 23, 2004).

RECALL DIANA DETTER

As you work through this chapter, keep in mind that Diana's primary goal in filing for bankruptcy protection is to relieve herself of some of the debt that she currently owes to creditors. This relief, known as "discharge" of debt, is an essential part of the bankruptcy code's goal of giving honest but unfortunate debtors a "fresh start." But should all debts be treated equally? Some of Diana's debts involve contractual obligations to pay and are secured by collateral—including her home mortgage and car payments. Others involve intentional injuries, such as the harm to Diana's boss and to his car. Others involve expenses owed to or in support of her children, such as child support obligations, her daughter's medical expenses, and her children's tuition payments. Remember that to the extent that these debts are discharged, the creditor owed the debt will not be paid on that obligation.

A. REVIEW OF CORE DOCTRINE OF TORTS

Black's Law Dictionary defines a tort as:

> A civil wrong, other than breach of contract, for which a remedy may be obtained, [usually] in the form of damages; a breach of a duty that the law imposes on persons who stand in a particular relation to one another. . . Tortious conduct is typically one of four types: (1) a culpable or intentional act resulting in harm; (2) an act involving culpable and unlawful conduct causing unintentional harm; (3) a culpable act of inadvertence involving an unreasonable risk of harm; and (4) a nonculpable act resulting in accidental harm for which, because of the hazards involved, the law imposes strict or absolute liability despite the absence of fault. . . .

Black's Law Dictionary (Bryan Garner ed., Westlaw 11th ed. 2019). *Black's* defines damages for such torts as "[m]onetary compensation for tangible and intangible harm to persons and property as the result of a tort." *Black's Law Dictionary*, (Bryan Garner ed., Westlaw 11th ed. 2019). Torts includes both intentional and non-intentional torts (primarily negligence).

As the definition from *Black's* notes, the types of torts fall into four categories. For the purpose of this book, however, the focus is on negligence and intentional torts. First consider the tort of negligence. The Restatement (Third) of Torts § 3 (2010) defines negligence as follows: "[a] person acts negligently if the person does not exercise reasonable care under all the circumstances. Primary factors to consider in ascertaining whether the person's conduct lacks reasonable care are the foreseeable likelihood that the person's conduct will result in harm, the foreseeable severity of any harm that may ensue, and the burden of precautions to eliminate or reduce the risk of harm." As learned in a Torts class, this definition can be broken down into elements that can be summarized as duty, breach, causation, and damages.

The Restatement explains the duty that the tortfeasor owes as typically "[a]n actor ordinarily has a duty to exercise reasonable care when the actor's conduct creates a risk of physical harm" and proximate cause as "[a]n actor's liability is limited to those harms that result from the risks that made the actor's conduct tortious." The Restatement (Third) of Torts §§ 7, 29 (2016 update).

In bankruptcy, intentional torts often serve as the basis for nondischargeability of debts. Recall that an intentional tort may constitute a claim for battery, assault, or another tort, which results in a recovery for the injured party. For example, the Restatement (Second) of Torts includes assault, battery, false imprisonment, and intentional infliction of emotional harm. *Black's Law Dictionary* makes a distinction by defining intentional tort as "[a] tort committed by someone acting with general or specific intent. . . . Examples include battery, false imprisonment, and trespass to land." *Black's Law Dictionary* (Bryan Garner ed., Westlaw 11th ed. 2019).

Liability also may arise from fraudulent conduct of a tortfeasor. Fraud results from the tortfeasor's conduct when the tortfeasor makes "[a] knowing misrepresentation or knowing concealment of a material fact made to induce another to act to his or her detriment." *Black's Law Dictionary* (Bryan Garner ed., Westlaw, 11th ed. 2019). "Additional elements in a claim for fraud may include reasonable reliance on the misrepresentation and damages resulting from this reliance." *Black's Law Dictionary* (Bryan Garner ed., Westlaw 11th ed. 2019). The Restatement (Second) of Torts § 525, *Liability for Fraudulent Misrepresentation,* explains that "[o]ne who fraudulently makes a misrepresentation of fact, opinion, intention or law for the purpose of inducing another to act or to refrain from action in reliance upon it, is subject to liability to the other in deceit for pecuniary loss caused to him by his justifiable reliance upon the misrepresentation."

Remember the role of intent with intentional torts. In the Restatement (Second) of Torts § 8A, "intent" is used to mean "that the actor desires to cause consequences of his act, or that he believes that the consequences are substantially certain to result from it." As you read through the cases in the next section, consider how the tortfeasor's intent or behavior is factored in by the bankruptcy court in determining whether to grant a discharge.

B. DISCHARGE OF DEBT (§§ 523, 524)

1. Accrual of Claims

In the bankruptcy context, a pre-petition tort may give rise to a claim against the debtor. As noted in Chapter 4, non-bankruptcy law governs the existence of a claim. Thus, whether a tort victim has a compensable claim against the debtor will typically depend upon state tort law. But how that claim will be treated in the bankruptcy case—and after the bankruptcy case is over—depends upon when the claim "accrued" and what type of tort occurred. The issue of how bankruptcy treats a negligence (or any other tort) claim becomes particularly complicated when the tortious act occurs long before the tort victim realizes she has a right to recovery from that act. This can occur in a variety of settings, such as diseases with a long latency period following exposure, environmental claims such as dumping of waste that impacts the environment over a long period of time, or manufacturing defects that come to light only after use by a consumer. Competing policies arise in these settings. On the one hand, bankruptcy seeks to handle claims during the life of the case; on the other hand, bankruptcy seeks to prevent some creditors or claims from holding up the distribution process for the remaining creditors. Balancing these competing goals in a situation where some potential claimants may not yet be known presents a challenge, particularly in the context of discharging unpaid debt.

At the conclusion of a bankruptcy case, debtors generally receive a discharge of debt. Each operating chapter of the Bankruptcy Code provides for discharge. 11 U.S.C. §§ 727, 944(b), 1141(d), 1228, 1328. Read 11 U.S.C. § 524(a), entitled "Effect of discharge." Note that the language in § 524(a) mirrors some of the language of § 362's automatic stay discussed in Chapter 3. How do these two sections work together to provide the debtor with a fresh start after bankruptcy?

Only bankruptcy claims are discharged at the end of the bankruptcy. Claims that arise after the bankruptcy case begins are dealt with outside of the bankruptcy system and are not subject to discharge.[2] Section 524(a) speaks in terms of discharge of "debt," which in turn is defined by § 101(12) as "liability on a claim." As noted in Chapter 4, the Code defines claims broadly, including rights that have not yet "matured." How the claimant fares when a delay exists between infliction of the harm and manifestation of an injury as a result of that harm depends on a determination of when

---

2. Note that some chapters of the Code provide that claims arising during the case can be dealt with in the bankruptcy case and discharged after successful completion of the plan. *See, e.g.,* 11 U.S.C. § 503 (administrative expenses), § 1305 (allowance of post-petition claims in Chapter 13 cases).

the claim *occurred* for purposes of the bankruptcy case. Consider the following case, which discusses the need to determine when the claim arose for purposes of both the automatic stay and the bankruptcy discharge.

Jeld-Wen, Inc. v. Van Brunt (In re Grossman's Inc.)

607 F.3d 114 (3rd Cir. 2010)

SLOVITER, Circuit Judge

... It is only on a rare occasion that we overrule a prior precedential opinion. We assemble en banc to consider whether this is such an occasion.

In the appeal before us, the Bankruptcy Court, affirmed by the District Court, followed our precedent in *Avellino & Bienes v. M. Frenville Co. (Matter of M. Frenville Co.)*, 744 F.2d 332 (3d Cir. 1984) ("*Frenville* "), to hold that a plan of reorganization did not discharge asbestos-related tort claims filed by Mary Van Brunt and her husband Gordon (the "Van Brunts") against Grossman's Inc. The underlying asbestos exposure occurred pre-petition but the injury manifested itself post-petition. ...

In 1977, Appellee Mary Van Brunt, who was remodeling her home, purchased products that allegedly contained asbestos. She purchased those products in upstate New York from Grossman's, a home improvement and lumber retailer. In April 1997, Grossman's filed petitions under Chapter 11 of the Bankruptcy Code.

The following are among the undisputed facts set forth in the Bankruptcy Court's Findings of Fact: "[a]t the time of the [bankruptcy], Grossman's had actual knowledge that it had previously sold asbestos containing products such as gypsum board and joint compound"; "Grossman's knew of the adverse health risks associated with exposure to asbestos"; it "was aware that asbestos manufacturers had been or were being sued by asbestos personal-injury claimants"; it "was aware that producers of both gypsum board and joint compound were being sued for asbestos-related injuries"; and it "was not aware of any product liability lawsuits based upon alleged exposure to asbestos-containing products that had been filed against [it]. . . ."

Grossman's proceeded to provide notice by publication of the deadline for filing proofs of claim. There was no suggestion in the publication notice that Grossman's might have future asbestos liability. Grossman's Chapter 11 Plan of Reorganization purported to discharge all claims that arose before the Plan's effective date. The Bankruptcy Court confirmed the Plan of Reorganization in December 1997.

Ms. Van Brunt did not file a proof of claim before confirmation of the Plan of Reorganization because, at the time, she was unaware of any "claim" as she manifested no symptoms related to asbestos exposure. It was only in 2006, almost ten years later, that Ms. Van Brunt began to manifest symptoms of mesothelioma, a cancer linked to asbestos exposure. She was diagnosed with the disease in March 2007.

Shortly after her diagnosis, the Van Brunts filed an action for tort and breach of warranty in a New York state court against JELD-WEN, the successor-in-interest to Grossman's, and fifty-seven other companies who allegedly manufactured the products that Ms. Van Brunt purchased from Grossman's in 1977. Ms. Van Brunt conceded that she did not know the manufacturer of any of the products that she acquired from Grossman's for her remodeling projects in 1977. After the Van Brunts filed their suit, JELD-WEN moved to reopen the Chapter 11 case, seeking a determination that their claims were discharged by the Plan. Ms. Van Brunt died in 2008 while the case was pending. Gordon Van Brunt has been substituted in her stead as the representative of her estate.

The Bankruptcy Court concluded that the 1997 Plan of Reorganization did not discharge the Van Brunts' asbestos-related claims because they arose after the effective date of the Plan. In so holding, the Bankruptcy Court relied on our decisions in *Frenville* and its progeny. *Frenville* held that a "claim," as that term is defined by the Bankruptcy Code, arises when the underlying state law cause of action accrues. The applicable New York law provides that a cause of action for asbestos-related injury does not accrue until the injury manifests itself. The Bankruptcy Court therefore reasoned that the Van Brunts had no "claim" subject to discharge in 1997 because Ms. Van Brunt did not manifest symptoms of mesothelioma — and thus the New York cause of action did not accrue — until 2006. The Bankruptcy Court entered judgment for the Van Brunts and against JELD-WEN, effectively allowing the Van Brunts to proceed with their claims in the New York state court.

* * *

In the case before us, the District Court and Bankruptcy Court correctly applied the [*Frenville* case's] accrual test in holding that the Van Brunts' tort claims were not discharged by the Plan of Reorganization. According to *Frenville,* the claims arose for bankruptcy purposes when the underlying state law cause of action accrued. The New York tort cause of action accrued in 2006 when Ms. Van Brunt manifested symptoms of mesothelioma. The claims were therefore post-petition under *Frenville.*

The question remains, however, whether we should continue to follow *Frenville* and its accrual test. We have recognized that "[s]ignificant authority [contrary to *Frenville*] exists in other circuits". A sister circuit has described our approach in *Frenville* as "universally rejected." The courts of appeals that have considered *Frenville* have uniformly declined to follow it.

* * *

Courts have declined to follow *Frenville* because of its apparent conflict with the Bankruptcy Code's expansive treatment of the term "claim." . . . The *Frenville* court focused on the "right to payment" language in § 101(5) and, according to some courts, "impos[ed] too narrow an interpretation on the term claim," . . . by failing to give sufficient weight to the words modifying it: "contingent," "unmatured," and "unliquidated." The accrual test in *Frenville* does not account for the fact that a "claim" can exist under the Code before a right to payment exists under state law.

* * *

Our decision to overrule *Frenville* leaves a void in our jurisprudence as to when a claim arises. That decision has various implications. One such implication involves the application of the automatic stay provided in § 362 of the Bankruptcy Code which operates to stay the commencement or continuation of any "action or proceeding" that was or could have been commenced against the debtor. . . It is applicable, however, only to stay a claim that arose pre-petition.

Principal among the effects of the determination when a claim arises is the effect on the dischargeability of a claim. Under 11 U.S.C. § 1141(d)(1)(A) of the Code, the confirmation of a plan of reorganization "discharges the debtor from any debt that arose before the date of such confirmation. . . ." A "debt" is defined as liability on a "claim," which in turn is defined as a "right to payment." This is consistent with Congress' intent to provide debtors with a fresh start, an objective, noted the Second Circuit, "made more feasible by maximizing the scope of a discharge." On the other hand, a broad discharge may disadvantage potential claimants, such as tort claimants, whose injuries were allegedly caused by the debtor but which have not yet manifested and who therefore had no reason to file claims in the bankruptcy. These competing considerations have not been resolved consistently by the cases decided to date.

Moreover, the determination when a claim arises has significant due process implications. If potential future tort claimants have not filed claims because they are unaware of their injuries, they might challenge the effectiveness of any purported notice of the claims bar date. Discharge of such claims without providing adequate notice raises questions under the Fourteenth Amendment.

The courts have generally divided into two groups on the decision as to when a claim arises for purposes of the Code, with numerous variations. One group has applied the conduct test and the other has applied what has been termed the pre-petition relationship test. Illustrative of the cases that have adopted the conduct test is the decision of the Fourth Circuit in *Grady*, 839 F.2d at 201.

. . . [The *Grady* Court] determined that the plaintiff's claim arose "when the acts giving rise to [the defendant's] liability were performed, not when the harm caused by those acts was manifested.". . .

In contrast, the Eleventh Circuit criticized a conduct test that would enable individuals to hold a claim against a debtor by virtue of their potential future exposure to "the debtor's product," regardless of whether the claimant had any relationship or contact with the debtor. . . Similarly, a commentator observed that under the conduct test, "[c]laimants who did not use or have any exposure to the dangerous product until long after the bankruptcy case has concluded would nonetheless be subject to the terms of a preexisting confirmed Chapter 11 plan."

Some of the courts concerned that the conduct test may be too broad have adopted what has been referred to as a pre-petition relationship test. Under this test, a claim arises from a debtor's pre-petition tortious conduct where there is also some pre-petition relationship between the debtor and the claimant, such as a purchase, use, operation of, or exposure to the debtor's product. . . .

* * *

Irrespective of the title used, there seems to be something approaching a consensus among the courts that a prerequisite for recognizing a "claim" is that the claimant's exposure to a product giving rise to the "claim" occurred pre-petition, even though the injury manifested after the reorganization. We agree and hold that a "claim" arises when an individual is exposed pre-petition to a product or other conduct giving rise to an injury, which underlies a "right to payment" under the Bankruptcy Code. Applied to the Van Brunts, it means that their claims arose sometime in 1977, the date Mary Van Brunt alleged that Grossman's product exposed her to asbestos.

That does not necessarily mean that the Van Brunts' claims were discharged by the Plan of Reorganization. Any application of the test to be applied cannot be divorced from fundamental principles of due process. Notice is "[a]n elementary and fundamental requirement of due process in any proceeding which is to be accorded finality. . . ." Without notice of a bankruptcy claim, the claimant will not have a meaningful opportunity to protect his or her claim. This issue has arisen starkly in the situation presented by persons with asbestos injuries that are not manifested until years or even decades after exposure.

* * *

. . . A court therefore must decide whether discharge of the Van Brunts' claims would comport with due process, which may invite inquiry into the adequacy of the notice of the claims bar date. The only open matter before the District Court is JELD-WEN's request for a declaration that the Van Brunts' claims had been discharged.

Whether a particular claim has been discharged by a plan of reorganization depends on factors applicable to the particular case and is best determined by the appropriate bankruptcy court or the district court. In determining whether an asbestos claim has been discharged, the court may wish to consider, inter alia, the circumstances of the initial exposure to asbestos, whether and/or when the claimants were aware of their vulnerability to asbestos, whether the notice of the claims bar date came to their attention, whether the claimants were known or unknown creditors, whether the claimants had a colorable claim at the time of the bar date, and other circumstances specific to the parties. . . .

* * *

Accordingly, we will reverse the decision of the District Court and remand this case to the District Court for further proceedings consistent with this opinion.

(Citations omitted.)

NOTES AND COMMENTS

1. The court clearly rejects its *Frenville* "accrual" standard. It discusses *Grady*'s conduct standard and the Eleventh Circuit's relationship standard. Consider this language from the court's opinion, and decide what type of test the court adopted:

> Irrespective of the title used, there seems to be something approaching a consensus among the courts that a prerequisite for recognizing a "claim" is that the claimant's exposure to a product giving rise to the "claim" occurred pre-petition, even though the injury manifested after the reorganization. We agree and hold that a "claim" arises when an individual is exposed pre-petition to a product or other conduct giving rise to an injury, which under-lies a "right to payment" under the Bankruptcy Code. . . . Applied to the Van Brunts, it means that their claims arose sometime in 1977, the date Mary Van Brunt alleged that Grossman's product exposed her to asbestos.

Grossman's, 607 F.3d at 125.

2. At the end of the excerpt, the court notes that determining when a claim arises does not end the inquiry as to whether a claim is discharged. The claimant must receive constitutionally sufficient notice of the bankruptcy proceedings in order to have a dischargeable claim. After the excerpt, the court discussed § 524(g), which allows for a "channeling injunction" to resolve some of the issues arising in the asbestos litigation context. The channeling injunction creates a trust fund in a Chapter 11 case that will be used to pay claims of claimants whose injuries manifest after the conclusion of the bankruptcy case. This remedy was originally used in the case of In the Matter of Johns-Manville Corp., 68 B.R. 618 (Bankr. S.D.N.Y. 1986). As the *Grossman's* court noted, this remedy helps to ensure that claimants receive their equitable share of the bankruptcy estate, while not undermining the successful reorganization of the bankruptcy debtor:

> It is apparent from the legislative history of § 524(g) that Congress was concerned that future claims by presently unknown claimants could cripple the debtor's reorganization. Senator Graham stated during floor debate on the bill that § 524(g) "provides companies who are seeking to fairly address the burden of thousands of current asbestos injury claims *and unknown future claims* . . . a method to pay their current asbestos claims and provide for equitable treatment of future asbestos claims." . . . The House of Representatives Committee on the Judiciary wrote in its report that § 524(g) was included in the bill "to offer similar certitude to other asbestos trust/injunction mechanisms that meet the same kind of high standards with respect to regard for the rights of claimants, present and future, ...

> By enacting § 524(g), Congress took account of the due process impli-
> cations of discharging future claims of individuals whose injuries were
> not manifest at the time of the bankruptcy petition.

Grossman's, 607 F.3d at 126-127.

2. Denial of Discharge of Individual Debts

Exceptions to the discharge occur in several ways. While §§ 524(b) and
(c) provide some limitations on debtor's discharge, the more important and
frequently used exceptions come in §§ 523 and 727 (with corresponding
sections in the other operating chapters). Many, but not all, of these exceptions arise in the context of fraud or other wrongful behavior by the debtor.
Most of this section will focus on denial of discharge when such wrongful
conduct occurs, but it is important to understand that discharge can be
denied even for the most "honest but unfortunate" debtor.

Section 523 allows the debtor to discharge some—often most—unpaid
debt, but excepts from discharge individual debts outlined in the Code.
Read § 523(a). You will quickly see that the exceptions protect creditors
because of a policy determination that the creditor deserves special treatment, either because of the debtor's bad behavior or the creditor's special
status (and sometimes both). Write a list of the types of debts excepted from
discharge under § 523(a), and identify each as falling within one policy or
the other (or both). In the special status category, for example, you might
include taxes (§ 523(a)(1)), domestic support obligations (§ 523(a)(5)),
student loan debt (§ 523(a)(8)), debt incurred to pay nondischargeable
taxes (§ 523(a)(14)), divorce settlements (§ 523(a)(15)), and homeowner
and condominium association fees (§ 523(a)(16)). Let's consider some of
those exceptions in more detail.

With regard to taxes, only some tax debts are nondischargeable.
Section 523(a)(1) provides that taxes are not dischargeable if they are the
types of claims given priority under §§ 507(a)(3) ["gap" claims in an involuntary bankruptcy filing] or (a)(8) [various taxes, normally due within a
few years before the bankruptcy filing]. It also provides for nondischargeability for any tax for which no return was filed or for which a return was
filed fraudulently. Section 523(a)(14) then goes on to protect a lender
who, essentially, pays off the nondischargeable debt by loaning the debtor
money—in turn making that lender's debt nondischargeable as well. This
prevents a debtor from bankruptcy planning by borrowing money from an
unsuspecting lender to pay off nondischargeable tax debt, and then wiping
out the new debt.

Many people proclaim that student loan debt can never be discharged in bankruptcy, but the Code actually allows for discharge of student loan debt when payment of the debt constitutes "undue hardship" for the debtor. But be warned—the standard for proving undue hardship is a high one. The Code does not define undue hardship. In Brunner v. New York State Higher Educ. Servs. Corp., 831 F.2d 395 (2nd Cir. 1987), the Second Circuit adopted a three-part test that has since been adopted by the majority of other courts considering discharge of student loan debt: (1) the debtor is unable to maintain a minimal standard of living, (2) that inability will likely continue for much of the loan repayment period, and (3) the debtor has tried in good faith to repay the loans.

While other tests have also developed, regardless of the test used, discharging student loan debt has proven to be challenging, and successful debtors frequently have severe and long-lasting illnesses that impair their abilities to meet the student loan obligations. In 2016, the Supreme Court denied certiorari to resolve the current circuit court split regarding the standard for undue hardship. Tetzlaff v. Educational Credit Mgmt., 136 S. Ct. 803 (2016) (involving law school graduate denied discharge under *Brunner* standard, but who argued for a different standard that might have allowed discharge in his case).

While the two exceptions discussed above do not necessarily require poor behavior, many of the exceptions to discharge revolve around fraud or other tortious behavior of the debtor prior to the bankruptcy filing. Consider three closely tied exceptions to discharge of debt found in §§ 523(a)(2), (a)(4), and (a)(6), highlighted in the following cases.

Archer v. Warner

538 U.S. 314 (2003)

BREYER, Justice

The Bankruptcy Code provides that a debt shall not be dischargeable in bankruptcy "to the extent" it is "for money . . . obtained by . . . false pretenses, a false representation, or actual fraud." 11 U.S.C. § 523(a)(2)(A). Can this language cover a debt embodied in a settlement agreement that settled a creditor's earlier claim "for money . . . obtained by . . . fraud"? In our view, the statute can cover such a debt, and we reverse a lower court judgment to the contrary.

. . . This case arises out of circumstances that we outline as follows: (1) *A* sues *B* seeking money that (*A* says) *B* obtained through fraud; (2) the parties settle the lawsuit and release related claims;

(3) the settlement agreement does not resolve the issue of fraud, but provides that *B* will pay *A* a fixed sum; (4) *B* does not pay the fixed sum; (5) *B* enters bankruptcy; and (6) *A* claims that *B*'s obligation to pay the fixed settlement sum is nondischargeable because, like the original debt, it is for "money . . . obtained by . . . fraud."

This outline summarizes the following circumstances: In late 1991, Leonard and Arlene Warner bought the Warner Manufacturing Company for $250,000. About six months later they sold the company to Elliott and Carol Archer for $610,000. A few months after that the Archers sued the Warners in North Carolina state court for (among other things) fraud connected with the sale.

In May 1995, the parties settled the lawsuit. . . The Warners paid the Archers $200,000 and executed a promissory note for the remaining $100,000. The Archers executed releases "discharg[ing]" the Warners "from any and every right, claim, or demand" that the Archers "now have or might otherwise hereafter have against" them . . . The releases, signed by all parties, added that the parties did not "admi[t] any liability or wrongdoing," that the settlement was "the compromise of disputed claims, and that payment [was] not to be construed as an admission of liability.". . . .

In November 1995, the Warners failed to make the first payment on the $100,000 promissory note. The Archers sued for the payment in state court. The Warners filed for bankruptcy. The Bankruptcy Court ordered liquidation under Chapter 7 of the Bankruptcy Code. And the Archers brought the present claim, asking the Bankruptcy Court to find the $100,000 debt nondischargeable, and to order the Warners to pay the $100,000. Leonard Warner agreed to a consent order holding his debt nondischargeable. Arlene Warner contested nondischargeability. The Archers argued that Arlene Warner's promissory note debt was nondischargeable because it was for "money . . . obtained by . . . fraud."

The Bankruptcy Court, finding the promissory note debt dischargeable, denied the Archers' claim. The District Court affirmed the Bankruptcy Court. And the Court of Appeals for the Fourth Circuit, dividing two to one, affirmed the District Court. The majority reasoned that the settlement agreement, releases, and promissory note had worked a kind of "novation." This novation replaced (1) an original potential debt to the Archers for money obtained by fraud with (2) a new debt. The new debt was not for money obtained by fraud. It was for money promised in a settlement contract. And it was consequently dischargeable in bankruptcy.

* * *

We agree with the Court of Appeals and the dissent that "[t]he settlement agreement and promissory note here, coupled with the broad language of the release, completely addressed and released each and every underlying state law claim." That agreement left only one relevant debt: a debt for money promised in the settlement agreement itself. To recognize that fact, however, does not end our inquiry. We must decide whether that same debt can *also* amount to a debt for *money obtained by fraud*, within the terms of the nondischargeability statute. Given this Court's precedent, we believe that it can.

Brown v. Felsen governs the outcome here. The circumstances there were the following: (1) Brown sued Felsen in state court seeking money that (Brown said) Felsen had obtained through fraud; (2) the state court entered a consent decree embodying a stipulation providing that Felsen would pay Brown a certain amount; (3) neither the decree nor the stipulation indicated the payment was for fraud; (4) Felsen did not pay; (5) Felsen entered bankruptcy; and (6) Brown asked the Bankruptcy Court to look behind the decree and stipulation and to hold that the debt was nondischargeable because it was a debt for money obtained by fraud.

* * *

This . . . Court conceded that the state law of claim preclusion would bar Brown from making any claim "'based on the same cause of action'" that Brown had brought in state court. Indeed, this aspect of res judicata would prevent Brown from litigating "all grounds for . . . recovery" previously available to Brown, whether or not Brown had previously "asserted" those grounds in the prior state-court "proceeding." But all this, the Court held, was beside the point. Claim preclusion did not prevent the Bankruptcy Court from looking beyond the record of the state-court proceeding and the documents that terminated that proceeding (the stipulation and consent judgment) in order to decide whether the debt at issue (namely, the debt embodied in the consent decree and stipulation) was a debt for money obtained by fraud.

As a matter of logic, *Brown's* holding means that the Fourth Circuit's novation theory cannot be right. The reduction of Brown's state-court fraud claim to a stipulation (embodied in a consent decree) worked the same kind of novation as the "novation" at issue here. . . If the Fourth Circuit's view were correct—if reducing a fraud claim to settlement definitively changed the nature of the debt for dischargeability purposes—the nature of the debt in *Brown* would have changed similarly, thereby rendering the debt dischargeable. . . .

Moreover, the Court's language in *Brown* strongly favors the Archers' position here. The Court said that "the mere fact that a conscientious creditor has previously reduced his claim to judgment should not bar further inquiry into the true nature of the debt.". . .

Finally, the Court's basic reasoning in *Brown* applies here. The Court pointed out that the Bankruptcy Code's nondischargeability provision had originally covered "only 'judgments' sounding in fraud." Congress later changed the language so that it covered all such "'liabilities.'" *Ibid.* This change indicated that "Congress intended the fullest possible inquiry" to ensure that "all debts arising out of" fraud are "excepted from discharge," no matter what their form. Congress also intended to allow the relevant determination (whether a debt arises out of fraud) to take place in bankruptcy court, not to force it to occur earlier in state court at a time when nondischargeability concerns "are not directly in issue and neither party has a full incentive to litigate them."

The only difference we can find between *Brown* and the present case consists of the fact that the relevant debt here is embodied in a settlement, not in a stipulation and consent judgment. But we do not see how that difference could prove determinative. The dischargeability provision applies to all debts that "aris[e] out of" fraud. A debt embodied in the settlement of a fraud case "arises" no less "out of" the underlying fraud than a debt embodied in a stipulation and consent decree. Policies that favor the settlement of disputes, like those that favor "repose," are neither any more nor any less at issue here than in Brown.

* * *

(Citations omitted.)

NOTES AND COMMENTS

1. Recall that one of the elements of a tort claim is causation. The Restatement uses the phrase "legal cause," which encompasses both proximate cause and factual cause.

2. Restatement (Second) of Torts § 9 explains "'legal cause' . . . to denote the fact that the causal sequence by which the actor's tortious conduct has resulted in an invasion of some legally protected interest of another is such that the law holds the actor responsible for such harm unless there is some defense to liability."

3. Justice Thomas's dissent focuses on the issue of proximate causation, a common issue in tort cases. Does the majority opinion ignore the causation issue, or does it consider causation in a different way? Do you agree with the dissent that settlement of the fraud claim constitutes a superseding cause?

4. What problems arise in determining whether a debt owed as a result of the settlement of a fraud claim can be discharged? The Supreme Court remanded the case for a determination of nondischargeability, holding only that "the Archers' settlement agreement and releases may have worked a kind of novation, but that fact *does not bar the Archers from showing* that the settlement debt arose out of 'false pretenses, a false representation, or actual fraud.'" What will the Archers need to show in determining nondischargeability? And what will be the standard of proof required? *See* Grogan v. Garner, 498 U.S. 279 (1991) (holding that fraud claims, like all claims for nondischargeability, must be proven by a preponderance of the evidence).

5. How does the Supreme Court opinion affect settlement negotiations on fraud claims? How might settlements of fraud claims have changed had the Court ruled in favor of the debtor instead?

CANONS OF STATUTORY CONSTRUCTION

NOSCITUR A SOCIIS—"known by its associates"
EJUSDEM GENERIS—"of the same kind"

Noscitur *a sociis* means that "a word may be defined by an accompanying word, and that, ordinarily, the coupling of words denotes an intention that they should be understood in the same general sense." Norman Singer & Shambie Singer, "Noscitur a Sociis," 2A Sutherland Statutory Construction, § 47:16 (7th ed.). *Ejusdem generis* provides "that, where general words follow specific words in an enumeration describing a statute's legal subject, the general words are construed to embrace only objects similar in nature to those objects enumerated by the preceding specific words." Norman Singer & Shambie Singer, "Ejusdem Generis", 2A Sutherland Statutory Construction, § 47:17 (7th ed.). Together, these canons help ascertain legislative intent by allowing an ambiguous term within a list to be clarified by the other terms within the list. But these canons of statutory construction should only be used when the meaning of a term or phrase cannot be ascertained by the clear language of the statute. In re Continental Airlines, Inc., 932 F.2d 282 (3d Cir. 1991).

Bullock v. BankChampaign, N.A.

569 U.S. 267 (2013)

B REYER, Justice

Section 523(a)(4) of the Federal Bankruptcy Code provides that an individual cannot obtain a bankruptcy discharge from a debt "for fraud or defalcation while acting in a fiduciary capacity, embezzlement, or larceny." 11 U.S.C. § 523(a)(4). We here consider the scope of the term "defalcation." We hold that it includes a culpable state of mind requirement akin to that which accompanies application of the other terms in the same statutory phrase. We describe that state of mind as one involving knowledge of, or gross recklessness in respect to, the improper nature of the relevant fiduciary behavior.

. . . In 1978, the father of petitioner Randy Bullock established a trust for the benefit of his five children. He made petitioner the (nonprofessional) trustee; and he transferred to the trust a single asset, an insurance policy on his life. The trust instrument permitted the trustee to borrow funds from the insurer against the policy's value.

In 1981, petitioner, at his father's request, borrowed money from the trust, paying the funds to his mother who used them to repay a debt to the father's business. In 1984, petitioner again borrowed funds from the trust, this time using the funds to pay for certificates of deposit, which he and his mother used to buy a mill. In 1990, petitioner once again borrowed funds, this time using the money to buy real property for himself and his mother. Petitioner saw that all of the borrowed funds were repaid to the trust along with 6% interest.

In 1999, petitioner's brothers sued petitioner in Illinois state court. The state court held that petitioner had committed a breach of fiduciary duty. It explained that petitioner "does not appear to have had a malicious motive in borrowing funds from the trust" but nonetheless "was clearly involved in self-dealing." It ordered petitioner to pay the trust "the benefits he received from his breaches" (along with costs and attorney's fees). The court imposed constructive trusts on petitioner's interests in the mill and the original trust, in order to secure petitioner's payment of its judgment, with respondent BankChampaign serving as trustee for all of the trusts. After petitioner tried unsuccessfully to liquidate his interests in the mill and other constructive trust assets to obtain funds to make the court-ordered payment, petitioner filed for bankruptcy in federal court.

BankChampaign opposed petitioner's efforts to obtain a bankruptcy discharge of his state-court-imposed debts to the trust.

And the Bankruptcy Court granted summary judgment in the bank's favor. It held that the debts fell within § 523(a)(4)'s exception "as a debt for defalcation while acting in a fiduciary capacity.". . . .

* * *

Petitioner sought certiorari. In effect he has asked us to decide whether the bankruptcy term "defalcation" applies "in the absence of any specific finding of ill intent or evidence of an ultimate loss of trust principal." The lower courts have long disagreed about whether "defalcation" includes a scienter requirement and, if so, what kind of scienter it requires. In light of that disagreement, we granted the petition.

. . . Congress first included the term "defalcation" as an exception to discharge in a federal bankruptcy statute in 1867. And legal authorities have disagreed about its meaning almost ever since. Dictionary definitions of "defalcation" are not particularly helpful. . . .

Similarly, courts of appeals have long disagreed about the mental state that must accompany the bankruptcy-related definition of "defalcation." Many years ago Judge Augustus Hand wrote that "the misappropriation must be due to a known breach of the duty, and not to mere negligence or mistake." But Judge Learned Hand suggested that the term "*may* have included innocent defaults." A more modern treatise on trusts ends its discussion of the subject with a question mark.

In resolving these differences, we note that this longstanding disagreement concerns state of mind, not whether "defalcation" can cover a trustee's failure (as here) to make a trust more than whole. We consequently shall assume without deciding that the statutory term is broad enough to cover the latter type of conduct and answer only the "state of mind" question.

. . . We base our approach and our answer upon one of this Court's precedents. In 1878, this Court interpreted the related statutory term "fraud" in the portion of the Bankruptcy Code laying out exceptions to discharge. Justice Harlan wrote for the Court:

> "[D]ebts created by 'fraud' are associated directly with debts created by 'embezzlement.' Such association justifies, if it does not impera-tively require, the conclusion that the 'fraud' referred to in that sec-tion means positive fraud, or fraud in fact, involving moral turpitude or intentional wrong, as does embezzlement; and not implied fraud, or fraud in law, which may exist without the imputation of bad faith or immorality."

We believe that the statutory term "defalcation" should be treated similarly.

Thus, where the conduct at issue does not involve bad faith, moral turpitude, or other immoral conduct, the term requires an intentional wrong. We include as intentional not only conduct that the fiduciary knows is improper but also reckless conduct of the kind that the criminal law often treats as the equivalent. Thus, we include reckless conduct of the kind set forth in the Model Penal Code. Where actual knowledge of wrongdoing is lacking, we consider conduct as equivalent if the fiduciary "consciously disregards" (or is willfully blind to) "a substantial and unjustifiable risk" that his conduct will turn out to violate a fiduciary duty. That risk "must be of such a nature and degree that, considering the nature and purpose of the actor's conduct and the circumstances known to him, its disregard involves *a gross deviation* from the standard of conduct that a law-abiding person would observe in the actor's situation."

. . . Several considerations lead us to interpret the statutory term "defalcation" in this way. First, as Justice Harlan pointed out in *Neal*, statutory context strongly favors this interpretation. Applying the canon of interpretation *noscitur a sociis*, the Court there looked to fraud's linguistic neighbor, "embezzlement." It found that both terms refer to different forms of generally similar conduct. It wrote that both are "'*ejusdem generis*,'" of the same kind, and that both are "'referable to the same subject-matter.'" 95 U.S., at 709. Moreover, embezzlement requires a showing of wrongful intent. Hence, the Court concluded, "fraud" must require an equivalent showing. And here, the additional neighbors. . . mean that the canon *noscitur a sociis* argues even more strongly for similarly interpreting the similar statutory term "defalcation."

Second, this interpretation does not make the word identical to its statutory neighbors. As commonly used, "embezzlement" requires conversion, and "larceny" requires taking and carrying away another's property. "Fraud" typically requires a false statement or omission. "Defalcation," as commonly used (hence as Congress might have understood it), can encompass a breach of fiduciary obligation that involves neither conversion, nor taking and carrying away another's property, nor falsity.

Nor are embezzlement, larceny, and fiduciary fraud simply special cases of defalcation as so defined. The statutory provision makes clear that the first two terms apply outside of the fiduciary context; and "defalcation," unlike "fraud," may be used to refer to *nonfraudulent* breaches of fiduciary duty.

Third, the interpretation is consistent with the long-standing principle that "exceptions to discharge 'should be confined to those plainly expressed.'" It is also consistent with a set of statutory exceptions that Congress normally confines to circumstances where strong, special policy considerations, such as the presence of fault, argue for preserving the debt, thereby benefiting, for example, a typically more honest creditor. In the absence of fault, it is difficult to find strong policy reasons favoring a broader exception here, at least in respect to those whom a scienter requirement will most likely help, namely *nonprofessional* trustees, perhaps administering small family trusts potentially immersed in intrafamily arguments that are difficult to evaluate in terms of comparative fault.

* * *

In this case the Court of Appeals applied a standard of "objectiv[e] reckless[ness]" to facts presented at summary judgment. We consequently remand the case to permit the court to determine whether further proceedings are needed and, if so, to apply the heightened standard that we have set forth. For these reasons we vacate the judgment of the Court of Appeals and remand the case for further proceedings consistent with this opinion.

(Citations omitted.)

NOTES AND COMMENTS

1. The Supreme Court considered one other argument that looked to the legislative history of § 523(a)(4):

> The Government has pointed to the fact that in 1970 Congress rewrote the statute, eliminating the word "misappropriation" and placing the term "defalcation" (previously in a different exemption provision) alongside its present three neighbors. . . . The Government believes that these changes support reading "defalcation" without a scienter requirement. But one might argue, with equal plausibility, that the changes reflect a decision to make certain that courts would read in similar ways "defalcation," "fraud," "embezzlement," and "larceny." In fact, we believe the 1970 changes are inconclusive.

Bullock v. BankChampaign, 133 S. Ct. at 1761. Do you agree that the modification of the code from misappropriation to defalcation is inconclusive? It was the government that used this change to argue against any scienter requirement, but how could the debtor have used the language to argue for a heightened scienter requirement?

2. The Model Penal Code defines reckless behavior as follows:

> A person acts recklessly with respect to a material element of an offense when he consciously disregards a substantial and unjustifiable risk that the material element exists or will result from his conduct. The risk must be of such a nature and degree that, considering the nature and purpose of the actor's conduct and the circumstances known to him, its disregard involves a gross deviation from the standard of conduct that a law-abiding person would observe in the actor's situation.

Model Penal Code § 2.02. Consider the facts of a case decided a decade before Bullock, Rutanen v. Baylis (In re Baylis), 303 F.3d 9 (1st Cir. 2002). Carl Baylis, an attorney, helped Antonia create a trust to hold real property. After Antonia's death, the trust was to pay to her children for a period of time and, at the end of that time, the property would be divided equally among them. Baylis served as a trustee along with Antonia's daughter, Estelle, who lived in and managed the real property. Though the property increased in value fivefold over 15 years, Antonia's other children did not receive significant benefit from the increased value and had to pay taxes on the capital gains from the property. Ultimately the children agreed to sell the properties, but Estelle refused to cooperate, holding up the sale. Baylis then agreed to sell some of the property to Estelle in order to garner her cooperation, but without the knowledge of the prospective purchasers—who then sued the trust and both trustees for fraud. As a result, the entire sale fell through, causing Antonia's other children to sue—successfully—for breach of fiduciary duties. Of course, Baylis filed for bankruptcy protection, and the children argued that their judgment against Baylis could not be discharged under § 523(a)(4). Despite Baylis's admission that he had basically allowed Estelle to control the trust, the First Circuit declined to find that Baylis's conduct rose to the level of "gross" recklessness, focusing on bankruptcy's fresh-start policy and finding defalcation to require something very close to fraud. Would that result change following the *Bullock* decision?

3. The gross recklessness standard has also been applied in the context of § 523(a)(2). *See* S.E.C. v. Bocchino (In re Bocchino), 794 F.3d 24 (3rd Cir. 2015). The *Bocchino* case involved trading by a stockbroker on behalf of his clients based on information that he learned from coworkers, but which turned out to be fraudulent investments that could easily have been uncovered by some basic investigation. *Id.* at 378. While there was no doubt that Bocchino's statements to his clients about the companies were not knowingly false, Bocchino was found liable to his clients, and those liabilities were determined to be nondischargeable under § 523(a)(2)'s "false written statement" exception; the court leaned extensively on the

allowance of the "gross recklessness" scienter standard in § 523(a)(4). *Id.* at 382.

Kawaauhau v. Geiger

523 U.S. 57 (1998)

GINSBURG, Justice

Section 523(a)(6) of the Bankruptcy Code provides that a debt "for willful and malicious injury by the debtor to another" is not dischargeable. 11 U.S.C. § 523(a)(6). The question before us is whether a debt arising from a medical malpractice judgment, attributable to negligent or reckless conduct, falls within this statutory exception. We hold that it does not and that the debt is dischargeable.

. . . In January 1983, petitioner Margaret Kawaauhau sought treatment from respondent Dr. Paul Geiger for a foot injury. Geiger examined Kawaauhau and admitted her to the hospital to attend to the risk of infection resulting from the injury. Although Geiger knew that intravenous penicillin would have been more effective, he prescribed oral penicillin, explaining in his testimony that he understood his patient wished to minimize the cost of her treatment.

Geiger then departed on a business trip, leaving Kawaauhau in the care of other physicians, who decided she should be transferred to an infectious disease specialist. When Geiger returned, he canceled the transfer and discontinued all antibiotics because he believed the infection had subsided. Kawaauhau's condition deteriorated over the next few days, requiring the amputation of her right leg below the knee.

Kawaauhau, joined by her husband Solomon, sued Geiger for malpractice. After a trial, the jury found Geiger liable and awarded the Kawaauhaus approximately $355,000 in damages. Geiger, who carried no malpractice insurance, moved to Missouri, where his wages were garnished by the Kawaauhaus. Geiger then petitioned for bankruptcy. The Kawaauhaus requested the Bankruptcy Court to hold the malpractice judgment nondischargeable on the ground that it was a debt "for willful and malicious injury" excepted from discharge by 11 U.S.C. § 523(a)(6). The Bankruptcy Court concluded that Geiger's treatment fell far below the appropriate standard of care and therefore ranked as "willful and malicious." Accordingly, the Bankruptcy Court held the debt nondischargeable. In an unpublished order, the District Court affirmed.

A three-judge panel of the Court of Appeals for the Eighth Circuit reversed and a divided en banc court adhered to the panel's position. Section 523(a)(6)'s exemption from discharge, the en banc court held, is confined to debts "based on what the law has for generations called an intentional tort." On this view, a debt for malpractice, because it is based on conduct that is negligent or reckless, rather than intentional, remains dischargeable.

The Eighth Circuit acknowledged that its interpretation of § 523(a)(6) diverged from previous holdings of the Sixth and Tenth Circuits. We granted certiorari to resolve this conflict and now affirm the Eighth Circuit's judgment.

. . . Section 523(a)(6) of the Bankruptcy Code provides:

"(a) A discharge under section 727, 1141, 1228(a), 1228(b), or 1328(b) of this title does not discharge an individual debtor from any debt—
. . . (6) for willful and malicious injury by the debtor to another entity or to the property of another entity."

The Kawaauhaus urge that the malpractice award fits within this exception because Dr. Geiger intentionally rendered inadequate medical care to Margaret Kawaauhau that necessarily led to her injury. According to the Kawaauhaus, Geiger deliberately chose less effective treatment because he wanted to cut costs, all the while knowing that he was providing substandard care. Such conduct, the Kawaauhaus assert, meets the "willful and malicious" specification of § 523(a)(6).

We confront this pivotal question concerning the scope of the "willful and malicious injury" exception: Does § 523(a)(6)'s compass cover acts, done intentionally,[3] that cause injury (as the Kawaauhaus urge), or only acts done with the actual intent to cause injury (as the Eighth Circuit ruled)? The words of the statute strongly support the Eighth Circuit's reading.

The word "willful" in (a)(6) modifies the word "injury," indicating that nondischargeability takes a deliberate or intentional *injury,* not merely a deliberate or intentional *act* that leads to injury. Had Congress meant to exempt debts resulting from unintentionally inflicted injuries, it might have described instead "willful acts that cause injury." Or, Congress might have selected an additional word

---

3. The word "willful" is defined in *Black's Law Dictionary* as "voluntary and intentional." *Black's Law Dictionary* 1434 (11th ed. 2019). Consistently, legislative reports note that the word "willful" in § 523(a)(6) means "deliberate or intentional."

or words, *i.e.,* "reckless" or "negligent," to modify "injury." Moreover, as the Eighth Circuit observed, the (a)(6) formulation triggers in the lawyer's mind the category "intentional torts," as distinguished from negligent or reckless torts. Intentional torts generally require that the actor intend "the *consequences* of an act," not simply "the act itself

The Kawaauhaus' more encompassing interpretation could place within the excepted category a wide range of situations in which an act is intentional, but injury is unintended, *i.e.,* neither desired nor in fact anticipated by the debtor. Every traffic accident stemming from an initial intentional act—for example, intentionally rotating the wheel of an automobile to make a left-hand turn without first checking oncoming traffic—could fit the description. A "knowing breach of contract" could also qualify. A construction so broad would be incompatible with the "well-known" guide that exceptions to discharge "should be confined to those plainly expressed."

Furthermore, "we are hesitant to adopt an interpretation of a congressional enactment which renders superfluous another portion of that same law." Reading § 523(a)(6) as the Kawaauhaus urge would obviate the need for § 523(a)(9), which specifically exempts debts "for death or personal injury caused by the debtor's operation of a motor vehicle if such operation was unlawful because the debtor was intoxicated from using alcohol, a drug, or another substance."

The Kawaauhaus heavily rely on *Tinker v. Colwell,* which presented this question: Does an award of damages for "criminal conversation" survive bankruptcy under the 1898 Bankruptcy Act's exception from discharge for judgments in civil actions for "'willful and malicious injuries to the person or property of another'"? The *Tinker* Court held such an award a nondischargeable debt. The Kawaauhaus feature certain statements in the *Tinker* opinion, in particular: "[An] act is willful . . . in the sense that it is intentional and voluntary" even if performed "without any particular malice," an act that "necessarily causes injury and is done intentionally, may be said to be done willfully and maliciously, so as to come within the [bankruptcy discharge] exception"

The exposition in the *Tinker* opinion is less than crystalline. Counterbalancing the portions the Kawaauhaus emphasize, the *Tinker* Court repeatedly observed that the tort in question qualified in the common law as trespassory. . . Criminal conversation, the Court noted, was an action akin to a master's "action of trespass and assault . . . for the battery of his servant." *Tinker* thus placed criminal conversation solidly within the traditional intentional tort category, and we so confine its holding. That decision, we clarify, provides no warrant for departure from the current statutory instruction that, to be nondischargeable, the judgment debt must be "for willful and malicious *injury.*"

Subsequent decisions of this Court are in accord with our construction. In *McIntyre v. Kavanaugh,* a broker "deprive[d] another of his property forever by deliberately disposing of it without semblance of authority." The Court held that this act constituted an intentional injury to property of another, bringing it within the discharge exception. But in *Davis v. Aetna Acceptance Co.,* the Court explained that not every tort judgment for conversion is exempt from discharge. Negligent or reckless acts, the Court held, do not suffice to establish that a resulting injury is "wilful and malicious."

Finally, the Kawaauhaus maintain that, as a policy matter, malpractice judgments should be excepted from discharge, at least when the debtor acted recklessly or carried no malpractice insurance. Congress, of course, may so decide. But unless and until Congress makes such a decision, we must follow the current direction § 523(a)(6) provides.

We hold that debts arising from recklessly or negligently inflicted injuries do not fall within the compass of § 523(a)(6). For the reasons stated, the judgment of the Court of Appeals for the Eighth Circuit is affirmed.

(Citations omitted.)

NOTES AND COMMENTS

1. The Supreme Court's opinion indicates that the "willful and malicious" standard suggests the need for an intentional tort. It also distinguishes the facts at hand from breach of contract actions, noting that under the Kawaauhaus's interpretation of § 523(a)(6), "a 'knowing breach of contract' could also qualify" for nondischargeability. Do these two statements suggest that a tort action is required to satisfy the willful and malicious standard, or simply that if a tort action is in question, it requires that the tort be intentional? Several courts have considered the question of whether non-tort actions can meet the willful and malicious standard. For a discussion of this question, *see* Theresa J. Pulley Radwan, *With Malice Toward One? Defining Nondischargeability of Debts For*

Willful and Malicious Injury Under Section 523(a)(6) of the Bankruptcy Code, 7 Wm. & Mary Bus. L. Rev. 151 (2016). Consider what type of circumstances might be a willful and malicious injury in the contract setting.

2. The *Kawaauhau* Court focused on intentional torts, but do all intentional torts automatically meet the nondischargeability standard—or is the Court simply saying that only intentional torts can possibly meet the standard? *See* First Weber Group, Inc. v. Horsfall, 738 F.3d 767 (7th Cir. 2013) (state law judgment on conversion and intentional interference, though intentional torts, did not automatically lead to nondischargeability under § 523); *cf.* Caruso v. Harmon (In re Harmon), 404 B.R. 521 (Bankr. W.D. Mo. 2009) (holding that state law finding of assault and battery precluded debtor from defending nondischargeability action because tort automatically included both intentional and willful elements).

3. Remember the discussion of intent. The Restatement (Third) of Torts § 1 (2010, Oct. 2016 update) defines "intent" as "[a] person acts with the intent to produce a consequence if: (a) the person acts with the purpose of producing that consequence; or (b) the person acts knowing that the consequence is substantially certain to result." Consider the Supreme Court's interpretation of the section of the statute in question in *Kawaauhau.* The Court found that "[t]he word 'willful' in (a)(6) modifies the word 'injury,' indicating that nondischargeability takes a deliberate or intentional *injury,* not merely a deliberate or intentional *act* that leads to injury." Is the Restatement then consistent with the Court's view of intent?

C. COMPLETE DENIAL OF DISCHARGE

In extraordinary cases, a debtor may be denied discharge of all of his or her debts. This extreme circumstance effectively eliminates the debtor's ability to receive a fresh start, as the debtor leaves bankruptcy burdened with any debt not paid through the bankruptcy case. Given its impact on the fresh start that is so crucial to the bankruptcy system, use of § 727's complete denial of discharge is limited to egregious situations. The case below considers behavior by the debtors that would likely be the basis of a complete denial of discharge—but a reconsideration by the court when the debtors reversed the transaction post-petition.

Village of San Jose v. McWilliams

284 F.3d 785 (7th Cir. 2002)

BAUER, Circuit Judge

The debtors filed for bankruptcy protection under Chapter 7 of the Bankruptcy Code. The Village of San Jose, a lien creditor, opposed the discharge on the ground that within one year of filing the petition the debtors hindered, delayed, or defrauded the Village by transferring or concealing property. 11 U.S.C. § 727(a)(2). The bankruptcy judge granted the discharge, finding the debtors' subsequent remedial conduct of disclosing and recovering the properties negated the pre-petition conduct. The Village then appealed to the district court, which affirmed the bankruptcy judge's ruling. Though the Village stated that the debtors have no discernable method to pay the amount owed, bankruptcy or not, the Village nevertheless seeks its "pound of flesh" in this court. After a thorough review, we find that the bankruptcy court erred, and reverse and remand for further proceedings not inconsistent with this opinion.

Background

The Village of San Jose, Mason County, Illinois, is a small enclave of some 696 people, located approximately twenty miles south of Pekin, Illinois. Daniel and Ida McWilliams owned a number of properties and buildings in the Village of San Jose. The main property at issue was a two-story brick building built in the late 1800s, which housed a restaurant at one time. . . .

In a letter dated January 4, 1999, Daniel McWilliams was notified that the building was condemned after inspection by a Village health officer. . . In a March 4, 1999 letter, the Village notified the McWilliamses that they must either repair or demolish the building, and if they failed to act, the Village would demolish it and charge the costs to them. The McWilliamses obtained an estimate that it would cost approximately $48,000 to repair the building. The McWilliamses neither repaired nor demolished the building, stating they were unable to pay for either action. On March 26, 1999, the Village moved to demolish the building and recover the costs of the demolition and attorney's fees incurred. . . An order was entered in state court on July 2, 1999, permitting the Village to demolish the building, effective July 22, 1999. The court also granted the Village a lien on the property to satisfy the costs of demolition.

On September 3, 1999, Daniel and Ida McWilliams conveyed several lots, by quitclaim deed, to their four grandchildren for "One ($1.00) Dollar and Love." Prior to transferring the properties, the McWilliamses satisfied the outstanding mortgages with the San Jose Tri-County Bank. The deeds were recorded as transferred to the grandchildren with the proper government officials, but the deeds were not physically delivered to the grandchildren.

In February 2000, the Village filed a supplemental motion in state court to set aside the transfers under the Uniform Fraudulent Transfer Act (UFTA). The McWilliamses voluntarily filed for bankruptcy protection on March 15, 2000. . . .

* * *

During the creditors' meeting, the Trustee inquired if the McWilliamses had sold, exchanged, or given away anything of value recently. Ida McWilliams responded "no." The Trustee then specifically asked about the lots conveyed to the grandchildren. Daniel McWilliams stated that they did convey the lots in September 1999, and that their value was $2,000 each. Daniel McWilliams added that they conveyed the lots "six months before we got a bill from San Jose lawyer on what we owed them that was the reason we had to file bankruptcy."

The Village filed an objection to the McWilliamses bankruptcy petition and discharge on April 10, 2000. On May 10, 2000, the grandchildren reconveyed the lots at issue back to Daniel and Ida McWilliams. A hearing was held on February 6, 2001, before the bankruptcy judge. The McWilliamses appeared *pro se* at the hearing, stating they could no longer afford an attorney. During the first few minutes of the hearing, the bankruptcy judge made his opinion of the case known to the Village's attorney.

> . . . I am not going to deny their discharge under 727(a)(2). . . . They have made no attempt to conceal anything to this Court or to the Bankruptcy Trustee. That's the purpose of the 727(a)(2) in my opinion. And you can pull out a number of cases . . . and I don't care what those say. . . .

After the hearing, consistent with his prior comments, the judge issued a ruling granting the McWilliams' petition. The Village appealed to the district court, which affirmed the bankruptcy court's ruling.

. . . The bankruptcy court interpreted 11 U.S.C. § 727(a)(2) as allowing a discharge even if the debtor violated the section, as long as the infraction was rectified and none of the creditors were harmed. . . .

* * *

A. Discharge in Bankruptcy

The purpose of the Code is to provide equitable distribution of the debtor's assets to the creditors and "to relieve the honest debtor from the weight of oppressive indebtedness and permit him to start afresh free from the obligations and responsibilities consequent upon business misfortunes." We construe the Bankruptcy Code "liberally in favor of the debtor and strictly against the creditor." Thus, consistent with the Code, bankruptcy protection and discharge may be denied to a debtor who was less than honest. If a creditor demonstrates by a preponderance of the evidence that the debtor actually intended to hinder, delay, or defraud a creditor, the court can deny the discharge. . . .

B. Objections to Discharge Based on Section 727(a)(2)

In order to succeed with an objection to discharge based on section 727(a)(2), the creditor must prove:

(1) that the act complained of was done at a time subsequent to one year before the date of the filing of the petition; (2) with actual intent to hinder, delay, or defraud a creditor or an officer of the estate charged with custody of property under the Bankruptcy Code; (3) that the act was that of the debtor or his duly authorized agent; (4) that the act consisted of transferring, removing, destroying or concealing any of the debtor's property, or permitting any of these acts to be done.

The facts show that three of the four elements were met. The issue was whether the second element, actual intent, had been met. Though actual intent is difficult to prove, it may be shown through circumstantial evidence, and the Fifth Circuit adopted a series of factors which, if proven, indicate actual fraud:

(1) the lack or inadequacy of consideration; (2) the family, friendship or close associate relationship between the parties; (3) the retention of possession, benefit or use of the property in question; (4) the financial condition of the party sought to be charged both before and after the transaction in question; (5) the existence or cumulative effect of the pattern or series of transactions or course of conduct after the incurring of debt, onset of financial difficulties, or pendency or threat of suits by creditors; and (6) the general chronology of the events and transactions under inquiry.

If the creditor can show that one or some of these factors are met, "[t]his creates a presumption of an intent to defraud establishing plaintiff's prima facie case and shifting . . . the burden [to the debtor-defendant] of demonstrating that he lacked fraudulent intent."

The McWilliamses did transfer the properties for $1.00 and love to their grandchildren, retained possession of the deeds, and transferred the properties after they had been notified that the Village demolished the building and would seek to recoup the costs from them. This circumstantial evidence demonstrates the McWilliamses transferred the properties to either conceal or prevent the Village from obtaining them to satisfy their debts. The bankruptcy court similarly found that several of these factors were met, yet concluded that the McWilliamses did not make the transfers "with the intent to hinder, delay, or defraud creditors." The bankruptcy court concluded that the McWilliamses cured the fraud and redeemed themselves by disclosing of the transfers and subsequently recovering the properties.

* * *

. . . Moreover, the McWilliamses disclosed the transfers and recovered the properties in March 2000, well after the Village discovered the transfers and filed a motion to set them aside under the UFTA in February 2000. Though they had disclosed the transfer in their petition, when asked by the Trustee if they had transferred anything in the past year, Ida McWilliams responded "no." It was not until the Trustee asked a second specific question about the properties did Daniel McWilliams acknowledge the transfers. . . .

* * *

. . . [W]e believe that the term "transfer" in the Code is defined broadly enough to encompass the transfer in this case. "Transfer" is defined as: "every mode, direct or indirect, absolute or conditional, voluntary or involuntary, of disposing of or parting with property or with an interest in property, including retention of title as a security interest and foreclosure of the debtor's equity of redemption." 11 U.S.C. § 101(54)

* * *

Whether the McWilliams' actions are defined as a "transfer" or "concealment," it is clear that they attempted to hide the property from their creditors. The recording, but failure to deliver the deeds, demonstrates the McWilliamses attempted to create the appearance that they no longer owned the property. Thus, even if the property was not found to have been "transferred," it could be found to have been "concealed." In this case, it is more likely that the disclosure was prompted by the fact that the Village had discovered the transfer and moved to have it set aside under the UFTA.

The McWilliamses are certainly unfortunate debtors, yet they are not exactly honest debtors either. . . . The McWilliamses appeared *pro se* at oral arguments before this court and we too were not unmoved by their plight, but the Village's objections are clearly valid under the law.

* * *

(Citations omitted.)

NOTES AND COMMENTS

1. Would the decision have been different if the McWilliamses had returned the property to the estate *before* the creditors discovered the transfer and sought recovery of the property under the Uniform Fraudulent Transfers Act? If so, is there a statutory argument under § 727(a)(2) for permitting discharge in those circumstances? Consider the facts of In re Adeeb, upon which the bankruptcy court relied in rendering its decision, which involved a pre-petition transfer of property for no consideration. When the debtor, Adeeb, consulted with a bankruptcy lawyer, the lawyer advised Adeeb to notify the creditors of the transfers and to reverse them. That notice then led the creditors to petition the debtor into an involuntary bankruptcy case. The bankruptcy court denied discharge to the debtor under § 727, but the Ninth Circuit reversed.

2. In the *Adeeb* case, creditors sought nondischargeability of debt under both § 523 and § 727. Which remedy would the creditor prefer that the court grant? Why would a creditor seek both options?

D. DISCHARGE IN CHAPTER 13

Section 1328(a) refers to § 523 for cases filed under Chapter 13. This section provides for a "superdischarge" when a debtor successfully completes a Chapter 13 plan, in theory a bonus discharge for the additional payments that should be made to creditors in a successful Chapter 13 case. The superdischarge was limited somewhat by the 2005 BAPCPA amendments, but still provides for a broader discharge than a Chapter 7 case. The following case considers the linguistic differences between § 523(a)(6)'s discharge exception for debts resulting from willful and malicious injury and § 1328(a)(4)'s discharge exception for personal injury debts arising from willful or malicious injury. Note that § 1328(a) cross-references directly to many of the discharge exceptions located in § 523(a) but does not include an express reference to § 523(a)(6).

Waag v. Permann (In re Waag)

418 B.R. 373 (9th Cir. BAP 2009)

MONTALI, Bankruptcy Judge

This appeal presents the panel with an issue of first impression in the Ninth Circuit: Does 11 U.S.C. § 1328(a)(4), which excepts from discharge certain debts for "restitution, or damages, awarded in a civil action against the debtor as a result of willful or malicious injury," require that a judgment for damages be rendered prior to the petition date? Concluding that section 1328(a)(4) does not require the existence of a prepetition judgment, the bankruptcy court denied the debtor's motion to dismiss a nondischargeability adversary proceeding against him. We AFFIRM.

. . . The relevant facts are undisputed. In 2006, DeVonna and John Permann ("Plaintiffs"), individually and as representatives of the estate of David J. Permann, filed a wrongful death action against Matthew Aaron Waag ("Debtor") and others in Montana state court. Before any trial in the state court action and before entry of any judgment, Debtor filed his chapter 13 case (on May 30, 2008) in Oregon.

On August 28, 2008, Plaintiffs filed a complaint alleging that their claim against Debtor was excepted from discharge pursuant to section 523(a)(6), averring that Debtor, acting in concert with others, engaged in a course of conduct (including assault and battery) resulting in the death of David J. Permann.

On September 22, 2008, Plaintiffs filed a second amended complaint alleging that their claim was excepted from discharge under both section 523(a)(6) and section 1328(a)(4).

In a motion to dismiss the nondischargeability adversary proceeding, Debtor argued that the language of section 1328(a)(4) excepting debts for damages "awarded in a civil action" required the existence of a prepetition judgment. . . .

Plaintiffs opposed the motion to dismiss, [arguing] that Congress' use of "awarded" in section 1328(a)(4) does not require the plaintiff to obtain a judgment before the petition date. At a hearing on the motion to dismiss, the bankruptcy court [concluded] that the plain language of section 1328(a)(4) does not require entry of a prepetition judgment.

* * *

Prior to BAPCPA, a chapter 13 debtor could discharge many of the debts which would have been nondischargeable in chapter 7 or chapter 11. Specifically, before BAPCPA, section 1328(a)(2) excepted from a chapter 13 discharge those debts specified in section 523(a)(5), (8), or (9). *See* 11 U.S.C. § 1328(a)(2) (2000). In 2005, acting to restrict the "superdischarge" of chapter 13, Congress expanded the list of nondischargeable debts in section 1328(a)(2) to include, *inter alia*, those described in section 523(a)(2), (a)(3), or (a)(4).

In addition to incorporating many of section 523's exceptions to discharge into section 1328(a)(2), Congress added another exception to a chapter 13 discharge: section 1328(a)(4), which excepts from the chapter 13 discharge a debt "for restitution, or damages, awarded in a civil action against the debtor as a result of willful or malicious injury by the debtor that caused personal injury to an individual or the death of an individual."

This subsection is similar to section 523(a)(6), which Congress chose not to incorporate into subsection 1328(a)(2). Section 523(a)(6) excepts from discharge a debt "for willful and malicious injury by the debtor to another entity or to the property of another entity[.]" *See* 11 U.S.C. § 523(a)(6).

Section 1328(a)(4) differs from section 523(a)(6) in three significant ways: (1) it applies to "willful *or* malicious" injuries instead of to "willful *and* malicious" injuries; (2) it applies to personal injuries or death and not to injuries to property; and (3) it applies to restitution and damages "awarded in a civil action against the debtor" as a result of such injuries.

. . .[O]nly two published cases, *Byrd* and *Taylor*, directly address the issue presented here, with diametrically opposed holdings. The court in *Byrd*, 388 B.R. at 877, held that a chapter 13 debtor can discharge a debt for willful or malicious personal injury or death if damages or restitution were not awarded on such a claim prior to the petition date. In contrast, the *Taylor* court held that a prepetition judgment is not a prerequisite to prevailing on a section 1328(a)(4) nondischargeability claim. In denying Debtor's motion to dismiss, the bankruptcy court here followed the holding of *Taylor*. We also find the reasoning of *Taylor* to be more persuasive, for the reasons set forth below.

. . . The courts in *Byrd* and *Taylor* disagreed about the grammatical role of "awarded" in section 1328(a)(4), with the *Byrd* court treating it as a past tense verb and the *Taylor* court treating it as a past participle modifying "restitution" and "damages." In *Byrd,* the court held that the "new section 1328(a)(4) *is worded in the past tense.* . . . Thus, a pre-petition award of restitution or damages for willful or malicious injury is a prerequisite to a finding of non-dischargeability under § 1328(a)(4)." The *Byrd* court also observed:

> Section 1328(a)(4) is clearly worded differently than 11 U.S.C. § 523(a)(6), and, had Congress intended a different meaning, it could easily have worded § 1328(a)(4) to include restitution or damages as being non-dischargeable regardless of the entry of a judgment in a civil proceeding prior to the filing of a Chapter 13 bankruptcy petition. Given the plain meaning of § 1328(a)(4), the Court must find that the debt of the Plaintiff in the instant case is simply a contingent, unliquidated debt that is allowable in the Debtor's Chapter 13 bankruptcy, and not subject to exception from discharge.

The *Taylor* court rejected the analysis of the *Byrd* and *Nuttall* courts:

> Whether Congress intended to distinguish between claims for personal injury that had been reduced to judgment before a petition is filed and claims that are disputed on the date of filing must be considered within the context of § 1328(a) as well as within the Bankruptcy Code as a whole. After analyzing this provision in the context of exceptions to discharge listed in § 1328(a) and the Code as a whole, I must disagree with the interpretation of § 1328(a)(4) that the *Nuttall* and *Byrd* courts find to be plain. Nuttall and Byrd hold that because Congress used the word "awarded," it must have intended to provide one treatment for a judgment entered before a petition is filed and a different treatment for a claim that is disputed or contingent on the date of the petition. However, I believe this interpretation is erroneous and ignores the grammatical structure of § 1328(a)(4).

The *Taylor* court then examined the use of the word "awarded" both grammatically and in the context of the entire subsection. Unlike the *Byrd* and *Nuttall* courts, the court found that "awarded"—like the "included" in subsection 1328(a)(3)—was not being used as a past tense verb, but as a past participial phrase as an adjective modifying the nouns "restitution" and "damages." "A past participle is simply the form of the verb used in the phrase and does not suggest past action." As noted in one leading grammar treatise, both present and past participles "can be used for referring to past present or future time" and the past participle "signifies 'perfectiveness' or completion, *but is not restricted to past time.*"

As a past participle, "awarded" merely signifies "completion" or an entry of a restitution or damages award at the time of the determination of nondischargeability. Nothing in phraseology of section 1328(a)(4) requires, either implicitly or explicitly, entry of a prepetition judgment. The contention by Debtor and the holding of *Byrd* that "awarded" is a past tense verb requiring a prepetition judgment is not convincing.

* * *

(Citations omitted.)

NOTES AND COMMENTS

1. Why didn't Congress simply cross-reference § 523(a)(6) in § 1328(a), as it did with so many other exceptions to discharge? What does this omission say about congressional intent in limiting the superdischarge previously available in Chapter 13 cases? In reviewing the debts that *are* deemed nondischargeable in Chapter 13, can you identify similarities between those debts?

2. Had the court determined that a pre-petition judgment is required to render a debt resulting from willful or malicious personal injury non-dischargeable in a Chapter 13, what effect might that have on personal injury litigation and bankruptcy filings? The court considered these issues as well in part of the case not included in the excerpt.

Even in situations where a debtor would not ordinarily be entitled to a discharge, Chapter 13 has been held to allow a debtor to discharge debt by writing it into the bankruptcy plan. This case provides a cautionary tale for creditors and their lawyers, reminding them to review the terms of repayment and reorganization plans carefully.

United Student Aid Funds, Inc. v. Espinosa

559 U.S. 260 (2010)

THOMAS, Justice

Under Chapter 13 of the Bankruptcy Code (Code), a debtor may obtain a discharge of certain government-sponsored student loan debts only if failure to discharge that debt would impose an "undue hardship" on the debtor and his dependents. 11 U.S.C. §§ 523(a)(8), 1328. The Federal Rules of Bankruptcy Procedure require bankruptcy courts to make this undue hardship determination in an adversary proceeding, see Rule 7001(6), which the party seeking the determination must initiate by serving a summons and complaint on his adversary, see Rules 7003, 7004, 7008. The debtor in this case filed a plan with the Bankruptcy Court that proposed to discharge a portion of his student loan debt, but he failed to initiate the adversary proceeding as required for such discharge. The creditor received notice of, but did not object to, the plan, and failed to file an appeal after the Bankruptcy Court subsequently confirmed the plan. Years later, the creditor filed a motion under Federal Rule of Civil Procedure 60(b)(4) asking the Bankruptcy Court to rule that its order confirming the plan was void because the order was issued in violation of the Code and Rules. We granted certiorari to resolve a disagreement among the Courts of Appeals as to whether an order that confirms the discharge of a student loan debt in the absence of an undue hardship finding or an adversary proceeding, or both, is a void judgment for Rule 60(b)(4) purposes.

... Between 1988 and 1989, respondent Francisco Espinosa obtained four federally guaranteed student loans for a total principal amount of $13,250. In 1992, Espinosa filed a bankruptcy petition under Chapter 13. That Chapter permits individual debtors to develop a plan to repay all or a portion of their debts over a period of time specified in the plan. A proposed bankruptcy plan becomes effective upon confirmation, and will result in a discharge of the debts listed in the plan if the debtor completes the payments the plan requires.

Espinosa's plan listed his student loan debt as his only specific indebtedness. The plan proposed to repay only the principal on that debt, stating that the remainder—the accrued interest—would be discharged once Espinosa repaid the principal.

As the Federal Rules of Bankruptcy Procedure require, the clerk of the Bankruptcy Court mailed notice and a copy of Espinosa's plan to petitioner United Student Aid Funds, Inc. (United), the creditor to whom Espinosa owed the student loan debt. In boldface type immediately below the caption, the plan stated: "WARNING IF YOU ARE A CREDITOR YOUR RIGHTS MAY BE IMPAIRED BY THIS PLAN." The plan also noted the deadlines for filing a proof of claim or an objection to the plan.

United received this notice and, in response, filed a proof of claim for $17,832.15, an amount representing both the principal and the accrued interest on Espinosa's student loans. United did not object to the plan's proposed discharge of Espinosa's student loan interest without a determination of undue hardship, nor did it object to Espinosa's failure to initiate an adversary proceeding to determine the dischargeability of that debt.

In May 1993, the Bankruptcy Court confirmed Espinosa's plan without holding an adversary proceeding or making a finding of undue hardship. One month later, the Chapter 13 trustee mailed United a form notice stating that "[t]he amount of the claim filed differs from the amount listed for payment in the plan" and that "[y]our claim will be paid as listed in the plan." The form also apprised United that if United "wishe[d] to dispute the above stated treatment of the claim," it had the "responsibility" to notify the trustee within 30 days. United did not respond to that notice.

In May 1997, Espinosa completed the payments on his student loan principal, as required by the plan. Shortly thereafter, the Bankruptcy Court discharged Espinosa's student loan interest.

In 2000, the United States Department of Education commenced efforts to collect the unpaid interest on Espinosa's student loans. In response, Espinosa filed a motion in 2003 asking the Bankruptcy Court to enforce its 1997 discharge order by directing the Department and United to cease all efforts to collect the unpaid interest on his student loan debt.

United opposed that motion and filed a cross-motion under Federal Rule of Civil Procedure 60(b)(4) seeking to set aside as void the Bankruptcy Court's 1993 order confirming Espinosa's plan. United made two arguments in support of its motion. First, United claimed that the provision of Espinosa's plan authorizing the discharge of his student loan interest was inconsistent with the Code, which requires a court to find undue hardship before discharging a student loan debt, and with the Bankruptcy Rules, which require the court to make the undue hardship finding in an adversary proceeding. Second, United argued that its due process rights had been violated because Espinosa failed to serve it with the summons and complaint the Bankruptcy Rules require as a prerequisite to an adversarial proceeding.

The Bankruptcy Court rejected both arguments, granted Espinosa's motion in relevant part, denied United's cross-motion, and ordered all claimants to cease and desist their collection efforts. United sought review in the District Court, which reversed. That court held that United was denied due process because the confirmation order was issued without service of the summons and complaint the Bankruptcy Rules require.

. . . The Court of Appeals concluded that by confirming Espinosa's plan without first finding undue hardship in an adversary proceeding, the Bankruptcy Court at most committed a legal error that United might have successfully appealed, but that any such legal error was not a basis for setting aside the confirmation order as void under Rule 60(b). In addition, the Court of Appeals held that although Espinosa's failure to serve United with a summons and complaint before seeking a discharge of his student loan debt violated the Bankruptcy Rules, this defect in service was not a basis upon which to declare the judgment void because United received actual notice of Espinosa's plan and failed to object.

* * *

A discharge under Chapter 13 "is broader than the discharge received in any other chapter." Chapter 13 nevertheless restricts or prohibits entirely the discharge of certain types of debts. As relevant here, § 1328(a) provides that when a debtor has completed the repayments required by a confirmed plan, a bankruptcy court "shall grant the debtor a discharge of all debts provided for by the plan or disallowed under section 502 of this title, except," inter alia, "any debt . . . of the kind specified in [§ 523(a)(8)]." § 1328(a)(2). Section 523(a)(8), in turn, specifies certain student loan debts "unless excepting such debt from discharge . . . would impose an undue hardship on the debtor and the debtor's dependents." As noted, the Bankruptcy Rules require a party seeking to determine the dischargeability of a student loan debt to commence an adversary proceeding by serving a summons and complaint on affected creditors. We must decide whether the Bankruptcy Court's order confirming Espinosa's plan is "void" under Federal Rule Civil Procedure 60(b)(4) because the Bankruptcy Court confirmed the plan without complying with these requirements.

. . . The Bankruptcy Court's order confirming Espinosa's proposed plan was a final judgment, from which United did not appeal. Ordinarily, "the finality of [a] Bankruptcy Court's orders following the conclusion of direct review" would "stan[d] in the way of challenging [their] enforceability." Rule 60(b), however, provides an "exception to finality," that "allows a party to seek relief from a final judgment, and request reopening of his case, under a limited set of circumstances,". Specifically, Rule 60(b)(4)—the provision under which United brought this motion—authorizes the court to relieve a party from a final judgment if "the judgment is void."

* * *

Federal courts considering Rule 60(b)(4) motions that assert a judgment is void because of a jurisdictional defect generally have reserved relief only for the exceptional case in which the court that rendered judgment lacked even an "arguable basis" for jurisdiction.

This case presents no occasion to engage in such an "arguable basis" inquiry or to define the precise circumstances in which a jurisdictional error will render a judgment void because United does not argue that the Bankruptcy Court's error was jurisdictional. First, § 523(a)(8)'s statutory requirement that a bankruptcy court find undue hardship before discharging a student loan debt is a precondition to obtaining a discharge order, not a limitation on the bankruptcy court's jurisdiction. Second, the requirement that a bankruptcy court make this finding in an adversary proceeding derives from the Bankruptcy Rules, see Rule Proc. 7001(6), which are "procedural rules adopted by the Court for the orderly transaction of its business" that are "not jurisdictional."

. . . Although United concedes that the Bankruptcy Court had jurisdiction to enter the order confirming Espinosa's plan, United contends that the court's judgment is void under Rule 60(b)(4) because United did not receive adequate notice of Espinosa's proposed discharge of his student loan interest. Specifically, United argues that the Bankruptcy Court violated United's due process rights by confirming Espinosa's plan despite Espinosa's failure to serve the summons and complaint the Bankruptcy Rules require for the commencement of an adversary proceeding. We disagree.

Espinosa's failure to serve United with a summons and complaint deprived United of a right granted by a procedural rule. United could have timely objected to this deprivation and appealed from an adverse ruling on its objection. But this deprivation did not amount to a violation of United's constitutional right to due process. Due process requires notice "reasonably calculated, under all the circumstances, to apprise interested parties of the pendency of the action and afford them an opportunity to present their objections." Here, United received actual notice of the filing and contents of Espinosa's plan. This more than satisfied United's due process rights. Accordingly, on these facts, Espinosa's failure to serve a summons and complaint does not entitle United to relief under Rule 60(b)(4).

. . . Unable to demonstrate a jurisdictional error or a due process violation, United and the Government, as amicus, urge us to expand the universe of judgment defects that support Rule 60(b)(4) relief. Specifically, they contend that the Bankruptcy Court's confirmation order is void because the court lacked statutory authority to confirm

Espinosa's plan absent a finding of undue hardship. In support of this contention, they cite the text of § 523(a)(8), which provides that student loan debts guaranteed by governmental units are not dischargeable "unless" a court finds undue hardship. They argue that this language imposes a "'self-executing' limitation on the effect of a discharge order" that renders the order legally unenforceable, and thus void, if it is not satisfied. In addition, United cites § 1325(a)(1), which instructs bankruptcy courts to confirm only those plans that comply with "the . . . applicable provisions" of the Code. Reading these provisions in tandem, United argues that an order confirming a plan that purports to discharge a student loan debt without an undue hardship finding is "doubly beyond the court's authority and therefore void."

We are not persuaded that a failure to find undue hardship in accordance with § 523(a)(8) is on par with the jurisdictional and notice failings that define void judgments that qualify for relief under Rule 60(b)(4). As noted, § 523(a)(8) does not limit the bankruptcy court's jurisdiction over student loan debts. Nor does the provision impose requirements that, if violated, would result in a denial of due process. Instead, § 523(a)(8) requires a court to make a certain finding before confirming the discharge of a student loan debt. It is true, as we explained in Hood, that this requirement is "'self-executing.' " But that means only that the bankruptcy court must make an undue hardship finding even if the creditor does not request one; it does not mean that a bankruptcy court's failure to make the finding renders its subsequent confirmation order void for purposes of Rule 60(b)(4).

* * *

United's response—that it had no obligation to object to Espinosa's plan until Espinosa served it with the summons and complaint the Bankruptcy Rules require is unavailing. Rule 60(b)(4) does not provide a license for litigants to sleep on their rights. United had actual notice of the filing of Espinosa's plan, its contents, and the Bankruptcy Court's subsequent confirmation of the plan. In addition, United filed a proof of claim regarding Espinosa's student loan debt, thereby submitting itself to the Bankruptcy Court's jurisdiction with respect to that claim. United therefore forfeited its arguments regarding the validity of service or the adequacy of the Bankruptcy Court's procedures by failing to raise a timely objection in that court.

Rule 60(b)(4) strikes a balance between the need for finality of judgments and the importance of ensuring that litigants have a full and fair opportunity to litigate a dispute. Where, as here, a party is notified of a plan's contents and fails to object to confirmation of the plan before the time for appeal expires, that party has been afforded a full and fair opportunity to litigate, and the party's failure to avail itself of that opportunity will not justify Rule 60(b)(4) relief. We thus agree with the Court of Appeals that the Bankruptcy Court's confirmation order is not void.

* * *

We are mindful that conserving assets is an important concern in a bankruptcy proceeding. We thus assume that, in some cases, a debtor and creditor may agree that payment of a student loan debt will cause the debtor an undue hardship sufficient to justify discharge. In such a case, there is no reason that compliance with the undue hardship requirement should impose significant costs on the parties or materially delay confirmation of the plan. Neither the Code nor the Rules prevent the parties from stipulating to the underlying facts of undue hardship, and neither prevents the creditor from waiving service of a summons and complaint. But, to comply with § 523(a)(8)'s directive, the bankruptcy court must make an independent determination of undue hardship before a plan is confirmed, even if the creditor fails to object or appear in the adversary proceeding.

* * *

(Citations omitted.)

NOTES AND COMMENTS

1. The *Espinosa* case involves a situation in which everyone erred in some manner—the debtor failed to properly seek discharge of student loan debt; the creditor failed to protect its rights; the court failed to make an undue hardship determination. What bankruptcy policies are promoted by granting the debtor's discharge in this situation?

2. One of the other arguments proffered by United involved the incentive for debtors to try to slip in discharge inappropriately. The Court addressed this concern:

   > We acknowledge the potential for bad-faith litigation tactics. . . . As we stated in Taylor v. Freeland & Kronz, 503 U.S. 638, . . . (1992), "[d]ebtors and their attorneys face penalties under various provisions for engaging in improper conduct in bankruptcy proceedings,". . . . The specter of such penalties should deter bad-faith attempts to discharge student loan debt without the undue hardship finding Congress required. And to the

extent existing sanctions prove inadequate to this task, Congress may enact additional provisions to address the difficulties United predicts will follow our decision.

E. REAFFIRMATION AGREEMENTS (§ 524)

Even if a debtor can discharge a debt, the debtor might choose to repay the debt in part. *See* § 524(f). A reaffirmation agreement constitutes a binding contract to pay the debt, and the Code views such an agreement with great suspicion. Section 524(c), cross-referencing §§ 524(d) and (k), provides the basic requirements for reaffirmation of a debt:

- The agreement must predate the discharge.
- The debtor must receive a variety of disclosures from the creditor before signing the agreement, including the amount reaffirmed, the annual percentage rate, disclosures under the Truth in Lending Act, a repayment schedule, and specific statements regarding the consequences of disclosure and the rights of the debtor.
- The agreement must be filed with the court.
- The debtor's attorney must provide an affidavit that the debtor understands what the agreement means, is voluntarily entering into the agreement, and was "fully advised" of the impact of the agreement, and the agreement will not be an "undue hardship" on the debtor or dependents.
- The debtor has not rescinded the agreement within the allowed time frame.
- A hearing is held to announce what debt will be discharged and, if the debtor is reaffirming debt, at which the court will ensure that the debtor has been advised by an attorney or will ensure that the debtor understands the consequence of reaffirmation.

To the extent that the debtor is not represented by an attorney, the court will also make an independent assessment that the agreement does not create an undue hardship and is in the debtor's best interest. Section 524(k)'s disclosure requirements are very specific—including form and language that must be used—and the creditor must follow them carefully to ensure the validity of the reaffirmation agreement.

Many court websites have guidance for debtors on reaffirming debt. Some even have form reaffirmation agreements. Check the website for your local bankruptcy court to see what is available regarding reaffirmation agreements. For an example from Florida, see http://www.flmb.uscourts .gov/faqs/documents/reaffirmationguide.pdf (created before the BAPCPA amendments but still available on the court website). Official bankruptcy forms include a cover sheet and a reaffirmation agreement; both are available at https://www.uscourts.gov/forms/bankruptcy-forms.

Venture Bank v. Lapides (In re Lapides)

800 F.3d 442 (8th Cir. 2015)

LOKEN, Circuit Judge

* * *

On August 30, 2007, Howard as President of his seafood import business signed a secured $400,000 promissory note evidencing a revolving line-of-credit loan by Venture Bank. Part of the collateral was a third mortgage on the Lapideses' home. Bank of America and Citizens Bank held the prior mortgages. In March 2008, the Lapideses signed a new $400,000 promissory note (number 12897) amending and restating the prior loan at a lower rate of interest. In September and November 2008, the Lapideses as borrowers signed Change in Terms Agreements extending the maturity date and modifying the credit terms of loan 12897. They signed a new promissory note (number 13317) in the amount of $357,456.35 in February 2009 providing that final payment was due three months later, and a new promissory note (number 13440) for $345,644 on June 30, 2009, payable on August 2, 2009. All notes and agreements were secured by the third mortgage on their home.

Howard filed for Chapter 7 bankruptcy protection on August 11, 2009. On October 12, Howard met with Venture Bank's president, Michael Zenk, and loan officer Nathan Urfer to discuss Venture Bank refinancing all three mortgages so the Lapideses could keep their home. Howard agreed to pay $3000 per month on loan 13440 to reestablish his credit with the Bank. On November 9, the Lapideses signed a Debt Re-Affirmation Agreement in which they promised to make five monthly payments of $3000, followed by payment of the outstanding principal and interest on May 9, 2010, and Venture Bank agreed to permit the Lapideses "the continued use and possession" of their home. Although Howard and Venture Bank knew the Re-Affirmation Agreement was unenforceable because Howard's bankruptcy attorney refused to sign the Agreement and it was never filed with the bankruptcy court, *see* 11 U.S.C. § 524(c), Howard continued to make regular loan payments to the Bank.

Howard's personal debts were discharged on November 16, 2009. On May 9, 2010, and November 9, 2010, the Lapideses executed

Change in Terms Agreements extending the maturity date of Note 13440 to Venture Bank by six months. Each Agreement provided for payment in five monthly installments of $3500 followed by a final payment of the unpaid balance. Howard testified that he understood these agreements reflected the understanding reached at the October 12, 2009, meeting that he would make regular loan payments to reestablish his credit with Venture Bank to induce the Bank to refinance his three mortgages. The Lapideses made twelve $3500 payments to Venture Bank between June 2010 and May 2011. During this time, loan officer Urfer sent Howard numerous emails reminding him that payments were due and asking him to pay additional principal and accrued interest. Venture Bank never refinanced the mortgages. Howard ceased making monthly payments in May 2011.

In July 2011, Venture Bank sued the Lapideses in state court, asserting a claim against borrower Holter–Lapides under the November 9, 2010, Change in Terms Agreement; foreclosure of the Bank's third mortgage on the Lapideses' home; and a declaratory judgment that the Change in Terms Agreement was enforceable against Howard. The Lapideses removed the case to bankruptcy court, and Howard filed a counterclaim for damages, alleging that Venture Bank's efforts to obtain loan payments after his debts were discharged violated the discharge injunction imposed by 11 U.S.C. § 524(a)(2). Citizens Bank, holder of the second mortgage, foreclosed on the Lapideses' home and it was sold at public auction in December 2012. Venture Bank received none of the sale proceeds.

After the bankruptcy court remanded Venture Bank's claim against Holter–Lapides and the foreclosure claim to state court, the parties filed cross motions for summary judgment on the retained claims. In denying Venture Bank's motion for summary judgment and setting the case for trial, the bankruptcy court ruled that, to be valid and enforceable, the post-discharge Change in Terms Agreements must *either* comply with the requirements of a reaffirmation agreement under 11 U.S.C. § 524(c), which they admittedly did not do, *or* they must contain "all of the essential elements of a contract" under state law. After trial, the court concluded that the post-discharge agreements did not meet two essential elements of a valid and enforceable contract, consideration and mutual assent. The court further found that all monthly payments made by Howard after the first Change in Terms Agreement were involuntary, *see* § 524(f), and Venture Bank's efforts to obtain those payments violated the discharge injunction. The district court affirmed, concluding the post-discharge agreements lacked consideration because Venture Bank did not provide the Lapideses new consideration and Venture Bank had violated the discharge injunction. Correcting an error in calculating the number of monthly payments, the district court increased the damage award to $42,000. Venture Bank appeals.

. . . A bankruptcy discharge extinguishes only the debtor's personal liability; a secured creditor's right to foreclose on loan collateral, such as a mortgage on the debtor's residence, "survives or passes through the bankruptcy." When a debtor's schedule of assets includes debts secured by property of the bankruptcy estate, the debtor must file a statement of his intent to surrender or retain the property and, if he elects to retain non-exempt property, whether he will redeem the property (i.e., pay off the secured loan before discharge) or "reaffirm debts secured by such property."

. . . "A reaffirmation agreement is one in which the debtor agrees to repay all or part of a dischargeable debt after a bankruptcy petition has been filed." Prior to 1978, the Bankruptcy Act looked to state law to determine the validity of reaffirmation agreements. In many States, the moral obligation to repay a discharged debt was regarded as sufficient consideration. In the 1978 Bankruptcy Code, Congress sought to equalize the unequal bargaining positions of experienced creditors and unsophisticated bankruptcy debtors by enacting § 524(c) of the Code, which provides in relevant part:

> (c) An agreement between a holder of a claim and the debtor, the consideration for which, in whole or in part, is based on a debt that is dischargeable in a case under this title is enforceable only to any extent enforceable under applicable nonbankruptcy law . . . only if—
>> (1) such agreement was made before the granting of the discharge . . .;
>> (2) the debtor received the disclosures described in subsection (k) . . .;
>> (2) such agreement has been filed with the court. . . .

Section 524(c) "reflects Congress's intent to . . . safeguard [] debtors against unsound or unduly pressured judgments about whether to attempt to repay dischargeable debts."

Under § 524(c), reaffirmation agreements are enforceable only if they are enforceable under state law *and* meet the requirements of federal law in § 524(c). Thus, the bankruptcy court erred in ruling that the Change in Terms Agreements are valid if either (1) "the post-petition agreements comply with the requirements of 11 U.S.C. section 524(c) *or* (2) all of the essential elements of a contract are present in the post-petition agreements." If the Agreements violate § 524(c), they are unenforceable as a matter of federal law, whether or not they would be enforceable under applicable state law contract principles.

It is undisputed that the post-discharge Change in Terms Agreements were not enforceable § 524(c) reaffirmation agreements, most obviously because they were entered into after Howard's bankruptcy discharge and were not filed with the bankruptcy court. Venture Bank argues, however, that the agreements are nonetheless valid because they are supported by consideration separate from Howard's discharged personal debt. The Bank had a right to foreclose on the family home after Howard's discharge lifted the automatic stay in bankruptcy, and its agreement not to foreclose was adequate consideration under Minnesota law and protected co-borrower Holter–Lapides (who did not file for bankruptcy) from a deficiency judgment.

As we have explained, we need not consider whether a promise not to foreclose on a mortgage is adequate consideration under Minnesota law if the Change in Terms Agreements were contrary to § 524(c). The Agreements served no purpose other than reaffirmation agreements in which Howard agreed to repay all of his discharged personal debt. . . . Like Howard's prior post-petition voluntary payments, the Agreements were entered into to induce Venture Bank to refinance the Lapideses' heavily mortgaged residence. They were not part of a complex refinancing; rather, they incorporated the terms of the parties' failed attempt to fashion an enforceable § 524(c) reaffirmation agreement prior to Howard's discharge. Instead of continuing to accept Howard's voluntary payments, a post-discharge arrangement both parties were free to continue, Venture Bank insisted that Howard again promise to repay the entire discharged personal debt in order to continue the refinancing negotiations.

When a post-discharge agreement does nothing but obligate a debtor to repay a discharged debt, it is inconsistent with § 524(c), a statute declaring that agreements removing specific personal debts from the benefits of discharge must be negotiated and filed with the court before discharge, when a debtor has the protection of his bankruptcy attorney and the bankruptcy court. . . .

* * *

(Citations omitted.)

NOTES AND COMMENTS

1. Not all agreements to pay a debt post-bankruptcy must meet the requirements of reaffirmation under § 524. One key element was the pressure provided by the bank to encourage repayment by the Lapideses:

> As the bankruptcy court and the district court recognized, Venture Bank did not necessarily violate the discharge injunction simply because it accepted monthly payments made pursuant to Change in Terms Agreements that are unenforceable. Discharge "operates as an injunction against . . . an act, to collect, recover or offset any [discharged] debt as a personal liability of the debtor." 11 U.S.C. § 524(a)(2). But discharge does not "prevent[] a debtor from voluntarily repaying any debt." § 524(f). After trial, the bankruptcy court concluded that Venture Bank violated the discharge injunction because the "Bank's communications and post-petition conduct were designed to obtain payments and enforce the debt" and therefore Howard's monthly payments under the post-discharge Change in Terms Agreements were involuntary.

In re Lapides, 800 F.3d at 447.

2. The debtor's bankruptcy attorney "refused to sign" the proposed reaffirmation agreement. On what basis do you think that the attorney refused to sign the agreement? What should an attorney consider when determining whether to sign the required affidavit for a valid reaffirmation agreement?

F. BANKRUPTCY IN PRACTICE

As Diana is considering a bankruptcy filing, she wonders what will happen to all of the debt that she owes if she doesn't pay it in the bankruptcy case. Consider all of the debts that Diana owes, and complete the following chart for her debts. If you determine that a debt falls in the "Maybe" dischargeable category, create your best argument in Diana's favor for discharging the debt. If you determine that a debt falls in the "No" discharge category, indicate the Code subsection that prohibits discharge under either Chapter 7 or Chapter 13. You can assume that she did not create any of the debt through fraud, embezzlement, defalcation, or the like, and that she would list all creditors in her schedules.

Debt	Dischargeable in Chapter 7? (Yes/No/Maybe)	Dischargeable in Chapter 13? (Yes/No/Maybe)	If "No," basis for non-dischargeability in either Chapter 7 or Chapter 13	If "Maybe," argument for discharging debt

6

Chapter 13 Bankruptcies: Bankruptcy Repayment Plans

> The instant bankruptcy is declared, laws on the federal, state, and
> local levels work in harmony to erode the condition. Some assets
> are exempted, others are sheltered. In order to maintain bank-
> ruptcy, fresh investments must be undertaken, and opportunities
> seized as they arise. A sharp eye on economic indicators must be
> kept lest the whole package slip back into the black. Being bankrupt
> is not a lazy man's game.[1]

Individuals generally file within Chapter 7 or Chapter 13. An attorney counseling a potential debtor must understand the differences between these
chapters to help the client determine which chapter (if the debtor has the
option to file under either chapter) best meets the client's needs. While
Chapter 13 bankruptcies differ from Chapter 7 bankruptcies in several
respects, keep in mind two fundamental differences that underlie most of
the provisions of Chapter 13:

- In a Chapter 13 bankruptcy case, the debtor uses future income as a
  primary means of paying creditors rather than using current assets.
- A Chapter 13 bankruptcy case is governed by a repayment plan, which
  must meet the requirements laid out by the Code.

---

1. John Updike, *The Bankrupt Man*, Esquire Magazine (Nov. 1, 1976).

> ### RECALL DIANA DETTER
>
> As you work through this chapter, consider how a Chapter 13 plan might impact Diana and her creditors differently than we have seen in a Chapter 7 liquidation. Presumably, Diana's creditors will be paid more from Diana's income during that period than her assets. Hopefully, the creditors are paid more than in a Chapter 7. What benefits does this provide for Diana as a debtor? Recall from Chapter 1 that Chapter 13 bankruptcies are sometimes filed by a debtor who would prefer to file a Chapter 7 but cannot do so because of the means test. Why might a debtor prefer a Chapter 7 over a Chapter 13, and vice versa?

A. ELIGIBILITY FOR CHAPTER 13 (§ 109)

Only individuals may file under Chapter 13. However, businesses that are synonymous with an individual—generally unincorporated businesses—may be part of the Chapter 13 filing. Chapter 13 filings also require that the debtor have "regular income" and limited debt.

1. Regular Income

The Bankruptcy Code defines "regular income" as "sufficiently stable and regular to enable such individual to make payments under a plan." 11 U.S.C. §101(30). As you read the following case, consider how that use of the future income to fund a plan has led to the definition of "regular income."

In re Robinson

535 B.R. 437 (Bankr. N.D. Ga. 2015)

SACCA, Bankruptcy Judge

The Court is faced with two questions that determine whether this Debtor is eligible to be a chapter 13 debtor pursuant to § 109(e). First, does this debtor have the requisite "regular income" since she lost her job shortly after the petition date, but received a large, lump sum severance payment equal to one year's salary, but otherwise remains unemployed? Second, does this debtor exceed the unsecured debt limit to be in chapter 13 when a large claim for attorneys' fees, to which she has asserted counterclaims in state court proceedings, is the difference between the debtor obtaining chapter 13 relief or not?

. . . Calita Elston Robinson ("Ms. Robinson") filed this chapter 13 case on January 27, 2015. On the date she filed the petition, Ms. Robinson was employed as an attorney with The Coca Cola Company ("Coca Cola") and had been employed there for the previous fourteen years. . . .

At least two weeks prior to the petition date, Coca Cola informed Ms. Robinson that it would be terminating her employment on March 15, 2015 and that she was eligible to receive one lump sum severance payment (the "Severance"). The Severance totaled $204,596.43, the equivalent of one year's salary. . . . Ms. Robinson received the Severance post-petition and her attorney is currently holding it in her trust account. Pursuant to order of this Court, the Severance is presently being used both to fund Ms. Robinson's chapter 13 plan payments and to pay Court-approved living expenses for her and her two children. Ms. Robinson previously testified that she has been and continues to search for employment, but is still unemployed.

The majority of Ms. Robinson's unsecured debt arises from long, contentious, and still on-going divorce and child custody proceedings. A large portion of the claims are attributable to attorneys' fees from those proceedings, both those of her ex-husband ("Mr. Robinson") and one of her own attorneys. . . .

* * *

Unlike a debtor in chapter 7 whose nonexempt assets may be liquidated in order to pay back creditors, a chapter 13 debtor may retain assets in exchange for committing all of her disposable income to a plan to pay back creditors over a three to five year commitment period. However, certain eligibility requirements exist in order for an individual to be a chapter 13 debtor. Of relevance here, "[o]nly an individual with regular income that owes, on the date of the filing of the petition, noncontingent, liquidated, unsecured debts of less than $383,175 and noncontingent, liquidated, secured debts of less than $1,149,5251" is eligible to be a chapter 13 debtor. 11 U.S.C. § 109(e). The Court is presented with the issue of whether Ms. Robinson is eligible to be a chapter 13 debtor within the meaning of the statute despite: (1) her current sole source of income being a lump sum severance payment and (2) having unsecured claims asserted against her that exceed $383,175.

. . . Section 109(e) only allows individuals with regular income, except stockbrokers and commodity brokers, to be chapter 13 debtors. An individual with regular income is one "whose income is sufficiently stable and regular to enable such individual to make payments under a plan." 11 U.S.C. § 101(30). The debtor has the burden in proving that he or she has regular income sufficient to be a chapter 13 debtor. . . .

Courts are split on the time at which it is determined whether a chapter 13 debtor is an individual with regular income. . . . Because this is an eligibility issue, the Court believes the proper focus is whether a debtor had regular income at the time the petition was filed. Although Ms. Robinson was still receiving her ordinary paycheck from her employment with Coca Cola on the date of the petition, it was known on the petition date that this would cease in the very near future, but that she would be provided with a lump sum payment to replace those wages equal to a period of 52 weeks. For the reasons set forth below, the Court concludes that the Severance is regular income sufficient for Ms. Robinson to be eligible to be a chapter 13 debtor.

Courts have interpreted regular income broadly, and "have recognized that congress intended a liberal interpretation of regular income." "That § 101(30) defines individual with regular income by reference to stability and regularity suggests that the existence of regular income is predominately a fact question answered by examining the flow of money available to the debtor."

The type or source of income is typically not the focus of this inquiry; instead, the test for regular income is its regularity and stability sufficient to allow the debtor to fund a plan. . . . Based on the particular circumstances of each case, regular income can include among other things gratuitous spousal and familial support, welfare, social security, unemployment compensation, child support, pension income, investment income, self-employment income, and disability. Because the meaning of "income" in the statute is so broad, the Court is satisfied that the Severance is a type of income sufficient to meet the eligibility requirement. Thus, the Court must focus its analysis on whether the Severance is sufficiently "stable" and "regular" to enable Ms. Robinson to make payments under a chapter 13 plan and fall within the statutory meaning of "regular income."

* * *

A lump sum severance payment arguably does not fit within the definition of regular because the debtor will only receive it once.

Although the Code does not provide definitions of what it means for income to be "stable" or "regular," the words of the applicable statute themselves provide that the purpose of the regular income requirement is to ensure that debtors are able to make payments under a chapter 13 plan. The statute defines an individual with regular income as one "whose income is sufficiently stable and regular *to enable such individual to make payments under a plan.*" 11 U.S.C. § 101(30) (emphasis added). The income does not have to be unequivocally stable and regular, only "sufficiently" stable and regular to ensure plan payments can be made. In addition, the legislative history explains that the purpose is to ensure debtors can make plan payments. That a chapter 13 debtor must be an "individual with regular income" was introduced in the Bankruptcy Reform Act of 1978 with the purpose of expanding the types of individuals that are eligible to be chapter 13 debtors beyond the pre–1978 restrictive "wage earner" standard. . . . This makes sense in considering the scheme of chapter 13 bankruptcy cases. If debtors are unable to make payments under a plan to pay back their creditors then they should not be eligible to receive the benefits of chapter 13, mainly retaining all of their assets. But in this case, the Severance is serving that purpose: it will allow Ms. Robinson to make her plan payments until she obtains another job.

Although a court must begin its analysis with the statutory language itself, a general principle of statutory construction is that "a statute should be interpreted and applied with an understanding and appreciation of the purpose it was intended to serve.". . . In construing a statute, courts should look at the entire statutory context, the whole law, and its policy.

In this case, to interpret the statute in a way to conclude Ms. Robinson does not have regular income leads both to an unjust and absurd result, and is also not an interpretation which serves the purpose of the requirement. First, it is not lost on this Court that had Ms. Robinson's former employer paid the severance out in regular installments just as though she were still being paid, which many former employers do, it would be considered regular income and this would not even be an issue. Second, it appears that in Georgia, Ms. Robinson had two options: (1) she could collect the Severance that was offered to her for the 52 weeks after her termination or (2) collect unemployment benefits for those same 52 weeks, but not both. If Ms. Robinson had decided to forgo her Severance and collect unemployment—which would undoubtedly have produced less money to her and her creditors—she would be an individual with regular income, but could possibly qualify for Chapter 13 relief. Instead,

Coca Cola provided a lump sum severance package. It seems wholly inequitable that Coca Cola's policy to provide her Severance in a lump sum instead of incremental payments should determine whether Ms. Robinson is eligible to receive the benefits of chapter 13 when she otherwise can potentially fund a plan. To interpret the statute in such a limited way would not coincide with the purpose of the regular income requirement.

The legislative history and case law further support that the usage of regularity and stability in § 101(30) should not be strictly construed to comport with that as defined by a dictionary. For example, the legislative history provides that both investment income and self-employment income are intended to be considered regular income so long as the debtor can make his or her plan payments. Both of those types of income may not easily fit within the constraints of the limitedly defined terms. Investment income in particular almost always comes with risk and may suddenly stop producing income for months at a time, or even result in a loss. The Severance in this case is essentially equivalent to an income that is only received once, but it is intended to cover an entire year. The Court cannot conclude that Congress intended to preempt individuals with income that is paid only annually or seasonally from being chapter 13 debtors, as long as they can fund a plan. . . .

Moreover, in this case, the Severance payment is being held in Ms. Robinson's attorney's trust fund account from which plan payments to the chapter 13 trustee are being made. In essence, "regularity" and "stability" in the strictest sense are being imposed by the Court. The Severance will last at least a year to make plan payments and the Court has set a restricted budget in which Ms. Robinson may use the money for living expenses. Because Ms. Robinson does not have possession of the Severance, the Court is not concerned it will be frivolously spent resulting in an inability to make plan payments.

Although a severance, whether in lump sum or allotted payments, does have a clear ending point in which it will no longer be available for plan payments, so too does unemployment compensation or contract labor, which courts have found to be regular income. Chapter 13 debtors always risk losing government benefits or losing their job, and indeed some lose multiple jobs throughout a chapter 13 case. . . .

Under the circumstances of this case, the Court believes Ms. Robinson has a legitimate need to restructure her debts in bankruptcy. Based on her qualifications and prior employment with Coca Cola for fourteen years, it appears to the Court that Ms. Robinson's should have the ability to obtain employment somewhere soon, albeit potentially at a lesser salary. Chapter 13 is meant to allow individuals to rehabilitate their financial situation and this debtor, who learned she will be losing her job on the eve of filing bankruptcy but was provided with a year's worth of wages with which she is able to make plan payments, is entitled to that financial rehabilitation.

Accordingly, the Court finds that Ms. Robinson is an individual with regular income, and may be eligible to be a chapter 13 if she can satisfy the other requirements of the Code. However, determining her eligibility on this issue is completely distinct from the determination of whether a plan is feasible. If Ms. Robinson continues to remain unemployed, the Court will have concerns about confirming *any* plan because it is unable to see how such plan will be feasible. At a certain point, if Ms. Robinson's future income is still unknown and the Court is unable to see sufficient progress in her obtaining employment, even if the Severance is still being used to make plan payments, it may decide that a plan is simply not feasible and convert the case to chapter 7 or, at her request, to chapter 11.

* * *

(Citations omitted.)

NOTES AND COMMENTS

1. What does it mean for income to be stable and regular, according to the court? How does that definition tie into the use of a repayment plan in Chapter 13?

2. Does regular income guarantee that a debtor will be able to make payments under a repayment plan?

3. Recall that BAPCPA added the means test to determine Chapter 7 eligibility. Should the means test requirement in Chapter 7 inform what qualifies as regular income in Chapter 13?

Section 109(e) also provides a limitation on the debt that a debtor can bring into Chapter 13. The numerical component of that limit changes every three years,[2] but only "noncontingent, unliquidated" debts count toward that limitation. The Code does not define either term. In the case you just read, after considering whether Ms. Robinson had regular income, the court went on to consider whether some of Ms. Robinson's unsecured debts

---

2. 11 U.S.C. § 104.

were noncontingent and liquidated, bringing her over the then-existing debt limit of $383,175 of unsecured debt.

In re Robinson

535 B.R. 437 (Bankr. N.D. Ga. 2015)

SACCA, Bankruptcy Judge

* * *

The Court will make a final determination on eligibility when Ms. Robinson's liability to Ms. Cohen is finally resolved.

In order to be eligible to be a chapter 13 debtor, as of the petition date the debtor must owe noncontingent, liquidated, unsecured debts less of than $383,175 and noncontingent, liquidated, secured debts of less than $1,149,525. 11 U.S.C. § 109(e). Because it is clear that Ms. Robinson's secured debt is less than $1,149,525, the Court will focus on the amount of her noncontingent, liquidated, unsecured debt.

The amount of debt is normally determined by the debtor's originally filed schedules, checking only to see if the schedules were made in good faith. . . .

The proofs of claims filed in this case result in a much larger amount of unsecured claims than do Ms. Robinson's schedules. The unsecured claims she scheduled total $381,279.97, some of which are disputed, which amount is just below the eligibility requirement. The unsecured claims filed in this case total $508,932.50, but that does not end the inquiry.

In this case, the claim of Beverly Cohen ("Ms. Cohen") was scheduled as a disputed claim for $100,000 and a proof of claim was filed for $185,217.41. Ms. Cohen was one of multiple attorneys that represented Ms. Robinson in her divorce proceedings. Prior to this bankruptcy case, Ms. Robinson and Ms. Cohen were involved in litigation in state court regarding the amount, if any, of the fees that are owed and the validity of the counterclaims. In addition, Ms. Robinson has objected to Ms. Cohen's claim in this case and disputes her liability as to the entire amount. If Ms. Cohen's claim is disallowed, or if it reduced sufficiently, Ms. Robinson's unsecured debt would be less than the statutory required amount and she would be eligible for relief in chapter 13. If most or all of the claim is allowed, she exceeds the statutory amount and would not be eligible. The issue is whether Ms. Cohen's claim is a noncontingent and liquidated debt.

"A debt is not contingent if all the events giving rise to liability have occurred prior to the filing of the bankruptcy petition." Ms. Cohen's claim is not contingent because all the events giving rise to Ms. Robinson's alleged liability occurred prior to the case being filed—Ms. Cohen was hired pursuant to a contract and some amount of hours were spent working and billed prepetition, so nothing else must occur for a liability in some amount to arise.

"A debt is liquidated if its amount is certain due to agreement of the parties or by operation of law." "[T]he concept of a liquidated debt relates to the amount of liability, not the existence of liability." *U.S. v. Verdunn,* 89 F.3d 799, 802 (11th Cir. 1996). "If the amount of the debt is dependent, however, upon a future exercise of discretion, not restricted by specific criteria, the claim is unliquidated." Generally, when a debt is owed pursuant to a contractual obligation it is liquidated, whereas a personal injury action, or something similar that would require an evidentiary hearing to determine that the amount owed, is unliquidated. . . .

It is worth mentioning that the situation in the instant case differs from a normal contract case or the situation in *Verdunn.* In a normal contract case, where it is clear that the debt is liquidated, the parties to the contract agree to a sum certain to be paid—either a specific contract amount (I will pay you $X according to certain terms) or a set amount of a product at a set price (I will buy five widgets at $50 each). . . . But in this case, neither party agreed to a sum certain, but instead only agreed on an hourly rate. Ms. Cohen, the party providing the services, unilaterally provided a billing statement based on the hours she asserts she spent on the case. The parties did not agree to a flat fee or a minimum fee. Thus, Ms. Cohen had complete control over and was solely able to determine the amount of the claim and that amount is not only disputed, but Ms. Robinson contends that Ms. Cohen actually damaged her by the performance of those services.

While *Verdunn* deals with the issue of whether or not a claim is liquidated, it does not address the specific question of whether a court should await determination of liability before deciding eligibility. . . . The language of § 109(e) states that a debtor cannot *owe* more *debts* than the statutory limit. . . . In this case, Ms. Robinson argues, for various reasons, that she does not *owe* Ms. Cohen anything. "The Bankruptcy Code expressly defines 'debt' as 'liability on a claim,' and the plain meaning of 'owe' is 'to be under an obligation to pay.'" A "claim," on the other hand, is defined more broadly as a "right to payment, whether or not such right is . . . disputed. . . ." [11 U.S.C. § 101(5)(a).] "The use of 'debt' in § 109(e) instead of 'claim,' together with the requirement that the debtor owe it, demonstrates that chapter 13 eligibility is properly based on the amount of the debtor's actual liability." Thus, Ms. Robinson's eligibility in this case depends on whether she was actually liable to Ms. Cohen for some or all of her claim as of the date of the petition. . . . Ms. Cohen's claim has been the subject of a counterclaim in state court, but has not yet been decided. In addition, Ms. Robinson objected to Ms. Cohen's claim in this case, but the objection to claim has yet to be decided.

"A debtor who does not owe an alleged debt that would otherwise render him ineligible should not be denied the right to proceed in chapter 13 merely because an adverse party asserts a claim." Otherwise, a creditor that wants to prevent a party from being a chapter 13 debtor, for example because its debt would be dischargeable in a chapter 13 but not the other chapters, could inflate its numbers in order keep a debtor out of chapter 13, even though those numbers are strongly contested. That a debtor would be denied the benefits of chapter 13 in such a scenario is wholly inequitable. The contrary is also true: it would be inequitable to give a debtor the benefits of chapter 13 relief merely because she disputes a claim. Under these facts, Ms. Robinson should be given an opportunity to litigate the issue of whether she does not owe all or a portion of that debt.

It is appropriate for a court to withhold confirmation of a plan allowing a debtor to obtain chapter 13 relief until it first determines that she is in fact an eligible chapter 13 debtor. . . . Because Ms. Robinson's liability to Ms. Cohen is contested, and a determination of the amount of the debt that she actually owes will result in whether or not she will be eligible to be a chapter 13 debtor, it is fair to allow the parties to finish the ongoing litigation regarding Ms. Cohen's claim before the Court makes an eligibility determination. . . . While the Court awaits a resolution, it will allow Ms. Robinson to remain in this chapter 13 proceeding, but will not confirm a plan. In doing so, the Court notes that this is appropriate because the creditors' interests can and will be protected by this result. Although the confirmation of the case will be delayed, the administration of the case will not: Ms. Robinson must continue making any adequate protection payments and plan payments, which this Court can authorize be disbursed to creditors, including distributions from Ms. Robinson's recently liquidated stock options, subject to proper reserves for objections to claims. . . .

* * *

(Citations omitted.).

NOTES AND COMMENTS

1. What type of debt would qualify as "contingent" debt?

2. Assume that another attorney, Smith, filed a proof of claim against Robinson for $185,000, alleging that as part of a contingent fee arrangement he had secured a settlement in Robinson's favor of $500,000 from the driver of a car that caused an accident harming Robinson. He and Robinson had signed a contingent fee agreement, but Robinson has defended on the basis that the agreement provides for payment of the contingency only if the attorney "successfully litigates" the case on Robinson's behalf. Would that constitute a noncontingent, liquidated debt?

B. THE CHAPTER 13 PLAN (§ 1322)

FILING A CHAPTER 13 PLAN

The repayment plan is filed by the debtor; no other party in interest may file a repayment plan. 11 U.S.C. § 1301. That plan may be filed at the time of filing of the bankruptcy petition, but (absent an extension) must be filed within two weeks of the petition date. Fed. R. Bankr. Proc. 3015(b).

1. Plan Contents (§ 1322)

Section 1322 provides what must and may be included in the repayment plan. As you read § 1322, you will see that the plan *must* include:

- Submission of income sufficient to fund the plan
- Payment in full of § 507 priority claims, except that § 507(a)(1)(B) claims may receive less than full payment if the debtor dedicates all projected disposable income to the plan for five years
- Equal treatment of the members in each class.

Classification of unsecured claims is permitted, but not required, in the plan. To the extent that the debtor chooses to group claims into classes, the debtor may not "discriminate unfairly against any class." 11 U.S.C. § 1322(b)(1).

The plan may modify creditors' rights, but cannot modify claims "secured only by a security interest in real property that is the debtor's principal residence." 11 U.S.C. § 1322(b)(2). In addition, the plan allows the debtor to make payments to all creditors concurrently, rather than paying secured and priority creditors in full before paying unsecured creditors. 11 U.S.C. § 1322(b)(4). This is possible because—if all goes according to the plan—the secured and priority creditors will be paid all that they are entitled to under the plan even if unsecured creditors also receive some payments during the plan period.

One of the most common issues regarding the repayment plan is the treatment of mortgage holders in bankruptcy and the prohibition on modifying their claims via the repayment plan.

Minnesota Housing Finance Agency v. Schmidt (In re Schmidt)

765 F.3d 877 (8th Cir. 2014)

COLLOTON, Circuit Judge

Jamey and Keeley Schmidt filed for bankruptcy under Chapter 13 of the bankruptcy code. Chapter 13 allows individuals with regular income to adjust their debts through flexible repayment plans funded primarily from future income. . . .

The bankruptcy court generally has authority to approve a debtor's Chapter 13 plan that modifies the rights of creditors. A plan may modify the rights of holders of unsecured claims; it also may modify the rights of holders of secured claims, "other than a claim secured only by a security interest in real property that is the debtor's principal residence." 11 U.S.C. § 1322(b)(2). In the bankruptcy context, a creditor's claim is a "secured claim" only to the extent of the value of the creditor's interest in the collateral that secures the claim. *Id.* § 506(a)(1).

This case involves a scenario in which a creditor holds a third mortgage that is secured only by the debtor's principal residence, but the value of the creditor's interest in the home is zero, because the value of the residence is insufficient to make whole the holders of the first and second mortgages. The question presented on this appeal is whether the debtor may engage in a practice known as "lien stripping," in which the debtor seeks to (1) have the creditor's claim reclassified from secured to unsecured, (2) modify the terms of the mortgage for the duration of the Chapter 13 plan, and (3) avoid the creditor's mortgage entirely upon discharge from bankruptcy. . .

In June 2012, the Schmidts filed for relief under Chapter 13 of the Bankruptcy Code. Their home, which has an appraised value of $140,000, is encumbered by three mortgages. The senior mortgage, in the amount of $154,578.20, is held by U.S. Bank Home Mortgage. The second-priority mortgage, also held by U.S. Bank Home Mortgage, is for $39,451.99. The Minnesota Housing Finance Agency holds the third-priority mortgage, in the amount of $26,469.31. The Schmidts' home is the only collateral that secures the debt owed to the Agency.

In November 2012, the Schmidts filed a "motion to value" in the bankruptcy court, seeking (1) a determination that there was no equity in their home to support the Agency's lien, (2) reclassification of the Agency's claim from secured to nonpriority unsecured, and (3) avoidance of the Agency's lien upon the Schmidts' successful completion of their Chapter 13 plan. They also filed a modified Chapter 13 plan that treats the Agency as an unsecured creditor and requires the Agency's mortgage lien to be removed from the home upon the Schmidts' bankruptcy discharge. . . .

The district court recognized that the "single legal issue presented by [the Agency's] appeals is whether a Chapter 13 debtor can strip off a lien on the debtor's principal residence if no equity exists to support the lien." The resolution of this issue, the court explained, turned on the interplay between § 506(a)(1) and the clause in § 1322(b)(2) that forbids a court to modify the rights of certain creditors who have a security interest in real property that is the debtor's principal residence.

* * *

The issue here is whether a bankruptcy court may strip off a valueless lien in a Chapter 13 proceeding. Each of our sister circuits that has addressed this question has answered in the affirmative.

Resolution of this appeal requires consideration of two statutes, 11 U.S.C. § 506(a)(1) and 11 U.S.C. § 1322(b)(2). Section 506(a)(1) divides a creditor's allowed claims against a debtor into secured and unsecured claims, based on the value of the underlying collateral. A creditor's claim is secured "to the extent of the value of [the] creditor's interest in . . . [the] property" and is unsecured "to the extent that the value of [the] creditor's interest . . . is less than the amount of [the creditor's] claim." 11 U.S.C. § 506(a)(1). . . .

Section 1322(b)(2) governs permissible modifications of a creditor's rights. As relevant here, it governs the "strip off" of a lien, which occurs when "there being no collateral value for a mortgage, the

entire lien is proposed to be avoided." Section 1322(b)(2) provides
that a debtor's Chapter 13 plan may "modify the rights of holders of
secured claims, other than a claim secured only by a security interest
in real property that is the debtor's principal residence, or of holders
of unsecured claims." We are concerned with the "other than" clause
of § 1322(b)(2)—the "antimodification provision"—which protects
certain claims from lien stripping.

The Supreme Court addressed the interplay of these two
statutes in [Nobelman v. American Savings Bank, 508 U.S. 324
(1993)]. The debtors there sought to strip off the unsecured
portion of a creditor's undersecured lien—the debtors owed the
creditor $71,335 on their home, which was valued at $23,500. . . .
The Court explained that the debtors "were correct in looking to
§ 506(a) for a judicial valuation of the collateral to determine the
status of the bank's secured claim." . . . Next, the Court observed
that "the bank is indisputably the holder of a claim secured by a
lien on [the debtors'] home," "because [the debtors'] home retains
$23,500 of value as collateral. The portion of the bank's claim
that exceeds $23,500 is an 'unsecured claim componen[t]' under
§ 506(a)."

The Court ultimately concluded that the debtors could not strip off
the unsecured portion of the bank's undersecured lien:

> [T]o give effect to § 506(a)'s valuation and bifurcation of secured
> claims through a Chapter 13 plan in the manner [the debtors] propose
> would require a modification of the rights of the holder of the security
> interest. Section 1322(b)(2) prohibits such a modification where, as
> here, the lender's claim is secured only by a lien on the debtor's prin-
> cipal residence.

. . . The Court explained that the debtors "cannot modify the payment and interest terms for the unsecured component, as they
propose to do, without also modifying the terms of the secured
component."

Nobelman held that as long as a creditor's lien is at least partially
secured, § 1322(b)(2) precludes stripping any part of that lien. The
Court had no occasion to address the question presented in this
case: What result if the creditor's lien is wholly unsecured under §
506(a)(1) because the creditor's interest in the collateral that secures
the lien has no value?

The Agency argues that because its lien is secured only by a
security interest in the Schmidts' principal residence, § 1322(b)(2)'s
antimodification provision protects it. Section 1322(b)(2) governs

B

when a bankruptcy court can "modify the rights of holders of secured claims" and the rights of "holders of unsecured claims." "Secured claim" and "unsecured claim" are terms of art in the Bankruptcy Code, so it is necessary first to consult § 506(a)(1) to determine which type of claim is involved. *Nobelman* "confirm[ed] that § 506(a) is the starting point in the analysis and is not rendered a nullity in the Chapter 13 context."

We agree with other circuits that when considering the rights of creditors who hold homestead liens, "the dividing line drawn by § 1322(b)(2) runs between the lienholder whose security interest in the homestead property has some 'value,' see § 506(a), and the lienholder whose security interest is valueless." "Section 1322(b)(2) protects a creditor's rights in a mortgage lien only where the debtor's residence retains enough value—after accounting for other encumbrances that have priority over the lien—so that the lien is at least partially secured under Section 506(a)."

Although the Agency acknowledges that its claim is not a secured claim under § 506(a)(1), the Agency relies on *Nobelman*'s conclusion that the antimodification provision of § 1322(b)(2) protects against modification any "claim secured . . . by" a debtor's principal residence, not merely a "secured claim." . . . On that basis, the Agency contends that § 1322(b)(2)'s antimodification provision applies to *all* claims "secured only by a secured interest in . . . the debtor's principal residence," whether or not the claim is a secured claim under § 506(a)(1).

In our view, the Agency reads too much into *Nobelman*'s discussion on this point. Because the creditor's claim in *Nobelman* was partially secured, the Court was not concerned with whether § 1322(b)(2)'s antimodification provision applies regardless of a claim's status under § 506(a)(1). The question in *Nobelman* was whether § 1322(b)(2) permits bifurcating a partially secured claim and stripping the lien from the unsecured portion of that claim. *Nobelman* thus made clear that if a creditor's claim is at least partially secured, none of the creditor's rights may be modified.

If, however, the creditor's claim is wholly unsecured, then the reasoning of *Nobelman* does not preclude modifying the creditor's rights under § 1322(b)(2). As the Third Circuit explained:

> If a mortgage holder's claim is wholly unsecured, then after the valuation that [the Court] said that debtors could seek under § 506(a), the bank is not in any respect a holder of a claim secured by the debtor's residence. The bank simply has an unsecured claim and the

antimodification clause does not apply. On the other hand, if any part of the bank's claim is secured, then, under [the Court's] interpretation of the term "claim," the entire claim, both secured and unsecured parts, cannot be modified. We think this reading reconciles the various parts of the Court's opinion.

* * *

The Agency complains that the bankruptcy court's interpretation of the statutes will have deleterious policy consequences. It says that a rule allowing modification of creditor rights in this situation places undue weight on the judicial valuation process and leads to arbitrary results. For example, a creditor with one dollar of equity in the debtor's home is accorded the full protection of § 1322(b)(2)'s antimodification provision under *Nobelman,* but the lien of a creditor with no equity (like the Agency here) may be avoided in full. . . . As other courts have observed, however, "[b]right-line rules that use a seemingly arbitrary cut-off point are common in the law," and "[s]imply pointing out that some arbitrariness occurs is not a compelling objection."

* * *

The Agency also urges that allowing modification of its rights would provide an unwarranted windfall to the debtors. If the debtor were allowed to strip liens attributable to junior mortgages and retain the property, the Agency says, the property might later increase in value, perhaps beyond the amount owed on the more senior mortgages that the debtor was not allowed to avoid. It is theoretically possible, of course, that a debtor might benefit from lien stripping in some circumstances. But "[t]here is always some theoretical potential for the value of the collateral to increase," and "if the possibility of property appreciation were to preclude lien avoidance, no final determination could ever be made in a bankruptcy case."

* * *

(Citations omitted.)

NOTES AND COMMENTS

1. Lien stripping involves two different possibilities—strip-down and strip-off. *Nobelman* involved a potential strip-down, where an undersecured creditor's lien would be bifurcated into a secured portion of the claim

and an unsecured portion of the claim; each claim would be treated accordingly based on its status. While *Nobelman* disallowed a strip-down on a residential mortgage lien in Chapter 13, a strip-down is still permitted in other situations. A strip-off, as was permitted in *Schmidt*, involves completely stripping the claim of its lien.

2. The *Schmidt* case involved three mortgage holders; the first mortgage holder's debt exceeded the value of the property. Could the debtors have sought to lien strip both the second and third mortgages, and, if so, why did the debtors seek to strip only the third mortgage?

3. After the *Schmidt* court's opinion, the Supreme Court rendered another decision regarding lien stripping in Bank of America, N.A. v. Caulkett, 135 S. Ct. 1995 (2015). *Caulkett* involved two Chapter 7 bankruptcy cases in which Bank of America held a junior lien and in which the senior mortgage lender's claim exceeded the value of the residence. The Supreme Court held that the Chapter 7 debtors could *not* treat the junior lien as an unsecured claim. It based that determination on the language of §§ 506(a) and (d), as well as the two prior Supreme Court cases—Dewsnup v. Timm, 502 U.S. 410 (1992) and Nobelman v. American Savings Bank, 508 U.S. 324 (1993). Since that decision, courts have held that *Caulkett* does not change the existing circuit-level precedent permitting lien stripping in the context of a Chapter 13 case. Given that § 506 applies to both Chapter 7 and Chapter 13 bankruptcy cases, should the end result on lien stripping be different in Chapter 13 than in Chapter 7? *See, e.g.,* In re Larson, 544 B.R. 883, 885-886 (Bankr. W.D. Wisc. 2016) ("The Supreme Court held in *Caulkett* that stripping a wholly underwater lien was not available in Chapter 7 because *Dewsnup* 'defined the term 'secured claim' in § 506(d) to mean a claim supported by a security interest in property, regardless of whether the value of that property would be sufficient to cover the claim.'. . . This does not address the directive that in a Chapter 13, the debtor should look 'to § 506(a) for a judicial valuation of the collateral to determine the status of the bank's secured claim.'. . . If value under section 506(a) establishes that there is any component of the claim that is secured, the debtor may not use 11 U.S.C. § 1322(b)(2) to modify the lien.").

2. Confirmation

Even if the repayment plan includes everything required under § 1322, it can only be confirmed if it passes the standards outlined by § 1325. In large part, confirmation requires that the debtor pay creditors minimum amounts designated by the Code:

- A secured claimant, unless the claimholder agrees otherwise, must either (a) retain its lien until paid in full or the debt is discharged AND be paid the full secured value of its claim under the plan, or (b) be given the property securing its interest. § 1325(a)(5).
- Domestic support obligations that came due during the bankruptcy case have been paid. § 1325(a)(8).
- Unsecured claims have been paid at least what they would have been paid if the debtor had filed under Chapter 7 (known as "the best interest test"). § 1325(a)(4). The unsecured creditors may also object if the debtor fails to put all projected disposable income into the plan. § 1325(b)(1).

In addition, the petition and plan must have been filed by the debtor in good faith, §§ 1325(a)(3) and (7), and the debtor must have paid all fees, § 1325(a)(2). Most importantly, even if the plan meets all requirements of § 1322 and proposes to pay the creditors as required under § 1325, the court may deny confirmation if the plan as proposed is not feasible. § 1325(a)(6).

a. Projected Disposable Income

In a Chapter 7 bankruptcy case, the trustee makes payments to creditors on the debtor's behalf by distributing property of the estate or proceeds of the sale of property of the estate. But in a Chapter 13 bankruptcy case, the trustee makes payments to creditors from future income. Since that future income will become part of the estate piecemeal, creditors cannot be certain what the ultimate payment will be. To add some level of certainty to a bankruptcy case that will last three to five years, the Code requires that the debtor draft a bankruptcy plan detailing how the anticipated future income will suffice to pay the claims as required by the Bankruptcy Code. In order to create that plan, the debtor must first determine his or her "projected disposable income"—the anticipated future income less permitted expenses—that will be used to repay claims. All of that projected disposable income must be devoted to paying creditors in the plan.[3] The process of determining projected disposable income largely mirrors the means test for determining Chapter 7 eligibility. However, because the means test determines eligibility, while projected disposable income looks into the future to determine ability to fund a plan, the two concepts are not always identical. Before reading the case, review bankruptcy schedules I and J, and Form 22C, each of which is available at https://www.uscourts.gov/forms/bankruptcy-forms; they provide

---

3. The debtor must sufficiently fund the plan payments. § 1322(a)(1). Either the trustee or an unsecured creditor can object if the creditors are not being paid in full and the debtor fails to put all projected disposable income into the plan. § 1325(b). Thus, the only time that the debtor can retain some projected disposable income is if the debtor is able to pay 100 percent on unsecured creditors' claims.

information regarding the debtor's income and expenses, which are relevant in calculating projected disposable income.

Hamilton v. Lanning

560 U.S. 505 (2010)

ALITO, Justice

Chapter 13 of the Bankruptcy Code provides bankruptcy protection to "individual[s] with regular income" whose debts fall within statutory limits. 11 U.S.C. §§ 101(30), 109I. Unlike debtors who file under Chapter 7 and must liquidate their nonexempt assets in order to pay creditors, see §§ 704(a)(1), 726, Chapter 13 debtors are permitted to keep their property, but they must agree to a court-approved plan under which they pay creditors out of their future income, see §§ 1306(b), 1321, 1322(a)(1), 1328(a). A bankruptcy trustee oversees the filing and execution of a Chapter 13 debtor's plan. § 1322(a)(1); see also 28 U.S.C. § 586(a)(3).

Section 1325 of Title 11 specifies circumstances under which a bankruptcy court "shall" and "may not" confirm a plan. § 1325(a), (b). If an unsecured creditor or the bankruptcy trustee objects to confirmation, § 1325(b)(1) requires the debtor either to pay unsecured creditors in full or to pay all "projected disposable income" to be received by the debtor over the duration of the plan.

We granted certiorari to decide how a bankruptcy court should calculate a debtor's "projected disposable income." Some lower courts have taken what the parties term the "mechanical approach," while most have adopted what has been called the "forward-looking approach." We hold that the "forward-looking approach" is correct.

* * *

BAPCPA left the term "projected disposable income" undefined but specified in some detail how "disposable income" is to be calculated. "Disposable income" is now defined as "current monthly income received by the debtor" less "amounts reasonably necessary to be expended" for the debtor's maintenance and support, for qualifying charitable contributions, and for business expenditures. § 1325(b)(2)(A)(i) and (ii) (2006 ed.). "Current monthly income," in turn, is calculated by averaging the debtor's monthly income during what the parties refer to as the 6-month look-back period, which generally consists of the six full months preceding the filing of the bankruptcy petition. See § 101(10A)(A)(i). The phrase "amounts reasonably necessary to be expended" in § 1325(b)(2) is also newly defined. For a debtor whose income is below the median for his or her State, the phrase includes the full amount needed for "maintenance or support," see § 1325(b)(2)(A)(i), but for a debtor with income that exceeds the state median, only certain specified expenses are included, see §§ 707(b)(2), 1325(b)(3)(A).

. . . Respondent had $36,793.36 in unsecured debt when she filed for Chapter 13 bankruptcy protection in October 2006. In the six months before her filing, she received a one-time buyout from her former employer, and this payment greatly inflated her gross income for April 2006 (to $11,990.03) and for May 2006 (to $15,356.42). . . . As a result of these payments, respondent's current monthly income, as averaged from April through October 2006, was $5,343.70—a figure that exceeds the median income for a family of one in Kansas. . . . Respondent's monthly expenses, calculated pursuant to § 707(b)(2), were $4,228.71. . . . She reported a monthly "disposable income" of $1,114.98 on Form 22C. . . .

On the form used for reporting monthly income (Schedule I), she reported income from her new job of $1,922 per month—which is below the state median. . . . On the form used for reporting monthly expenses (Schedule J), she reported actual monthly expenses of $1,772.97. . . . Subtracting the Schedule J figure from the Schedule I figure resulted in monthly disposable income of $149.03.

Respondent filed a plan that would have required her to pay $144 per month for 36 months. . . . Petitioner, a private Chapter 13 trustee, objected to confirmation of the plan because the amount respondent proposed to pay was less than the full amount of the claims against her, see § 1325(b)(1)(A), and because, in petitioner's view, respondent was not committing all of her "projected disposable income" to the repayment of creditors, see § 1325(b)(1)(B). . . . [P]etitioner calculated that creditors would be paid in full if respondent made monthly payments of $756 for a period of 60 months. There is no dispute that respondent's actual income was insufficient to make payments in that amount. . . .

. . . The Bankruptcy Court endorsed respondent's proposed monthly payment of $144 but required a 60-month plan period. . . . The court agreed with the majority view that the word "projected" in § 1325(b)(1)(B) requires courts "to consider at confirmation the debtor's *actual* income as it was reported on Schedule I.". . . [The 10th Circuit Bankruptcy Appellate Panel and 10th Circuit Court of Appeals each affirmed.]

* * *

. . . The parties differ sharply in their interpretation of § 1325's reference to "projected disposable income." Petitioner, advocating the mechanical approach, contends that "projected disposable income" means past average monthly disposable income multiplied by the number of months in a debtor's plan. Respondent, who favors the forward-looking approach, agrees that the method outlined by petitioner should be determinative in most cases, but she argues that in exceptional cases, where significant changes in a debtor's financial circumstances are known or virtually certain, a bankruptcy court has discretion to make an appropriate adjustment. Respondent has the stronger argument.

First, respondent's argument is supported by the ordinary meaning of the term "projected.". . . Here, the term "projected" is not defined, and in ordinary usage future occurrences are not "projected" based on the assumption that the past will necessarily repeat itself. For example, projections concerning a company's future sales or the future cashflow from a license take into account anticipated events that may change past trends. . . . On the night of an election, experts do not "project" the percentage of the votes that a candidate will receive by simply assuming that the candidate will get the same percentage as he or she won in the first few reporting precincts. And sports analysts do not project that a team's winning percentage at the end of a new season will be the same as the team's winning percentage last year or the team's winning percentage at the end of the first month of competition. While a projection takes past events into account, adjustments are often made based on other factors that may affect the final outcome. . . .

Second, the word "projected" appears in many federal statutes, yet Congress rarely has used it to mean simple multiplication. For example, the Agricultural Adjustment Act of 1938 defined "projected national yield," "projected county yield," and "projected farm yield" as entailing historical averages "adjusted for abnormal weather conditions," "trends in yields," and "any significant changes in production practices."

By contrast, we need look no further than the Bankruptcy Code to see that when Congress wishes to mandate simple multiplication, it does so unambiguously—most commonly by using the term "multiplied." *See, e.g.,* 11 U.S.C. § 1325(b)(3) ("current monthly income, when multiplied by 12"); §§ 704(b)(2), 707(b)(6), (7)(A) (same); § 707(b)(2) (A)(i), (B)(iv) ("multiplied by 60"). Accord, 2 U.S.C. § 58(b)(1)(B) ("multiplied by the number of months in such year"); 5 U.S.C. § 8415(a) ("multiplied by such individual's total service"); 42 U.S.C. § 403(f)(3) ("multiplied by the number of months in such year").

Third, pre-BAPCPA case law points in favor of the "forward-looking" approach. Prior to BAPCPA, the general rule was that courts would multiply a debtor's current monthly income by the number of months in the commitment period as the first step in determining projected disposable income. . . . But courts also had discretion to account for known or virtually certain changes in the debtor's income. . . .

Pre-BAPCPA bankruptcy practice is telling because we "'will not read the Bankruptcy Code to erode past bankruptcy practice absent a clear indication that Congress intended such a departure.'" Congress did not amend the term "projected disposable income" in 2005, and pre-BAPCPA bankruptcy practice reflected a widely acknowledged and well-documented view that courts may take into account known or virtually certain changes to debtors' income or expenses when projecting disposable income. In light of this historical practice, we would expect that, had Congress intended for "projected" to carry a specialized—and indeed, unusual—meaning in Chapter 13, Congress would have said so expressly. Cf., e.g., 26 U.S.C. § 279(c)(3)(A), (B) (expressly defining "projected earnings" as reflecting a 3-year historical average).

. . . The mechanical approach also clashes repeatedly with the terms of 11 U.S.C. § 1325.

First, § 1325(b)(1)(B)'s reference to projected disposable income "to be received in the applicable commitment period" strongly favors the forward-looking approach. There is no dispute that respondent would in fact receive far less than $756 per month in disposable income during the plan period, so petitioner's projection does not accurately reflect "income to be received" during that period. . . . The mechanical approach effectively reads this phrase out of the statute when a debtor's current disposable income is substantially higher than the income that the debtor predictably will receive during the plan period. . . .

Second, § 1325(b)(1) directs courts to determine projected disposable income "as of the effective date of the plan," which is the date on which the plan is confirmed and becomes binding, see § 1327(a). Had Congress intended for projected disposable income to be nothing more than a multiple of disposable income in all cases, we see no reason why Congress would not have required courts to determine that value as of the *filing* date of the plan. . . . In the very next section of the Code, for example, Congress specified that a debtor shall commence payments "not later than 30 days after the *date of the filing of the plan*." § 1326(a)(1) (emphasis added). Congress' decision to require courts to measure projected disposable income "as of the *effective* date of the plan" is more consistent with the view that Congress expected courts to consider postfiling information about the debtor's financial circumstances. . . .

Third, the requirement that projected disposable income "will be applied to make payments" is most naturally read to contemplate that the debtor will actually pay creditors in the calculated monthly amounts. § 1325(b)(1)(B). But when, as of the effective date of a plan, the debtor lacks the means to do so, this language is rendered a hollow command.

. . . The arguments advanced in favor of the mechanical approach are unpersuasive. Noting that the Code now provides a detailed and precise definition of "disposable income," proponents of the mechanical approach maintain that any departure from this method leaves that definition "'with no apparent purpose.'" This argument overlooks the important role that the statutory formula for calculating "disposable income" plays under the forward-looking approach. As the Tenth Circuit recognized in this case, a court taking the forward-looking approach should begin by calculating disposable income, and in most cases, nothing more is required. It is only in unusual cases that a court may go further and take into account other known or virtually certain information about the debtor's future income or expenses.

* * *

In order to avoid or at least to mitigate the harsh results that the mechanical approach may produce for debtors, petitioner advances several possible escape strategies. He proposes no comparable strategies for creditors harmed by the mechanical approach, and in any event none of the maneuvers that he proposes for debtors is satisfactory.

. . . Petitioner first suggests that a debtor may delay filing a petition so as to place any extraordinary income outside the 6-month look-back period. We see at least two problems with this proposal.

First, delay is often not a viable option for a debtor sliding into bankruptcy. . . .

Second, even when a debtor is able to delay filing a petition, such delay could be risky if it gives the appearance of bad faith. See

11 U.S.C. § 1325(a)(7) (requiring, as a condition of confirmation, that "the action of the debtor in filing the petition was in good faith"). . . .

* * *

(Citations omitted.)

NOTES AND COMMENTS

1. Shortly after the *Lanning* decision, the Supreme Court rendered a decision in Ransom v. FIA Card Servs., N.A., 562 U.S. 61 (2011). While *Lanning* focused on whether the debtor's income could be modified within the calculation of disposable income, *Ransom* questioned whether the debtor's expenses could be modified within that calculation. The debtor deducted expenses for ownership of a car based on the Code's calculation of expenses, even though the debtor had paid for his car in full prior to the bankruptcy filing. The trustee argued that his projected disposable income should be increased to reflect the reality that the debtor would not be making a car payment during the bankruptcy case. *Ransom*, 562 U.S. 66-67. The Court agreed with the trustee, based on its reading of § 707 (from which disposable income is determined). That section provides that the debtor may deduct "applicable" expenses from income. The Court held that applicable requires that the debtor actually have such an expense. *Ransom*, 562 U.S. at 69.

2. In rendering its decision, the Court focuses on post-filing changes to income that are "known or virtually certain." *Lanning*, 560 U.S. at 524. Why does the Court limit modification of income to such circumstances? What types of income changes will meet this requirement?

APPLICABLE COMMITMENT PERIOD

Section 1325(b) requires that the debtor commit all projected disposable income for the "applicable commitment period." Subsection 1325(b)(4) defines the applicable commitment period as either three or five years. The five-year commitment period applies when the debtor's current monthly income (combined with that of the debtor's spouse) equals or exceeds the median state income for a household of that size. 11 U.S.C.

§1325(b)(4)(A)(ii);   *see also* 11 U.S.C. § 1322(d). The applicable commitment period can only be shortened if unsecured creditors are paid in full. 11 U.S.C. § 1325(b)(4)(B).

b. Social Security Income and Projected Disposable Income

Social Security is a complex program that provides benefits to several groups of people. Briefly, Social Security is actually three programs, formally known as Old Age, Survivors and Disability Insurance. The three programs consist of retirement income for the worker and the worker's dependents; survivors' benefits for those who survive the worker such as the spouse, former spouse, or dependent children; and disability benefits for those individuals who meet the criteria for eligibility for the program.

Typically when thinking about Social Security, one thinks of retirement benefits. Eligibility for Social Security retirement is tied to work history. Social Security uses a time frame measurement of work, something known as "quarters of coverage." Social Security looks at whether the worker earned a specific minimum amount during a quarter of work and has accumulated at least 40 quarters of coverage. In addition to work history, Social Security also looks at a worker's age. There are three relevant ages for retirement benefits: age 62, known as early retirement, is the earliest age at which a worker can begin to draw Social Security retirement, assuming the worker meets all of the other eligibility requirements. One important point regarding early retirement is the benefit amount the worker receives is permanently reduced. The second relevant age is the full retirement age, which is 66 for those born between 1943-1954.[4] The final relevant age for Social Security retirement for the worker is age 70, which is known as "delayed retirement."

A worker's dependents may draw on the worker's earnings record in certain circumstances and, if the worker has died, the survivors (typically a spouse, former spouse and dependent children (or even grandchildren)) may draw on the worker's earnings record as survivors. There are specific eligibility requirements for each program.

---

4. Previously the retirement age for Social Security was 65, and many may still think that is true. The full retirement age for Social Security has been increasing in increments over a number of years and will gradually increase to age 67. The full retirement age for a worker is determined by the worker's date of birth. *See* https://www.ssa.gov/planners/retire/retirechart.html.

The amount of the Social Security payment a beneficiary receives is based on earnings history. Workers (whether through their employers, or if self-employed, themselves) pay taxes on their wages that are placed in the Social Security Trust Fund. Social Security offers an online calculator for those who want to estimate the amount of their benefits. Social Security is not a welfare program; recipients do not have to be means-tested. A person who meets the criteria (work and age, etc.) is entitled to Social Security regardless of the person's other income and assets. More information about Social Security benefits and eligibility requirements are available on the Social Security website.

For an individual who is retired, Social Security benefits are an important part of the individual's retirement (or income) security. When planning for retirement, sources of income are typically referred to as the "three-legged stool," with one leg being Social Security retirement income; the second, savings; and the third, pension income. As noted below, Social Security benefits have some special protections, known as anti-alienation of benefits.

Unlike Social Security, Supplemental Security Income (SSI) is means-tested. SSI is a welfare program designed to provide a very low level of income for those who meet the eligibility criteria. Among other criteria, SSI eligibility looks at a person's income and assets as well as whether the person falls into a certain category, such as being old, blind, or disabled. SSI, an entitlement program, is sometimes referred to as a public benefits or welfare program, since it is a program to provide income to certain individuals who are poor. SSI is what is known as a means-tested program. Unlike Social Security, SSI is not based on a person's earnings record or work history; rather, it looks at a person's income and assets. Thus for a person to be eligible for SSI, among the criteria, the person has to meet the limits on income and assets (thus testing the person's means for eligibility).

NOTES AND COMMENTS

1. Why do you think the Social Security program is structured the way it is?

2. The solvency of the Social Security program is frequently in the news and is often the subject of debate during the election cycle. The debate revolves around whether and how to change Social Security to make it more solvent. Do you think Social Security will be available in its current form when you reach retirement age? If you think Social Security should be revised, what changes would you recommend? To learn more about the solvency issue, see the Social Security Trustees' Report (issued annually) at https://www.ssa.gov/oact/tr/.

3. To get an estimate of the amount of your Social Security benefit, go to www.ssa.gov and use the retirement calculator.

4. Social Security is not the only source of retirement income. Beyond Social Security, a debtor may have savings, investments, and pensions. To learn more about retirement benefits and bankruptcy, see Tara Twomey and Todd F. Maynes, *Protecting Nest Eggs and Other Retirement Benefits in Bankruptcy*, 90 Am. Bankr. L.J. 235 (2016).

THE ELDER IN BANKRUPTCY: HOW SOCIAL SECURITY FALLS INTO THE BANKRUPTCY SCHEME

An individual's decision to file for bankruptcy protection often follows months—and maybe years—of financial distress and difficulty. For the elderly, underlying medical issues, the need for long-term care, or other realities of aging may cause such financial distress. As the population ages, bankruptcy practitioners are likely to find seniors among their clientele. *See* Deborah Thorne, Pamela Foohey, Robert M. Lawless, and Katherine M. Porter, *Graying of U.S. Bankruptcy: Fallout from Life in a Risk Society*, available at https://papers.ssrn.com/sol3/papers .cfm?abstract_id=3226574 (rate of filing among elders has doubled). The Bankruptcy Code and Rules are not different for seniors, but they may impact seniors differently than the general population. As suggested by the pieces cited below, more elderly clients find themselves facing the question of whether to file for bankruptcy protection than ever before; what triggers those bankruptcy filings helps dictate how the attorney represents this increasing population of debtors.

Several studies have sought to determine the reasons why debtors file for bankruptcy protection. A landmark study determined that half or more of bankruptcy filings are "medical bankruptcies"—filing precipitated by a medical diagnosis or event. Since publication of that study, commentators have divided on the prevalence of medical bankruptcy.

Some of the follow-up studies have focused on seniors and the reasons why they file for bankruptcy protection. Surprisingly, the studies find that seniors are not more likely to file for medical reasons than the general population. The studies have found the prevalence of credit card debt due to the challenges of living on a limited income to be more problematic for seniors. *See* John A.E. Pottow, *The Rise in Elder Bankruptcy Filings and the Failure of U.S. Bankruptcy Law*, 19 Elder L.J. 119 (2011); Theresa J. Pulley Radwan and Rebecca C. Morgan, *The Elderly in Bankruptcy and Health Reform*, 18 Geo. J. on Poverty L. & Pol'y 1 (Fall 2010).

Determining projected disposable income can be challenging, particularly for a debtor who receives Social Security payments or other benefits that are normally exempt from creditor collection. Part of the difficulty stems from the various bankruptcy schedules used in different bankruptcy calculations. Form 22C, used in the means test calculation from which "disposable income" is derived, *excludes* Social Security. Schedule I provides the debtor's current income, and is often the starting point for the Chapter 13 plan; Schedule I specifically *includes* Social Security. Once the debtor proposes the plan, the court determines whether the plan is confirmed—the final step to make the plan effective—based on the requirements listed in the Bankruptcy Code.

Beaulieu v. Ragos (In re Ragos)

700 F.3d 220 (5th Cir. 2012)

DAVIS, Circuit Judge

Chapter 13 of the Bankruptcy Code provides bankruptcy protection to individuals with regular income whose debts fall within statutory limits. Unlike bankruptcy debtors who file under Chapter 7 and must liquidate their assets, Chapter 13 debtors are permitted to keep their property subject to a court-approved plan under which they agree to pay creditors out of their future income. This appeal presents the question of whether social security benefits are included in a debtor's projected disposable income in the formulation of a Chapter 13 plan and the calculation of the future payments the debtor will be required to make to creditors. Because we find that social security benefits are not included in the projected disposable income calculation, we AFFIRM the bankruptcy court's order.

I.

Benjamin and Stella Ragos ("Debtors") voluntarily filed a joint Chapter 13 bankruptcy petition on February 22, 2011. On schedule I (Current Income of Individual Debtors), Debtors itemized their monthly income, including a $200.00 portion of their monthly social security benefits. Debtors' actual monthly receipt of social security benefits totals $1,854.00. Pursuant to a Chapter 13 reorganization, the Debtors filed a proposed payment plan. Under the terms of the plan, creditors would receive all of Debtors' declared monthly net income. However, the Debtors would retain the undeclared balance of their social security benefits, $1,654.00 each month.

S.J. Beaulieu, Jr., the Chapter 13 Trustee ("Trustee"), objected to confirmation of the Debtors' plan because Debtors did not dedicate 100% of their social security income to the plan for payment to creditors. Trustee additionally argued that Debtors' willful failure to commit their social security income to the repayment of creditors indicated that their plan had not been proposed in good faith. After a hearing, the bankruptcy judge rejected both of Trustee's arguments. The bankruptcy court based its ruling primarily on the language of provisions of both the Bankruptcy Code and the Social Security Act, reflecting a congressional intent to exclude social security benefits in calculating projected disposable income. . . .

* * *

Trustee argues first that the bankruptcy court erred by allowing Debtors to exclude their social security benefits from the Debtors' projected disposable income dedicated to the payment of creditors.

. . . Although Debtors' plan complies with § 1325(a), Trustee nonetheless relies upon a separate provision of the Bankruptcy Code to challenge the plan. Trustee bases his objection upon § 1325(b)(1)(B), which states:

> If the trustee . . . objects to the confirmation of the plan, then the court may not approve the plan unless, as of the effective date of the plan—
>
> . . . .
>
> (B) the plan provides that all of the debtor's *projected disposable income* to be received in the applicable commitment period . . . will be applied to make payments to unsecured creditors under the plan.

Id. (emphasis added).

According to Trustee, the bankruptcy court should not have approved the plan because it allows Debtors to withhold social security benefits. This appeal thus asks us to decide whether a Chapter 13 debtor's social security income must be included in "projected disposable income."

The Trustee contends that the term "all of the debtor's projected disposable income" includes *all* sources of income and does not exclude social security benefits. Under this view, because Debtors are receiving social security benefits which they are keeping for themselves, they are withholding a portion of their projected disposable income and "the court may not approve the plan." *Id.*

Although projected disposable income is not defined *per se,* we are guided in this inquiry by two statutes. The first statute relevant here is the Bankruptcy Code itself. Though "projected disposable income" is not defined in § 1325(b)(1), the term "disposable income" is defined in the statute's very next provision: "[T]he term 'disposable income' means *current monthly income* received by the debtor . . . less amounts reasonably necessary" for certain enumerated expenses. *Id.* § 1325(b)(2) (emphasis added). "Current monthly income," in turn, is elsewhere defined as the average of "all sources" of the debtor's monthly income during the previous six-month period. *See id.* § 101(10A)(A). Importantly, the statutory definition of "current monthly income" explicitly "excludes benefits received under the Social Security Act." *Id.* § 101(10A)(B). Trustee's argument thus rests on the uncertain premise that although social security benefits are not included in "current monthly income," which is the starting point for determining "disposable income," "projected disposable income" should nonetheless include a debtor's social security income.

We cannot square Trustee's argument with the apparent intent of Congress. If Congress excluded social security income from current monthly income and disposable income, it makes little sense to circumvent that prohibition by allowing social security income to be included in *projected* disposable income. . . .

The conclusion that Congress exempted social security benefits from projected disposable income is also bolstered by two independently enacted provisions of the Social Security Act. The first provision, Social Security Act § 407(a), was enacted in 1935, long before the enactment of the Bankruptcy Code. That section provides:

> (a) . . . [N]one of the moneys paid or payable or rights existing under this subchapter shall be subject to execution, levy, attachment, garnishment, or other legal process, or *to the operation of any bankruptcy or insolvency law.*

42 U.S.C. § 407(a) (emphasis added). Section 407(a) thus makes it clear that social security benefits such as the Debtors' are not subject to the operation of *any* bankruptcy law. Despite this explicit statutory language, some courts however failed to read the § 407(a) as exempting social security benefits from income available to pay creditors in Chapter 13 bankruptcy proceedings.

According to a 1983 House Conference Report,

> Based on the legislative history of the Bankruptcy Reform Act of 1978, some bankruptcy courts ha[d] considered social security and [Social

Security Income] benefits listed by the debtor to be income for purposes of a Chapter XIII bankruptcy.

The 1983 House Committee then made clear its intent to legislatively overrule these cases and protect social security benefits by enacting a second provision in § 407(b) of the Social Security Act, which states:

> No other provision of law, enacted before, on, or after April 20, 1983, may be construed to limit, supersede, or otherwise modify the provisions of this section except to the extent that it does so by express reference to this section.

42 U.S.C. § 407(b). According to the modified statute, even laws enacted after § 407 was enacted must expressly cite to § 407 if they wish to overcome social security income's exemption from the operation of any bankruptcy law. *Id.* These two independently enacted provisions of the Social Security Act, read together with the Bankruptcy Code, express the clear intent of Congress to protect Social Security payments from bankruptcy process.

* * *

In response, Trustee argues that the Supreme Court's recent decision in *Hamilton v. Lanning* requires a different result. . . . The Court held that "when a bankruptcy court calculates a debtor's projected disposable income, the court may account for changes in the debtor's income or expenses that are known or virtually certain at the time of confirmation."

Trustee is correct that Debtors' social security benefit payments are amounts certain to recur in the future and this fact is known to the debtors. However, the facts before the *Lanning* Court and the issue those facts raised are completely different from the issue in this case. Because of a material change of circumstances, Lanning's current income was not a reliable predictor of her future income. . . . Here, however, there has been no change in the Debtors' circumstances or in any income stream. Trustee simply seeks to circumvent the exemption granted to social security income by accounting for it in the future income (projected disposable income) calculation. However, the mere existence of a statutorily exempt income stream the debtor has been receiving for some time is not a change in circumstances, and *Lanning* does not undermine our analysis.

* * *

The problem with Trustee's argument ... is that it completely ignores the final clause in the sentence, "absent a clear indication that Congress intended such a departure." As explained above, Congress made such a clear indication in 2005 when it passed the Bankruptcy Abuse Prevention and Consumer Protection Act ("BAPCPA"), which amended the Bankruptcy Code in many respects. Part of the BAPCPA's revision included the modification of the definition of "current monthly income" in 11 U.S.C. § 101(10A)(A)—the starting point for projected disposable income—to explicitly exclude social security benefits. We consider this a "clear indication that Congress intended . . . a departure" from the practice of including social security benefits in projected disposable income. . . .

* * *

(Citations omitted.)

NOTES AND COMMENTS

1. Inherent tension exists between Social Security's anti-alienation clause, 42 U.S.C. § 407, and the Bankruptcy Code. Early courts determined that the Bankruptcy Code, enacted after the anti-alienation clause, "repealed by implication" the anti-alienation clause. Toson v. United States, 18 B.R. 371, 373 (Bankr. N.D. Ga. 1982). Congress responded to this line of cases by amending the anti-alienation provision to provide that "No other provision of law, enacted before, on, or after April 20, 1983, may be construed to limit, supersede, or otherwise modify the provisions of this section except to the extent that it does so by express reference to this section." 42 U.S.C. § 407(b). The House Report referred to the earlier line of cases, indicating that:

> [s]ome bankruptcy courts have considered social security and SSI benefits listed by the debtor to be income for purposes of a chapter XIII bankruptcy and have ordered SSA in several hundred cases to send all or part of a debtor's benefit check to the trustee in bankruptcy. Your committee's bill specifically provides that social security and SSI benefits may not be assigned notwithstanding any other provisions of law, including P.L. 95-598, the 'Bankruptcy Reform Act of 1978'. This provision would be effective upon enactment.

H.R. 98-25(I) §336 (1983). Even with this amendment, however, the debate continued regarding when a debtor *must* use Social Security payments to pay creditors in a Chapter 13 plan. *See, e.g.,* Hildebrand v. Social Security Administration (In re Buren), 725 F.2d 1080 (6th

Cir. 1984) (denying mandatory use of Social Security in a Chapter 13 plan); In re Baxter, 34 B.R. 911 (Bankr. E.D. Tenn. 1983) (suggesting that the anti-assignment clause may be an unconstitutional denial of equal protection because it could prevent Social Security recipients from utilizing Chapter 13 of the bankruptcy code). Courts have, however, always allowed Social Security recipients to *voluntarily* use the proceeds of Social Security to fund a Chapter 13 repayment plan. Hagel v. Drummond (In re Hagel), 184 B.R. 793, 797 (9th Cir. BAP 1995). Why might a debtor *want* to use Social Security income to fund a Chapter 13 plan if the debtor would be allowed to retain the income for himself or herself?

2. While Social Security payments are expressly excluded from calculation of the means test, courts have considered them in determining abuse of the bankruptcy system by filing of a Chapter 7 bankruptcy petition. Failing the means test is a presumed form of abuse, but a court may find "actual" abuse even for a debtor who passes the means test. 11 U.S.C. §707(b)(1). *See, e.g.,* In re Calhoun, 396 B.R. 270 (Bankr. D.S.C. 2008):

> testimony and other evidence establishes the Debtors' ability to make a substantial payment to their creditors. . . . Debtors admit to $133.00 per month of disposable income. The Debtors report and then subtract income from Social Security, shielding it from creditors. This is not proper. In two instances Social Security benefits are specifically excluded from income calculations by the Bankruptcy Code. Income received under the Social Security Act is excluded from "current monthly income" in computing the means test for the purpose of determining whether a presumption of abuse arises under § 707(b)(2). *See* § 101(10A)(B). Social Security income is also excluded from the calculation of disposable income for above median income chapter 13 debtors. *See* §§ 1325(b)(2); 101(10A) (B). . . . Congress clearly knew how to exclude benefits under the Social Security Act from consideration but did not do so in connection with the § 707(b)(3)(B) totality of the circumstances test. Because this test was added to the Bankruptcy Code at the same time exclusions of Social Security Act income were added to other sections of the Bankruptcy Code the failure to exclude the benefits is even more significant. Such income should not therefore be excluded from consideration in analyzing ability to pay as a component of the totality of the debtor's financial circumstances under § 707(b)(3). This is consistent with pre amendment caselaw in which courts recognized Social Security benefits as income. . . .

Id. at 276. *Cf.* In re Suttice, 487 B.R. 245 (Bankr. C.D. Cal. 2013) (refusing to follow *Calhoun* and similar precedent, and finding congressional intent to exclude Social Security income from determination of abuse).

c. Feasibility

The following case also considers the question of how Social Security income fits into the Chapter 13 scheme, specifically whether SSI may be considered in determining the feasibility of a Chapter 13 plan.

Mort Ranta v. Gorman

721 F.3d 241 (4th Cir. 2013)

GREGORY, Circuit Judge

Robert D. Mort Ranta filed a voluntary petition for bankruptcy under Chapter 13 of the Bankruptcy Code. . . . The bankruptcy court denied confirmation of his proposed Chapter 13 plan on the grounds that it did not accurately reflect his disposable income and that it was unfeasible if Mort Ranta's Social Security income was excluded from his "projected disposable income," as Mort Ranta urged. The district court affirmed. We hold that the plain language of the Bankruptcy Code excludes Social Security income from the calculation of "projected disposable income," but that such income nevertheless must be considered in the evaluation of a plan's feasibility. For these reasons, we vacate and remand to the district court with instructions to remand the case to the bankruptcy court for further proceedings consistent with this opinion.

. . . At the time he filed the Chapter 13 petition, Mort Ranta owed $20,000 in arrears on his home mortgage loan, $12,981 in individual credit card debt, and $8,295 in joint credit card debt with his wife. On Form B22 (C), Mort Ranta reported a "current monthly income" of $3,097.46, a figure derived from the couple's combined average monthly income from employment over the previous six months.

On Form B6I ("Schedule I"), however, Mort Ranta reported his "combined average monthly income" as $7,492.10. That figure reflected the couple's current monthly take-home pay from employment, plus an additional $3,319 in combined monthly Social Security benefits. His monthly expenses were reported on Form B6J ("Schedule J") as $6,967.24. Subtracting that figure from his "combined average monthly income," his "monthly net income" per Schedule J was $524.86.

Mort Ranta proposed a plan requiring payments of $525 per month for five years, for a total of $31,500. From that amount, the plan would pay off in full his mortgage arrears and joint credit card debt. However, his individual credit card debt would be paid off at less than one percent.

* * *

In a colloquy with the parties, the bankruptcy court determined that if Mort Ranta's monthly payments were increased to reflect his actual net income, including Social Security, the total payments under the plan would be approximately $50,000. That amount would allow for full repayment of all debts, including the individual credit card debt that would be paid off at less than one percent under Mort Ranta's proposed plan. Thus, the Trustee noted, the holder of that unsecured debt would either "get paid pretty much in full like everybody else or [under Mort Ranta's proposed plan] they get nothing."

* * *

We next address whether the district court erred when it disregarded Mort Ranta's Social Security income for purposes of evaluating whether his plan was feasible. The "feasibility" requirement is expressed in § 1325(a)(6), which states that the plan shall be confirmed if "the debtor will be able to make all payments under the plan and to comply with the plan."

The bankruptcy court reasoned that if Social Security income is excluded from "disposable income," then it must also be excluded when evaluating whether the plan is feasible. But nothing in the Code supports this conclusion. Section 1325(a)(6) simply states that a debtor must be able to make the payments required by the plan; it does not state that only "disposable income" may be used to make payments. Further, it has long been established that Social Security income may be used to fund a Chapter 13 plan. *See* 11 U.S.C. § 109(e) (allowing individuals with "regular income" to be debtors under Chapter 13). . . . According to the bankruptcy court's interpretation of the Code, however, it is unlikely that a debtor whose primary source of income is Social Security could ever propose a confirmable plan, for the debtor would be unable to prove feasibility. There is no indication Congress intended to throw this kind of obstacle to relief in the way of Social Security recipients when it revised the definition of "projected disposable income" with the BAPCPA.

We therefore hold, in agreement with the Sixth Circuit, that "a debtor with zero or negative projected disposable income may propose a confirmable plan by making available income that falls outside of the definition of disposable income—such as . . . benefits under the Social Security Act—to make payments under the plan." . . . Thus, in evaluating whether a debtor will be able to make all payments under the plan and comply with the plan, the bankruptcy court must take into account any Social Security income the debtor proposes to rely upon, and may not limit its feasibility analysis by considering only the debtor's "disposable income." If the debtor's actual net income, including Social Security income, is sufficient to cover all the required payments, the plan is feasible.

* * *

(Citations omitted.)

NOTES AND COMMENTS

1. The decision indicates that a court can "consider" Social Security income in determining feasibility. What does that mean?

2. Other than adding additional income to the plan, how else might a debtor make a plan feasible if a court determines that it fails to meet that requirement?

MODIFICATION OR REVOCATION OF CHAPTER 13 PLAN FOLLOWING CONFIRMATION

A Chapter 13 plan may be modified after confirmation, but the plan must of course still meet the requirements applicable under §§ 1322 and 1325. While the modified plan can change the payment totals and schedule, it cannot generally extend the overall length of the plan. 11 U.S.C. § 1329.

In addition, the confirmation order can be revoked for a period of six months after confirmation if the confirmation occurred through the use of fraud. 11 U.S.C. § 1330.

C. CONVERSION FROM CHAPTER 13

Section 1307 allows a debtor to convert from Chapter 13 to Chapter 7 "at any time." It also allows the debtor to dismiss a case. 11 U.S.C. § 1307(b). A party in interest may also request conversion to Chapter 7, but, unlike a request by a debtor to convert, a party-in-interest must provide a basis for the conversion. The Code provides some examples of cause sufficient to support such a request; most of the illustrative list of reasons involves the failure of the debtor to meet requirements such as paying fees or filing a plan. Neither the debtor nor a party-in-interest can seek a conversion into a chapter for which the debtor is ineligible. 11 U.S.C. § 1307(g). Thus, a debtor denied the ability to file under Chapter 7 due to the means test may not skirt that prohibition by filing under Chapter 13 and converting into Chapter 7. The following case considers some of the implications of conversion into a Chapter 7.

Harris v. Viegelahn

135 S. Ct. 1829 (2015)

GINSBURG, Justice

This case concerns the disposition of wages earned by a debtor *after* he petitions for bankruptcy. The treatment of postpetition wages generally depends on whether the debtor is proceeding under Chapter 13 of the Bankruptcy Code (in which the debtor retains assets, often his home, during bankruptcy subject to a court-approved plan for the payment of his debts) or Chapter 7 (in which the debtor's assets are immediately liquidated and the proceeds distributed to creditors). In a Chapter 13 proceeding, postpetition wages are "[p]roperty of the estate," 11 U.S.C. § 1306(a), and may be collected by the Chapter 13 trustee for distribution to creditors, § 1322(a)(1). In a Chapter 7 proceeding, those earnings are not estate property; instead, they belong to the debtor. See § 541(a)(1). The Code permits the debtor to convert a Chapter 13 proceeding to one under Chapter 7 "at any time," § 1307(a); upon such conversion, the service of the Chapter 13 trustee terminates, § 348(e).

When a debtor initially filing under Chapter 13 exercises his right to convert to Chapter 7, who is entitled to postpetition wages still in the hands of the Chapter 13 trustee? Not the Chapter 7 estate when the conversion is in good faith, all agree. May the trustee distribute the accumulated wage payments to creditors as the Chapter 13 plan required, or must she remit them to the debtor? That is the question this case presents. We hold that, under the governing provisions of the Bankruptcy Code, a debtor who converts to Chapter 7 is entitled to return of any postpetition wages not yet distributed by the Chapter 13 trustee.

* * *

Chapter 7 allows a debtor to make a clean break from his financial past, but at a steep price: prompt liquidation of the debtor's assets.

When a debtor files a Chapter 7 petition, his assets, with specified exemptions, are immediately transferred to a bankruptcy estate. § 541(a)(1). A Chapter 7 trustee is then charged with selling the property in the estate, § 704(a)(1), and distributing the proceeds to the debtor's creditors, § 726. Crucially, however, a Chapter 7 estate does not include the wages a debtor earns or the assets he acquires *after* the bankruptcy filing. § 541(a)(1). Thus, while a Chapter 7 debtor must forfeit virtually all his prepetition property, he is able to make a "fresh start" by shielding from creditors his postpetition earnings and acquisitions.

Chapter 13 works differently. A wholly voluntary alternative to Chapter 7, Chapter 13 allows a debtor to retain his property if he proposes, and gains court confirmation of, a plan to repay his debts over a three- to five-year period. § 1306(b), § 1322, § 1327(b). Payments under a Chapter 13 plan are usually made from a debtor's "future earnings or other future income." § 1322(a)(1). . . . Accordingly, the Chapter 13 estate from which creditors may be paid includes both the debtor's property at the time of his bankruptcy petition, and any wages and property acquired after filing. § 1306(a). A Chapter 13 trustee is often charged with collecting a portion of a debtor's wages through payroll deduction, and with distributing the withheld wages to creditors.

* * *

Many debtors, however, fail to complete a Chapter 13 plan successfully. . . . Recognizing that reality, Congress accorded debtors a nonwaivable right to convert a Chapter 13 case to one under Chapter 7 "at any time." § 1307(a). To effectuate a conversion, a debtor need only file a notice with the bankruptcy court. Fed. Rule Bkrtcy. Proc. 1017(f)(3). No motion or court order is needed to render the conversion effective.

Conversion from Chapter 13 to Chapter 7 does not commence a new bankruptcy case. The existing case continues along another track, Chapter 7 instead of Chapter 13, without "effect[ing] a change in the date of the filing of the petition." § 348(a). Conversion, however, immediately "terminates the service" of the Chapter 13 trustee, replacing her with a Chapter 7 trustee. § 348(e).

* * *

In February 2010, petitioner Charles Harris III filed a Chapter 13 bankruptcy petition. At the time of filing, Harris was indebted to multiple creditors, and had fallen $3,700 behind on payments to Chase Manhattan, his home mortgage lender.

Harris' court-confirmed Chapter 13 plan provided that he would immediately resume making monthly mortgage payments to Chase. The plan further provided that $530 per month would be withheld from Harris' postpetition wages and remitted to the Chapter 13 trustee, respondent Mary Viegelahn. Viegelahn, in turn, would distribute $352 per month to Chase to pay down Harris' outstanding mortgage debt. She would also distribute $75.34 per month to Harris' only other secured lender, a consumer-electronics store. Once those secured creditors were paid in full, Viegelahn was to begin distributing funds to Harris' unsecured creditors.

Implementation of the plan was short lived. Harris again fell behind on his mortgage payments, and in November 2010, Chase received permission from the Bankruptcy Court to foreclose on Harris' home. Following the foreclosure, Viegelahn continued to receive $530 per month from Harris' wages, but stopped making the payments earmarked for Chase. As a result, funds formerly reserved for Chase accumulated in Viegelahn's possession.

On November 22, 2011, Harris exercised his statutory right to convert his Chapter 13 case to one under Chapter 7. By that time, Harris' postpetition wages accumulated by Viegelahn amounted to $5,519.22. On December 1, 2011—ten days after Harris' conversion—Viegelahn disposed of those funds by giving $1,200 to Harris' counsel, paying herself a $267.79 fee, and distributing the remaining money to the consumer-electronics store and six of Harris' unsecured creditors.

Asserting that Viegelahn lacked authority to disburse funds to creditors once the case was converted to Chapter 7, Harris moved the Bankruptcy Court for an order directing refund of the accumulated wages Viegelahn had given to his creditors. The Bankruptcy Court granted Harris' motion, and the District Court affirmed.

The Fifth Circuit reversed. . . . Notwithstanding a Chapter 13 debtor's conversion to Chapter 7, the Fifth Circuit held, a former Chapter 13 trustee must distribute a debtor's accumulated postpetition wages to his creditors.

The Fifth Circuit acknowledged that its decision conflicted with the Third Circuit's decision . . . which held that a debtor's undistributed postpetition wages "are to be returned to the debtor at the time of conversion [from Chapter 13 to Chapter 7]." We granted certiorari to resolve this conflict, and now reverse the Fifth Circuit's judgment.

* * *

Prior to the Bankruptcy Reform Act of 1994, courts divided . . . on the disposition of a debtor's undistributed postpetition wages following conversion of a proceeding from Chapter 13 to Chapter 7. . . .

Congress addressed the matter in 1994 by adding § 348(f) to the Bankruptcy Code. Rejecting the rulings of several Courts of Appeals, § 348(f)(1)(A) provides that in a case converted from Chapter 13, a debtor's postpetition earnings and acquisitions do not become part of the new Chapter 7 estate:

> "[P]roperty of the [Chapter 7] estate in the converted case shall consist of property of the estate, as of the date of filing of the [initial Chapter 13] petition, that remains in the possession of or is under the control of the debtor on the date of conversion."

In § 348(f)(2), Congress added an exception for debtors who convert in bad faith:

> "If the debtor converts a case [initially filed] under chapter 13 . . . in bad faith, the property of the estate in the converted case shall consist of the property of the estate as of the date of the conversion."

Section 348(f), all agree, makes one thing clear: A debtor's postpetition wages, including undisbursed funds in the hands of a trustee, ordinarily do not become part of the Chapter 7 estate created by conversion. Absent a bad-faith conversion, § 348(f) limits a converted Chapter 7 estate to property belonging to the debtor "as of the date" the original Chapter 13 petition was filed. Postpetition wages, by definition, do not fit that bill.

* * *

By excluding postpetition wages from the converted Chapter 7 estate, § 348(f)(1)(A) removes those earnings from the pool of assets that may be liquidated and distributed to creditors. Allowing a terminated Chapter 13 trustee to disburse the very same earnings to the very same creditors is incompatible with that statutory design. We resist attributing to Congress, after explicitly exempting from Chapter 7's liquidation-and-distribution process a debtor's postpetition wages, a plan to place those wages in creditors' hands another way.

* * *

Section 348(e) also informs our ruling that undistributed postpetition wages must be returned to the debtor. That section provides: "Conversion [from Chapter 13 to Chapter 7] terminates the service of [the Chapter 13] trustee." A core service provided by a Chapter 13 trustee is the disbursement of "payments *to creditors*." § 1326(c) (emphasis added). The moment a case is converted from Chapter 13 to Chapter 7, however, the Chapter 13 trustee is stripped of authority to provide that "service." § 348(e).

* * *

Viegelahn cites two Chapter 13 provisions in support of her argument that the Bankruptcy Code *requires* a terminated Chapter 13 trustee "to distribute undisbursed funds to creditors." Brief for Respondent 21. The first, § 1327(a), provides that a confirmed Chapter 13 plan "bind[s] the debtor and each creditor." The second, § 1326(a)(2), instructs a trustee to distribute "payment[s] in accordance with the plan," and that, Viegelahn observes, is just what she did. But the cited provisions had no force here, for they ceased to apply once the case was converted to Chapter 7.

* * *

We acknowledge the "fortuit[y]," as the Fifth Circuit called it, that a "debtor's chance of having funds returned" is "dependent on the trustee's speed in distributing the payments" to creditors. A trustee who distributes payments regularly may have little or no accumulated wages to return. When a trustee distributes payments infrequently, on the other hand, a debtor who converts to Chapter 7 may be entitled to a sizable refund. These outcomes, however, follow directly from Congress' decisions to shield postpetition wages from creditors in a converted Chapter 7 case, § 348(f)(1)(A), and to give Chapter 13 debtors a right to convert to Chapter 7 "at any time," § 1307(a). Moreover, creditors may gain protection against the risk of excess accumulations in the hands of Chapter 13 trustees by seeking to include in a Chapter 13 plan a schedule for regular disbursement of funds the trustee collects.

For the reasons stated, the judgment of the United States Court of Appeals for the Fifth Circuit is reversed, and the case is remanded for further proceedings consistent with this opinion.

(Citations omitted.)

NOTES AND COMMENTS

1. The *Harris* Court notes one exception to the rule that, upon conversion, property of the Chapter 7 estate does not include post-filing property. That exception involves "bad-faith" conversion to Chapter 7. Given that the debtor has an absolute right to convert from Chapter 13 to Chapter 7, how can the debtor do so in bad faith? As an example, *see* In re Siegfried, 219 B.R. 581 (Bankr. D. Colo. 1998), in which the court held that the debtor's conversion was in bad faith. The alleged bad-faith behavior included:

> . . . the conversion occurred on the eve of the hearing set before this Court to consider (1) objections to confirmation of Debtor's Chapter 13 Plan . . . and (2) the Trustee's Motion to Dismiss premised on Debtor's ineligibility for relief under 11 U.S.C. § 109(e) based on the amount of his unsecured debt. Additionally, . . . Debtor failed to disclose all of his debts in his bankruptcy schedules, failed to commit all of his disposable income to the Plan as required by 11 U.S.C. § 1325(b)(1)(B), and failed to reveal funds to which Debtor was entitled from an overbid on a foreclosure of property in which Debtor had an interest. Further, . . . Debtor knew or should have known all along that his unsecured debts exceeded the unsecured debt threshold . . . under 11 U.S.C. § 109(e).

In re Siegfried, 219 B.R. at 582-583.

2. The court found that the debtor's behavior "evidences a pattern of dissembling, failure to fully or accurately disclose financial affairs, disingenuous explanations of wrongful conduct and unfair manipulation of the bankruptcy system to the detriment of his creditors. This continuing pattern of lack of disclosure and procedural gymnastics, combined with an eleventh-hour conversion to another chapter to avoid imminent . . . is sufficient to find that this case was converted in bad faith." In re Siegfried, 219 B.R. 581 at 585–86.

D. BANKRUPTCY IN PRACTICE

Assume that Diana filed a Chapter 13 bankruptcy petition on December 1 of last year. In the six months preceding her filing, she made $0 per month in June and July because, as a teacher, she is on a ten-month contract. She earns $5,000 per month, but takes home $4,000 after taxes during each of the months of her contract. Her debts include monthly child support of $500; Catie's medical expenses of approximately $500 per month; her boss's claim for $300,000 for intentional infliction of emotional distress; the insurance companies' claims for $25,000 for the boss's car and $30,000 for the boss's medical expenses. Of course, she also has monthly food expenses (about $300), her monthly mortgage payment of $1,500, gas and other automobile expenses of about $300 monthly. Is Diana eligible for Chapter 13? If so, will she need to file a three-year or five-year plan? Can she create a feasible plan? If so, do her creditors have any other argument against confirmation of a Chapter 13 plan?

7

Business Law and Bankruptcy: Chapter 11 Reorganizations

> The object of Chapter 11 of the Bankruptcy Code is to empower
> a debtor with going concern value to reorganize its operations to
> become solvent once more.[1]

Under Chapter 7 of the Bankruptcy Code, business entities that enter bankruptcy are liquidated and ultimately cease to exist. By contrast, under Chapter 11 of the Bankruptcy Code, businesses may file a bankruptcy proceeding with the goal of being reorganized and continuing on as a viable entity. Recall that bankruptcy law is driven by the Bankruptcy Code, and continued reference to that code is essential. Pursuant to the Bankruptcy Code, in a Chapter 11 bankruptcy, debtors work with creditors to draft a plan of reorganization. That plan, if and when approved by the bankruptcy court, becomes the roadmap for how the entity will emerge from bankruptcy to continue being a viable enterprise. Chapter 11 of the Bankruptcy Code is designed, at least in part, to help businesses make a "fresh start."

Chapter 11 reorganizations have been the subject of much debate over the past several decades.[2] Some scholars have argued that Chapter 11 would not be necessary if enterprises simply specified in their contracts with creditors what exactly would happen in the event of a default. Others argue that the reorganization process can be abused to disenfranchise otherwise entitled creditors from their rightful recovery from a debtor. It has also

---

1. Justice Kennedy, N.C.P. Mktg. Grp., Inc. v. BG Star Prods., Inc., 556 U.S. 1145 (2009).
2. For a discussion of the critiques of the modern Chapter 11 bankruptcy reorganization, see Douglass Baird and Robert K. Rassmusen, *The End of Bankruptcy*, 55 Stan L. Rev. 751 (2002).

been observed that many large enterprises are using Chapter 11 merely as a means to sell their assets in a "363 sale" (discussed below) and then divide up the proceeds. Empirically, the vast majority of distressed businesses do not opt to enter a Chapter 11 bankruptcy reorganization, and the vast bulk that do, do not end up with a successful reorganization. Nevertheless, Chapter 11 reorganizations remain an available device for troubled enterprises hoping to remain viable. Moreover, many large enterprises continue to file for protection under Chapter 11, even if it is with the goal of selling the bulk of their business' assets.

As with other areas of the law, the business law that governs outside of bankruptcy is still very relevant inside of bankruptcy. Business law generally is designed to strike a balance between encouraging business development and protecting investors and the public. Likewise, Chapter 11 is designed to encourage businesses that have faltered to reorganize and continue to be productive, while protecting creditors and the public more generally.

DIANA DETTER AND HER BUSINESS'S BANKRUPTCY

First, as you review the material in this chapter, recall again our hypothetical scenario with our debtor, Diana. Developments in her case implicate business law as it intersects with the law of bankruptcy. Consider this hypothetical scenario as you learn in this chapter about, among other things: (1) fiduciary duties in bankruptcy, (2) the development of a plan of reorganization, and (3) use of the debtor's property. Finally, consider (4) any possibility that the Chapter 11 reorganization discussed here might be either dismissed or converted to a Chapter 7 liquidation.

Diana holds 1,000 shares of BigCo, Inc., a company that manufactures electronics. As a minority shareholder, Diane is not involved in the business in any way. BigCo had great success in the early 2000s, working closely with manufacturers of personal digital assistants (PDAs). But PDAs became obsolete with the introduction of smartphones, and BigCo had trouble transitioning its business to meet modern technology. Several newspaper articles even suggested that BigCo's board of directors had an ulterior motive because several of the board members had significant investments in companies developing smartphones.

BigCo filed for Chapter 11 bankruptcy protection six months ago and put forward a plan of reorganization almost immediately. Under the plan, trade creditors will receive 98 percent of their claim amounts. However, the minority shareholders will receive nothing under the plan, and the general unsecured creditors will receive just 10 percent of their claim amounts. The majority shareholders will receive stock in the newly

> reorganized BigCo in exchange for new capital contributions to the new company.
>
> A liquidation analysis suggests that, had BigCo been liquidated, unsecured creditors would have received no more than $.05 on the dollar. But the liquidation analysis fails to account for a copyright infringement lawsuit that BigCo brought against a competing company, which has yet to be resolved.

Because basic business law principles are still very much relevant, this chapter will begin in Section A with a review of some core business law concepts. Section B will then introduce the heart of a Chapter 11 bankruptcy: the plan of reorganization. The plan is the roadmap that outlines how the debtor will be able to emerge from the bankruptcy as a viable, productive business. Section C will examine special rules for small or single-asset debtors. Section D will discuss the lease, use, or sale of the debtor's property. Finally, Section E will examine how a reorganization under Chapter 11 can, if ultimately necessary, be dismissed or converted to a liquidation under Chapter 7.

A. REVIEW OF CORE DOCTRINE: BUSINESS LAW

This section will review some core areas of business law, including business organization, ownership and management, and fiduciary duties. It will also present some case materials as examples of how that core business law is implicated in bankruptcy.

1. Organization and Management

Entrepreneurs have a wide *choice of business entities* with which to organize their business. Generally, that choice is driven by a desire for *limited liability* and the most *optimal tax situation* possible. The *management structure* of each business entity is largely dictated by the business entity chosen.

a. Choice of Business Entity

Limited liability refers to the notion that the owners of the business entity will not be personally liable for the debts of the business. Owners will only be liable for the amount they invested into the business. This principle is qualified by the idea of *piercing the corporate veil*. Pursuant to that doctrine, in certain limited circumstances, plaintiffs can get a court to disregard the business entity and hold the owners of the business personally liable for the debts of the business. Courts considering whether to pierce the corporate veil take into account a variety of factors including whether there is some unfairness in the way the business entity has been used, undercapitalization, lack of following business formalities, or a co-mingling of the business's assets with the assets of the owners or other businesses.[3] While the doctrine is most frequently described using the word "corporate," it also applies to other limited liability business entities such as limited liability companies.

The concept of limited liability is particularly important in the context of bankruptcy. It means that creditors in the bankruptcy will not be able to recover from any of the owners of the business entity, absent some personal guaranty given by an owner or a successful piercing the veil claim. This is exactly why owners choose entities that provide them with limited liability.

Sophisticated creditors are aware of the principle of limited liability, of course. They can protect themselves when contracting with a limited liability business entity by demanding personal guaranties from an owner or owners, or by taking a security interest of some sort to protect their position. Recall that a security interest provides a creditor with access to specific property or cash flow if the debtor defaults on the debt. Security interests will be discussed more fully later in this chapter.

There are generally two distinct types of *tax treatment* that business entities receive in the United States: (1) partnership-like tax treatment, perhaps more commonly known as "pass-through tax treatment," and (2) corporate tax treatment. With pass-through tax treatment, the income or loss of the business passes directly through to the income of the owners. Where there is more than one owner, the income or loss passes through in accordance with owner's percentage interest in the business.

With corporate tax treatment, there are two levels of tax. The business is first taxed on its profits or losses. Then, when income is distributed to owners in the form of dividends, those owners are taxed on the dividends at 0, 15, or 20 percent, depending on each owner's income. Individuals with higher incomes have their dividends taxed at the higher rate.[4]

Note, however, that corporations also can be organized as S corporations. Such corporations still are entitled to pass-through tax treatment. In

---

3. For a discussion of piercing the corporate veil and a variety of the factors courts use to make their determination, *see* DeWitt v. W. Ray Flemming Fruit, 540 F.2d 681 (4th Cir. S.C. May 13, 1976).

4. For example, in 2019 individuals filing taxes with less than $39,375 in income pay 0 percent on dividend income; individuals with more than $39,375, but less than $434,550, pay 15 percent; and individuals with more than $434,550 pay 20 percent.

order to be an S corporation, certain requirements must be followed. For example, an S corporation must have fewer than 100 shareholders, have only one class of stock, and have no aliens or artificial entities as shareholders. The double taxation that is characteristic of corporate tax treatment is afforded to C corporations, which are not restricted by the requirements of the S corporation.

Historically, pass-through tax treatment was considered very favorable because losses from the business could offset other income of the owners. In addition, the ultimate rate of tax under pass-through tax treatment was typically lower than under corporate tax treatment because there was only one level of tax, not two.

At the end of 2017, however, the United States passed the Tax Cuts and Jobs Act of 2017 (the 2017 Tax Reform Act). The 2017 Tax Reform Act lowered corporate tax rates from a high marginal rate of 35 percent to essentially a flat rate of 21 percent. This is dramatically lower than the higher individual tax rates that can apply if pass-through tax treatment is used. Indeed, in 2019 the highest marginal rate of tax for individuals is 37 percent.

The C corporation is often chosen because it provides the business owners with the desired limited liability and because the tax situation, especially now in the wake of the 2017 Tax Reform Act, can be very favorable. Moreover, the corporate form has such a long track record that the laws and regulations that relate thereto are relatively well understood with the outcomes of disputes being relatively predictable. Because of these desirable attributes, the C corporation is the dominant form of business organization for large business in the United States.

CHOICE OF BUSINESS ENTITY — LIMITED LIABILITY AND TAXES Here is a review of some of the most commonly used business entities:				
Type of entity	**Ownership**	**Registration**	**Liability for owners**	**Tax treatment**
Sole proprietorship	Single owner	None required	No limited liability	Pass-through taxation
General partnership	Two or more owners	None required	No limited liability	Pass-through taxation
Limited partnership	Two types of partners (general and limited)	State registration required	Limited liability for limited partners only	Pass-through taxation

CHOICE OF BUSINESS ENTITY — LIMITED LIABILITY AND TAXES

Here is a review of some of the most commonly used business entities:

Type of entity	Ownership	Registration	Liability for owners	Tax treatment
Limited liability partnership	Two or more owners	State registration required	Limited liability for all partners	Pass-through taxation
Limited liability company	One or more owners	State registration required	Limited liability for all owners	Choice of tax treatment
S corporation	One or more owners	State registration required	Limited liability for all owners	Pass-through taxation
C corporation	One or more owners	State registration required	Limited liability for all owners	Corporate tax treatment

b. Management

The different business entities have different management structures. Sole proprietors, since there is only one owner, are managed by their owner, the sole proprietor. General partnerships are managed by all the partners jointly, and each partner has joint and several liability with the other partners. Limited partnerships are managed by the general partners. In fact, if limited partners take on any management roles, they might be deemed general partners and thus exposed to unlimited personal liability for the debts of the business.

Limited liability companies are a bit more complex. They can be managed in a dispersed management structure by all the owners (called "members"). Alternatively, they can be managed by a select group of members (called "managing members") to achieve a more centralized management structure.

Corporations are managed hierarchically by corporate officers who operate under the supervision of a board of directors. The equity owners of the corporation (the shareholders) do not participate in management as shareholders at all, though the officers and directors may be shareholders themselves. The shareholders elect the directors. Thus, the corporate management structure reflects a corporate democracy. The directors, who are not necessarily employees of the corporation, meet regularly and review corporate operations to provide broad oversight and goals for the corporation. The officers, by comparison, are corporate employees who run the daily affairs of the corporation.

In a Chapter 11 reorganization, ironically, many or all of the managers who led the debtor into the bankruptcy are often retained to help see the debtor through the bankruptcy process. While most bankruptcy filings lead to the appointment of a panel trustee, Chapter 11 bankruptcy cases[5] allow a "debtor-in-possession" to oversee the bankruptcy case. The debtor-in-possession is indeed the incumbent management team of the debtor. The role of the debtor-in-possession largely mirrors that of the trustee. 11 U.S.C. § 1107 ("a debtor in possession shall have all the rights, other than the right to compensation . . . and powers, and shall perform all the functions and duties . . . of a trustee").

While the idea of allowing management to continue for a company that has filed bankruptcy may seem odd, keep in mind that a reorganization effort has more chance of succeeding if management has some expertise in the business. A panel trustee may not have the expertise necessary to run a particular business or the time needed to learn the business in order to ensure a successful reorganization. Concerns regarding the business acumen or honesty and good faith of management can be taken care of through court oversight, appointment of an examiner, or even appointment of a trustee in extreme cases.[6]

2. Fiduciary Duties

The members of the board of directors and the officers of a corporation owe fiduciary duties to the business, and those duties continue during the bankruptcy process. The two clear pillars of fiduciary duties under state corporate law are (1) the duty of care and (2) the duty of loyalty. These duties are also required of partners in a partnership and any members who act as management in a limited liability company.

a. The Duty of Care

The *duty of care* is exactly what it sounds like. It is a process-oriented duty to act with due care in managing a business entity. There are two contexts

---

5. *See also* 11 U.S.C. §§ 1203, 1304 (permitting debtor-in-possession in cases under Chapter 12, and continuation of business operations by a Chapter 13 individual debtor engaged in business operations).

6. A trustee or examiner may be appointed for cause or if such an appointment serves the interest of creditors. 11 U.S.C. § 1104.

for the duty of care: the first requires the board members and officers to act with good faith and diligence in conducting the affairs of the business; the second requires diligence in the oversight context.[7]

In the first context, the duty of care requires that the managers have or gain the requisite knowledge to make informed decisions on behalf of the company. In the famous Smith v. Van Gorkom case, the board members were deemed to have violated the duty of care when they approved a sale of the company without having had the time to fully consider the transaction and its details.[8]

The defense to a duty of care claim is the deferential *business judgment rule*. That rule provides that judges give deference to the good faith business judgment of business managers. Thus, if a business judgment does not prove successful for a business, it is still not a violation of the duty of care. Instead, courts will defer to the managers' good faith business judgment as long as that judgment was the product of an appropriate and diligent process. Indeed, shareholders elect board members, who in turn hire executive officers especially for their ability to make potentially risky business decisions. Accordingly, the fact that a business decision turns out to create losses for shareholders is not sufficient to allow for a successful cause of action against the decision makers.

In handling the second type of cases—those involving managerial supervision—the Delaware Court of Chancery looked to whether "reporting systems exist in the organization that are reasonably designed to provide to senior management and to the board itself timely, accurate information sufficient to allow management and the board, each within its scope, to reach informed judgments concerning both the corporation's compliance with law and its business performance."[9] Assuming such reporting systems are put into place and are monitored, the business managers have acted with due care in their supervisory capacity.

Note that in an effort to protect business managers from personal liability resulting from a duty of care violation, states have adopted so-called raincoat statutes. Such statutes allow companies to specifically state in their charters that managers will not be personally liable for any unintentional violations of a duty of care. Insurance covering officer and director conduct can also be purchased by companies to reimburse managers for any personal liability where there was no intentional misconduct.

---

7. In re Caremark Intern. Inc. Derivative Litigation, 698 A.2d 959, 967-8 (Del. Ch. 1996).
8. Smith v. Van Gorkom, 488 A.2d 858 (Del. 1985).
9. *Caremark,* 698 A.2d at 970.

b. The Duty of Loyalty

Directors and officers must put the interests of the corporation ahead of their own interests in handling business transactions. This *duty of loyalty* ensures that directors and officers do not use their position of trust to personally gain at the expense of the business.[10] The duty of loyalty is often invoked because an officer or director is engaged in self-dealing, such as being on both sides of a transaction (for example, selling assets of the company to another company owned or controlled by the same director).

A duty of loyalty is also owed by business entities that are the parents of subsidiaries. In that case, a violation might be triggered where parent management stands on both sides of a transaction and puts its interests ahead of the interests of its subsidiary.

While such self-dealing is not per se invalid, an officer, director, or parent company engaged in self-dealing has the burden of showing the "entire fairness" of the transaction.[11] Entire fairness includes both procedural and substantive fairness. Procedural fairness relates to fair dealing. Substantive fairness often is judged by the pricing of any particular transaction.[12]

Consider the *Brook Valley* case, excerpted below, as an example of a bankruptcy case where the court clearly explained, examined, and enforced the core fiduciary duties of business managers to a bankruptcy estate. While the court discusses the duty of care, the violation in this case involved the duty of loyalty.

In re Brook Valley VII, Joint Venture

496 F.3d 892 (8th Cir. 2007)

COLLOTON, Circuit Judge

Rick D. Lange, the bankruptcy trustee for debtors . . . brought suit against Robert C. Schropp, Leo E. Dahlke, and several entities controlled by Schropp and/or Dahlke. Lange alleges that Schropp and Dahlke breached their fiduciary duties to the bankruptcy estates and converted property of the estates. After a two-day trial, the bankruptcy court concluded that Schropp and Dahlke had violated their fiduciary duties. To remedy this breach, the court imposed a constructive trust on their gains from the sale of the properties and awarded damages. . . . the Eighth Circuit Bankruptcy Appellate Panel

---

10. Guth v. Loft, Inc., 5 A.2d 503, 510 (Del. 1939).
11. Weinberger v. UOP, Inc., 457 A.2d 701, 710-711 (Del. 1983).
12. *Id.*

(BAP) . . . affirmed the bankruptcy court's finding. . . . We affirm the ruling of the BAP.

I.

Schropp and Dahlke were partners in thirteen commercial real estate partnerships with Prime Realty, an entity controlled by James McCart. The debtors . . . were two of these partnerships, with each owning a single commercial property in Omaha. In September 2001, a dispute arose between the partners in the Brook Valley joint ventures. In response to this falling out, McCart's company (Prime Realty) filed suit to dissolve all thirteen partnerships, including the two at issue in this appeal. By March 2002, several lenders had foreclosed on the partnerships' properties, causing Schropp, Dahlke, and Prime Realty to lose substantial sums of money. As a result, Prime Realty filed for bankruptcy protection in March 2002.

The Brook Valley partnerships suffered a similar fate. . . . In addition to the mortgage with First National, the properties were allegedly encumbered by liens held by Darland Construction Company and Prime Realty. . . . After filing for bankruptcy, both partnerships acted as debtors in possession under the exclusive control of Schropp and Dahlke.

Seventeen days after filing for bankruptcy protection, Schropp and Dahlke, acting on behalf of the bankruptcy estates, consented to a foreclosure sale of the two Brook Valley properties. Prime Realty, the entity controlled by McCart and a partner in both ventures, objected to the sale, arguing that it did not serve the interests of the bankruptcy estates. McCart argued that the properties had substantial equity and produced sufficient rents to service the debt to First National. Concerned that Schropp and Dahlke were unwilling to act in the estates' interests, Prime Realty requested the appointment of a trustee. After the bankruptcy court denied this request, McCart remained convinced that the properties were more valuable than Schropp and Dahlke had acknowledged, and he attempted to buy the properties at the foreclosure sale. Because of Prime Realty's precarious financial position, McCart could not raise the necessary capital.

The foreclosure sale occurred on September 24, 2002. The winning bidder, at a combined cost of $2,406,430 for both properties, was Phoenix Properties LLC, an entity controlled by Schropp and Dahlke. Schropp and Dahlke did not disclose their controlling interest in Phoenix Properties. At the time of the sale, both Great Western Bank and First National conducted appraisals of the properties. Great Western appraised the properties at $3,310,105, while First National valued them between $2,480,000 and $3,700,000. These appraisals suggest that Phoenix purchased the properties at a considerable discount. Thus, the decision to consent to the foreclosure sale had proved lucrative for Schropp and Dahlke, if not for the bankruptcy estates and the creditors.

Schropp and Dahlke financed most of the acquisition with a loan from Great Western Bank, while an entity called Phoenix Brook Valley Re–Cap provided an additional $600,000. The terms of the foreclosure sale required all bidders other than First National to pay in cash the amount of the estates' debt to First National. Any amount beyond this would be paid to the bankruptcy court pending a determination of the priority of the remaining liens. Phoenix Properties failed to abide by this stricture, purporting to "credit bid" the amount of the Darland lien, rather than pay this amount to the bankruptcy court, as required by the terms of the sale.

Shortly after the foreclosure sale, in November 2002, McCart discovered that Schropp and Dahlke had been on both sides of the foreclosure sale as controlling partners of both Phoenix Properties and the Brook Valley partnerships. Upon learning this fact, Prime Realty filed another motion requesting the appointment of a trustee, and accused Schropp and Dahlke of secretly buying estate property. . . .

Th[eir] response, of course, did not acknowledge that Schropp and Dahlke had controlling interests in both the debtors in possession and Phoenix Properties. The bankruptcy court found it "misleading," and concluded that "Mr. Schropp and Mr. Dahlke, through their counsel, who were also counsel for the debtors, went to a lot of trouble to keep the ownership of Phoenix Properties a secret from the court and from counsel for Prime Realty."

On June 10, 2004, all of the debtors' assets having been sold, the bankruptcy court converted the case to a Chapter 7 proceeding and appointed the Appellee, Rick Lange, as trustee of both estates. . . .

After a two-day trial, the bankruptcy court found in the trustee's favor and imposed a constructive trust on the net proceeds of the sale. In addition, the court found that $146,862.35, which Schropp and Dahlke "credit bid" at the foreclosure sale but never paid, was property of the bankruptcy estates and had been converted by Schropp and Dahlke. The bankruptcy court also found that the net cash flow earned by the partnerships in the period between the filing for bankruptcy and the foreclosure sale ($86,581.32, plus interest) was property of the estate, and the court awarded that amount to the trustee. The court nonetheless concluded that the last two amounts would not be due if Schropp and Dahlke complied with the order establishing a constructive trust. The court also declined to award damages for operating profits generated by the properties after the sale to Phoenix Properties.

* * *

Schropp and Dahlke argue that the trustee's action against them is an impermissible collateral attack on the bankruptcy court's order allowing the debtors to proceed with the foreclosure sale. In their view, property interests acquired at a foreclosure sale are "good against the world" and thus are not subject to later attack by the trustee.

Once a sale of assets has been approved by a final order of the bankruptcy court, it is "a judgment that is good as against the world, not merely as against parties to the proceeding." Under this standard, property rights acquired at a foreclosure sale cannot be challenged unless the procedural rules allow for a collateral attack. *See* Fed. R. Civ. P. 60(b); Fed. R. Bankr. P. 9024. Thus, if the trustee discovers that the order permitting a foreclosure sale has been obtained wrongfully, Rule 60(b) governs his ability to obtain relief from the otherwise final judgment.

We conclude, however, that Rule 60(b) does not apply in this circumstance. This action does not directly attack the validity of the foreclosure sale. Instead, the trustee alleges a breach of fiduciary duty and requests that the gains enjoyed by Schropp and Dahlke be placed in a constructive trust, to be conveyed to the estates. The court need not set aside the judgment approving the foreclosure sale to effect a disgorgement of these allegedly ill-gotten gains. Thus, the trustee's action is not an impermissible collateral attack on a final sale, because he does not seek to abrogate the foreclosure sale. Rather, he seeks a remedy for an alleged breach of fiduciary duty, where the remedy presumes the continued validity of the foreclosure sale itself.

* * *

. . . because the properties were part of the estates at the time of the foreclosure sale, we must decide whether Schropp and Dahlke acted improperly by bidding. The bankruptcy court held that there is a *per se* prohibition on debtors in possession purchasing estate property at a foreclosure sale. On appeal, the BAP ruled that while there was no *per se* prohibition, Schropp and Dahlke violated their fiduciary duties in this case by consenting to the foreclosure sale and then bidding. In this appeal, Schropp and Dahlke argue that there is no blanket prohibition on such bidding, and that they did not act improperly by bidding at the foreclosure sale.

Debtors in possession and those who control them owe fiduciary duties to the bankruptcy estate. Thus, the partners in a bankrupt partnership, acting as a debtor in possession, must run the business as agents of the bankruptcy estate, and not for their own personal gain. The fiduciary obligation consists of two duties: the duty of care and the duty of loyalty. The duty of care requires the fiduciary to make good-faith decisions that can be attributed to a rational business purpose. In general, courts do not second-guess business decisions made in good faith.

The duty of loyalty comes into play when there appears to be a conflict between the interests of the fiduciary and the entity to which he owes loyalty. For a debtor in possession, this duty "includes an obligation to refrain from self-dealing, to avoid conflicts of interests and the appearance of impropriety, to treat all parties to the case fairly and to maximize the value of the estate." "Courts have held that managers of debtors in possession breached their duty of loyalty by . . . participating as an undisclosed bidder at an auction of estate property."

Though some courts—including the bankruptcy court in this case—have held that bidding for estate property always violates the debtor in possession's duty of loyalty, we need not adopt this blanket rule to conclude that Schropp and Dahlke violated their duties here. Only seventeen days after filing the bankruptcy petitions, Schropp and Dahlke consented to relief from the automatic stay. This consent implicitly represented to the court that Schropp and Dahlke believed foreclosure to be in the estates' interests. This could be the case only if the properties could not be operated profitably on the estates' behalf. In fact, the properties remained profitable after the partnerships filed for bankruptcy, and the appraisals of the property revealed substantial equity. Schropp and Dahlke proceeded to bid secretly at the foreclosure sale and take possession of the properties unencumbered by any duties to the bankruptcy estates. Rather than searching for financing to make their own purchase of the properties, Schropp and Dahlke "should have been making efforts to obtain financing on behalf of the *Debtors* to salvage the properties."

When a transaction involving an insider is challenged as breaching the insider's duty of loyalty, the fiduciary must prove that the transaction was fair and reasonable. Schropp and Dahlke have failed to carry this burden. Initially, they caused the debtors to consent to relief from the automatic stay. Then, they secretly bid at the foreclosure sale, paying considerably less than the appraised value of the properties. After Prime Realty objected, Schropp and Dahlke misled the court about their holdings in Phoenix Properties. The actions of Schropp and Dahlke support the BAP's conclusion that they were looking out for themselves rather than the estates.

* * *

(Citations omitted.)

NOTES AND COMMENTS

1. To whom does the debtor-in-possession owe fiduciary duties? *See* Commodity Futures Trading Commission v. Weintraub, 471 U.S. 343, 355 (1985) ("[I]f a debtor remains in possession . . . the debtor's directors bear essentially the same fiduciary obligation to creditors and shareholders as would the trustee. . . . [T]he management of a debtor-in-possession would have to exercise control . . . consistently with this obligation to treat all parties, not merely the shareholders, fairly.").

2. What should the debtor-in-possession's attorney do when faced with possible breach of a fiduciary duty by the debtor-in-possession? Consider the case of Zeisler & Zeisler, P.C. v. Prudential Ins. Co. of America (In re JLM, Inc.), 210 B.R. 19 (2d Cir. 1997). In *JLM*, the actions arose from the potentially improper dismissal by a controlling creditor of the management of the debtor company. No evidence was presented regarding whether counsel for the debtor-in-possession attempted to counsel the parties as to their fiduciary obligations. The court discussed the attorney's obligations:

> In the nonbankruptcy context, absent ongoing fraud or criminal activity, an attorney's obligation is to advise the client and, if the client disagrees, resign. Conn. Rules of Professional Conduct Rules 1.13(C), 1.16, & 3.3. But because "[b]ankruptcy causes fundamental changes in the nature of corporate relationships," *Commodity Futures Trading Comm'n v. Weintraub*, 471 U.S. 343, 355 (1985), obligating the corporation's board of directors to consider the best interests of creditors, and because counsel for the debtor in possession has fiduciary obligations not ordinarily foisted upon the attorney-client relationship, the attorney for the debtor in possession may not simply resign where the client refuses the attorney's advice concerning the client's fiduciary obligations to the estate and its creditors. Counsel must do more, informing the court in some manner of derogation by the debtor in

> possession. . . . It is to ensure this integrity of the bankruptcy process where, by definition, a debtor in possession is not disinterested, that counsel for the debtor in possession must be disinterested, free of any adverse entanglements which could cloud its judgment respecting what is best for the estate.

In re JLM at 26.

B. THE PLAN OF REORGANIZATION

At the heart of a Chapter 11 reorganization is a reorganization plan. The basic idea of a Chapter 11 reorganization is that the debtor still has valuable business assets that can be reorganized in a way that will allow the overall business to be viable and productive. Part of the Chapter 11 bankruptcy, therefore, is a reorganization plan that details how the business will be restructured to achieve viability going forward. This section will address how such plans are created and proposed, then move to how they are approved and confirmed. But first, we will consider first day orders, court orders that allow the debtor in a Chapter 11 case to continue day-to-day operations long enough to get through to at least the creation, if not also confirmation, of a detailed reorganization plan.

TIMELINE OF A CHAPTER 11 REORGANIZATION

Chapter 11 cases are complicated because no two cases are alike. Unlike a Chapter 13 case, in which some districts have a form repayment plan used by all debtors, each Chapter 11 case plan is a unique creation tailored to the situation of that debtor. Even so, the general timeline of a Chapter 11 case involves the following steps:

1. Filing the petition and schedules

2. Deciding on first day motions, which are designed to ensure that basic business functions (such as paying employees) continue as the reorganization begins

3. Forming the committee of unsecured creditors and other committees as needed

4. Operating the debtor throughout the bankruptcy case, often including:

   a. Determining whether to accept or reject executory contracts

b. Obtaining credit or other financing

c. Deciding which property to use, sell, or lease

5. Providing additional documentation as required by the Bankruptcy Code; most of the documentation will be financial documents detailing the ongoing operations of the company

6. Creating the plan of reorganization

7. Approving and confirming the plan of reorganization, or, if not confirmed, considering alternative plans, converting to liquidation, or dismissing the case

8. If confirmed, closing the case and beginning operations under the confirmed plan

Some cases, even in Chapter 11, involve the liquidation of the debtor company or a sale of the company as a going concern. This liquidation/sale may take place pursuant to Section 363 of the bankruptcy code, which allows the sale of assets outside of the ordinary course of business with court approval.

1. First Day Orders

In order for a business to operate, it has to meet its basic obligations. It must pay employees, suppliers, and utility companies. While the automatic stay of bankruptcy prevents creditors from suing the company to collect on obligations owed, it does not mandate that these parties continue to work with the debtor. But if these parties refuse to work with the debtor, successful reorganization is jeopardized.

In order to ensure that these parties continue to work with the debtor-in-possession, courts often issue *first day orders* allowing for payment of these parties. The Code does not provide express authority for such orders; the authority of the court comes from the Code's general equity provision, 11 U.S.C. § 105, which states that "[t]he court may issue any order, process, or judgment that is necessary or appropriate to carry out the provisions of this title." The process begins with one or more first day motions submitted by the debtor for the court's approval.

The following case provides an example of a court considering first day motions. Note, once again, the primacy of the Bankruptcy Code itself wherein the court finds the standards relevant to the approval of those motions.

In re The Colad Group, Inc.

324 B.R. 208 (Bankr. W.D.N.Y. 2005)

Bucki, Bankruptcy Judge

This case provides an unusual opportunity to consider standards for the approval of first day motions in a case filed under chapter 11.

The Colad Group, Inc. ("Colad") is a specialty printer, whose primary business involves the production and sale of custom folders, binders and other stationery products. On the evening of Thursday, February 3, 2005, Colad electronically filed a petition for relief under chapter 11 of the Bankruptcy Code. The following day, debtor's counsel contacted the court to schedule an opportunity on an emergency basis to seek the court's approval of "first day orders." . . .

Daniel Williams is the largest creditor in the chapter 7 bankruptcy case of William P. Brosnahan, Jr., an individual who at one time was affiliated with Colad. In the present context, it is not necessary to relate the complex and contentious issues that the Brosnahan case has presented. Rather, it suffices to note that Colad identifies the bankruptcy estate of Brosnahan as its largest unsecured creditor, and that Brosnahan's trustee has named Colad as a defendant in various adversary proceedings. For these reasons, this court directed that the Brosnahan trustee and its largest creditor receive notice of the conference and hearing relative to any first day motions in the Colad case. Mr. Williams participated in those proceedings, and his objections have served to focus the court's attention on a number of issues that have long had need for explication.

In bankruptcy practice, the phrase "first day motions" refers generally to any of a variety of requests made shortly after the filing of a chapter 11 petition, for prompt authorizations needed to facilitate the operation of the debtor's business. On February 7th, the debtor presented eight such motions, as follows:

1. a motion to authorize payment of pre-petition employee compensation and benefits;

2. a motion to authorize payment of pre-petition sales and use taxes;

3. a motion to specify adequate assurance of payment for post-petition utility services and to prohibit utilities from discontinuing, altering or refusing service;

4. a motion to authorize the debtor to implement a key employee retention and incentive program for non-insiders;

5. a motion to approve the employment of a restructuring consultant, whose services would include those of a chief restructuring officer;

6. a motion to approve the retention of bankruptcy counsel;

7. a motion to authorize the debtor to maintain an existing cash management system and bank accounts, and to authorize the clearing of checks in transit; and

8. an application for emergency and final authority to obtain post-petition financing to be secured by a priming lien with administrative super-priority.

As of the present moment, this court has already rendered an oral decision with respect to all aspects of the above motions, with the exception of the application for final authority to obtain post-petition financing. . . . With respect to post-petition financing, the debtor presently operates with benefit of an interim financing order. Primarily, the instant decision must address issues that relate to the terms of the final financing arrangement. However, to place the outstanding issues into context and to clarify the appropriate standard for first day orders, the court wishes to identify relevant principles and briefly recite the rationale for its ruling as to each of the motions. In attempting to justify the grant of many first day orders, debtors will urge reliance upon the so-called "Doctrine of Necessity." . . . [T]he Doctrine of Necessity finds support from section 105(a) of the Bankruptcy Code, which authorizes the bankruptcy court to "issue any order, process, or judgment that is necessary or appropriate to carry out the provisions of this title." Nonetheless, section 105(a) does not create authority and rights that do not otherwise arise from the express provisions of the Bankruptcy Code. In the Second Circuit, the Court of Appeals stated the controlling interpretation of section 105(a) in its decision in *F.D.I.C. v. Colonial Realty Co.*, 966 F.2d 57, 59 (1992): "By its very terms, Section 105(a) limits the bankruptcy court's equitable powers, which 'must and can only be exercised within the confines of the Bankruptcy Code[,]' and 'cannot be used in a manner inconsistent with the commands of the Bankruptcy Code'." Within this spirit, this court has discerned four principles that should apply to consideration of first day motions.

First, the requested relief should be limited to that which is minimally necessary to maintain the existence of the debtor, until such time as the debtor can effect appropriate notice to creditors and parties in interest. In particular, a first day order should avoid substantive rulings that irrevocably determine the rights of parties.

Second, first day orders must maintain a level of clarity and simplicity sufficient to allow reasonable confidence that an order will effect no unanticipated or untoward consequences.

Third, first day orders are not a device to change the procedural and substantive rights that the Bankruptcy Code and Rules have established. In particular, first day orders should provide no substitute for the procedural and substantive protections of the plan confirmation process.

Fourth, no first day order should violate or disregard the substantive rights of parties, in ways not expressly authorized by the Bankruptcy Code.

Other principles may also apply with respect to certain first day motions, but the above list will help to explain the court's rulings with respect to the eight motions that the debtor presented in the instant case.

Payments to Employees and to Taxing Authorities

The debtor's first motion sought authority to pay pre-petition wages and benefits; its second motion sought to approve payment of pre-petition use and sales taxes. In papers filed with these motions, the debtor represented that nearly all of these wages, benefits and taxes would constitute priority claims; that the debtor had incurred these obligations in its ordinary course of operations; that the outstanding wages and benefits were pre-petition obligations that were not yet payable; that a disruption of wage and benefit payments could affect its ability to maintain its work force; and that the outstanding tax liabilities were ordinary obligations for use taxes and for sales taxes that the debtor had collected from its customers. In considering these two motions, the court was principally concerned for prejudice to the rights of other creditors. As against the interests of general unsecured creditors, the tax claims and nearly all of the employee claims held priority. No other priority claims appeared to be outstanding. Secured creditors might typically hold a superior interest in the cash that would be paid to the employees and taxing authorities, but here, the secured creditor consented to the debtor's proposed distribution. Based upon that consent and upon the various representations made on behalf of the debtor, the court granted both motions in substantial part. With respect to employee wages and benefits, however, the distribution could not exceed the priority limits of 11 U.S.C. § 507(a)(3) and (4). . . .

Post-petition Utility Services

Without prior notice to utilities, the debtor also moved for an order specifying adequate assurance of payment for post-petition utility services and to prohibit utilities from discontinuing, altering or refusing service. Concerned that a lack of notice had denied due process to the affected utilities, this court refused to consider such an *ex parte* application. Moreover, the motion sought extraordinary relief with respect to issues that Congress had already addressed in section 366 of the Bankruptcy Code. Section 366 protects a debtor's access to utility service during the first twenty days after the filing of a bankruptcy petition. Then, on "request of a party in interest and after notice and a hearing, the court may order reasonable modification of the amount of deposit or other security necessary to provide adequate assurance of payment." 11 U.S.C. § 366(b). By its first day motion, the debtor essentially sought to disregard the procedural requirements of section 366 for a notice and hearing. Nor was such special relief necessary, in light of the protection of utility access for twenty days. For these reasons, the court denied the debtor's motion, but without prejudice to a future application under section 366.

Key Employee Retention and Incentive Program

The debtor next moved for authority to implement a key employee retention and incentive program for non-insider personnel. Specifically, the debtor proposed to offer a bonus to key employees who would remain with the company through the completion of the anticipated sale of the debtor's operating assets. Contemplating a typical bonus equal to 133 percent of an individual's bi-weekly pay, the debtor estimated a total cost to the estate of less than $25,000. In support of its request, the debtor represented that it required the services of these key employees; that the debtor had no ability on the short term to replace these key employees; and that in light of the debtor's precarious financial condition, these employees might accept other employment unless they received sufficient financial incentive to remain with the company.

The retention and incentive program represents the type of operational decision for which this court will generally give reasonable deference to the sound discretion of management. In the present instance, to the satisfaction of this court, the debtor has demonstrated an immediate danger to its personnel requirements and hence, that it has an urgent need for the proposed program. The projected payments appear to be reasonable in amount. The court discerns nothing in the program that would violate any substantive rights of parties in interest. For these reasons, the court granted this first day motion to authorize a key employee retention and incentive program.

Restructuring Consultant

Pursuant to 11 U.S.C. § 363(b), Colad asked the court to approve the continued employment of Getzler Henrich & Associates LLC ("Getzler Henrich") as a restructuring consultant. As part of this engagement, Getzler Henrich will also provide the services of a chief restructuring officer. In its moving papers, the debtor acknowledged that prior to the bankruptcy filing, its secured creditor had requested that Colad retain the services of a restructuring firm. Colad's president further represented that the debtor needed these consulting services "in order to maximize recovery for all parties in interest."

This court realizes that the designation of a particular restructuring manager may define the likely course of events in a bankruptcy proceeding. . . . [T]he continued retention of the firm will involve the use of resources outside the ordinary course of the debtor's business. . . .

Section 363(b) provides that a debtor in possession "after notice and a hearing, may use, sell, or lease, other than in the ordinary course of business, property of the estate." By reason of the requirement for notice, this court denied the first day motion for final approval of the retention of Getzler Henrich. Instead, the court approved an interim retention, with direction for final hearing on notice to the twenty largest creditors and others who might request service. At that final hearing, debtor's counsel demonstrated the need for a consultant and that Colad had exercised sound discretion in its selection of Getzler Henrich. For these reasons, the court then gave its final approval to the retention proposal.

Retention of Counsel

In the absence of opposition from the office of the United States Trustee, this court will normally grant a first day motion for the appointment of counsel for the debtor in possession. In the present instance, however, the proposed firm had previously represented William J. Brosnahan, as well as two of the debtor's creditors on unrelated matters. Section 327(c) of the Bankruptcy Code provides that such prior representation does not preclude employment by the debtor, "unless there is objection by another creditor or the United States trustee, in which case the court shall disapprove such employment if there is an actual conflict of interest." To allow creditors to assert any such opposition, this court requires that creditors receive appropriate notice of the proposed and prior representations. Accordingly, as a first day order, I approved only an interim appointment of counsel.

Cash Management System

Prior to its bankruptcy filing, Colad had established a cash management system, which required the deposit of receipts into a lockbox and the transfer of those funds to Continental, on account of its secured position. Essentially, this system facilitated the debtor's revolving credit agreement, under which Colad would direct all receipts toward payment on account of its secured obligations and Continental would continuously advance new funds into Colad's operating accounts. If continued on a post-petition basis, this arrangement would cause the gradual but inevitable satisfaction of the debtor's pre-petition obligation and a corresponding re-extension of credit with administrative priority. . . .

Colad represented to the court that the Office of the United States Trustee was insisting that the debtor close all existing bank accounts; that it open new accounts in the name of the debtor in possession; that it maintain a separate account for cash collateral; and that all checks bear the description "debtor in possession", as well as the bankruptcy case number and a designation of the purpose of the account. Arguing that these measures would unduly disrupt its operations, Colad sought a first day order that would allow it to maintain its pre-petition system of cash management. Further, Colad represented that at least some payroll checks were still in float. In light of the first day order allowing payment of priority wage claims, a closing of the existing payroll account would cause the dishonor of existing checks and would thereby impact adversely upon the debtor's relationship with its employees. . . .

In comparison to the debtor in possession financing agreement, the cash management system has only tangential significance to the administration of this case. For reasons of convenience, I granted the debtor's request to maintain all of its existing accounts, but on condition that the debtor order new checks indicating Colad's status as a debtor in possession. Additionally, I allowed the processing of extant checks, in order to avoid disruption of relationships with employees who in any event would have claimed priority for the amount of their uncashed checks.

* * *

(Citations omitted.)

NOTES AND COMMENTS

1. Consider the court's detailed analysis regarding its approval or disapproval of the various first day orders. Note that the court identifies four principles that are important when considering first day orders: (1) limiting relief to that necessary to maintain debtor's existence, (2) clarity and simplicity to avoid unintended consequences, (3) no modification to procedural and substantive protections afforded by the Code and Rules, and (4) no violation of parties' substantive rights except as permitted by the Code. Which of these factors does the court consider most in determining whether such orders are appropriate?

2. How does the court's decision fit with the business judgment rule discussed earlier in this chapter? Are there areas in which business judgment is called into question by the court's decision? Is there a reason why the court might be more critical of business managers' judgment in the Chapter 11 context?

2. Creating and Proposing the Plan — General Rules

Every plan of reorganization is different, and creating such a plan can be a time-consuming and expensive process. The Bankruptcy Code contains guidance on *when* such a plan must be submitted to the court and then approved, *who* is allowed to propose such a plan, and *what* the plan must and may address. Reference to the Bankruptcy Code is therefore, once again, crucial.

Section 1121 provides an "exclusivity period" for the debtor to file a plan of reorganization. This period allows the debtor a time in which only the debtor may propose a plan (per § 1121(b), 120 days from the order for relief for non-small-business cases unless modified per § 1121(d)) and, if proposed within that time, gives additional time (per § 1121(c)(3), 180 days from the order for relief for non-small-business cases unless modified per § 1121(d)) for the debtor to achieve confirmation.

If the debtor fails to propose a plan during the exclusivity period or fails to achieve confirmation on a timely basis, other parties may propose competing plans of reorganization. The other parties to a Chapter 11 bankruptcy case often include various committees of creditors. The most common of those, commonly known as the "creditors committee," is the committee of the largest unsecured creditors willing to serve in the case. Code § 1102 provides that the U.S. Trustee shall appoint such a committee, as well as other appropriate committees (such as committees of equity holders, employees, trade creditors, and so on). The Code suggests that committees include the seven largest claimants of the type represented by the committee. 11 U.S.C. § 1102(b). The committees are entitled to hire counsel and other professionals—at the bankruptcy estate's expense—and are entitled to fully participate in the bankruptcy case, including consulting with the debtor-in-possession and conducting investigations. 11 U.S.C. § 1103.

Section 1123 sets some parameters for the contents of a plan, both on what *must* and what *may* be included in the plan. The plan must indicate how each class will be treated under the plan, § 1123(a)(3), and must indicate how the plan will be put into effect, § 1123(a)(5). It must also provide for the distribution of power among the various classes of shares, § 1123(a)(6). Sections 1123(a) and (b) also allow the plan to do many other things, including classify claims, impair the rights (or not) of any class of claims, dictate the treatment of executory contracts, and sell property of the estate.

A business may have thousands of claims, and individualized treatment of each claim may be impractical. For that reason, the party proposing a plan of reorganization is permitted to—and usually does—place each claim into a class. As the following subsections will discuss, classification holds special importance (and strategy) in the plan voting process. In order to place claims in the same class, the Code requires that they be "substantially similar," but it also allows all unsecured claims to be classified together if they are of small value, and such classification provides for efficiency and convenience. 11 U.S.C. § 1122. Claims within the same class must be treated the same under the plan, unless the claimant agrees otherwise. 11 U.S.C. § 1123(a)(4).

3. Acceptance and Confirmation of the Plan (§§ 1124, 1125, 1126, 1129, 1141, 1144)

The process for acceptance and confirmation is complex and can be thought of in two stages. In the first stage, the plan is voted upon for *acceptance* by the creditors. In a second later stage, the court will consider whether to *confirm* the plan.

In advance of the creditors voting to *accept* a plan, the plan proponent creates and distributes a *disclosure statement* for creditors. The disclosure statement provides a history of the debtor and the bankruptcy, and information about the plan. As long as the disclosure statement adequately and fairly describes the history and plan, the court can approve the disclosure statement, it can be distributed, and voting may occur. 11 U.S.C. § 1125. Upon receipt of the plan and disclosure, each claim is permitted a vote to either accept or reject the plan. However, any claimant whose rights are not "impaired" (meaning altered) under the plan is automatically deemed to vote to accept the plan. 11 U.S.C. § 1124. Further, any claimant receiving nothing under the plan is automatically deemed to vote to reject the plan. 11 U.S.C. § 1124 (f), (g).

While each creditor votes individually on a plan, the vote tally is done by class. A class accepts the plan if more than one-half of the number of creditors in the class *and* at least two-thirds of the value of the claims held by members of the class vote in favor of the plan. 11 U.S.C. § 1126(c). This ensures that (in most cases) one lone creditor cannot prevent confirmation. Assuming that the creditor does not have a large claim and is in a class with several other creditors, one creditor voting against the plan can be outvoted by the remainder of the class. If all classes vote in favor of the plan, it is approved and can move to the confirmation stage. 11 U.S.C. § 1129(a)(8).

If any impaired class votes against the plan, confirmation requires an additional step—"cramdown" of the plan. A cramdown occurs under 11 U.S.C. § 1129(b) where there is one or more classes of creditors voting against the plan, but at least one class of impaired creditors has approved of the plan, and the court approves the plan as "fair and equitable" regardless of those creditors objections. An impaired class, per § 1124, means that the rights of the class have been changed under the plan.

Confirmation of a plan by the court binds the debtor and all claimants. 11 U.S.C. § 1141(a). The case closes after confirmation of the plan. The property of the estate becomes property of the debtor under § 1141(b). Moreover, the plan can be enforced as a contract under state law. National City Bank v. Troutman Enterprises, Inc. (In re Troutman Enterprises, Inc.), 253 B.R. 8, 11 (6th Cir. BAP 2000). Confirmation of a plan also discharges the debtor from pre-petition debts. 11 U.S.C. § 1141(d). A confirmation order may only be revoked if obtained by fraud, and only within 180 days after the order is entered. 11 U.S.C. § 1144.

Confirmation is governed by § 1129. This section imposes several requirements that are only considered at the confirmation stage. But the plan proponent should consider these requirements when proposing the plan in order to achieve confirmation at the end of the process.

In reviewing § 1129, pay particular attention to the following requirements:

- the plan is proposed in good faith (§ 1129(a)(3));
- each impaired claimant (not just class) has accepted the plan or will receive at least what the claimant would have received if the case had been filed as a Chapter 7, known as "the best interest test" (§ 1129(a)(7));
- each class of claims has voted in favor of the plan (§ 1129(a)(8)); or one impaired class has accepted the plan (§ 1129(a)(10)) and the plan is "fair and equitable" (§ 1129(b)(1)), known as a "cramdown";
- the plan provides for full payment of priority claims as listed in § 1129(a)(9); and
- the plan is likely to be feasible (§ 1129(a)(11)).

The easiest path to confirmation is creating a plan in which every class votes in favor of the plan—making composition of each class particularly important. But if a class dissents, the plan can still be confirmed through the cramdown process if at least one "impaired" class approves of the plan, and the plan treats the other classes in a fair and equitable manner. Section 1129(b) provides the parameters for fair and equitable treatment.

As to secured claims, the plan proponent has several options: allow the creditors to retain their liens on the estate assets and pay them in full over the course of the plan; sell the collateral and transfer the proceeds of the sale to the lien holder; or provide the "indubitable equivalent" of the other options. As to unsecured claims, the plan must pay the class in full or not pay anything to classes below that class in priority (known as the "absolute priority rule").

GOOD FAITH IN BUSINESS AND IN BANKRUPTCY

Good faith is a pervasive concept throughout business law. Contracts must be entered into in good faith. Likewise, business managers must make good faith business decisions to be protected against a claim for a violation of the duty of care.

With respect to a Chapter 11 reorganization, confirmation of a plan requires that the plan be submitted "in good faith." Similarly, creditors voting on reorganization plans must do so in good faith. If a creditor has not voted in good faith, then that vote may be discounted in determining acceptance of the plan.

Consider, for example, the facts in DISH Network Corp. v. DBSD North America, Inc. (In re DBSD North America, Inc.), 634 F.3d 79 (2d

Cir. 2011). In that case, the bankruptcy court found that DISH Network did not vote in good faith. DISH had purchased its claims against DBSD in the hopes of having an impact on the bankruptcy case and, ultimately, purchasing spectrum licenses issued by the Federal Communications Commission in DBSD's favor. The bankruptcy court deemed DISH's not to have voted in good faith because DISH was not voting to maximize payment on its debt in the case but "to establish control" over the licenses.

Consider the following two very recent federal appellate cases and how they differ on the intersection of the good faith requirement and the requirement that at least one class of impaired creditors vote to approve the plan. The Sixth Circuit takes a flexible approach to interpreting the Bankruptcy Code, while the Fifth Circuit takes a more literal approach.

In re Village Green I, GP

811 F.3d 816 (6th Cir. 2016)

KETHLEDGE, Circuit Judge

In order for a bankruptcy court to approve a plan of reorganization under Chapter 11 of the Bankruptcy Code, the debtor must propose the plan in good faith and at least one class of creditors whose interests are impaired by the plan must vote to accept it. Here, the only creditors who voted in favor of Village Green's plan were its own former lawyer and accountant, whom Village Green owed less than $2,400 in total, and whose interests were impaired only because Village Green proposed to pay them (in full) over 60 days rather than up front. That arrangement, the district court found, was merely an artifice to circumvent the Code's requirement that an impaired class of creditors approve the plan. The district court therefore reversed the bankruptcy court's confirmation of the plan, holding that Village Green had not proposed the plan in good faith. We agree with the district court and affirm its judgment.

Village Green owes Fannie Mae $8.6 million pursuant to loan agreements executed when Village Green purchased an apartment building in Memphis. Under those agreements, Village Green's mortgage payment is about $55,000 per month. Village Green missed its payment in December 2009; four months later it filed for bankruptcy under Chapter 11 of the Bankruptcy Code. The bankruptcy court promptly stayed any creditor action against Village Green, *see* 11 U.S.C. § 362(a), which prevented Fannie Mae from foreclosing on the apartment building. The building itself is worth $5.4 million and is Village Green's only asset in the bankruptcy. Apart from Fannie Mae, Village Green's only creditors are its former lawyer and accountant. (We call their claims the "minor claims.")

Village Green's proposed plan of reorganization has several features relevant here. First, Village Green would pay down Fannie Mae's claim relatively slowly, leaving a balance of $6.6 million after 10 years. (In contrast, if Fannie Mae foreclosed on the property, it would reduce its balance to $3.2 million right away.) The plan would also strip Fannie Mae of several protections in the parties' loan agreements, including the requirements that Village Green properly maintain the building and obtain adequate insurance for it. Finally, though Village Green would pay the minor claims in full under the plan, it would do so in two payments (of roughly $1,200 each) over 60 days.

* * *

Two of the bankruptcy court's determinations are at issue here. The first is that, under Village Green's plan, the minor claims were "impaired" for purposes of § 1129(a)(10). Section 1124(1) provides, in relevant part, that "a class of claims . . . is impaired under a plan unless" the plan "leaves unaltered the legal, equitable, and contractual rights to which such claim or interest entitles the holder of such claim or interest[.]" Here, the plan undisputedly would alter the minor claimants' rights, because these claimants are legally entitled to payment immediately rather than in two installments over 60 days. That this impairment seems contrived to create a class to vote in favor of the plan is immaterial. Section 1124(1) by its terms asks only whether a plan would alter a claimant's interests, not whether the debtor had bad motives in seeking to alter them. The debtor's motives instead are expressly the business of § 1129(a)(3), which requires that "the plan has been proposed in good faith and not by any means forbidden by law." And given that § 1129(a)(3) expressly requires an inquiry into the debtor's motives in proposing the plan, there is no reason to graft that inquiry onto the plain terms of § 1124(1).

So we turn to the question whether Village Green proposed its plan in good faith, which is the second of the determinations at issue here. The bankruptcy court found that the plan was proposed in good faith, reasoning that "Village Green was economically justified in rationing every dollar" under the plan. But that rationale is undermined by Village Green's own projections in support of the plan's feasibility, see § 1129(a)(11), which were that Village Green would earn roughly

$857,000 in net operating income during its first year after the plan's confirmation. That averages out to net income of $71,400 per month, which renders dubious at best Village Green's assertion that it could not safely pay off the minor claims (total value: less than $2,400) up front rather than over 60 days. On these points—the projections, and the assertion—Village Green cannot have it both ways. Moreover, that the minor claimants (Village Green's former lawyer and accountant) are closely allied with Village Green only compounds the appearance that impairment of their claims had more to do with circumventing the purposes of § 1129(a)(10) than with rationing dollars. And the "rationing" rationale falls away altogether when one considers that, during litigation regarding the plan's confirmation, Fannie Mae itself sought to pay the minor claimants up front— by tendering each of them checks for full payment of their claims—and yet the minor claimants refused to accept that payment. On this record, the minor claims' impairment was transparently an artifice to circumvent the purposes of § 1129(a)(10). We therefore agree with the district court that the bankruptcy court clearly erred when it found that Village Green proposed its plan in good faith.

(Citations omitted.)

In re Village at Camp Bowie I, L.P.

710 F.3d 239 (5th Cir. 2013)

HIGGINBOTHAM, Circuit Judge

* * *

The appellee, Village at Camp Bowie I, LLC ("the Village"), owns a parcel of real estate in west Fort Worth, Texas. The real estate includes unimproved land as well as several buildings, which the Village leases out for retail and office space. The Village itself has no employees, and a third-party independent contractor handles the day-to-day management of the property on a fee basis.

The Village acquired and improved the property in 2004, investing approximately $10,000,000 of its own equity capital and obtaining the balance of the necessary financing by executing short-term promissory notes ("the Notes") in favor of SouthTrust Bank and Texas Capital Bank. The Notes were secured by the property. Neither of the original lenders is a party to this suit. By a series of mergers, Wells Fargo National Bank—also not a party to this case—succeeded the original lenders as owner of the Notes.

The Notes were originally scheduled to mature on January 22, 2008. . . . [T]he Village entered into a series of modification agreements with Wells Fargo that postponed maturity until February 11, 2010. On that date, the Village defaulted on the Notes. Thereafter, the Village negotiated a series of forbearance agreements by which Wells Fargo agreed to temporarily forego its state law remedies. After the final forbearance period expired on July 9, 2010, Wells Fargo auctioned off the Notes to Western, the appellant, at a discount from their face value.

Western purchased the Notes with an eye toward displacing the Village as owner of the underlying real estate. Pursuant to this objective, Western posted the Village for a non-judicial foreclosure immediately after acquiring the Notes. On August 2, 2010—the day before the scheduled foreclosure sale—the Village filed its Chapter 11 petition, staying the foreclosure proceedings. As of the petition date, the outstanding principal on the Notes was $32,112,711. The Village also owed $59,398 in unsecured pre-petition debt to thirty-eight miscellaneous trade creditors. . . .

* * *

On November 29, 2010, the Village filed its original plan of reorganization. The bankruptcy court indicated that the plan was unconfirmable because the proposed equity infusion from the Village's pre-petition owners was too small to stabilize the property. Thereafter, the Village filed a series of amendments and modifications to its original plan, culminating in the filing of its modified second amended plan. The plan designated only two voting, impaired creditor classes, one consisting of Western's secured claim and the other consisting of the unsecured trade debt. Under the plan, Western would receive a new five-year note in the amount of its secured claim, with interest accruing at 5.84% per annum, and with a balloon payment of the remaining principal and accrued interest due at maturity. Moreover, the plan proposed to pay the class of unsecured trade claims in full within three months from the effective date, without interest. Finally, the plan provided that the Village's pre-petition owners and related parties would make a capital infusion of $1,500,000 in exchange for newly issued preferred equity.

While all thirty-eight unsecured trade creditors voted to accept the plan, Western voted its much larger secured claim against it. The bankruptcy court held a three-day hearing to determine whether it could confirm the plan under 11 U.S.C. § 1129 notwithstanding Western's objection. During the hearing, Western complained that the Village's plan failed a number of the conditions for confirmation set forth in § 1129. Among other things, Western argued that the plan offended § 1129(a)(10), which requires that a plan garner the vote of "at least one class of claims that is impaired under the plan." Here, Western observed, the Village's plan minimally impaired the unsecured trade creditors by proposing to pay them in full, but over a period of three months after plan confirmation without interest. Western argued that the Village impaired the trade claims solely to create an accepting impaired class, pointing to the undisputed fact that the Village had the cash flow to pay off the trade claims in full at plan confirmation. As the trade claims were thus "artificially" impaired, Western reasoned, their acceptance could not satisfy § 1129(a)(10). In the alternative, Western argued, the Village's tactics constituted an abuse of the bankruptcy process that violated the good faith requirement of § 1129(a)(3).

The bankruptcy court agreed that the Village had the financial wherewithal to leave its trade creditors unimpaired. However, it rejected Western's theory that § 1129(a)(10) distinguishes between artificial and economically driven impairment, observing that:

> [As] the definition of impairment in Code § 1124 is clear—and broad—and [as] Congress did not, as it might have, condition the accepting class requirement of section 1129(a)(10) on meaningful impairment of that class, the latter section cannot be read to require any particular degree of impairment.

Moreover, while the court suggested that artificial impairment is a factor to consider in determining whether a plan proponent has satisfied its duty of good faith under § 1129(a)(3), it concluded that "in the usual case, artificial impairment does not amount per se to a failure of good faith." Here, the court observed, the Village had proposed its plan for the legitimate bankruptcy purposes of reorganizing its debts, continuing its real estate venture, and preserving its non-trivial equity in its real estate. Moreover, the court determined, the Village would likely be able to stay current on its restructured obligations. Thus, the court concluded, the Village satisfied § 1129(a)(3).

* * *

On appeal, Western reasserts its theory that a plan proponent cannot "artificially" impair a friendly class of creditors solely to create the impaired accepting class necessary to satisfy § 1129(a)(10). Western predicates its theory on both § 1129(a)(10) as well as the separate good faith requirement of § 1129(a)(3). As Western's arguments raise questions of statutory construction, we review de novo.

We begin by examining the relevant provisions of the Bankruptcy Code. Section 1129(a)(10) prohibits a court from confirming a plan of reorganization unless "at least one class of claims that is impaired under the plan has accepted the plan." Section 1124 explains that a plan impairs a class of claims unless it "leaves unaltered the legal, equitable, and contractual rights" of the claim holders. Section 1123(b)(1) provides that "a plan may impair or leave unimpaired any class of claims." Lastly, § 1129(a)(3) requires a plan proponent to "propose [its plan] in good faith and not by any means forbidden by law."

Circuits have divided over the question of whether § 1129(a)(10) draws a distinction between artificial and economically driven impairment. At the one end of the spectrum, the Eighth Circuit held in *Matter of Windsor on the River Associates, Ltd.* that "a claim is not impaired [for purposes of § 1129(a)(10)] if the alteration of the rights in question arises solely from the debtor's exercise of discretion." Under the Eighth Circuit's approach, § 1129(a)(10) recognizes impairment only to the extent that it is driven by economic "need."

At the other end of the spectrum, the Ninth Circuit held in *Matter of L & J Anaheim Associates* that § 1129(a)(10) does not distinguish between discretionary and economically driven impairment, observing that "the plain language of section 1124 says that a creditor's claim is 'impaired' unless its rights are left 'unaltered' by the [p]lan," and that "[t]here is no suggestion here that only alterations of a particular kind or degree can constitute impairment." However, the Ninth Circuit left open the possibility that discretionary impairment could offend a plan proponent's duty of good faith under § 1129(a)(3).

For its part, this Circuit has yet to stake out a clear position in the debate over artificial impairment. In *Matter of Sun Country Development, Inc.,* we rejected the concept of artificial impairment altogether, both as a matter of the good faith requirement of § 1129(a)(3), and—at least implicitly—as a matter of the voting requirement of § 1129(a)(10). However, as we ultimately concluded that the impairment before us was economically motivated, we deprived our analysis of artificial impairment of precedential force. Moreover, in our subsequent decision in *Matter of Sandy Ridge Development Corp.,* we voiced concern with artificial impairment in a single-asset reorganization analogous to the case at bar, remanding to the bankruptcy court to "consider the issue in light, *inter alia,* of the requirement of good faith."

Today, we expressly reject *Windsor* and join the Ninth Circuit in holding that § 1129(a)(10) does not distinguish between discretionary and economically driven impairment. As the *Windsor* court itself acknowledged, § 1124 provides that "any alteration of a creditor's rights, no matter how minor, constitutes 'impairment.'" By shoehorning a motive inquiry and materiality requirement into § 1129(a)(10), *Windsor* warps the text of the Code, requiring a court to "deem" a claim unimpaired for purposes of § 1129(a)(10) even though it plainly qualifies as impaired under § 1124. *Windsor* 's motive inquiry is also inconsistent with § 1123(b)(1), which provides that a plan proponent "*may* impair or leave unimpaired any class of claims," and does not contain any indication that impairment must be driven by economic motives.

The *Windsor* court justified its strained reading of §§ 1129(a)(10) and 1124 on the ground that "Congress enacted section 1129(a)(10) . . . to provide some indicia of support [for a cramdown plan] by affected creditors," reasoning that interpreting § 1124 literally would vitiate this congressional purpose. But the Bankruptcy Code *must* be read literally, and congressional intent is relevant only when the statutory language is ambiguous. Moreover, even if we were inclined to consider congressional intent in divining the meaning of §§ 1129(a)(10) and 1124, the scant legislative history on § 1129(a)(10) provides virtually no insight as to the provision's intended role, and the Congress that passed § 1124 considered and rejected precisely the sort of materiality requirement that *Windsor* has imposed by judicial fiat.

The *Windsor* court also reasoned that condoning artificial impairment would "reduce [§ 1129](a)(10) to a nullity." But this logic sets the cart before the horse, resting on the unsupported assumption that Congress intended § 1129(a)(10) to implicitly mandate a materiality requirement and motive inquiry. Moreover, it ignores the determinative role § 1129(a)(10) plays in the typical single-asset bankruptcy, in which the debtor has negative equity and the secured creditor receives a deficiency claim that allows it to control the vote of the unsecured class. In such circumstances, secured creditors routinely invoke § 1129(a)(10) to block a cramdown, aided rather than impeded by the Code's broad definition of impairment.

Western insists that "the real issue here is not one of statutory construction," urging that "courts do not apply a plain meaning test to the provisions of the . . . Code where the issue is one of manipulating the bankruptcy process." Specifically, Western points to our decision in *Matter of Greystone III Joint Venture,* in which we held that a plan proponent cannot gerrymander creditor classes solely for purposes of obtaining the impaired accepting class necessary to satisfy § 1129(a)(10). Western reads *Greystone* to enunciate a broad, extrastatutory policy against "voting manipulation" and urges that prohibiting artificial impairment is merely the next logical extension of this policy. However, Western brushes over the fact that *Greystone* 's anti-gerrymandering principle resolves an ambiguity left open by the classification rules set forth in § 1122. *Greystone* does not stand for the proposition that a court can ride roughshod over affirmative language in the Bankruptcy Code to enforce some Platonic ideal of a fair voting process.

As we suggested in *Sandy Ridge,* a plan proponent's motives and methods for achieving compliance with the voting requirement of § 1129(a)(10) must be scrutinized, if at all, under the rubric of § 1129(a)(3), which imposes on a plan proponent a duty to propose its plan "in good faith and not by any means forbidden by law." Good faith should be evaluated "in light of the totality of the circumstances surrounding establishment of [the] plan," mindful of the purposes underlying the Bankruptcy Code. Generally, "[w]here [a] plan is proposed with the legitimate and honest purpose to reorganize and has a reasonable hope of success, the good faith requirement of § 1129(a)(3) is satisfied." We review a bankruptcy court's § 1129(a)(3) analysis only for clear error.

Here, the bankruptcy court determined that the Village had not run afoul of § 1129(a)(3), as it had proposed a feasible cramdown plan for the legitimate purposes of reorganizing its debts, continuing its real estate venture, and preserving its non-trivial equity in its properties. Western does not dispute that the Village will be able to stay current on its restructured obligations or that it has significant equity in its properties, instead relying wholly on the theory that artificial impairment constitutes bad faith as a matter of law—a theory that has no basis in the Code or our precedents. On this record, we cannot conclude that the district court clearly erred in its § 1129(a)(3) analysis, particularly as we have recognized that a single-asset debtor's desire to protect its equity can be a legitimate Chapter 11 objective.

We emphasize, however, that our decision today does not circumscribe the factors bankruptcy courts may consider in evaluating a plan proponent's good faith. In particular, though we reject the concept of artificial impairment as developed in *Windsor,* we do not suggest that a debtor's methods for achieving literal compliance with § 1129(a)(10) enjoy a free pass from scrutiny under § 1129(a)(3). It bears mentioning that Western here concedes that the trade creditors are independent third parties who extended pre-petition credit to the Village in the ordinary course of business. An inference of bad faith might be stronger where a debtor creates an impaired accepting class out of whole cloth by incurring a debt with a related party, particularly if there is evidence that the lending transaction is a sham. Ultimately, the § 1129(a)(3) inquiry is fact-specific, fully empowering the bankruptcy courts to deal with chicanery. We will continue to accord deference to their determinations.

* * *

(Citations omitted.)

NOTES AND COMMENTS

1. Does creation of an impaired class that will almost certainly vote in favor of the plan necessarily violate the good faith requirement for confirmation of a plan? What factors will be most critical to a court in determining whether an "artificial" impaired class violates the good faith requirement?

2. How does a single asset real estate (SARE) case differ factually and legally from other cases, and what impact do those differences have on the good faith standard?

3. The cases view "good faith" differently. What standard does each use for good faith? Had the *Village Green* court utilized the *Camp Bowie* standard, would the court have reached a different result?

C. SPECIAL PLAN RULES FOR SMALL AND SINGLE-ASSET DEBTORS

No two businesses are alike, and Chapter 11 provides a great deal of flexibility for each business to determine how best to reorganize. As you have just read, Chapter 11 centers around a plan of reorganization. While the Code provides some standards that must be met to finalize (or "confirm") the plan, the debtor-in-possession, creditors, committees, and other parties in interest negotiate the plan and, ultimately, have a say in whether the plan is approved.

All of this negotiation comes at a cost, both in terms of fees and expenses and in terms of the time it takes to resolve the case. For some businesses, that additional cost and lost time may doom the reorganization to failure. In an effort to create more efficient procedures for such bankruptcy cases, Congress has enacted different rules for two types of bankruptcy debtors: (1) small businesses and (2) single-asset real estate debtors. The two types of debtors are defined in 11 U.S.C. §§ 101(51)(B-D). A small business debtor is defined primarily by a cap on the amount of debt held by the business debtor. A single-asset real estate debtor has assets consisting primarily of one parcel of real property or project relating to real property that generates substantially all of the debtor's income.

SMALL BUSINESS AND SINGLE-ASSET REAL ESTATE DEBTORS' PLANS OF REORGANIZATION

The Code provisions differ for small business debtors and single-asset real estate debtors, especially when it comes to creating and confirming the plan. Sections 308 and 1116 provide additional reporting requirements for small businesses—including initial and periodic financial statements and assurances of compliance with the Code requirements—and mandate attendance of executives at the creditors' meeting to help ensure that the business is on track for an effective reorganization.

Section 362(n) limits the automatic stay available to a small business debtor with successive filings in a two-year period. Section 362(d)(3) provides that a single-asset real estate debtor must file a plan of reorganization within 90 days of the date of the order for relief (or 30 days after the determination that the debtor qualifies as a SARE, if later) or risk losing the protection of the automatic stay.

The exclusivity period for a small business debtor to file a plan of reorganization is extended to 180 days from the order for relief, but extensions for filing the plan are less liberally granted and absolutely capped at 300 days, per § 1121(e). However, the small business debtor may be relieved of the requirement to create and gain approval of a disclosure statement. 11 U.S.C. § 1125(f). Finally, § 1129(e) mandates that a court approve a plan within 45 days of filing, absent extension of that deadline.

Consider the following cases that discuss these types of debtors and the reasons that Congress modified the rules for such cases.

In re Roots Rents, Inc.

420 B.R. 28 (Bankr. D. Idaho 2009)

MYERS, Chief Judge

* * *

On September 10, 2008, Roots Rents, Inc., an Idaho corporation ("Debtor"), filed a voluntary petition for relief under chapter 11. It has consistently served as debtor in possession since filing, and no trustee has been appointed.

On its petition, Debtor checked a box designating that "Debtor is a small business debtor as defined in 11 U.S.C. § 101(51D)." That section provides in pertinent part:

> The term "small business debtor" . . . means a person engaged in commercial or business activities . . . that has aggregate noncontingent liquidated secured and unsecured debts as of the date of the petition . . . in an amount not more than $2,190,000 . . . for a case in which the United States trustee has not appointed under section 1102(a)(1) a committee of unsecured creditors[.]

Section 101(51D)(A).

On September 25, 2008, Debtor filed an amended petition. The amended petition also contained Debtor's self-designation as a small business debtor, and it provided, as attachments, the financial statements and tax returns required of small business debtors by § 1116(1)(A). . . .

In October, 2008, Debtor filed its schedules. They established a total of $1,740,433.38 in secured and unsecured debt, of which $49,843.17 was marked on schedule D as contingent, thus yielding a total of $1,690,590.21 in "aggregate noncontingent liquidated secured and unsecured" debt for purposes of § 101(51D)(A).

On February 24, 2009, Debtor filed a disclosure statement. This disclosure statement notes on its first page that Debtor's case is a small business case, and the same notation appears on the first page of an appended proposed chapter 11 plan.

Debtor filed its proposed plan on March 15, 2009. As discussed below, this is a significant date given the language of the Bankruptcy Code as amended in 2005.

On March 25, 2009, the Court issued a notice of hearing on approval of the disclosure statement. . . .

On April 27, at the scheduled hearing, and after hearing from Debtor, several creditors, and the United States Trustee ("UST"), the Court denied approval of the proposed disclosure statement.

. . . the UST filed a motion to convert or dismiss the case under § 1112(b) on July 28.

The UST's Dismissal Motion noted the requirement of § 1129(e) that:

> In a small business case, the court shall confirm a plan that complies with the applicable provisions of this title and that is filed in accordance with section 1121(e) not later than 45 days after the plan is filed unless the time for confirmation is extended in accordance with section 1121(e)(3).

The UST observed that no extension of time under § 1121(e) had been sought or granted, and that the 45 days from the Plan's March 15 filing expired on April 29, 2009. It argued that the failure to timely confirm, or to have properly requested and obtained an extension of the confirmation deadline, constituted cause for dismissal or conversion of the case.

The following day, Debtor filed an amended small business plan of reorganization . . . ("Amended Plan") and an amended small business disclosure statement . . . ("Amended Disclosure").

Then, on August 2, Debtor responded to the UST's Dismissal Motion by filing the following:

1. An "amended" petition for relief . . . ("Amended Petition") that checked the box designating Debtor as "not a small business debtor as defined in 11 U.S.C. § 101(51D)."

2. An objection to the Dismissal Motion.

3. A "Motion for Extension of Time for Confirmation" under § 105 and § 1129(e) . . . ("Extension Motion"), related to the Amended Plan and asking for 60 days after September 8 within which to obtain confirmation of that Plan under the small business case requirements.

4. A "Motion for Determination of Small Business Status" under Fed. R. Bankr. P. 1020(d) . . . ("Status Motion"), seeking a ruling that Debtor is not a small business debtor and that, therefore, the requirements of the BAPCPA-amended Code related to such debtors are inapplicable.

Debtor did not withdraw its Amended Plan and Amended Disclosure Statement which asserted it *was* a small business debtor in a small business case. . . .

* * *

Prior to BAPCPA a chapter 11 debtor elected whether to proceed as a small business and incur the burdens and benefits associated with such an election. BAPCPA eliminated any "election" by the debtor by amending former § 101(51 C) and defining a "small business case" as "a case filed under chapter 11 of this title in which the debtor is a small business debtor." *See* § 101(51C). As material to the present matter, the definition of a small business debtor requires not more than $2,190,000 in aggregate, noncontingent, liquidated, secured and unsecured debt as of the date of the petition. *See* § 101(51D)(A). If a debtor satisfies the requirements of § 101(51D), its bankruptcy case is a small business case and the BAPCPA-amended Code's small business timing provisions and deadlines are applicable.

At the time of filing the petition, Debtor affirmed it was a small business debtor, and its case was a small business case. This declaration was consistent with Debtor's scheduled $1,690,590.21 in qualifying debt. According to Debtor's schedules, it was $499,409.79 shy of no longer qualifying as a small business debtor.

. . . Every chapter 11 debtor is faced with a plethora of deadlines. Those for a small business debtor vary from those for other chapter 11 debtors.

For example, under § 1121(e), a small business debtor—such as Debtor here—is the only entity that may file a plan in the first 180 days of the case (unless that period of exclusivity is extended or the court orders otherwise). *See* § 1121(e)(1). This is a longer period of exclusivity than the 120 days a non-small business debtor enjoys. *See* § 1121(c)(2). But the statute gives the small business debtor burdens as well. The small business debtor has an outside bar of 300 days from the order for relief (here, the petition date) within which it must file a disclosure statement and plan. *See* § 1121(e)(2). There is no similar Code-imposed bar for non-small business debtors.

Additionally, as noted above, § 1129(e) now provides that "*the court shall confirm a plan . . . that is filed in accordance with section 1121(e) not later than 45 days after the plan is filed* unless the time for confirmation is extended in accordance with section 1121(e)(3)." (Emphasis added).

This is a plainly-worded, express deadline. It effectively mandates that any small business debtor choosing to follow a "traditional" disclosure statement approach, rather than asking the Court to waive the need for a disclosure statement or to conditionally approve a disclosure statement under § 1125(f)(1) or (3), *must* file a § 1121(e)(3) motion, to be heard on notice, and establish grounds for a timely-entered order extending the 45-day confirmation deadline.

. . . In this case, while Debtor filed an Extension Motion, on its face, that Motion only requests relief from deadlines arising from the filing of Debtor's *Amended Plan.* Debtor appears to ignore or discount the Code's express timing requirements as they pertain to its *original Plan.* Debtor's Amended Plan and related Extension Motion do not negate Debtor's failure to properly extend the 45-day deadline. However, since Debtor did file the Extension Motion and make arguments at the September 8 hearing, which, if liberally construed, could be viewed as a request for extension of the 1129(e) deadline arising from the filing of the original March 15 Plan, the Court will analyze such a request.

Section 1129(e) expressly provides that § 1121(e)(3) controls the granting of any extension of the 45-day period within which confirmation must occur. That section requires:

(e) In a small business case—
   . . .

(3) the time periods specified in paragraphs (1) and (2), and the time fixed in section 1129(e) within which the plan shall be confirmed, may be extended only if—
    (A) the debtor, after providing notice to parties in interest (including the United States trustee), demonstrates by a preponderance of the evidence that it is more likely than not that the court will confirm a plan within a reasonable period of time;
    (B) a new deadline is imposed at the time the extension is granted; and
    (C) the order extending time is signed before the existing deadline has expired.

Section 1121(e)(3).

There are three parts to § 1121(e)(3). They are conjunctively stated, meaning that each must be satisfied. Thus, the deadlines of, *inter alia,* § 1129(e) "may be extended *only if*" all three of those statutory conditions are met. *See* § 1121(e)(3).

Given the requirements of the Code and construing Debtor's Extension Motion as a request to extend the deadline pertaining to its March 15 Plan, the Court must deny that request on a number of grounds. First, while there is little case law on § 1121(e)(3), what there is tends to focus on the evidentiary burden imposed on debtors under § 1121(e)(3)(A). The Court concludes that neither the allegations within the Extension Motion nor Debtor's presentation at the September 8 hearing meet the burden imposed on debtors under § 1121(e)(3)(A).

Second, the plain language of § 1121(e)(3)(C) requires the order be obtained *before* the period expires. Here, Debtor did not request an extension, and the Court did not enter an order, before the 45-day period ran from the filing of Debtor's March 15 Plan.

Nor can Debtor rely on this Court's equitable powers or any Federal Bankruptcy Rules to enlarge such time limitations. While, in certain circumstances, Rule 9006(b)(1) allows the Court to grant requests made after the period in question has expired given a showing of excusable neglect, 28 U.S.C. § 2075 provides that the Bankruptcy Rules "shall not abridge, enlarge, or modify any substantive right." This statute has been interpreted to require any conflicts between the Code and Rules to be settled in favor of the Code. Thus, where the Code requires an act to be completed within a specific time, the Court cannot apply a Rule to circumvent that deadline.

The various constructions of the Code urged by Debtor to circumvent its failure to timely seek and obtain an extension to confirm the Plan would require the Court to ignore the plain language of the Code and interpret it in a way that renders meaningless the express deadlines imposed.

Therefore, the Court finds and concludes Debtor failed to confirm its Plan within the time fixed by § 1129(e), and that cause therefore exists to dismiss or convert this case under § 1112(b)(4)(J).

. . . As an alternative response to the UST's Dismissal Motion, Debtor filed its Amended Petition asserting it was not a small business debtor. It also filed the Status Motion. Both are problematic.

. . . Though the prior process of "election" of small business changed to a statutory qualification based on amount of debt, both BAPCPA and pre-BAPCPA approaches are clearly (a) aimed at addressing the status as of the petition date and (b) designed to achieve a prompt determination. Under the former regime, the election had to be made within 60 days of the date of filing. Under the present approach, the debtor is obligated to establish a position as to its status in the petition itself.

The reasons are self-evident. Small business cases impose different obligations and requirements (see § § 1116, 1121(e), 1125(f) and 1129(e)), and it is critical to know at the outset of the case if those Code provisions apply. Indeed, § 1116(1) requires certain financial documents to be provided by the small business debtor with the petition or within 7 days thereafter, illustrating the time-critical nature of the inquiry.

Rule 1020 echoes the early-in-the-case approach. It provides:

(a) SMALL BUSINESS DEBTOR DESIGNATION. In a voluntary chapter 11 case, the debtor shall state in the petition whether the debtor is a small business debtor. In an involuntary chapter 11 case, the debtor shall file within 15 days after entry of the order for relief a statement as to whether the debtor is a small business debtor. Except as provided in subdivision (c), the status of the case as a small business case shall be in accordance with the debtor's statement under this subdivision, unless and until the court enters an order finding that the debtor's statement is incorrect.

* * *

Thus, clearly the Code and Rules contemplate that issues of proper characterization of small business debtors and cases must be promptly resolved. The time-sensitive nature of the designation, and the imposition of a deadline for objections to and for prompt resolution of an initial self- designation weigh against Debtor's approach in this case. It was not until almost a full year after its September, 2008 filing that Debtor filed its request for determination of Debtor's small business status.

However, the issue is muddied because Rule 1020(b) allows for objections to the debtor's small business designation within the *later* of 30 days after the "statement" in the petition or "*within 30 days after any amendment to the statement.*" *Id.* (emphasis added). There are no time limitations on, or further provisions for, amendments found within Rule 1020. However, Rule 1009(a) provides: "A voluntary petition, list, schedule, or statement may be amended by a debtor as a matter of course at any time before the case is closed." *Id.* Thus, Debtor's attempt to amend its designation almost a year after its bankruptcy filing, while in conflict with the goal of prompt resolution, would appear to be allowed under the Rules.

. . . Even given Rule 1020(b)'s apparent allowance of amendment without express time limit and Rule 1009's directive to liberally allow amendments, such an amended designation is not a fait accompli merely upon its filing. As the Ninth Circuit Bankruptcy Appellate Panel noted in considering Rule 1009's liberal amendment approach in the context of exemptions, "the mere fact that [Debtors] can [amend to] *claim* the exemption does not necessarily mean that they are *entitled* to it." Moreover, Rule 1020 states that "the status of the case as a small business case *shall* be in accordance with the debtor's statement under this subdivision *unless and until* the court enters an order finding that the debtor's statement is incorrect." Thus, while a debtor may amend its designation, it may not be entitled to operate under that amended statement until it demonstrates that its original statement was incorrect.

* * *

Like a debtor's bankruptcy schedules, the first self-designation by Debtor as a small business debtor, at the time of the filing of the petition in September, 2008, was made under penalty of perjury. It controlled the conduct of the case through the disclosure statement hearing and past the § 1129(e) deadline for confirmation. That Debtor filed an amended statement in the Amended Petition in August, 2009, did not nullify the first statement. The initial assertion of small business debtor status retains evidentiary effect. This presents, of course, a disputed issue of fact and a conflict in the evidence. Debtor's first assertion in September, 2008, is that it was almost $500,000.00 below the cutoff point for mandatory application of the small business debtor provisions of the BAPCPA-amended Code. Debtor now argues that, as of the time of filing this case, it was over the threshold by some amount. Debtor was required to prove the proposition it now advances—that it was over the $2,190,000 aggregate debt cap of § 101(51D)(A) as of September 10, 2008.

Rule 1020(d) indicates that a "request for determination" such as that advanced under Debtor's Status Motion is a contested matter "governed by Rule 9014." Rule 9014(d) establishes that testimony of witnesses on disputed issues of fact shall be taken in the same manner as in adversary proceedings. But Debtor offered no testimony at the September 8, 2009 hearing. It also offered no documentary exhibits. Its Status Motion referenced the "claims register" but Debtor provided nothing to explain what the filed claims purported to establish as far as aggregate qualifying debt.

Debtor's arguments at hearing relied solely on the total amount shown on the Clerk's claims register. However, Debtor provided no analysis as to any of the claims filed. Thus, it failed to establish that the Clerk's summary total was accurate, or that none of the proofs filed included contingent or unliquidated claims, which § 101(51D)(A) excludes.

* * *

(Citations omitted.)

In re Meruelo Maddux Properties, Inc.

667 F.3d 1072 (9th Cir. 2012)

GOULD, Circuit Judge

Chapter 11 debtor Meruelo Maddux Properties–760 S. Hill Street LLC ("MMP Hill"), one of more than 50 subsidiaries of Meruelo Maddux Properties, Inc. ("MMPI"), filed a motion seeking a determination that it and other subsidiaries were not subject to the single asset real estate provisions of the Bankruptcy Code, 11 U.S.C. §§ 101(51B) and 362(d)(3). Creditor Bank of America filed a cross motion seeking to apply the single asset real estate provisions to MMP Hill and another subsidiary not at issue in this case. The bankruptcy court concluded that MMP Hill "appears to have the characteristics of a [single asset real estate] case" but decided that it would not apply the single asset real estate provisions because of the consolidated, interrelated nature of the business operations of MMPI and its subsidiaries. Bank of America appealed to the district court, which reversed the bankruptcy court's determination regarding MMP Hill, holding that MMP Hill should be treated as a single asset real estate debtor because there is no "whole enterprise exception" to the single asset real estate provisions in the plain language of the statute. MMP Hill now appeals, arguing that Congress did not intend the single asset real estate provision to apply to debtors like MMP Hill and that the district court erred by holding that Bank of America was entitled to relief from the automatic stay. We have jurisdiction under 28 U.S.C. § 158(d), and we affirm the district court's holding that the single asset real estate provisions apply to MMP Hill.

. . . MMPI owns and develops real property in the Los Angeles area through a network of subsidiaries. MMPI has a centralized management team that operates MMPI and its subsidiaries, including MMP Hill. The business is operated on a consolidated basis: revenues from operation of MMPI's subsidiaries' properties each day are swept into a single general operating account that is used to pay expenses for MMPI and its subsidiaries. MMPI and its subsidiaries file consolidated financial reports with the SEC and consolidated tax returns with the IRS. MMP Hill owns a 92–unit apartment complex commonly known as "Union Lofts." Bank of America loaned MMP Hill $28.72 million in 2006 to renovate Union Lofts, taking a security interest in the real estate. Bank of America is also an unsecured creditor of MMPI based on guaranty agreements in connection with the loan to MMP Hill and loans to other MMPI subsidiaries.

In March 2009, MMPI and fifty-three of its subsidiaries, including MMP Hill, each filed voluntary Chapter 11 petitions, which were jointly administered under Fed. R. Bankr.P. 1015, but not substantively consolidated, by the bankruptcy court. . . .

* * *

To determine whether MMP Hill is a single asset real estate debtor we look to the plain language of the statute. . . . Single asset real estate by statute is defined as real property that meets three elements: that the property be, first, "a single property or project, other than residential real property with fewer than [four] residential units"; second, that the property "generates substantially all of the gross income of a debtor who is not a family farmer"; and, third, that "no substantial business is being conducted by a debtor other than the business of operating the real property and activities incidental thereto." 11 U.S.C. § 101(51B).

The single asset real estate provisions at first applied only to debtors who owed four million dollars or less, but Congress removed this cap in 2005. Bankruptcy Abuse Prevention and Consumer Protection Act of 2005, Pub. L. No. 109–8, § 1201(5)(B), 119 Stat. 23, 193 (2005). If the single asset real estate provisions apply, the bankruptcy court "shall grant relief from [the automatic stay], such as by terminating, annulling, modifying, or conditioning such stay" to any creditor whose claim is secured by single asset real estate, unless:

> Not later than [90 days from the filing of the bankruptcy petition] or 30 days after the court determines that the debtor is subject to this paragraph, whichever is later—
>
>   (A) the debtor has filed a plan of reorganization that has a reasonable possibility of being confirmed within a reasonable time; or
>
>   (B) the debtor has commenced monthly payments [equal to the interest at the non-default contract rate of interest]

11 U.S.C. § 362(d)(3). The bankruptcy court concluded that MMP Hill "appears to have the characteristics of a [single asset real estate] case," suggesting that it found that Union Lofts meets the elements of § 101(51B). We agree. Union Lofts is (1) a single property that (2) generates all or substantially all of MMP Hill's gross income and (3) MMP Hill's only business activities involve operating and collecting rents from Union Lofts. In the absence of any evidence that MMP Hill received funds from MMPI or its sister subsidiaries in exchange for labor or services, or as profit from MMP Hill investments, or that any money received from those entities otherwise qualified as "income," we reject MMP Hill's argument that the consolidated management team and cash management system of MMPI and its subsidiaries allow MMP Hill to claim income generated by other MMPI entities, as well as the contention that any cash transferred to MMP Hill from MMPI or related entities should be characterized as "income" rather than as an equity investment by MMPI.

The bankruptcy court held MMP Hill is "part of a whole business enterprise to which it would not be appropriate to apply the [single asset real estate] provisions." The district court reversed, holding that Union Lofts is single asset real estate because it meets the elements of § 101(51B) and that there was no basis for the bankruptcy court's holding absent substantive consolidation. We agree with the district court, and we hold that the plain language of § 101(51B) gives no basis for a "whole business enterprise" exception. Absent a substantive consolidation order, we must accept MMP Hill's chosen legal status as a separate and distinct entity from its parent corporation and sister subsidiaries, and look only to its assets, income, and operations in determining whether Union Lofts is single asset real estate.

MMP Hill contends that we should "look to the substance and not the form" of the single asset real estate provisions because Congress did not intend to include entities that were part of complicated financial and organizational structures within the single asset real estate provisions. . . . Whatever the merits of a non-literal approach, we conclude that this is not one of those "rare cases." We presume that Congress said what it meant in the language it drafted. *Int'l Ass'n of Machinists & Aerospace Workers*, 387 F.3d at 1051. Congress could amend § 101(51B) to insert the "whole business enterprise" exception that MMP Hill champions, but it has not done so. We here apply the statute as it is written.

* * *

(Citations omitted.)

NOTES AND COMMENTS

1. As the cases note, some of the Code provisions regarding small business bankruptcies and single-asset real estate cases changed with the 2005 BAPCPA amendments. Why did Congress feel that these two types of bankruptcy cases merited different rules? Consider these statements from the National Bankruptcy Review Commission's 1997 report recommending changes to the Bankruptcy Code.

   That report found that "a moribund business generally has little to lose by seeking relief in bankruptcy. By filing under Chapter 11, the debtor gets the immediate benefit of the automatic stay, retains control of the business, and is under no requirement to pay creditors or file a plan promptly. Chapter 11 thus lures many small business debtors who have no realistic hope of confirming a plan." National Bankruptcy Review Commission, *Bankruptcy: The Next Twenty Years*, at 612 (Oct. 20, 1997), available at http://govinfo.library.unt.edu/nbrc/reportcont .html.

   As to single-asset cases, it focused on concerns of abuse of the bankruptcy system: "Two concerns are voiced most frequently by those who contend that abuse is rampant and must be stamped out. First, the automatic stay enables the debtor to prevent foreclosure for an extended period of time without filing a plan or making post-petition payments. This gives the debtor substantial leverage over the secured lender by imposing the principal costs of delay on that creditor. Second, SARE debtors sometimes attempt to use the provisions of Chapter 11 to keep overencumbered property without either paying the mortgage in full or obtaining the assent of a majority of creditors.

   These concerns are heightened because, many contend, SARE cases fulfill few of the recognized goals of Chapter 11. Reorganization is not generally necessary to preserve jobs and going-concern value in SARE cases. Whether the debtor keeps the real property or the secured creditor takes it back, the property will be operated in the same manner, creating the same jobs and economic activity." NBRC Report at 661.

2. Note that the American Bankruptcy Institute's Commission to Study the Reform of Chapter 11 has submitted a proposed amendment to Chapter 11 making a Chapter 11 reorganization a more viable option for small and medium-sized enterprises (SMEs). SMEs are defined in the proposed amendment, generally speaking, as companies that do not have publicly traded securities and whose assets or liabilities are less than $10 million. The proposal was brought because of research showing that these SMEs have been avoiding Chapter 11 and instead opting for liquidation under Chapter 7. Among other changes, the proposal would

make deadlines and reporting requirements easier to meet for SMEs under chapter 11.[13]

D. USE, SALE, OR LEASE OF PROPERTY OF THE ESTATE

Just as with any business, a debtor running a business needs to use its property to make money to pay creditors. But the use of that property in the bankruptcy context comes with a risk. If the debtor uses cash to pay employees, for example, the cash cannot be used to pay creditors, and there is no guaranty that the employees' efforts will yield additional cash that can be paid to creditors. As the debtor uses equipment in its manufacturing processes, the equipment faces wear and tear that makes the equipment less valuable. But if the debtor does not pay employees or use its equipment, it certainly won't make money to pay claims. To balance the competing goals of preserving property of the estate and using property of the estate to create more value for the estate, 11 U.S.C. § 363 provides guidance for the use, lease, or sale of the property of the estate. Before turning specifically to a discussion of that provision, it is important to have a basic understanding of secured transactions.

1. Basics of Secured Transactions

You have encountered secured creditors—those with collateral supporting their claims— throughout this book. Businesses typically have both real property and personal property. Real property includes land and buildings attached to land. Security interests in real property are referred to as "mortgages." Personal property includes the wide array of other assets owned by a business, including equipment such as the machines used to produce products, or the desks that workers use, inventory that becomes the business's final products, intangible items such as patents and licenses, and other valuable property such as stock holdings, bank accounts, and accounts receivable. A creditor can take an interest in almost any type of personal property owned by a business or individual. Article 9 of the Uniform Commercial Code (the UCC) governs security interests in personal (as opposed to real) property.

---

13. For the text of the proposed amendment and testimony from the Commission's co-chair, see: American Bankruptcy Institute, *Chapter 11 Commission Co-Chair Proposes Legislation for Viable Reorganizations for Small and Medium Sized Enterprises,* available at https://www.abi.org/newsroom/press-releases/chapter-11-reform-commission-co-chair-proposes-legislation-for-viable

A creditor becomes secured by *attaching* collateral and then *perfecting* its interest in that collateral. *Attachment* causes the creditor to have superior rights to the debtor in the collateral upon default.

Attachment

Attachment causes the creditor to have superior rights to the debtor in the collateral upon default. In order to attach to collateral, three requirements must be met:

(1) the debtor must have rights in the collateral (after all, the debtor cannot transfer rights to the creditor that the debtor does not have in the first place);

(2) the creditor must give value to the debtor in return for the transfer of those rights (i.e., consideration); and

(3) the parties must authenticate the transfer of the collateral, typically done through a signed security agreement.

For a simple example, consider a typical loan transaction. The creditor promises to loan the debtor $1 million. As part of the documentation of the loan, the debtor signs an agreement promising the creditor a security interest in all of the debtor's inventory and equipment. The loan itself (in fact, the binding commitment to make the loan qualifies) constitutes the value given by the creditor. The debtor has rights in its own inventory and equipment. And the parties sign an agreement documenting not just the loan itself, but the granting of a security interest in the collateral. Once all three pieces are in place, the creditor has attached the inventory and equipment and, upon the debtor's default, will be entitled to the collateral. When a creditor takes a security interest in all of the debtor's personal property,[14] the creditor is said to have a "blanket lien."

Creditors often seek a security interest in property to be acquired in the future in addition to property in which the debtor currently has an interest. That protects the creditor even in the event that the debtor's property interests change. For example, the inventory held by the debtor today may not be in inventory for long, and in a year most of the inventory may turn over. By including an "after-acquired" property clause in the security agreement, the creditor can ensure that it is protected by debtor's assets now and into the future.

---

14. Per U.C.C. § 9-108(c), the security agreement cannot simply say that the creditor has an interest in "all personal property." Rather, the security agreement must provide a more detailed list of the personal property. That list typically lists all categories of collateral recognized by the UCC.

Attachment only gives a creditor rights that are superior to those of the debtor, and generally only upon default by the debtor. But one debtor can allow multiple creditors to attach to the same collateral. **Perfection** provides notice of a security interest to the rest of the world and is typically accomplished by the filing of a *financing statement* in a state registry.[15] Generally speaking, the first creditor to file the financing statement or "perfect" a security interest has priority over later creditors. This first-in-time rule works because other creditors have constructive notice of the existence of competing creditors. There are many exceptions to the first-in-time rule. Perhaps the most notable is the purchase-money-security-interest (PMSI) exception, which allows a creditor who loaned money for the purpose of buying the collateral at issue to have priority as to that collateral.[16] Consider a few examples:

Perfection

Perfection provides notice of a security interest to the rest of the world, and is typically accomplished by the filing of a *financing statement* in a state registry.

Generally, the first creditor to file the financing statement or "perfect" a security interest has priority over later creditors.

The purchase-money-security-interest (PMSI) exception allows a creditor who loaned money for the purpose of buying certain collateral to have priority as to that collateral.

Example 1: Bank A loans Debtor $1 million, attaching and perfecting on all of the debtor's equipment (including after-acquired equipment) on January 1. Bank B loans Debtor $500,000, attaching and perfecting on all of the debtor's equipment (again, including after-acquired equipment) on February 1. Both banks have a security interest in the equipment, but Bank A has priority over Bank B because Bank A was first in time.

Example 2: Bank A loans Debtor $1 million, attaching on all of the debtor's equipment (including after-acquired equipment) on

---

15. Remember that priority among secured creditors under the UCC is different than bankruptcy priority under 11 U.S.C. § 507. Bankruptcy priority deals with priority among unsecured creditors and is based on congressional decisions regarding which creditors should be paid in what order among the assets allocated to pay unsecured claims.

16. A creditor seeking to take advantage of the PMSI exception must comply with specific filing dates based on the type of collateral in which the creditor seeks to have a PMSI and the date on which the debtor acquires that collateral. See U.C.C. § 9-324.

January 1. Bank B loans Debtor $500,000, attaching and perfecting on all of the debtor's equipment (again, including after-acquired equipment) on February 1. Bank A perfects on the debtor's equipment on March 1. Both banks have a security interest in the equipment, but Bank B has priority over Bank A because Bank B was first to file (and to perfect). While Bank A loaned money first, Bank B had no way of knowing about Bank A's interest in the equipment when Bank B loaned the debtor money. By failing to file a financing statement right away, Bank A had failed to put the world on notice of its interest and Bank B can jump in and create that notice of its interest first.

Example 3: Bank A loans Debtor $1 million, attaching and perfecting on all of the debtor's equipment (including after-acquired equipment) on January 1. Bank B loans Debtor $500,000 for the purpose of purchasing new equipment. Bank B gives the loan on February 1; the equipment is purchased on February 2; Bank B attaches and perfects its security interest on February 3. Both banks have a security interest in the equipment, but Bank B has priority over Bank A. Even though Bank A is first in time, Bank B can use the exception for a PMSI to take priority over Bank A. Without the PMSI exception, Bank B would likely not have loaned the money to Debtor to acquire the needed equipment since it would not have been willing to accept only a second priority interest in the equipment behind Bank A. So, the debtor is better off as it gets its equipment. Bank A is theoretically better off because the debtor is in a stronger business position with its new equipment, and Bank B is comfortable with its first priority security interest in that new equipment.

Another protection available to a creditor under the UCC is an interest in the proceeds of collateral. U.C.C. § 9-315. Attachment or perfection in a piece of collateral transfers to any "proceeds" of that collateral, ensuring that if the debtor sells, exchanges, or otherwise transfers the secured party's collateral, the secured party can have an interest in whatever the debtor receives in return. If the proceeds of the disposition of collateral include cash and the debtor then files for bankruptcy protection, that cash becomes "cash collateral" in the bankruptcy case—a category of collateral entitled to additional bankruptcy protection.

2. Use of Cash Collateral

Section 363(c) allows the trustee (or debtor-in-possession, per § 1107) to use property of the estate *in the ordinary course of business* without the need for notice and a hearing. That section provides an exception:

requiring notice and a hearing for the use of "cash collateral" even in the ordinary course of business. *Cash collateral* is a term of art in bankruptcy, defined by § 363(a) to include "cash,. negotiable instruments, documents of title, securities, deposit accounts, or other cash equivalents whenever acquired in which the estate and an entity other than the estate have an interest and includes the proceeds, products, offspring, rents, or profits of property and the fees, charges, accounts or other payments [related to room rentals in hotels and the like]. . .". Thus, cash collateral has two components: (1) it must be cash or a similar type of collateral, including the proceeds of property, and (2) a party other than the debtor must have an interest in it.

The following case considers how closely the cash must be related to collateral in order to constitute cash collateral.

In re Premier Golf Properties, LP

477 B.R. 767 (9th Cir. BAP 2012)

HOLLOWELL, Bankruptcy Judge

* * *

Premier Golf Properties, L.P. (the Golf Club) owns and operates the Cottonwood Golf Club in El Cajon, California. The Golf Club has two 18–hole golf courses, a driving range, pro shop, and club house restaurant. The Golf Club maintains the golf courses and operates a golf course business on the real property (Land). Its income comes from green fees, range fees, annual membership sales, golf lessons, golf cart rentals, pro shop clothing and equipment sales, and food and beverage services.

The Bank financed the Golf Club's business. In December 2007, the Bank loaned the Golf Club $11,500,000. The loan is secured by a Deed of Trust, Security Agreement, Assignment of Leases and Rents and Fixture Filing (Security Documents). According to the Security Documents, the Bank was granted a blanket security interest in all of the Golf Club's real and personal property. The Security Documents state, in part, that the Bank holds a security interest in all of the following described property "and all proceeds thereof":

> All accounts, contract rights, general intangibles, chattel paper, documents, instruments, inventory, goods, equipment . . . , including without limitation . . . all revenues, receipts, income, accounts, customer obligations, installment payment obligations . . . accounts receivable and other receivables, including without limitation license fees, golf club and membership initiation fees, green fees, driving range fees, golf cart fees, membership fees and dues, revenues, receipts, . . . and profits . . . arising from (i) rentals,. . . . license, concession, or other grant

of right of possession, use or occupancy of all or any portion of the Land, and . . . (ii) the provision or sale of any goods and services. . . .

Additionally, the Security Documents included an Assignment of Rents and Leases assigning the Bank an interest in:

all agreements affecting the use, enjoyment or occupancy of the Land now or hereafter entered into (the "Leases") and all rents, prepayments, security deposits, termination payments, royalties, profits, issues and revenues from the Land . . . accruing under the Leases. . . .

The Bank filed UCC–1 Financing Statements listing the same collateral as that in the Security Documents.

On May 2, 2011, the Golf Club filed a chapter 11 bankruptcy petition. It continued to operate its business as debtor in possession. The Golf Club opened a new bank account designated for cash collateral and segregated in that account its prepetition cash and receivables from goods and inventory sold, but did not segregate the revenue received from green fees and driving range fees.

On May 13, 2011, the Bank filed an emergency motion to prohibit the Golf Club from using cash collateral. The Bank asserted that the Golf Club was using the Bank's cash collateral in its ordinary course of business without the Bank's consent and without providing adequate protection.

On May 22, 2011, the Golf Club filed an opposition, asserting that it was not using the Bank's cash collateral but was operating the estate from its own postpetition income. The Golf Club argued that the postpetition income from the sale of golf memberships, green fees, cart rentals, the sale of buckets of balls for the driving range, and food and beverage service was not the proceeds, profits, or products of the Bank's collateral.

In its reply, the Bank focused its argument on the revenue from the green fees and driving range fees. It argued the fees were cash collateral because they were rents derived from the use of the Land. Alternatively, the Bank argued that if the green fees and driving range fees were not rents, they were still cash collateral because they were proceeds or profits of its personal property collateral.

. . . The bankruptcy court held that the revenue received by the Golf Club for green fees and driving range fees was not the rents or proceeds of the Bank's security and therefore, was not cash collateral. The Bank timely appealed.

* * *

A debtor in possession is prohibited from using cash collateral absent authorization by the court or consent from the entity that has an interest in the collateral. 11 U.S.C. § 363(c)(2). Cash collateral consists of "cash, negotiable instruments . . . deposit accounts, or other cash equivalents whenever acquired in which the estate and an entity other than the estate have an interest." 11 U.S.C. § 363(a).

As a general rule, postpetition revenue is not cash collateral. Under § 552(a), a creditor's prepetition security interest does not extend to property acquired by the debtor postpetition even if there is an "after acquired" clause in the security agreement. 11 U.S.C. § 552(a). The purpose of § 552(a) is "to allow a debtor to gather into the estate as much money as possible to satisfy the claims of all creditors."

Section 552(b) provides an exception to this rule. Section 552(b)(1) allows a prepetition security interest to extend to the postpetition "proceeds, products, offspring, or profits" of collateral to be covered by a security interest if the security agreement expressly provides for an interest in such property and the interest has been perfected under applicable nonbankruptcy law. Additionally, § 552(b)(2) provides similar treatment for "amounts paid as rents of such property or the fees, charges, accounts, or other payments for the use or occupancy of rooms and other public facilities in hotels, motels, or other lodging properties." Read together, the provisions of § 363(c)(2) and § 552(b) protect a creditor's collateral from being used by a debtor postpetition if the creditor's security interest extends to one of the categories set out in § 552(b). Put another way, a creditor is not entitled to the protections of § 363(c)(2) unless its security interest satisfies § 552(b). . . .

. . . the Bank was required to show that (1) its security agreement extended to the Golf Club's postpetition revenue from green fees and driving range fees and (2) the green fees and driving range fees were proceeds, products, rents or profits of its prepetition collateral.

. . . In 1987, the Ninth Circuit Bankruptcy Appellate Panel (BAP) articulated a general test for determining whether income from real property constitutes rents: If the income is produced by the real property, it is considered rents; but if the income is the result of services rendered or the result of the specific business conducted on the property, then it does not constitute rents. *In re Zeeway Corp.*, 71 B.R. at 211–12. In applying its test, the BAP concluded that gate receipts generated by postpetition races at the debtor's racetrack were not within the scope of rents subject to the creditor's deed of trust because the income was not produced by the occupancy or use of the real property, but by the services that the raceway provided.

* * *

Courts have used the *Zeeway* test to determine whether revenue from green fees and similar use fees is rents constituting cash collateral. The first of those decisions, *In re GGVXX, Ltd.*, 130 B.R. 322, 326 (Bankr. D. Colo.1991), held that revenue from green fees and use fees was not directly tied to or wholly dependent on the use of the real property, but was the result of the operation of the golf course business, and therefore, was not rents. The court determined that "a temporary right to enter upon real property and partake of the services offered thereon is not the same as an interest in real property." Thus, it concluded that the relationship to the real property was "too attenuated from the actual real estate to reasonably be considered as directly derived from the use of the land."

Similarly, the court in *In re Everett Home Town Ltd. P'ship*, 146 B.R. 453, 456 (Bankr.D.Ariz.1992) held that although revenue from green fees was produced in part by the use of the real property, the income was the result of the services provided by the golf club business. However, it further held that revenue from suite fees was rents because, like a hotel room, the main charge was for the occupancy of the suite.

The Bank asserts that the Ninth Circuit's opinion in *Fin. Sec. Assurance, Inc. v. Days Cal. Riverside Ltd. P'ship (In re Days Cal. Riverside Ltd. P'ship)*, 27 F.3d 374 (9th Cir. 1994) altered the *Zeeway* test. The Bank argues that *Days* created a new approach to determining whether income was rents by focusing on the economics of the case from the perspective of the *source* of the revenue and the bargain of the parties. Thus, the Bank argues that determining if revenue is rents must take into account the perspective of the lender, the contractual and economic intent of the parties at the time the loan was made, and the economic consequences on the financing market if § 552(b) is read too narrowly.

The Bank contends that revenue from the green fees and driving range fees is a primary component of the value of the Land. It argues that "[l]ike hotels, the value of golf courses, both for financing and investment purposes, is principally based on the net operating income of the golf course, a principal component of which is green fees and driving range fees." To give meaning to the benefit of the parties' agreement, the Bank asserts that the Golf Club's income from green fees and driving range fees must be considered rents generated from the Land.

The Bank's argument is unpersuasive. The Ninth Circuit in *Days* concluded that hotel room charges were rents based on its determination that under California law, room rent is "produced by the property." 27 F.3d at 377. Its conclusion was "buttressed by, although . . . not dependent upon, the distinction made in *In re Bering Trader, Inc.,* 944 F.2d at 502, between income that is derivative from the secured property and income that is derived from services." *Id.* Thus, the *Days* court did not erode the *Zeeway* test in favor of a different approach. The *Days* court was mindful that hotel financing depended on access to the stream of revenue produced by the hotels and that excluding hotel receipts from the scope of rents would cut against the bargain made by the parties. However, it based its decision on the premise that room rent was generated from the occupancy of real property and differentiated between revenue from occupancy of rooms and revenue that was generated by other services provided by the hotel. *Id.* Consequently, the *Zeeway* test remains a viable guideline for determining if revenue constitutes rents.

* * *

The bankruptcy court noted that the key to a golf club's generation of income is due to the regular planting, seeding, mowing, repositioning holes, watering, fertilizing, and maintaining the golf course. Based on *Zeeway* and *Days,* we agree with the bankruptcy court and conclude that the Golf Club's revenue from green fees and driving range fees is not produced from the Land as much as generated by other services that are performed on the Land, and therefore, is not rents. Unlike hotel cases where the revenue from room rental derives primarily from the usage of real property as shelter or occupancy, a golf course derives its revenue primarily from the usage of real property as entertainment. As a result, the bankruptcy court did not err in determining that the Golf Club's green fees and driving range fees were not rents subject to the Bank's real property security interest.

. . . The Bank alternatively argues that if the Golf Club's postpetition green fees and driving range fees are not rents, they are proceeds of the Bank's security interest in the Golf Club's intangible property.

As discussed above, distinguishing between after-acquired property and what may fall within § 552(b)'s exceptions is key to determining what is cash collateral. A creditor's interest in proceeds, products, offspring, or profits are secured "to the extent provided by . . . applicable nonbankruptcy law." Thus, Congress intended to defer to state law, namely, the Uniform Commercial Code (UCC), in making the determination of what constitutes proceeds.

UCC § 9–102(a)(64) defines proceeds as:

> (A) whatever is acquired upon the sale, lease, license, exchange, or other disposition of collateral;
>
> (B) whatever is collected on, or distributed on account of, collateral;
>
> (C) rights arising out of collateral . . .

Accordingly, postpetition proceeds, products, offspring, or profits are subject to an after-acquired property clause only if they *derive from* prepetition collateral.

Here, the Bank holds a perfected security interest in general intangibles, including the Golf Club's personal property, licenses, payment obligations and receipts. A "general intangible" means:

> any personal property, including things in action, other than accounts, chattel paper, commercial tort claims, deposit accounts, documents, goods, instruments, investment property, letter-of-credit rights, letters of credit, money, and oil, gas, or other minerals before extraction. The term includes payment intangibles and software.

UCC § 9–102(a)(42). "General intangibles" is a "residual" category of personal property, and includes rights that arise under a license and payment intangibles. *See* Official Comment 5(d). The question we must answer is whether the revenue from the Golf Club's green fees and driving range fees was acquired on the disposition of, or collected on, the Golf Club's general intangible property making them proceeds of the Bank's collateral.

. . . A license is a contract that authorizes the use of an asset without an accompanying transfer of ownership. There is no real dispute that the Golf Club licenses the use of the Land to golfers who pay for "a temporary right to enter upon real property and partake of the services offered thereon." Thus, "[g]olfers, by paying a greens fee, become mere licensees, entitled to the non-exclusive use of the golf course for a short period of time."

* * *

The Golf Club asserts that because the licenses belonged to the *golfers,* not the Golf Club, they were not part of the Bank's security interest. That argument is unpersuasive. The Golf Club, as licensor, collects payment in exchange for providing a license to golfers to use its facilities. . . .

However, the BAP has noted that "revenue generated by the operation of a debtor's business, post-petition, is not considered proceeds if such revenue represents compensation for goods and services rendered by the debtor in its everyday business performance. . . . Revenue generated post-petition solely as a result of a debtor's labor is not subject to a creditor's pre-petition interest." Section 552(b) is "intended to cover after-acquired property that is directly attributable to prepetition collateral, *without addition of estate resources.*"

The Golf Club must maintain the Land regularly as part of its business operation by mowing, planting, watering, fertilizing, and repairing the grass, raking sand traps, repositioning the holes, and retrieving golf balls from the range. Thus, the revenue that the Golf Club generates postpetition on the licenses is not merely from issuing a license to its customers but is largely the result of the Golf Club's labor and own operational resources, which make the license valuable to golfers. Consequently, although the green fees and driving range fees may be "collected on" the Golf Club's licenses, they are not proceeds generated from the Bank's collateral.

* * *

In *In re Northview Corp.,* 130 B.R. at 548, the BAP noted that the term "profits" in § 552(b) refers to the sale of real property to which a perfected security interest attached. Thus, profits arise out of the ownership of real property and derive from conversion of the property into some other property. We already concluded that the green fees and driving range fees are not derivative of the Bank's security interest in the Land when we determined that the fees were not in the nature of rents. As a result, the green fees and driving range fees are not profits of the Bank's security interest in the Land.

. . . The postpetition revenue from the Golf Club's green fees and driving range fees is not the rents, proceeds or profits of the Bank's security interest within the exceptions of § 552(b). Accordingly, we conclude that the green fees and driving range fees are not the Bank's cash collateral. Therefore, we AFFIRM.

(Citations omitted.)

NOTES AND COMMENTS

1. The court distinguishes the post-petition revenues received by a golf club from those received by a hotel chain. How are the two different? Does it

matter that the hotel staff must maintain and service the rooms between guests? Would the post-petition revenues received by a hotel continue to be proceeds of the hotel property if repairs had to be done on the rooms? What if the hotel underwent a complete renovation?

2. How does § 552(b) fit with § 363(c)? The court states that before § 363(c) can create cash collateral, the creditor must have an interest under § 552(b). Do you agree?

When cash collateral is used, or when other types of property of the estate are used, sold, or leased outside of the ordinary course of business, the court must approve such use following notice and a hearing. The following case provides an example of a court considering which Bankruptcy Code standard governs whether to allow the use of cash collateral. Notice the recurrence of the notion of deference to the business judgment of business managers. Recall that the "Business Judgment Rule" was described and discussed above as a defense to a duty of care claim.

In re ASARCO, L.L.C.

650 F.3d 593 (5th Cir. 2011)

STEWART, Circuit Judge

The bankruptcy court in this case issued an order that authorized the debtor, ASARCO LLC ("ASARCO"), to reimburse qualified bidders for expenses incurred in connection with the sale of a substantial asset of the debtor's estate. The bankruptcy court determined that such reimbursements were proper under the business judgment standard in section 363(b) of the Bankruptcy Code. . . .

* * *

ASARCO is a mining conglomerate that was purchased by Grupo Mexico, S.A.B. de C.V. in 1999. ASARCO's assets at the time included a controlling number of shares in Southern Peru Copper Company ("SCC"). Grupo Mexico transferred the SCC shares to a holding company it created as a wholly-owned subsidiary of ASARCO, and it created AMC as its own wholly-owned subsidiary. After financial troubles beset ASARCO, Grupo Mexico decided to sell the SCC shares in 2003 by transferring them to AMC. ASARCO was unable to escape its financial difficulties, however, and in 2005 it filed for Chapter 11 bankruptcy.

While its bankruptcy proceeding was pending, ASARCO brought an adversary action in the district court against AMC. ASARCO, proceeding in its capacity as debtor-in-possession, alleged that AMC wrongfully caused ASARCO to transfer the SCC shares. The district court conducted a four-week bench trial in 2008 and ultimately found AMC liable for actual fraudulent transfer, aiding and abetting a breach of fiduciary duty, and conspiracy. In April 2009, the district court awarded damages and entered final judgment. The final judgment ("SCC Judgment") ordered AMC to transfer approximately 260 million shares of SCC common stock to ASARCO and pay nearly $1.4 billion in damages for past dividends and interest.

. . . In the bankruptcy proceeding, ASARCO and the Parent submitted competing plans of reorganization under Chapter 11. ASARCO's plan proposed to be partially funded with the SCC Judgment, which was the most substantial asset of the debtor's estate. Given the difficulty of valuing the SCC Judgment, ASARCO decided to sell the asset via a two-part bid solicitation process, subject to a topping auction. Such a process, ASARCO believed, would maximize the value of the SCC Judgment. ASARCO engaged the services of its financial advisor, Barclays Capital Inc., to help identify potential bidders for all or a portion of the SCC Judgment.

In July 2009, while Barclays was conducting the first phase of the bid solicitation process, ASARCO moved the bankruptcy court for the order at the heart of this dispute. ASARCO requested authorization to reimburse certain expenses incurred by bidders selected to proceed to the second phase of the bid process. In its motion, ASARCO explained that after consulting with its advisors, it had decided to invite a select group of bidders to proceed to the second phase of the process. During the second phase, the bidders would have the opportunity to conduct additional due diligence relating to the SCC Judgment. That due diligence would entail highly sophisticated legal analysis—and thus substantial legal costs—and ASARCO believed it necessary to provide bidders with an incentive to undertake this investment. ASARCO thus sought authorization under section 363 of the Bankruptcy Code to reimburse qualified bidders for their due diligence expenses.

On July 29, 2009, after a hearing, the bankruptcy court issued an order granting ASARCO's motion (the "Reimbursement Order"). The bankruptcy court concluded that ASARCO had demonstrated a "compelling and sound business justification" for the authorization requested. . . .

* * *

Appellants raise three challenges to the Reimbursement Order. First, they contend that the bankruptcy court applied the wrong standard under the Bankruptcy Code to ASARCO's motion for authorization to pay reimbursement expenses. They argue that the bankruptcy court should have considered ASARCO's motion under section 503(b), which applies to administrative expenses, and not under section 363(b), the business judgment standard. Section 503(b) is the more stringent of the two, and Appellants contend that under that standard the Reimbursement Order was in error. Second, Appellants argue that even assuming section 363(b) was the correct standard to apply, the bankruptcy court erred in finding that ASARCO's motion satisfied the business judgment standard.

* * *

Section 363 of the Bankruptcy Code addresses the debtor's use of property of the estate and incorporates a business judgment standard. Subsection 363(b) provides that "a debtor-in-possession, 'after notice and hearing, may use, sell, or lease, other than in the ordinary course of business, property of the estate.'" In such circumstances, "for the debtor-in-possession or trustee to satisfy its fiduciary duty to the debtor, creditors and equity holders, there must be some articulated business justification for using, selling, or leasing the property outside the ordinary course of business."

The business judgment standard in section 363 is flexible and encourages discretion. "Whether the proffered business justification is sufficient depends on the case. . . . [T]he bankruptcy judge 'should consider all salient factors pertaining to the proceeding and, accordingly, act to further the diverse interests of the debtor, creditors and equity holders, alike.'"

In contrast, the narrower standard in section 503 of the Bankruptcy Code pertains to entities that have incurred administrative expenses and wish to request payment from the estate. Claims under this section "generally stem from voluntary transactions with third parties who lend goods or services necessary to the successful reorganization of the debtor's estate." Subsection 503(b) allows parties to recover administrative expenses "including the actual, necessary costs and expenses of preserving the estate." 11 U.S.C. § 503(b)(1). But as used in this section, "[t]he words 'actual' and 'necessary' have been construed narrowly: 'the debt must benefit [the] estate and its creditors.'"

Appellants argue that the bankruptcy court erred in relying on section 363(b) to issue the Reimbursement Order. They assert that the business judgment standard in section 363(b) is too broadly worded to address what they contend is the salient issue here: whether third parties such as the Intervenors may recover expenses incurred in the course of due diligence. In Appellants' view, the correct and applicable standard—the one the bankruptcy court should have applied—appears in section 503(b)(1). Under that standard for administrative expenses, Appellants argue, the Reimbursement Order was in error because the requested reimbursements were not actually necessary to preserve the value of the estate.

In support of their argument Appellants cite two Third Circuit decisions where the court applied section 503(b) and not 363(b) to requests for break-up fees. *See In re Reliant Energy Channelview LP,* 594 F.3d 200 (3d Cir.2010); *In re O'Brien Envtl. Energy, Inc.,* 181 F.3d 527 (3d Cir.1999). In both *Reliant* and *O'Brien,* the bankruptcy court refused to approve break-up fees to unsuccessful stalking-horse bidders in bankruptcy auctions. . . .

We are not persuaded that *Reliant* and *O'Brien* are apt where, as here, a debtor requests the authority to reimburse expense fees "for second-round 'qualified' bidders in a multiple stage auction for a very unique and very valuable but possibly worthless asset." For one, the break-up fee provisions at issue in *Reliant* and *O'Brien* significantly differ from the due diligence reimbursement fees at issue in this case. The break-up fees were to be paid only if the prospective bidder was unsuccessful. Here, in contrast, prospective (and qualified) bidders could be reimbursed regardless of whether they were ultimately successful. Moreover, in both *O'Brien* and *Reliant Energy* the bankruptcy court refused to approve the break-up fee in part due to the concern that the fee would "chill . . . the competitive bidding process." No such concern arises in this context, where ASARCO sought to *increase* competition by providing bidders an incentive to undertake the costly but necessary due diligence.

On this record, we conclude that the business judgment standard is the better fit for assessing ASARCO's reimbursement motion. Section 363 addresses the debtor's use of the estate property, and in its motion ASARCO sought authorization to make discretionary use of the estate's funds. Section 503, in contrast, generally applies to third parties that have already incurred expenses in connection to the debtor's estate. The unsuccessful bidders in *O'Brien* and *Reliant Energy* sought payment for expenses incurred without the court's pre-approval for reimbursement, and thus section 503 was the proper channel for requesting payment. In ASARCO's case, however, the bankruptcy court issued the Reimbursement Order *before* any potential qualified bidders, including the Intervenors, had incurred due diligence and work fees. In this context, application of the business judgment standard is appropriate.

. . . Appellants argue that even if section 363(b) applies in this case, there was insufficient evidence in the record to support the bankruptcy court's finding that the requested expense reimbursements had sound business justification. As stated in the Reimbursement Order, the bankruptcy court found that ASARCO's proposed reimbursement of expenses was designed to maximize the value of ASARCO's estate, and was fair, reasonable, and appropriate. The bankruptcy court further determined that the Reimbursement Order was "in the best interests of ASARCO and its estate, creditors, interest holders, stakeholders, and all other parties in interest." On this basis, the bankruptcy court concluded that ASARCO had demonstrated a compelling and sound business justification for the reimbursement authority. Finding no clear error in the bankruptcy court's findings of fact, we defer to its findings.

* * *

NOTES AND COMMENTS

1. Where in § 363 is the business judgment standard found? Why do the courts uniformly accept the business judgment of the trustee or debtor-in-possession as the appropriate standard for use, sale, or lease of estate property?

2. Is the business judgment standard, as articulated by the bankruptcy court in the ASARCO case, the same as the business judgment rule outlined in the general discussion of fiduciary duties above? If not, how is it different?

3. 363 sales

One transaction that is clearly outside of the ordinary course of business is the sale of all or substantially all of the assets of the company. However, such "363 sales" have become increasingly more common in Chapter 11 bankruptcy cases. The following case explores the rights of creditors to ensure that such a sale (here, written into the plan of reorganization) does not negatively impact the creditors' rights to collateral. The case also illustrates standards used when courts consider whether to confirm a so-called cramdown plan, discussed above.

RadLAX Gateway Hotel, LLC v. Amalgamated Bank

132 S. Ct. 2065 (U.S. 2012)

Scalia, Justice

We consider whether a Chapter 11 bankruptcy plan may be confirmed over the objection of a secured creditor pursuant to 11 U.S.C. § 1129(b)(2)(A) if the plan provides for the sale of collateral free and clear of the creditor's lien, but does not permit the creditor to "credit-bid" at the sale.

. . . In 2007, petitioners RadLAX Gateway Hotel, LLC, and RadLAX Gateway Deck, LLC (hereinafter debtors), purchased the Radisson Hotel at Los Angeles International Airport, together with an adjacent lot on which the debtors planned to build a parking structure. To finance the purchase, the renovation of the hotel, and construction of the parking structure, the debtors obtained a $142 million loan from Longview Ultra Construction Loan Investment Fund, for which respondent Amalgamated Bank (hereinafter creditor or Bank) serves as trustee. The lenders obtained a blanket lien on all of the debtors' assets to secure the loan.

Completing the parking structure proved more expensive than anticipated, and within two years the debtors had run out of funds and were forced to halt construction. By August 2009, they owed more than $120 million on the loan, with over $1 million in interest accruing every month and no prospect for obtaining additional funds to complete the project. Both debtors filed voluntary petitions for relief under Chapter 11 of the Bankruptcy Code.

A Chapter 11 bankruptcy is implemented according to a "plan," typically proposed by the debtor, which divides claims against the debtor into separate "classes" and specifies the treatment each class will receive. See 11 U.S.C. § 1123. Generally, a bankruptcy court may confirm a Chapter 11 plan only if each class of creditors affected by the plan consents. See § 1129(a)(8). Section 1129(b) creates an exception to that general rule, permitting confirmation of nonconsensual plans—commonly known as "cramdown" plans—if "the plan does not discriminate unfairly, and is fair and equitable, with respect to each class of claims or interests that is impaired under, and has not accepted, the plan." Section 1129(b)(2)(A), which we review in further depth below, establishes criteria for determining whether a cramdown plan is "fair and equitable" with respect to secured claims like the Bank's.

In 2010, the RadLAX debtors submitted a Chapter 11 plan to the United States Bankruptcy Court for the Northern District of Illinois.

The plan proposed to dissolve the debtors and to sell substantially all of their assets pursuant to procedures set out in a contemporaneously filed "Sale and Bid Procedures Motion." Specifically, the debtors sought to auction their assets to the highest bidder, with the initial bid submitted by a "stalking horse"—a potential purchaser who was willing to make an advance bid of $47.5 million. The sale proceeds would be used to fund the plan, primarily by repaying the Bank. Of course the Bank itself might wish to obtain the property if the alternative would be receiving auction proceeds that fall short of the property's full value. Under the debtors' proposed auction procedures, however, the Bank would not be permitted to bid for the property using the debt it is owed to offset the purchase price, a practice known as "credit-bidding." Instead, the Bank would be forced to bid cash. Correctly anticipating that the Bank would object to this arrangement, the debtors sought to confirm their plan under the cramdown provisions of § 1129(b)(2)(A).

The Bankruptcy Court denied the debtors' Sale and Bid Procedures Motion, concluding that the proposed auction procedures did not comply with § 1129(b)(2)(A)'s requirements for cramdown plans. The Bankruptcy Court certified an appeal directly to the United States Court of Appeals for the Seventh Circuit. That court accepted the certification and affirmed, holding that § 1129(b)(2)(A) does not permit debtors to sell an encumbered asset free and clear of a lien without permitting the lienholder to credit-bid. . . .

. . . A Chapter 11 plan confirmed over the objection of a "class of secured claims" must meet one of three requirements in order to be deemed "fair and equitable" with respect to the nonconsenting creditor's claim. The plan must provide:

"(i)(I) that the holders of such claims retain the liens securing such claims, whether the property subject to such liens is retained by the debtor or transferred to another entity, to the extent of the allowed amount of such claims; and (II) that each holder of a claim of such class receive on account of such claim deferred cash payments totaling at least the allowed amount of such claim, of a value, as of the effective date of the plan, of at least the value of such holder's interest in the estate's interest in such property;

"(ii) for the sale, subject to section 363(k) of this title, of any property that is subject to the liens securing such claims, free and clear of such liens, with such liens to attach to the proceeds of such sale, and the treatment of such liens on proceeds under clause (i) or (iii) of this subparagraph; or

"(iii) for the realization by such holders of the indubitable equivalent of such claims." 11 U.S.C. § 1129(b)(2)(A).

. . . Under clause (ii), the property is sold free and clear of the lien, "subject to section 363(k)," and the creditor receives a lien on the proceeds of the sale. Section 363(k), in turn, provides that "unless the court for cause orders otherwise the holder of such claim may bid at such sale, and, if the holder of such claim purchases such property, such holder may offset such claim against the purchase price of such property"—*i.e.,* the creditor may credit-bid at the sale, up to the amount of its claim. Finally, under clause (iii), the plan provides the secured creditor with the "indubitable equivalent" of its claim.

The debtors in this case have proposed to sell their property free and clear of the Bank's liens, and to repay the Bank using the sale proceeds—precisely, it would seem, the disposition contemplated by clause (ii). Yet since the debtors' proposed auction procedures do not permit the Bank to credit-bid, the proposed sale cannot satisfy the requirements of clause (ii). Recognizing this problem, the debtors instead seek plan confirmation pursuant to clause (iii), which—unlike clause (ii)—does not expressly foreclose the possibility of a sale without credit-bidding.

According to the debtors, their plan can satisfy clause (iii) by ultimately providing the Bank with the "indubitable equivalent" of its secured claim, in the form of cash generated by the auction.

We find the debtors' reading of § 1129(b)(2)(A)—under which clause (iii) permits precisely what clause (ii) proscribes—to be hyperliteral and contrary to common sense. A well established canon of statutory interpretation succinctly captures the problem: "[I]t is a commonplace of statutory construction that the specific governs the general." That is particularly true where, as in § 1129(b)(2)(A), "Congress has enacted a comprehensive scheme and has deliberately targeted specific problems with specific solutions."

The general/specific canon is perhaps most frequently applied to statutes in which a general permission or prohibition is contradicted by a specific prohibition or permission. To eliminate the contradiction, the specific provision is construed as an exception to the general one. But the canon has full application as well to statutes such as the one here, in which a general authorization and a more limited, specific authorization exist side-by-side. There the canon avoids not contradiction but the superfluity of a specific provision that is swallowed by the general one, "violat[ing] the cardinal rule that, if possible, effect shall be given to every clause and part of a statute." The terms of the specific authorization must be complied with. . . .

Here, clause (ii) is a detailed provision that spells out the requirements for selling collateral free of liens, while clause (iii) is a broadly worded provision that says nothing about such a sale. The general/specific canon explains that the "general language" of clause (iii), "although broad enough to include it, will not be held to apply to a matter specifically dealt with" in clause (ii).

Of course the general/specific canon is not an absolute rule, but is merely a strong indication of statutory meaning that can be overcome by textual indications that point in the other direction. The debtors point to no such indication here. One can conceive of a statutory scheme in which the specific provision embraced within a general one is not superfluous, because it creates a so-called safe harbor. The debtors effectively contend that that is the case here—clause (iii) ("indubitable equivalent") being the general rule, and clauses (i) and (ii) setting forth procedures that will always, *ipso facto*, establish an "indubitable equivalent," with no need for judicial evaluation. But the structure here would be a surpassingly strange manner of accomplishing that result—which would normally be achieved by setting forth the "indubitable equivalent" rule first (rather than last), and establishing the two safe harbors as provisos to that rule. The structure here suggests, to the contrary, that (i) is the rule for plans under which the creditor's lien remains on the property, (ii) is the rule for plans under which the property is sold free and clear of the creditor's lien, and (iii) is a residual provision covering dispositions under all other plans—for example, one under which the creditor receives the property itself, the "indubitable equivalent" of its secured claim. Thus, debtors may not sell their property free of liens under § 1129(b)(2)(A) without allowing lienholders to credit-bid, as required by clause (ii).

* * *

(Citations omitted.)

NOTES AND COMMENTS

1. What constitutes the "indubitable equivalent" of either retaining a lien on collateral or being allowed to credit-bid at a sale of the collateral? *See* In re East River Plaza, LLC, 669 F.3d 826 (7th Cir. 2012) (giving lien on Treasury bonds to creditor to replace lien on real property not indubitable equivalent of retaining lien on real property). *Cf.* In re Scrub Island Development Group Ltd., 523 B.R. 862, 877 (Bankr. M.D.

Fla. 2015) ("*River East Plaza* does not stand for the proposition that substitute collateral cannot satisfy the 'indubitable equivalent' standard, only that it fails to do so when the substitute collateral is less valuable or more volatile than the original collateral.").

2. Some commentators have suggested the credit-bidding is also a constitutional right of secured lenders because use of bankruptcy laws to deny a creditor its contracted-for property rights would constitute a taking of property. *See, e.g.,* Geoffrey K. McDonald, *The Road Not Taken:* RadLax *and the Unstated Constitutional Basis and Limits of a Secured Creditor's Right to Credit Bid at a Bankruptcy Sale of Its Collateral,* 2014 Norton Ann. Survey of Bankr. Law 9 (2014).

3. Some scholars have criticized the use of Section 363 sales as a manipulative device that has undercut the established priority rules that have characterized bankruptcy law for the past 100 years. See, e.g., Ralph Brubaker and Charles Jordan Tabb, *Bankruptcy Reorganizations and the Troubling Legacy of Chrysler and GM,* 2010 U. Ill. L. Rev. 1375.

4. Obtaining Credit as a Debtor in Bankruptcy

Not surprisingly, businesses trying to reorganize under Chapter 11 of the Bankruptcy Code sometimes need an additional influx of capital in order to successfully reorganize. Traditional corporations in need of funding have several options open to them, including borrowing money, finding additional equity investors, or selling assets. But finding lenders, equity investors, or purchasers of assets for a company in bankruptcy is far more challenging. Further, the sale of assets might not be in the best interests of the company if those assets are needed to successfully reorganize. And, in bankruptcy, as noted above, the sale of assets outside of the ordinary course of business requires judicial notice and a hearing.

Most Chapter 11 debtors seek financing, known as "debtor-in-possession financing," to finance bankruptcy operations. But the lender providing that financing will need assurances that it will be repaid or, if not repaid, will have collateral to take instead. This can put the debtor-in-possession financer in conflict with previously existing secured creditors who stand to lose their first-in-time priority on property of the estate. But without such financing, unsecured creditors with no collateral to lean on run the risk of little to no payment when the reorganization fails.

Section 364 provides guidelines for how a debtor may incur additional debt (including smaller debt, such as purchasing new inventory on credit). That section provides that the debtor may incur debt as follows:

- Incurring unsecured debt in the ordinary course of business: permitted, and the creditor holds status as an administrative expense with § 507 priority (§ 364(a)).
- Incurring unsecured debt outside of the ordinary course of business: requires notice and a hearing and, if permitted, the creditor holds status as an administrative expense with § 507 priority (§ 364(b)).
- If the debtor cannot incur debt with simple administrative expense status: requires notice and a hearing and, if permitted, the creditor may (1) hold status as an administrative expense with priority over all other administrative expense claimants, or (2) be secured by unencumbered property of the estate, or (3) be secured by already-encumbered property but hold a lien junior to previously existing secured creditors with a claim on that property (§ 364(c)).

Note that the first two options are detrimental to general unsecured creditors as well as to any priority creditors who rank below administrative claims. The third option not only harms those creditors but also harms all other administrative expense claims. And, if the new creditor is given a security interest, it removes value that would otherwise be available to pay even the highest priority unsecured creditors.

At times, there is no unencumbered or underencumbered property in which to give a security interest or no creditor willing to provide credit with simple administrative priority or a junior lien on assets. In those cases, § 364(d) comes into play. This subsection requires notice and a hearing, but if successful, allows the party granting credit to a debtor-in-possession to trump an existing lien—to take UCC first-in-time priority away from an existing creditor. To effectuate this extreme remedy, the debtor-in-possession and creditor seeking to prime an existing lien must show that the debtor-in-possession cannot otherwise obtain credit and that the existing lienholder is "adequately protected." Consider again the *Colad* case, part of which was excerpted above, as an example.

In re The Colad Group, Inc.

324 B.R. 208 (Bankr. W.D.N.Y. 2005)

BUCKI, Bankruptcy Judge

* * *

The most important of the first day motions was the application for authority to obtain post-petition financing. Like most debtors in chapter 11, Colad had pledged nearly all of its assets as collateral to secure a pre-petition credit facility. Among these assets were

Colad's inventory, receivables, and the proceeds of its inventory and receivables, all of which are deemed to constitute "cash collateral," as defined by section 363(a) of the Bankruptcy Code. Pursuant to 11 U.S.C. § 363(c)(2), a debtor in possession may not use cash collateral unless either "(A) each entity that has an interest in such cash collateral consents; or (B) the court, after notice and a hearing, authorizes such use, sale, or lease in accordance with the provisions of this section." Hence, without either consent or court authorization, Colad would have had no access to most of the cash that would have been generated through its normal business operations. To satisfy its cash needs, Colad moved under 11 U.S.C. § 364 for emergency and final authority to obtain post-petition financing from Continental, the current holder of Colad's pre-petition loan facility.

Continental and Colad have proposed to link the post-petition financing facility to the debtor's pre-petition revolver loan. Under their agreement, proceeds of collateral would be applied first to the satisfaction of the balance due on the pre-petition loan. Meanwhile, Continental would fund the debtor's post-petition activities through new advances under the post-petition facility. Providing that post-petition advances would be secured by all assets of the debtor, the proposed facility would also create an obligation that would receive administrative and super priority status, as allowed under 11 U.S.C. § 364(c).

In a competitive and adversarial environment, one cannot fault a creditor for seeking an outcome that will maximize the return for itself. For this reason, this court has often approved the post-petition use of a revolving credit facility. From the lender's perspective, such an arrangement avoids the various legal problems of cross-collateralization. In a cross-collateralization arrangement, a lender advances new credit on condition that an enhanced set of collateral will secure both pre-petition and post-petition loans. Instead, the revolver arrangement permits a satisfaction of the pre-petition loan, so that an increasing percentage of the lender's total exposure will receive the security and benefits of the new post-petition credit facility. Although this court will approve a proper-post petition revolver facility, it will not allow a disregard of the procedural and substantive rights of other parties in interest.

Bankruptcy Rule 4001 imposes procedural rules for consideration of a motion for authority to obtain credit. Subdivision (c)(1) of this rule requires that the court treat such a motion as a contested matter under Rule 9014, and that notice of such a motion be served upon the members of the Official Committee of Unsecured Creditors, or if no committee has been appointed, then upon the twenty largest unsecured creditors. In a typical case, this requirement of notice presents practical challenges, in as much as most debtors have an immediate need for financing. For this reason, the following text of Bankruptcy Rule 4001(c)(2) attempts to find a balance that will accommodate both financial necessity and concerns for due process:

> The court may commence a final hearing on a motion for authority to obtain credit no earlier than 15 days after service of the motion. If the motion so requests, the court may conduct a hearing before such 15 day period expires, *but the court may authorize the obtaining of credit only to the extent necessary to avoid immediate and irreparable harm to the estate pending a final hearing.*

(emphasis added). Pursuant to this rule, therefore, the court may consider a first day motion to approve an emergency lending facility, but only if two conditions are satisfied. First, any emergency authorization must be limited only "to the extent necessary to avoid immediate and irreparable harm." Second, the authorization may be effective only until a final hearing on appropriate notice to creditors as required under Rule 4001(c)(1).

In support of its first day motion for authority to obtain post-petition financing, the debtor represented that it could not operate without a post-petition line of credit and that it had no ability to obtain such credit from any source other than Continental. Conceptually, this Court found that these representations were adequate to justify an appropriate form of emergency lending until the scheduled hearing for final approval. However, in the form that the debtor proposed, the emergency funding order was unacceptable for the following four reasons:

1. The order failed to reflect any effort to limit the conditions of credit only to those which would be absolutely necessary to avoid immediate and irreparable harm. *See* Bankruptcy Rule 4001(c)(2). Rather, the proposed order would have approved an interim loan agreement with terms essentially identical to those contemplated for the final loan agreement. The only difference between the two agreements was their effective date. Without a showing of any compelling reason for identical terms, the debtor appeared to treat the interim order as a mere formality of procedure on a one-way street to approval of a final order.

2. The interim order was inappropriately complex, and thereby denied to the court a sufficient basis of confidence in the reasonableness of its terms. On an emergency basis, the debtor wanted the court to

sign a twenty-six page order, which incorporated the terms of a loan agreement that filled 93 pages of single space text, including exhibits. This court appreciates the dollar value of the proposed lending facility, and accepts the need for a comprehensive agreement. For this reason, as hereafter discussed, the court has carefully examined the terms of the final loan agreement. A first day order is inherently different, however. Without benefit of opportunities for comment from creditors on notice, the court must view with skepticism the exigent submission of any such complex instrument.

3. Based on its cursory review, the court discovered that the proposed order would change substantive and procedural rights, without allowing any reasonable opportunity for creditor objection. For example, the interim loan arrangement included a grant of relief from the automatic stay in the event of default, limitations on the debtor's right to propose a plan of reorganization, and a waiver of various claims that the debtor might assert against Continental. Particularly troublesome were the provisions of section 11.6 of the Loan Agreement, which purported to require, as a condition for interim funding, the disavowal and waiver of various "rights and remedies provided under the Bankruptcy Code, the Federal Rules of Civil Procedure, and the Bankruptcy Rules." Furthermore, paragraphs 2.1 and 11.1 of the Loan Agreement seemingly attempted to grant administrative priority to the pre-petition claims of Continental. Later in this opinion, the court will discuss whether certain of these terms are appropriately included into an order that authorizes lending on a final basis. As part of a first day order, where unsecured creditors have had no opportunity to object, such terms are unacceptable.

4. As originally submitted, the first day lending order proposed to authorize a potential violation of state law and to waive the substantive rights of other creditors without prior notice to them. By its terms, the proposed loan agreement contemplated a post-petition advance of $500,000, for a term of approximately 90 day [sic]. In addition to interest at the rate of 4.5 percent over prime, Colad was to pay loan fees totaling in excess of $135,000. Based upon these facts, the court questioned whether the cost of borrowing would exceed New York State's criminal usury rate of 25 percent. Additionally, the debtor's proposed order would approve a loan that was conditioned upon a waiver of all marshaling obligations. Without deciding these issues, this court refused on an emergency basis to approve the loan charges or to consider a waiver of rights, where the affected creditors had yet to receive notice of the debtor's proposal.

At the hearing to consider the debtor's first day motions, the respective attorneys for Colad and Continental responded to the above concerns, by asserting that the proposed lending arrangement represented the best and only terms available to the debtor. In my view, this position seemed disingenuous. Continental had recently acquired its secured position, with the stated desire to effect a purchase of assets as a going concern under section 363 of the Bankruptcy Code. With this objective, Continental would be obviously disinclined to compel a distressed liquidation of its position. As holder of a first lien in the debtor's inventory and receivables, Continental was positioned to dictate terms. Consequently, the proposed loan did not represent terms negotiated in any form of open market. Although the reality of circumstances might compel acceptance of these terms after a final hearing, this court was unwilling to disregard the above mentioned concerns until at least after the twenty largest unsecured creditors had opportunity to object.

The resolution of the motion for interim financing confirmed the court's perception of disingenuousness with regard to the assertion that the debtor could obtain no better terms of lending. After this court refused to approve an order in the form that the debtor had first presented, the parties negotiated an arrangement that the court could accept on an interim basis. Ultimately, I signed a simpler order authorizing the debtor to borrow funds needed to pay necessary expenditures. With respect to these advances, the lender received a super-priority administrative expense claim secured by a lien on all of the debtor's assets. Without rejecting the possibility of eventual approval under the terms of a final lending order, the interim order deferred consideration of the various provisions which the court had found to be troublesome. In particular, the parties agreed that most of the proposed loan fees would be charged not in connection with the interim loan, but only if authorized under the terms of a final loan agreement.

The interim lending order authorized the debtor to borrow funds on an emergency basis, until such time as the court would decide the request to approve a final lending order. As required by Bankruptcy Rule 4001(c), the court also directed that the debtor give to the twenty largest creditors a fifteen day notice of the hearing to consider a final DIP lending facility. That hearing was initially scheduled for February 24, but on consent of all parties, was adjourned to March 8. A further hearing with respect to the terms of a possible order was then conducted on March 28, 2005.

. . . The debtor seeks authority to borrow funds under the terms of a final lending facility, whose present form incorporates changes designed to address some of the concerns that the court expressed to the parties at the hearing to approve interim lending. Appointed subsequent to the consideration of interim authorization, the Official Committee of Unsecured Creditors now supports the debtor's motion for final authority. However, Daniel Williams opposes the request. Primarily, he contends that the proposed facility entails excessive risk, particularly in light of the fact that the debtor's financial history indicates the improbability of a successful reorganization. The court might give greater consideration to this objection, if the debtor intended to reorganize as a going concern. In the present instance, however, the debtor has candidly indicated an intent to liquidate, most likely through a sale of assets under 11 U.S.C. § 363. Thus, the borrowing is designed only to maintain operations as a going concern for the short term, until a sale can be completed. Under these circumstances, the court is prepared to authorized [sic] borrowing under terms of an appropriate facility. However, the court cannot approve lending in the form that Colad and Continental have proposed. In addition to his general opposition, Daniel Williams presented 27 objections to specific terms of the debtor's lending proposal. Except as stated herein, these objections are overruled. Due to the need for a timely decision, the court will not now comment about those provisions of the lending agreement that are acceptable. Rather, this opinion will discuss five fatal defects that preclude approval of the proposed order in its current form.

. . . The debtor seeks to borrow a maximum of $494,000.00 for a term of less than ninety days. On this loan, the debtor would pay interest at an annual rate of four and one-half percent over "the Chase Bank Rate." In addition, however, the debtor would pay a non-refundable loan commitment fee of $50,000, a closing fee of $50,000, collateral management fees of $10,000 at closing and $1,500 per month thereafter, and an unused line fee based on a formula that would be calculated each month. All of these various fees would be deducted from the amount that the debtor proposes to borrow. Thus, the debtor would actually receive operating funds of less than $381,000 dollars. Because the term of the loan is less than ninety days, the fees alone would represent charges equivalent to an interest rate in excess of 100 percent per annum.

New York law exempts corporate borrowings from the penalties of civil usury. N.Y. Gen. Oblig. L. § 5–521(1). However, pursuant to General Obligations Law § 5–521(3), this exemption does not extend to the prohibitions against criminal usury in Penal Law § 190.40. This latter section provides generally that a person or entity commits criminal usury in the second degree when it "knowingly charges, takes or receives any money or other property as interest on the loan or forbearance of any money or other property, at a rate exceeding twenty-five per centum per annum or the equivalent rate for a longer or shorter period."

Paragraph 10.6 of the proposed loan agreement would obligate Colad to pay "all out-of-pocket costs and expenses" that Continental may incur. Consequently, the various loan fees do not represent any reimbursement of reasonable costs and expenses. With no evidence of a contrary purpose or effect, the court can only view the fees as the collection of additional interest. *See* N.Y. Gen. Oblig. L. § 5–501(2). Unless some other statutory exception applies, therefore, the proposed loan agreement would violate the criminal usury provisions of New York law.

Subdivision (6)(b) of New York General Obligations Law § 5–501 states that the criminal usury statute shall not apply to any loan or forbearance in the amount of $2,500,000 or more. In its application for interim borrowing authority, Colad asked the court to approve an agreement that would allow a loan amount for "up to the maximum of $494,000." Now, in the application for final borrowing authority, Colad seeks to approve a restructured loan agreement. Although the restructured agreement also seeks a similar advance of new credit, it defines the "Post–Petition Loan Amount" as "up to the aggregate of $3,252,000.00, consisting of (a) the renewal of the pre-petition revolving line of credit and (b) the over-line facility in the amount of $494,000.00. . . ." The issue for this court is whether such wordsmithery and linguistic legerdemain can transform the proposed post-petition loan into a transaction that is exempt from New York's usury prohibition.

This court believes that it must treat the post-petition advances as a separate loan that is subject to the prohibitions against criminal usury. Section 364 speaks only to court approval of post-petition indebtedness, and not to any ratification of pre-petition obligations. If Continental and Colad had so wanted, they could have proposed a new loan whose proceeds would be used to discharge the pre-petition loan and to fund post-petition activity. For good reason, however, the parties chose to preserve the pre-petition indebtedness. As against other secured debt, the pre-petition loans retain priority that relates to the earlier date of perfection. . . . Preservation of the pre-petition debt also serves to avoid the risk of a loss of priority, in the event of a demonstration of bad faith after a reversal on appeal of any lending authorization. *See* 11 U.S.C. § 364(e). . . . Despite its reference to the pre-petition obligation, the modified loan agreement created a new loan of only $494,000. . . .

* * *

The debtor seeks an order which would give to Continental a priming lien over all other secured creditors. In my view, however, the present circumstances do not justify such relief under the applicable standard of 11 U.S.C. § 364(d)(1):

> The court, after notice and a hearing, may authorize the obtaining of credit or the incurring of debt secured by a senior or equal lien on property of the estate that is subject to a lien only if—(A) the trustee is unable to obtain such credit otherwise; and (B) there is adequate protection of the interest of the holder of the lien on the property of the estate on which such senior or equal lien is proposed to be granted.

In the present instance, Continental seeks the benefit of a generalized priming as against the positions of all other secured creditors. However, the moving papers fail to identify any secured creditors whose liens would be primed. Under these circumstances, a priming lien of any kind would be inappropriate for two reasons. First, the notice requirement of section 364(d)(1) must necessarily inure to the benefit of superior lienors. Without an identification of those superior lienors, the court cannot possibly confirm the adequacy of notice. The debtor has satisfied the requirements of Bankruptcy Rule 4001, which mandates notice either to the twenty largest unsecured creditors or to a committee appointed under 11 U.S.C. § 1102. This notice, however, does not necessarily reach the holders of secured debt. Seeking to modify the rights of parties *in absentia,* the generalized priming lien cannot possibly satisfy the notice requirements of section 364(d)(1). Second, as required by section 364(d)(1)(B), in order to grant a priming lien, the court must make a finding of adequate protection of all senior or equal interests. With no identification of those interests, the court cannot begin to assess the adequacy of protection. Contrary to the mandate of 11 U.S.C. § 364(d)(2), therefore, the debtor has failed to meet its burden of proof on this issue.

. . . Any extension of secured credit will usually impact the interests of other creditors. In bankruptcy, the court may authorize the debtor to exacerbate this impact in several narrowly defined ways. For example, under section 364(c) of the Bankruptcy Code, the court may grant priority over other administrative creditors. As noted earlier in this opinion, section 364(d) permits a priming lien in certain limited circumstances. Generally, however, the Bankruptcy Code gives to post-petition secured creditors only the same rights that a secured creditor could acquire outside bankruptcy. Unless the Bankruptcy Code expressly provides, this court has no power to diminish the rights of third parties as against a secured creditor.

Colad has asked the court to approve an order which provides that Continental "will not be subject to the equitable doctrine of 'marshaling' or any other similar doctrine with respect to any of the Collateral." Conversely, section 11.7 of the proposed loan agreement would preserve Continental's right to seek the equitable remedy of marshaling for its own benefit. These contrasting provisions obviously violate the maxim, that one who seeks equity must do equity. But more fundamentally, equitable principles like marshaling have potential application to every secured indebtedness. While the debtor may seek authority to waive its own rights, it cannot waive the marshaling rights of parties who have not consented and may not even have received notice of the debtor's motion. Under the present procedural circumstances, this court can discern no basis to eviscerate the equitable doctrine of marshaling.[17]

. . . The debtor and its secured creditor do not constitute a legislature. Thus, they have no right to implement a private agreement that effectively changes the bankruptcy law with regard to the statutory rights of third parties. In three important respects, Colad and Continental have proposed terms that would impermissibly modify the laws and rules of bankruptcy.

First, the proposed order would prohibit any surcharge of collateral under section 506(c) of the Bankruptcy Code.[18] This section provides that a trustee "may recover from property securing an allowed secured claim the reasonable, necessary costs and expenses of preserving, or disposing of, such property to the extent of any benefit to the holder of such claim." For example, if a sprinkler system extinguishes a fire that would otherwise have destroyed Continental's collateral, section 506(c) would allow the trustee to recover the resulting water bill. Instead, Colad and Continental would either deny the means to pay such charges, or would impose such costs on funds available for

---

17. Marshaling of assets is an equitable doctrine that comes into play when a senior lienholder on a particular asset also has liens on other assets, but the junior lienholder's interest is only on that particular asset. It requires the senior lienholder to seek its interest on the other assets first so that the junior lienholder has a better chance at recovery from its only collateral. See, e.g., Great Lakes Agri-Services, LLC v. State Bank of Newburg (In re Enright), 474 B.R. 854, 861 (Bankr. E.D. Wisc. 2012) ("Marshaling is traditionally used to prevent a junior lienholder with a security interest in a single property from being squeezed out by a senior lienholder with security interest not only in that property, but also in one or more additional properties."), quoting 53 Am. Jur. 2d *Marshaling Assets* § 3.

18. Section 506(c) allows the trustee to recover "the reasonable, necessary costs and expenses of preserving, or disposing of, such property to the extent of any benefit to the holder of such claim", known as a "surcharge" on the property. It is based in the equitable notion that a creditor should not benefit from the trustee's actions to the detriment of the unsecured creditors. See In re Codesco, Inc., 18 B.R. 225, 230 (Bankr. S.D.N.Y. 1982) (discussing rationale for surcharge).

distribution to unsecured creditors. By its language, section 506(c) speaks only to the payment of reasonable and necessary costs. This court can discern no basis to allow a secured creditor to ignore its application.

Second, to the detriment of any future trustee, the proposed order would change the procedural requirements for stay relief. Section 362(d) of the Bankruptcy Code provides that the court may grant relief from the automatic stay "[o]n request of a party in interest and after notice and a hearing." Instead, the proposed order would create a default procedure, whereby the stay would automatically lift upon a failure by any interested party to demand a hearing within five business days following notice of an event of default. To the extent that the debtor and creditors' committee consent, this court would approve such a procedure for purposes of notice to the consenting parties. However, the court will not sanction a waiver of the controlling standard for a hearing on notice to any trustee that may hereafter be appointed.

Third, the proposed order would repudiate the provisions of 11 U.S.C. § 546(a), which sets time limitations for commencement of an action to enforce the avoiding powers of sections 544, 545, 547, 548, and 553 of the Bankruptcy Code. Pursuant to section 546(a), unless a case is sooner closed or dismissed, the trustee may commence any avoidance action within the latter of 2 years after the entry of an order for relief, or one year after the appointment or election of a first trustee within the period of two years after entry of an order for relief. Instead, paragraph 26 of the proposed order would more severely limit the commencement of an avoidance action. For example, it would provide that upon conversion of the case to chapter 7, the trustee would be compelled to commence any avoidance action within the earlier of sixty days after appointment or thirty days after delivery of various documentation. Bankruptcy Rule 9006 allows an enlargement or reduction of many of the time limits in the Bankruptcy Rules. However, section 546(a) is a statute, not a rule. Consequently, this court lacks authority to approve the shorter time limits that Continental would impose.

. . . Section 364(e) of the Bankruptcy Code provides generally that a reversal or modification on appeal of an order authorizing secured debt "does not affect the validity of any debt so incurred, or any priority or lien so granted, to an entity that extended such credit in good faith. . . ." For this obvious reason, the debtor has proposed an order which includes a finding that Continental is extending credit in good faith. At the hearing on this motion, the debtor offered only one witness and his statements about good faith were conclusory.

Moreover, the order's other defects cause uncertainty about intent, particularly with respect to any attempt to discourage competitive bidding. Any finding of good faith is more appropriately made with the benefit of testimony and argument after a reversal or modification on appeal. This is not to say that the debtor would not be able to establish good faith at a future hearing. At this time, however, the court simply lacks an adequate basis to reach any conclusion about Continental's good faith.

. . . For the reasons stated above, this court will not approve the form of the debtor's proposed order. Nonetheless, the court would sign an appropriate order authorizing a post-petition loan that avoids the various defects identified herein. With hope that the parties will negotiate the necessary changes, I will continue the interim financing authorization until further order of the court.

* * *

(Citations omitted.)

NOTES AND COMMENTS

1. How would Continental benefit by providing debtor-in-possession financing, if the court had approved the proposed arrangement? How would the debtor benefit? What is the risk to other creditors?

2. The court approved several first day orders, but Bankruptcy Rule 4001(c)(2) limited its ability to approve debtor-in-possession financing as a first day order. Why does a rule exist for debtor-in-possession financing but not for the other types of first day issues? Why allow even temporary authority for such financing?

3. How does the court's analysis on the *final* debtor-in-possession financing proposal differ from its analysis on the *first day* order for debtor-in-possession financing?

E. DISMISSAL OR CONVERSION

As the *Czyzewski* court, opinion excerpted below, mentions, if a Chapter 11 reorganization plan cannot be agreed to by the relevant parties, then the court might not confirm the plan. The court may, instead, either dismiss the case, or convert it to a Chapter 7 liquidation.

1. Dismissal

Dismissal typically entails restoring the debtor to the position that it was in before the bankruptcy filing. That is not always possible or prudent, however, and courts may dismiss a case with orders to the debtor that involve certain debt restructuring. 11 U.S.C. § 349(b).

Recall that as a matter of corporate law, creditors have certain *inherent priorities in bankruptcy*. The equity owners of a business (shareholders in a corporation, members in a limited liability company, or partners in a partnership) contribute capital to the business and, in turn, expect a share of the profits of the business. While equity holders have a claim against the business, those claims are junior to the claims of general unsecured creditors. Likewise, unsecured creditors' claims are junior to secured creditors'—at least with regard to the collateral securing those claims. There may be intercreditor agreements whereby parties have agreed to certain priorities of payment in bankruptcy. Complicating matters even further, equity holders may also be debt holders in the pre-petition debtor; or they may provide debt to the new debtor. Thus, equity holders might be subordinated to the extent of their equity interest but be given priority status with respect to their debt holdings.[19]

It is clear that those priorities for repayment need to be respected in the bankruptcy context, but it was not entirely clear whether those priorities needed to be respected if a bankruptcy case were dismissed with restructuring orders. The following very recent Supreme Court case gives guidance.

Czyzewski v. Jevic Holding Corp.

2017 WL 1066259, at *3–16 (U.S. 2017)

Breyer, Justice

Bankruptcy Code Chapter 11 allows debtors and their creditors to negotiate a plan for dividing an estate's value. See 11 U.S.C. §§ 1123, 1129, 1141. But sometimes the parties cannot agree on a plan. If so, the bankruptcy court may decide to dismiss the case. § 1112(b). The

---

19. For an interesting case examining the rights of a holder of equity in a Chapter 11 bankrupt debtor to acquire equity in the new debtor, *see* Bank of America Nat'l Trust & Savings Assn. v. 203 N. LaSalle St. Partnership, 526 U.S. 434 (1999) (recognizing that equity holders have a "junior" interest to general unsecured creditors and requiring that, for old equity holders to contribute to and receive equitable interest in new debtor, other creditors had to be given same opportunity to invest).

Code then ordinarily provides for what is, in effect, a restoration of the prepetition financial status quo. § 349(b).

In the case before us, a Bankruptcy Court dismissed a Chapter 11 bankruptcy. But the court did not simply restore the prepetition status quo. Instead, the court ordered a distribution of estate assets that gave money to high-priority secured creditors and to low-priority general unsecured creditors but which skipped certain dissenting mid-priority creditors. The skipped creditors would have been entitled to payment ahead of the general unsecured creditors in a Chapter 11 *plan* (or in a Chapter 7 liquidation). See §§ 507, 725, 726, 1129. The question before us is whether a bankruptcy court has the legal power to order this priority-skipping kind of distribution scheme in connection with a Chapter 11 *dismissal.*

In our view, a bankruptcy court does not have such a power. A distribution scheme ordered in connection with the dismissal of a Chapter 11 case cannot, without the consent of the affected parties, deviate from the basic priority rules that apply under the primary mechanisms the Code establishes for final distributions of estate value in business bankruptcies.

* * *

It is important to keep in mind that Chapter 11 foresees three possible outcomes. The first is a bankruptcy-court-confirmed plan. Such a plan may keep the business operating but, at the same time, help creditors by providing for payments, perhaps over time. See §§ 1123, 1129, 1141. The second possible outcome is conversion of the case to a Chapter 7 proceeding for liquidation of the business and a distribution of its remaining assets. §§ 1112(a), (b), 726. That conversion in effect confesses an inability to find a plan. The third possible outcome is dismissal of the Chapter 11 case. § 1112(b). A dismissal typically "revests the property of the estate in the entity in which such property was vested immediately before the commencement of the case"—in other words, it aims to return to the prepetition financial status quo. § 349(b)(3).

Nonetheless, recognizing that conditions may have changed in ways that make a perfect restoration of the status quo difficult or impossible, the Code permits the bankruptcy court, "for cause," to alter a Chapter 11 dismissal's ordinary restorative consequences. § 349(b). A dismissal that does so (or which has other special conditions attached) is often referred to as a "structured dismissal," defined by the American Bankruptcy Institute as a "hybrid dismissal and confirmation order . . . that . . . typically dismisses the case while, among other things, approving certain distributions to creditors, granting certain third-party releases, enjoining certain conduct by creditors, and not necessarily vacating orders or unwinding transactions undertaken during the case." American Bankruptcy Institute Commission to Study the Reform of Chapter 11, 2012–2014 Final Report and Recommendations 270 (2014).

* * *

The Code also sets forth a basic system of priority, which ordinarily determines the order in which the bankruptcy court will distribute assets of the estate. . . .

The Code makes clear that distributions of assets in a Chapter 7 liquidation must follow this prescribed order. §§ 725, 726. It provides somewhat more flexibility for distributions pursuant to Chapter 11 plans, which may impose a different ordering with the consent of the affected parties. But a bankruptcy court cannot confirm a plan that contains priority-violating distributions over the objection of an impaired creditor class. §§ 1129(a)(7), 1129(b)(2).

The question here concerns the interplay between the Code's priority rules and a Chapter 11 dismissal. Here, the Bankruptcy Court neither liquidated the debtor under Chapter 7 nor confirmed a Chapter 11 plan. But the court, instead of reverting to the prebankruptcy status quo, ordered a distribution of the estate assets to creditors by attaching conditions to the dismissal (*i.e.*, it ordered a structured dismissal). The Code does not explicitly state what priority rules—if any—apply to a distribution in these circumstances. May a court consequently provide for distributions that deviate from the ordinary priority rules that would apply to a Chapter 7 liquidation or a Chapter 11 plan? Can it approve conditions that give estate assets to members of a lower priority class while skipping objecting members of a higher priority class?

. . . In 2006, Sun Capital Partners, a private equity firm, acquired Jevic Transportation Corporation with money borrowed from CIT Group in a "leveraged buyout." In a leveraged buyout, the buyer (B) typically borrows from a third party (T) a large share of the funds needed to purchase a company (C). B then pays the money to C's shareholders. Having bought the stock, B owns C. B then pledges C's assets to T so that T will have security for its loan. Thus, if the selling price for C is $50 million, B might use $10 million of its own money, borrow $40 million from T, pay $50 million to C's shareholders, and then pledge C assets worth $40 million (or more) to T as security for T's $40 million loan. If B manages C well, it might make enough money to pay T back the $40 million and earn a handsome profit on its own $10 million investment. But, if the deal sours and C descends into bankruptcy, beware of what might happen: Instead of C's $40 million in assets being distributed to its existing creditors, the money will go to T to pay back T's loan—the loan that allowed B to buy C. (T will receive what remains of C's assets because T is now a secured creditor, putting it at the top of the priority list.) Since C's shareholders receive money while C's creditors lose their claim to C's remaining assets, unsuccessful leveraged buyouts often lead to fraudulent conveyance suits alleging that the purchaser (B) transferred the company's assets without receiving fair value in return. . . . This is precisely what happened here. Just two years after Sun's buyout, Jevic (C in our leveraged buyout example) filed for Chapter 11 bankruptcy. At the time of filing, it owed $53 million to senior secured creditors Sun and CIT (B and T in our example), and over $20 million to tax and general unsecured creditors.

The circumstances surrounding Jevic's bankruptcy led to two lawsuits. First, petitioners, a group of former Jevic truckdrivers, filed suit in bankruptcy court against Jevic and Sun. Petitioners pointed out that, just before entering bankruptcy, Jevic had halted almost all its operations and had told petitioners that they would be fired. Petitioners claimed that Jevic and Sun had thereby violated state and federal Worker Adjustment and Retraining Notification (WARN) Acts—laws that require a company to give workers at least 60 days' notice before their termination. See 29 U.S.C. § 2102; N.J. Stat. Ann. § 34:21–2 (West 2011). The Bankruptcy Court granted summary judgment for petitioners against Jevic, leaving them (and *this* is the point to remember) with a judgment that petitioners say is worth $12.4 million. Some $8.3 million of that judgment counts as a priority wage claim under 11 U.S.C. § 507(a)(4), and is therefore entitled to payment ahead of general unsecured claims against the Jevic estate.

* * *

Second, the Bankruptcy Court authorized a committee representing Jevic's unsecured creditors to sue Sun and CIT. The Bankruptcy Court and the parties were aware that any proceeds from such a suit would belong not to the unsecured creditors, but to the bankruptcy estate. The committee alleged that Sun and CIT, in the course of their leveraged buyout, had "hastened Jevic's bankruptcy by saddling it with debts that it couldn't service." In 2011, the Bankruptcy Court held that the committee had adequately pleaded claims of preferential transfer under § 547 and of fraudulent transfer under § 548.

Sun, CIT, Jevic, and the committee then tried to negotiate a settlement of this "fraudulent-conveyance" lawsuit. By that point, the depleted Jevic estate's only remaining assets were the fraudulent-conveyance claim itself and $1.7 million in cash, which was subject to a lien held by Sun.

The parties reached a settlement agreement. It provided (1) that the Bankruptcy Court would dismiss the fraudulent-conveyance action with prejudice; (2) that CIT would deposit $2 million into an account earmarked to pay the committee's legal fees and administrative expenses; (3) that Sun would assign its lien on Jevic's remaining $1.7 million to a trust, which would pay taxes and administrative expenses and distribute the remainder on a pro rata basis to the low-priority general unsecured creditors, *but which would not distribute anything to petitioners* (who, by virtue of their WARN judgment, held an $8.3 million mid-level-priority wage claim against the estate); and (4) that Jevic's Chapter 11 bankruptcy would be dismissed.

* * *

. . . Petitioners and the U.S. Trustee objected, arguing that the settlement's distribution plan violated the Code's priority scheme because it skipped petitioners—who, by virtue of their WARN judgment, had mid-level priority claims against estate assets—and distributed estate money to low-priority general unsecured creditors.

The Bankruptcy Court agreed with petitioners that the settlement's distribution scheme failed to follow ordinary priority rules. But it held that this did not bar approval. That, in the Bankruptcy Court's view, was because the proposed payouts would occur pursuant to a structured dismissal of a Chapter 11 petition rather than an approval of a Chapter 11 plan. The court accordingly decided to grant the motion in light of the "dire circumstances" facing the estate and its creditors. Specifically, the court predicted that without the settlement and dismissal, there was "no realistic prospect" of a meaningful distribution for anyone other than the secured creditors. A confirmable Chapter 11 plan was unattainable. And there would be no funds to operate, investigate, or litigate were the case converted to a proceeding in Chapter 7. [The District Court and Third Circuit affirmed the bankruptcy court's decision.]

* * *

Respondents initially argue that petitioners lack standing because they have suffered no injury, or at least no injury that will be remedied by a decision in their favor. . . .

The reason, respondents say, is that petitioners would have gotten nothing even if the Bankruptcy Court had never approved the structured dismissal in the first place, and will still get nothing if the structured dismissal is undone now. . . .

This argument, however, rests upon respondents' claims (1) that, without a violation of ordinary priority rules, there will be no settlement, and (2) that, without a settlement, the fraudulent-conveyance lawsuit has no value. In our view, the record does not support either of these propositions. As to the first, the record indicates that a settlement that respects ordinary priorities remains a reasonable possibility. It makes clear . . . that Sun insisted upon a settlement that gave petitioners nothing only because it did not want to help fund petitioners' WARN lawsuit against it. But, Sun has now won that lawsuit. If Sun's given reason for opposing distributions to petitioners has disappeared, why would Sun not settle while permitting some of the settlement money to go to petitioners?

As to the second, the record indicates that the fraudulent-conveyance claim could have litigation value. CIT and Sun, after all, settled the lawsuit for $3.7 million, which would make little sense if the action truly had no chance of success. The Bankruptcy Court could convert the case to Chapter 7, allowing a Chapter 7 trustee to pursue the suit against Sun and CIT. Or the court could simply dismiss the Chapter 11 bankruptcy, thereby allowing petitioners to assert the fraudulent-conveyance claim themselves. Given these possibilities, there is no reason to believe that the claim could not be pursued with counsel obtained on a contingency basis. Of course, the lawsuit—like any lawsuit—*might* prove fruitless, but the mere *possibility* of failure does not eliminate the value of the claim or petitioners' injury in being unable to bring it.

* * *

We turn to the basic question presented: Can a bankruptcy court approve a structured dismissal that provides for distributions that do not follow ordinary priority rules without the affected creditors' consent? Our simple answer to this complicated question is "no."

The Code's priority system constitutes a basic underpinning of business bankruptcy law. Distributions of estate assets at the termination of a business bankruptcy normally take place through a Chapter 7 liquidation or a Chapter 11 plan, and both are governed by priority. In Chapter 7 liquidations, priority is an absolute command—lower priority creditors cannot receive anything until higher priority creditors have been paid in full. See 11 U.S.C. §§ 725, 726. Chapter 11 plans provide somewhat more flexibility, but a priority-violating plan still cannot be confirmed over the objection of an impaired class of creditors. See § 1129(b).

The priority system applicable to those distributions has long been considered fundamental to the Bankruptcy Code's operation. See H.R. Rep. No. 103–835, p. 33 (1994) (explaining that the Code is "designed to enforce a distribution of the debtor's assets in an orderly manner . . . in accordance with established principles rather than on the basis of the inside influence or economic leverage of a particular creditor"). . . .

. . . we would expect to see some affirmative indication of intent if Congress actually meant to make structured dismissals a backdoor means to achieve the exact kind of nonconsensual priority-violating final distributions that the Code prohibits in Chapter 7 liquidations and Chapter 11 plans.

We can find nothing in the statute that evinces this intent. The Code gives a bankruptcy court the power to "dismiss" a Chapter 11 case. § 1112(b). But the word "dismiss" itself says nothing about the power to make nonconsensual priority-violating distributions of estate value. Neither the word "structured," nor the word "conditions," nor anything else about distributing estate value to creditors pursuant to a dismissal appears in any relevant part of the Code.

Insofar as the dismissal sections of Chapter 11 foresee any transfer of assets, they seek a restoration of the prepetition financial status quo. See § 349(b)(1) (dismissal ordinarily reinstates a variety of avoided transfers and voided liens); § 349(b)(2) (dismissal ordinarily vacates certain types of bankruptcy orders); § 349(b)(3) (dismissal ordinarily "revests the property of the estate in the entity in which such property was vested immediately before the commencement of the case"); see also H.R. Rep. No. 95–595, p. 338 (1977) (dismissal's "basic purpose . . . is to undo the bankruptcy case, as far as practicable, and to restore all property rights to the position in which they were found at the commencement of the case").

Section 349(b), we concede, also says that a bankruptcy judge may, "for cause, orde[r] otherwise." H.R. Rep. No. 95–595, at 338. . . . But, read in context, this provision appears designed to give courts the flexibility to "make the appropriate orders to protect rights acquired in reliance on the bankruptcy case." Nothing else in the Code authorizes a court ordering a dismissal to make general end-of-case distributions of estate assets to creditors of the kind that normally take place in a Chapter 7 liquidation or Chapter 11 plan—let alone final distributions that do not help to restore the *status quo ante* or protect reliance interests acquired in the bankruptcy, and that would be flatly impermissible in a Chapter 7 liquidation or a Chapter 11 plan because they violate priority without the impaired creditors' consent. That being so, the word "cause" is too weak a reed upon which to rest so weighty a power.

* * *

We recognize that the Third Circuit did not approve nonconsensual priority-violating structured dismissals in general. To the contrary, the court held that they were permissible only in those "rare case[s]" in which courts could find "sufficient reasons" to disregard priority. Despite the "rare case" limitation, we still cannot agree.

For one thing, it is difficult to give precise content to the concept "sufficient reasons." That fact threatens to turn a "rare case" exception into a more general rule. Consider the present case. The Bankruptcy Court feared that (1) without the worker-skipping distribution, there would be no settlement, (2) without a settlement, all the unsecured creditors would receive nothing, and consequently (3) its distributions would make some creditors (high- and low-priority creditors) better off without making other (mid-priority) creditors worse off (for they would receive nothing regardless). But, as we have pointed out, the record provides equivocal support for the first two propositions. And, one can readily imagine other cases that turn on comparably dubious predictions. The result is uncertainty. And uncertainty will lead to similar claims being made in many, not just a few, cases.

The consequences are potentially serious. They include departure from the protections Congress granted particular classes of creditors. They include changes in the bargaining power of different classes of creditors even in bankruptcies that do not end in structured dismissals. They include risks of collusion, *i.e.,* senior secured creditors and general unsecured creditors teaming up to squeeze out priority unsecured creditors. And they include making settlement more difficult to achieve.

For these reasons, as well as those set forth in Part III, we conclude that Congress did not authorize a "rare case" exception. . . . The judgment of the Court of Appeals is reversed, and the case is remanded for further proceedings consistent with this opinion.

* * *

(Citations omitted.)

NOTES AND COMMENTS

1. Would the result of this case have been different if the truck drivers' claims against Sun Capital had not been dismissed but were still ongoing at the time of the dismissal?

2. Read 11 U.S.C. § 349(b). What is the Court's statutory language argument? Why did the Court not accept the argument that the language "[u]nless the court, for cause, orders otherwise" permits a bankruptcy court to allow a structured dismissal in violation of the Code's priority rules? The House Report, cited by the Court, provides the following:

> Subsection (b) specifies that the dismissal reinstates proceedings or cus-todianships that were superseded by the bankruptcy case, reinstates avoided transfers, reinstates voided liens, vacates any order, judgment, or transfer ordered as a result of the avoidance of a transfer, and revests the property of the estate in the entity in which the property was vested at the commencement of the case. The court is permitted to order a different result for cause. The basic purpose of the subsection is to undo the bankruptcy case, as far as practicable, and to restore all property rights to the position in which they were found at the commencement of the case. This does not necessarily encompass undoing sales of property from the estate to a good faith purchaser. Where there is a question over the scope of the subsection, the court will make the appropriate orders to protect rights acquired in reliance on the bankruptcy case.

3. In language omitted from the excerpt, the Court contrasts its refusal to allow judicial discretion in violating the priority rule through a structured dismissal with other well-accepted instances of judicial discretion that may impact priority distributions:

> Courts, for example, have approved "first-day" wage orders that allow payment of employees' prepetition wages, "critical vendor" orders that allow payment of essential suppliers' prepetition invoices, and "roll-ups" that allow lenders who continue financing the debtor to be paid first on their prepetition claims. In doing so, these courts have usually found that the distributions at issue would "enable a successful reorganization and make even the disfavored creditors better off." By way of contrast, in a structured dismissal like the one ordered below, the priority-violating dis-tribution is attached to a final disposition; it does not preserve the debtor as a going concern; it does not make the disfavored creditors better off; it does not promote the possibility of a confirmable plan; it does not help to restore the *status quo ante*; and it does not protect reliance interests.

Jevic at *12. Section 349 only covers dismissal. Where does a court obtain authority to pay some creditors early in the bankruptcy case in potential violation of the priority distribution scheme? See 11 U.S.C. § 105. Do you agree that the discretion of the judge in such circumstances is valid?

2. Conversion (§ 1112)

Not all Chapter 11 bankruptcies lead to a confirmed plan of reorganization. The exact percentage that end in a "successful" reorganization plan is the subject of debate, with figures ranging from about 17 percent to 34 percent.[20] At some point, a case may need to be dismissed (just discussed), or convert from a Chapter 11 reorganization into a Chapter 7 liquidation. While debtors often recognize the need to convert and do so voluntarily, in other situations, another party-in-interest moves to convert in the best interest of the creditors.

In the following case, the U.S. Trustee filed a motion to convert a Chapter 11 bankruptcy into a Chapter 7 liquidation. A motion to convert the case involuntarily requires that the movant demonstrate that conversion is in the best interest of the creditors and should be done for cause. Section 1112(b)(4) provides an illustrative list of cause; review that list to gain a sense of the types of situations that will lead a court to order conversion or dismissal.

In re Hoover

828 F.3d 5 (1st Cir. 2016)

KAYATTA, Circuit Judge

* * *

As an individual and doing business as "Halloween Costume World," Hoover filed a voluntary petition for bankruptcy under Chapter 11 of the United States Bankruptcy Code. The United States Trustee ("the Trustee") filed a motion pursuant to 11 U.S.C. § 1112(b) ("section 1112") to dismiss or convert the case to a liquidation proceeding under Chapter 7 of the Bankruptcy Code.

Hoover was the sole witness at the July 30, 2014, evidentiary hearing. After direct and cross-examination about his business, his finances, and the prospects for rehabilitation and reorganization, the bankruptcy court granted the Trustee's motion, finding that cause existed to convert the case to Chapter 7 under three separate provisions of section 1112(b)(4):

> "substantial or continuing loss to or diminution of the estate and the absence of a reasonable likelihood of rehabilitation" under (b)(4)(A);

---

20. For a discussion of the various studies and their methodologies and results, *see* Elizabeth Warren & Jay Lawrence Westbrook, *The Success of Chapter 11: A Challenge to the Critics*, 107 Mich. L. Rev. 603 (Feb. 2009).

"unauthorized use of cash collateral substantially harmful to 1 or more creditors" under (b)(4)(D); and "unexcused failure to satisfy timely any [pertinent] filing or reporting requirement" under (b)(4)(F). The district court affirmed, concluding that cause to convert existed under (b)(4)(A) and without discussing the alternative grounds for cause found by the bankruptcy court under (b)(4)(D) and (b)(4)(F).

* * *

When an interested party files a motion to convert or dismiss a Chapter 11 case, the bankruptcy court inquires as follows: Does "cause" exist to convert or dismiss the case; and, if so, is conversion or dismissal in the best interests of creditors and the estate? See 11 U.S.C. § 1112(b)(1).

Hoover argues that the bankruptcy court erred both in finding that "cause" to convert existed and in finding that conversion was in the best interests of the creditors. We address each argument in turn.

* * *

Cause exists under section 1112(b)(4)(A) if there has been a "substantial or continuing loss to or diminution of the estate and the absence of a reasonable likelihood of rehabilitation." 11 U.S.C. § 1112(b)(4)(A). The bankruptcy court's finding of diminution in this case was simple and straightforward: Hoover conceded that he was selling inventory without replacing it, and his monthly operating reports ("MORs") showed insufficient profit to account for (or replace) the sold inventory. In short, the estate was diminishing. As for the likelihood of rehabilitation, the court again pointed to the MORs, showing insufficient cash flow to pay costs and debts. The court concluded: "This debtor barely makes it. That's what the numbers tell me and barely makes it only by not paying people . . . and that's no recipe for a reorganization."

* * *

. . . Hoover baldly asserts that there was no evidence of diminution "other than possibly the fact that Hoover was continuing to conduct business." But as Hoover's own records unmistakably reveal, he was "conducting business" by selling inventory without replacing it with new inventory or retaining cash sufficient to offset the diminution.

Hoover next argues that his proposed plan of reorganization was not "patently unconfirmable," that the state tax authorities would "hopefully" write off much of his debt, and that it was "too early" to tell whether a zero dividend was "ineluctable." The issue before us, though, is whether the bankruptcy court abused its discretion in determining that there did not exist "a reasonable likelihood of rehabilitation." 11 U.S.C. § 1112(b)(4)(A).

We see no such abuse. The Profit and Loss Statement revealed that in 2013, Hoover's business lost over $135,000, and the [Monthly Operating Reports] showed that, since filing for bankruptcy, the business had generated only minimal profits despite selling off its inventory and not paying anything to secured creditors. The court described, in detail, its view of the evidence regarding whether there was a reasonable likelihood of rehabilitation, noting a lack of sufficient funds and income to pay monthly expenses under a Chapter 11 plan. The court, in its broad discretion, supportably declined to credit Hoover's testimony that he had plans for generating more income, finding those plans both speculative and optimistic.

Although the question of rehabilitation under section 1112(b)(4)(A) is not synonymous with reorganization (i.e., the debtor need not have a confirmed reorganization plan in place to avoid conversion), the debtor still must have "sufficient business prospects," to "justify continuance of [a] reorganization effort[.]" . . .

* * *

Once the bankruptcy court determined that there was cause to convert the case, it had broad discretion to do so if it concluded that conversion was in the best interests of creditors and the estate. 11 U.S.C. § 1112(b)(1). Given the court's findings on diminution and rehabilitation, its conclusion that conversion was in the interest of creditors and the estate was hardly surprising.

Hoover argues to us, nevertheless, that the creditors will mostly get nothing on liquidation after both the administrative fees and his Massachusetts tax obligation (in part) are paid. Therefore, he reasons, even a long shot at making a go of it under Chapter 11 is worth it for the creditors. Hoover, though, did not make this argument to the bankruptcy court; therefore, we can consider the argument waived. Even if not waived, this argument would fail. Confronted with two likely bleak alternative outcomes, the bankruptcy court had ample discretion to conclude that a prompt conversion rather than further diminution was in the best interests of creditors, especially where no creditor opposed conversion as hostile to its interests.

* * *

(Citations omitted.)

NOTES AND COMMENTS

1. A study by the U.S. Trustee's Office comparing pre-BAPCPA and post-BAPCPA results in Chapter 11 cases found that slightly less than one-quarter of Chapter 11 cases (those filed from mid-2004 through mid-2006) studied ended in conversion to Chapter 7. One-third of cases ended in a confirmed plan, one-third were dismissed, and the remainder remained pending. Cases that were converted took an average of nine months from filing until conversion. *See* Ed Flynn and Phil Crewson, *Chapter 11 Filing Trends in History and Today,* available at https://www.justice.gov/sites/default/files/ust/legacy/2011/07/13/abi_200905.pdf, pgs. 6-7.

2. The court relied heavily on the debtor-in-possession's monthly operating reports. The debtor-in-possession must file monthly operating reports, which include several other documents providing information regarding cash receipts, disbursements, the company's balance sheet, a profit and loss statement, bank statements, information about taxes and insurance, information about accounts receivable and accounts payable, information about payment to professionals and corporate executives, and a narrative description of the business activities. These documents are available at https://www.justice.gov/sites/default/files/ust-regions/legacy/2011/07/13/mor.pdf.

F. BANKRUPTCY IN PRACTICE

Return to the hypothetical presented at the outset of this chapter concerning Diana Detter and her business's bankruptcy. For this review question, you represent the committee of equity holders, which is arguing against confirmation of the plan. The committee has a competing plan of reorganization, but because the debtor-in-possession filed and obtained approval of its plan within the exclusivity period, the committee's plan has not been proposed. Craft arguments against confirmation of the debtor-in-possession's plan of reorganization.

8

Professional Responsibility in Bankruptcy

In the long run men inevitably become the victims of their wealth.
They adapt their lives and habits to their money, not their money to
their lives.[1]

Issues of professional responsibility in bankruptcy practice follow the same general guidelines as the state-law Rules of Professional Conduct. However, when discussed in the bankruptcy courts, they generally arise in conjunction with motions to hire an attorney or with fee applications—applications made to the bankruptcy court to be paid from property of the estate for legal services. And they frequently involve sections of the Bankruptcy Code that supplement an attorney's existing state-law responsibilities.

RECALL DIANA DETTER

As a bankruptcy lawyer, you will be representing people facing financial difficulty. How will you be paid by your clients, and how does your payment affect the debtor's other creditors (who, after all, likely existed as a creditor before you)? And, given the complexities of bankruptcy practice, how do you ensure that you can adequately represent Ms. Detter without depleting all financial resources?

---

1. Herbert Croly, *The Promise of American Life* (Princeton Univ. Press 2014).

A. COMPETENCY

It is no coincidence that the the first rule of the Model Rules of Professional Conduct is the rule which requires an an attorney to be competent. Model Rule 1.1 states: "A lawyer shall provide competent representation to a client. Competent representation requires the legal knowledge, skill, thoroughness and preparation reasonably necessary for the representation."

The competency of an attorney is not measured merely based on experience.[2] A very experienced lawyer can lack competence, and a very inexperienced attorney can attain competence. Comments to Rule 1.1 make it clear that an attorney "need not necessarily have special training or prior experience to handle legal problems of a type with which the lawyer is unfamiliar. A newly admitted lawyer can be as competent as a practitioner with long experience."[3] However, as a New York court in *Law Office of Thaniel J. Beinert v. Litinskaya* recognized, "It is totally inappropriate for a lawyer to learn his or her craft at the total expense of his or her client."[4] In the bankruptcy context, the lawyer would be operating not only at the expense of his or her client, but potentially at the expense of the bankruptcy estate that impacts so many other parties.

Anne E. Wells, *Navigating Ethical Minefields on the Bankruptcy Bandwagon*

31 Cal. Bankr. J. 767 (2011)

. . . As bankruptcy filings continue to climb, attorneys continue to flock to the bankruptcy practice, representing debtors, trustees and creditors under all chapters of the Bankruptcy Code. However, jumping on the bankruptcy bandwagon is not without its unique ethical perils. In addition to requiring not only the skills of both litigators and business lawyers, the bankruptcy practice requires a specialized body of knowledge that has its own terms of art, quirks, nuances, idiosyncrasies, deadlines and numerous statutory, procedural, administrative and local requirements. While the applicable rules of professional conduct generally governing attorneys also apply in bankruptcy cases, in many respects, the ethical bar is higher in

---

2. ABA Model Rules of Professional Conduct R. 1.1 Cmt .2 (2011).

3. *Id.*

4. Law Office of Thaniel J. Beinert v. Litinskaya, 43 Misc.3d 1205(A), N.Y. City Civ. Ct., 2014. March 31, 2014 (where the court found a violation of New York's competence rule when a three-year associate and law student were assigned a "simple" landlord-tenant matter to retake possession of a condominium and spent "an inordinate amount of time and even tried to file the case in the wrong state").

the bankruptcy practice than in general practice. As one bankruptcy court has warned, "bankruptcy lawyers often find themselves faced with complex ethical situations unique to the practice that call on them to apply standards that exceed the minimum for acceptable conduct."[5]

* * *

The duty of competency is one of an attorney's most basic duties. In any legal matter, an attorney's incompetence or inattention is generally unacceptable. However, in a bankruptcy matter, incompetence can have even more serious consequences. The client in such circumstances is already in severe financial difficulty, and assets and rights may be irrevocably lost if a matter is mishandled, regardless of whether the client subsequently hires new, and more competent, counsel. For example, the failure to assume a lease within the statutory timeline of Bankruptcy Code § 365(d)(4) results in its deemed rejection, potentially causing the irrevocable loss of an estate asset. Similarly, a debtor can be denied their discharge, the very reason for which bankruptcy is generally filed, if counsel fails to provide adequate representation.

* * *

"Bankruptcy is a highly technical practice that mandates particular expertise in order to adequately represent clients." Because bankruptcy is such a specialized area of the law, there are serious risks for attorneys who jump into the area without understanding the technicalities and requirements unique to the practice. Thus, the first decision an attorney contemplating a bankruptcy representation must make is whether he or she has the requisite competency to take on the matter.

Attorneys who venture into the bankruptcy arena without the necessary appreciation for the knowledge or background that is required may find themselves in serious trouble not only with their clients but with the bankruptcy courts. . . . Indeed, bankruptcy judges are becoming increasingly frustrated with the increasing number of counsel unfamiliar with bankruptcy law who are attempting to practice before the bankruptcy court. The Honorable Margaret Murphy of the United States Bankruptcy Court for the Northern District of Georgia expressed her frustration in a recent opinion: "Many attorneys who are expert in other legal specialties, such as commercial litigation,

---

5. In re Alvarado, 363 B.R. 484, 490 (Bankr. E.D. Va. 2007).

tax law or securities law, mistakenly assume they can enter the bankruptcy arena with little experience or preparation and still perform competently; however, malpractice is not uncommon."[6] Similarly, the Honorable Alan Jaroslovsky, the Chief Bankruptcy Judge for the Northern District of California, in a notice posted on his official court website notes that "[t]here has been a recent spate of individual chapter 11 cases filed by attorneys who have neither the experience nor the education nor the competence to venture into Chapter 11."[7]

The competency bar is particularly high in Chapter 11 representations. "An attorney hoping to represent a Chapter 11 debtor must have more than just integrity; that counsel must also have a strong knowledge of the technical requirements under the Bankruptcy Code."[8] Further,

> In a Chapter 11 case, an attorney can provide competent representation to the estate only if the attorney is thoroughly familiar with the Bankruptcy Code, the Bankruptcy Rules, and the Local Rules. Bankruptcy, particularly Chapter 11 bankruptcy, is a highly specialized area of law. An attorney for a debtor in possession must have expert knowledge of bankruptcy law in order to achieve a successful result. Experience indicates that a business that files for Chapter 11 is already in trouble. . . . Only an attorney with expert knowledge of bankruptcy can properly aid in the administration of the case.[9]

Bankruptcy judges have broad powers to discipline incompetent attorneys who appear before them, including the power to suspend and even disbar attorneys from practice before bankruptcy courts. These broad powers come from multiple sources. First, bankruptcy courts have "inherent powers to manage their cases and courtrooms and to maintain the integrity of the judicial system."[10] This inherent authority includes the power to suspend or disbar attorneys from appearing before them, as long as the attorney receives due process. Bankruptcy courts also have civil contempt authority under 11 U.S.C. § 105(a) to impose penalties, including suspending an attorney, as

---

6. *See, e.g.,* In re Taylor Quality Concrete, Inc., 359 B.R. 273, 278 (Bankr. D. Idaho 2007) (noting that the Bankruptcy Code and Bankruptcy Rules "apply equally to all professionals, regardless of experience" and no allowance should be made for practitioners who are unfamiliar with the requirements of bankruptcy law); In re Mattinson, 2010 WL 4102293, at *3 (Bankr. N.D. Ga. Oct. 1, 2010) ("The practice of bankruptcy law does not lend itself to holding a case in abeyance for any significant period of time while an attorney . . . learns bankruptcy law").

7. *Mattinson,* 2010 WL 4102293, at *2.

8. In re Vettori, 217 B.R. 242, 245 (Bankr. N.D. Ill. 1998).

9. In re Doors and More, Inc., 126 B.R. 43, 45 (Bankr. E.D. Mich. 1991).

10. In re Brooks-Hamilton, 400 B.R. 238, 246047 (B.A.P. 9th Cir. 2009); Hale v. U.S. Trustee, 509 F.3d 1139, 1148 (9th Cir. 2007) (bankruptcy courts have inherent authority to run their courtrooms and to supervise the attorneys who appear before them).

well as powers under Federal Rule of Bankruptcy Procedure 9011. Pursuant to Rule 9011, faced with incompetent representation, a bankruptcy court may "impose an appropriate sanction . . . limited to what is sufficient to deter repetition" of improper conduct,[11] which again may include suspension from practice, or take the form of other sanctions. Lastly, under Bankruptcy Code § 329(b) and § 330, which gives courts the power to review and approve fees, if a bankruptcy court finds that an attorney failed to competently perform his or her duties, the court may disallow or order disgorgement of counsels' fees.

* * *

Similarly, another bankruptcy court was so concerned by a perceived pattern of "what appeared to be incompetent and wrongful conduct by the lawyers in the firm" by one law firm that regularly appeared before it in Chapter 11 and Chapter 13 cases that the court entered an order: (1) suspending the firm from filing any new debtor cases in *any* bankruptcy court in the United States until further order of the court; (2) directing the firm to retain at its expense a "Consumer Bankruptcy Reviewing Attorney" and a "Business Bankruptcy Reviewing Attorney" to undertake a complete review of the firm's operating procedures and to report to the court in regards to any readmission application by the attorneys; (3) directing lawyers in the firm to take 30 hours of basic and intermediate level consumer bankruptcy continuing legal education and 30 hours of basic and intermediate level business bankruptcy continuing legal education before making application to be readmitted to file new cases before the court; (4) directing the firm to subscribe to a treatise on Chapter 13 practice; and (5) requiring the individual lawyers in the firm to demonstrate competency in bankruptcy law to the court's satisfaction before readmitting and allowing them to file new bankruptcy cases.[12]

* * *

(Citations omitted.)

NOTES AND COMMENTS

1. One of the duties of competence includes keeping abreast of changes in the law. Consider the facts in In re Alvarado, 363 B.R. 484 (Bankr. E.D.

---

11. Bankruptcy Rule 9011 provides for the imposition of sanctions against a party who signs or files petitions or other bankruptcy papers for improper purposes or without any factual or legal merit. Fed. R. Bankr. P. 9011.

12. In re Moon Thai & Japanese, Inc., 448 B.R. 576, 590-591, (Bankr. S.D. Fla. 2011).

Va. 2007). The attorney, Mr. Jones, failed to pay filing fees on behalf of his client, leading to dismissal of her bankruptcy case. Though an experienced bankruptcy practitioner, he filed another bankruptcy case for the client, which had significant negative consequences:

> It was apparent from Mr. Jones' testimony that he was unfamiliar with the 2005 amendments to the Bankruptcy Code. He was unaware that the automatic stay under § 362 of the Bankruptcy Code would automatically expire in the second bankruptcy case 30 days following the petition date. See 11 U.S.C. § 362(c)(3)(A). As of the hearing, Mr. Jones had taken no affirmative action on the Debtor's behalf in the second case to extend the automatic stay. He was unaware that as a result of the 2005 amendments to § 707 of the Bankruptcy Code, his signature on a petition certified that he had performed a reasonable investigation into the circumstances surrounding the filing of the petition and that he had concluded that the filing of the petition did not constitute an abuse. He was unaware that he was required to make reasonable inquiry into the information contained in the documents filed with the Court. 11 U.S.C. § 707(b)(4)(C). The Debtor never subsequently signed the second bankruptcy petition. It is of great concern to the Court that the Debtor may not have authorized Mr. Jones to file the second petition.

Id. at 489. The lack of awareness of the Bankruptcy Code provisions, along with his failure to meet other ethical obligations of trust and competent representation, led to sanctioning of the attorney.

2. Prior poor performance can be considered in determining competence in bankruptcy practice. In In re Vettori, the court looked at prior incidents involving bankruptcy counsel, including lack of understanding that a scheduled claim in Chapter 11 is treated as a filed proof of claim unless scheduled as contingent, unliquidated, or disputed. The prior incidents sufficed to question the debtor's competence as a Chapter 11 attorney, and the court mandated use of co-counsel. In re Vettori, 217 B.R. 242 (Bankr. N.D. Ill. 1998).

3. While lack of knowledge of the Bankruptcy Code frequently impacts the client, it can also have a direct and devastating impact on the attorneys' ability to be paid. In In re Taylor Quality Concrete, Inc., the attorneys were unaware of the requirement that their employment as debtor's counsel be approved by the Bankruptcy Court. Ultimately, the attorneys were denied compensation for seven months of work on behalf of the debtor:

> . . . while the Court does not doubt the benefit of Counsel's services to the estate, if the attorneys representing Debtor were "unaware" of the legal requirement that their employment be approved, that lack of knowledge resulted from their failure to consult the Code or Rules, and the cases construing the applicable provisions. Surely, an attorney's self-imposed

lack of awareness of the legal requirements of chapter 11 should not justify avoidance of the consequences of failure to comply with the law.

In re Taylor Quality Concrete, Inc., 359 B.R. 273, 276 (Bankr. D. Idaho 2007).

B. SCOPE OF REPRESENTATION

Traditionally, a debtor's attorney represents the debtor from filing of the petition through discharge. However, that traditional model of representation has given way to a newer trend of "unbundling" legal services. This unbundling model can benefit both the attorney and the client. But it also presents several issues to the courts, including whether the client understands the scope of the attorney's services, promoting freedom of contract, and helping bankruptcy debtors with limited financial capacity afford legal assistance. Model Rule 1.2 provides guidance regarding the scope of an attorney's representation of a client:

> (a) Subject to paragraphs (c) and (d), a lawyer shall abide by a client's decisions concerning the objectives of representation and, as required by Rule 1.4, shall consult with the client as to the means by which they are to be pursued. . . .

* * *

> (b) A lawyer may limit the scope of the representation if the limitation is reasonable under the circumstances and the client gives informed consent.

* * *

Unbundling provides a means of limiting the cost of representation for a client in the bankruptcy system, and make attorney services more available for financially strapped debtors. But it also creates the risk of ineffective representation of clients, as is seen in the following case.

In re Seare

493 B.R. 158 (Bankr. D. Nev. 2013)

MARKELL, Bankruptcy Judge

. . . When a consumer consults a lawyer, there is a reasonable expectation that the lawyer's advice will address the consumer's concerns. Here, that didn't happen. Although the consumers here—debtors Wayne Seare and Marinette Tedoco—gave their attorney what any attorney would need to identify their problem, the attorney gave bad advice. When the bad advice was discovered, the attorney, Anthony J. DeLuca, doubled down. He refused to assist Seare and Tedoco further, whether or not they had the money to pay him for it, which, as Chapter 7 debtors, they did not. DeLuca justified his inaction by pointing to provisions in his standard form retainer agreement that Seare and Tedoco had signed. For the reasons given in this opinion, that conduct was wrong. . . .

Seare's legal odyssey began in December 2010 when he filed a complaint in the United States District Court for the District of Nevada alleging employment discrimination against his former employer, St. Rose Dominican Health Foundation ("St. Rose"), the plaintiff in this adversary proceeding. . . . Ultimately, the district court ordered sanctions against Seare, dismissed his lawsuit with prejudice, and ordered him to pay St. Rose's attorney's fees.

In awarding these attorney's fees, the district court found that Seare knowingly provided false information to the court, allowed his attorney to file an amended complaint based upon the false information, and instituted and conducted litigation in bad faith—amounting to "fraud upon the court.". . .

. . . By January 2012, St. Rose had obtained a writ of execution and served the related writ of garnishment on Seare's current employer. . . . Seare's desire to have the garnishment permanently stopped drove Marinette Tedoco (his wife) and him (collectively, the "Debtors") to DeLuca to seek legal counsel about whether to file for bankruptcy.

. . . On February 13, 2012, Seare and Tedoco consulted with DeLuca at his law office. . . . They met personally with DeLuca, which, as it turned out, was the only direct contact they had with him during the entire case. Among other documents, they gave DeLuca copies of both the Order for Wage Garnishment and Wage Sanctions. According to the Debtors, DeLuca flipped through the court papers and stated that hospital bills are dischargeable.

After the short meeting with DeLuca, the Debtors were placed in a small room to sign and initial the 19–page retainer agreement (the "Retainer Agreement") under which they hired DeLuca. DeLuca's staff periodically checked to see if they had completed the forms, but no one sat with them to explain any part of the Retainer Agreement.

The Debtors proceeded to execute the Retainer Agreement and retain DeLuca with a $200 down payment. In addition, DeLuca provided them with a 19–page "Frequently Asked Questions" document (the "FAQ"). The Debtors signed every relevant page and initialed every relevant paragraph of the Retainer Agreement. At the bottom of every page (right above the Debtors' signatures) is the statement: "I have read, understand, and agree to this page and its contents." On the last page (right above the Debtors' signatures) is the statement: "I have read and received the foregoing NINETEEN (19) pages and I understand and agree to its terms and conditions."

Notably, DeLuca did not sign or initial the Retainer Agreement. The first page, a welcome page of sorts that thanks prospective clients for their business and instructs them to sign and initial the following pages, is a form letter with DeLuca's printed signature. It states that the Retainer Agreement is only valid if the Debtors sign and initial at every location indicated. The Retainer Agreement is evidently the same for all clients, with only a few differences in fees depending on whether the case is filed under Chapter 7 or Chapter 13. For the Debtors' Chapter 7 case, DeLuca's flat fee was $1,999.99.

The Retainer Agreement separates basic services from those services that require additional fees:

BASIC SERVICES: Services to be performed by DeLuca & Associates include:

a. Analysis of debtor's financial situation and assistance in determining whether to file a petition under the United States Bankruptcy code whether in Chapter 7 or chapter 13....

b. Review, preparation and filing of the petition, schedules, statement of affairs, and other documents required by the bankruptcy court;

c. Representation at the meeting of creditors.

d. Reasonable in person and telephonic consultation with the client....

ADDITIONAL FEES: There are circumstances which may require additional fees. Additional attorney fees will be charged for additional services including but not limited to: [1] Addressing allegations of fraud or nondischargeability; . . . [13] . . . Adversary Proceedings. . . .

The Retainer Agreement does not explain the relationship between items [1] and [13].

The Retainer Agreement includes a fraud disclaimer: "DEBTS THAT DO NOT GO AWAY: Non-dischargeable debts (debts you must re-pay), or debts not affected by client's bankruptcy, include but are not limited to the following: . . . debts incurred through fraud. . . ." It also includes a request for copies of "ALL LAWSUITS you have been involved in within the last (2) years. . . ." The FAQ also explains that debts incurred through fraud are nondischargeable.

. . . On February 29, 2012, DeLuca filed the Debtors' Chapter 7 bankruptcy petition. The St. Rose Debt is listed as a garnishment on Schedule F in the amount of $67,431.00. . . .

On May 24, 2012, St. Rose filed its adversary complaint against Seare (the "Complaint"), claiming nondischargeability under Section 523(a)(4) and (a)(6). On May 30, the court granted the Debtors' discharge with respect to all other debts. . . .

Within several days, on June 4, 2012, DeLuca sent the Debtors an e-mail informing them of their discharge and that, as of the discharge date, their case was completed. The e-mail appears to be a form message. It does not mention the particulars of the Debtors' bankruptcy or the then-recently filed adversary proceeding. It states, "we are very happy to inform you that you can now move forward with a fresh start on life, free from the stress of excessive debt. Now you can place your financial situation back on the right track."

Also on June 4, the Debtors responded via e-mail to DeLuca's communication. . . .

They asked whether the St. Rose Debt was discharged, since they understood that St. Rose was going to pursue the adversary proceeding against them. . . .

On June 5, 2012, DeLuca's office responded. They reminded the Debtors that St. Rose had expressed its intention to pursue the Judgment against the Debtors at the Section 341 meeting of creditors. The e-mail also stated that on April 16, 2012 DeLuca had received a "fax cover letter . . . with an attached Stipulation and Order regarding the discharge-ability [sic] of subject debt in question as to Mr. Sear [sic] only.". . . It then informed the debtors that DeLuca had responded to the fax by advising St. Rose's counsel that he "would not sign off on any [s]tipulation regarding the discharge-ability [sic] of any debt listed in the schedules.". . . Put more bluntly, DeLuca rejected the proposed stipulation and order without consulting with Seare. It is unclear whether DeLuca informed St. Rose that he was not representing Seare in the adversary proceeding. The e-mail then explained that DeLuca had performed all the duties for which he was contracted and that DeLuca would not represent Seare in the adversary proceeding. It recommended that Seare retain another attorney, Mr. Terry Leavitt, to handle the adversary proceeding.

On June 6, 2012, the Debtors replied to the e-mail. They admitted to understanding that DeLuca was hired only to "do our bankruptcy," but were very upset and frustrated that the fax containing the proposed stipulation and order was never sent to them. They asserted that they were never even aware that DeLuca had received those documents from St. Rose; "[n]ot informing your clients of very important documents and failing to return phone calls are unacceptable and unprofessional customer service."

Also on June 6, DeLuca sent a letter to the Debtors informing them that he would not represent Seare in the adversary proceeding. . . .

On June 27, 2012, Seare filed his answer pro se in the adversary proceeding. He argued that the debt was dischargeable "due to the hardship on the dependents of debtor.". . .

On August 2, 2012, the court held a scheduling conference for the adversary proceeding. DeLuca did not appear on behalf of Seare, who explained that DeLuca told him that DeLuca does not represent clients in adversary proceedings. St. Rose's counsel stated that she had informed DeLuca shortly after the Debtors filed their petition of St. Rose's intent to file a nondischargeability action.

* * *

These facts present the legal issue of when consumer bankruptcy attorneys such as DeLuca may limit the scope of their representation, a practice colloquially referred to as "unbundling." While unbundling is permissible, it must be done consistent with the rules of ethics and professional responsibility binding on all attorneys. Those rules allow a lawyer to limit his or her representation only when it is reasonable under the circumstances to do so, and only when the client gives informed consent to the limitation. In this case, DeLuca met neither of these requirements. As a defense, DeLuca asserts that his retainer overrides such mandatory rules. As will be seen, his position is incorrect; to the extent his retainer is inconsistent with the applicable rules of professional responsibility, his retainer is unenforceable, and his abandonment of his clients violated norms applicable to lawyers generally.

***

. . . [DeLuca] argues that the decision to unbundle all adversary proceedings, regardless of their relation to the relief requested or needed by a debtor was reasonable, and that the reasonable assumption of any attorney would be that a debt owed to a hospital is for medical care rather than a fraud judgment. He claims that he undertook representation based on "incomplete, inaccurate, or intentionally omitted information regarding the fraudulent nature of a significant portion of the Debtors' debt." He further argues, using the benefit of hindsight, that it is reasonable to limit services when the client is a known liar.

* * *

DeLuca's next argument is that the Debtors gave informed consent to the exclusion of adversary proceedings. He asserts that the Retainer Agreement "specifically excludes adversary proceedings as part of the services provided . . . for the basic fee.". . . He argues that the Debtors had ample warning of the likelihood of an adversary proceeding because St. Rose communicated its intent to enforce its rights under the Judgment at the Section 341 meeting. He further argues that the Debtors were "clearly advised of what services were to be covered under the agreement," and testified that a staff member "go[es] through" the Retainer Agreement, paragraph-by-paragraph, with clients. . . . He points out that the Debtors signed the page that contains the "DEBTS THAT DO NOT GO AWAY" paragraph, which includes "[d]ebts incurred through fraud.". . . Moreover, he argues, the FAQ also explains that debts incurred through fraud are nondischargeable. Lastly, he claims that the Retainer Agreement made clear that the representation ended "by operation of law" when the clients obtained their discharge. In short, his argument is that the Debtors executed the Retainer Agreement with the knowledge that (1) such debts are nondischargeable; (2) St. Rose would likely bring an adversary proceeding; (3) adversary proceedings were excluded from the flat fee; and (4) his representation ended when the clients obtained their discharge.

* * *

Seare claims that he understood that the flat fee did not cover adversary proceedings, but also that, at the time of the initial consultation, he did not even know what an adversary proceeding was. The Debtors assert that DeLuca did not explain anything about adversary proceedings at the consultation — either what they are or whether one was likely in their case. . . .

* * *

The court finds that DeLuca failed to inquire about the nature of the Judgment during the consultation. If the Debtors did mention any of the facts underlying the Judgment, either the facts as presented did not clearly amount to fraud or DeLuca was not sufficiently attentive to reach that conclusion on his own. If he did know it was for fraud, then he surely would have told the Debtors that St. Rose would likely seek to have the debt found nondischargeable in an adversary proceeding.

The court believes Seare's testimony that DeLuca did not explain anything about adversary proceedings during the consultation—what they are, whether one was likely in this case, or what the potential consequences could be. Because DeLuca did not carefully review the district court documents, he did not realize that an adversary proceeding was a near certainty. Moreover, DeLuca does not have a standard practice of explaining adversary proceedings to prospective clients, other than to point out that they are not covered under the flat fee in his standard form retainer agreement.

* * *

Lawyers are not plumbers. They cannot indiscriminately dismiss clients at their whim, or even if their clients don't pay on time. Lawyers are professionals that owe fiduciary duties to their individual clients, and must continue to represent them even if initially rosy predictions turn sour. A profession such as law is different from other occupations in that (1) "its practice requires substantial intellectual training and the use of complex judgments;" (2) it places clients in a position of trust because they typically cannot evaluate the quality of service; and (3) "the client's trust presupposes that the practitioner's self-interest is overbalanced by devotion to serving both the client's interest and the public good[.]" These traits justify the special privileges that lawyers, as members of a profession, enjoy; among the most noteworthy are a monopoly on representing others in court, and the enhanced ability to earn a livelihood that such a monopoly provides.

The duties that a lawyer owes her client also flow from this understanding of what it means to a be a "professional"—that a lawyer's superior knowledge and training place clients in a position of trust and dependence such that the lawyer has obligations to individual clients beyond that of two equal parties to a transaction or contract. Instead, a lawyer is a fiduciary that owes the duties of candor, good faith, trust, and care to a client. ABA Handbook 91.

* * *

Before assessing the specific rules and statutes at issue, a thorough discussion of unbundling is necessary. Unbundling is the practice of limiting the scope of services that an attorney will provide—"dividing comprehensive legal representation into a series of discrete tasks, only some of which the client contracts with the lawyer to perform." It is growing ever more common in general, and in family law and bankruptcy law in particular. In bankruptcy cases, for example, the client and attorney may agree that not everything that could be done should be done by the attorney; some things might be left to the client or to other professionals. In effect, this *unbundling* excludes services that might aid or further the client's goals, but with the expectation and assumption that the items excluded can be accomplished by the client acting alone, or with another, presumably less expensive, attorney. The practice can benefit clients by giving them access to legal services that would otherwise be too expensive, and clients may feel a greater sense of satisfaction "flowing from the collaborative effort of achieving the client's desired goals." Pro bono attorneys may be more willing to volunteer their time and effort if the representation has clear boundaries. Attorneys who work for fees may likewise find the representation more predictable, as well as more profitable.

The practice of unbundling also recognizes that the attorney-client relationship need not fit an identical mold for each client; parties have the right to contract for the services they deem appropriate to the situation. Clients are given autonomy—the freedom to "choose one or more tasks that will involve legal representation and . . . pay only for legal services related to those specific tasks." The courts may also benefit from unbundling; where the choice is between pro se litigation and limited representation, the latter should increase the quality of pleadings and better focus the issues.

Unbundling raises concerns, however. The push to limit representation may come from the attorney, who often benefits from and has superior knowledge of the possible ramifications of excluding certain services.

> There are strong reasons for protecting those who entrust vital concerns and confidential information to lawyers. Clients inexperienced in such limitations may well have difficulty understanding important implications of limiting a lawyer's duty. Not every lawyer who will benefit from the limitation can be trusted to explain its costs and benefits fairly. In the long run, moreover, a restriction could become a standard practice that constricts the rights of clients without compensating benefits. The administration of justice may suffer from distrust of the legal system that may result from such a practice. Those reasons support special scrutiny of noncustomary contracts limiting a lawyer's duties, particularly when the lawyer requests the limitation.

Restatement (Third) of Law Governing Lawyers § 19 (2000).

There is a particular concern in consumer bankruptcy practice that attorneys will unbundle services that are essential or fundamental to bankruptcy cases and clients' objectives.

> . . . some lawyer services are so fundamental and essential to effective representation, no amount of disclosure and consent will suffice.

> Instructing a debtor to "go it alone" in any significant aspect of the
> bankruptcy case exposes counsel to possible criticism, and worse yet,
> a potential for sanction.

Hon. Jim D. Pappas, *Simple Solution = Big Problem,* 46 Advocate
(Idaho) 31, 33 (2003).

An additional concern is that limited representation may not
afford a client full protection against direct contact by opposing
counsel. If opposing counsel does not know the extent of a party's
representation, opposing counsel may inadvertently communicate
with the party about matters for which the party is represented.
The ABA official comment to Model Rule 4.2, which is identical to
Nevada Rule 4.2, states that communication with a represented party
is prohibited even if "the represented person initiates or consents
to the communication." ABA Model Rule 4.2 cmt. 3. Unless the
attorney has either seen that party's retainer agreement, which is
highly unlikely, or otherwise has knowledge of the relevant scope of
representation, the attorney is unlikely to respond because to do so
could risk a violation of Nevada Rule 4.2. . . .

In spite of the concerns that unbundling raises, the ABA
amended Model Rule 1.2(c) in 2002 to expressly allow limited-scope
representation and provide a mechanism to regulate it. . . . ABA Model
Rule 1.2, which Nevada has adopted verbatim, states that "[a] lawyer
may limit the scope of representation if the limitation is *reasonable
under the circumstances* and the client gives *informed consent.*" Nev.
Rule of Prof'l Conduct 1.2(c) (2011) (emphasis supplied).

Shortly after the ABA amended the rule, the ABA published the
ABA Handbook, a report on limited scope legal assistance. . . .

The *ABA Handbook* lists various factors that lawyers should
consider when determining whether unbundling is appropriate, and
a series of specific steps that lawyers should take when considering
whether to provide unbundled services to a particular client.
Although the court does not adopt these measures, it agrees with the
ABA's view that the focus should be client-centered; the decision to
unbundle is specific to the particular circumstances of the client, the
legal problem, and the court (or other decision-making forum). One-
size-fits-all is not appropriate.

If limited representation is selected, "the lawyer must also alert
the client to reasonably related problems and remedies that are
beyond the scope of the limited-service agreement." . . . .

* * *

Under Nevada Rule 1.1, which is identical to ABA Model Rule 1.1, "[a] lawyer shall provide competent representation to a client . . . the legal knowledge, skill, thoroughness and preparation reasonably necessary for the representation." Nev. Rule of Prof'l Conduct 1.1 (2011). "Competent handling of a legal matter includes inquiry into and analysis of the factual and legal elements of the problem, and use of methods and procedures meeting the standards of competent practitioners." ABA Model Rule 1.1 cmt. 5. "The level of competency heightens as the complexity and specialized nature of the matter increase." *In re Slabbinck*, 482 B.R. at 590.

Whether a lawyer fulfilled the duty of competence depends on the client's objectives. The lawyer's duty is to competently attain the client's goals of representation. In the absence of a valid limitation on services, a lawyer must provide the bundle of services that are reasonably necessary to achieve the client's reasonably anticipated result, unless and until grounds exist for the lawyer's withdrawal.

Nevada Rule 1.2(c), which is identical to ABA Model Rule 1.2(c), explicitly permits a lawyer to limit the scope of representation. Nev. Rule of Prof'l Conduct 1.2(c) (2011). The ABA comments shed light on the relationship between the duty of competence and agreements to limit the scope of representation. "Although an agreement for a limited representation does not exempt a lawyer from the duty to provide competent representation, the limitation is a factor to be considered when determining the legal knowledge, skill, thoroughness and preparation necessary for the representation." ABA Model Rule 1.2 cmt. 7 (citing ABA Model Rule 1.1).

In other words, the duty of competence both informs and survives any and all limitations on the scope of services. The baseline obligation to inquire into the facts and circumstances of a case and analyze the possible legal issues is not changed when the scope of services is limited. The bottom line is that an agreement to unbundle services constitutes a breach of the duty of competence if the agreement excludes the services reasonably necessary to achieve the client's reasonable objectives. The duty of competence informs the agreement to unbundle by mandating the inclusion of those services reasonably necessary to achieve the client's reasonable objectives. Nev. Rule of Prof'l Conduct 1.1 (2011). If those services are excluded, the client's goals cannot be met regardless of how knowledgeable, skilled, thorough, and prepared the lawyer may be. . . .

To determine the client's objectives, a lawyer must properly communicate with the client to understand the client's expectations, learn about the client's particular legal and financial situation, and independently investigate any "red flag" areas. A bankruptcy lawyer cannot assume that a client knows what a bankruptcy will or will not do for her. . . .

A lawyer who holds himself out as a bankruptcy expert or specialist should explain the limits of the specialty. For example, a potential client that wants to discharge her student debts should be informed that student debts are nondischargeable absent undue hardship, and the lawyer should inquire into her circumstances to determine the likelihood of prevailing on a claim of undue hardship. The lawyer should perform the same inquiry and explanation for all potentially nondischargeable debts, such as those incurred through fraud.

. . . A bankruptcy lawyer should inquire into a potential debtor's situation to determine if any of the debts were incurred by fraud and whether a nondischargeability proceeding is likely. The lawyer should also ascertain to what extent any nondischargeable debts are the driving force behind the potential client's decision to seek counsel. . . .

. . . The consumer bankruptcy attorney's role is to determine how bankruptcy may assist the client and whether some of the client's goals may be left unmet through bankruptcy, and effectively communicate this to the client. The client then decides whether and how to proceed. If the attorney and the client have different understandings of the goals of representation, viewed objectively, then the lawyer has not fulfilled the duty of competence.

* * *

DeLuca's first failure—the root cause of his other failings—was to not define the goals of the representation, which resulted from a lack of communication with the Debtors at the initial consultation. He apparently treats all debtors the same, as if the discharge of all dischargeable debts is always the primary goal. Here, however, the Debtors' goal was to permanently stop the wage garnishment resulting from the St. Rose Debt. While a discharge of their other debts is of some benefit, the reason they sought counsel was the wage garnishment. DeLuca was aware of the garnishment and was given copies of various district court documents. He did not inquire into the nature of the Judgment, either at the initial consultation or thereafter. He apparently assumed that, because the debt was from a hospital, it was for medical services. He argues that any reasonable attorney would make the same assumption. The court disagrees. Competently attaining the Debtors' goals of representation mandated an independent inquiry into the nature of the Judgment.

DeLuca argues that the Debtors had the burden to inform him that the debt was incurred through fraud, as the Retainer Agreement states that debts incurred through fraud "do not go away" and requests copies of all lawsuits within the last two years. Because the Debtors knew that the Judgment was based on fraud, so DeLuca argues, the burden was on them to communicate that fact to him. DeLuca's argument fails, however, because he improperly placed the burden on the Debtors to make the legal conclusion that fraud, as defined in the Bankruptcy Code, includes the fraudulent act that Seare committed in the district court. A layperson cannot be reasonably expected to connect those dots—that a Judgment under Civil Rule 11 for fabricating evidence ("fraud on the court") may be nondischargeable as fraud under bankruptcy law. In addition, the Debtors complied with the request in the Retainer Agreement to provide copies of all lawsuits. While they did not give DeLuca hard copies of the entire district court docket, they provided sufficient documents to inform him of the existence of the district court case. Once DeLuca was aware of a garnishment connected to a prior judgment, he had the affirmative duty to investigate. DeLuca is the bankruptcy expert, not the Debtors.

Either DeLuca did not understand the Debtors' primary objective or he negligently assumed that the St. Rose Debt was dischargeable and thus the Debtors' objective would be met. Either way, he did not exercise the legal knowledge, skill, and thoroughness reasonably necessary for the representation. He was not thorough, either in reviewing the documents given to him or in undertaking any independent review of the district court proceedings. He did not apply the knowledge and skill he has acquired through many years of consumer bankruptcy practice to the Debtors' needs.

* * *

In the attorney-client relationship, the client sets the objectives and the attorney determines the means to fulfill them in consultation with the client. Without understanding the Debtors' goals of representation, DeLuca could not determine which legal services were reasonably necessary to attain those goals. Nor could the Debtors properly evaluate DeLuca's choice of means because the Debtors did not understand that filing a petition would likely result in an adversary proceeding—a proceeding in which DeLuca, the lawyer they reasonably understood to represent them for the entire bankruptcy matter, refused to represent them. The Debtors' choice to file was colored by DeLuca's failure to properly advise them. With sufficient information, the Debtors may have chosen not to file or sought an attorney that had a different fee structure concerning adversary proceedings.

DeLuca did not reach an understanding of the Debtors' goals or explain to them the challenges they were likely to face in trying to achieve those goals by filing for bankruptcy. In the absence of such guidance, he had the duty to offer the services reasonably necessary to achieve a permanent cessation of the wage garnishment. Because an adversary proceeding was a near certainty in light of what DeLuca should have known at the time of the initial consultation—that the Judgment was based on fraud—representing the Debtors at an adversary proceeding was not only reasonably necessary to achieve their goal of stopping the garnishment but likely the only way to stop the garnishment. Consequently, DeLuca's decision to unbundle representation in adversary proceedings violated the duty of competence.

. . . Unbundling is permissible only if "the limitation is reasonable under the circumstances and the client gives informed consent." Nev. Rule of Prof'l Conduct 1.2(c).

. . . "'Reasonable' . . . denotes the conduct of a reasonably prudent and competent lawyer." Nev. Rule of Prof'l Conduct 1.0(h) (2011). . . . The *Restatement* declares that a limitation is reasonable if the benefits supposedly obtained by the waiver, such as reduced legal fees or the ability to obtain a particularly able lawyer, could reasonably be considered to outweigh the potential risks posed by the limitation. Restatement (Third) of Law Governing Lawyers § 19 (2000). . . .

The ABA has stated that a limitation is unreasonable if it would violate another ethics rule or a provision of substantive law. . . .

Reasonableness is assessed at the time the client agreed to unbundled services; neither party has the benefit of hindsight. Nev. Rule of Prof'l Conduct 1.2(c) (2011). . . .

* * *

The second element of Nevada Rule 1.2(c)—informed consent—is "the agreement by a person to a proposed course of conduct after the lawyer has communicated adequate information and explanation about the material risks of and reasonably available alternatives to the proposed course of conduct." Nev. Rule of Prof'l Conduct 1.0(e) (2011). The analysis involves two questions: (1) whether the information disclosure was sufficient; and (2) whether the consent was valid. "Consent involves a clear understanding on the part of the debtor as to these factors and the possible results of a debtor proceeding without an attorney being present."

* * *

The nature of the required disclosure is fact-specific and depends on the client's particular situation. For example, the risks of proceeding without representation in adversary proceedings depend on the likelihood of an adversary proceeding, which in turn depends on the nature of the client's debts and the identity of the creditors (e.g., whether a particular creditor has a propensity for filing adversary complaints).

The ABA also has endorsed the view that attorneys have a dual obligation to explain the inherent risks of unbundling and the specific risks of a particular case.

> Although there is no one-size-fits all explanation for clients, it might include a general description of limited representation, a specific description of the type of limited representation the lawyer will provide to the client, what the lawyer and client each will do, what the lawyer will *not* do under the agreement (a little redundancy here helps), whether the lawyer will enter an appearance and when and how the lawyer will withdraw or strike that appearance (making it clear the client will be required to support the withdrawal), whether and how the lawyer and client can modify the initial agreement if they need or want to do so, and identification of the risks of limited representation.

ABA Handbook 71 (emphasis in original). The lawyer must start with the big picture—explaining what unbundling is—and then go into more detail about the risks of limited representation and the responsibilities of the lawyer and the client.

* * *

A particular risk of limited representation is that the client may find herself in a position of diminished bargaining power if unbundled services become necessary during the course of representation.

Because the required information that a lawyer must provide is situation-specific, boilerplate disclosures in contracts of adhesion are highly suspect. Such disclosures may sufficiently communicate what unbundling is and the general risks associated with it, but a boilerplate disclosure cannot be expected to capture the specific risks that a client will face if her lawyer does not perform certain services. . . .

* * *

DeLuca failed both aspects of informed consent. First, he did not adequately communicate the material risks of unbundling adversary proceedings—either in general or in the Debtors' situation—or the available alternatives to such unbundling. Without adequate information upon which to base a decision, valid consent was impossible. Second, the means of the consent—initialing and signing DeLuca's contract of adhesion—did not sufficiently demonstrate that the Debtors understood the import of proceeding without representation in adversary proceedings.

* * *

Even if a limitation is reasonable and the client gives informed consent, the lawyer is not discharged of all duties surrounding the unbundled matter. The lawyer still has the duty to communicate under Nevada Rule 1.4, which is identical in pertinent part to ABA Model Rule 1.4. Nev. Rule of Prof'l Conduct 1.4 (2011); ABA Model Rule 1.4 (2002). The lawyer shall "[r]easonably consult with the client about the means by which the client's objectives are to be accomplished; . . . [k]eep the client reasonably informed about the status of the matter; [and] . . . [p]romptly comply with reasonable requests for information. . . ." Nev. Rule of Prof'l Conduct 1.4(a) (2011).

. . . DeLuca first violated Nevada Rule 1.4 by failing to reasonably consult with the Debtors about the means to achieve their objectives. Nev. Rule of Prof'l Conduct 1.4(a)(2) (2011). Because he did not understand that their primary goal was to permanently stop the garnishment, to the near exclusion of discharging other debts, a meaningful consultation about which means best served the Debtors' goals was rendered impossible.

DeLuca's failure to forward the proposed stipulation and order that he received via fax from St. Rose one month before St. Rose filed the Complaint also violated Nevada Rule 1.4. Even if DeLuca had properly unbundled representation in the adversary proceeding, which he did not, he had the ongoing duty to "keep the client reasonably informed about the status of the matter." Nev. Rule of Prof'l Conduct 1.4(a)(3) (2011). There is no doubt that the Debtors' "matter" included a judgment creditor's communication concerning the possible settlement of its claim. To make matters worse, DeLuca told St. Rose that he would not sign off on the proposed stipulation without consulting first with the Debtors, a consultation which apparently never happened. (Ex. H.)

DeLuca also violated Nevada Rule 1.4 by failing to timely respond to requests for information by the Debtors. Nev. Rule of Prof'l Conduct 1.4(a)(4) (2011). Tedoco argues that throughout the representation, DeLuca's office was nonresponsive and failed to keep the Debtors informed of the progress in their case. . . . She further argues that DeLuca's staff returned messages that specifically requested for DeLuca to call. Even when DeLuca's office returned the call, it often took two or three messages to prompt DeLuca's office to act. While a busy attorney is not required to return all calls directed at him or her, especially if the matter can be addressed by a staff member, the primary relationship is between the attorney and client. DeLuca could not simply ignore the requests for direct communication. The Debtors paid for DeLuca's ongoing professional legal counsel, not just for a one-time meeting.

* * *

(Citations omitted.)

COMMUNICATION

One of the issues that arises in unbundling is the duty to communicate sufficient information to allow the client to make an informed decision. Model Rule 1.4 defines the communication duties of an attorney. It states that:

(a) A lawyer shall:

(1) promptly inform the client of any decision or circumstance with respect to which the client's informed consent, as defined in Rule 1.0(e), is required by these Rules;

(2) reasonably consult with the client about the means by which the client's objectives are to be accomplished;

(3) keep the client reasonably informed about the status of the matter;

(4) promptly comply with reasonable requests for information; and

(5) consult with the client about any relevant limitation on the lawyer's conduct when the lawyer knows that the client expects assistance not permitted by the Rules of Professional Conduct or other law.

(b) A lawyer shall explain a matter to the extent reasonably necessary to permit the client to make informed decisions regarding the representation.

NOTES AND COMMENTS

1. The court declines to adopt the *ABA Handbook*'s considerations for unbundling. Those considerations include: "[1] the capabilities of the client, [2] the nature [i.e., complexity] and importance of the legal problem, [3] the degree of discretion that decision-makers exercise in

resolving the problem, [4] the type of dispute-resolution mechanism, and [5] the availability (or not) to the client of other self-help resources." In re Seare, 493 B.R. at 186 n. 20. How do these factors limit the ability to unbundle services in bankruptcy cases?

2. The court discusses the need for the attorney to understand the client's goals. What does it mean for an attorney to understand the client's goals? If the debtors had indicated a goal of "filing bankruptcy," would that suffice, or would the attorney need to ask more questions? What about a goal of "discharging debt"? A goal of "getting a creditor off my back"?

3. What type of consultation does the court ask of the attorney in order to create informed consent? If it is not enough to mention that adversary proceedings are not included, what does the court want?

4. How does the requirement of attorney competence discussed by the *Seare* court differ from the competence discussed in the prior section of this textbook?

5. Another common unbundling scenario involves the separation of pre-petition services and post-petition services. In such situations, the debtor hires the attorney solely for the purpose of filing the bankruptcy petition. The debtor may hire another attorney (or even the same attorney) to represent her post-petition. But the debtor does not have to hire an attorney post-petition, and the attorney does not have to represent the debtor post-petition. Why might the attorney and client structure the relationship this way? What unbundling considerations need to be considered in such a scenario?

C. CONFLICTS OF INTEREST (§ 327)

Conflicts of interest can present challenges in the bankruptcy context because of the sheer number of parties involved in a bankruptcy case. It is not unusual for an attorney to represent two different creditors independently who suddenly find themselves in conflict with each other over limited resources once a bankruptcy case has been filed. In addition, some attorneys are hired to represent a group of people—such as a creditors' committee—that operates as one unit but consists of members with divergent interests. And in some cases, the attorney had represented one or more of the creditors before being tasked to represent the committee as a whole.

CONFLICT OF INTEREST ANALYSIS
COMMENT 2 OF RULE 1.7

1. Identify the client or clients and the nature of the representation (current; former; prospective);

2. Determine whether a conflict of interest exists;

3. Decide whether the conflict is consentable; and

4. Obtain informed consent, confirmed in writing.

The prohibitions against conflicts of interest are based on two very important values of the legal profession. The first core value is loyalty; the importance of loyalty to the client is emphasized consistently in the Model Rules of Professional Conduct, even to the extent of protecting former clients (*see* Model Rule 1.9) and individuals who merely seek advice but do not subsequently hire the attorney (prospective clients under Model Rule 1.18). Loyalty on the part of the attorney can create trust within the attorney-client relationship that allows the client to be confident in the attorney's advice and actions. As Comment 1 to Rule 1.7 provides, "[l]oyalty and independent judgment are essential elements in the lawyer's relationship to a client." Additionally, the conflict rules are intended to add further protection to confidential information. The rules stress the concept that when a lawyer represents multiple clients concurrently or even sequentially, confidential information may be disclosed either intentionally or unintentionally. The rules not only prohibit the use of confidential information but also prohibit representation when the risk of disclosure of confidential representation is too high.

Read 11 U.S.C. § 327, which provides that professionals hired by the trustee (or debtor-in-possession) may not have a conflict of interest with the bankruptcy estate. This section mirrors the ABA's Model Rule of Professional Conduct 1.7(a), which provides that ". . . a lawyer shall not represent a client if the representation involves a concurrent conflict of interest. A concurrent conflict of interest exists if (1) the representation of one client will be directly adverse to another client or (2) there is a significant risk that the representation of one or more clients will be materially limited by the lawyer's responsibilities to another client, a former client or a third person or by a personal interest of the lawyer." One of the challenges of representing a debtor is in having an interest in being paid by that debtor—an interest that may be at odds with the best interest of the debtor or with the debtor's duties in bankruptcy.

CONFIDENTIALITY

As you consider conflicts of interest, keep in mind the attorney's duty of confidentiality. The Rules of Professional Conduct in every state contain provisions for protecting confidential information. These rules provide for the basis of attorney discipline if an attorney reveals information covered by the definition of confidential information. Additionally, the evidentiary privilege rules protect privileged information from being admitted as evidence in court. It is important to understand the differences between these two protections.

Significantly more information is protected by the Rules of Professional Conduct than the evidentiary privilege. Model Rule 1.6(a) contains the definition of *confidential information*. Although the exceptions to the confidentiality rules vary greatly from state to state, the definition is generally the same throughout the United States. Model Rule 1.6(a) defines the protected information as "information relating to the representation of a client."

The Model Rules definition of confidentiality is broad in scope. Rule 1.6 notes that confidential information includes all information related to the representation—whether the information was gained prior to the representation, during the representation, or even after the representation. Confidentiality is not affected by the way in which the information is obtained; it is confidential in that it relates to the representation of the client.

In re Pillowtex, Inc.

304 F.3d 246 (3d Cir. 2002)

SLOVITER, Circuit Judge

The U.S. Trustee appeals from the District Court's order authorizing the retention of Jones, Day, Reavis and Pogue ("Jones Day") as Pillowtex, Inc.'s Chapter 11 bankruptcy counsel. The U.S. Trustee argues that payments of fees by Pillowtex to Jones Day within the 90 days before bankruptcy may have constituted an avoidable preference and that the receipt of such a preference by Jones Day would constitute a conflict of interest with Pillowtex's creditors and its bankruptcy estate. The U.S. Trustee maintains that because the Bankruptcy Code provides that debtor's counsel may not "hold or represent an interest adverse to the estate" or "an interest materially adverse to the interest of . . . any class of creditors," Jones Day may have been disqualified from serving as Pillowtex's bankruptcy counsel. Without ruling on the U.S. Trustee's preference allegation, the District Court approved Jones Day's retention on condition, proposed by Jones Day, that if Jones Day is determined to have received a preference, it return the amount of the preference to Pillowtex's bankruptcy estates and waive any resulting claim. . . .

Pillowtex Corporation and its subsidiaries (referred to collectively as Pillowtex) manufacture pillows, blankets, towels and other textiles. Jones Day has represented and advised Pillowtex since 1996 in a variety of matters, including corporate, financial, securities, real property, litigation, environmental, intellectual property, labor, employee benefits and tax affairs. Prior to filing its bankruptcy petition, Pillowtex retained Jones Day to assist it with contingency planning and bankruptcy preparation.

Pillowtex declared bankruptcy on November 14, 2000 by filing a petition under Chapter 11 of the Bankruptcy Code. . . .

On November 16, 2000, Pillowtex filed an application with the Bankruptcy Court to retain and employ Jones Day as its bankruptcy counsel pursuant to section 327 of the Bankruptcy Code. As part of Jones Day's retention application, Jones Day set forth the date and amount of each payment that Pillowtex made to the firm during the year immediately preceding the filing for bankruptcy. The disclosure by Jones Day showed that Pillowtex made the following payments to Jones Day for services rendered:

11/29/99	$203,520.69	
12/27/99	450,573.79	
12/30/99	155,912.06	
2/23/00	181,550.01	
3/31/00	67,482.73	
4/30/00	146,520.71	
6/30/00	180,585.22	
7/7/00	132,299.71	
9/11/00	78,652.94	
11/3/00	40,759.09	
11/10/00	778,157.33	
11/13/00	300,000.00	(retainer-approx. $100,000 toward prepetition fees)

The last payment listed, that on November 13, 2000, was made the day before Pillowtex filed its petition for bankruptcy and was a retainer of $300,000 for services rendered or to be rendered by Jones Day and for reimbursement of expenses. Including the applied portion of the retainer, Pillowtex paid Jones Day $2,516,014 in the year before it declared bankruptcy. Of those payments $997,569.36 were made in the ninety days before Pillowtex filed its petition for bankruptcy.

* * *

A debtor in possession, such as Pillowtex, may, with bankruptcy court approval, employ one or more attorneys to represent it and to assist it in fulfilling its duties. *See* 11 U.S.C. § 327(a). The attorneys selected may not be persons who "hold or represent an interest adverse to the estate," and must be "disinterested persons." *Id.* The Bankruptcy Code includes as a "disinterested person," someone who "does not have an interest materially adverse to the interest of the estate or of any class of creditors or equity security holders, by reason of any direct or indirect relationship to, connection with, or interest in, the debtor . . . , or for any other reason." 11 U.S.C. § 101(14)(E). Prior representation of the debtor does not, of itself, merit disqualification. See 11 U.S.C. § 1107(b) ("[A] person is not disqualified for employment under section 327 of this title by a debtor in possession solely because of such person's employment by or representation of the debtor before the commencement of the case.").

We have considered the statutory requirements for retention of counsel in several opinions. In *In re BH&P, Inc.,* 949 F.2d 1300 (3d Cir.1991), the bankruptcy court had disqualified counsel after finding that the law firm had an actual conflict of interest by representing both the trustee for the debtor in its chapter 7 proceeding and the two principals of the debtor who had also filed chapter 7 proceedings. In affirming the disqualification of counsel (as well as the trustee), we stated that a conflict is actual, and hence per se disqualifying, if it is likely that a professional will be placed in a position permitting it to favor one interest over an impermissibly conflicting interest

We again considered the standards applicable to retention of trustee's counsel in *In re Marvel Entertainment Group, Inc.,* 140 F.3d 463 (3d Cir. 1998). Because the parties urged "conflicting interpretations of *BH&P*, we expressly reiterat[ed]" our earlier holding that:

(1) Section 327(a), as well as § 327(c), imposes a per se disqualification as trustee's counsel of any attorney who has an *actual conflict of interest*; (2) the district court may within its discretion-pursuant to § 327(a) and consistent with § 327(c)-disqualify an attorney who has a

potential conflict of interest and (3) the district court may not disqualify an attorney on the *appearance of conflict* alone.

Id. at 476 (emphases added). . . .

Although the retention of counsel for the trustee was at issue in
both *BH&P* and *Marvel Entertainment*, the same standards apply to
the retention of counsel for the debtor in possession. *See* 11 U.S.C.
§ 1107(a).

In *In re First Jersey Securities, Inc.,* 180 F.3d 504 (3d Cir. 1999),
the U.S. Trustee objected to retention of the counsel proposed by
the debtor in possession on the ground that counsel had received
a preferential payment, constituting an interest adverse to the
estate. Notwithstanding that both the bankruptcy court and
the district court had approved counsel's retention, this court
reversed. We stated that "[w]here there is an actual conflict of
interest . . . disqualification is mandatory." Then, in language that
the U.S. Trustee here emphasizes, we stated that "[a] preferential
transfer to [debtor's counsel] would constitute an *actual conflict
of interest* between counsel and the debtor, and would require the
firm's disqualification."

* * *

In this case, the District Court never decided whether Jones Day
received an avoidable preference from Pillowtex when it accelerated
billing for and received payment for past due bills during the ninety
days before Pillowtex declared bankruptcy. An avoidable preference
is defined in section 547(b) of the Bankruptcy Code as

> any transfer of an interest of the debtor in property-(1) to or for the
> benefit of a creditor; (2) for or on account of an antecedent debt
> owed by the debtor before such transfer was made; (3) made while
> the debtor was insolvent; (4) made-(A) on or within 90 days before
> the date of the filing of the petition; . . . (5) that enables such credi-
> tor to receive more than such creditor would receive [in a Chapter 7
> distribution].

11 U.S.C. § 547(b).

The preference rule prevents debtors from depleting the estate
to pay favored creditors with assets that otherwise would have
been apportioned among creditors according to the prioritization
scheme of the Bankruptcy Code. When the debtor becomes
insolvent, a payment to one creditor from the estate's limited assets
is necessarily paid at the expense of another creditor. The receipt

of a preference by a creditor thus creates a conflict with unpaid creditors, whose share of the remaining assets is diminished by the payment.

In this court, Jones Day explained that it sought payment from Pillowtex of its outstanding bills in order that it would not be a creditor at the time of the bankruptcy, as that would have disqualified it from retention as counsel. The record does not show how much of the fee Jones Day received within the 90 days before bankruptcy was for bankruptcy preparation, how much was for legal work done years earlier, and what the ordinary practice was in Jones Day's billings to Pillowtex and Pillowtex's payments.

Jones Day did not make a proffer of such information. Instead, it argued merely that a hearing was expensive and unnecessary, and proposed that the court could avoid any possible conflict by authorizing retention of Jones Day subject to the conditions that (1) Jones Day return any preference it is determined to have received, and (2) Jones Day waive any claim resulting from the preference.

We agree with the U.S. Trustee that the court's order incorporating the two conditions does not resolve the question whether Jones Day received an avoidable preference and was therefore not disinterested and whether it should have been disqualified. If payments to Jones Day were determined to be preferences, Jones Day would, in any event, be obliged to return the funds to the estate. . . .

Nor does its undertaking to waive the claims resulting from the preference resolve the issue of its possible disqualification if the fee payment was an avoidable preference. Jones Day cites a series of cases to illustrate that a professional can eliminate an adverse interest by waiving any claim it has against the estate, but it is not in the same position as the professionals in these cases.

In each of the cited cases, the professional waived its fees *prior* to being approved for retention under section 327(a). Here, Jones Day has not actually waived any fees as there has been no determination that there was a preference and its amount, but Jones Day was retained nonetheless.

* * *

At the heart of the U.S. Trustee's objection to retention of Jones Day as counsel before the preference issue was decided is the improbability that Jones Day, as counsel to the debtor-in-possession, would bring an action against itself to recover any preference. As the U.S. Trustee states in its brief, "[b]ecause Jones Day has taken and retained payments that may be preferential and it 'will not be advising the Debtors to seek to recover payments made to Jones Day' . . . the conflict of interests, if any, has been in place since Jones Day's retention was approved and is an actual conflict of interest today."

* * *

At the oral argument, Jones Day contended that all bankruptcy lawyers find themselves with past due bills from putative debtors on the eve of bankruptcy and seek to clear the accounts so that they are qualified to serve as counsel for the debtor. It suggested that if this court were to hold that such payments may be avoidable preferences which must be determined before retention can be approved, we will disrupt the already hectic period after bankruptcy filing when the bankruptcy court is occupied with first day orders and the parties are meeting to form creditors committees. We believe that some accommodation can undoubtedly be made between the need of counsel for payment of appropriate fees and the explicit provisions of the Code. The U.S. Trustee agrees that counsel are entitled to receive fees for the bankruptcy preparation, although we reserve the issue how this can be done consistently with the provisions of the Code. The U.S. Trustee maintained before the District Court that "professionals entering bankruptcy cases protect themselves from the preference issue by obtaining a retainer, and they . . . draw down on the retainer during the 90 day period so as to avoid raising the issue of whether or not they received preferential payments." It also argues that many preference claims may be insubstantial and that bankruptcy counsel typically waive past fees due. The U.S. Trustee focuses on Jones Day's receipt of payments for past bills which enabled it to receive 100% of all past due bills rather than waiving those for earlier work. It argues that "[p]aying hundreds of thousands of dollars of accrued fees on the eve of bankruptcy was not typical."

The record does not show which view is accurate. The parties may choose to present evidence at the hearing on remand that would permit the District Court to make a finding of fact on the matter.

Because there has never been a judicial determination whether Jones Day received a preference, it is unclear at this time whether the preference, if there were one, presents a conflict which would require Jones Day's disqualification. We hold that when there has been a facially plausible claim of a substantial preference, the district court and/or the bankruptcy court cannot avoid the clear mandate of the statute by the mere expedient of approving retention conditional on a later determination of the preference issue.

The District Court in this case could not adequately evaluate the alleged conflict and was not in a position to conclude that any preference did not pose a conflict with Pillowtex's estate or a material conflict with the other creditors. We therefore agree with the U.S. Trustee that the District Court must hold a hearing on whether Pillowtex [sic] received a preference, and will remand for that purpose.

(Citations omitted.)

NOTES AND COMMENTS

1. Why is the U.S. Trustee involved in this case? *See* 11 U.S.C. § 307.

2. Remember that in a Chapter 11 case, a debtor-in-possession generally takes on the role of a panel trustee and thus Pillowtex would be responsible for seeking recovery of preferential transfers. *See* 11 U.S.C. §§ 547, 1107. Do you think that the court would have been more inclined to the law firm's position if a trustee were appointed in the case?

3. The law firm also argued that the debtor-in-possession was not the only party able to recover preferential transfers. The ability of creditors' committees and other parties-in-interest to seek recovery of preferential transfers has been a hotly debated issue and is generally limited to situations in which the trustee or debtor-in-possession has "unjustifiably" refused to bring such an action. *See* Hyundai Translead, Inc. v. Jackson Truck & Trailer Repair, Inc. (In re Trailer Source, Inc.), 555 F.3d 231 (6th Cir. 2009); PW Enter., Inc. v. North Dakota Racing Comm'n (In re Racing Srvcs., Inc.), 540 F.3d 892 (8th Cir. 2008). Assuming that the creditors' committee or another party-in-interest *could* bring a preferential transfer action against the law firm, would the conflict be remedied?

4. Are bankruptcy boutique firms—generally small or midsized firms that practice exclusively bankruptcy law—in a better position to avoid disqualification due to potential preferential transfers than a large firm that engages in multiple areas of law?

EXCEPTIONS TO THE DUTY OF CONFIDENTIALITY

In addition to the duty not to defraud the court, the attorney may in some circumstances circumvent the duty of confidentiality to ensure that the client does not engage in fraud upon the court. The Model Rules of Professional Responsibility contain a total of eight exceptions to confidentiality that permit (but do not require) attorney disclosure, including:

***

(2) to prevent the client from committing a crime or fraud that is reasonably certain to result in substantial injury to the financial interests or property of another and in furtherance of which the client has used or is using the lawyer's services;

(3) to prevent, mitigate or rectify substantial injury to the financial interests or property of another that is reasonably certain to result or has resulted from the client's commission of a crime or fraud in furtherance of which the client has used the lawyer's services;

(4) to secure legal advice about the lawyer's compliance with these Rules. . . .

***

Model Rule 1.6(b).

The exceptions enumerated under Rule 1.6(b)(2) and (3) deal with financial harm to another person. Rule 1.6(b)(2) requires four circumstances be present in order for the attorney to disclose. They are:

1. The *client* (not a third party) is involved;

2. The client is committing a *crime or a fraud;*

3. The crime or fraud will result in *reasonably certain substantial financial harm to anther;*

4. The client has used, or is using, the *lawyer's services.*

The exception under 1.6(b)(2) also deals with financial harm but deals with disclosure to rectify or mitigate harm that has already occurred. Again the elements of this exception require that the client be involved in the crime of fraud, that the harm be substantial, and that the client used the lawyer's services to commit the crime or fraud.

The following case also concerns the potential that prior representation of the debtor might prohibit an attorney from representing other parties in the bankruptcy case—this time the creditors' committee.

Hofmeister v. Official Comm. Of Unsecured Creditors (In re Revstone Indus., LLC)

551 B.R. 745 (D. Del. 2015)

ROBINSON, District Judge

* * *

. . . Debtors filed a voluntary bankruptcy petition under title 11 of the United States Code, §§ 101-1532. On December 17, 2012, the Office of the United States Trustee appointed the Official Committee of Unsecured Creditors of Revstone Industries, LLC ("the Committee"), pursuant to 11 U.S.C. § 1102(a)(1). On January 15, 2013, the Committee submitted an application seeking approval to retain and employ Womble Carlyle Sandridge & Rice, LLP ("WCSR"), as counsel for the Committee *nunc pro tunc* to December 17, 2012 ("the Application"). On January 30, 2013, George S. Hofmeister, the individual who founded Revstone in 2008 and who was the Chairman of Revstone and/or a member of its Board of Managers, filed an objection to the Application based on his assertion that WCSR had a conflict of interest because it had previously provided legal advice to Revstone in connection with the domestication of a judgment by Boston Finance Group, a member and chair of the Committee.

* * *

. . . Section 1103(b) of the bankruptcy code governs a committee's retention of counsel and provides that "an attorney . . . employed to represent a committee . . . may not, while employed by such committee, represent any other entity having an adverse interest in connection with the case. . . ." 11 U.S.C. § 1103(b). Disqualification under the code, therefore, requires the existence of an actual, ongoing conflict between a law firm's representation of a committee and its representation of an entity with an adverse interest. *See, e.g., In re Muma Servs., Inc.,* 286 B.R. 583, 590–91 (Bankr.D.Del.2002). . . . Even if I were to embrace Mr. Hofmeister's version of the facts, i.e., that WCSR gave advice to Revstone regarding the ability of Boston Finance (a member of the Committee) to enforce its judgment in South Carolina against Revstone, and even if (unidentified) confidential documents were shared in this regard, the record is undisputed that: (1) no formal engagement was entered into; (2) the advice was given in connection with a discrete matter unrelated to the bankruptcy cases; and (3) the advice was given (i.e., the "representation" ended) before the filing of the bankruptcy case.

. . . Under any reading of the statute or the case law, the bankruptcy court did not err in approving the retention of WCSR as the Committee's counsel over the objection of Mr. Hofmeister. An order will issue.

(Citations omitted.)

The debtor need not be one of the parties represented to create a conflict. In the following case, the potential conflict involved representation of one creditor when the attorney's former firm represented a different creditor—who also happened to be one of the debtor's shareholders.

In re ProEducation Int'l, Inc.

587 F.3d 296 (5th Cir. 2009)

KING, Circuit Judge

* * *

Attorney Kirk A. Kennedy seeks to represent Dr. Mark D'Andrea in his efforts to collect a judgment from ProEducation International, Inc. (ProEducation). Kennedy worked in the bankruptcy section of the Houston firm of Jackson Walker L.L.P. from February 2003 to November 2004. His office was located down the hall from Lionel Schooler, who also worked in the bankruptcy section. Unbeknownst to Kennedy, since 1999 Schooler had been representing MindPrint, Inc. (MindPrint) in a state court case against ProEducation. Several shareholders of ProEducation, including D'Andrea, intervened in the state court suit and took positions adverse to MindPrint. In November 2000, during the pendency of the state court case, ProEducation filed for Chapter 7 bankruptcy. The state court case was removed to bankruptcy court as an adversary proceeding shortly thereafter. Schooler continued to represent MindPrint throughout the adversary proceeding and in all matters pertaining to the ProEducation bankruptcy. D'Andrea was represented in the adversary proceeding by attorney Tom Schmidt.

While Kennedy worked at Jackson Walker, Schooler provided legal services to MindPrint in connection with the bankruptcy case and the adversary proceeding. At the conclusion of the adversary proceeding in July 2005, the bankruptcy court entered judgment in favor of both MindPrint and the shareholders (including D'Andrea) against ProEducation. MindPrint moved for sanctions against the shareholders, which the bankruptcy court denied. MindPrint appealed the denial of sanctions.

After Kennedy left Jackson Walker in November 2004, the Gulf Coast Cancer Center—where D'Andrea works as medical director—hired Kennedy as general counsel. In November 2005, during the appeal from the denial of sanctions in the adversary proceeding, Schmidt informed Schooler that he was planning to withdraw from representing D'Andrea and that Kennedy would replace him. MindPrint objected to Kennedy's involvement because of his previous association with Jackson Walker. Kennedy did not officially enter an appearance as D'Andrea's attorney at this point; but despite MindPrint's objections, Kennedy contributed to a brief filed on D'Andrea's behalf.

In July 2006, MindPrint discovered that Kennedy was attempting to conduct discovery about the appeal from the adversary proceeding. Schooler emailed Kennedy on two occasions, objecting to his representation of D'Andrea on the ground of imputed conflict of interest. Kennedy did not respond to either email, and he continued to work on behalf of D'Andrea in his collection efforts and in the appeal. On September 29, 2006, Kennedy filed a notice to appear on behalf of D'Andrea in the main bankruptcy case.

* * *

The Fifth Circuit's approach to ethical issues has remained "sensitive to preventing conflicts of interest." *Id.* at 611. Under this approach, a "[d]istrict [c]ourt is *obliged* to take measures against unethical conduct occurring in connection with any proceeding before it." *Id.* (emphasis and alterations in original; internal quotation marks omitted). Yet, "[d]epriving a party of the right to be represented by the attorney of his or her choice is a penalty that must not be imposed without careful consideration." *U.S. Fire Ins.,* 50 F.3d at 1313. Because of the severity of disqualification, we do not apply disqualification rules "mechanically," but we consider "[a]ll of the facts particular to [the] case . . . in the context of the relevant ethical criteria and with meticulous deference to the litigant's rights.". . . .

Texas Rule 1.09 states:

(a) Without prior consent, a lawyer who personally has formerly represented a client in a matter shall not thereafter represent another person in a matter adverse to the former client:
(1) in which such other person questions the validity of the lawyer's services or work product for the former client;
(2) if the representation in reasonable probability will involve a violation of Rule 1.05 [dealing with confidential client information]; or
(3) if it is the same or a substantially related matter.

(b) Except to the extent authorized by Rule 1.10, when lawyers are or have become members of or associated with a firm, none of them shall knowingly represent a client if any one of them practicing alone would be prohibited from doing so by paragraph (a).

(c) When the association of a lawyer with a firm has terminated, the lawyers who were then associated with that lawyer shall not knowingly represent a client if the lawyer whose association with that firm has terminated would be prohibited from doing so by paragraph (a)(1) or if the representation in reasonable probability will involve a violation of Rule 1.05.

. . . Under Texas Rule 1.09(b), the personal conflicts of one attorney are imputed to all other members of a firm. *Id.* 1.09(b). Comment 7 to Rule 1.09 states that this imputation can be removed when an attorney leaves a firm, stating that "should . . . other lawyers cease to be members of the same firm as the lawyer affected by paragraph (a) *without personally coming within its restrictions,* they thereafter may undertake the representation against the lawyer's former client unless prevented from doing so by some other of these Rules." *See id.* 1.09 cmt. 7 (emphasis added). . . .

The relevant Model Rule, Rule 1.9(b), uses slightly different language than the Texas Rule:

A lawyer shall not knowingly represent a person in the same or a substantially related matter in which a firm with which the lawyer formerly was associated had previously represented a client (1) whose interests are materially adverse to that person; and (2) about whom the lawyer had acquired information protected by Rules 1.6 and 1.9(c) that is material to the matter; unless the former client gives informed consent, confirmed in writing.

Model Rules of Prof'l Conduct R. 1.9(b) (2006). Regardless of linguistic differences, the two codes produce the same result in application—they both require that a departing lawyer must have actually acquired confidential information about the former firm's client or personally represented the former client to remain under imputed disqualification. . . .

* * *

Under Texas Rule 1.09(b), Kennedy was conclusively disqualified by imputation from representing D'Andrea only while he remained at Jackson Walker. When Kennedy ended his affiliation with Jackson Walker without personally acquiring confidential information about MindPrint, his imputed disqualification also ended. . . .

The evidence reflects that while at Jackson Walker, Kennedy never personally represented MindPrint, nor did he gain any actual knowledge of MindPrint. At the evidentiary hearing before the bankruptcy court,

Kennedy testified that he never heard of MindPrint while he was at Jackson Walker and that he never attended any firm meetings where the representation of MindPrint was discussed. He further testified that he had never met Al Winters, the principal of MindPrint, and that he first learned that Schooler was representing MindPrint in "May or June of 2005," about six months after he left Jackson Walker.

* * *

(Citations omitted.)

NOTES AND COMMENTS

1. The case involved a potential conflict between a shareholder or the debtor and a creditor. If D'Andrea had not been a shareholder, could a conflict still exist? In other words, could representation of two creditors create a conflict of interest? How, then, does an attorney represent a creditors' committee composed of many creditors?

2. What level of knowledge of MindPrint representation during Kennedy's time at Jackson Walker would have sufficed to disqualify him from representing D'Andrea? Would it be enough if Kennedy had known MindPrint was a client? Had he known that MindPrint was involved in a case against ProEducation?

D. CREDIBILITY

An attorney is required to refrain from dishonest conduct by a variety of the Rules of Professional Conduct.

HONESTY TO THE TRIBUNAL

Rule 3.3 rules requires an attorney to be honest to the tribunal. It states:

> (a) A lawyer shall not knowingly:
> (1) make a false statement of fact or law to a tribunal or fail to correct a false statement of material fact or law previously made to the tribunal by the lawyer;
> (2) fail to disclose to the tribunal legal authority in the controlling jurisdiction known to the lawyer to be directly adverse to the position of the client and not disclosed by opposing counsel; or

(3) offer evidence that the lawyer knows to be false. If a lawyer, the lawyer's client, or a witness called by the lawyer, has offered material evidence and the lawyer comes to know of its falsity, the lawyer shall take reasonable remedial measures, including, if necessary, disclosure to the tribunal. A lawyer may refuse to offer evidence, other than the testimony of a defendant in a criminal matter, that the lawyer reasonably believes is false.

(b) A lawyer who represents a client in an adjudicative proceeding and who knows that a person intends to engage, is engaging or has engaged in criminal or fraudulent conduct related to the proceeding shall take reasonable remedial measures, including, if necessary, disclosure to the tribunal.

HONESTY TO OTHER PARTIES

Rule 4.1 discusses honesty in regard to other parties:
In the course of representing a client a lawyer shall not knowingly:

(a) make a false statement of material fact or law to a third person; or
(b) fail to disclose a material fact to a third person when disclosure is necessary to avoid assisting a criminal or fraudulent act by a client, unless disclosure is prohibited by Rule 1.6.

Additionally, Rules 1.2(d) and 8.4 prohibit dishonest conduct, specifically counseling a client to engage in fraudulent behavior or engaging in dishonest behavior.

1. Candor

Honesty is a pillar of professional behavior, particularly honesty to the court. Candor comes up in a variety of contexts, including the hiring of bankruptcy professionals discussed earlier in this chapter. Recall that § 327 provides that a professional hired in the bankruptcy case cannot have a conflict of interest with the bankruptcy estate. The professional to be hired must disclose any potential conflicts of interest under Bankruptcy Rule 2014. The following case is just a small piece of a bigger drama involving two major restructuring firms that work in the Chapter 11 restructuring context.

In re Alpha Natural Resources, Inc.

556 B.R. 249 (Bankr. E.D. Va. 2016)

HUENNEKENS, Bankruptcy Judge

On August 3, 2015 (the "Petition Date"), Alpha Natural Resources, Inc., and 1491 of its direct and indirect subsidiaries (the "Debtors") commenced these bankruptcy cases by each filing a separate voluntary petition for relief under chapter 11 of the Bankruptcy Code in the United States Bankruptcy Court for the Eastern District of Virginia. . . . On June 2, 2016, following the Court's approval of a disclosure statement in accordance with § 1125 of the Bankruptcy Code, the Debtors filed solicitation versions of their proposed Second Amended Joint Plan of Reorganization of Debtors and Debtors in Possession (the "Second Amended Plan") and Second Amended Disclosure Statement.

. . . The Court found that it could confirm the Second Amended Plan under § 1129(b) of the Bankruptcy Code . . . .

Before the Court is the motion of Mar-Bow Value Partners LLC ("Mar-Bow") asking the Court to stay the effectiveness of the Confirmation Order (the "Motion"). Mar Bow had filed a substantive objection to the confirmation of the Plan on June 29, 2016 ("Mar-Bow's Plan Objection"). . . . Mar-Bow contends that the Court erred in approving certain release and exculpation provisions in the Confirmation Order with respect to McKinsey Recovery & Transformation Services U.S., LLC ("McKinsey RTS") in contravention of law and public policy. . . .

***

The Debtors are one of the largest domestic producers of coal in the United States. . . .

To assist the Debtors in the reorganization of their business affairs, the Debtors filed an application to employ McKinsey RTS as its turnaround advisor. McKinsey RTS is an affiliate of McKinsey & Company, Inc. ("McKinsey & Company") a global consulting firm. The Debtors sought to engage McKinsey RTS to support their management team's development of a business plan that would improve the Debtors' financial performance and optimize the Debtors' business operations. The Debtors also sought to engage McKinsey RTS to analyze the Debtors' position in the domestic coal markets. In support of McKinsey RTS' employment application, the Debtors filed the declaration of Kevin Carmody ("Carmody"), a practice leader at McKinsey RTS (the "First Declaration").

The First Declaration sets forth bases for a finding that McKinsey was a "disinterested party" under § 101(14) of the Bankruptcy Code and therefore eligible to be employed under § 327 of the Bankruptcy Code. In accordance with Bankruptcy Rule 2014, the First Declaration disclosed a number of connections McKinsey RTS had to interested parties in the Debtors' Bankruptcy Case that were unrelated to their representation of the Debtors. McKinsey RTS chose to disclose its connections not on an individual basis but instead by category of interested party (e.g. "Material Sureties," "Revolving Facility

Lenders," "Lenders Under A/R Facility," Major Competitors, Major Unsecured Note holders, Major Customers, etc.).

The First Declaration detailed the process that McKinsey RTS employed to detect potential conflicts among its own clients and among the clients of McKinsey & Company as a whole. McKinsey & Company began its conflict check by cross-referencing the Interested Parties List with McKinsey & Company's global database of clients—which included clients of McKinsey RTS as well as any other McKinsey affiliate. If McKinsey & Company provided services to an entity included on the Interested Parties List or to an entity potentially adverse to any listed entity, McKinsey RTS sent a follow up email to determine the nature of the relationship McKinsey & Company had with the interested party. McKinsey RTS also sent an email to all of the employees of McKinsey RTS and all of its affiliates to determine if any employee had a relationship to the Debtors, the United States Trustee, this Court, or an equity ownership in the Debtors. The First Declaration represents that McKinsey RTS would continue to review its client files in order to ensure no disqualifying conflicts arose during the pendency of the case and that it would make supplemental disclosures as necessary to comply with the Bankruptcy Code and the Federal Rules of Bankruptcy Procedure. Based on its conflict check, Carmody declared in the First Declaration that he believed McKinsey RTS to be disinterested as defined by § 101(14) of the Bankruptcy Code and eligible to be employed. No party objected to the employment of McKinsey RTS, or requested the opportunity to cross-examine Carmody based on the First Declaration. By order entered September 17, 2015, the Court found McKinsey RTS was disinterested within the meaning of Bankruptcy Code section 101(14) and authorized the Debtors to retain McKinsey RTS pursuant to the terms of the engagement letter attached to the Debtors' application (the "McKinsey RTS Retention Order"). . . .

McKinsey RTS made three additional public disclosures after the disclosures set forth in its First Declaration. On November 9, 2015, McKinsey RTS filed its first supplemental disclosure (the "First Supplemental Disclosure"). The First Supplemental Disclosure identified additional connections that McKinsey RTS had with other entities on the Interested Parties List. The additional connections were once again disclosed not on an individual basis but instead by category. On March 25, 2016, McKinsey RTS filed with the Court its second supplemental declaration (the "Second Supplemental Disclosure"). The Second Declaration disclosed additional connections that McKinsey RTS had with other interested parties. Like the First Declaration and First Supplemental Disclosure, the Second Supplemental Declaration did not disclose the individual names of the interested parties, but instead disclosed the interested parties only by category.

On May 3, 2016, the U.S. Trustee filed a motion to compel McKinsey RTS to comply with the requirements of Bankruptcy Rule 2014 (the "U.S. Trustee's Motion to Compel"). The U.S. Trustee's Motion to Compel sought the disclosure of the names of the entities on the Interested Parties List that McKinsey RTS had previously identified only by category. It also sought the disclosure of a general description of the work performed for each of the identified entities. The U.S. Trustee's Motion to Compel acknowledged that the U.S. Trustee was working with McKinsey RTS to resolve the pending issues.

On May 19, 2016, McKinsey RTS filed its third supplemental disclosure of Carmody pursuant to a stipulation resolving the United States Trustee's Motion to Compel (the "Third Supplemental Disclosure."). The Third Supplemental Disclosure identified by name many (but not all) of the current and former clients of McKinsey RTS who were on the Interested Parties List that McKinsey RTS had previously identified only by category. Carmody confirmed in the Third Supplemental Disclosure that the representation of these entities by McKinsey RTS was unrelated to the Debtors' chapter 11 case. The Third Supplemental Disclosure also identified by name employees of McKinsey RTS who had previously been employed by any entity included on the Interested Party List. Finally, the Third Supplemental Disclosure discussed the existence of an entity named MIO ("MIO") that offered investment products for McKinsey RTS' partners and pension plans. Although McKinsey RTS and MIO were independent from each other, it was disclosed that a member of MIO's board of directors also served as an employee of McKinsey RTS.

On June 6, 2016, Mar-Bow filed a Motion to Compel McKinsey RTS to comply with Bankruptcy Rule 2014. Mar-Bow claimed that McKinsey RTS had failed to disclose by name all of the entities with which it had connections on the Interested Parties List. Mar-Bow maintained that identification of connections by category was far too generic a description. . . .

In support of the Motion to Compel, Mar-Bow submitted the declaration of Jay Alix ("Alix"). Alix is the beneficial owner of Mar-Bow. Alix founded the restructuring advisory firm AlixPartners. AlixPartners competes with McKinsey RTS in the turnaround consulting business. Mar-Bow claimed that it had standing in this Court to file the Motion to Compel because it had acquired 7.5% of bonds due August 1, 2020, having a face amount of $1.25 million (the "Bonds"). Mar-Bow filed its proof of claim in the Debtors' bankruptcy case on March 23, 2016.

McKinsey RTS filed a response to Mar-Bow's allegations, painting the Motion to Compel as an anticompetitive strike by Alix to force McKinsey RTS out of the restructuring advisory business. McKinsey

RTS suggested that Alix bought the Bonds after the Petition Date at a substantial discount in order to obtain standing as a creditor for the sole purpose of challenging the employment of McKinsey RTS. . . .

***

On July 1, 2016, the Court entered an order granting most (but not all) of the relief requested by Mar-Bow in its Motion to Compel. . . . The Order Compelling Compliance tasked the Debtors, Mar-Bow, the Unsecured Creditors Committee, the U.S. Trustee, and McKinsey RTS to negotiate in good faith a confidentiality order whereunder the U.S. Trustee, the Debtors and the Unsecured Creditors Committee could review the In Camera Disclosures provided to the Court. . . .

Mar-Bow filed a motion to clarify the Order Compelling Compliance. Mar-Bow asked that it be allowed to review the In Camera Disclosures following the entry of a confidentiality order. By order entered July 15, 2016, the Court denied Mar-Bow's motion to clarify, declining to revisit the Order Compelling Compliance (the "Clarification Order"). The Court's Clarification Order did invite the U.S. Trustee to file a recommendation with the Court whether any portion of the In Camera Disclosures should be made public (the "Clarification Order"). . . .

***

The Court noted at the Confirmation Hearing that it had received the In Camera Disclosures from McKinsey RTS and was satisfied with them. In light of the In Camera Disclosures, the Court found that McKinsey RTS was disinterested and could receive the benefit of the Plan's release and exculpation provisions. The Court also found that the release and exculpation provisions contained in the Plan were negotiated in good faith, narrowly tailored, reasonable, and appropriate for all of the parties. Accordingly, the Court overruled Mar-Bow's Plan Objection.

. . . Section 327 of the Bankruptcy Code provides that the Trustee may employ professionals to assist in the bankruptcy case so long as the professionals are "disinterested persons" that do not hold or represent an interest adverse to the Debtor. 11 U.S.C. § 327. The Bankruptcy Code defines the term "distinterested person" to mean a person that:

(A) is not a creditor, an equity security holder, or an insider;
(B) is not and was not, within 2 years before the date of the filing of the petition, a director, officer, or employee of the debtor; and
(C) does not have an interest materially adverse to the interest of the estate or of any class of creditors or equity security holders, by reason of any direct or indirect relationship to, connection with, or interest in, the debtor, or for any other reason.

11 U.S.C. § 101(14). "While the Bankruptcy Code does not define an 'interest adverse to the estate,' bankruptcy courts have widely held that an adverse interest means either (1) the possession or assertion of any economic interest that would tend to lessen the value of the bankruptcy estate or create an actual or potential dispute with the estate as a rival claimant, or (2) a predisposition of bias against the estate."

Bankruptcy Rule 2014 facilitates the implementation of § 327 and § 101(14) of the Bankruptcy Code. The Rule requires that an application of a debtor in possession for an order approving the employment of a professional person must state "to the best of the applicant's knowledge, all of the person's connections with the debtor, creditors, any other party in interest, their respective attorneys and accountants, the United States trustee or any person employed in the office of the United States trustee." Fed. R. Bankr. P. 2014(a). The application must be accompanied by a verified statement of the person to be employed setting forth that very same information. "The duty to disclose under Bankruptcy Rule 2014 is considered sacrosanct because the complete and candid disclosure by [a professional person] seeking employment is indispensable to the court's discharge of its duty to assure the attorney's eligibility for employment under section 327(a) and to make an informed decision on whether the engagement is in the best interest of the estate." Disclosure under Rule 2014 must be clear enough for the Court, the U.S. Trustee and for other parties in interest to gauge the disinterestedness of the professional.

* * *

In the context of the Mar-Bow/McKinsey dispute, the Court kept a keen focus on the ultimate issue before it. The Court recognized the interests of the Debtors, their creditors other than Mar-Bow who numbered in the tens of thousands, and their 8000 employees who, along with various state and Federal regulatory agencies, had steadfastly worked in good faith to steer this Bankruptcy Case in a successful direction. . . . The Court was torn with a choice between its duty to move the Debtors' case forward to a prompt and fair conclusion for the benefit of all the constituencies involved in the Bankruptcy Case on the one hand and its duty to enforce Rule 2014 on the other.

In balancing the competing concerns presented by the Mar-Bow/ McKinsey dispute over the implementation of Rule 2014, the Court turned its focus on assuring the disinterestedness of the professionals whose employment it approved. Sections 105(a) and 107(b) of the Bankruptcy Code provided the Court with the means to tailor its enforcement of Rule 2014 to this end.

The Court agreed that additional disclosures needed to be made under Rule 2014. But delaying the Confirmation Hearing risked a post-petition financing default and a very real possibility for the unraveling of the web of interrelated settlements that had been painstakingly woven together to support the Debtors' Plan. The Court's Order Compelling Compliance and its Clarification Order were both carefully crafted to permit the Court and a limited number of key parties who were most intimately involved in the Bankruptcy Case to have timely access to all the information necessary to dispel any concerns over the disinterestedness of McKinsey RTS while protecting the legitimate business concerns of McKinsey RTS.

McKinsey RTS fully complied with the Court's Order Compelling Compliance and delivered the In Camera Disclosures to the Court the day before the Confirmation Hearing. The Court thoroughly reviewed the In Camera Disclosures, and it was satisfied that McKinsey RTS had complied in good faith with the Order Compelling Compliance and that McKinsey RTS was a "disinterested person" under the Bankruptcy Code.

***

Mar-Bow's public policy argument is premised on the facts that McKinsey RTS failed to comply with Bankruptcy Rule 2014 and such failure adversely impacts Mar-Bow. McKinsey RTS has publically disclosed all its connections. Mar-Bow's initial complaint was that McKinsey RTS identified its connections by category of interested party, instead of by name. The names are now public. As the record shows, McKinsey RTS' disclosures were more than adequate for the Court to find that McKinsey RTS is a disinterested person. Mar-Bow's current point of contention concerns the fact that it was excluded from the list of key parties that received the In Camera Disclosures. In light of the concerns expressed by McKinsey RTS about Mar-Bow's private agenda, further dissemination of the In Camera Disclosures to Mar-Bow would not have been an aid to the Court in its determination of disinterestedness. It only would have served to foster protracted litigation of the Mar-Bow/McKinsey dispute.

***

(Citations omitted.)

NOTES AND COMMENTS

1. The U.S. Supreme Court declined to hear an appeal by Mar-Bow of the decision in McKinsey's favor, after its appeals were dismissed by

the district court and those dismissals were affirmed per curiam by the Fourth Circuit Court of Appeals. Mar-Bow Value Partners, LLC v. McKinsey Recovery, 587 U.S. ___, Case No. 18-974 (*Cert. Denied* Apr. 22, 2019).

2. The drama between Mar-Bow and McKinsey did not end with this case. In May of 2018, Jay Alix sued McKinsey in the District Court for the Southern District of New York, alleging racketeering, breach of contract, tortious interference with business expectancy, and bankruptcy fraud. Jay Alix v. McKinsey & Co., Inc., et al., Case 1:18-cv-04141 (S.D.N.Y. May 9, 2018). Other cases have been filed in other courts with similar allegations. In recent years, McKinsey has paid millions in settlements with the U.S. Trustee's office in connection with allegations of insufficient disclosures under Bankruptcy Rule 2014. https://www.justice.gov/opa/pr/us-trustee-program-reaches-15-million-settlement-mckinsey-company-remedy-inadequate.

Bankruptcy Rule 2014 mandated specific disclosures to the court. But, of course, attorneys provide information to the courts outside of specific bankruptcy rules; candor is required in every communication with the courts. The following case considers the consequences of a lack of candor to the court.

Baker v. Harrington (In re Hoover)

827 F.3d 191 (1st Cir. 2016)

* * *

KAYATTA, Circuit Judge

Baker is a very experienced bankruptcy practitioner who regularly appears before the U.S. Bankruptcy Court. In this case, he represented the Debtor, John E. Hoover, III ("Hoover"), who sought relief under Chapter 11 of the U.S. Bankruptcy Code. Hoover, through Baker, filed his bankruptcy petition on March 15, 2014, four days before the day on which Bank of America, N.A. ("BOA") was to sell his business property in foreclosure. Hoover's petition was also prompted by the significant tax debt that he owed to the Massachusetts Department of Revenue.

In the wake of Hoover's March 15 filing for bankruptcy protection, BOA did not proceed with the foreclosure sale as previously scheduled. Instead, BOA continued the sale to June 18, 2014, sending Hoover on April 7 a written notice of the rescheduled date. BOA also suggested to Hoover its intent to file a motion for relief from the automatic stay. Seven days later, on April 14, Baker on behalf of Hoover filed a motion seeking sanctions against BOA for violating the automatic stay provisions of the U.S. Bankruptcy Code. See 11 U.S.C. § 362. In that motion, Baker argued that rescheduling the foreclosure sale constituted an improper continuation of debt collection activity under § 362 that warranted sanctions and a cancellation of the rescheduled sale.

In support of this motion, Baker wrote as follows:

8. Where a creditor has notice, continuation of a mortgage foreclosure sale post-petition, without obtaining relief from the automatic stay, is a willful violation. *See* In re Lynn–Weaver, 385 B.R. 7 (Bkrtcy.D.Mass. 2008), *citing* In re Heron Pond, LLC, 258 B.R. 529 (Bkrtcy.D. Mass. 2001) (both by Hillman, J.); Hart v. GMAC Mortgage Corp., 246 B.R. 709 (Bkrtcy.D.Mass. 2000) (Feeney, J.).

9. The cases cited in the previous paragraph held, in essence, that a single continuance of a foreclosure sale is not a stay violation *so long as* the creditor seeks relief from the stay prior to the sale date. However, Judge Hillman's holding in Heron Pond was based on "the obscurity of the prevailing legal rule (at least prior to this decision)". That decision was about 13 years ago, and the Lynn–Weaver decision was 6 years ago. The "prevailing legal rule" is no longer obscure. *See also* In re Derringer, 375 B.R. 903 (10th Cir. BAP, 2007).

(citation formatting and spacing as in original).

On April 18, four days after Hoover filed this motion, BOA filed a motion seeking relief from the automatic stay. Hoover, nonetheless, persisted with his claim that, by continuing the sale for several months without having first obtained relief from the stay, BOA violated the stay. On June 2, 2014, the bankruptcy court issued an order denying Hoover's motion for sanctions against BOA.

Separately, Baker also filed on Hoover's behalf an objection to a motion filed by the U.S. Trustee (the "Trustee") to convert Hoover's bankruptcy case to a case filed under Chapter 7 of the U.S. Bankruptcy Code, or to dismiss it. The Trustee's motion concerned cash that the debtor was spending even though the cash was subject to a tax lien. The Trustee argued that this cash constituted "cash collateral" under 11 U.S.C. § 363(a), and, therefore, could not be spent without the permission of the court.

Baker's attempt to parry the Trustee's motion focused on a claim that "cash collateral" only consists of cash or other property that is subject to a consensual lien. As Baker now admits, no case law so holds. Nevertheless, Baker claimed that the statute itself supported the argument. In his objection that he filed with the bankruptcy court, he wrote that "'cash collateral' means cash or other property 'subject to a security interest as provided in section 552(b) ...'." Having thus limited the meaning of "cash collateral" to cash subject to a security interest under 11 U.S.C. § 552(b), Baker argued that such a security interest can only arise by agreement; hence, cash in which a creditor has an interest by an involuntary lien is not "cash collateral." The applicable statute, though, plainly does not read as Baker's hybrid paraphrase and partial quote portrayed it (that cash collateral "means" cash or other property subject to a "security interest"). To the contrary, it provides that cash collateral "means cash . . . or other cash equivalents . . . in which the estate and an entity other than the estate have an interest and includes [certain other things] subject to a security interest as provided in section 552(b)." 11 U.S.C. § 363(a) (emphasis supplied).

* * *

On June 2, 2014, the bankruptcy court ordered Baker to show cause why he should not be sanctioned under Federal Rule of Bankruptcy Procedure 9011(b)(2). As grounds for its order, the court quoted from Paragraph 8 of Baker's motion for sanctions against BOA, observing that the statement Baker made in that paragraph was not a correct statement of law and was not supported by the cases Baker cited therein. The bankruptcy court also pointed to Paragraph 12 of Baker's objection to the Trustee's motion to convert or dismiss, finding that Baker had "misquot[ed] the definition of cash collateral" and "misstat[ed] the law by claiming that the obligation of a debtor to obtain authority to use cash collateral applies only where the lien on cash is a consensual lien."

In his written response to the order to show cause, Baker argued that the bankruptcy court read Paragraph 8 "out of context." He offered, though, no alternative reading of Paragraph 8, in or out of context. Instead, he pointed to the fact that the first sentence of Paragraph 9 correctly summarized existing law. He then described the rest of Paragraph 9 as a type of "nonfrivolous argument for the extension [or] modification . . . of existing law" permissible under Rule 9011. See Fed. R. Bankr. 9011(b)(2). The "modification" Baker claims to have had in mind was a requirement that, in order to comply with the automatic stay provisions, a creditor must not only move for relief from the automatic stay before the rescheduled sale date, but must file such a motion "promptly."

Next, in addressing the bankruptcy court's charge that he misquoted the definition of "cash collateral" and misstated the law in his objection to the Trustee's motion to convert or dismiss, Baker doubled down on his prior arguments. First, he disputed the bankruptcy court's characterization that he "misquot[ed]" the definition of "cash collateral," maintaining that, "at worst, I paraphrased it and omitted words that are not relevant to the context of the motion and objection." Second, after opining that the bankruptcy court's "real issue" with his objection was the merits of his argument, Baker proceeded to explain why the argument that one must possess a consensual security interest over cash or other property in order for that cash or property to be protected as "cash collateral" was not frivolous. In his analysis, Baker argued that he had only found two cases on point after "thoroughly research[ing]" the issue, and that although both of those cases interpreted the statute as including non-consensual security interests, they were non-binding and unsatisfactory to him. He also argued that dictum in another case implied support for his position, and that the "rule of the last antecedent"—whereby a modifier is attributed to the last term before it—is not necessarily controlling and, in this case, is overcome by "textual indications of contrary meaning."

The bankruptcy court rejected Baker's explanations on both counts. . . .

The bankruptcy court went on to observe that this conduct was not uncharacteristic of Baker. It explained that on at least three prior occasions Baker had been sanctioned by different sessions of the court for conduct that included asserting frivolous defenses, advancing arguments contrary to express statutory provisions, and filing a meritless motion for sanctions.

. . . the bankruptcy court observed that the "hefty" monetary penalties imposed on Baker in those prior cases had not deterred Baker from repeating such conduct. The court thus decided to impose a non-monetary penalty "in the hope of effecting a more lasting behavioral modification." It ordered Baker to "enroll in and attend in person (not on-line) a one semester, minimum three credit-hour class on legal ethics or professional responsibility in an ABA accredited law school to be completed within 13 months of this order."

* * *

The sanction in this case was based on the bankruptcy court's finding that Baker transgressed the dictates of Bankruptcy Rule 9011(b)(2). That Rule is substantively identical to Federal Rule of Civil Procedure 11(b)(2). By certifying that the papers he filed with the bankruptcy court complied with Rule 9011, Baker was obligated to believe, after reasonable inquiry, that the legal contentions he advanced in those papers were not advanced for an improper purpose, such as misleading the court. See Fed. R. Bankr. P. 9011(b).

. . . We turn our attention first to Paragraphs 8 and 9 of Baker's motion for sanctions against BOA. Paragraph 8 is a flat out misstatement of the cases cited therein. To put a fine point on it, even now Baker is unable to make any argument that the statement he made in Paragraph 8 is supported by the cases he cited.

Instead, he argues that the inaccuracy disappears if one reads Paragraph 8 in conjunction with Paragraph 9, the first sentence of which does accurately state what the cited cases say. The remainder of Paragraph 9, though, clearly suggests that the first sentence is itself no longer the law. At best, the two paragraphs are unintelligible, saying in form: "X, although not X when the law was obscure, and now the law is not obscure." In theory, one might hazard a guess that Paragraph 8 should be ignored entirely. Indeed, this is how Baker asks us to read that paragraph, in substance. He makes no claim, though, that he intended it to be ignored, even now claiming it properly stands "in context."

The bankruptcy court was familiar with Baker and his writings. The inference that the pertinent misstatement was the product not of reasonable mistake, but of something worse, strikes us as reasonable.

Baker's explanation of how we should read his submission suffers, too, from the lack of fit between what he wrote then and what he says now. He argues now that Paragraphs 8 and 9 simply advanced an argument that the case law should be extended or changed so as to include a requirement that the creditor move for relief from the automatic stay not just before the rescheduled sale, but also "promptly." The problem, though, is that Baker filed his motion for sanctions over two months before the rescheduled sale date, even after BOA indicated to him that it intended to file a motion for relief from the automatic stay, and he still persisted even when BOA within days filed the motion. More to the point, if Baker had wanted to argue that BOA had waited too long to seek relief, Paragraph 8 of his motion would have been entirely irrelevant to the motion. The bankruptcy court therefore reasonably read it as an attempt to sow confusion by misleading the reader into thinking that existing authority supported sanctioning BOA merely for rescheduling the sale without first obtaining relief from the stay. Such an attempt transgressed the boundary of permissible argument and, here, adequately supported the bankruptcy court's decision to impose a Rule 9011 sanction.

. . . Baker fares no better, and perhaps worse, in defending the arguments he advanced in his objection to the Trustee's motion to convert or dismiss. As we have described it above, he fashioned support for an otherwise unsupported position by materially mischaracterizing what the statute says, and by leaving out the most relevant, and to his argument, the most discrediting, portion of it. He took a statute that, in effect, said "A means B, and includes C," and rewrote it to say "A means C."

. . . Bankruptcy courts often need to act quickly, and should be able to assume that counsel are truthful. Even when they fail to deceive a court, filings supported only by artifice serve to delay the proceedings and impose costs on the other parties. Here, moreover, the misleading assertions were not merely erroneous detours made in pursuit of otherwise well-grounded filings. Rather, Baker, in each instance, marshalled artifice to provide illusory support for positions that were otherwise without an apparent basis. As the bankruptcy court observed, he has a record of using his knowledge and skills for improper purposes. The bankruptcy court thus confronted, in short, not a lack of ability by counsel but rather an excess of zeal. Sanctioning artifice that is the product of such zeal was well within the bankruptcy court's discretion.

* * *

(Citations omitted.)

NOTES AND COMMENTS

1. The court characterizes the first transgression—misstating the law in paragraph 8—as "at best . . . unintelligible." Does lack of clarity violate Rule 9011? If not, should the court give the benefit of the doubt to the attorney, or do the circumstances here suggest that intentional deceit rather than a lack of clarity in writing caused the error?

2. While the *Hoover* case involves mischaracterization of the law, mischaracterization of facts also suffices as the basis for Rule 9011 sanctions. In re Young involved misstatements about payment of domestic support obligations, including listing the obligations as pre-petition rather than post-petition, indicating that the debtor would "continue" to pay alimony when he had never actually paid alimony, and indicating that debtor was current on domestic support obligations. Young v. Young (In re Young), 789 F.3d 872 (8th Cir. 2015). The attorney was fined $1,000 and suspended from practice for six months for Rule 9011 violations.

3. Rule 9011 applies in situations beyond misrepresentations to the court; it requires a good faith basis for any pleading signed by the attorney. *See* In re Armstrong, 487 B.R. 764 (E.D. Tex. 2012) (upholding sanction of attorney for filing procedural objections to proofs of claim knowing that no substantive basis for objection existed).

4. The court characterizes the attorney's conduct as an "excess of zeal." The Model Rules do not actually require "zealous representation" as a rule. Rather, the idea of zeal appears in the preamble to the Rules:

> . . . As advocate, a lawyer zealously asserts the client's position under the rules of the adversary system. . . .
> . . . and in the comments to Rule 1.3, Diligence:
> A lawyer should pursue a matter on behalf of a client despite opposition, obstruction or personal inconvenience to the lawyer, and take whatever lawful and ethical measures are required to vindicate a client's cause or endeavor. A lawyer must also act with commitment and dedication to the interests of the client and with zeal in advocacy upon the client's behalf. A lawyer is not bound, however, to press for every advantage that might be realized for a client. . . . The lawyer's duty to act with reasonable diligence does not require the use of offensive tactics or preclude the treating of all persons involved in the legal process with courtesy and respect.

How do these two mentions of zealous advocacy within the Model Rules dictate a balance between candor to the Court and zealous advocacy for one's client?

While the *Hoover* case involved intentional misrepresentations to the court, neither Rule 9011 nor the Model Rules of Professional Responsibility require such intent to find a violation of the attorney's ethical responsibilities. The following case involves—at least initially—unintentional misrepresentations that the attorney failed to correct upon learning the truth.

In re Taylor

655 F.3d 274 (3d Cir. 2011)

FUENTES, Circuit Judge

* * *

This case is an unfortunate example of the ways in which overreliance on computerized processes in a high-volume practice, as well as a failure on the part of clients and lawyers alike to take responsibility for accurate knowledge of a case, can lead to attorney misconduct before a court. It arises from the bankruptcy proceeding of Mr. and Ms. Niles C. and Angela J. Taylor. The Taylors filed for a Chapter 13 bankruptcy in September 2007. In the Taylors' bankruptcy petition, they listed the bank HSBC, which held the mortgage on their house, as a creditor. In turn, HSBC filed a proof of claim in October 2007 with the bankruptcy court.

We are primarily concerned with two pleadings that HSBC's attorneys filed in the bankruptcy court—(1) the request for relief from the automatic stay which would have permitted HSBC to pursue foreclosure proceedings despite the Taylors' bankruptcy filing and (2) the response to the Taylors' objection to HSBC's proof of claim. We are also concerned with the attorneys' conduct in court in connection with those pleadings. We draw our facts from the findings of the bankruptcy court.

. . . To preserve its interest in a debtor's estate in a personal bankruptcy case, a creditor must file with the court a proof of claim, which includes a statement of the claim and of its amount and supporting documentation. . . . In October 2007, HSBC filed such a proof of claim with respect to the Taylors' mortgage. To do so, it used the law firm Moss Codilis. Moss retrieved the information on which the claim was based from HSBC's computerized mortgage servicing database. No employee of HSBC reviewed the claim before filing.

This proof of claim contained several errors: the amount of the Taylors' monthly payment was incorrectly stated, the wrong mortgage note was attached, and the value of the home was understated by about $100,000. It is not clear whether the errors originated in HSBC's database or whether they were introduced in Moss Codilis's filing.

. . . At the time of the bankruptcy proceeding, the Taylors were also involved in a payment dispute with HSBC. HSBC believed the Taylors' home to be in a flood zone and had obtained "forced insurance" for the property, the cost of which (approximately $180/month) it passed on to the Taylors. The Taylors disputed HSBC's position and continued to pay their regular mortgage payment, without the additional insurance costs. HSBC failed to acknowledge that the Taylors were making their regular payments and instead treated each payment as a partial payment, so that, in its records, the Taylors were becoming more delinquent each month.

Ordinarily, the filing of a bankruptcy petition imposes an automatic stay on all debt collection activities, including foreclosures. . . . However, pursuant to 11 U.S.C. § 362(d)(1), a secured creditor may file for relief from the stay . . . in order to permit it to commence or continue foreclosure proceedings. Because of the Taylors' withheld insurance payments, HSBC's records indicated that they were delinquent. Thus, in January 2008, HSBC retained the Udren Firm to seek relief from the stay.

Mr. Udren is the only partner of the Udren Firm; Ms. Doyle, who appeared for the Udren Firm in the Taylors' case, is a managing attorney at the firm, with twenty-seven years of experience. HSBC does not deign to communicate directly with the firms it employs in its high-volume foreclosure work; rather, it uses a computerized system called NewTrak (provided by a third party, LPS) to assign individual firms discrete assignments and provide the limited data the system deems relevant to each assignment. The firms are selected and the instructions generated without any direct human involvement. The firms so chosen generally do not have the capacity to check the data (such as the amount of mortgage payment or time in arrears) provided to them by NewTrak and are not expected to communicate with other firms that may have done related work on the matter. Although it is technically possible for a firm hired through NewTrak to contact HSBC to discuss the matter on which it has been retained, it is clear from the record that this was discouraged and that some attorneys, including at least one Udren Firm attorney, did not believe it to be permitted.

In the Taylors' case, NewTrak provided the Udren Firm with only the loan number, the Taylors' name and address, payment amounts, late fees, and amounts past due. It did not provide any correspondence with the Taylors concerning the flood insurance dispute.

In January 2008, Doyle filed the motion for relief from the stay. This motion was prepared by non-attorney employees of the Udren Firm, relying exclusively on the information provided by NewTrak. The motion said that the debtor "has failed to discharge arrearages on said mortgage or has failed to make the current monthly payments on said mortgage since" the filing of the bankruptcy petition. It identified "the failure to make . . . post-petition monthly payments" as stretching from November 1, 2007 to January 15, 2008, with an "amount per month" of $1455 (a monthly payment higher than that identified on the proof of claim filed earlier in the case by the Moss firm) and a total in arrears of $4367. . . . It stated that the Taylors had "inconsequential or no equity" in the property. The motion never mentioned the flood insurance dispute.

Doyle did nothing to verify the information in the motion for relief from stay besides check it against "screen prints" of the NewTrak information. She did not even access NewTrak herself. In effect, she simply proofread the document. It does not appear that NewTrak provided the Udren Firm with any information concerning the Taylors' equity in their home, so Doyle could not have verified her statement in the motion concerning the lack of equity in any way, even against a "screen print."

***

In February 2008, the Taylors filed a response to the motion for relief from stay, denying that they had failed to make payments and attaching copies of six checks tendered to HSBC during the relevant period. Four of them had already been cashed by HSBC.

. . . In March 2008, the Taylors also filed an objection to HSBC's proof of claim. The objection stated that HSBC had misstated the payment due on the mortgage and pointed out the dispute over the flood insurance. . . .

***

. . . In May 2008, the bankruptcy court held a hearing on both the motion for relief and the claim objection. HSBC was represented at the hearing by a junior associate at the Udren Firm, Mr. Fitzgibbon. At that hearing, Fitzgibbon ultimately admitted that, at the time the motion for relief from the stay was filed, HSBC had received a mortgage payment for November 2007, even though both the motion for stay and the response to the Taylors' objection to the proof of claim stated otherwise. Despite this, Fitzgibbon urged the court to grant the relief from stay . . . .

***

After the hearing, the bankruptcy court directed the Udren Firm to obtain an accounting from HSBC of the Taylors' prepetition payments so that the arrearage on the mortgage could be determined correctly. At the next hearing, in June 2008, Fitzgibbon stated that he could not obtain an accounting from HSBC, though he had repeatedly placed requests via NewTrak. He told the court that he was literally unable to contact HSBC—his firm's client—directly to verify information which his firm had already represented to the court that it believed to be true.

. . . Thereafter, the court entered an order *sua sponte* dated June 9, 2008, directing Fitzgibbon, Doyle, Udren, and others to appear and give testimony concerning the possibility of sanctions.

* * *

The bankruptcy court held four hearings over several days, making in-depth inquiries into the communications between HSBC and its lawyers in this case, as well as the general capabilities and limitations of a system like NewTrak.

Ultimately, it found that the following had violated Rule 9011: Fitzgibbon, for pressing the motion for relief based on claims he knew to be untrue; Doyle, for failing to make reasonable inquiry concerning the representations she made in the motion for relief from stay and the response to the claim objection; Udren and the Udren Firm itself, for the conduct of its attorneys; and HSBC, for practices which caused the failure to adhere to Rule 9011.

Because of his inexperience, the court did not sanction Fitzgibbon. However, it required Doyle to take 3 CLE credits in professional responsibility; Udren himself to be trained in the use of NewTrak and to spend a day observing his employees handling NewTrak; and both Doyle and Udren to conduct a training session for the firm's relevant lawyers in the requirements of Rule 9011 and procedures for escalating inquiries on NewTrak. The court also required HSBC to send a copy of its opinion to all the law firms it uses in bankruptcy proceedings, along with a letter explaining that direct contact with HSBC concerning matters relating to HSBC's case was permissible.

. . . the District Court, . . . ultimately overturned the order. The District Court's decision was based on three considerations: that the confusion in the case was attributable at least as much to the actions of Taylor's counsel as to Doyle, Udren, and the Udren Firm; that the bankruptcy court seemed more concerned with "sending a message" to the bar concerning the use of computerized systems than with the conduct in the particular case; and that, since Udren himself did not sign any of the filings containing misrepresentations, he could not be sanctioned under Rule 9011. . . .

* * *

Rule 9011 of the Federal Rules of Bankruptcy Procedure, the equivalent of Rule 11 of the Federal Rules of Civil Procedure, requires that parties making representations to the court certify that "the allegations and other factual contentions have evidentiary support or, if specifically so identified, are likely to have evidentiary support." Fed. R. Bank. P. 9011(b)(3). A party must reach this conclusion based on "inquiry reasonable under the circumstances." Fed. R. Bank. P. 9011(b). The concern of Rule 9011 is not the truth or falsity of the representation in itself, but rather whether the party making the representation reasonably believed it at the time to have evidentiary support. In determining whether a party has violated Rule 9011, the court need not find that a party who makes a false representation to the court acted in bad faith. "The imposition of Rule 11 sanctions . . . requires only a showing of objectively unreasonable conduct.". . .

In this opinion, we focus on several statements by appellees: (1) . . . statements suggesting that the Taylors had failed to make payments on their mortgage since the filing of their bankruptcy petition and the identification of the months in which and the amount by which they were supposedly delinquent; (2) . . . the statement that the Taylors had no or inconsequential equity in the property; (3) . . . the statement that the figures in the proof of claim were accurate. . . . As discussed above, all of these statements involved false or misleading representations to the court.

. . . As an initial matter, the appellees' insistence that Doyle's and Fitzgibbon's statements were "literally true" should not exculpate them from Rule 9011 sanctions. First, it should be noted that several of these claims were not, in fact, accurate. There was no literal truth to the statement in the request for relief from stay that the Taylors had no equity in their home. Doyle admitted that she made that statement simply as "part of the form pleading," and "acknowledged having no knowledge of the value of the property and having made no inquiry on this subject." Similarly, the statement in the claim objection response that the figures in the original proof of claim were correct was false.

* * *

In particular, even assuming that Doyle's and Fitzgibbon's statements as to the payments made by the Taylors *were* literally accurate, they were misleading. In attempting to evaluate whether HSBC was justified in seeking a relief from the stay on foreclosure, the court needed to know that at least partial payments had been made and that the failure to make some of the rest of the payments was due to a bona fide dispute over the amount due, not simple default. Instead, the court was told only that the Taylors had "failed to make regular mortgage payments" from November 1, 2007 to January 15, 2008, with a mysterious notation concerning a "suspense balance" following. A court could only reasonably interpret this to mean that the Taylors simply had not made payments for the period specified. . . . Therefore, Doyle's and Fitzgibbon's statements in question were either false or misleading.

. . . We must, therefore, determine the reasonableness of the appellees' inquiry before they made their false representations. Reasonableness has been defined as "an objective knowledge or belief at the time of the filing of a challenged paper that the claim was well-grounded in law and fact.". . . The requirement of reasonable inquiry protects not merely the court and adverse parties, but also the client. The client is not expected to know the technical details of the law and ought to be able to rely on his attorney to elicit from him the information necessary to handle his case in the most effective, yet legally appropriate, manner.

In determining reasonableness, we have sometimes looked at several factors: "the amount of time available to the signer for conducting the factual and legal investigation; the necessity for reliance on a client for the underlying factual information; the plausibility of the legal position advocated; . . . whether the case was referred to the signer by another member of the Bar . . . [; and] the complexity of the legal and factual issues implicated.". . . However, it does not appear that the court must work mechanically through these factors when it considers whether to impose sanctions. Rather, it should consider the reasonableness of the inquiry under all the material circumstances.

Central to this case, then, is the degree to which an attorney may reasonably rely on representations from her client . . . In making statements to the court, lawyers constantly and appropriately rely on information provided by their clients, especially when the facts are contained in a client's computerized records. It is difficult to imagine how attorneys might function were they required to conduct an independent investigation of every factual representation made by a client before it could be included in a court filing.

. . . a lawyer need not routinely assume the duplicity or gross incompetence of her client in order to meet the requirements of Rule 9011. It is therefore usually reasonable for a lawyer to rely on information provided by a client, especially where that information is superficially plausible and the client provides its own records which appear to confirm the information.

However, Doyle's behavior was unreasonable, both as a matter of her general practice and in ways specific to this case. First, reasonable reliance on a client's representations assumes a reasonable attempt at eliciting them by the attorney. That is, an attorney must, in her independent professional judgment, make a reasonable effort to determine what facts are likely to be relevant to a particular court filing and to seek those facts from the client. She cannot simply settle for the information her client determines in advance—by means of an automated system, no less—that she should be provided with.

Yet that is precisely what happened here . . . By working solely with NewTrak, a system which no one at the Udren Firm seems to have understood, much less had any influence over, Doyle permitted HSBC to define—perilously narrowly—the information she had about the Taylors' matter. That HSBC was not providing her with adequate information through NewTrak should have been evident to Doyle from the face of the NewTrak file. She did not have any information concerning the Taylors' equity in the home, though she made a statement specifically denying that they had any.

More generally, a reasonable attorney would not file a motion for relief from stay for cause without inquiring of the client whether it had any information relevant to the alleged cause, that is, the debtor's failure to make payments. Had Doyle made even that most minimal of inquiries, HSBC presumably would have provided her with the information in its files concerning the flood insurance dispute, and Doyle could have included that information in her motion for relief from stay — or, perhaps, advised the client that seeking such a motion would be inappropriate under the circumstances.

With respect to the Taylors' case in particular, Doyle ignored clear warning signs as to the accuracy of the data that she did receive. In responding to the motion for relief from stay, the Taylors submitted documentation indicating that they had already made at least partial payments for some of the months in question. In objecting to the proof of claim, the Taylors pointed out the inaccuracy of the mortgage payment listed and explained the circumstances surrounding the flood insurance dispute. Although Doyle certainly was not obliged to accept the Taylors' claims at face value, they indisputably put her on notice that the matter was not as simple as it might have appeared from the NewTrak file. At that point, any reasonable attorney would have sought clarification and further documentation from her client, in order to correct any prior inadvertent misstatements to the court and to avoid any further errors. Instead, Doyle mechanically affirmed facts (the monthly mortgage payment) that *her own prior filing* with the court had already contradicted.

Doyle's reliance on HSBC was particularly problematic because she was not, in fact, relying directly on HSBC. Instead, she relied on a computer system run by a third-party vendor. She did not know where the data provided by NewTrak came from. She had no capacity to check the data against the original documents if any of it seemed implausible. And she effectively could not question the data with HSBC. In her relationship with HSBC, Doyle essentially abdicated her professional judgment to a black box.

None of the other factors . . . affect our analysis of the reasonableness of appellees' actions. This was not a matter of extreme complexity, nor of extraordinary deadline pressure. Although the initial data the Udren Firm received was not, in itself, wildly implausible, it was facially inadequate. In short, then, we find that Doyle's inquiry before making her representations to the bankruptcy court was unreasonable.

In making this finding, we, of course, do not mean to suggest that the use of computerized databases is inherently inappropriate.

However, the NewTrak system, as it was being used at the time of this case, permits parties at every level of the filing process to disclaim responsibility for inaccuracies. HSBC has handed off responsibility to a third-party maintainer, LPS, which, judging from the results in this case, has not generated particularly accurate records. LPS apparently regards itself as a mere conduit of information. Appellees, the attorneys and final link in the chain of transmission of this information to the court, claim reliance on NewTrak's records. Who, precisely, can be held accountable if HSBC's records are inadequately maintained, LPS transfers those records inaccurately into NewTrak, or a law firm relies on the NewTrak data without further investigation, thus leading to material misrepresentations to the court? It cannot be that all the parties involved can insulate themselves from responsibility by the use of such a system. In the end, we must hold responsible the attorneys who have certified to the court that the representations they are making are "well-grounded in law and fact."

* * *

We appreciate that the use of technology can save both litigants and attorneys time and money, and we do not, of course, mean to suggest that the use of databases or even certain automated communications between counsel and client are presumptively unreasonable. However, Rule 11 requires more than a rubber-stamping of the results of an automated process by a person who happens to be a lawyer. Where a lawyer systematically fails to take any responsibility for seeking adequate information from her client, makes representations without any factual basis because they are included in a "form pleading" she has been trained to fill out, and ignores obvious indications that her information may be incorrect, she cannot be said to have made reasonable inquiry. . . .

* * *

(Citations omitted.)

NOTES AND COMMENTS

1. Which statements to the court were intentionally false? Had those statements not been made, would the court still have imposed sanctions? Was the issue the false statements made in the original filings based on the NewTrak system's information or the failure to correct those misstatements after the Taylors disputed the facts?

2. The attorneys were "literally unable to contact HSBC." Whose fault is the lack of communication? If attorneys should contact their client for information but cannot do so, what options do they have?

3. The bankruptcy court required HSBC to let all of its law firms know that they could contact someone at HSBC with regard to the case. Does that sanction go far enough to prevent future issues? Does that sanction comport with the statement in prior cases that Rule 9011 does not put strict liability on the attorneys?

4. Should the Taylors' counsel have been sanctioned for failure to respond to the Requests for Admissions?

5. The court indicates that "no one at the Udren Firm seems to have understood" the NewTrak system. What does the court mean by that statement?

While the *Hoover* and *Taylor* cases focused on the consequences under Bankruptcy Rule 9011, lack of candor toward the bankruptcy court can also lead to state disciplinary action. *See, e.g.,* In re Henry, 2006 WL 4667138 (Bankr. D. Md. 2006) (bankruptcy court referred action to the state disciplinary board after the attorney knowingly filed petition for debtors ineligible to file for bankruptcy protection using a fictitious debtor name); In re Minsk, 296 Ga. 152(2014)(attorney disbarred for numerous violations of the Georgia Rules of Professional Conduct, including making false statements).

2. Ghostwriting

Torrens v. Hood (In re Hood)

727 F.3d 1360 (11th Cir. 2013)

WILSON, Circuit Judge

* * *

On January 24, 2012, Hood met with Adrian Reyes, a member of the Torrens Law Firm, to discuss foreclosure defense services provided by the firm. At this time, Hood allegedly considered hiring the firm to attempt to extend the February 22, 2012 sale date for the state-court foreclosure proceedings concerning his Hollywood, Florida business. Reyes also discussed bankruptcy with Hood, the impact it would have on the foreclosure process, and the firm's fees for both foreclosure defense work and bankruptcy representation. On February 21, 2012, Hood, apparently unable to afford representation for both his bankruptcy and foreclosure needs, paid a $1,000 retainer to the firm to provide foreclosure defense work. On that same date, a courier filed a pro se Chapter 13 petition via a power of attorney on Hood's behalf in the bankruptcy court for the Southern District of Florida. The circumstances behind the petition's preparation and filing are highly disputed.

Before the bankruptcy court, Hood contended that he had no knowledge that he had filed for bankruptcy. The bankruptcy court found Hood's contention to be untruthful, yet still held that Appellants fraudulently prepared and filed a pro se petition on behalf of Hood. Appellants maintain that the firm's secretary acted as a scrivener when she prepared the petition at Hood's request. Appellants also argue that, at Hood's request, the secretary wrote his oral responses into the corresponding blanks on the petition. A courier then filed the petition on behalf of Hood via a power of attorney notarized by Luis Torrens, a partner at the firm.

On February 28, 2012, one of Hood's largest business clients contacted him regarding his involvement in the bankruptcy proceeding and expressed concern over Hood's continued ability to perform work for them. Hood, seemingly leery of losing business, informed the client that he had no knowledge of the bankruptcy proceeding. On April 3, 2012, with what the bankruptcy court characterized as "buyer's remorse," Hood, represented by counsel, filed a motion for order to show cause against Appellants.

The bankruptcy court granted Hood's motion and held an evidentiary hearing on April 16, 2012. The court noted that despite Hood's remorse, he "signed several documents containing the word bankruptcy in multiple places." Regardless, on June 7, 2012, the bankruptcy court held that Appellants violated 11 U.S.C. §§ 527 and 528(a)(1), Florida Rules of Professional Conduct 4–3.3(a)(1) and 4–8.4(c), and "appear[ed] to have violated 18 U.S.C. § 157(3)." The bankruptcy court found that Appellants acted as ghostwriters by failing to sign the Chapter 13 petition, and thus perpetrated fraud on the court.

The bankruptcy court suspended Torrens from practice before the United States Bankruptcy Court for the Southern District of Florida for six months, barred Reyes from applying for admission to practice before the United States Bankruptcy Court for the Southern District of Florida before December 31, 2012, prohibited both Torrens and Reyes from filing any papers in bankruptcy court during their period of suspension, and held that all employees, associates and business affiliates of the firm were enjoined from acting as bankruptcy petition preparers under 11 U.S.C. § 110 or as a "debt relief agency" as defined by 11 U.S.C. § 101(12A). The court also referred the matter to the office of the United States Attorney for possible criminal prosecution and to the Florida Bar for further disciplinary proceedings. The district court affirmed the bankruptcy court's decision, concluding that the surrounding circumstances revealed at the evidentiary hearing supported the bankruptcy court's findings. Appellants only appeal the holding that they perpetrated fraud on the court by ghostwriting Hood's Chapter 13 petition in violation of Florida Rules of Professional Conduct 4–3.3(a)(1) and 4–8.4(c), and 18 U.S.C. § 157(3).

* * *

. . . Attorneys who practice before Florida courts are governed by the Florida Rules of Professional Conduct. . . . The Florida Rules provide that "[a] lawyer shall not . . . make a false statement of fact or law to a tribunal," *id.* at 4–3.3(a)(1), and "shall not . . . engage in conduct involving dishonesty, fraud, deceit, or misrepresentation," *id.* at 4–8.4(c). The Rules explain, however, that "a lawyer and client may agree to limit the objectives or scope of the representation if the limitation is reasonable under the circumstances and the client gives informed consent in writing." *Id.* at 4–1.2(c). In practice then, "[i]f the lawyer assists a pro se litigant by drafting any document to be submitted to a court, the lawyer is not obligated to sign the document." *Id.* at 4–1.2(c) cmt. But "the lawyer must indicate 'Prepared with the assistance of counsel' on the document to avoid misleading the court, which otherwise might be under the impression that the person, who appears to be proceeding pro se, has received no assistance from a lawyer." *Id.* Rule 4–1.2(c) reflects the Florida Bar's stance on the issue of attorney ghostwriting, or more simply put, the undisclosed assistance of counsel in the drafting of a pro se document filed with the court.

Here, the bankruptcy court held that Appellants violated Florida Rules of Professional Conduct 4–3.3(a)(1) and 4–8.4(c) by perpetrating fraud on the court through a ghostwritten pro se Chapter 13 petition. Yet, the bankruptcy court failed to cite Rule 4–1.2(c), the specific Florida Rule of Professional Conduct regulating the practice of ghostwriting. . . . *Hunter v. United States*, 101 F.3d 1565, 1574 (11th Cir. 1996) (en banc). We first note that while this court has not addressed the propriety of ghostwriting, we do so today only as ghostwriting applies to the factual circumstances of the present case.

Rule 4–1.2(c) explains that when an attorney assists "by drafting" a pro se document to be submitted to the court, the attorney must identify the document as "[p]repared with the assistance of counsel.". . . . To "draft" is defined as "[t]o write or compose." *Black's Law Dictionary* (9th ed. 2009). It is apparent to us that under the plain language of the rule, Appellants did not "draft" a document for Hood. . . . They did not "write or compose" the pre-formatted Chapter 13 petition. . . . To the contrary, Appellants recorded answers on a standard fill-in-the-blank Chapter 13 petition based on Hood's verbal responses. Moreover, Hood personally signed the petition. That Hood attempted to attain the best of both worlds by claiming that he had no knowledge of the petition only after the bankruptcy proceeding effectively stalled the foreclosure on his property is patent. Regardless, a Chapter 13 petition stands in stark contrast to a ghostwritten pro se brief, such as the brief drafted by the undisclosed attorney in *Duran,* 238 F.3d at 1273, and noted by the court in *Ellis,* 448 F.2d at 1328. A legal brief is a substantive pleading that requires extensive preparation; much more than is necessary for the completion of a basic, fill-in-the-blank bankruptcy petition.

* * *

. . . we see no fraudulent intent in this record by Appellants. Rather, they were attempting to assist Hood with the completion of a straightforward pro se Chapter 13 petition for which there was no unfair advantage to be gained. Who, within the firm, filled out the petition is a distinction without a difference. A Chapter 13 petition is a publicly available form that is designed in a manner that lends itself to a pro se litigant. Hood could have personally completed the petition at issue in the exact same manner and likely obtained the same result. . . .

* * *

(Citations omitted.)

NOTES AND COMMENTS

1. The Eleventh Circuit follows the Second Circuit's precedent in In re Fengling Liu, 664 F.3d 367 (2d Cir. 2011). The *Liu* court reached the following conclusion:

   In light of this Court's lack of any rule or precedent governing attorney ghostwriting, and the various authorities that permit that practice, we conclude that Liu could not have been aware of any general obligation to disclose her participation to this Court. We also conclude that there is no evidence suggesting that Liu knew, or should have known, that she was withholding material information from the Court or that she otherwise acted in bad faith. The petitions for review now at issue were fairly simple and unlikely to have caused any confusion or prejudice. Additionally, there is no indication that Liu sought, or was aware that she might obtain, any unfair advantage through her ghostwriting. Finally, Liu's motive in preparing the petitions—to preserve the petitioners' right of review by satisfying the thirty-day jurisdictional deadline—demonstrated concern for her clients rather than a desire to mislead this Court or opposing parties. Under these circumstances, we conclude that Liu's ghostwriting did not constitute misconduct and therefore does not warrant the imposition of discipline.

Id. at 372-373. Are the *Liu* and *Hood* cases substantially similar? Does the *Liu* decision support the holding in *Hood*?

2. Prior to Hood's bankruptcy filing, he had discussed bankruptcy and other options with the law firm. Should that discussion be disclosed to the court? At what point would the firm move from simply ghostwriting the Chapter 13 petition in a way that does not need to be disclosed to actually representing the debtor or at least helping draft the petition in a manner that must be disclosed to the court?

3. Bankruptcy Fraud

Closely related to credibility toward the court and other parties in interest in the case is the obligation of the attorney not to be involved in fraudulent behavior of the client.

RULE 1.2 SCOPE OF REPRESENTATION AND ALLOCATION OF AUTHORITY BETWEEN CLIENT AND LAWYER

(d) A lawyer shall not counsel a client to engage, or assist a client, in conduct that the lawyer knows is criminal or fraudulent, but a lawyer may discuss the legal consequences of any proposed course of conduct with a client and may counsel or assist a client to make a good faith effort to determine the validity, scope, meaning, or application of the law.

Rule 8.4 Misconduct

It is professional misconduct for a lawyer to:

***

(b)   commit a criminal act that reflects adversely on the lawyer's honesty, trustworthiness or fitness as a lawyer in other respects;

(c)   engage in conduct involving dishonesty, fraud, deceit or misrepresentation;

(d)   engage in conduct that is prejudicial to the administration of justice;

* * *

Matter of Disciplinary Proceedings Against Webster

217 Wis. 2d 371 (1998)

We review the stipulation, by the Board of Attorneys Professional Responsibility (Board) and Attorney Leslie J. Webster, concerning Attorney Webster's professional misconduct that resulted in his conviction in federal court of one count of aiding and abetting the fraudulent concealment of a debtor's property from a bankruptcy trustee. The parties stipulated that the appropriate discipline to impose for that professional misconduct is the suspension of Attorney Webster's license to practice law for two years. . . .

We approve the stipulation and adopt the facts and conclusions of law set forth in it. . . . Using his professional position, Attorney Webster counseled his client to make a fraudulent representation in the bankruptcy, which led to the client's criminal conviction and incarceration, and participated actively in a fraud on the bankruptcy court. Moreover, as the federal court determined, Attorney Webster gave false testimony during his trial regarding his participation in the fraud.

* * *

The facts to which the parties stipulated concern Attorney Webster's conduct in representing the owner of a bar and the owner's wife beginning in January, 1991. The owner, who also managed the bar, retained Attorney Webster to incorporate the business in order to limit his liability. The business was incorporated February 1, 1991, and the owner and his wife received stock in exchange for the assets of the business and became the corporation's only directors. In the course of that matter, Attorney Webster advised the clients to review their finances and debts and to consider filing a bankruptcy petition to have their debts discharged.

On Attorney Webster's advice and with his representation, the clients filed for bankruptcy March 25, 1991. In the schedules and statement of financial affairs specified for a debtor not engaged in a business that he drafted, Attorney Webster stated that in January,

1991, the owner voluntarily had surrendered the bar business to the vendor of a land contract in exchange for his release from the unpaid balance on that contract. Those papers did not advert, however, to the facts that the bar recently had been incorporated and that the owner's assets in it had been conveyed to the corporation and did not report any ownership of stock in the business. The papers reported "zero" stock ownership and no real property, and Attorney Webster told the bankruptcy trustee that this was a "no asset" case. The bankruptcy court granted the owner and his wife a discharge July 16, 1991.

Thereafter, the bar was destroyed by fire, and Attorney Webster initially represented the clients in attempting to collect insurance proceeds. Having discovered the owner's bankruptcy and the statement in it that the bar had been surrendered to the land contract vendor in January, 1991, the insurance company investigators questioned whether the client was in fact the owner of the bar at the time of the fire. Attorney Webster tried to clarify a sworn statement given by the client to the insurance company concerning his ownership of the bar and asserted that the client had not understood the difference between pledging and transferring stock and that what the client in fact had done was give the land contract vendor a lien on the stock, which did not transfer the stock to him. The client's testimony and documentary evidence demonstrated that the client had purchased the bar in 1986 and owned it continuously until it was destroyed by fire in May, 1992.

The client then was charged with federal bankruptcy fraud and was convicted on a guilty plea of one count of making a false oath, for which he was sentenced to three months in prison. Attorney Webster was charged with one count of aiding and abetting the fraudulent concealment of the debtors' property from the bankruptcy trustee and was found guilty by a jury and sentenced to 15 months' imprisonment, fined $4000, and placed on three years' supervised release. . . .

Attorney Webster and the Board stipulated that the conduct for which he was convicted of a federal felony violated SCR 20:8.4(b), as it constituted a criminal act that reflects adversely on his honesty, trustworthiness and fitness as a lawyer. The parties also stipulated that, pursuant to SCR 11.03(5), the conviction constitutes conclusive evidence of Attorney Webster's guilt of the crime. As aggravating factors to be considered, the parties stipulated to Attorney Webster's active participation in the fraud, conclusion [sic], based on the federal court's statement, that his advice and counsel to the client contributed significantly to that client's participation in the fraud and his conviction and incarceration for it, the federal court's conclusion that Attorney Webster gave false testimony during the trial, and his prior discipline. In mitigation, the parties stipulated to the facts that the client's creditors had not been deprived of assets, as the debtor had no equity in the bar, that Attorney Webster did not benefit personally from the fraudulent conduct, that he has assisted charities and civic groups in his community, and that he fully cooperated during the Board's investigation of this matter.

We adopt the facts and legal conclusions to which the parties have stipulated concerning Attorney Webster's professional misconduct in this matter. We determine that the seriousness of the misconduct, in light of the aggravating and mitigating factors set forth in the parties' stipulation, warrants the suspension of Attorney Webster's license to practice law for two years as discipline. We impose that license suspension commencing the date on which we summarily suspended Attorney Webster's license following exhaustion of his remedies on appeal of his conviction.

* * *

(Citations omitted.)

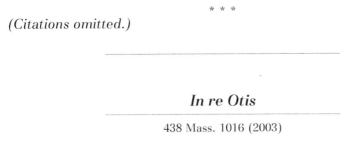

In re Otis

438 Mass. 1016 (2003)

Susan P. Otis appeals from a judgment of a single justice of this court disbarring her from the practice of law. We affirm.

The respondent was convicted in the United States District Court for the District of Massachusetts of one count of conspiracy to commit bankruptcy fraud, 18 U.S.C. §§ 2 and 152 (2000), in violation of 18 U.S.C. § 371 (2000). Thereafter, bar counsel filed a petition for discipline with the Board of Bar Overseers (board). Both the committee hearing the matter and the board recommended that the respondent be disbarred, retroactive to the date of her temporary suspension. After a hearing, the single justice entered a judgment of disbarment. The only issue on appeal is whether the respondent should be "disbarred or given the lesser sanction of indefinite suspension." *Matter of Kennedy,* 428 Mass. 156, 156, 697 N.E.2d 538 (1998).

* * *

We begin with the premise that disbarment is the "usual and presumptive sanction" for conviction of a serious crime. *Matter of Concemi,* 422 Mass. 326, 330, 662 N.E.2d 1030 (1996). In *Matter of Concemi, supra,* we quoted with approval § 5.11(a) of the ABA Standards on Imposing Lawyer Sanctions (1986), which provides that disbarment is appropriate where a necessary element of the crime for which the respondent was convicted "includes intentional . . . misrepresentation [or] fraud . . . or an attempt or conspiracy or solicitation of another to commit any of these offenses." *Matter of Concern, Supra* at 329–330, 662 N.E.2d 1030.

Although deviation from the "usual and presumptive sanction of disbarment" may be justified where a respondent shows a "special mitigating circumstance," . . . such circumstances have not been demonstrated here. . . . The fact that a single felony conviction was involved, particularly where that felony concerned fraud on a court, . . . and occurred over a period of years, neither changes our analysis nor mitigates the sanction. We share the committee's "particular" concern with the respondent's "cavalier attitude about her wrongdoing," as reflected in her testimony at the hearing before it.

. . . Here, the respondent's conviction was based on various acts perpetuating a fraud over the course of several years, and the fraud cannot fairly be characterized as "isolated.". . . In the circumstances, and giving substantial deference to the board's recommendation, we cannot say that disbarment is a markedly disparate sanction.

* * *

(Citations omitted.)

In re Zodrow

43 A.3d 943 (D.C. 2012)

PER CURIAM

In 2010, in the United States District Court for the District of Colorado, respondent pleaded guilty to the felony offense of knowingly and fraudulently making a false oath and account in relation to a bankruptcy petition, in violation of 18 U.S.C. § 152(2). He was sentenced on December 20, 2010. . . .

After being notified of respondent's conviction, we suspended respondent pursuant to D.C. Bar R. XI, § 10(c), and directed the Board on Professional Responsibility ("Board") to institute a formal proceeding to determine the nature of the offense and whether it involves moral turpitude within the meaning of D.C. Code § 11–2503(a) (2001).

    . . . if an offense "manifestly involve[s] moral turpitude by virtue of [its] underlying elements," disbarment is mandatory without inquiry into the specific conduct that led to the conviction. . . . This court has held that the crime of bankruptcy fraud, in violation of 18 U.S.C. § 152(1) and (2), inherently involves moral turpitude. Respondent's disbarment is, therefore, mandatory under D.C. Code § 11–2503(a).

* * *

(Citations omitted.)

NOTES AND COMMENTS

1. As these cases demonstrate, attorneys who help perpetrate such fraud are in danger of criminal conviction and disbarment or other sanctions. For more on the crime of bankruptcy fraud, see Chapter 7.

2. In *Webster* and *Otis*, the courts start from the presumption that suspension or disbarment is appropriate when an attorney commits bankruptcy fraud, but allow for the possibility of mitigating circumstances. In *Zodrow*, the court cites the District of Columbia's decisions stating that bankruptcy fraud automatically warrants disbarment. Should mitigating factors be considered and, if so, what type of factors would suffice to provide for a less-harsh penalty? *See, e.g.*, People v. Brown, 841 P.2d 1066 (Colo. 1992) (fact that the fraud conviction was the attorney's first offense not sufficient mitigation, though the court would allow for mitigating factors).

E. FEE APPLICATIONS

The Model Rules of Professional Responsibility provide guidance for attorneys in setting fees. The Bankruptcy Code augments those Rules in the context of attorneys and other professionals who will be paid from the bankruptcy estate. In order to be paid in the bankruptcy case, professionals must submit a fee application outlining the services provided and the time incurred. That fee application must be approved by the court before the professional may be paid from the bankruptcy estate.

While not truly a question of attorney professional responsibility, because the issues frequently arise in the context of a fee application, bankruptcy professionals need to understand the nuances of seeking fees from property of the estate. Attorneys seeking to be paid from the estate must be providing a benefit in the bankruptcy case—representing debtors, trustees, or committees. The attorney must file a detailed fee application for court approval, and while the attorney might be compensated for preparing the application, the attorney cannot be compensated for time spent *defending* that fee application if needed.[13] Fee applications can be time consuming for counsel and the court, and the following cases discuss some alternative arrangements used by courts to minimize the time and energy spent preparing and reviewing them.

RULE 1.5 FEES

(a) A lawyer shall not make an agreement for, charge, or collect an unreasonable fee or an unreasonable amount for expenses. The factors to be considered in determining the reasonableness of a fee include the following:

(1) the time and labor required, the novelty and difficulty of the questions involved, and the skill requisite to perform the legal service properly;

(2) the likelihood, if apparent to the client, that the acceptance of the particular employment will preclude other employment by the lawyer;

(3) the fee customarily charged in the locality for similar legal services;

(4) the amount involved and the results obtained;

(5) the time limitations imposed by the client or by the circumstances;

(6) the nature and length of the professional relationship with the client;

(7) the experience, reputation, and ability of the lawyer or lawyers performing the services; and

(8) whether the fee is fixed or contingent.

(b) The scope of the representation and the basis or rate of the fee and expenses for which the client will be responsible shall be communicated to the client, preferably in writing, before or within a reasonable time after commencing the representation, except when the lawyer will charge a regularly represented client on the same basis or rate. Any changes in the basis or rate of the fee or expenses shall also be communicated to the client.

***

---

13. Baker Botts L.L.P. v. Asarco LLC, 135 S. Ct. 2158, 2167 (2015).

(e) A division of a fee between lawyers who are not in the same firm may be made only if:

(1) the division is in proportion to the services performed by each lawyer or each lawyer assumes joint responsibility for the representation;

(2) the client agrees to the arrangement, including the share each lawyer will receive, and the agreement is confirmed in writing; and

(3) the total fee is reasonable.

CRG Partners Group, L.L.C. v. Neary
(In re Pilgrim's Pride Corp.)

690 F.3d 650 (5th Cir. 2012)

ELROD, Circuit Judge

* * *

On December 1, 2008, Pilgrim's Pride Company and six of its affiliates (collectively, the "Debtors") filed for chapter 11 bankruptcy protection. At that time, the Debtors' prospects for a successful reorganization were far from promising. They had lost approximately $1 billion in the fiscal year preceding their bankruptcy filing and were operating at a negative annual cash flow of over $300 million. The Debtors anticipated that unsecured creditors would receive, at best, a debt for equity swap, and that pre-petition shareholders would be left empty-handed.

Upon receiving the bankruptcy court's approval, the Debtors retained CRG Partners Group, LLC to provide William Snyder as their chief restructuring officer and other personnel to assist in their chapter 11 restructuring process. . . .

With CRG's assistance, the Debtors prepared a bankruptcy plan that was confirmed by the bankruptcy court on December 10, 2009, just over a year after the petition date. The plan was an absolute success. It provided for a 100% return to all of the Debtors' secured and unsecured creditors, and the Debtors' pre-petition shareholders received $450 million in new equity interests.

Once the plan was confirmed, CRG sought the bankruptcy court's approval of $5.98 million in fees calculated in accordance with the lodestar method. CRG also requested approval of a $1 million fee enhancement that the Debtors' board of directors had recommended be paid to CRG. No party objected to the $5.98 million fee request, and that request was approved by the bankruptcy court. The United States Trustee did object, however, to the $1 million fee enhancement . . . .

After holding an evidentiary hearing, the bankruptcy court found that CRG had provided superior services that contributed to the outstanding results in the Debtors' bankruptcy case. Specifically, the court stated that:

> [T]he result in this case [was] rare and exceptional. One hundred percent dividend cases are rare in Chapter 11, and rarer still in large cases such as this. And what made this case truly exceptional was that it emerged from bankruptcy in about a year, and the Court can't begin to estimate how much was saved in administrative costs due to this quick emergence from bankruptcy.

It also concluded "the evidence showed that Mr. Snyder contributed significantly to the superior results in" the case. Nonetheless, the bankruptcy court denied CRG's enhancement request because CRG failed to satisfy the strict requirements of the Supreme Court's 2010 holding in *Perdue,* 130 S. Ct. at 1662.

CRG appealed the decision to the district court, which held that the bankruptcy court erred in treating the federal fee-shifting decision in *Perdue* as binding authority in a bankruptcy proceeding. The district court reversed the bankruptcy court's decision and remanded the case for further proceedings.

On remand, the bankruptcy court . . . awarded CRG the $1 million fee enhancement. . . .

* * *

We begin with a brief review of the relevant precepts that have governed the compensation of professionals employed by the estate for over three decades. First, in the year preceding the enactment of the Bankruptcy Code in 1978, we held that bankruptcy courts must address the following twelve *Johnson* factors when determining reasonable attorney's fees under the Bankruptcy Act of 1898:

> (1) The time and labor required; (2) The novelty and difficulty of the questions; (3) The skill requisite to perform the legal service properly; (4) The preclusion of other employment by the attorney due to acceptance of the case; (5) The customary fee; (6) Whether the fee is fixed or contingent; (7) Time limitations imposed by the client or other circumstances; (8) The amount involved and the results obtained; (9) The experience, reputation, and ability of the attorneys; (10) The "undesirability" of the case; (11) The nature and length of the professional relationship with the client; (12) Awards in similar cases. . . .

We also recognized, however, that the unique nature of proceedings under the Bankruptcy Act of 1898 merited consideration of two additional factors. First, in light of the "strong policy of the Bankruptcy Act that estates be administered as efficiently as possible," bankruptcy courts were required to award fees that were "at the lower end of the spectrum of reasonableness." Second, we advised bankruptcy courts to remain vigilant that there were "a number of peculiarities of bankruptcy practice such as the award of ad interim allowances and the possibility that some officers of the court may be furnishing services to the estate in more than one capacity which could lead to the award of duplicative fees or compensation for non-legal services if overlooked."

Next, in another case decided under the Bankruptcy Act, we held that the lodestar method for calculating reasonable attorney's fees applied in the bankruptcy arena. The lodestar amount "is equal to the number of hours reasonably expended multiplied by the prevailing hourly rate in the community for similar work." We further explained that, after calculating the lodestar, bankruptcy courts retained the discretion to adjust the lodestar upwards or downwards to reflect their consideration of the *Johnson* factors.

This framework was then slightly modified for cases governed by the Bankruptcy Code. In addition to considering the lodestar and the *Johnson* factors, bankruptcy courts became required to consult 11 U.S.C. § 330(a), the Bankruptcy Code provision governing compensation of professionals employed by the estate. . . .

The current version of § 330(a) provides, in relevant part, that a bankruptcy court may award "a professional person employed under section 327 or 1103 . . . reasonable compensation for actual, necessary services." 11 U.S.C. § 330(a)(1)(A). It also sets forth a non-exclusive list of factors for courts to examine when determining the reasonableness of fees requested by professionals:

***

(A) the time spent on such services;

(B) the rates charged for such services;

(C) whether the services were necessary to the administration of, or beneficial at the time at which the service was rendered toward the completion of, a case under this title;

(D) whether the services were performed within a reasonable amount of time commensurate with the complexity, importance, and nature of the problem, issue, or task addressed;

(E) with respect to a professional person, whether the person is board certified or otherwise has demonstrated skill and experience in the bankruptcy field; and

(F) whether the compensation is reasonable based on the customary compensation charged by comparably skilled practitioners in cases other than cases under this title.

11 U.S.C. § 330(a)(3).

Following the Bankruptcy Code's enactment, we made clear that the lodestar, *Johnson* factors, and § 330 coalesced to form the framework that regulates the compensation of professionals employed by the bankruptcy estate. Under this framework, bankruptcy courts must first calculate the amount of the lodestar. After doing so, bankruptcy courts "then may adjust the lodestar up or down based on the factors contained in § 330 and [their] consideration of the twelve factors listed in *Johnson*." We also have emphasized that bankruptcy courts have "considerable discretion" when determining whether an upward or downward adjustment of the lodestar is warranted.

However, as we held in *Fender,* bankruptcy courts must remain mindful that "[f]our of the *Johnson* factors—the novelty and complexity of the issues, the special skill and experience of counsel, the quality of the representation, and the results obtained from the litigation—are presumably fully reflected in the lodestar amount.". . . Accordingly, those four *Johnson* factors may only form the basis for an upwardly adjusted fee in rare and exceptional circumstances. . . .

* * *

We now address the focal point of this case: whether the Supreme Court's fee-shifting decision in *Perdue* unequivocally, *sub silentio* overruled our circuit's bankruptcy precedent.

. . . In *Perdue,* the Supreme Court analyzed "whether the calculation of an attorney's fee, *under federal fee-shifting statutes,* based on the 'lodestar' . . . may be increased due to superior performance and results." The underlying case dealt with a class action lawsuit commenced by approximately 3,000 children in the Georgia foster care system against the Governor of Georgia and various state officials, alleging violations of their constitutional and statutory rights. The plaintiffs reached a favorable settlement and their attorneys sought to recover their fees from the defendants pursuant to 42 U.S.C. § 1988, which provides, in pertinent part, that "the court, in its discretion, may allow the prevailing party . . . a reasonable attorney's fee as part of the costs." [The Supreme Court did not allow adjustments to the lodestar calculation.]

* * *

The Trustee argues that we should extend *Perdue* to the bankruptcy arena because the decision clarifies how to apply the lodestar method, cabins the discretion of bankruptcy judges, and leads to more uniform and predictable results. We decline this invitation because *Perdue* did not unequivocally, *sub silentio* overrule our legion of precedent in the field of bankruptcy.

* * *

The question thus becomes whether *Perdue* unequivocally, *sub silentio* overruled our bankruptcy framework, which currently permits bankruptcy courts to: (1) consider the *Johnson* factors after calculating the lodestar; and (2) award fee enhancements in situations that fall outside of the three specific circumstances set forth in *Perdue*. . . We cannot say that it did.

We begin with the obvious: *Perdue* is a federal fee-shifting case. The opinion neither explicitly touched on bankruptcy law nor indicated that the Supreme Court intended *Perdue* to extend to non-fee-shifting cases. . . .

There is also textual support for our decision. Unlike § 1988, which "[u]nfortunately . . . does not explain what Congress meant by a 'reasonable' fee," . . . § 330(a) provides specific considerations (i.e. the nature, extent, and value of the services) and six factors for bankruptcy courts to consider when determining a reasonable fee. *See* 11 U.S.C. § 330(a)(3). Section 330(a)(3)'s text also indicates that its list of factors is not exclusive: bankruptcy courts may consider "all relevant factors," including factors not specified in the statute. . . . Accordingly, given the factors that bankruptcy courts are expected to consider under § 330(a)'s plain language, it is inappropriate to automatically extend *Perdue* into the bankruptcy arena.

We are also persuaded by the fact that the Court's justifications for the holding in *Perdue* do not transfer to this case. Unlike cases under § 1988, where fee enhancements often come at the expense of the taxpayer, the public's purse is left untouched in bankruptcy proceedings. The Trustee's related argument—that the enhancement comes at the expense of creditors—is similarly unavailing where, as here, all creditors receive a 100% return on their claims. The Debtors are the only party whose bottom-line was reduced by the enhancement and, because their own board of directors recommended paying the enhancement, we can hardly compare the Debtors' situation to that of the non-consenting taxpayers.

* * *

(Citations omitted.)

NOTES AND COMMENTS

1. How does the lodestar calculation, combined with the *Johnson* factors and the factors listed in § 330, meet the goals of Model Rule of Professional Responsibility 1.5 in determining appropriate attorney's fees?

2. Unlike the Model Rules of Professional Responsibility, § 330 applies to *any* bankruptcy professional.

The calculation of fees and the determination of the appropriateness of those fees by a court can be a time-consuming process. In an effort to create more efficiency, some courts have created guidelines or presumed fee structures for bankruptcy cases. The next case considers the application of those guidelines in conjunction with the lodestar method of calculating appropriate fees.

Boone v. Derham-Burk (In re Eliapo)

468 F.3d 592 (9th Cir. 2006)

FLETCHER, Circuit Judge

This appeal concerns the appropriate standards and procedures for awarding attorney's fees in connection with Chapter 13 bankruptcy petitions. The Bankruptcy Court for the Northern District of California has established three means by which a debtor's attorney may obtain a fee award in a Chapter 13 case. The attorney may (1) submit a fee application under "no-look" guidelines that establish presumptive fees for a "basic case" and specified variations thereon, (2) submit a detailed fee application based on the hours actually spent on the case, or (3) first submit a no-look application and later submit a detailed application seeking additional fees based on the hours actually spent.

In this case, Appellant Law Offices of David A. Boone ("Boone") initially submitted a fee application under the no-look guidelines. Boone later submitted a second fee application in which he sought additional fees based on the hours actually spent. In ruling on the second application, the bankruptcy court allowed a fee for a "basic case" based on the no-look guidelines and some additional fees according to the hours actually spent, but it refused to allow the full amount of fees requested. The BAP affirmed. We affirm in part, reverse in part, and remand.

. . . On January 18, 2001, Filiae and Judy Eliapo ("the Eliapos") hired Boone to assist them in filing for bankruptcy. On January 22, Boone filed a Chapter 13 petition on their behalf. A plan was first filed on February 2. The plan was amended and re-filed on April 10. The plan was amended a second time and re-filed on April 18.

On May 30, Boone signed a one-page application for attorney's fees under the bankruptcy court's no-look guidelines, reproduced *infra,* in the amount of $2,350. This figure included $1,400 for the "basic case," $750 because the case "involve[d] real property claims," and $200 because the case "involve[d] vehicle loans or leases." The bankruptcy court approved the Eliapos' second amended plan on June 21 and approved Boone's $2,350 no-look fee application on the same day.

On February 27, 2002, Boone filed a second fee application requesting an additional $1,248. This application included time sheets describing the tasks performed and hours spent by Boone. Boone had already been provided compensation, pursuant to his no-look application, for some of the work described in the time sheets. Boone did not place under separate headings the work he had performed on the "basic case," or the work involving "vehicle loans or leases" or "real property claims." Most, perhaps all, of the work for which Boone sought additional compensation was performed after the date on which the no-look fees were awarded. The bankruptcy court initially scheduled a hearing on the second application, but took the matter under submission when no objection to the application was filed.

The bankruptcy court ruled on Boone's second fee application on August 2, 2002, without a hearing. The court divided the tasks performed by Boone into two categories. The first category was compensation for work involving "normal preparation of the petition, schedules and statement of affairs and the moving of the case to confirmation." The court concluded that Boone was seeking $2,254 for this work, based on 9.6 hours of work.

The court wrote that, absent "extraordinary circumstances," compensation for this work should not exceed the $1,400 Boone had already been paid for the "basic case" under the no-look guidelines. The court held that there were no extraordinary circumstances, and it refused to award additional fees beyond the $1,400 already awarded.

Pursuant to his no-look application, Boone had been awarded $200 for work involving "vehicle loans or leases." Even though Boone did not list work under that heading in his second application, it is apparent from the confirmed plan and the second fee application that Boone had indeed done such work. . . . Boone's second fee application lists various tasks pertaining directly to this secured claim. . . . The application lists other tasks, such as "Prepare schedules and

Statement of Financial Affairs" for 1.4 hours, that obviously include work relating to the secured loan on the vehicle. . . . The court added nothing to the $1,400 "basic case" guideline fee to take into account Boone's work involving this vehicle loan.

The second category of tasks Boone performed involved motions for relief from the automatic stay brought by the first and second mortgage holders. Pursuant to his no-look application, Boone had been awarded an additional $750 for work involving "real property claims." The court concluded that Boone was seeking $1,219 for this work, based on 5.2 hours of work related to these motions. The court wrote that this work "appears suspect." However, "given the debtors['] problems with their mortgage payments," the court declined to "second guess" the time spent on these motions. It therefore awarded the full $1,219 for the work related to motions for relief from the automatic stay.

The court awarded a total attorney's fee of $2,744 based on the second application—$1,400 for the basic case, an additional $1,219 for work on the stay motions, and an additional $125 for preparation of the second application. The court did not award the $200 guideline amount for work involving "vehicle loans or leases." Because Boone had already been awarded $2,350 based on his no-look application, the net award based on his second application was $394. This amount was $854 less than the net amount Boone had requested in the second application. . . . Boone now appeals to this court, listing numerous questions in his brief. The questions overlap to a considerable extent and may be reduced to four: First, do the no-look presumptive fee guidelines violate 11 U.S.C. § 330? Second, did the bankruptcy court's criterion for awarding additional fees beyond the no-look presumptive fees violate § 330? Third, did the bankruptcy court abuse its discretion in ruling on Boone's second application without a hearing? Fourth, did the bankruptcy court abuse its discretion in refusing to give Boone $200 credit for having performed work involving "vehicle loans or leases"? All but the fourth question were raised in Boone's appeal to the BAP.

* * *

A bankruptcy court in a Chapter 13 case "may allow reasonable compensation to the debtor's attorney for representing the interests of the debtor in connection with the bankruptcy case based on a consideration of the benefit and necessity of such services to the debtor and the other factors set forth in this section." 11 U.S.C. § 330(a)(4)(B). The "other factors" are listed in § 330(a)(3).

* * *

The bankruptcy court has *sua sponte* authority to "award compensation that is less than the amount of compensation that is requested." *Id.* § 330(a)(2).

Local Bankruptcy Rule 9029–1 for the Northern District of California allows the bankruptcy court to adopt guidelines for attorney's fees. . . . As authorized by Local Rule 9029–1, bankruptcy judges for the Northern District have adopted guidelines establishing presumptive fees for routine services in Chapter 13 cases. The guidelines in effect when Boone represented the Eliapos provided as follows:

* * *

2. The maximum fee which can be approved through the procedure described in Paragraph 1 is:
    $1400 for the basic case; and an additional
    $750 if the case involves real property claims;
    $400 if the case involves state or federal tax claims;
    $200 if the case involves vehicle loans or leases;
    $1200 if the case involves an operating business;
    $300 if the case involves support arrears claims; and
    $300 if the case involves student loans.

* * *

3. If counsel elects to be paid other than pursuant to these Guidelines, all fees including the retainer shall be approved by the court whether or not the fees are payable through the Chapter 13 Trustee's Office and whether or not fees are paid for services in connection with the Chapter 13 case.

* * *

Boone argues that the bankruptcy court's presumptive fee guidelines are inconsistent with 11 U.S.C. § 330. We disagree.

The customary method for assessing an attorney's fee application in bankruptcy is the "lodestar," under which "the number of hours reasonably expended" is multiplied by "a reasonable hourly rate" for the person providing the services. However, the lodestar method is not mandatory.

We see nothing in § 330 that prevents a bankruptcy court from issuing and then relying on guidelines establishing presumptive fees for routine services in Chapter 13 cases. Such presumptive fees, if set at an appropriate level, have a number of virtues. First, use of presumptive fees in a no-look application saves attorney time that would otherwise be spent preparing detailed applications using the lodestar method. Saving attorney time has the potential, perhaps even likely, consequence of lowering attorney's fees.

Second, use of presumptive fees encourages efficient use of attorney time by providing fair compensation to efficient practitioners and by preventing inefficient practitioners from passing on the cost of their inefficiency. . . .

Third, the presumptive fee guidelines benefit attorneys by providing for earlier payment of fees. In this case, Boone was awarded the $2,350 requested in his no-look fee application several months before he even filed his second fee application. Indeed, since a no-look fee is intended to cover all services required in the usual case, an attorney who opts to file a no-look application may receive full payment even before all the services covered by that payment have been performed.

Fourth, use of presumptive fees saves time that a busy bankruptcy court would otherwise be required to spend dealing with detailed fee applications. . . .

As the BAP noted in this case, bankruptcy courts around the country have been experimenting for several years with presumptive fees for routine services in Chapter 13 cases, based on guidelines issued by the Executive Office of the United States Trustee. The Fifth Circuit has recently approved the use of a "precalculated lodestar" as a basis for awarding attorney's fees in "typical" Chapter 13 cases. The Seventh Circuit has also approved the use of presumptive fees in routine Chapter 13 cases. . . .

We emphasize that the no-look guidelines establish only presumptive fees. If a Chapter 13 practitioner does not wish to apply for fees under the no-look guidelines, he or she is free not to do so and to submit instead a detailed fee application using the lodestar method. Or, if the practitioner has already submitted a no-look application and received presumptive fees, he or she is free to seek additional fees using the lodestar method if the presumptive fees have not provided fair compensation for the time spent on the case. Of course, a practitioner who chooses the latter approach must accept the possibility that the bankruptcy court may take a fresh look at his entire fee application, not just that portion of the application relating to "additional" fees.

We therefore conclude that reliance on presumptive guideline fees for routine services in Chapter 13 cases is consistent with § 330.

* * *

It is apparent from its order that the bankruptcy court declined to award more than the presumptive guideline amount of $1,400 for a "basic case" because it concluded that there was nothing out of the ordinary about the Eliapos' case. That is, as stated by the court, the problems in the Eliapos' case were "no more difficult than those faced by Chapter 13 practitioners on a regular basis." It might have been preferable for the court to have avoided the word "extraordinary" because of the potential for misinterpretation, but we do not understand the court to have required that there be extremely unusual circumstances. In context, it is apparent that court used the word "extraordinary" to mean merely "out-of-the-ordinary" or "atypical"—that is, extra-ordinary—circumstances. So understood, the bankruptcy court's criterion for awarding additional fees was proper.

* * *

(Citations omitted.)

NOTES AND COMMENTS

1. Not all bankruptcy courts utilize a guideline system as an alternative to standard fee applications. Review your local bankruptcy court rules to determine whether guidelines exist in your area.

2. The case discusses a Chapter 13 bankruptcy guideline. Would such guidelines be appropriate in Chapter 7 cases? Chapter 11 cases?

3 If an attorney files a standard fee application in a jurisdiction that utilizes guidelines, can the court look to the guidelines in determining reasonableness of the fee application? *See* In re Williams, 357 B.R. 434 (6th Cir. BAP 2007) (the court must conduct lodestar analysis and provide specific information regarding which expenses are denied when counsel submits fee application).

F. BANKRUPTCY IN PRACTICE

Diana would like you to represent her in her bankruptcy case, but she cannot afford your (very reasonable!) fees. She chose you because you handled her ex-husband's bankruptcy case eight years ago, before he and Diana were married. His case was a simple no-asset Chapter 7; you just helped him put together the petition and schedules and obtain the discharge. There were basically no issues in the case.

She asks you whether you can help her to file her bankruptcy case, and she will try to handle everything after filing on her own. Alternatively, she asks whether you can help walk her through filing on her own, and she can then hire you as needed on post-filing matters. Draft a letter to Diana outlining any concerns that you have with these two arrangements and with the prior representation of her ex-husband.

9

Criminal Law and Bankruptcy:
Bankruptcy Crime and Punishment

Too many people spend money they haven't earned, to buy things
they don't want, to impress people that they don't like.[1]

RECALL DIANA DETTER

This chapter considers how actions taken by the debtor and/or her attorneys might give rise to criminal actions. If Diana had valuable property that she hid from the trustee, should that constitute a crime? What if she cannot explain the disappearance of assets before commencement of the bankruptcy case? What if she can account for assets, but those assets were sold or given as a gift to a friend or family member shortly before commencement of the bankruptcy case?

Title 18 of the U.S. Code lists a variety of crimes related to bankruptcy cases. Most of these crimes involve hiding assets or information from the court or trustee. While the panel trustee often uncovers the evidence of bankruptcy crimes, the trustee refers bankruptcy crimes to the U.S. Trustee's Office. In fact, anyone can report a suspected bankruptcy crime to the U.S. Trustee. *See* https://www.justice.gov/ust/report-suspected-bankruptcy-fraud. Prosecution of bankruptcy crimes occurs through the Office of the

---

1. This quote is often attributed to Will Rogers, including when it was quoted by Will Smith in his 2010 biography. Actually, the original quote was written in a June 4, 1928 column by syndicated humorist Robert Quillen when he labeled the expression "Americanism." Robert Quillen, Paragraphs, The Detroit Free Press, Quote Page 6, Column 4 (Newspapers.com) as reported in the Quote Investigator https://quoteinvestigator.com/2016/04/21/impress/ (contains a complete history of the quote).

United States Attorney. As reported by the Executive Office for the United States Trustees:

> The United States Trustee Program (Program or USTP) made 2,131 bankruptcy and bankruptcy-related criminal referrals during Fiscal Year (FY) 2015. This represents a 2.5 percent increase from the 2,080 criminal referrals made during FY 2014. The five most common allegations contained in the FY 2015 criminal referrals involved tax fraud, false oath or statement, concealment of assets, bankruptcy fraud scheme, and identity theft or use of false/multiple Social Security numbers.
>
> Of the 2,131 criminal referrals, as of January 7, 2016, formal criminal charges had been filed in connection with 10 of the referrals, 1,276 of the referrals remained under review or investigation, and 845 of the referrals were declined for prosecution.

United States Department of Justice, Executive Office for United States Trustees, *Report to Congress: Criminal Referrals by the United States Trustee Program Fiscal Year 2015*, available at https://www.justice.gov/ust/file/criminal_report_fy2015.pdf/download.

A. BASICS OF CRIMINAL LAW

It is important to consider three core criminal concepts: first, the required elements of a crime including the *mens rea* (mental state) and *actus reus* (acts); second, the kinds of proof that are used to prove crimes; and third, the purpose and application of sentencing laws to bankruptcy crimes.

Crimes are defined by their elements. The prosecution must prove each element of the crime beyond a reasonable doubt in order for a defendant to be found guilty of the crime. The elements of bankruptcy crimes are contained in Title 18 of the U.S. Code. However, bankruptcy crimes are based in part on non-bankruptcy crimes such as perjury and criminal fraud. As a result, the Model Penal Code is a good place to begin a review of the elements of crimes. The Model Penal Code §1.13(9) broadly defines the elements of a crimes as:

> (9) "elements of an offense" means (i) such conduct or (ii) such attendant circumstances or (iii) such result of conduct as
> > (a) is included in the description of the forbidden conduct in the definition of the offense: or
> > (b) establishes the required kind of culpability; or
> > (c) negatives an excuse or justification for such conduct; or

(d) negatives a defense under the statute of limitations; or

(e) establishes jurisdiction or venue.

The elements of the crime can usually be divided into four categories.

ELEMENTS OF A CRIME

Action (Actus Reus)
Mental State (Mens Rea)
Attendant circumstances
Consequences of the action/Causation

The prosecutor must prove that all the elements are concurrent. The act must occur at the same time as the mental state and the required attendant circumstances. The mental state cannot occur after the action that is required.

B. *ACTUS REUS*

In order for a person to be criminally liable, there must be a physical act that is accompanied by the required mental state under statutorily defined circumstances and result in a specific consequence. Therefore, the elements of every crime prosecuted in the United States fit into one of these four categories. However, not every crime will include all four elements, although all crimes require that there be an action and a mental state. The elements of the crime define the mental state of the actor, the actions of the actor, the attendant circumstances, and the consequences of the action. In many crimes, the action and the consequence may be combined, for example, murder, which requires the action to cause the death of another.

ACTIONS

Conduct of the defendant
Voluntary
Consciously

The action of the actor is called the *actus reus,* otherwise known as the "wrongful act." The Model Penal Code §2.01(1) defines that the action required to be "conduct which includes a voluntary act or the omission to perform an act of which he is physically capable." Timing of the act is critical to the proof of the crime. The act must be performed in relation to the condition of the defendant (conscious) the mental state of the defendant (*mens rea*) and the presence of an attendant circumstance (which, though not required in all crimes, must occur in the context of or in contemplation of a bankruptcy case in all bankruptcy crimes). Additionally, some crimes require that the act cause a certain result in order for a crime to be committed.

1. False Oath/Perjury (18 U.S.C. § 152(2, 3))

When a debtor files a bankruptcy case, the debtor submits the schedules under penalty of perjury. *See* Official Form 106Dec, *Declaration About an Individual Debtor's Schedules* (eff. Dec. 1, 2015) (indicating "[u]nder penalty of perjury, I declare that I have read the summary and schedules filed with this declaration and that they are true and correct."); Official Form 202, *Declaration Under Penalty of Perjury for Non-Individual Debtors* (eff. Dec. 1, 2015) (requiring officer of company to review schedules and "declare under penalty of perjury" that "I have a reasonable belief that the information is true and correct"). In addition, 18 U.S.C. §§ 152(2) and (3) make it a bankruptcy crime to "knowingly and fraudulently" commit perjury in a bankruptcy case.

THE ELEMENTS OF PERJURY

The bankruptcy crimes of false oaths and declarations in a bankruptcy case follow closely from the concept of perjury in criminal law. The Model Penal Code § 241 defines "perjury" as follows (the elements of perjury are italicized):

(1) **Offense Defined.** A person is guilty of perjury, a felony of the third degree, if in any *official proceeding* he makes a *false statement under oath or equivalent affirmation*, or swears or affirms the truth of a statement previously made, when the *statement is material* and he *does not believe it to be true.*

(2) **Materiality.** Falsification is material, regardless of the admissibility of the statement under rules of evidence, if it *could have affected the course or outcome of the proceeding.* It is no defense that the declarant mistakenly believed the falsification to be immaterial. Whether a falsification is material in a given factual situation is a question of law.

United States v. Marston

694 F.3d 131 (1st Cir. 2012)

BOUDIN, Judge

Ramie Marston appeals her convictions, after a jury trial, for two counts of bankruptcy fraud. The convictions stemmed from a pro se petition for bankruptcy that Marston filed in March 2009 under Chapter 7 of the Bankruptcy Code, 11 U.S.C. § 701 et seq. (2006). The prosecution alleged that Marston failed to include in the petition information related to her past fraudulent use of credit cards that she obtained under the names of two acquaintances—Susan Blake and Kristy Kromer.

A debtor who files such a bankruptcy petition has to identify "All Other Names used by the Debtor in the last 8 years (include married, maiden, and trade names)." Marston wrote "Marston, Robbi" in answer to that question, but she did not mention the names of Susan Blake or Kristy Kromer. She then signed under penalty of perjury that the information she provided in the petition was "true and correct."

A debtor must also identify creditors of different classes in separate schedules. In Schedule E, which asks for all creditors with unsecured priority claims, Marston listed Susan Blake as holding a $50,000 claim incurred on February 3, 2009, of which $46,000 was entitled to priority. In Schedule F, which asks for all creditors holding unsecured nonpriority claims, Marston listed Susan Blake as holding a disputed $50,000 claim incurred on September 22, 2007. Marston made no reference to the credit card issuers that had issued the cards in Susan Blake's name. Again, Marston's signature under penalty of perjury represented that the information in the schedules was "true and correct to the best of my knowledge, information, and belief."

Eventually, the petition was dismissed on Marston's own motion after the United States Trustee challenged her right to a discharge. On April 27, 2011, Marston was charged with five counts of bankruptcy fraud, 18 U.S.C. § 152, each count alleging that she had made a false statement in her application or schedule. The two counts ultimately submitted to the jury alleged as follows:

—Count One: that Marston had used the names Kristy Kromer and Susan Blake but knowingly and fraudulently failed to disclose this as required in the petition.

—Court Four: that Marston knowingly and fraudulently failed and refused to disclose debts to Bank of America, BMW Bank of North America, and American Express.

The government's theory as to the first count was that Marston had used the names of her two friends, Blake and Kromer, in credit card applications without their approval in order to secure cards with which Marston then made unauthorized purchases in their names; as to the fourth count, its theory was that the credit card issuers had claims against Marston for purchases made with those accounts. The jury convicted on both counts and Marston was ultimately sentenced to concurrent terms of 37 months imprisonment and three years supervised release for each count, as well as a statutory $100 special assessment imposed separately for each count.

Marston now appeals, contending that the evidence was insufficient for a reasonable jury to convict on either count. . . .

A false oath conviction under 18 U.S.C. § 152(2) requires the government to prove (1) the existence of a bankruptcy proceeding; (2) that the defendant made a false statement in that proceeding under penalty of perjury; (3) that the false statement concerned a material fact; and (4) that the defendant made the false statement knowingly and fraudulently.

Although Marston now attacks the adequacy of the evidence in several different ways, she does not deny that she fraudulently secured credit cards by listing her friends, without their permission, as the applicants or co-applicants and that she made purchases with those accounts. . . .

Marston apparently met Kristy Kromer while both women were working at an insurance agency in Nevada. Kromer thereafter discovered, among other things, that a Chase Visa card had been taken out in her name with an address corresponding to Marston's residence in Henderson, Nevada and that a Certegy loan credit card had been issued under her name with Marston listed as the co-borrower. A later search of Marston's home in New Hampshire revealed that several other credit cards had also been opened in Kromer's name but mailed to Marston's addresses in Nevada and New Hampshire.

The evidence as to Susan Blake is more circumscribed because the government, instead of presenting a full scale case, accepted a stipulation in which Marston admitted *inter alia* that she had possessed credit cards bearing the names of both Marston and Blake, that she made purchases with those cards never authorized by Blake, and that the "fraudulent liabilities incurred in Blake's name by Marston totaled approximately $61,545." Specific credit card issuers were identified in the stipulation, including the ones named in the indictment on Count Four.

* * *

With respect to Count One, Marston's attack is several-fold: even positing that Marston had fraudulently applied for and also used credit cards in the names of her two friends, she argues that (1) this did not call for the listing of such names as ones "used by" Marston; (2) the omissions were immaterial since they would not have lead [sic] to discovery of assets relevant in bankruptcy; and (3) the evidence of fraudulent intent in omitting the names was insufficient.

The first objection rests on the view that the language of the petition did not call for Marston to reveal other people's names that she had entered on fraudulent credit card applications and then presented as her own when using the cards she received or, at least, that the question in the bankruptcy application was wholly unclear as to whether such a deployment of another's name was "use." In our view, both branches of this attack fail: the language did call for Blake and Kromer's names and it was in no way fatally ambiguous.

True, "use" is a word that has various layers of meaning, but certainly an individual literally "uses" another person's name by entering it on a credit card application or presenting it as one's own in making purchases. This is not so different than using another person's name as a trade name—say, the deceased founder of one's company—save that this "use" is fraudulent and that one permissible. The parenthetical's reference to trade names, however, is neither necessary to our conclusion nor helpful to Marston although she urges the contrary.

Marston argues that the parenthetical references to "married, maiden, and trade names" confine the meaning of "use" under the *ejusdem generis* canon; but the canon is weakest, and only dubiously applicable, whereas here the general term comes first. Indeed, as already noted, the more specific examples in the question can be used effectively against Marston herself by way of analogy to trade names.

Neither is Marston's proposed interpretation saved by her argument that the petition only asked for names "used by the Debtor in the last 8 years," and that it therefore could be read only to include the names under which she might have previously filed for bankruptcy, as a means to enforce the prohibition on successive discharges. *See* 11 U.S.C. § 727(a)(8). Obviously the requirement for listing alias names has various uses in bankruptcy, including the tracing of assets obtained or concealed under other names. Anyway, the question literally called for her to disclose Blake and Kromer's names without limiting it to names used in bankruptcy petitions.

There is an outer limit to confusing or misleading questions and courts do regard some questions as so inherently ambiguous as to defeat a false statement prosecution without regard to the defendant's state of mind. One formulation distinguishes ordinary ambiguity from "fundamental ambiguity," the latter barring conviction outright; we have also said a conviction is improper if the answer given is literally correct even if it could be regarded as misleading.

The answer here was not literally correct nor was the question fundamentally ambiguous. This follows from the commonly understood breadth of the term "use," only slightly narrower than words like "do" or "make," combined with the fact that using the name of another on a credit card application or making purchases with the resulting credit card is plainly portraying oneself as that other person. True, even a reasonably clear question can be innocently misunderstood; but no conviction for making a false statement is complete without a finding of scienter.

The remaining wrinkle is, as Marston points out, that some of the cards bore her own name in addition to those of Kromer or Blake, but this also is of no help to her. Whether or not one could distinguish *dubitante* between using another's name without more and using it fraudulently along with one's own, the evidence includes correspondence seized from Marston's home that clearly supported the inference that at least some of the cards Marston secured and used bore *only* the names "Kristy Kromer" or "Susan Blake."

Marston also suggests that her answer, true or false, was immaterial. As the bankruptcy trustee in this case explained at trial, finding all names used by the debtor in any capacity in the last eight years serves as a tool for locating additional assets to distribute to the debtor's creditors. That the *particular* appropriation of Kristy Kromer and Susan Blake's names here would have lead [sic] rather to more claims against the estate than to more assets matters not.

Finally, the evidence was sufficient for the jury to conclude that Marston's failure to reveal the aliases she had used was done with the kind of dishonest or fraudulent awareness required by the statute. The language reasonably called for disclosure of Blake and Kromer's names as ones previously assumed by Marston in credit card applications, and Marston had an affirmative motive to falsify her answers by omitting their names.

The first point is covered by our earlier discussion. The second is obvious: to reveal her use of the names would have pointed directly to Marston as the perpetrator of credit card fraud. She responds that investigators were already looking into the matter; but it is one thing to be subject to suspicion and another to make admissions that would go far toward conviction. Of course, Marston did not have to make any such admissions; but once she chose to file for bankruptcy she could not then represent under penalty of perjury that she had accurately answered the questions on her petition.

***

[The Court found insufficient evidence as to Count Four, based on the prosecution's failure to prove that the debts the Defendant had incurred under Blake's name were still extant claims against her.]

(Citations omitted.)

NOTES AND COMMENTS

1. Compare the elements of perjury under the Model Penal Code, as listed in the textbox above, with the elements of false declaration provided in the case. Are there any differences?

2. Would a false statement in documents filed in a bankruptcy case be criminal without a signature page on the documents? Consider the case of United States v. Naegele, 367 B.R. 1 (D.D.C. 2007), in which the court granted a motion to dismiss when debtor's Statement of Financial Affairs (known as a "SOFA") and schedules contained false statements of the debtor's assets and liabilities but the signature page was missing:

   Trial in this case was scheduled to begin on January 29, 2007. On January 16, 2007, the government and the defendant exchanged trial exhibits in compliance with this Court's scheduling order. At that time, the government included . . . a five-page copy of defendant's SOFA that forms the basis of the false statement charge in Count 7. . . . The first page of the SOFA is date stamped as having been filed on May 4, 2000 in the United States Bankruptcy Court for the District of Columbia, as alleged in the indictment. . . . What the defendant discovered in reviewing the proposed exhibit, however, was that the last page of the SOFA, containing defendant's signature and declaration under penalty of perjury . . . was Bates-stamped "SHER01839." It therefore is identifiable as having come from the files of Jeffrey Sherman, the bankruptcy attorney who represented the defendant in the underlying bankruptcy proceeding. Documents from Mr. Sherman's files were not produced to the government by Mr. Sherman until January 10, 2007, after Mr. Sherman's assertion of the attorney-client privilege to withhold them was overruled by the Court. . . .

. . . The defendant requested that the Court unseal the grand jury transcripts and minutes to determine how Naegele could have been indicted on the counts alleging violations of 18 U.S.C. § 152(3) relating to the SOFA when the government did not have in its possession the signature page of the SOFA at the time of the grand jury proceedings. . . .

Although it opposed the motion to unseal the grand jury transcript and to dismiss Count 7, the government conceded that at the time the indictment was returned, neither the government nor the grand jury had possession of page 5 of the SOFA, containing the signature portion of the SOFA signed by Naegele. The government also conceded that it had never seen Naegele's signed SOFA signature page until Mr. Sherman produced his files. . . .

Naegele, 367 B.R. at 4-5.

3. Is harm a requirement for a false oath conviction? *See* U.S. v. O'Donnell, 539 F.2d 1233 (9th Cir. 1976) (even if debtor's misstatement regarding employment did not harm creditors in the bankruptcy case, misstatement was material because it involved debtor's financial situation).

2. Hiding Assets and Conspiracy (18 U.S.C. § 152 (1, 7))

Sections 1 and 7 prohibit various forms of concealing property, whether of the estate or of the debtor. The following case involved not only the debtor, but the debtor's sister (and attorney), leading to the addition of conspiracy charges.

CONSPIRACY

Title 18 does not provide a specific bankruptcy crime of conspiracy, but conspiracy to commit a crime is itself a crime under the Model Penal Code, § 5.03:

(1) **Definition of Conspiracy.** A person is guilty of conspiracy with another person or persons to commit a crime if with the purpose of promoting or facilitating its commission he:
  (a) agrees with such other person or persons that they or one or more of them will engage in conduct that constitutes such crime or an attempt or solicitation to commit such crime; or
  (b) agrees to aid such other person or persons in the planning or commission of such crime or of an attempt or solicitation to commit such crime.

United States v. Ledee

772 F.3d 21 (1st Cir. 2014)

LIPEZ, Judge

Appellants in this consolidated appeal are a brother and sister who were found guilty of multiple bankruptcy-related crimes designed to conceal the brother's assets and thereby avoid his obligations to creditors. The pair assert a host of trial and sentencing errors, none of which we find meritorious. Accordingly, we affirm both siblings' convictions and sentences.

* * *

In August 2002, Edgardo Colón Ledée, a plastic surgeon, and his sister, Astrid Colón Ledée, a bankruptcy attorney, collaborated on the transfer of Edgardo's oceanfront residence and office to Investments Unlimited ("IU"), a corporation wholly owned and controlled by Edgardo. Astrid drafted the deed and represented IU in the transaction as its president. The property, known as Málaga # 1, had an outstanding mortgage of about $720,000, and the deed states that Edgardo sold it to IU to extinguish a $40,000 debt. Edgardo reported in his later filings in bankruptcy court that he leased the property from the corporation after the transfer, but the mortgage remained in his name and he continued to take the mortgage interest deduction on his personal tax return.

In May 2003, approximately nine months after the transfer of Málaga # 1, Edgardo filed a voluntary petition for Chapter 7 bankruptcy, with Astrid serving as his attorney. At that time, he reported a debt of $100,000 to the Puerto Rico Treasury Department and faced about twenty malpractice suits. In the Statement of Financial Affairs ("SOFA") filed with his bankruptcy petition, Edgardo did not disclose his ownership of IU and Málaga # 1 or that he had transferred the property to IU less than a year earlier. In October 2003, Edgardo filed an amended petition whose supporting documents disclosed some additional properties, but he again failed to report the Málaga # 1 transaction or his ownership of IU. The newly disclosed properties were heavily encumbered, and therefore did not add to the funds available for creditors. Astrid also signed the amended petition as Edgardo's legal representative in the bankruptcy. In both the original and amended petitions, Edgardo reported that he rented Málaga # 1 from IU.

In November 2003, Edgardo lied under oath at a meeting of his creditors convened by the bankruptcy trustee, testifying that IU's stockholders lived in Chicago and were not related to him. He also reported that his only relationship with IU was an agreement to rent Málaga # 1. Astrid, who attended the meeting as Edgardo's attorney, subsequently gave the trustee copies of commercial and residential leases that purported to show that Edgardo was renting Málaga # 1 from IU. Based on Edgardo's filings and his representations at the creditors' meeting, the trustee found that there were no assets that could be liquidated to obtain funds to pay creditors and, on December 28, 2004, the trustee filed a Report of No Distribution.

In July and August 2006, during the pendency of the bankruptcy case and without notice to the trustee or bankruptcy court, Edgardo arranged for IU to purchase three pieces of property: a penthouse condominium known as Laguna Gardens V PHP (for $195,000), a building known as El Convento (for $490,000), and an adjacent lot next to El Convento identified as Antonsanti (for $68,000). Edgardo deposited cash into IU's bank account to fund the purchases, and Astrid paid the amounts due at the closings with manager's checks drawn on IU's account. Astrid represented IU as its president for each of the three transactions, executing the deeds at each closing.

The deception began to unravel in late 2006 when a creditor's objection to the Report of No Distribution led the bankruptcy trustee to look more closely at the Málaga # 1 property. A realtor hired by the trustee discovered a "for sale" sign on the property and, upon inquiring, learned that the seller was Edgardo. The trustee's ensuing investigation revealed Edgardo's prior sale of the property to IU and Astrid's role in the transaction, prompting the filing of an adversary complaint in the bankruptcy case on December 14. The trustee alleged in the complaint that Edgardo had transferred the property to IU "with an actual intent to hinder, delay or defraud" creditors, and he demanded that the transfer be set aside and the property declared part of Edgardo's bankruptcy estate. The trustee also sought sanctions against Astrid, including damages and attorney's fees in favor of the bankruptcy estate, and filed a notice in the real property registry alerting third parties to the title claim against Málaga # 1. Later in the month, Astrid, as IU's president, signed annual reports for the company for the years 2001 to 2005.

Developments on two fronts quickly followed the filing of the adversary proceeding. On January 5, 2007, Astrid withdrew from the bankruptcy case and informed the bankruptcy court that she had resigned her position as IU's president. Meanwhile, Edgardo arranged a hurried sale of Málaga # 1 to his girlfriend's parents, with the closing taking place on January 6, Three Kings Day, a significant holiday in Puerto Rico and an unusual day for such a transaction. Representing IU at the closing was Myrna Cintrón Estrada ("Cintrón"), Edgardo's cousin who served as his housekeeper and who had been newly installed as IU's president to replace Astrid. The sales price was $1.1 million, with $410,000 due from the buyers, Luis Santiago Aponte ("Santiago") and Yolanda Lebrón Matos ("Lebrón"), the latter figure being roughly the amount in excess of the outstanding mortgage on the property.

On January 8 and 12, manager's checks totaling $410,000 and made out to Investments Unlimited were deposited into IU's bank account, one in the amount of $205,000 on the earlier date and two for $102,500 on the later date. The larger check and one of the two smaller ones was obtained in Santiago's name, and the third check was obtained in Lebrón's name. On each of the two days the deposits were made, or shortly thereafter, Edgardo wrote four checks on IU's account for $51,250 each—a total of eight checks—to the following individuals: Cintrón, Rafael Vaquer, Maria Bonilla Hernández, and Reynaldo Cordero Cintrón. Each of the eight IU checks was used to purchase a manager's check in the same amount made out to the same individuals. Although the manager's checks contained endorsement signatures on the back, all four payees—all family members of Edgardo—denied receiving or endorsing the checks. All of the checks apparently were returned to the accounts of Santiago and Lebrón.

The adversary proceeding in Edgardo's bankruptcy case was resolved in March 2008. Edgardo and Astrid both accepted a Partial Settlement Agreement finding that Málaga # 1 was property of the bankruptcy estate and requiring Edgardo to rescind the sale to Santiago and Lebrón. Edgardo further agreed that, if the proceeds from the trustee's sale of Málaga # 1 did not suffice to pay all claims and costs, the trustee could reactivate the adversary proceeding and seek the shortfall from sale of the properties Edgardo purchased in 2006—the Laguna Gardens VPHP, El Convento, and Antonsanti. Edgardo subsequently filed amended schedules with the bankruptcy court that reported, inter alia, his 100 percent ownership of IU.

A year later, in April 2009, Edgardo and Astrid were charged in an eight-count indictment with various bankruptcy-related crimes, including conspiracy to conceal property belonging to Edgardo's bankruptcy estate and to fraudulently conceal and transfer his and IU's property with the intent to defeat the bankruptcy laws, as well as a substantive offense alleging that they concealed the property. *See* 18 U.S.C. §§ 371, 152(1) & (7). The first five counts cited the siblings' concealment of Edgardo's ownership interests in IU and

Málaga # 1 and the transfer of funds through IU to purchase the three properties in 2006. Count Six charged Edgardo alone with the fraudulent transfer of Málaga # 1 in January 2007, in violation of 18 U.S.C. § 152(7). Count Seven charged him with laundering the proceeds of the Málaga # 1 "sale" in January 2007 by converting the two $205,000 payments into eight cashier's checks payable to four individuals who "had no financial interest in the transaction or Investments Unlimited," in violation of 18 U.S.C. § 1956. Count Eight was based on conduct unrelated to the activities at issue in this appeal.

After a seventeen-day trial in January and February 2012, a jury found Edgardo guilty on Counts One through Seven and Astrid guilty on all five counts against her. Edgardo was acquitted of the fraudulent transfer alleged in Count Eight. The district court sentenced Edgardo to sixty months' imprisonment on each of Counts One through Six and seventy-two months' imprisonment on Count Seven, the money-laundering crime, all to be served concurrently. The court sentenced Astrid to a term of thirty-six months. The district court granted Astrid's request for release on bail pending appeal so that she could care for her ailing mother, conditioned on her mother's continuing need for help. Edgardo began serving his term in May 2013.

On appeal, appellants challenge both their convictions and sentences, each asserting multiple claims of error. They insist that the evidence was insufficient to support their convictions on some or all counts, and their common claims also include an objection to the district court's sixteen-level increase in their base offense levels under the sentencing guidelines. Edgardo includes among his claims a contention that the Partial Settlement Agreement, which brought Málaga # 1 into his bankruptcy estate, constituted a waiver by the government of all charges based on conduct that was cured by his corrective actions. Astrid includes among her claims a contention that the district court abused its discretion by denying her motion in limine to exclude prejudicial evidence relating to her own bankruptcy proceedings in 2000.

* * *

Both appellants claim that the evidence presented by the government at trial fell short of establishing a conspiracy between them to conceal and fraudulently transfer Edgardo's assets in violation of the bankruptcy laws. *See* 18 U.S.C. § 152(1), (7). Astrid attempts to distance herself from Edgardo's conduct, claiming that she had nothing to do with his actions before the transfer of the Málaga # 1 property to IU and, hence, no conspiracy could have been in place at the time of that transaction. She also minimizes the significance of her role as president of IU, pointing to evidence that other individuals who held that position were uninvolved in the business and citing Edgardo's admission that IU was his alter ego. For his part, Edgardo complains that the government relied on improper hearsay evidence, and he asserts that the jury necessarily drew impermissible inferences from appellants' brother-sister relationship.

We find none of appellants' arguments persuasive. To sustain a conspiracy conviction, the government must show that the defendant knowingly agreed with at least one other person to commit a crime, intending that the underlying offense be completed. The indictment charges a conspiracy that extended from about August 17, 2002—the date Málaga # 1 was transferred from Edgardo to IU—through mid-January 2007—following the Three Kings Day sale of Málaga # 1, and after Astrid withdrew from the bankruptcy case and relinquished the presidency of IU. The record shows continuous collaboration by the siblings throughout that period. Both were involved in the 2002 transfer: Edgardo was the seller and, in effect, the buyer as well, and Astrid drafted the deed and formally represented IU in the transaction as its president. When Edgardo filed for bankruptcy about ten months later without disclosing the sale of Málaga # 1 or his ownership interest in IU, Astrid signed the bankruptcy petition as his attorney. Both attended the creditors' meeting in November 2003, when Edgardo falsely stated that IU was owned by Chicago investors. At that time, Astrid was still acting as IU's president (as well as Edgardo's attorney). Both also signed the amended bankruptcy schedules that continued to omit Málaga # 1, and Astrid acted as IU's president in the multiple real estate deals that Edgardo initiated for IU in 2006. Later in 2006, Astrid signed five years' worth of IU's late annual reports.

This evidence of the siblings' activities is sufficient to permit a reasonable jury to conclude that the pair worked jointly throughout the period charged in the indictment to unlawfully conceal and transfer property belonging to Edgardo's bankruptcy estate. Appellants attempt to discount the import of their obvious collaboration by claiming a lack of proof that their actions were taken pursuant to a conspiratorial agreement. The government, however, need not produce "evidence of an explicit agreement to ground a conspiracy conviction." Rather, "[a]n agreement to join a conspiracy 'may be express or tacit . . . and may be proved by direct or circumstantial evidence.'"

Based on the evidence described above, a jury reasonably could infer that the siblings had agreed to mislead the bankruptcy court about Edgardo's assets, including his ownership of IU, and took numerous steps designed to protect his resources, beginning with the transfer of Málaga # 1 in anticipation of the bankruptcy filing....

. . . Both appellants claim that judgments of acquittal should have been entered on the three counts charging them with the fraudulent transfers of Laguna Gardens V PHP (Count Three), El Convento (Count Four), and Antonsanti (Count Five), in violation of 18 U.S.C. § 152(7). Section 152(7) provides, in relevant part, that it is unlawful for a person, "with intent to defeat the provisions of [the Bankruptcy Code], knowingly and fraudulently [to] transfer[] or conceal[] any of his property." Appellants argue that the government failed to prove that the properties were purchased with funds belonging to the bankruptcy estate and, hence, the jury could not properly find that they acted with the intent to defeat the provisions of the Bankruptcy Code. Although the government acknowledges that, "[d]ue to Appellants' actions," the bankruptcy trustee could not exclude the possibility that the properties were purchased with post-petition earnings, it asserts that § 152(7) does not demand that the fraudulent transfers at issue involve property of the bankruptcy estate.

We agree with the government, whose position is supported by the plain language of the statute. Unlike § 152(1), which addresses the concealment of "any property belonging to *the estate of a debtor,*" 18 U.S.C. § 152(1) (emphasis added), § 152(7) covers the transfer or concealment of "*any of [a debtor's] property* or the property of [any] other person or corporation," *id.* § 152(7) (emphasis added). Hence, although the transfer or concealment prohibited by § 152(7) must relate to a bankruptcy case—i.e., it must be intended to defeat the provisions of the Bankruptcy Code—the statute reaches beyond the bankruptcy estate itself.

The facts here illustrate why the fraud provisions of the Bankruptcy Code reach post-petition earnings. The jury reasonably could have found that Edgardo used post-petition earnings to fund IU's account—a bankruptcy estate asset that should have been disclosed initially—and then used that IU account to acquire the three properties. It is inconceivable that such a blatant scheme to manipulate an estate asset could be insulated from criminal consequences simply because the funds at issue derived from postpetition earnings. Indeed, because IU should have been included in the bankruptcy estate, appellants presumably were obliged to bring to the trustee's attention any funds moving through the company.

Ultimately, however, appellants' challenge to their convictions under Counts Three through Five does not depend on the source of the funds used to purchase the three properties. Regardless of how the acquisitions were financed, the jury could have found that the transactions were deliberately structured to conceal assets from the trustee and, hence, were done "with intent to defeat the provisions of [the Bankruptcy Code]." 18 U.S.C. § 152(7). Appellants were therefore not entitled to judgments of acquittal on Counts Three through Five.

* * *

(Citations omitted.)

NOTES AND COMMENTS

1. On the conspiracy charge, how does the fact that the debtor and attorney are siblings play into the government's case? Could a nonrelated attorney also be involved in a conspiracy to commit bankruptcy fraud?

2. As the court notes, § 152(7) prohibits the transfer of property of the *debtor* without notice to the court. Why should the debtor's transfer of its own property be a crime? Is any transfer of debtor's property without permission of the court a crime?

3. Crimes Involving Non-debtor Defendants (18 U.S.C. § 152(4, 5))

As with the conspiracy charges in the *Ledee* case, several of the bankruptcy crimes implicate non-debtor defendants. These crimes can involve the debtor as well, as in the case below, which considers both the receipt of fraudulently transferred property and the filing of a false claim in the bankruptcy case.

United States v. Arthur

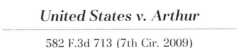

582 F.3d 713 (7th Cir. 2009)

BAUER, Judge

Ronald Arthur ("Ronald") filed a Chapter 7 bankruptcy petition to discharge various debts incurred over a period of time. Ronald claimed to have few assets to satisfy the various claims. The fact was, however, he had transferred, prior to the proceeding, assets not listed in the petition to his wife Mary Arthur ("Mary"). More assets were transferred to Mary after the petition had been filed. The matters were presented to a grand jury, which charged both Ronald and Mary with various counts of bankruptcy fraud and money laundering. After a bench trial, the district court found that the couple conspired to conceal Ronald's assets from both the trustee and the bankruptcy's creditors, in an attempt to have all of his debt discharged while retaining the money.

Ronald attacks all aspects of his convictions and sentence, claiming constitutional violations and various district court trial errors. Mary challenges the sufficiency of the evidence as to her convictions. We affirm.

. . . After Barbara Doyle obtained a judgment for $125,000 against Ronald based on damages to her property by loggers affiliated with Ronald, he filed a Chapter 7 bankruptcy petition and accompanying schedules to discharge the debt in the United States Bankruptcy Court for the Eastern District of Virginia. The proceedings were later transferred to the Eastern District of Wisconsin.

In the course of these proceedings, it became apparent to the trustee that Ronald had more assets than he had disclosed in his petition; that he had transferred virtually all of his income and assets to his wife Mary through various marital property agreements. And several of his entities, such as the Xtant Foundation, had received considerable earnings that had not been disclosed in his petition. (Mary served as a director of Xtant, a business that purportedly sold recycled paper.)

Mary, with the help of her husband, filed a claim for $650,000 against Ronald's bankruptcy estate. This claim was filed as a stipulation, signed by Ronald and Mary, acknowledging that Ronald was indeed indebted to Mary for her various managerial, charitable and legal services.

The bankruptcy trustee, suspicious of the couple's transfers, filed an adversary action against Ronald. Ultimately, Ronald agreed to waive the discharge of Doyle's judgment and settled the trustee's action for $25,000. This, in the couple's view, put the matter to rest.

The circumstances of the bankruptcy proceeding, however, had not gone unnoticed. A grand jury indicted Ronald on 26 counts of bankruptcy fraud and money laundering conspiracies, as well as various substantive fraud and money laundering offenses based on his and Mary's efforts to conceal his assets from the bankruptcy trustee and his creditors; Mary was charged on eleven of these counts. Ronald and Mary each agreed to waive their right to a jury trial.

During the trial, the couple mounted a joint defense, claiming that the transfers of the assets were legitimate and not an effort to hide assets. According to the couple, Ronald transferred his interests in most individually and jointly owned assets, as well as after-acquired assets and income, to Mary pursuant to a marital agreement executed on January 2, 1995, and subsequent agreements executed on August 1, 1995, and January 2, 1997.

The district court, in a 48–page "Findings of Fact and Verdict" order, found that Ronald had utilized the bankruptcy system in an attempt to discharge the Doyle judgment and foil other creditors. The court found that, with the assistance of his wife Mary, Ronald created and used "phony" entities, as well as "sham[]" marital agreements, to hide his assets and income from the trustee, Doyle, and his other creditors, and repeatedly lied during the course of the bankruptcy proceeding. The court found that the couple had deposited funds, which should have been disclosed in the bankruptcy petition, into the bank accounts of the corporations; deposited assets into Mary's personal accounts; used the entities, such as Xtant, to conceal assets; and engaged in other unusual financial moves in an effort to conceal assets. Also, the court found that Mary inflated Ronald's liabilities by filing a false claim.

Specifically, the court found Mary guilty of bankruptcy fraud — receiving debtor property illegally and filing a false claim. This finding was based on: (1) Mary's deposit of a check, issued by a Thompson Consulting Ltd. to Ronald for work previously rendered, into their firm's business account titled "Arthur & Arthur"; (2) the purchase of a SEA DOO, a personal watercraft, for personal use with a Xtant check; and (3) Mary's deposit of a check, representing the proceeds of Ronald's interest in another business, G & K Investment, into her own bank account.

The money laundering convictions were based on the transfer of Ronald's assets and the proceeds of the bankruptcy fraud into the bank accounts of the "dummy corporations", and Mary's personal accounts, to hide Ronald's income.

* * *

The court found Mary guilty of nine counts of the eleven charged and sentenced her to twelve months and one-day of imprisonment.

The district court then ordered Ronald and Mary to forfeit the assets listed in the indictment, as well as a personal money judgment in an amount equal to the total of the laundered funds. The judgment against Ronald totaled $87,395.93; Mary's judgment totaled $40,806.49.

***

Ronald and Mary each raise issues distinct to their own appeal. Mary argues that the evidence presented to the district court was insufficient to convict her of conspiracy to commit money laundering, money laundering, receipt of debtor property and filing a false claim in the bankruptcy proceeding. Ronald argues that a variety of constitutional, trial, and sentencing errors were committed by the district court. The appeals have been consolidated, and we begin with Mary's appeal.

. . . "[W]e will overturn a conviction based on insufficient evidence only if the record is devoid of evidence from which a reasonable [trier of fact] could find guilt beyond a reasonable doubt.". . .

. . . The indictment charged Mary with five counts of receipt of debtor property, all in violation of 18 U.S.C. § 152(5). The district court found her guilty on three of these counts, relating to: (1) her deposit of a Thompson Consulting check (representing an account receivable for work previously rendered by Ronald) into the bank account of Arthur & Arthur; (2) the purchase of a SEA DOO with a check from the Arthurs' foundation Xtant; and (3) her deposit of the G & K check into her bank account. The district court found that in these three instances, assets, which should have been included in Ronald's estate and subject to creditors' claims, were intentionally removed and concealed from the bankruptcy trustee and creditors.

For these convictions to stand, the evidence must be such that a rational trier of fact could have found beyond a reasonable doubt that: (1) Mary received a material amount of property from Ronald after the filing of Ronald's bankruptcy case; (2) Mary received such property with the intent to defeat the provisions of Title 11; and (3) Mary received this property knowingly and fraudulently. See 18 U.S.C. § 152(5). Mary argues that the evidence presented by the government did not prove these elements beyond a reasonable doubt. Specifically, Mary argues that the assets received were legitimately hers and not Ronald's, pursuant to marital agreements entered into by the couple, which directed the distribution of the couple's assets from Ronald to Mary. In her view, she simply deposited checks that were hers under the agreements, and so could not have had the requisite mental state required for the convictions.

The district court found that the marital agreements were a sham—essentially efforts to divest Ronald of his interests in the assets to avoid creditors. The court determined that, although some marital agreements may be valid, these bore many "badges of fraud." The agreements did not surface until after the bankruptcy proceeding had been initiated. When the trustee demanded that Ronald reveal documents related to the transfer of his assets to Mary within four years of the bankruptcy filing, the first agreement was tendered, indicating that it had been entered into five years before. Although the agreement had purportedly been entered into five years before the bankruptcy filing, Ronald had not transferred any real property to Mary until the Doyle judgment had been entered against him, three years before the filing. So, in fact, nothing was transferred pursuant to the agreements until a state court ordered Ronald to pay Doyle $125,000. Although this agreement, and others, were ultimately produced at the bankruptcy proceeding, they were never publicly filed until roughly a year after Ronald filed his bankruptcy proceeding, around the time when the couple's relationship was claimed to have soured, evidenced by a filing of a legal separation petition. In fact, the couple still lived together after the "legal separation." Moreover, funds that Mary claims were legitimately hers were never given to her, but deposited into bank accounts, accessible to Ronald. And, Ronald and Mary's tax returns did not reflect any of the transfers from Ronald to Mary, or that Ronald's income belonged to Mary. This is more than enough evidence to support a factual finding that the agreements were entered into fraudulently.

Finding the marital agreements fraudulent, the facts are sufficient to establish that Mary received Ronald's assets with an intent to defeat the bankruptcy code. For example, the SEA DOO was purchased by a check drawn on Xtant's account and titled in the name of the foundation. The district court found that Xtant had no legitimate business reason for a personal watercraft since recreational use of the vehicle does not comport with selling recycled paper. Although Mary testified that, by buying the watercraft, she was merely "taking back" money that she had loaned to Xtant, there was no evidence of a personal loan to the foundation. The district court noted that the evidence proved that Xtant was a shell corporation used by the couple to conceal income and assets, and to pay personal expenses. Viewing these facts in the light most favorable to the government, there was enough evidence to lead a rational trier of fact to find that Mary intentionally received the property fraudulently.

Next, she challenges the sufficiency of the evidence that led to her conviction for filing a false claim against Ronald's bankruptcy estate. Under 18 U.S.C. § 152(4), the government had to prove beyond a reasonable doubt that Mary personally, or by an agent, knowingly and fraudulently presented a false claim against her husband's estate in his Title 11 bankruptcy proceeding.

Mary filed a claim for $650,000 in her husband's bankruptcy for managerial, charitable and legal work previously performed. Despite the fact that the claim was stipulated to and signed by Ronald and Mary, the district court rejected this take-our-word-for-it document. It found that she had been employed on a full-time basis as a nursing home administrator from 1997 to 2004, and "it is incredible that she was also performing legal work for her husband worth hundreds of thousands of dollars during this time." It is reasonable to conclude that the sheer amount of work-hours claimed could not have been amassed while working full time for another organization. This alone is enough for a rational trier of fact to find her guilty of filing a false claim.

* * *

(Citations omitted.)

NOTES AND COMMENTS

1. A debtor is likely to give property to loved ones after a bankruptcy filing, such as birthday or holiday gifts. Would simple gifts suffice as the basis of criminal activity? If not, how does a court distinguish between these gifts and the types of transfers that constitute criminal activity under § 152(5)?

2. Several courts have considered whether § 152(4) can create a private right of action by the debtor (if, unlike the present case, the debtor is not party to creating the false claim but is, instead, a victim of it). They have consistently held that § 152(4) does not create a private right of action. *See, e.g.*, Davis v. Orion Fed. Credit Union (In re Davis), 558 B.R. 222, 224 (Bankr. W.D. Tenn. 2015).

ATTORNEYS CONVICTED OF BANKRUPTCY CRIMES

Attorneys who have been convicted of bankruptcy crimes also face disbarment. Several state courts have upheld disbarment of an attorney based on conviction of a bankruptcy crime. *See, e.g.*, In re Greenspan, 683 A.2d 158 (D.C. App. 1996) (conviction of attorney-trustee for embezzlement from estate under 18 U.S.C. § 153); In re Hattier, 894 So. 2d 1123 (La. 2005) (conviction for knowing and fraudulent concealment of assets); In re Otis, 438 Mass. 1016 (Mass. 2003) (conviction for bankruptcy fraud).

C. *MENS REA*

The mental state of the defendant is called the *mens rea*. At common law, the *mens rea* element was divided into two categories: specific intent and general intent. The difficulty in distinguishing between general and specific and the lack of gradation in culpability led to the Model Penal Code's four categories of mental states. They include purposefully, knowingly, recklessly, and negligently. *See* Model Penal Code § 2.02.

MENTAL STATES

Purposeful/intentional
Knowingly
Recklessly
Negligently

Each of the mental states is defined in the Model Penal Code §2.02 as follows:

(a) Purposely.[2] A person acts purposely with respect to a material element of an offense when:

(i) if the element involves the nature of his conduct or a result thereof, it is his conscious object to engage in conduct of that nature or to cause such a result; and

(ii) if the element involves the attendant circumstances, he is aware of the existence of such circumstances or he believes or hopes that they exist.

(b) Knowingly. A person acts knowingly with respect to a material element of an offense when:

(i) if the element involves the nature of his conduct or the attendant circumstances, he is aware that his conduct is of that nature or that such circumstances exist; and

(ii) if the element involves a result of his conduct, he is aware that it is practically certain that his conduct will cause such a result.

(c) Recklessly. A person acts recklessly with respect to a material element of an offense when he consciously disregards a substantial and unjustifiable risk that the material element exists or will result from his conduct. The risk must be of such a nature and degree that, considering the nature

---

2. The Model Penal Code defines "intentional" to mean "purposeful."

and purpose of the actor's conduct and the circumstances known to him, its disregard involves a gross deviation from the standard of conduct that a law-abiding person would observe in the actor's situation.

(d) Negligently. A person acts negligently with respect to a material element of an offense when he should be aware of a substantial and unjustifiable risk that the material element exists or will result from his conduct. The risk must be of such a nature and degree that the actor's failure to perceive it, considering the nature and purpose of his conduct and the circumstances known to him, involves a gross deviation from the standard of care that a reasonable person would observe in the actor's situation.

Notice that the bankruptcy crimes generally require that the defendant act "knowingly and fraudulently." While the knowing standard finds its roots in criminal law, bankruptcy crimes add an element of fraudulent intent that lacks a parallel in the Model Penal Code. The short excerpt from a very complicated and lengthy court opinion considers the evidence needed to determine a defendant's fraudulent intent.

United States v. Knight

25 F. Supp. 3d 1104 (W.D. Ark. 2014) *aff'd in part, rev'd in part,* 800 F.3d 491 (8th Cir. 2015)

BEAM, Judge

[Knight represented Barber in a series of complicated real estate transactions. In addition to serving as Barber's attorney, Knight repeatedly facilitated financial transactions using his trust account. Ultimately, these transactions shielded money from creditors in Barber's ensuing bankruptcy case. Knight was convicted of various bankruptcy crimes, and appealed those convictions.]

* * *

In order to aid its determination of whether a conspiracy to commit bankruptcy fraud existed, as charged in Count 1, the jury was instructed as follows as to the elements of the substantive offense of bankruptcy fraud:

1. The defendant voluntarily and intentionally devised or intended to devise a scheme or plan to defraud, with the scheme being to conceal income, assets, and funds from creditors and the bankruptcy court by transferring income, assets, and funds belonging to Brandon Barber into and through accounts belonging to defendant and James Van Doren;

2. The defendant did so with the intent to defraud; and

3. The defendant made a material false or fraudulent representation, claim, or promise concerning, or in relation to, a Title 11

bankruptcy proceeding for the purpose of concealing the scheme or plan to defraud.

* * *

Certain emails admitted into evidence tended to show that Knight knew that Barber was using his trust account as an alternative to a traditional bank account so that Barber did not have to keep large sums of money in any account in Barber's name for any length of time. Other emails indicated that Knight knowingly allowed his trust account to be used as a pass-through to disguise Barber as the source of money paid to creditors. . . . At no time did Knight refuse to accept Barber's money into his trust account or counsel Barber that he could not act as Barber's personal banker simply because Barber did not want to keep large sums of money in his own account. Knight accepted large sums of money into his trust account even after he was aware that Barber had bank accounts available to him.

At the time that Legacy Bank propounded post-judgment discovery in the foreclosure proceeding, Knight had some of Barber's money left in his trust account. That money, however, was quickly depleted before Barber served untimely answers to the interrogatories. After the money ran out and Legacy Bank was making every effort to collect on its judgment, Barber filed for personal bankruptcy with Knight as his attorney. Neither Barber nor Knight disclosed that large sums of Barber's money had passed through Knight's trust account in the year previous to the filing, although such disclosures were arguably required.

Taking all of this evidence together and making numerous inferences in favor of the verdict, the Court finds that the evidence submitted by the Government was sufficient to show a pattern of conduct intended to defraud the bankruptcy court and to convict Knight of conspiracy to commit bankruptcy fraud as charged in Count 1. "While the government's proof was less than overwhelming, the jury's verdict must be upheld if there is an interpretation of the evidence that would allow a reasonable-minded jury to conclude guilt beyond a reasonable doubt."

. . . Although the evidence presented was sufficient, by a thin margin, to support Knight's conviction as to Count 1, the Court finds that the evidence weighs heavily enough against the verdict that a miscarriage of justice may have occurred. The Court finds, therefore, that Knight's motion for new trial as to Count 1 should be granted.

The Government presented a lot of evidence as to Barber's activities. However, any evidence as to the extent of Knight's knowledge of and involvement in Barber's schemes was largely speculative and based generally on the fact that Knight was Barber's lawyer. The testimony revealed that the witnesses, except for Knight himself, had little to no direct or personal knowledge of the extent of Knight's knowledge of or involvement with any conspiracy to commit bankruptcy fraud. . . . No witness testified to having personal knowledge of a conversation between Barber and Knight where a fraudulent scheme, an intention to defraud, or even a specific intent by Barber to file personal bankruptcy was discussed. The only two people that would have had personal knowledge of any private conversations between Barber and Knight not memorialized by documentary evidence are Barber and Knight. Knight testified in his defense and denied his guilt as to all counts. Barber did not testify. While the Court recognizes that proof of the existence of a conspiracy may be based on circumstantial evidence, the evidence in this case was so speculative as to raise a real concern as to whether Knight had either knowledge of the purpose of any conspiracy or the requisite intent to carry out the essential object of a conspiracy to commit bankruptcy fraud.

Furthermore, in the civil context, the Eighth Circuit has found that, even where a debtor is facing loan defaults or demands on personal guarantees and has specifically sought the advice of bankruptcy counsel, that there must be extrinsic indicia of fraud in order to find an intent to defraud creditors. The transfers of Barber's money through Knight's trust account were not *per se* contrary to law. The transfers would only be contrary to law, at least as to Knight, if Knight acted with an intent to defraud and—in this case—specifically an attempt to defraud Barber's creditors and the bankruptcy court. Merely putting money beyond the reach of creditors, even on the eve of bankruptcy, is not enough to find an intent to defraud, as the intent to keep value away from creditors is not automatically impermissible. Therefore, the fact that Knight knew that Barber was in a precarious financial condition, offered his legal services, and allowed Barber to pass money through his trust account—even knowing that Barber wanted to keep money away from his creditors—are not facts that weigh heavily in favor of finding that Knight had the requisite intent to defraud Barber's bankruptcy creditors or the bankruptcy court. Although the record is replete with documentary evidence, no email or other document was admitted that would otherwise tip the scales in the Government's favor as to this Count.

* * *

The Court finds that Knight's motion for a new trial should be granted as to Count 2 [concealment of assets] on the alternative grounds that the evidence presented at trial preponderated sufficiently heavily against a finding that Knight possessed an intent to defraud in relation to allowing Barber to pass funds through his trust account. As evidence of fraudulent intent, the Government presented testimony and documentary evidence regarding Knight's use of his trust account; Knight's involvement in the . . . real estate transactions; false disclosure and nondisclosures in relation to the Legacy Bank proceeding and Barber's personal bankruptcy filing; Barber's use of the entity NWARE; and Knight's receipt of attorney's fees for his representation of Barber. . . .

. . . Between April 2008 and January 2009, approximately $1,200,000 was transferred through Knight's trust account on Barber's behalf. A lot of argument and testimony was presented at trial as to whether a lawyer's trust account was a good hiding spot to keep money from creditors or whether a lawyer's trust account is subject to garnishment. This testimony was all largely irrelevant except to the extent that it could have shed light on the mindset of Knight in allowing Barber's money to be transferred into or out of the trust account. The important consideration is not whether, in hindsight, Barber or Knight actually kept money from bankruptcy creditors through their use of the trust account. Rather, it is whether, at the time the transfers were made, Knight allowed those transfers with the requisite intent to defraud and in contemplation of Barber's eventual bankruptcy.

* * *

The Government presented evidence at trial as to the amount of fees Knight received for his representation of Barber, with the implication being that perhaps these fees were not deserved, and that Knight was gaining a benefit from a scheme to commit bankruptcy fraud. . . . During the month-and-a-half covered by the first bill Knight sent to Barber, dated March 6, 2008, Knight billed Barber for 191 hours at a rate of $200 per hour for a total of $37,400. The time was accounted for on the bill in a detailed manner. It was at that point that Knight testified he proposed charging Barber a flat rate of $17,000 a month. Knight then later billed separately for his firm's representation of Barber during Barber's personal bankruptcy proceedings.

Beginning in early 2009, it appears that Barber got behind in his payments to Knight. Any funds that Barber had in Knight's trust account had been depleted. When Barber decided to go ahead and file for personal bankruptcy in July of 2009, Barber and Knight entered into a separate representation agreement. The agreement contemplated that Barber would pay the Knight Law Firm a total of $20,000 (a non-refundable fee of $19,701.00 plus $299.00 for a filing fee). It was "expressly understood" by the parties to the agreement that the $20,000 was paid only for work involved up to the first meeting of creditors and that, "in event [sic] Client desires for attorney to assist with any further representation (including, but not limited to, adversarial proceedings), then Client agrees to pay Attorneys their current hourly rate for such services." This $20,000 retainer was paid by others on Barber's behalf.

No party disputed that Barber was fighting numerous lawsuits at the time that Knight began his representation of Barber. Knight's initial detailed bill also shows that Knight was spending a lot of time on Barber's various legal issues. . . . Knight also stated that he would have to hire another associate, or possibly even partner with someone, if Barber was going to be fighting his various lawsuits for months.

The Court cannot find that either an hourly rate of $200 or a monthly rate of $17,000 was unreasonable under the circumstances. Despite the fact that the Government had numerous bank records at its disposal, no evidence was presented that Knight was transferring undue amounts of attorney's fees from his trust account to himself. Nor was any convincing evidence presented that Knight was otherwise receiving such sums of attorney's fees so as to legitimately raise an inference of an unlawful motive in his representation of Barber.

* * *

The evidence regarding Knight's mindset at the time the transfers were made was far from overwhelming in regard to whether he had any general intent to defraud in allowing Barber to pass money through his trust account. The circumstantial evidence relied on by the Government, as discussed above, analyzed either separately or as a whole, was not strong. There are arguably only two people that could have testified as to the purpose of Knight allowing Barber to use his trust account—Knight and Barber. No other witness had direct knowledge of what Knight knew or intended, and the documentary evidence presented required numerous inferential leaps to presume that Knight acted with fraudulent intent. Knight testified, as would be expected, that he did not intend to defraud Barber's bankruptcy creditors. Barber did not testify to rebut Knight's testimony. While the jury could legitimately have found that Knight's testimony was not credible, the burden remains on the government to produce proof beyond a reasonable doubt to satisfy each element of each offense. The evidence as to Knight's intent in allowing Barber to pass funds through his trust account preponderated sufficiently heavily against a verdict of guilty on Count 2, such that a miscarriage of justice may have occurred. Because a conviction based on aiding and abetting requires a finding of shared criminal intent of the principal, the Court likewise finds that a new trial should be granted on this alternative basis even if considering that Knight's conviction may have been based on a theory of aiding and abetting.

* * *

(Citations omitted.)

NOTES AND COMMENTS

1. The court notes that intent to defraud must often be proven via circumstantial evidence. What type of evidence would have sufficed for the government to meet its burden in this type of case?

2. How does the evidence of intent in this case differ from the evidence of intent to conspire and conceal assets in the *Arthur* case from the prior section?

3. Why do the bankruptcy crimes involve a fraudulent intent in addition to a knowing intent?

D. ATTENDANT CIRCUMSTANCES

Some criminal statutes also require that certain circumstances exist at the time of the actions of the defendant. In bankruptcy crimes, the initiation or existence of a bankruptcy case is always an element of the crime. While most bankruptcy crimes also require materiality, the following case provides an example of a bankruptcy crime that does not require materiality.

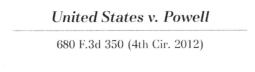

United States v. Powell

680 F.3d 350 (4th Cir. 2012)

FLOYD, Judge

* * *

On January 5, 2010, the grand jury indicted Powell on one count of a fifteen-count indictment for making, or aiding and abetting his co-defendant, Michael Pavlock, in making, a false entry in a bankruptcy-related document, in violation of 18 U.S.C. §§ 2, 1519. The indictment charged Pavlock with twelve counts of wire fraud and three counts of making, or aiding and abetting the making of, a false entry in a bankruptcy-related document.

The charges arose from a fraudulent scheme directed by Pavlock. Under this scheme, Pavlock established companies and maintained control over them by installing his associates as their nominal heads. He then convinced individuals to invest in the companies through loans that he represented would be repaid with interest. But these companies in fact had no legitimate business activity, and he misappropriated the invested funds for personal use. Relevant to the present appeal, Pavlock installed Powell as the managing member of one such company, Fayette Investment Acquisitions, LLC (FIA).

Golden Investment Acquisitions, LLC (GIA), although nominally owned and managed by Craig Golden, was also under Pavlock's control. On March 31, 2006, at Pavlock's direction, GIA signed a contract of sale to purchase the assets of a limousine service, including a number of limousines (the Gratz limousines), from Charles and Trudy Gratz for $175,000. But the Gratzes did not sign title to the limousines to GIA at that time.

Instead, in December 2006, Powell met with the Gratzes' accountant, Wallace McCarrell, in McCarrell's office in Washington, Pennsylvania. Powell represented that he had authority to receive the limousines on behalf of FIA. Without questioning Powell's authority or FIA's entitlement, McCarrell signed the titles of the limousines to FIA—not GIA—and delivered the vehicles to Powell. Although Charles Gratz was not present, McCarrell signed Mr. Gratz's name to the certificates of title and notarized the signatures. There is no evidence, however, that Powell or FIA paid for these vehicles at any time, and Golden later testified that GIA never transferred ownership to FIA.

By June 2007, GIA was severely over-leveraged, and Pavlock directed his associate, Stephen Graham, to put GIA into Chapter 11 bankruptcy. As a result, without Golden's knowledge or consent, Graham filed a Chapter 11 bankruptcy petition and schedules for GIA. Thomas Fluharty was appointed as GIA's bankruptcy trustee. GIA's bankruptcy schedules failed to reflect its acquisition or ownership of the Gratz limousines, so Fluharty initially was unaware that GIA had purchased the vehicles.

Pavlock then directed Powell to contact Fluharty to open negotiations for the purchase of GIA's assets by FIA. Fluharty ultimately agreed to the sale, but the deal fell through in May 2008 after several checks Powell sent to complete the purchase bounced. Powell and Fluharty did not discuss the Gratz limousines during these negotiations.

Fluharty first learned of the transaction involving the Gratz limousines when Charles Gratz's attorney contacted him in summer 2008. Fluharty then began to investigate whether the limousines were the subject of a fraudulent transfer. Thereafter, in a letter dated January 29, 2009, Powell wrote Fluharty regarding the Gratz limousines. . . . The letter contained two allegedly false statements. First, Powell claimed that Pavlock and Graham, through FIA and another of Pavlock's companies, "loaned over $500,000 to GIA to fund acquisitions including the Gratz Limousine Service." Second, he stated, "With the exception of . . . two Lincoln limousines, all of the physical assets of Mr. Gratz's limousine service[,] approximately twelve aged and nonserviceable limousines and other vehicles[,] were transferred to the ownership of [FIA] on December 12, 2006." These statements form the basis of the charge against him.

. . . At the close of evidence, Powell requested several jury instructions, three of which are relevant here. First, he asked that in instructing on the elements of an offense under 18 U.S.C. § 1519, the district court inform the jury that the government was required to prove the materiality of the false statement. Second, he sought an instruction on an advice-of-counsel defense. Finally, he asked the district judge to direct the jury that the statement in the January 29 letter regarding FIA's ownership of the Gratz limousines was true as a matter of law based on the signed, notarized certificates of title. The judge declined to give each instruction. The jury subsequently found Powell guilty of the charged offense.

* * *

Section 1519 of Title 18 of the United States Code establishes criminal penalties for any person who "knowingly . . . makes a false entry in any record, document, or tangible object with the intent to impede, obstruct, or influence the investigation or proper administration of . . . any case filed under title 11." 18 U.S.C. § 1519. Powell asserts that, to obtain a conviction under this provision, the government must prove that the false entry was material, meaning that it had "a natural tendency to influence, or [was] capable of influencing, the decision of the decisionmaking body to which it was addressed." [United States v. Wells, 519 U.S. 482, 489 (1997)]. Thus, he claims the district court erred in failing to instruct the jury that materiality was an element of the offense.

When interpreting a statutory provision, "we 'first and foremost strive to implement congressional intent by examining the plain language of the statute.'" . . .

A plain reading of the pertinent language of § 1519 requires the government to prove the following elements: (1) the defendant made a false entry in a record, document, or tangible object; (2) the defendant did so knowingly; and (3) the defendant intended to impede, obstruct, or influence the investigation or proper administration of a case filed under Title 11 (i.e., a bankruptcy action). *See* 18 U.S.C. § 1519. Because "[n]owhere does it further say that a material fact must be the subject of the false statement or so much as mention materiality," a "natural reading of the full text" demonstrates that "materiality would not be an element of" § 1519. *Wells,* 519 U.S. at 490 . . . (finding that materiality is not an element of an offense under 18 U.S.C. § 1014, which criminalizes knowingly making a false statement to a federally insured bank for the purpose of influencing a loan application).

Our interpretation accords with those of our sister circuits, which, when construing § 1519, have omitted a materiality requirement. . . .

Accordingly, we hold that the government need not prove the materiality of the falsification for an offense under 18 U.S.C. § 1519 and that the district court did not err in failing to instruct the jury on such an element.

* * *

Likewise, we find no abuse of discretion in the district court's refusal to instruct the jury that Powell's statement that FIA acquired ownership of the Gratz limousines was true as a matter of law. The parties agree that, because the title transfers occurred in Pennsylvania, Pennsylvania law controls the issue of ownership of the vehicles. Powell contends that, under this law, the signed certificates of title established that FIA became the vehicles' owner as reported in the January 29 letter.

Pennsylvania law provides:

> In the event of the sale or transfer of the ownership of a vehicle within this Commonwealth, the owner shall execute an assignment and warranty of title to the transferee in the space provided on the certificate or as the department prescribes, sworn to before a notary public ... and deliver the certificate to the transferee at the time of the delivery of the vehicle.

Pa. Cons. Stat. § 1111(a). Pennsylvania courts have clarified, however, that "a certificate of title is merely evidence of ownership . . . and is not conclusive." [*Wasilko v. Home Mut. Cas. Co.,* 210 Pa. Super. 322 (1967)].

As the district court explained in declining to provide the jury instruction and, more thoroughly, in denying Powell's motions for judgment of acquittal and for a new trial, there was sufficient evidence from which a reasonable jury could conclude that Powell obtained title to the limousines on behalf of FIA by fraud or theft by deception, so the titles did not, in fact, establish ownership. Specifically, the government submitted evidence that McCarrell, the Gratzes' accountant, signed title to FIA based on Powell's false representation that FIA was entitled to the vehicles. The jury could further infer that Powell knew FIA was not the owner of the limousines. Based on our review of the record and in light of the superior position of the district court to consider the evidence, we accept the district court's well-reasoned and considered analysis. . . .

* * *

For the foregoing reasons, the judgment of the district court is

AFFIRMED.

(Citations omitted.)

NOTES AND COMMENTS

1. Why does § 1519 apply absent a materiality determination, while other bankruptcy crimes require materiality (such as § 152(2))? How does § 1519 differ from perjury, which (at least in § 152(2)) requires materiality?

2. Besides materiality, what are the attendant circumstances elements we have seen in the other bankruptcy statutes?

E. CAUSATION

Some crimes require a specific consequence as one of the elements of the crime. This is called "causation." Just as in tort litigation, there are two causation requirements. The prosecution must show legal causation, sometimes referred to as "but-for causation." But-for causation means that but for the actions of the defendant, the harm that resulted would not have happened. The Michigan Supreme Court in People v. Zak, 457 N.W. 2d 59 (1990), made the distinction between the defendant creating a condition under which the harm occurred and the defendant actually causing the harm. It suggested that it would defy legal reasoning to blame a mother for the homicide of her child merely because she gave birth to the homicide victim and the victim could not have died had he not been born.

Legal causation is a cause that is a direct and substantial factor in bringing about the injury or harm required. The prosecutor must also prove that the defendant's actions were the proximate cause of the crime. In order for a defendant to be convicted of a crime requiring specific consequences, his or her actions must be the predominate cause without which the result would not have occurred. But even when the crime does not require that an act cause a specific consequence, there must be a causal link between the defendant's actions and the crime itself.

United States v. Heavrin

144 F. Supp. 2d 769 (W.D. Ky. 2001)

HEYBURN, Judge

Defendant, Donald M. Heavrin, an attorney, was charged in the Third Superceding Indictment with 14 separate criminal counts, all of which relate to an alleged scheme to defraud the bankrupt estate of Triple S Restaurants, Inc. ("TSR") of over $252,000 in life insurance proceeds and deceive the United States Bankruptcy Court. Heavrin admits that one purpose of his actions during the summer of 1994 was to obtain these proceeds for himself and his stepsister through his father's trust. The essential question of this case is whether the means he used to achieve this admitted goal amounts to a crime.

* * *

In 1988, Michael Macatee and Robert Harrod formed TSR, a Kentucky corporation. TSR operated Sizzler Restaurants. . . . Heavrin, Harrod's step-son, served as the attorney for TSR from its inception.

Shortly after Harrod and Macatee formed TSR, they sought financing from McDonnell Douglas Finance Corporation ("MDFC"). MDFC agreed to loan TSR approximately $3.5 million to obtain franchise rights to operate eight to ten additional Sizzler restaurants. As additional security for the loan, MDFC required TSR to purchase "key man" life insurance policies on Macatee and Harrod. TSR, Harrod, and Macatee were jointly and severally liable to MDFC on the loan.

Harrod's insurance was a single policy, originally issued by Trans America, but converted in 1991 to a $2 million policy issued by Jackson

National Life Insurance Company ("Jackson National"). . . . TSR was both the owner and beneficiary of the Harrod Policy. On November 21, 1991, Harrod and Macatee, on behalf of TSR, executed a collateral assignment to MDFC as security for its indebtedness to MDFC (the "Collateral Assignment"). The Collateral Assignment transferred to MDFC all rights, title, and interest in the Harrod Policy. Since the assignment was collateral and not general, TSR retained the rights to any policy proceeds remaining after satisfaction of the MDFC debt. However, until the debt was satisfied, MDFC had the exclusive right to collect the Harrod Policy proceeds. TSR, as the owner, retained the right to change the beneficiary. TSR's limited right did not affect MDFC's other rights under the Harrod Policy.

By the summer of 1992, TSR faced severe financial problems. Harrod thought that TSR might need to file for bankruptcy. Heavrin persuaded Harrod that such a course of action was premature. Heavrin then began to negotiate with creditors to restructure TSR's debts. Shortly thereafter, in September 1992, Harrod created the Robert Harrod Irrevocable Trust (the "Harrod Trust") and transferred his shares of TSR stock to the Harrod Trust. . . .

In late 1992, MDFC restructured its loan and reduced TSR's monthly payments. Despite this restructuring, TSR continued to experience significant financial problems. In late 1993, TSR stopped making the premium payments on both the Harrod and Macatee policies and MDFC took over the premium payments to prevent their lapse. About the same time, Harrod became increasingly upset with MDFC's treatment of TSR. Heavrin initiated discussions concerning various legal claims of TSR and Harrod against MDFC. In March 1994, Harrod was diagnosed with lung cancer and he immediately began treatment. Harrod renewed his insistence that Heavrin pursue Harrod's claims against MDFC for the benefit of Heavrin and his step-sister. Though Heavrin served as TSR's counsel, he also stood to gain personally from the settlement demands on behalf of Harrod individually.

On June 17, 1994, TSR transferred ownership of the Harrod Policy to the Harrod Trust. As company president, Macatee authorized the transfer on behalf of TSR. TSR also authorized a change in the beneficiary from TSR to the Harrod Trust. Heavrin recommended the transfer and prepared the legal documentation for the transaction. . . .

In June 1994, Heavrin continued to press his step-father's various legal claims against MDFC. Heavrin pursued these claims throughout the summer. By August 1994, MDFC had tentatively agreed that at Harrod's death, it would pay $250,000 to the Harrod Trust from the proceeds of the Harrod Policy. MDFC also agreed to release Harrod of all further individual liability to MDFC. . . .

In the midst of the negotiations, Robert Harrod died on September 2, 1994. Several weeks after Harrod's death, Bell Atlantic, a large judgment creditor, executed a lien on various TSR bank accounts, essentially stopping normal corporate operations. At this point, bankruptcy became almost unavoidable. . . .

On September 30, 1994, TSR filed a Chapter 11 petition in the United States Bankruptcy Court for the Western District of Kentucky. . . . The Chapter 11 petition and schedules neither listed nor otherwise disclosed the June 1994 transfer of the Harrod Policy from TSR to the Harrod Trust. . . .

During September and October, Heavrin continued to negotiate the final details settling Harrod's claims against MDFC. As a result of those negotiations, MDFC ultimately agreed to authorize a payment to the Harrod Trust from the Harrod Policy proceeds. . . . About the same time, MDFC filed a claim with the bankruptcy court, listing its secured claims without deducting or referring to any monies received from the Harrod Policy.

On December 13, 1994, the bankruptcy court converted the TSR bankruptcy from a Chapter 11 to a Chapter 7 proceeding. TSR filed a new Chapter 7 petition and additional schedules. Neither TSR nor Chinn [the bankruptcy attorney] listed the transfer of the Harrod Policy to MDFC on the new filings. Likewise, Heavrin said nothing about the receipt of $252,712.33 from the Harrod Policy. . . .

Sometime after 1995, Baxter Schilling, in his capacity as Trustee for the bankrupt estate of TSR, took a variety of legal actions against Heavrin to recover the MDFC insurance proceeds and to disgorge well over $100,000 of Heavrin's legal fees charged to TSR. . . . The Trustee charged Heavrin with all manner of Bankruptcy Code violations. . . .

On September 22, 1999, the grand jury returned a five-count indictment that charged Heavrin with transferring, concealing, and laundering money that should have been part of the bankrupt estate. On May 17, 2000, just over three weeks before the then scheduled trial date, the grand jury returned a superceding indictment that added counts of concealment, money laundering, perjury, and contempt. . . .

Count One of the Indictment charges Heavrin with knowingly and fraudulently transferring and concealing the Harrod Policy in violation of 18 U.S.C. § 2(b) and 18 U.S.C. § 152(7).

To convict Heavrin on Count One the government must present evidence from which a reasonable jury could find beyond a reasonable doubt that: (1) Heavrin transferred, willfully caused to be transferred, concealed, or willfully caused to be concealed property belonging to the estate of the debtor, TSR; (2) in transferring, willfully causing the transfer, concealing, or willfully causing the concealment of the policy Heavrin acted knowingly and fraudulently with the intent to defraud creditors or the bankruptcy court; and (3) Heavrin acted in contemplation of bankruptcy or with the intent to defeat the provisions of title 11. 18 U.S.C. § 2(b), 152(7). . . .

* * *

The government's primary theory is that transferring the Harrod Policy in June was part of Heavrin's plan ultimately calculated to deceive. . . .

The government's theory faces a stunning and insurmountable roadblock: the government admits that it presented no evidence whatsoever to suggest, let alone prove, that Heavrin facilitated, encouraged, or caused Chinn, Macatee, MDFC or anyone else to conceal the Harrod Policy transfer on the bankruptcy petition. Had Heavrin a hand in influencing the actions of Chinn, Macatee or MDFC, evidence of it might be readily available from several sources. The government's case fails, however, due not just to the absence of incriminating evidence, but also due to the presence of other evidence.

Chinn had an independent duty to perform due diligence and examine TSR's books. There is no evidence that Heavrin hid records of the Harrod Policy or its transfer. The government did not call Chinn to testify, leaving one only to speculate why he did not disclose the transfer. Macatee knew of and had no objection to the transfer, the negotiations between Heavrin and MDFC, and MDFC's payment to the Harrod Trust. He testified that in his view no legal transfer occurred in June because MDFC retained their absolute right to the Harrod Policy proceeds. Finally, no evidence connects Heavrin to MDFC's non-disclosure of the full transaction.

In the criminal context, proximate causation requires a close relationship between the defendant's act and the crime. As explained here, the Trustee and the bankruptcy court were ignorant of the Harrod life insurance proceeds only because three entities with probable independent duties to report the transactions—Chinn, Macatee and MDFC—each failed to do so. Without a closer causal connection tying Heavrin's actions to the actions or omissions of any one of these three entities one cannot conclude that Heavrin caused a fraudulent or deceptive act.

What seems to exist here is a facially plausible theory without actual evidence from which jurors could find an unlawful scheme beyond a reasonable doubt. Far too many intervening decisions, actions, omissions, and obligations of third parties prevent the June transfer from causing or showing the intent to cause the September concealment. The concealment itself is far too indirectly related to the transfer to support a reasonable finding of willful causation or intent to conceal. Under any reasonable definition of "cause or bring about," this proof fails. Without evidence of willful intent or causation, no reasonable jury could find beyond a reasonable doubt that Heavrin acted fraudulently in transferring property belonging to TSR.

* * *

(Citations omitted.)

NOTES AND COMMENTS

1. The court determines that causation is required to establish criminal liability. Given that the criminal statute (18 U.S.C. § 152(7)) does not discuss causation, where does this requirement come from? What type of causation is required—but-for or proximate (legal) causation?

2. If the bankruptcy attorney, Mr. Chinn, had testified that he asked Mr. Heavrin about other assets and Mr. Heavrin failed to disclose the existence of the insurance policies, would that suffice to establish criminal liability? If Mr. Chinn did not ask Mr. Heavrin about the policies, could Mr. Chinn face criminal liability?

F. PROOF OF THE CRIME

The American criminal justice system is called an "adversary system." The foundation of that system is that the burden of proof is always on the prosecution. The prosecution determines what offenses will be charged and prosecuted. Therefore, it is required to prove every element of the charged offenses beyond a reasonable doubt. The Supreme Court in In re Winship found that "[d]ue [p]rocess protects the accused against conviction except as upon proof beyond a reasonable doubt of every fact necessary to constitute the crime with which he is charged." The reasonable doubt standard, it found, "provides concrete substance for the presumption of innocence—that bedrock 'axomatic and elementary' principle whose 'enforcement lies at the foundation of the administration of criminal law.'"[3]

United States v. Naegele

537 F. Supp. 2d 36 (D.D.C. 2008)

FRIEDMAN, Judge

* * *

Defendant Timothy Naegele is an attorney licensed to practice law in California and in the District of Columbia. Naegele owns his own law firm as a sole proprietorship. On or about March 29, 2000, Naegele filed a Chapter 7 petition for personal bankruptcy in the United States Bankruptcy Court for the District of Columbia. On or about May 4, 2000, he filed with the Bankruptcy Court additional documents relating to his bankruptcy case.

On May 23, 2000, the bankruptcy trustee conducted a creditors' meeting pursuant to 11 U.S.C. § 341, at which Naegele was questioned under oath by the trustee and several creditors about the information provided in the documents filed with the Bankruptcy Court and about his financial situation in general. On September 5, 2000, the Bankruptcy Court granted Naegele a discharge from bankruptcy under 11 U.S.C. § 727. The bankruptcy case was closed on September 20, 2000.

On April 28, 2005, a grand jury returned an eleven-count indictment against Naegele, alleging that he had made numerous misstatements on his bankruptcy forms and in the creditors' meeting. He was charged in three counts with testifying falsely under oath at the creditors' meeting (18 U.S.C. § 152(2)), in seven counts with making false declarations or statements under penalty of perjury in documents he used in connection with his bankruptcy proceeding (18 U.S.C. § 152(3)), and in one count with bankruptcy fraud (18 U.S.C. § 157). Before trial, the Court dismissed Counts 1, 2, 3 and 7 of the indictment—all relating to alleged false statements made on the Statement of Financial Affairs filed in the Bankruptcy Court—and Count 9, relating to false testimony under oath at the creditors' meeting.

Naegele was tried before a jury on the remaining counts of the indictment—Counts 4, 5, 6, 8, 10 and 11—beginning on September 19,

3. 397 U.S. 358, 363 (1970) (quoting Coffin v. U.S., 156 U.S. 394, 453 (1895)).

2007. On October 17, 2007, the jury returned a verdict of not guilty on Counts 4, 6, 10 and 11 of the indictment, and reported that they were unable to reach a unanimous verdict with respect to Counts 5 and 8 of the indictment. On October 18, 2007, after further deliberation, the jury reported that they were still unable to reach a unanimous verdict on Counts 5 and 8 of the indictment. The Court declared a mistrial as to those counts.

The defense orally moved for judgment of acquittal on all counts. . . . For the reasons explained below, the Court will grant the motion and will order the entry of a judgment of acquittal on Counts 5 and 8 of the indictment.

. . . Rule 29(a) of the Federal Rules of Criminal Procedures provides that "[a]fter the government closes its evidence or after the close of all the evidence, the court on the defendant's motion must enter a judgment of acquittal of any offense for which the evidence is insufficient to sustain a conviction." Fed. R. Crim. P. 29(a). "If the jury has failed to return a verdict, the Court may enter a judgment of acquittal." Fed R. Crim. P. 29(c)(2).

In ruling on a motion for judgment of acquittal, the Court must "consider [] the evidence in the light most favorable to the government and determin[e] whether, so read, it is sufficient to permit a rational trier of fact to find all of the essential elements of the crime beyond a reasonable doubt." In so doing, the Court must "accord[] the government the benefit of all legitimate inferences." The question is whether the evidence is sufficient for a rational juror to have found the defendant guilty. Put another way, the Court may grant a motion for judgment of acquittal only when "a reasonable juror *must necessarily* have had a reasonable doubt as to the defendant['s] guilt." "If the evidence reasonably permits a verdict of acquittal or a verdict of guilt, the decision is for the jury to make."

. . . Count 5 of the indictment charges Naegele with making a material false statement in violation of 18 U.S.C. § 152(3), alleging that on his Bankruptcy Schedule B he stated "[t]hat he had no contingent claims of any nature when, in truth and in fact as he then well knew, he had contingency fee agreements with clients of his law practice."

Count 8 charges Naegele with making material false statements at the creditors' meeting in violation of 18 U.S.C. § 152(2), alleging that at the May 23, 2000 creditors' meeting, Naegele "[f]alsely testif[ied] under oath that he had listed all of his assets in his bankruptcy documents when, in truth and in fact as he then well knew, he had at least one asset that he had not listed, specifically, at least one contingent claim." The contingent claim to which this count related was a contingency fee arrangement Naegele had with his clients, Mr. and Mrs. Albers.

. . . As the defense exhaustively points out in its memorandum of law, however, the parties and the Court proceeded through extensive pretrial litigation and the trial itself on the basis that the false statement charged in Count 8 was the oral equivalent of the false statement charged in Count 5—namely, the exclusion from the disclosures Naegele made during his bankruptcy of the defendant's contingency fee agreement with his clients, Mr. and Mrs. Albers.

* * *

Defendant presents three arguments in his memorandum of law, one of which is that the evidence presented at trial was insufficient to sustain a jury verdict of guilty on Count 5 and on Count 8. That is the argument addressed by this Opinion. . . .

Schedule B requires a debtor to list his personal property. Line 20 of Schedule B requires a debtor to list "Other contingent and unliquidated claims of every nature, including tax refunds, counterclaims of the debtor, and rights to setoff claims." The instructions on Schedule B at the time that Naegele (with the assistance of his bankruptcy counsel, Jeffrey Sherman) completed it provided:

> Except as directed below, list all personal property of the debtor of whatever kind. If the debtor has no property in one or more of the categories, place an "X" in the appropriate position in the column labeled "None." If additional space is needed in any category, attach a separate sheet properly identified with the case name, case number, and the number of the category.... *Do not list interests in executory contracts and unexpired leases on this Schedule. List them in Schedule G—Executory Contracts and Unexpired Leases.* If the property is being held for the debtor by someone else, state that person's name and address under "Description and Location of Property."

Schedule B (emphasis provided).

In order to sustain a conviction on Count 5, the government has to have presented evidence sufficient for a reasonable jury to conclude beyond a reasonable doubt, among other things, that Naegele's answer on Line 20 of Schedule B—"None"—was false, and that instead he should have listed his contingency fee agreement with the Albers there. The defendant argues that "[o]n the threshold issue of falsity, the sole evidence that the government offered that the Albers' agreement should have been listed on Line 20 was Ms. [expert witness Tamara] Ogier's opinion that this is so." It is undisputed, as the defense notes, that Naegele's contingency fee agreement with the Albers was an executory contract, and that the instructions at the top of Schedule B instruct debtors not to list "interests in executory contracts" on Schedule B. Defendant argues that Ms. Ogier's opinion testimony is "flatly inconsistent with the instruction on Schedule B" and that, if that's all there is, "[n]o rational juror could find it sufficient to conclude ***beyond a reasonable doubt*** that Mr. Naegele's answer on Line 20 was false, much less knowingly so."

The government responds:

> [T]he defense continues to argue that, as a matter of law, the Albers' fee agreement is *only* an executory contract, that the analysis of the contingent portion of the fee agreement need go no further, and that, therefore, Naegele did not have to disclose as property his contingent claim for attorneys fees which that fee agreement represented. The United States again urges the Court to reject this flawed reasoning because it runs counter to the definition of property under the Bankruptcy Code and disregards the *property interest* that an attorney holds in the client's cause of action in a contingency fee case.

Opp. at 2 (emphasis added).

From the testimony and argument at trial, and again from the government's opposition brief, it became clear what the government's theory of falsity is. As Ms. Ogier testified, and as the government continues to maintain, while the Albers fee agreement was indeed an executory contract, Naegele had an interest—a personal property interest—in the executory contract and in the Albers' cause of action because he had a right to attorneys' fees, albeit a contingent right, if the Albers were successful in their lawsuit. The government argues that this interest is a contingent claim that is required to be disclosed on Line 20 of Schedule B because Schedule B requires the disclosure of "all personal property ... of whatever kind." The government fails in its brief to address the specific issue raised by the defense—that the instructions on Schedule B specifically instruct debtors not to list "interests in executory contracts"—whether they are property interests or some other kind of interest. The government presented evidence during its case-in-chief from Ms. Ogier that Naegele's interest in the Albers fee agreement was indeed an interest in an executory contract, but it never offered any evidence as to how a debtor could be convicted for failing to list an interest in an executory contract on Schedule B when the instructions specifically say not to.

Despite the government's argument to the contrary, the *only* evidence at trial that remotely supports its position is the testimony of Ms. Ogier. And what did she say? The government elicited testimony from Ms. Ogier during her direct examination that, in her opinion, "Mr. Naegele's right to receive fees in this case [of the Albers] should have been disclosed in Schedule B, Question 20." Ms. Ogier continued: "Once you filled out Schedule A and Schedule B, Schedule A is the previous schedule to the disclosed real property, like land, you should have disclosed everything you owned. Mr. Naegele had a right to receive money based on his representation of the Albers. It was contingent on them ultimately recovering something, so it was a contingent *interest,* which is exactly what Question 20 asks for." The basis for this opinion seemed to be that every asset of a debtor must be either real property or personal property, and so everything must be listed either on Schedule A or on Schedule B. But that premise—for which, a careful review of the transcript shows, Ogier had absolutely no basis other than her own unsupported statement—is inconsistent both with the instructions on Schedule B and the very existence of Schedule G. That can hardly be the basis for a criminal conviction.

On cross examination, Ms. Ogier testified that "[a]n attorney representing a client is [sic] an executory contract. His right to fees is a *property interest.*" Ms. Ogier then testified as follows:

Q: My question is, you've testified before that a fee agreement that has both an hourly as well as a contingency fee component to it is an executory contract; do you recall?
A: I don't recall exactly what I said, but I would agree with that with the addition that his right to fees is a property interest.
Q: Right. But-so we're in agreement that that is an executory contract in your view; is that right?
A: Yes.
Q: Okay. And what you've said is that his interest, that is to say, in the contingency portion, his interest should be disclosed on Schedule B; is that right?
A: His right to fees, yes.
Q: So his right to fees in the—arising out of the fee agreement; is that right?
A: Yes. His contract with the Albers.
Q: Right. And it's not just any contract, it's an executory contract, right?
A: Yes, but that doesn't mean the fee interest doesn't belong in Schedule B. It is an executory contract and he has a right to fees that should be disclosed to the trustee so the trustee can liquidate it for the benefit of creditors.
Q: I'm just trying to make sure I'm understanding your view. Which is that his interest in the executory contract should be disclosed on Schedule B?
A: Yes.

The defense then repeatedly asked Ms. Ogier to explain the basis for her opinion that this particular interest in an executory contract should be listed on Schedule B, Line 20, when the Schedule B instructions direct that interests in executory contracts *not* be listed on Schedule B. Ms. Ogier had no articulable explanation for her opinion that this was so. In fact, she testified that in her ten years of experience as a bankruptcy trustee in over 7500 bankruptcies, she had never seen a contingency fee agreement reported on Schedule B, and had never seen a government publication, court decision or treatise that states that a contingency fee agreement belongs on Schedule B. And there was absolutely no other evidence before the jury from which it could conclude that it was false not to include the interest in the contingency fee agreement on Line 20 of Schedule B.

Based on the evidence at trial, and giving the government the benefit of all legitimate inferences, the Court concludes that the evidence presented to the jury was insufficient to support a guilty verdict on Count 5, alleging that Naegele's answer to the question posed in Line 20 of Schedule B was false. Any reasonable juror necessarily must have had a reasonable doubt of the defendant's guilt on Count 5. . . .

(Citations omitted.)

NOTES AND COMMENTS

1. The standard for a jury to convict a defendant of a crime is "beyond a reasonable doubt." How is that standard worked into the standard for a judge to order acquittal of a defendant?

2. The debtor, Timothy Naegele, ended up suing his former clients who were the subject of the missing contingency fee agreement. Mr. Naegele alleged that the Albers failed to pay his fees for an appeal of their case to the Ninth Circuit Court of Appeals. The lawsuit was filed after Mr. Naegele filed his bankruptcy petition but before he was indicted for bankruptcy fraud. Ultimately, his claims were dismissed. Naegele v. Albers, 110 F. Supp. 3d 126 (D.D.C. 2015).

G. SENTENCING FOR THE CRIME

The purposes for sentencing can be roughly divided into utilitarian purposes and non-utilitarian purposes. A utilitarian theory of sentencing is the belief that the function of prosecution and sentencing is to reduce the risk of future crimes.[4] Deterrence and rehabilitation are considered utilitarian purposes for prosecution of crimes and sentencing convicted wrongdoers. Retribution is considered a non-utilitarian theory.

PURPOSES FOR SENTENCING

Deterrence (General and Specific)
Rehabilitative
Retributive

The deterrence theory of sentencing suggests that an individual will be less likely to commit a crime if he sees that others have been punished for that same or similar behavior (general deterrence). Specific deterrence, on the other hand, is based on the notion that the individual sentenced will be deterred from committing additional crimes because the individuals is either incarcerated or is dissuaded by the previous punishment meted out for his behavior.

Rehabilitation is also considered utilitarian. The theory is that punishment should serve as method of rehabilitating an individual so he "he is a better person and better citizen"[5] and therefore he will choose to not commit a crime in the future. The rehabilitative theory of sentencing is based on the belief that people can be reformed and move forward to become contributing members of society.

On the other hand, retribution is not based on a utilitarian theory. The purpose of sentencing under this theory is to punish the wrongdoer in proportion to the harm he committed. The purpose for retributive sentencing is to see that the convicted defendant "gets what he deserves."[6] Punishment is based on the idea of the defendant "paying back" for the wrong that was committed. Determining what is necessary to "repay society" is a combination of looking at the "wrongfulness of the act, the degree of harm caused and the mental state of the defendant at the time of the act."[7]

The courts have struggled with the right balance between utilitarian and non-utilitarian purposes of sentencing. Because bankruptcy crimes are

---

4. Ellen S. Podgor, Peter L. Henning, Andrew E. Taslitz, & Alfredo Garcia, *Criminal Law: Concepts and Practice* 4-5 (3d ed. Carolina Press 2013).
    5. *Id.*
    6. *Id.*
    7. *Id* at 6.

prosecuted by federal prosecutors, the U.S. Sentencing Guidelines apply. The U.S. Sentencing Guidelines were produced by the U.S. Sentencing Commission, a body that was under the judicial branch. It was created under the Sentencing Reform Act of 1984 (Act), as amended.[8] Originally, the guidelines were mandatory and required to be followed in all federal sentences. In United States v. Booker,[9] the Supreme Court found that the guidelines were merely guidelines and subject to appellate review. The guidelines utilize a matrix to calculate the sentence, using the criminal history of the defendant and the offense level as assigned by the commission, based on amount of the fraud and any harm to victims. After calculating the sentence by using the chart, the court can make adjustments based on mitigating and aggravating factors, including victim-related adjustments, role in the offense, obstruction and related adjustments, multiple counts, and acceptance of responsibility.[10] Courts continue to debate whether bankruptcy is a fraud offense or a perjury-related offense. The following case exemplifies why bankruptcy fraud does not fit squarely under a fraud case when no money is actually "lost."

United States v. Free

839 F.3d 308 (3d Cir. 2016)

FUENTES, Judge

This case raises the question of how to calculate "loss" under the Sentencing Guidelines when a defendant commits bankruptcy fraud but all of his creditors receive payment in full.

The defendant, Michael Free, made the bizarre decision to file for bankruptcy even though he had more than sufficient assets to pay his debts. He then, having filed for bankruptcy unnecessarily, hid assets worth hundreds of thousands of dollars from the Bankruptcy Court. Free's actions eventually led to criminal charges and convictions for multiple counts of bankruptcy fraud. The oddity of this entire situation is best summarized by the fact that, despite all of Free's prevarications, his creditors received 100 cents on the dollar from Free's bankruptcy estate.

The Sentencing Guidelines increase a fraudster's recommended sentence based on the amount of loss he causes, or intends to cause, to his victims. The District Court therefore had to decide whether Free caused or intended to cause any loss at all. Recognizing the

---

8. 18 U.S.C. § 3551 *et seq.* (1982 ed., Supp. IV), and 28 U.S.C. §§ 991-998 (1982 ed., Supp. IV).
9. 680 F.3d 350 (4th Cir. 2012)
10. United States Sentencing Commission, *Guidelines Manual*, §3E1.1 (Nov. 2016).

novelty of the situation, the District Court chose to treat the estimated value of the assets that Free concealed from the Bankruptcy Court and the amount of debt sought to be discharged as the relevant "loss" under the Guidelines. In doing so, the District Court did not clearly find whether Free intended to deprive his creditors of this, or of any, amount. While we appreciate the District Court's reasoning, we ultimately conclude that treating the value of Free's concealed assets as "loss," at least on the rationale articulated by the District Court, is out-of-step with the structure of the Guidelines and inconsistent with our own precedent. Instead, the District Court must determine whether Free intended to cause a loss to his creditors or what he sought to gain from committing the crime, per *United States v. Feldman*, 338 F.3d 212, 221–23 (3d Cir. 2003). . . . However, even if the District Court finds no such intended loss, this is not to say that Free would necessarily receive a lower sentence on remand. Free's repeated lying to the Bankruptcy Court and his manifest disrespect for the judicial system may well merit an upward departure or variance from the Guidelines. The District Court may consider whether such an upward departure is appropriate.

For the reasons that follow, we will vacate the judgment of the District Court and remand this case for resentencing.

. . . Free filed a voluntary bankruptcy petition in July of 2010 in his capacity as the sole proprietor of Electra Lighting & Electric Company, one of the businesses he owns. He also owns Freedom Firearms, a company that specializes in the sale of rare WWII-era guns. After Free fell behind on payments on two business-related properties, the lender purchased them in foreclosure, and Free purportedly filed for bankruptcy in an effort to "stay" the sale and "possibly to work out an agreement with" the lender.

Filing a bankruptcy petition requires a debtor to complete several forms. These include "Schedule A," which requires an accounting of the debtor's real estate assets, and "Schedule B," which requires an accounting of the debtor's personal property. A debtor certifies that both documents are correct under penalty of perjury. On Free's Schedule A, he disclosed over $1.3 million in real estate assets. On Free's Schedule B, he listed $368,990 worth of personal property, including 27 firearms collectively valued at $250,000. The District Court later concluded that, at the time he filed for bankruptcy, Free had liabilities of approximately $671,166, meaning that his disclosed assets exceeded his debts by several hundred thousand dollars.

Free initially filed for bankruptcy under Chapter 13 of the Bankruptcy Code. . . . The Bankruptcy Court later converted Free's proceeding into a Chapter 7 action, meaning that the focus shifted from "confirmation and completion of a reorganization plan" to "liquidation of assets and distribution to creditors.". . . The trustee in this case was James Walsh. . . .

. . . During Free's creditors' meeting, which took place in March of 2011, Free indicated that he was "trying to" sell weapons he owned by "put[ting] them on the internet." Walsh immediately told Free to stop. . . .

Over the course of the ensuing months, Free became increasingly uncooperative with Walsh and progressively more disrespectful towards the Bankruptcy Court. Less than a month after the creditors' meeting, Walsh asked the Bankruptcy Court to compel Free to turn over certain assets and to cease operation of his businesses, both of which Free had refused to do. On another occasion, Free raised suspicions by purchasing several of his own assets during a court-supervised auction, falsely claiming that he had the money to do so through the generosity of friends and relatives. In fact, Free actually made such purchases with the proceeds of his surreptitious sales of weapons, after he had specifically been told he could not sell his weapons. Free also refused to cooperate with Walsh's efforts to obtain paperwork that was necessary to sell the firearms that Free had disclosed in Schedule B of his bankruptcy petition.

Convinced that Free had concealed assets and violated court orders, Walsh filed a motion for sanctions in October of 2011. The Bankruptcy Court granted Walsh's motion in February of 2012, ordering Free to provide a full accounting of his assets or face monetary penalties. The Bankruptcy Court also threatened to incarcerate Free if he failed to comply. In doing so, it expressed its profound frustration with Free's conduct:

> [Free] has acted willfully, vexatiously, wantonly, and in bad faith. His inappropriate conduct has negatively impacted the entire bankruptcy case. . . . [He] has persisted in his willful misconduct despite the attempts of three bankruptcy judges to dissuade him from future misconduct. The failure to cooperate and comply while [Free] is facing sanctions for civil contempt is shocking to the Court.

Events finally came to a head a few weeks later when Walsh filed an emergency motion for civil contempt. Walsh claimed that Free had, in various ways, failed to comply with the Bankruptcy Court's February 2012 orders. In particular, Walsh said that he had recently been contacted by a man who had tried to purchase a WWII-era firearm from Free for a price of $13,500. The man told Walsh that

Free had sold other firearms since entering Chapter 7 proceedings. Walsh responded by asking the Bankruptcy Court to enter an order directing a third-party auction company "to take physical possession of [Free's guns] as soon as possible."

The Bankruptcy Court convened a hearing on the matter, after which it entered an order directing the local sheriff "to take possession of all of [Free's] firearms." A few days later, on March 26, 2012, Free filed a declaration with the Bankruptcy Court in which he claimed, again under penalty of perjury, that he had not "sold or transferred" any estate assets—including firearms—since his bankruptcy case was converted into a Chapter 7 proceeding. By the time Free filed his declaration, the government claims that he had sold at least 20 firearms worth more than $400,000.

Local sheriff's deputies, acting on the Bankruptcy Court's order, searched Free's house on March 27, 2012—the day after Free filed his declaration with the Bankruptcy Court. They found 49 guns in various locations throughout the home. When they questioned Free, he said he had no additional firearms in his possession. Later that afternoon, Free filed a revised declaration with the Bankruptcy Court that included a handwritten list of dozens of firearms, along with a copy of the Schedule B from his original bankruptcy petition. Because Free did not list any serial numbers in these two documents, Walsh was unable to determine the degree of overlap between the two lists.

The depth of Free's fraud on the Bankruptcy Court became increasingly apparent in the ensuing months. In April of 2012, Walsh filed a status report in which he informed the Bankruptcy Court that Free "ha[d] received at least $90,000.00 in funds from third parties whom he offered to sell firearms which constitute property of the estate during the pendency of this Chapter 7 proceeding." The day after Walsh filed his status report, the Bankruptcy Court ordered the United States Marshal to take Free into custody until such time as he paid over $26,000 in fines and rent then owing to the Bankruptcy Court and to the estate.

It was around this time that the FBI became involved. Having reviewed certain firearms registration records, FBI agents came to believe that Free was continuing to conceal firearms from the Bankruptcy Court. The FBI obtained a warrant to search Free's residence a second time. During that search, which took place in March of 2013, federal agents discovered an additional 55 firearms.

. . . Federal prosecutors eventually initiated a criminal case against Free for committing bankruptcy fraud. The grand jury returned an indictment in January of 2014 that charged Free with six counts relating to (i) false statements in Free's Schedule A relating to real property; (ii) false statements in Free's Schedule B relating to his ownership of firearms; (iii) false statements in Free's declaration of March 26, 2012; (iv) false statements in Free's supplemental declaration of March 27, 2012; (v) concealment of additional assets from the Bankruptcy Court, including real property, motor vehicles, farm implements, and cash; and (vi) false statements that Free made under oath at the March 2011 creditors' meeting.

Counts I through IV arose under 18 U.S.C. § 157, which outlaws various forms of bankruptcy fraud. Counts V and VI arose under 18 U.S.C. § 152, which makes it a crime to conceal assets or to commit perjury in the context of a bankruptcy proceeding. Both statutes set a maximum term of imprisonment of five years for each violation.

After a five-day trial, a jury convicted Free on all counts.

. . . Under the Sentencing Guidelines, a bankruptcy fraudster's recommended term of imprisonment depends on a number of factors. "Section 2B1.1 of the Guidelines governs the calculation of the offense level for crimes involving, among other things, fraud and deceit." Subsection (a) of that provision "provides the base offense level, which is either seven, if the offense has a maximum term of imprisonment of twenty years or more, or six." Subsection (b) "provides an extensive list of adjustments for offense-specific characteristics," including "the adjustment for the amount of loss." As the loss amount increases, so too does the defendant's offense level.

At Free's sentencing hearing, the District Court therefore needed to make a determination as to the amount of loss caused by Free's crimes. The issue here is that, by the time of Free's sentencing, it had become clear that Free had (and perhaps always had) sufficient assets to pay off his creditors in full. Given this odd factual posture, the parties disputed the correct loss amount under the Guidelines.

The government argued that the District Court should take at least three numbers into account to calculate loss, all relating to the value of Free's concealed guns. First, it identified fifteen firearms, valued at $357,460, that Free unlawfully sold during the pendency of his bankruptcy proceedings. Second, it pointed to the fact that, at an auction supervised by the Bankruptcy Court, ten additional guns concealed by Free were sold for $640,000 (although, by the date of the sentencing hearing, that sale had not yet been finalized). Third, it asked the District Court to consider an additional cache of guns that had not yet been sold at auction and remained in the

FBI's possession. Based on an appraisal from the same buyer who purchased the second lot of guns, the government estimated the value of the unsold lot at $833,000. Altogether, these figures indicated that Free concealed firearms worth approximately $1.83 million from the Bankruptcy Court.

* * *

. . . the government argued that Free should have 16 levels added to his offense level. It derived this figure from the Sentencing Guidelines' stepwise scheme for calculating loss. . . . If the fraudster's conduct causes over $1 million but less than $2.5 million in loss, the Guidelines add 16 levels to his offense level. . . .

Free's position, by contrast, was that he "should only be held accountable for a loss amount that's consistent with what he could have deprived creditors of receiving back during the bankruptcy." Since all of Free's creditors were paid back in full, Free asserted that the loss amount in his case was, in fact, $0.

In a colloquy with Free's counsel, the District Court challenged Free's arguments in favor of a $0 loss calculation. It pointed out that courts rely on honesty from litigants:

> But then, as I thought about it, read Feldman, one of the things that we rely on people doing is, when they come to Court, whether it's this Court or the Bankruptcy, particularly, the Bankruptcy Court, they have to deal the cards faced up, because we don't have a cavalry of investigators to go out snooping around everyone that runs through the tens of thousands of bankruptcy cases just filed here in Pittsburgh, let alone around the country. We absolutely rely on people telling the truth because we can't ferret it out any other way.

In addition, the District Court expressed the view that, under the Guidelines, there is a difference between a debtor who conceals $100 in assets and a debtor who conceals $1 million in assets. . . .

* * *

The District Court . . . concluded that "it was certainly Mr. Free's intention to conceal from the United States Bankruptcy Court and to cause a loss, to the extent that it was needed, materially in excess of a million dollars." The District Court did *not*, however, explicitly state that Free intended to cause pecuniary harm to his creditors. . . .

* * *

Somewhat curiously, even though the District Court concluded that the loss amount in Free's case was more than $1 million, it only added 14 levels to Free's base offense level of 6. That 14-level enhancement is consistent with a loss amount of between of between $400,000 and $1 million, whereas a loss amount greater than $1 million normally triggers a 16-level enhancement. The discrepancy appears to have arisen because the Presentence Investigation Report only recommended a 14-level enhancement, and the District Court tentatively adopted that recommendation before Free's sentencing hearing and then adhered to its prior decision at the hearing itself.

In addition to the 14-level enhancement resulting from the District Court's loss calculation, the Guidelines state that "[i]f the offense involved . . . a misrepresentation or other fraudulent action during the course of a bankruptcy proceeding," or "a violation of any prior, specific judicial or administrative order," the district court should "increase [the offense level] by 2 levels." The District Court applied this 2-level enhancement as well.

Combining Free's base offense level of 6, his loss causation enhancement of 14, and his 2-level enhancement for bankruptcy fraud, Free's total offense level was 22. This resulted in a Guidelines Range of 41–51 months' imprisonment on each count. The District Court then varied downward, concluding that an offense level of 16 was "more appropriate" given the facts of Free's case. This led to a Guidelines range of 21–27 months' imprisonment. The District Court ultimately sentenced Free to 24 months' incarceration on each count, to run concurrently, and to a term of supervised release of three years.

* * *

There are essentially two ways to think about loss in this case. Under one view, the goal of the Sentencing Guidelines is to calibrate a fraudster's punishment so that it reflects the extent of the economic harm inflicted or intended to be inflicted on the fraudster's victims. This is Free's position. Free argues that there were no victims here because Free's creditors received 100 cents on the dollar in Free's bankruptcy proceeding.

Under the alternative view proffered by the government, the Guidelines provide district courts with broad discretion to conceptualize the harm caused by a defendant based on the facts of any particular case. In the context of bankruptcy fraud, then, it is appropriate to think about harm in terms of the value of any assets that a debtor conceals from the bankruptcy court—not only because concealing assets can harm creditors, but also because it harms the integrity of the judicial system itself. The District Court ultimately embraced this view.

We begin with the Sentencing Guidelines themselves, which we think favor Free's argument. The application notes define the following key terms:

- **Actual loss:** "Actual loss" means the reasonably foreseeable pecuniary harm that resulted from the offense.

- **Intended Loss:** "Intended loss" (I) means the pecuniary harm that was intended to result from the offense; and (II) includes intended pecuniary harm that would have been impossible or unlikely to occur (*e.g.*, as in a government sting operation, or an insurance fraud in which the claim exceeded the insured value).

- **Pecuniary harm:** "Pecuniary harm" means harm that is monetary or that otherwise is readily measurable in money. Accordingly, pecuniary harm does not include emotional distress, harm to reputation, or other non-economic harm.

In our view, the application notes to § 2B1.1, which discuss these definitions in further detail, suggest that the District Court's rationale for Free's sentence was inconsistent with the structure of the Guidelines. The notes focus extensively on *pecuniary* harm, explicitly stating that the proper way to punish a defendant who causes *non-pecuniary* but otherwise serious harm is to impose an upward departure. This guidance implies that the gravamen of any loss calculation is concrete, monetary harm to a real-world victim. In other words, while it may indeed be appropriate to punish a bankruptcy fraudster more severely when that person conceals assets of greater value, the Guidelines seem to indicate that, in the absence of any pecuniary harm to a victim, the mechanism for realizing that goal is an upward departure rather than a more severe loss calculation in the first instance.

Our Court's leading case regarding loss calculation and bankruptcy fraud is *United States v. Feldman*. The defendant there, like Free, committed fraud on the bankruptcy court by concealing large quantities of assets. His main argument on appeal, like Free's, focused on the lack of any concrete harm or intended pecuniary harm to his creditors. . . .

The *Feldman* Court began its analysis by observing that loss calculations under the Guidelines can turn on either actual loss or intended loss. Thus, "even if Feldman could not have caused any loss by concealing exempt assets, he could still be subject to a sentencing enhancement if he *thought* he would cause a loss by concealing the assets." The government, by contrast, urged the *Feldman* Court to go even further by adopting "a bright line rule that '[i]ntended loss includes the value of assets concealed from creditors and the bankruptcy court.'" We declined to do so, stating that the key question in these cases is not the value of the assets concealed, but rather "what [a defendant] sought to gain from committing the crime."

* * *

Importantly, however, we did not say in *Feldman* that the concealment of large quantities of assets *always* proves a fraudster's intent to short-change his creditors. Instead, we emphasized that there were other facts tending to show that Feldman *in particular* intended to inflict such a loss. We emphasized that, in addition to the real estate he owned with his wife, Feldman concealed two Jaguar vehicles "that were not even arguably exempt from bankruptcy." In our view, this conduct supported the conclusion "that Feldman intended to inflict a loss in the amount of the entire debt from which he sought to be discharged."

* * *

The District Court, however, seemed to select a different approach and thus did not make a factual finding regarding the government's view. The government, both in its briefing and at oral argument, argues that the District Court drew the explicit inference that Free intended to cause *pecuniary harm* to his creditors, among other victims. Reviewing the record on appeal, we simply disagree. The District Court relied primarily on the notion that Free harmed the judicial system by concealing assets. We believe that rationale is inconsistent with the Guidelines and incompatible with *Feldman*. Thus, we disagree with the District Court's view that the concept of "loss" under the Guidelines is broad enough to cover injuries like abstract harm to the judiciary. In our view, "loss" has a narrower meaning—i.e., pecuniary harm suffered by or intended to be suffered by victims.

* * *

It is true that the District Court stated at Free's sentencing hearing "that it was certainly Mr. Free's intention to conceal from the United States Bankruptcy Court and to cause a loss, to the extent that it was needed, materially in excess of a million dollars." However, the District Court also stated, somewhat cryptically, that "Free had his reasons for both filing and persisting in the bankruptcy proceeding, [and] that Mr. Free had his reasons that were of value to him in not causing any of his lawyers to attempt to resolve the matter earlier."

In our view, this is something short of an explicit factual finding that Free intended to harm his creditors by concealing assets. It is, at most, a finding that Free wanted to protect certain assets—especially his firearms—from the bankruptcy process.... Any ambiguity on this point is clarified by the District Court's opinion regarding Free's motion for bail pending appeal. The District Court there said that "the *principal basis* for the sentence [it] imposed" was "harm [] [to] the integrity of the judicial process"—not pecuniary harm, actual or intended, to Free's creditors, or what he sought to gain from committing the crime. *Feldman* requires such a factual finding, and we thus remand to allow the District Court to determine what, if any, loss to creditors Free intended, or the gain he sought by committing the crime.

* * *

(Citations omitted.)

NOTES AND COMMENTS

1. The Federal Sentencing Guidelines apply to various types of cases under federal law. How does the court consider the policies of the Bankruptcy Code versus the policies of the Sentencing Guidelines in reaching its conclusion?

2. On remand, what must the government show to establish a case for an increase in Free's sentence? How might Free respond?

3. As the court noted, the Sentencing Guidelines also provide mitigating factors for reduction of a sentence. In the United States v. Powell case discussed earlier in this chapter, the defendant argued for mitigation on the basis that his part in the fraudulent scheme "makes him substantially less culpable" under Sentencing Guideline 3B1.2:

> Powell urges that the evidence plainly demonstrates that he was minimally culpable in Pavlock's fraudulent scheme. We have declared, however, that the "critical inquiry" for a sentencing court, in considering a § 3B1.2 adjustment, is "not just whether the defendant has done fewer 'bad acts' than his codefendants, but whether the defendant's conduct is material or essential to committing the offense." . . . That is, the sentencing court must measure the defendant's "individual acts and relative culpability against the elements of the offense of conviction," not merely against the criminal enterprise as a whole. . . .
>
> Regardless of whether Powell may have played only a small role in Pavlock's overall scheme, the district court could reasonably find that as

to the offense of conviction—making a false entry in a bankruptcy-related document—his conduct was essential and material. The jury found Powell signed the January 29 letter and submitted it to Fluharty with knowledge that it contained at least one false statement and with intent to obstruct, impede, or influence the bankruptcy. Thus, the district court did not clearly err in rejecting this adjustment.

Powell, 680 F.3d at 358.

H. BANKRUPTCY IN PRACTICE

A few weeks before Diana's discharge hearing, the trustee received a call from Diana's ex-husband. During the call, the ex-husband related to the trustee that while he and Diana were married, Diana inherited a large sum of money from her aunt as well as a property in the Florida Keys. According to the husband, the money was invested in a start-up venture, and Diana continued to use the property—vacationing there with her children as recently as six months before the bankruptcy filing. Upon further investigation, the trustee found that the start-up venture had itself gone bankrupt three years before Diana filed for bankruptcy protection, paying only a fraction of Diana's investment to her in the process. Diana sold the Key West property to her brother, Charlie, one year before the bankruptcy filing; Charlie had allowed her to continue to vacation there on occasion. Diana's ex-husband also mentioned that Diana continues to refer to the Key West property as "her vacation home," and their children mentioned to him that Diana said "it's our home, but right now, Uncle Charlie is holding onto it for us."

When the trustee spoke with Diana's attorney about the money and the property, the attorney offered the following explanations:

- Diana put the money distributed in the start-up venture's bankruptcy into her checking account and spent it before she filed her own bankruptcy case. Her checking account was used to buy the types of things that people buy—groceries, trips, furniture, house payments, and so on.
- Diana sold the property to her brother at a discounted price (40 percent of market value) because she needed to sell the property quickly in order to pay off some of her debts, and because she wanted it to remain in the family. She has no legal or equitable interest in it at this time.

Consider whether any bankruptcy crimes might have occurred and what types of evidence might be necessary to establish those crimes.

10

Probate Law and Bankruptcy: The Probate Exception, Inheritances, and Trusts

Death is a debt we all must pay.[1]

Probate is a process where a decedent's property that does not otherwise pass outside of probate is distributed according to the terms of the decedent's testamentary documents or in cases without a will, per the terms of the intestacy statute. *Black's Law Dictionary* defines probate as "[t]o admit (a will) to proof . . .[t]o administer (a decedent's estate)." (Bryan Garner ed., Westlaw 11th ed. 2019).

The property that makes up the probate estate depends on how the property is titled because some property will pass outside of probate, such as, for example, property titled jointly with the right of survivorship. The property that does not pass outside of probate thus makes up the probate estate. A "probate estate" means the "decedent's property [that is] subject to administration by a personal representative. . . . The probate estate comprises property owned by the decedent at the time of death and property acquired by the decedent's estate at or after the time of death. . . ." *Black's Law Dictionary* (Bryan Garner ed., Westlaw 11th ed. 2019).

How does a probate matter show up in a bankruptcy proceeding? While you might initially think of the debtor dying after filing for bankruptcy

---

1. Euripedes, http://www.finestquotes.com/author_quotes-author-Euripides-page-0.htm.

protection, often probate arises because the beneficiary of a probate estate is a debtor filing for bankruptcy.

RECALL DIANA DETTER

While Diana is working through her bankruptcy, she will face issues that are not necessarily bankruptcy related. Consider what might happen if Diana's mother dies during the time of Diana's bankruptcy. What happens with the inheritance that Diana receives after her mother's death? What if her mother set up a trust for Diana, or Diana is entitled to the proceeds of a life insurance policy? Should Diana have to use those funds to pay creditors in her bankruptcy case, or should Diana be able to keep those funds?

A. THE PROBATE EXCEPTION TO JURISDICTION

The first inquiry regarding the intersection of probate and bankruptcy is jurisdiction. 28 U.S.C. §157(b)(1) provides that "Bankruptcy judges may hear and determine all cases under title 11 and all core proceedings arising under title 11, or arising in a case under title 11, referred under subsection (a) of this section, and may enter appropriate orders and judgments, subject to review under section 158 of this title." When dealing with probate matters, there is something known as the probate exception to the district court's—and thus the bankruptcy court's—jurisdiction. The primary case on the probate exception is Markham v. Allen, 326 U.S. 490 (1946).

Markham v. Allen

326 U.S. 490 (1946)

STONE, Chief Justice

* * *

It is true that a federal court has no jurisdiction to probate a will or administer an estate, the reason being that the equity jurisdiction conferred by the Judiciary Act of 1789, 1 Stat. 73, and §24(1) of the

Judicial Code, which is that of the English Court of Chancery in 1789, did not extend to probate matters. But it has been established by a long series of decisions of this Court that federal courts of equity have jurisdiction to entertain suits 'in favor of creditors, legatees and heirs' and other claimants against a decedent's estate 'to establish their claims' so long as the federal court does not interfere with the probate proceedings or assume general jurisdiction of the probate or control of the property in the custody of the state court.

Similarly while a federal court may not exercise its jurisdiction to disturb or affect the possession of property in the custody of a state court, it may exercise its jurisdiction to adjudicate rights in such property where the final judgment does not undertake to interfere with the state court's possession save to the extent that the state court is bound by the judgment to recognize the right adjudicated by the federal court.

Although in this case petitioner sought a judgment in the district court ordering defendant executor to pay over the entire net estate to the petitioner upon an allowance of the executor's final account, the judgment declared only that petitioner 'is entitled to receive the net estate of the late Alvina Wagner in distribution, after the payment of expenses of administration, debts, and taxes. The effect of the judgment was to leave undisturbed the orderly administration of decedent's estate in the state probate court and to decree petitioner's right in the property to be distributed after its administration. This, as our authorities demonstrate, is not an exercise of probate jurisdiction or an interference with property in the possession or custody of a state court.

* * *

The judgment is reversed and the cause remanded to the Circuit Court of Appeals for further proceedings in conformity to this opinion.

* * *

(Citations omitted.)

Probably the most famous case recently involving the probate exception is Marshall v. Marshall, 547 U.S. 293 (2006), where the Court considered the breadth of the exception. It was the first of two Supreme Court decisions involving the estate of J. Howard Marshall. In Chapter 2 you read the second decision, Stern v. Marshall, in considering the jurisdiction of

Article I courts. The lower court in *Marshall* set the stage in discussing the origins of the probate exception in Marshall v. Marshall, 264 B.R. 609 (C.D. Calif. 2001):

> It is commonly understood that the "probate exception" bars federal courts from probating a will. While at first glance this proposition may seem unremarkable, both the origin and scope of the exception are not entirely clear. As the Seventh Circuit has noted, "The probate exception is one of the most mysterious and esoteric branches of the law of federal jurisdiction." In particular, the origins of the exception are rather murky. A historical explanation, involving the exclusive jurisdiction of the ecclesiastical courts in England at the time the Judiciary Act of 1789 was passed, is frequently proffered. However, there are potential problems with this explanation. Further, the historical explanation does not offer a compelling reason or rationale for why the exception should be continued today.
>
> Other possible explanations include the idea that probating a will is not a "case or controversy" within the meaning of Article III, or that the Tenth Amendment reserves probate matters to the states. These rationales may be more satisfying than the historical explanation as justifications for the probate exception today. However, the Supreme Court has never formally adopted one of these rationales. Also, these rationales conflict with authority that states that the doctrine is "judicially created." If the doctrine stems from the Constitution itself, it is not judicially created.
>
> It is also possible that while not being constitutionally compelled, the doctrine is a result of the principles of comity attendant to our federal system.

Id. at 619-620.

Now consider this excerpt from the first *Marshall* case, in which the Supreme Court discusses the probate exception.

Marshall v. Marshall

547 U.S. 293 (2006)

GINSBURG, Justice

In Cohens v. Virginia, Chief Justice Marshall famously cautioned: "It is most true that this Court will not take jurisdiction if it should not: but it is equally true, that it must take jurisdiction if it should. . . . We have no more right to decline the exercise of jurisdiction which is given, than to usurp that which is not given." Among longstanding limitations on federal jurisdiction otherwise properly exercised are the so-called "domestic relations" and "probate" exceptions. Neither is compelled by the text of the Constitution or federal statute. Both are judicially created doctrines stemming in large measure from misty understandings of English legal history. In the years following

Marshall's 1821 pronouncement, courts have sometimes lost sight of his admonition and have rendered decisions expansively interpreting the two exceptions. In Ankenbrandt v. Richards, this Court reined in the "domestic relations exception." Earlier, in Markham v. Allen, the Court endeavored similarly to curtail the "probate exception."

Nevertheless, the Ninth Circuit in the instant case read the probate exception broadly to exclude from the federal courts' adjudicatory authority "not only direct challenges to a will or trust, but also questions which would ordinarily be decided by a probate court in determining the validity of the decedent's estate planning instrument." The Court of Appeals further held that a State's vesting of exclusive jurisdiction over probate matters in a special court strips federal courts of jurisdiction to entertain any "probate related matter," including claims respecting "tax liability, debt, gift, [or] tort." We hold that the Ninth Circuit had no warrant from Congress, or from decisions of this Court, for its sweeping extension of the probate exception.

* * *

[I]n the Texas Probate Court, [E. Pierce Marshall ("Pierce"), the decedent's son,] sought a declaration that the living trust and his father's will were valid. [Vickie Lynn Marshall ("Vickie"), the widow and Pierce's step-mother], in turn, challenged the validity of the will and filed a tortious interference claim against Pierce, but voluntarily dismissed both claims once the Bankruptcy Court entered its judgment. Following a jury trial, the Probate Court declared the living trust and J. Howard's will valid.

Back in the federal forum, Pierce sought district-court review of the Bankruptcy Court's judgment. While rejecting the Bankruptcy Court's determination that Pierce had forfeited any argument based on the probate exception, the District Court held that the exception did not reach Vickie's claim. The Bankruptcy Court "did not assert jurisdiction generally over the probate proceedings . . . or take control over [the] estate's assets," the District Court observed, "[t]hus, the probate exception would bar federal jurisdiction over Vickie's counterclaim only if such jurisdiction would 'interfere' with the probate proceedings". Federal jurisdiction would not "interfere" with the probate proceedings, the District Court concluded, because: (1) success on Vickie's counterclaim did not necessitate any declaration that J. Howard's will was invalid, and (2) under Texas law, probate courts do not have exclusive jurisdiction to entertain claims of the kind asserted in Vickie's counterclaim.

* * *

Federal jurisdiction in this case is premised on 28 U.S.C. § 1334, the statute vesting in federal district courts jurisdiction in bankruptcy cases and related proceedings. Decisions of this Court have recognized a "probate exception," kin to the domestic relations exception, to otherwise proper federal jurisdiction. Like the domestic relations exception, the probate exception has been linked to language contained in the Judiciary Act of 1789.

* * *

. . . Thus, the probate exception reserves to state probate courts the probate or annulment of a will and the administration of a decedent's estate; it also precludes federal courts from endeavoring to dispose of property that is in the custody of a state probate court. But it does not bar federal courts from adjudicating matters outside those confines and otherwise within federal jurisdiction.

. . . As the Court of Appeals correctly observed, Vickie's claim does not "involve the administration of an estate, the probate of a will, or any other purely probate matter." Provoked by Pierce's claim in the bankruptcy proceedings, Vickie's claim . . . alleges a widely recognized tort. Vickie seeks an in personam judgment against Pierce, not the probate or annulment of a will. Nor does she seek to reach a res in the custody of a state court.

Furthermore, no "sound policy considerations" militate in favor of extending the probate exception to cover the case at hand. Trial courts, both federal and state, often address conduct of the kind Vickie alleges. State probate courts possess no "special proficiency . . . in handling [such] issues."

* * *

For the reasons stated, the judgment of the Court of Appeals for the Ninth Circuit is reversed, and the case is remanded for further proceedings consistent with this opinion.

It is so ordered.

* * *

(Citations omitted.)

NOTES AND COMMENTS

1. Thinking back to the later Supreme Court case of Stern v. Marshall, how do the two cases fit together? *Stern* held that bankruptcy courts do not have jurisdiction to hear traditionally state-law claims even if they are deemed "core" proceedings under 28 U.S.C. § 157, but *Marshall* allows the district court to decide on Vickie Lynn Marshall's tort claim.

2. Can you list the circumstances when the probate exception applies according to the *Marshall* Court? The court in In re: Robin Horvath, 572 B.R. 864 (Bankruptcy N.D. Ohio 2017) noted the application of the probate exception in the Sixth Circuit:

   Since *Marshall*, the Sixth Circuit has stated that "the probate exception is narrowly limited to three circumstances: (1) if the plaintiff 'seek[s] to probate . . . a will'; (2) if the plaintiff 'seek[s] to . . . annul a will'; and (3) if the plaintiff 'seek[s] to reach the *res* over which the state court had custody.'" *Chevalier v. Estate of Barnhart*, 803 F.3d 789, 801 (6th Cir. 2015) (citing *Lee Graham Shopping Ctr., LLC v. Estate of Kirsch*, 777 F.3d 678, 681 (4th Cir.2015) ("[The probate exception] applies only if a case actually requires a federal court to perform one of the acts specifically enumerated in *Marshall*: to probate a will, to annul a will, to administer a decedent's estate; or to dispose of property in the custody of a state probate court. A case does not fall under the probate exception if it merely impacts a state court's performance of one of these tasks.")).

Id. at 871.

Sometimes the debtor is a defendant in a state-court proceeding and then files a petition for bankruptcy. If the debtor asserts a counterclaim in an adversary proceeding that was not asserted in state court, the bankruptcy court has to decide whether to allow the claim to proceed in bankruptcy.

Capuccio v. Capuccio

558 B.R. 461 (Bankr. W.D. Okla. 2016)

LOYD, Bankruptcy Judge

. . . This adversary proceeding arises from a family dispute regarding management of the estate of an incapacitated woman, Anna Marie Capuccio ("Mother"). The plaintiff is Anthony Capuccio (the "Plaintiff") who is the son of Mother, and her current court-appointed guardian. The Defendant is Elena Marie Capuccio (the "Debtor"), the debtor in the underlying bankruptcy case. . . .

[A dispute between the brother (Plaintiff) and sister [debtor] ultimately led to the plaintiff filing a court action to be appointed as mother's guardian, with debtor's consent. As guardian, plaintiff filed suit against debtor who was mother's agent under power of attorney for stealing mother's assets. After filing an answer, debtor filed for bankruptcy.]

* * *

Plaintiff filed this adversary proceeding seeking to bar Debtor's discharge as to the approximately $300,000.00 based upon fraud under § 523(a)(2) and defalcation in a fiduciary relationship under § 523(a)(4). . . . Debtor filed her Answer and Counterclaim in which she essentially denied all the material allegations of the Plaintiff's Complaint.

* * *

Plaintiff argues this Court lacks jurisdiction to entertain the Debtor's Counterclaim because Oklahoma state statutes pertaining to guardianship grant exclusive jurisdiction to the court in which the guardianship petition is filed. A reading of those statutes makes clear that such jurisdiction is exclusive as to specific matters such as (1) "the need for a guardian or other order and (2) how the estate of the ward shall be managed, expended or distributed to or for the use of the ward or the dependents of the ward". Similarly, the other statute upon which Plaintiff relies provides, in pertinent part, that "in all cases the court making the appointment of a guardian has exclusive jurisdiction to control such guardian in the management and disposition of the person and property of the ward". It is clear that this Court's exercise of jurisdiction over the Counterclaim against the guardianship estate does not interfere with the care of the ward (Mother), management of the guardianship estate nor any *res* therein.

While not stated as such, Plaintiff's argument is analogous to arguing the so-called "probate exception" to federal jurisdiction which establishes that "a federal court has no jurisdiction to probate a will or administer an estate". The probate exception is a judicially created doctrine that limits federal jurisdiction. The exception has been construed narrowly. In *Markham*, the leading Supreme Court decision on the scope of the probate exception before *Marshall*, the Supreme Court noted as follows:

> "It is true that a federal court has no jurisdiction to probate a will or administer an estate. . . . But it has been established by a long series of decisions of this Court that federal courts of equity have jurisdiction to entertain suits in favor of creditors, legatees and heirs and other claimants against a decedent's estate 'to establish their claims' so long

as the federal court does not interfere with the probate proceedings or assume general jurisdiction of the probate or control of the property in the custody of the state court."

In *Marshall* the Supreme Court narrowed the probate exception stating that it:

"[R]eserves to state probate courts the probate or annulment of a will and the administration of a decedent's estate; it also precludes federal courts from endeavoring to dispose of property that is in the custody of a state probate court. *But it does not bar federal courts from adjudicating matters outside those confines and otherwise within federal jurisdiction.*" (Emphasis added).

The probate exception prevents federal courts from exercising *in rem* jurisdiction over a *res* when a state court is simultaneously doing the same. Therefore, federal courts may not exercise jurisdiction to dispose of property that is in the custody of a state probate court.

Here, the bankruptcy court is not asserting jurisdiction generally over the Mother's guardianship proceedings or taking control over the guardianship's estate assets, which are part of the *in rem* jurisdiction of the state district court. All the Counterclaim seeks is the possible establishment of a claim against Plaintiff as guardian. While a federal court may not exercise its jurisdiction to disturb or affect the possession of property in the custody of a state court, "it may exercise its jurisdiction to adjudicate rights in such property where the final judgment does not undertake to interfere with the state court's possession save to the extent that the state court is bound by the judgment to recognize the right adjudicated by the federal court". Therefore, Mother's pending guardianship proceeding does not preclude the Bankruptcy court from exercising jurisdiction in this adversary proceeding.

* * *

For the above-stated reasons, the Plaintiff's Amended Motion to Dismiss Counterclaim Combined with Affidavit and Brief in Support [Doc. 8] is hereby DENIED, and Plaintiff is ORDERED to file its answer to the Counterclaim within fifteen (15) days from the entry of this Order.

(Citations omitted.)

B. INHERITANCES AND BEQUESTS IN BANKRUPTCY

A pre-petition interest in a probate estate is property of the estate and must be disclosed on Schedule A/B. Recall that any "bequest, devise, or inheritance" or proceeds "as a beneficiary of a life insurance policy or of a death benefit plan" that the debtor obtains a right to within the six months post-petition is included in property of the estate. 11 U.S.C. § 541(a)(5). A failure to disclose these property interests may be considered fraudulent intent, which would be grounds to dismiss a case or revoke a discharge.

Gebhardt v. Cooper (In re Cooper)

2017 WL 945085 (Bankr. N.D. Ga. 03/09/2017)

DRAKE, Bankruptcy Judge

* * *

The Debtor filed her Chapter 7 case on June 30, 2015. On July 23, 2015, the Debtor filed her Statement of Financial Affairs (hereinafter "SOFA"), Schedules A through J, and her Chapter 7 Statement of Current Monthly Income (hereinafter "Means Test Form"). The Debtor's SOFA and Means Test Form both bear her signature attesting to their correctness under penalty of perjury. The Debtor also signed and submitted a Declaration Concerning Debtor's Schedules, swearing, under penalty of perjury, that her Schedules were correct to the best of her knowledge, information, and belief.

The meeting of creditors was held on September 18, 2015. On October 19, 2015, the Debtor filed an Amended Schedule B, in which she disclosed a potential personal injury settlement—the Debtor had been in an automobile accident in May of 2015. On October 21, 2015, the Debtor received a discharge. Her case remains open.

On March 31, 2016, the Debtor filed a petition initiating a Chapter 13 case. On May 5, 2016, the U.S. Trustee filed a motion seeking permission to conduct a Rule 2004 examination of the Debtor, as the U.S. Trustee had learned that the Debtor had failed to timely disclose one or more assets. Specifically, the U.S. Trustee had been contacted on April 29, 2016, by an attorney who had information concerning the Debtor's undisclosed interest in a probate estate (the Debtor's mother passed away on March 15, 2015) as well as in certain real property.

On May 5, 2016, the same day the U.S. Trustee filed his motion for an examination, the Debtor filed amended Schedules A and C in her Chapter 7 case. In this filing, the Debtor disclosed her interest in real property known as 3716 Treebark Trail, Decatur, Georgia (hereinafter "the Property").

. . . The U.S. Trustee's complaint contains six counts: (I) the Debtor concealed or falsified papers from which financial situation could be ascertained; (II) the Debtor knowingly and fraudulently made false oaths; (III) the Debtor concealed property of the estate; (IV) the Debtor concealed property of the estate and made false oaths in her Chapter 13 case; (V) the Debtor acquired or became entitled to property of the estate without reporting her acquisition or entitlement; and (VI) the Debtor failed to produce recorded information regarding the receipt and disposition of the life insurance proceeds. These six counts all lead to one prayer for relief, i.e., the U.S. Trustee's requests that the Court revoke the Debtor's discharge pursuant to § 727(d).

A. Revoking the Discharge Generally

Section 727(d) allows the U.S. Trustee to request revocation in four situations, two of which the U.S. Trustee asserts are relevant here: (1) the "discharge was obtained through the fraud of the debtor, and the [party requesting revocation] did not know of such fraud until after the granting of such discharge;" and (2) "the debtor acquired property that is property of the estate, or became entitled to acquire property that would be property of the estate, and knowingly and fraudulently failed to report the acquisition of or entitlement to such property, or to deliver or surrender such property to the trustee." In the instant proceeding, the U.S. Trustee seeks revocation under both subsections (1) and (2) of § 727(d). The Court notes that revocation is an extraordinary remedy, and, therefore, courts should liberally construe the provisions of § 727(d) in favor of debtors. The U.S. Trustee bears the burden of proving the application of § 727(d) by a preponderance of the evidence.

B. Timeliness of the Complaint

The U.S. Trustee may request revocation under subsection (1) "within one year after the discharge is granted," and may request revocation of the discharge under subsection (2) "before the later of—(A) one year after the granting of such discharge; and (B) the date the case is closed."

Here, the Debtor received her discharge on October 21, 2015, but her case remains open. The U.S. Trustee filed his complaint on October 19, 2016, and filed his amended complaint on October 20, 2016. Consequently, the U.S. Trustee's complaint is timely under either subsection.

C. Revocation Under § 727(d)(1)

As stated above, subsection (d)(1) empowers a court to revoke a debtor's discharge if the debtor obtained the discharge through fraud and the party seeking revocation did not have knowledge of the fraud prior to the entry of the discharge. Courts applying subsection (d)(1) have looked for three criteria: "(1) the debtor obtained the discharge through fraud; (2) the creditor possessed no knowledge of the debtor's fraud prior to the granting of the discharge; and (3) the fraud, if known, would have resulted in the denial of the discharge under 11 U.S.C. § 727(a)."

A complaint seeking revocation of the discharge may be based on conduct falling under § 727(a)(4). That statute denies a debtor a discharge if the debtor "knowingly and fraudulently, in or in connection with the case—(A) made a false oath or account." Thus, the Court will focus on Count II of the U.S. Trustee's complaint, which alleges that the Debtor knowingly and fraudulently made false oaths.

A "false oath" for the purposes of § 727(a)(4) may include intentional omissions from the debtor's schedules and SOFA. The omission must be made with actual fraud, but that fraud may be inferred from the circumstances. For example, evidence of a series of omissions has been found particularly condemnatory. Subsequent disclosure does not mitigate the initial fraud. . . .

In addition to being fraudulent, the omission must also relate to subject matter that is "material." The subject of an omission is "'material' . . . if it bears a relationship to the [debtor's] business transactions or estate, or concerns the discovery of assets, business dealings, or the existence and disposition of his property." This is a broad definition, and serves to promote the debtors "uncompromising duty to disclose."

In the instant proceeding, the Debtor is alleged to have made false oaths by failing to disclose her interest in the life insurance policy, her personal injury claim, that she was involved in the probate filing, and that she had an interest in her mother's estate. The Debtor was required to disclose these assets and involvements, which are "material" as that term is used here, but did not. While failing to disclose one of her assets could be seen as inadvertent, the multiplicity of the Debtor's omissions indicates that the Debtor acted with fraudulent intent. That she subsequently disclosed the existence of her assets and her involvement in her mother's probate estate does not diminish that initial fraudulent intent. Consequently, the Court concludes that the Debtor fraudulently omitted those assets and involvements from her Schedules and SOFA filed on July 23, 2015.

Having concluded that the Debtor's conduct would have constituted a violation of § 727(a)(4), the only thing remaining for the Court to determine is whether the U.S. Trustee, as the party seeking revocation, "did not know of such fraud until after the granting of such discharge." "A party seeking revocation has 'knowledge,' as that term is used in relation to § 727(d)(1), when the party 'knows facts such that he or she is put on notice of a possible fraud.'"

In the instant proceeding, the facts as stated in the U.S. Trustee's complaint show that the U.S. Trustee did not have knowledge of the Debtor's failure to disclose her involvement with her mother's probate estate, the Debtor's interest in that estate, or the Debtor's receipt of the $43,000 in life insurance proceeds. The U.S. Trustee first learned of the probate estate on April 29, 2016, and first learned of the insurance proceeds at the 2004 examination held on July 14, 2016—both well after the Debtor received her discharge.

Therefore, the U.S. Trustee's complaint states sufficient facts to find that the Debtor's discharge should be revoked pursuant to § 727(d)(1).

* * *

(Citations omitted.)

In some cases, a debtor may wish to renounce an inheritance, presumably for the benefit of loved ones who will receive the inheritance instead. This is particularly relevant when the renunciation prevents creditors from receiving the inheritance. Consider the following case, which discussed whether such a renunciation constitutes a fraudulent transfer.

Laughlin v. Nouveau Body and Tan, L.L.C. (In re Laughlin)

602 F.3d 417 (5th Cir. 2010)

KING, Circuit Judge

Thomas J. Laughlin appeals the district court's order affirming the bankruptcy court's judgment denying discharge pursuant to 11 U.S.C. § 727(a)(2). The bankruptcy court determined that Laughlin fraudulently transferred property under § 727(a)(2) by renouncing his interest in his father's estate before filing his Chapter 7 petition, and the district court affirmed. For the following reasons, we REVERSE the bankruptcy court's judgment and REMAND for further proceedings.

[Debtor had outstanding judgments. During the same time frame. Debtor's father died and debtor renounced his statutory share of his father's estate so his mother could ultimately receive it.]

* * *

[Subsequently] Laughlin filed a Chapter 7 bankruptcy petition, in which he disclosed the renunciation of his interest in his father's estate. Nouveau filed an adversary action against Laughlin and objected to Laughlin's discharge of debt, pursuant to 11 U.S.C. § 727(a)(2), arguing that Laughlin's renunciation of his interest in his father's estate was a transfer of property made within one year of the bankruptcy petition that was made with the intent to delay, hinder, or defraud his creditors.

In an oral ruling, the bankruptcy court determined that . . . Laughlin's renunciation of his interest in his father's estate was a fraudulent transfer under § 727(a)(2). Specifically, the bankruptcy court concluded that Laughlin "had the power to channel [his inheritance interest]" and he thus transferred that interest by renouncing his inheritance; that Laughlin had the intent to delay, hinder, or defraud his creditors when he made the transfer; and that Laughlin's intent in transferring this interest was sufficient to deny discharge under § 727(a)(2).

Laughlin appealed the denial of his discharge under § 727(a)(2). The district court [affirmed]. . . .

* * *

Here, the parties dispute whether the pre-petition renunciation of Laughlin's succession rights constituted a "transfer" of property for the purposes of § 727(a)(2) and, if a transfer of property did occur, whether the transfer was done with intent to hinder, delay, or defraud creditors.

. . . The bankruptcy code defines "transfer" to include "each mode, direct or indirect, absolute or conditional, voluntary or involuntary, of disposing of or parting with—(i) property; or (ii) an interest in property." 11 U.S.C. § 101(54)(D). "'What constitutes a transfer and when it is complete' is a matter of federal law . . . since . . . the statute itself provides a definition of 'transfer.' " However, "property" and "interest in property" are not defined in the code. "In the absence of any controlling federal law, [property and] interests in property are [] creature [s] of state law."

* * *

Under the Louisiana Civil Code, "[a] successor is not obligated to accept rights to succeed [inheritance rights]. He may accept some of those rights and renounce others." "To the extent that a successor renounces rights to succeed, *he is considered never to have had them.*". . . .

These provisions in the Louisiana Civil Code are comparable to the Texas law at issue in *Simpson* and the Arizona law at issue in *Costas* because Louisiana law also treats a renouncing successor as never having had an interest in property. As such, Laughlin urges that, as in *Simpson,* we should hold that Laughlin's pre-petition renunciation of his interest in his father's estate was not a "transfer" of "property" or an "interest in property" under § 727(a)(2).

Nouveau responds that the Louisiana law is different [because] Louisiana law allows a creditor to reopen the succession to accept a debtor's renounced interest, with the result that there is a creditor's "interest in property" sufficient to support the denial of Laughlin's discharge under § 727(a)(2). We disagree.

Under Louisiana law:

> A creditor of a successor may, with judicial authorization, accept succession rights in the successor's name if the successor has renounced them in whole or in part to the prejudice of his creditor's rights. In such a case, the renunciation may be annulled in favor of the creditor to the extent of his claim against the successor, but it remains effective against the successor.

The Louisiana Supreme Court has interpreted this article as requiring "a creditor [to] prove that an heir renounced his inheritance fraudulently or with an intent to wrongfully deprive the creditor of his claim on the debtor's property in order for the creditor to have a right to have the renunciation annulled and to accept the inheritance in the heir's stead."

We determine that, for the purposes of our inquiry today, Louisiana law is indistinguishable from the Texas law at issue in *Simpson,* and we hold that, under Louisiana law, a valid pre-petition renunciation of an inheritance interest is not a transfer of the debtor's property under § 727(a)(2). . . .

To analyze this issue, we first look to the text of the Louisiana Civil Code. . . . The text does not suggest that a renouncing successor gains an interest in the inheritance because, even if the annulment action is successful, article 967 specifies that the successor's renunciation *remains effective* against him. . . . [W]e read article 967 together with articles 954 and 947 to mean that a successful annulment of a renunciation does not disturb the fiction that the renouncing successor predeceased the decedent and thus never had rights in the inheritance interest. . . .

*   *   *

REVERSED AND REMANDED.

(Citations omitted.)

NOTES AND COMMENTS

1. Is it too late for the debtor to renounce an inheritance when the debtor files for bankruptcy? *See* Lowe v. Sanflippo (In re Schmidt), 362 B.R. 318 (Bankr. W.D. Tex. 2007) (debtor inherited property pre-petition, and thus post-petition renunciation was ineffective even though state law allowed renunciation to be effective as of date of decedent's death because at time of renunciation, property was part of estate and under control of trustee); *cf.* Gaughan v. The Edward Dittlof Revocable Trust (In re Costas), 555 F.3d 790 (9th Cir. 2009) (post-petition renunciation of pre-petition inheritance not a fraudulent transfer).

2. If the debtor files for bankruptcy protection, family members are free to modify a will to prevent the debtor from receiving an inheritance that could fall into the bankruptcy estate—the debtor has no property interest in the inheritance until the testator's death. *See* In re McGuire, 209 B.R. 580, 582 (Bankr. D. Mass. 1997)("This Court finds that the Debtor had no more than an expectation of inheriting property from

his mother at the time of her death. His mother could have revoked her will at any time and disinherited both her son and her daughter. The execution of the codicil was within her prerogative as she had no duty to underwrite the creditors of her son's bankruptcy estate.").

C. NONDISCHARGEABILITY ISSUES IN PROBATE

Trusts are becoming more popular than wills as a vehicle to pass ownership of property. A trust has great flexibility and can take many forms. When considering the use of a trust by an individual to pass ownership of property, the trust is a private trust, rather than a charitable trust. The creator of the trust is known as the settlor, the one who holds legal title is known as the trustee, and the one who has equitable title is known as the beneficiary. In probate, it is not unusual to see a will contest based on fraud or undue influence. For trusts, litigation may occur on the basis that the trustee breached a fiduciary duty in the administration of a trust. If the debtor is responsible for wrongdoing, such as fraud or breach of fiduciary duty, are claims against a debtor arising from the wrongdoing dischargeable in bankruptcy? Consider the excerpt from the lengthy opinion in In re Whitaker addressing these issues.

Whitaker v. Whitaker (In re Whitaker)

564 B.R. 115 (Bankr. D. Mass. 2017)

BAILEY, Bankruptcy Judge

[The debtor was named as the agent for his mother and father under a power of attorney as well as trustee of their trusts. His siblings claimed fraud and breach of fiduciary duty by their sibling and asserted that their claims against him were exempt from discharge. The court then discussed the Debtor's departure from the investment strategy.]

* * *

42. Sometime after December 31, 2008, the Debtor submitted his final report regarding the Trust to his siblings the "Third Report"). The precise date of this report is unclear. The Debtor testified it was probably before April 15, 2009, because in the report he stated that he had not yet finished the Parents' tax returns for 2008. Still, it is unclear precisely how early in the year it was made and whether it

was made before the Debtor made his decision to begin trading Trust monies in options.

43. Regarding financial assets (the investment and the bank accounts), the Third Report states only the following: "Financial assets totaled $904,551. At 12/31/08 including bank accounts. [sic] This is after distributing $120,000 to the children and grandchildren."

44. In the Third Report, the Debtor also indicated that he had finally sold the Euclid house in May 2008, for $58,000.

45. When the Debtor issued the Third Report, he had already departed from the investment strategy that he had previously told his siblings he would follow: at the very least, he had, after the fall of the stock market in 2008, sold some or all of the Trusts' conservative investments and, with the proceeds, purchased what he called "high-quality stock issues." The Debtor deliberately omitted any mention of this change of strategy from this report.

46. It is unclear whether, by the date of this report, he had also sold that stock at a gain and begun investing a portion of the portfolio in options. I cannot find by a preponderance of the evidence that, by the date of this report, he had begun trading in options or decided to do so, and therefore that the Debtor had anything to disclose to his siblings about option trading *in this report.*

47. Nonetheless, the Debtor did eventually decide to invest Trust funds in options. The Debtor acknowledged, and in any event I find, that this constituted a material change in investment strategy and that he did not update his siblings as to that material change. This withholding of information from his siblings was not merely negligent—he did not simply forget—but intentional and deliberate.

48. In the three reports he made to his siblings, he did not indicate that he planned to depart from his father's wish of conservative investment of the Trust Assets.

49. The Debtor acknowledged that he did not intend to keep supplying reports to his siblings because he did not want to report negative results to them and did not want them to find out what was going on with the Trust.

* * *

50. On April 27, 2009 and on May 1, 2009, the Debtor wrote two checks against the Fidelity investment account in which he maintained the Trusts' investments, both payable to himself: the first for $58,500 and the second for $49,000. He used the funds thereby transferred

to pay for a timeshare in Mexico that he purchased and owned jointly with his wife.

* * *

[The court discussed further the Debtor's actions as well as the losses incurred.]

80. At the time that the Trusts' funds were rapidly dissipating, the Debtor did not report any of this to his siblings. Though he had sent them year-end reports for 2006, 2007, and 2008, and notwithstanding his promise in the first report to inform them if his investment strategy were to change, he sent his siblings no reports for 2009, 2010, and 2011. Nor did the siblings ask him for information when none was forthcoming.

* * *

83. The Debtor testified and admitted that if he had continued to invest conservatively as his father desired, the Fidelity Account would be worth $1,200,000 or $1,300,000 today. . . .

* * *

88. The Plaintiffs have not established by a preponderance of the evidence that the Debtor's investment of Trust funds in options was substantially certain to lead to loss of the funds. The evidence shows that his options investments resulted in both losses and gains. Had he stopped after his first month, it would have resulted in modest gains. In the end, losses greatly outnumbered gains. The strategy was reckless, but it was not substantially certain to lead to loss.

* * *

92. In or about June of 2012, the weekend of their mother's passing, the Debtor notified the Plaintiffs of the massive losses to the investment account for the very first time, and they were shocked by the news.

93. The Debtor resigned as trustee of each Family Trust in June of 2012. He signed the documents effecting his resignation as trustee on November 6, 2012. The Debtor conceded that the resignation had been forced upon him: "they [his siblings] probably fired me, but—we didn't have very much conversation." At the time of his resignation, there was approximately $500,000 in the Fidelity Account. He was succeeded as trustee of each trust by each of his three siblings.

* * *

98. Joan and Ben both testified that, had they known about the risky investment strategy that the Debtor adopted, and of the losses that strategy soon began to generate, they would have sought to remove him as trustee. Both testified that they had relied on representations he had made in his report of January 31, 2007: that he was investing in accordance with their father's wishes and would notify them if this changed.

* * *

The Plaintiffs assert counts under 11 U.S.C. § 523(a)(2)(A), (a)(4), and (a)(6). A party seeking to except a debt from discharge bears the burden of proving each element by a preponderance of the evidence. In furtherance of the Bankruptcy Code's "fresh start" policy, exceptions to discharge are narrowly construed.

* * *

. . . the Plaintiffs contend that the Debtor's liability to them for failing to invest the funds as a "prudent investor" is excepted from discharge under § 523(a)(4) as a debt for a defalcation while acting in a fiduciary capacity. . . . [T]he Plaintiffs contend that the Debtor's liability to them for his unauthorized appropriation for his own use of $107,500 that he used to purchase a time share and $38,000 that he transferred to his personal investment account should be excepted from discharge under § 523(a)(4) as debts "for embezzlement or larceny" within the meaning of that subsection. . . . [T]he Plaintiffs contend that the Debtor's failure to inform them of the declining balances in his trust accounts amounted to, and should be excepted from discharge under § 523(a)(4) as, fraud or defalcation while acting in a fiduciary capacity.

. . . In their first sub-count under § 523(a)(4), the Plaintiffs contend that the Debtor's liability to them for failing to invest the funds as a "prudent investor" is excepted from discharge under § 523(a)(4) as a debt for a defalcation while acting in a fiduciary capacity. The gravamen of this count is the Debtor's loss of Trust funds by investment of those monies in options. The Plaintiffs contend that this investment strategy was highly risky and for this reason both reckless and inconsistent with the Debtor's fiduciary obligations to the Trusts and their beneficiaries.

* * *

The sole disputed issue is whether the conduct in question amounted to a defalcation within the meaning of § 523(a)(4). "[Defalcation] is not defined in the Bankruptcy Code, and though the term was carried into § 523(a)(4) of the present Bankruptcy Code from § 17a(4) the Bankruptcy Act of 1898 and predates even that act, the legislative history sheds no light on its meaning." Two principal questions arise about its meaning in § 523(a)(4). What kinds of acts constitute defalcations? And with what scienter, fault, or intent must the act have been performed?

Courts have long puzzled over the precise meaning and scope of "defalcation" as it has been used in the Bankruptcy Code and in earlier federal bankruptcy statutes. To understand its meaning, courts have examined defalcation's dictionary definitions and its context in the statute.

Congress first used the term 'defalcation' in an exception to discharge in a federal bankruptcy statute in 1867. The Supreme Court's recent survey of its dictionary definitions, both in 1867 and more recently, show its meaning to be broad:

[A] law dictionary in use in 1867 defines the word "defalcation" as "the act of a defaulter," which, in turn, it defines broadly as one "who is deficient in his accounts, or fails in making his accounts correct." Modern dictionaries contain similarly broad definitional language. Black's Law Dictionary, for example, defines "defalcation" first as "Embezzlement," but, second, as "[l]oosely, the failure to meet an obligation; a nonfraudulent default."

Dictionary definitions thus clearly include the misappropriation of money held in a fiduciary capacity and the failure to account for any such monies. However, the dictionary definitions also encompass, more broadly, "default," "failure to meet an obligation," and "monetary deficiency through breach of trust": that is, any monetary deficiency resulting from a breach by a trustee of his or her fiduciary obligation.

The context and use of defalcation in subsection 523(a)(4) supports the conclusion that Congress intended for defalcation to have this broader meaning.

Defalcation carries a different meaning than the other behaviors listed in § 523(a)(4): embezzlement, larceny, and fraud. Typically, embezzlement requires conversion, larceny requires carrying away another's property, and fraud requires a false statement. By contrast, "defalcation" "can encompass a breach of fiduciary obligation that involves neither conversion, nor taking and carrying away another's property, nor falsity." Rather, "defalcation" requires only a "nonfraudulent breach[] of fiduciary duty."

While defalcation is construed as conduct "of the same kind" as its statutory neighbors in § 523(a)(4) (fraud while acting in a fiduciary capacity, embezzlement, and larceny), it should also be construed to "not make the word identical to its statutory neighbors." I therefore conclude that it includes breaches of fiduciary duty other than those that would amount to embezzlement of trust assets. Provided there exists the necessary level or type of intent, risk, or scienter (about which more below), defalcation encompasses any breach of fiduciary duty that results in a monetary deficiency. It includes conduct of the type on which the present complaint is predicated, imprudent investing of trust funds. It follows, as the Court of Appeals has held, that "[i]nherent in 'defalcation' is the requirement that there be a breach of fiduciary duty; if there is no breach, there is no defalcation."

There is nonetheless a limitation on the kind of intent, risk, or scienter that will suffice for a particular breach to constitute a defalcation. As the Supreme Court held in *Bullock,* a defalcation in § 523(a)(4) requires either (i) moral turpitude, bad faith, or other immoral conduct or (ii) in lieu of these, an intentional wrong, which includes not only conduct that the fiduciary knows is improper but also reckless conduct of the kind that the criminal law often treats as the equivalent, such as where the fiduciary consciously disregards, or is willfully blind to, a substantial and unjustifiable risk that his conduct will turn out to violate a fiduciary duty. That risk "must be of such a nature and degree that, considering the nature and purpose of the actor's conduct and the circumstances known to him, its disregard involves a gross deviation from the standard of conduct that a law-abiding person would observe in the actor's situation."

In view of these rulings, I must decide, with respect to each instance in which the Debtor invested Trust funds in options, whether the conduct at issue amounted to a breach of the Debtor's fiduciary obligations under the Trusts, and, if so, whether he committed the breach with the requisite intent or scienter.

While the existence or not of a fiduciary relationship, and the breach or not of a trustee's duty in such a relationship, are questions of federal law, they are informed in large measure by state law.

* * *

For these reasons—the high risk of investing in options, the Debtor's known inadequacy as an options trader, his failure to limit the amount that he might invest in options, and his inability to cope with a loss other than by throwing good money after bad—I conclude that it was imprudent under Florida law, and beyond the scope of any reasonable business judgment, for the Debtor to have invested even the first $200,000, or any sum, in options. This too constituted a breach of fiduciary duty.

Did the Debtor commit these breaches with the requisite intent or scienter? I find that he did. Under the Supreme Court's decision in *Bullock*, the necessary intent will be present when the defalcation is "an intentional wrong, which includes . . . conduct that the fiduciary knows is improper." Here, the Debtor fully appreciated that he was subjecting the Trusts' assets to a degree of risk that he could not justify. From personal experience, he knew he did not have the wherewithal to finesse this risky practice or to limit the damage. He knowingly placed himself in a position in which he felt he could not stop with losses. And, as is evident from the fact that he had already converted portions of the account to his own use, he knew himself to be acting on his own interests as a residual beneficiary and not on the concerns appropriate to a fiduciary. For all these reasons, and each of them separately, I conclude that the Debtor acted with the requisite scienter and intent and that his breaches of fiduciary duty were defalcations within the meaning of § 523(a)(4).

* * *

For the reasons set forth above, the Court will, by separate judgment, declare that the Debtor's liability to the Plaintiffs for the conduct that forms the basis of Counts II.i, II.ii, II.iii, III.ii, and III.iii is excepted from discharge and dismiss the remaining counts on their merits.

(Citations omitted.)

D. BANKRUPTCY IN PRACTICE

Assume Diana's mother recently died and her estate is currently in probate. Diana is slated to receive a lump sum of money and some of her mother's personal property when the estate is settled. Diana wonders whether any of her creditors can attach these gifts in the probate proceeding. What if Diana has filed for bankruptcy? What is the effect of her doing so on anything she may receive through probate?

584   Chapter 10   Probate Law & Bankruptcy: The Probate Exception, Inheritances, & Trusts

Instead of leaving Diana a bequest in her will, Diana's mother created a support trust for herself, and on her death, Diana is named the co-trustee and the beneficiary. The distribution standard for Diana to use is for her health, maintenance, and support. If Diana files for bankruptcy, could any of Diana's creditors force her to make distributions from the trust to the creditors to pay her debts?

11

Alternatives to Bankruptcy: Consumer Protection Laws and State Collections

What good is money if it can't buy happiness?[1]

A. CONSUMER PROTECTION REMEDIES FOR DEBTORS

RECALL DIANA DETTER

Before Diana filed for bankruptcy protection, she owed debt, and creditors likely sought to collect that debt. Maybe they used debt collectors; maybe they notified credit reporting agencies if Diana fell behind on payments; maybe they filed suits against Diana. To what extent is Diana protected from actions that may cross the line of normal commercial behavior by a creditor or an agent of the creditor seeking to collect a debt?

Consumer protection includes state and federal laws and regulations designed to protect consumers by promoting fair trade, competition, and accurate information in the marketplace. Some arise from common law principles of tort and contract, but increasingly consumer protection falls within the jurisdiction of federal and state agencies, guided by legislation and regulation. But regardless of the source of the law, the goal remains the same: ensuring that consumers have access to accurate information about what is being offered on the market to make an informed decision about

---

1. Agatha Christie, *The Man in the Brown Suit.*

how to spend their money. Those with precarious financial positions can be particularly vulnerable because they lack a variety of alternatives available to those with strong credit.

CAVEAT EMPTOR

The doctrine of *caveat emptor*, "let the buyer beware," likely originated in the 1500s, but became more prevalent in the 1700s. But even in its early stages, caveat emptor did not allow sellers to engage in fraud. Walton H. Hamilton, *The Ancient Maxim Caveat Emptor*, 40 Yale L.J. 1133, 1164, 1169, 1173 (1931). But absent fraud, buyers were protected only to the extent that the buyer specifically contracted for such protection. Maronda Homes of Fla., Inc. v. Lakeview Reserve Homeowners Assn., ___ So.3d ___ (Fla. 2013); 2013 WL 3466814, *3. This doctrine placed the burden upon buyers to ask questions and contract for additional protections.

The Federal Trade Commission (FTC) was established in 1914 with the mission to protect consumers in the marketplace.[2] The FTC's consumer protection mission became more prominent in 1930 when the agency's primary statute was amended to declare unlawful "unfair or deceptive acts or practices."[3] Since then the philosophy of consumer protection in the United States has been to encourage consumers to make smart choices by requiring sellers to make information available to consumers prepurchase as necessary, and to punish deceptive acts which prevent consumers from making informed decisions. Since 1930, all 50 states have adopted laws against deceptive and unfair acts or practices, using language identical or substantially identical to the FTC Act.[4] One of the strengths of consumer protection in the United States is the uniformity of federal and state law. The model state consumer protection act includes a provision affording binding or persuasive authority to cases arising under the deception standard in any state or under federal law. While not every state has adopted all the model act language, most require consistency with interpretations by the FTC of the deception standard that have been upheld in federal court.

Enforcement of consumer protection laws is powerful and diffuse. The FTC has primary jurisdiction over consumer protection law, although other

---

2. 15 U.S.C. §41. Title 15 is commonly known as the FTC Act.

3. 15 U.S.C. § 45 (a)(1).

4. *See* Mark D. Bauer, *The Licensed Professional Exemption in Consumer Protection: At Odds With Antitrust History and Precedent,* 73 Tenn. L. Rev. 131, 144 (2006).

federal agencies are also involved, including the Department of Justice, the Consumer Financial Protection Bureau (CFPB), and the Federal Communications Commission. The CFPB has many of the same powers of the FTC, but is specifically focused on consumer protection in financial transactions, including mortgages, bank accounts, pay day lending, and car loans.

At the state level, all state's attorneys general are empowered to enforce consumer protection laws, although some states additionally have a consumer protection agency specifically focused on enforcement. Some states also permit counties and cities to enforce the consumer protection laws, as well as other state agencies that interact with consumers.

All states also permit private suits by consumers against sellers of allegedly deceptive products. Many states encourage private suits because state budgets do not allow for vigorous enforcement against every single deceptive act that may befall a consumer. To sweeten the pot, most states authorize attorney's costs and fees if the consumer wins, as well as exemplary or multiple damage awards. In addition, many states permit class action consumer lawsuits.

State consumer protection laws are an example of the "Private Attorney General" doctrine. If someone is the victim of a deceptive act or practice, it is unlikely they were the only one impacted. While the individual consumer may recover damages in a lawsuit, a judgment against a bad actor benefits the public at large. In that capacity every consumer protection complainant is acting as a private attorney general protecting the citizens of the state.

B. CREDIT REPORTS

Credit reports provide information to potential creditors and others[5] with a justifiable interest with information regarding the potential borrower's credit and repayment history. The Fair Credit Reporting Act[6] (FCRA) provides that the credit reporting agencies must provide, upon request, one free copy of the consumer's credit report to the consumer every 12 months. The only official source of this free report is annualcreditreport.com, a site

---

5. The ability to view someone's credit report is limited under federal law to specific situations. 15 U.S.C. § 1681b. Outside of a court order, the few parties that may view a consumer credit report include current or potential creditors, and potential employers, landlords, and insurance companies. *Id.*

6. 15 U.S.C. § 1681.

developed by the Federal Trade Commission in conjunction with the three major credit-report providers: Experian, Equifax, and TransUnion.[7]

Most creditors (and substantially all large creditors) provide Experian, Equifax, and TransUnion with consumers' payment histories monthly. A credit report is simply a list of every credit or loan account held by a consumer, along with the consumer's payment history. Consumer credit reports do not evaluate the consumer or assess risk; credit reports are essentially raw data concerning the timeliness of debt payments to be used or interpreted by the authorized viewer. The three major credit report providers sell many different types of credit reports. In addition to payment histories, most also include public records of bankruptcy, court judgments, and crimes.

Failure to pay debt or the filing of a bankruptcy case can be reported to the credit reporting agencies, and will remain on the credit report for up to seven years, or ten years in the case of a bankruptcy filing. Title 15 of the U.S. Code, which governs Commerce and Trade, includes the provisions governing credit reports. The provisions below come from the Fair Credit Reporting Act, 15 U.S.C. § 1681 et seq.

---

15 U.S.C. § 1681c

(a) Information excluded from consumer reports

Except as authorized under subsection (b) of this section, no consumer reporting agency may make any consumer report containing any of the following items of information:

(1) Cases under Title 11 or under the Bankruptcy Act that, from the date of entry of the order for relief or the date of adjudication, as the case may be, antedate the report by more than 10 years.

(2) Civil suits, civil judgments, and records of arrest that, from date of entry, antedate the report by more than seven years or until the governing statute of limitations has expired, whichever is the longer period.

(3) Paid tax liens which, from date of payment, antedate the report by more than seven years.

(4) Accounts placed for collection or charged to profit and loss which antedate the report by more than seven years.

(5) Any other adverse item of information, other than records of convictions of crimes which antedates the report by more than seven years.

* * *

---

7. http://www.consumer.ftc.gov/articles/0155-free-credit-reports. There are many websites that purport to supply free credit reports, but there are often strings attached, including a charge for the so-called free report.

(d) Information required to be disclosed
  (1) Title 11 information
  Any consumer reporting agency that furnishes a consumer report
that contains information regarding any case involving the consumer
that arises under Title 11 shall include in the report an identification
of the chapter of such Title 11 under which such case arises if provided by
the source of the information. If any case arising or filed under Title 11 is
withdrawn by the consumer before a final judgment, the consumer reporting agency shall include in the report that such case or filing was withdrawn
upon receipt of documentation certifying such withdrawal.

* * *

As noted, when a bankruptcy case is withdrawn, the credit report must so
indicate. The following case discusses the responsibilities of a credit reporting agency when notified of a withdrawal.

Childress v. Experian Info. Sols., Inc.

790 F.3d 745 (7th Cir. 2015)

POSNER, Circuit Judge

The Fair Credit Reporting Act, 15 U.S.C. §§ 1681 *et seq.,* provides
that "if any case arising or filed under Title 11 [the Bankruptcy Code]
is withdrawn by the consumer before a final judgment, the consumer
reporting agency shall include in the report that such case or filing
was withdrawn upon receipt of documentation certifying such
withdrawal." 15 U.S.C. § 1681c(d)(1). The Act further provides that
"whenever a consumer reporting agency prepares a consumer report
it shall follow reasonable procedures to assure maximum possible
accuracy of the information concerning the individual about whom
the report relates." § 1681e(b).

The plaintiff and her husband (they are now divorced, and he is
not participating in this litigation) had filed a petition for bankruptcy
under Chapter 13 of the Bankruptcy Code, but later they filed a timely
motion in the bankruptcy court to dismiss the petition, and the court
granted the motion. That was in 2006. The defendant, a consumer
credit-reporting agency, receives copies of judgments in bankruptcy
cases from Lexis (which in turn retrieves them from PACER—short
for Public Access to Court Electronic Records, a service that provides
online access to federal court and docket information) and notes them
in the credit reports of persons who have filed bankruptcy petitions.
The agency reported the plaintiff's bankruptcy petition "dismissed,"
which was what the judgment terminating the bankruptcy case had
caused to be done.

In 2009 the's [sic] lawyer demanded that the agency remove all reference to her bankruptcy because it had been dismissed at her behest. The agency refused. In 2012 she told the agency: "my bankruptcy was not dismissed. It was voluntarily withdrawn prior to plan approval." The agency then purged the reference to the bankruptcy from her file, but did so because it would soon be seven years since she had filed her bankruptcy petition and the agency deletes reference to a bankruptcy in a consumer credit report after seven years have elapsed since the petition for bankruptcy was filed. (The Fair Credit Reporting Act requires that reporting agencies purge bankruptcy records ten years after the filing date, but the major credit-reporting agencies purge them after seven years instead.) There is no indication that had it not been for the lapse of time the agency would have added to her credit report a notation that the petition for bankruptcy had been withdrawn. But since the bankruptcy was purged from her file we needn't decide whether her letter alerting the reporting agency that the dismissal had been voluntary would count as "documentation certifying . . . withdrawal" of the petition for bankruptcy. 15 U.S.C. § 1681c(d)(1).

* * *

. . . The key provisions of the two sections of the Fair Credit Reporting Act that we quoted at the outset of this opinion are that the agency must report that the bankruptcy petition was withdrawn "upon receipt of documentation certifying such withdrawal" and must "follow reasonable procedures to assure maximum possible accuracy of the information concerning the" person who had filed for bankruptcy. In 2006, when the plaintiff's bankruptcy petition was withdrawn, no documentation certifying such withdrawal was or had been submitted to the agency. The plaintiff argues that the agency shouldn't (despite the statute) require such documentation, but instead should monitor all dismissals of bankruptcy petitions and investigate to determine whether they were dismissed at the request of the petitioner. A Lexis representative testified, however, that the variance in bankruptcy docket entries from bankruptcy court to bankruptcy court is so great—and there are 94 bankruptcy courts—that Lexis has been unable to develop reliable computer algorithms for determining the basis on which a particular bankruptcy case has been dismissed. What the plaintiff wants would thus require a live human being, with at least a little legal training, to review every bankruptcy dismissal and classify it as either voluntary or involuntary. That's a lot to ask—too much when one considers the alternative, which is for the agency to act only upon receiving information from the bankruptcy petitioner indicating that the petition has indeed been voluntarily dismissed.

That approach is not only consistent with but implied by the phrase "upon receipt of documentation certifying such withdrawal."

We noted at the outset of this opinion that the Fair Credit Reporting Act requires only that the procedures adopted by credit-reporting agencies be "reasonable" in relation to the goal of accurate credit reporting. The procedure urged by the plaintiff is not "reasonable." It would put an enormous burden on the consumer credit-reporting agencies. . . .

There is more that is wrong with her case. Every bankruptcy case that is "withdrawn" at the request of the petitioner is dismissed. There was therefore no inaccuracy in the statement in the plaintiff's credit report that her bankruptcy petition had been dismissed. Nor is the fact that such a petition is dismissed at the petitioner's request a reliable sign that she decided not to stiff her creditors by seeking a discharge—she may have dismissed the petition because she thought she'd be denied a discharge. To make a consumer credit report fully precise would require an investigation that went far beyond merely noting whether the petition for bankruptcy had been dismissed at the petitioner's request. The plaintiff does not want that; nor has she shown that it would be a feasible task to lay on the consumer credit-reporting agencies.

(Citations omitted.)

NOTES AND COMMENTS

1. What does the *Childress* opinion suggest about the burden on the person who is the subject of a credit report? What is the burden on the credit reporting agency?

2. The court determined that the statement that the bankruptcy case had been withdrawn was technically accurate. What impact did that have on the case? Consider the list of elements for a FCRA claim, as provided by Smith v. LexisNexis Screening Sols., Inc., 138 F. Supp. 3d 872 (E.D. Mich. 2015), *aff'd in part, rev'd in part*, 837 F.3d 604 (6th Cir. 2016):

   FCRA is not a strict liability statute. While a showing of inaccuracy is an essential element of a § 1681e(b) claim, a FCRA plaintiff must allege and prove more to establish the prima facie case: "(1) the defendant reported inaccurate information about the plaintiff; (2) the defendant either negligently or willfully failed to follow reasonable procedures to assure maximum possible accuracy of the information about the plaintiff; (3) the plaintiff was injured; and (4) the defendant's conduct was the proximate cause of the plaintiff's injury." Reasonableness is measured against "what a reasonably prudent person would do under the circumstances."

Smith v. Lexis Nexis Screening Sols., Inc., 138 F. Supp. 3d at 878 (citations omitted). If you represented a client with an inaccurate credit report, what proof might meet this standard? Consider that as many as 20 percent of Americans or more may have an error in their credit report that makes them look riskier than they are. CNBC, *The Real Problem with Credit Reports is the Astounding Number of Errors* at https://www.cnbc.com/2017/09/27/the-real-problem-with-credit-reports-is-the-astounding-number-of-errors-equifax-commentary.html (last accessed September 1, 2018).

3. How can you help a client fix errors in the client's credit report? One way to answer the question is to experience the process yourself. Go to annualcreditreport.com and get copies of your own credit report from Experian, Equifax, and TransUnion. If there is an error, follow the instructions to dispute the incorrect information. Even if there are no errors, read carefully the process to dispute information and visit the websites required to initiate a dispute. What did you learn, and what would you tell a client about your own experience?

ADVICE FOR CONSUMERS, AND PARTICULARLY FOR LAW STUDENTS

It is important to review your credit report annually. There is considerable debate about the precise accuracy of credit reports, but it is incontrovertible that the credit report database contains a large number of errors. Sometimes a mistake can be fixed quickly, but the correction often takes much longer. Because of this, the time to check your credit report is not in the days before you apply for a car loan or mortgage. Additionally, all state bars review law students' credit reports as a part of the character and fitness examination required for admission to the bar. It is therefore very important for law students to review their credit reports from all three major reporting agencies well before applying for bar admission.

The only way to get a free copy of your credit report is a website managed by the FTC at www.annualcreditreport.com.

After reviewing a credit report and finding an error, submit an online dispute with the credit reporting agency that supplied the incorrect information. That agency must respond within 30 days, or the information must be removed from your credit report. (15 U.S.C. § 1681i(a)(1)(A) and (a)(5).)

If the credit reporting agency notifies you that the information was correct or at least was reported precisely as a creditor supplied it, then you need to follow up with the creditor supplying the erroneous information. The credit reporting agencies are required to notify you of who supplied the information and how to contact them to continue your dispute.

Finally, a word about identity theft, a serious crime affecting millions of Americans every year. The only way to be sure that you are not a victim of identity theft is to check your credit report annually.

C. CREDIT SCORES

Accurate assessment and interpretation of credit reports takes training. When applying for a mortgage and many auto loans, you can be fairly certain that an employee of the creditor will actually read and review your credit report. But most businesses, including most credit card companies, do not find it cost effective to carefully read every credit report.

Credit scores provide an alternative. Fair Isaac & Co (FICO), the primary vendor of credit scores, uses an algorithm applied to your credit history and creates a three-digit credit score. For many credit decisions the only factor is whether your credit score is above or below a specific number, which varies by creditor and the specific type of credit applied for. For many years, most credit scores were generated by FICO, even if it came from a credit reporting agency or credit card company. In 2006 the three credit reporting agencies partnered to create VantageScore, which uses a three-digit credit score similar to FICO but with a slightly different range and criteria. VantageScore provides credit scores to several organizations that provide free credit scores to consumers, including Credit Karma. But FICO is more commonly used by lenders than is VantageScore.

FICO makes no secret of its basic criteria for credit scores, although it does not make available the precise algorithm to compute your score:[8]

- 35 percent is based on your payment history; late payments, collection actions, and bankruptcies negatively impact your score.

---

8. *What's In My FICO Score?*, Fair Isaac & Co. at https://www.myfico.com/credit-education/whats-in-your-credit-score (last accessed September 3, 2019).

- 30 percent reflects the amount of available credit that you are using. For example, you may have a credit card with a $15,000 limit, but you are only using $1,000 of the available credit. For the best score, FICO recommends keeping each credit card below 10 percent of the available credit.
- 15 percent is the length of your relationship with creditors. The longer you maintain accounts in good standing, the higher your credit score.
- 10 percent is impacted by inquiries. There are two types of inquiries: hard and soft. Hard inquiries are when you initiate a credit check and give permission. A hard inquiry impacts your credit score, but by category. For example, if you apply for a mortgage, your credit score will not be further reduced by applying for mortgages with other lenders for about two weeks. Soft inquiries are when creditors pay the credit reporting agencies to find potential customers meeting certain qualifications; soft inquiries are not included in this calculation.
- 10 percent of your score relates to your mix of credit. The score is increased by having a mix of credit (e.g. credit cards and a mortgage) and also by the types of credit cards (many are harder to get than are others).

DO I NEED TO BUY MY CREDIT SCORE? YES AND NO

There is considerable advertising to entice people to purchase their credit score. And credit scores do determine many lending decisions, including most decisions by banks to issue credit cards. But is it necessary to buy a credit score?

The most widely used credit score used by lenders is the FICO score, and FICO charges a fee to consumers for a copy of their credit score. But purchasing a credit score shortly before applying for credit may not be helpful. While it may be interesting to know your credit score, by the time you are applying for credit there is little one can do to change the credit score.

All Americans should review their credit report annually and can do so at no charge at the FTC's website: annualcreditreport.com. Ensuring there are no mistakes on your credit report, and learning what factors are important will improve your credit score over time. Reviewing your credit report is also the best way to avoid identity theft.

VantageScores are often available for free from many credit card companies and sent to customers monthly, as well as through organizations like Credit Karma. While a VantageScore and a FICO score are not identical, either will let consumers know generally whether they are likely to receive the best rates for credit, or whether they need to work to improve their credit history.

THE CONSUMER FINANCIAL PROTECTION BUREAU

The CFPB was formed in 2010 as part of the Dodd-Frank Wall Street Reform and Consumer Protection Act of 2010. The CFPB has had a rocky history because many members of Congress were against establishing the agency and have continued to fight against its statutory mission. In the meantime, the CFPB has assisted over 1.2 million consumers by responding to complaints regarding specific financial products and actions by financial services companies. The CFPB website (www.consumerfinance .gov) contains information that may be helpful to consumers seeking information about financial products. The CFPB responds promptly to consumer complaints about financial products and companies, and can often help resolve disputes. To file a complaint with the CFPB, visit www.consumerfinance.gov/complaint.

NOTES AND COMMENTS

1. Different attorneys have different styles. While some bankruptcy attorneys provide valuable assistance to clients by counseling them through bankruptcy proceedings, other attorneys are also interested in helping their client avoid future financial distress. Financial literacy in the United States is generally quite poor, with many Americans having little understanding of bank accounts, credit cards, mortgages, and interest. What counseling can you provide a client considering bankruptcy or in bankruptcy to improve the client's chances for financial success in the future?

2. If a client tells you they have a low credit score, what specific advice can you give them to help raise their score in the future?

SPEAKING OF FINANCIAL LITERACY . . .

For many years, American high schools required a course in Economics or some related course teaching basic financial literacy. While many schools are reinstituting these requirements, for several decades most Americans received no financial training in public schools. The result is most Americans are unable to understand or correctly use credit, loans, banks, and other financial instruments. Only 24 percent of a relevant sample of millennial generation adults passed a basic financial literacy test administered by the National Endowment for Financial Education. Thirty-five percent of adults with a credit history have at least one account in collections. Slightly more than half of all Americans could pay for a hypothetical $400 medical emergency.

When Congress amended the Bankruptcy Code in 2005, it required most bankruptcy filers to undergo credit counseling in a government-approved program. At the conclusion of a bankruptcy proceeding, filers must participate in a government-approved financial management education program before any debt can be discharged. 11 U.S.C. § 109(h)(1).

The creation of this requirement led to the development of a large number of businesses focused on credit counseling and, in some cases, so-called credit repair. Particularly with credit repair, debtors seeking counseling may just as easily become victims of a scam.

Each bankruptcy court maintains a list of approved counseling programs, which can be found on the court's website. Regardless of whether your client is considering bankruptcy, anyone disadvantaged by financial illiteracy may benefit from such a program. The best choice of a program is likely one that a bankruptcy court has vetted and approved.

Debtors may find the best experience with counseling from a nonprofit organization that has been engaged in counseling for at least seven years. The organization should be willing to waive fees for those who cannot afford the counseling. And of course the organization should be listed on the local bankruptcy court website.

D. FAIR DEBT COLLECTION PRACTICES ACT

The Fair Debt Collection Practices Act (FDCPA) is part of the Consumer Credit Protection Act, Title 15 of the U.S. Code. The Federal Trade Commission and Consumer Financial Protection Bureau enforce the FDCPA.[9] Violations of the FDCPA may lead to actual damages as well as statutory damages of up to $1,000 for each violation.

Under the FDCPA, a debt collector (including lawyers who regularly engage in debt collection) cannot engage in unfair, deceptive, and abusive

---

9. The CFPB enforces the FDCPA against financial institutions, and the FTC enforces the Act against all other organizations, including third-party debt collectors.

practices when collecting a consumer debt. Most of these prohibitions consider the time, place, or manner of collecting a debt. Some of the prohibited practices include:

- Use or threat of violence
- Harassment
- Intimidation, including the use of obscene language
- Deception, including lying about the amount of debt or the legal consequences of failure to repay
- Calling the debtor at odd times (times outside 9 A.M. to 8 P.M.) without the debtor's permission
- Calling the debtor at work if asked not to do so
- Engaging in unusual or unfair collection practices, such as overcollection or soliciting postdated checks

In passing the FDCPA, Congress found that "[a]busive debt collection practices contribute to the number of personal bankruptcies, to marital instability, to the loss of jobs, and to invasions of individual privacy."[10]

One area of frequent confusion is to whom the FDCPA applies. The Act applies primarily to third-party entities that do not loan money but instead collect money. The FDCPA does not apply to creditors that extended the credit or that were otherwise a party to creating the debt. In other words, if a bank loans a consumer money, and the debtor falls behind on payments, any efforts by that bank to collect its own debt are not covered by the FDCPA.[11] The Act was drafted this way because Congress believed that creditors that deal directly with the public have a reputation to protect and are unlikely to engage in abusive practices.[12] An important exception to the rule is if a debt issuer attempts to collect a debt under a different name. So, for example, assume the fictional Acme National Bank gave a mortgage to a consumer and the consumer fell behind on payments. If Acme telephoned the consumer to inquire about payments as Acme National Bank, then the FDCPA does not apply. If Acme decided it might have better results if the calls came from a group at the bank called "Acme Payment Collections," then the FDCPA does apply.

When the FDCPA does apply, if the debtor is known to be represented by an attorney with regard to the debt being collected, the debt collector must communicate with the attorney rather than the debtor. In addition,

---

10. 15 U.S.C. § 1692a.
11. 15 U.S.C. § 1692b.
12. This approach remains controversial. There is currently a split between the U.S. courts of appeal regarding whether creditors are ever covered by the FDCPA. The CFPB announced in 2013 that it would promulgate rules to bring banks under the collection harassment standards of the FDCPA, but that effort is currently on hold. The FTC has filed amicus briefs in specific cases arguing that banks originating debt are also under some circumstances debt collectors covered by the Act.

the debt collector must provide to the consumer information regarding the amount of the debt being collected and the identity of the creditor to whom the debt is owed.

WHAT ARE DEBT COLLECTORS?

Many businesses try to focus on what they do best. For example, a bank's greatest skill may be lending money, not collecting debts. Debt collection requires a specialized staff, the cost of which only increases a bank's financial losses on an uncollectable debt. Additionally, there can be certain tax advantages when a business declares a debt as a total loss rather than continuing to try to collect the money.

Third-party debt collectors buy debt from creditors, usually through a bidding process. Because debts are difficult to collect, debt collectors pay an average of four cents on the dollar. In other words, if a creditor was owed $1,000 on a debt unlikely to be collected, the creditor may sell that debt to the third-party collector for $40. At that point the debt is owed to the third-party collector and not to the original creditor. And anything the third-party collector receives from the debtor over $40 is profit, at least after paying ordinary business expenses.

Debt collection has often been associated with abusive practices because debt collectors are only in business to collect money, and almost anything they are paid is profitable. The system can be particularly frustrating for consumers who claim they do not owe some part or any of the debt. The original creditor is no longer involved, and the debt collector may have little or no information about how the original debt was generated.

The FDCPA requires debt collectors to notify debtors of the name of the original creditor, and debtors have 30 days to dispute or question the validity of the debt. 15 U.S.C. § 1692h. The law does not provide for any assistance in erroneous collections if the consumer fails to notify the debt collector in writing within 30 days.

If the debtor no longer owes the debt, the debtor may notify the debt collector in writing to cease collection action on the debt, indicating that the debtor has paid the debt. If the debtor actually does owe the debt, he or she may still notify the debt collector in writing to cease all further communications regarding the debt. Though most communication must then stop, the debt collector will still have some ability to notify the debtor of other available remedies for debt collection. Of course, if it is a valid debt, the debtor remains responsible for it. But rather than trying to collect through direct contact with the debtor, the debt collector will instead need to use judicial process to collect the debt once the debtor sends a cease-communication notice. In the following case the Supreme Court considers the issue of whether it is lawful to collect a debt that has statutorily expired.

FDCPA RULES REGARDING THIRD PARTY COMMUNICATIONS

15 U.S.C. § 1692(b)

A debt collector may contact a third person (someone other than the debtor or the debtor's spouse, or a person legally responsible for the debtor such as a parent or guardian) for the sole purpose of obtaining information regarding how to contact the debtor. The third party does not have to provide such information, and in most cases the third party should only be contacted one time. In contacting a third person, the debt collector should not discuss the debt owed but merely seek to obtain contact information. And, of course, the debt collector cannot engage in any of the deceptive, unfair, or abusive practices listed above in communications with the third party.

Midland Funding, LLC v. Johnson

137 S. Ct. 1407 (2017)

BREYER, Justice

The Fair Debt Collection Practices Act, 91 Stat. 874, 15 U.S.C. § 1692 et seq., prohibits a debt collector from asserting any "false, deceptive, or misleading representation," or using any "unfair or unconscionable means" to collect, or attempt to collect, a debt, §§ 1692e, 1692f. In this case, a debt collector filed a written statement in a Chapter 13 bankruptcy proceeding claiming that the debtor owed the debt collector money. The statement made clear, however, that the 6-year statute of limitations governing collection of the claimed debt had long since run. The question before us is whether the debt collector's filing of that statement falls within the scope of the aforementioned provisions of the Fair Debt Collection Practices Act. We conclude that it does not.

* * *

In March 2014, Aleida Johnson, the respondent, filed for personal bankruptcy under Chapter 13 of the Bankruptcy Code (or Code), 11 U.S.C. § 1301 et seq., in the Federal District Court for the Southern

District of Alabama. Two months later, Midland Funding, LLC, the petitioner, filed a "proof of claim," a written statement asserting that Johnson owed Midland a credit-card debt of $1,879.71. The statement added that the last time any charge appeared on Johnson's account was in May 2003, more than 10 years before Johnson filed for bankruptcy. The relevant statute of limitations is six years. See Ala. Code § 6–2–34 (2014). Johnson, represented by counsel, objected to the claim; Midland did not respond to the objection; and the Bankruptcy Court disallowed the claim.

Subsequently, Johnson brought this lawsuit against Midland seeking actual damages, statutory damages, attorney's fees, and costs for a violation of the Fair Debt Collection Practices Act. See 15 U.S.C. § 1692k. The District Court decided that the Act did not apply and therefore dismissed the action. The Court of Appeals for the Eleventh Circuit disagreed and reversed the District Court. 823 F.3d 1334 (2016). . . . We granted the petition. We now reverse the Court of Appeals.

. . . Like the majority of Courts of Appeals that have considered the matter, we conclude that Midland's filing of a proof of claim that on its face indicates that the limitations period has run does not fall within the scope of any of the five relevant words of the Fair Debt Collection Practices Act. We believe it reasonably clear that Midland's proof of claim was not "false, deceptive, or misleading." Midland's proof of claim falls within the Bankruptcy Code's definition of the term "claim." A "claim" is a "right to payment." 11 U.S.C. § 101(5)(A). State law usually determines whether a person has such a right. The relevant state law is the law of Alabama. And Alabama's law, like the law of many States, provides that a creditor has the right to payment of a debt even after the limitations period has expired.

Johnson argues that the Code's word "claim" means "enforceable claim." She notes that this Court once referred to a bankruptcy "claim" as "an enforceable obligation." And, she concludes, Midland's "proof of claim" was false (or deceptive or misleading) because its "claim" was not enforceable.

But we do not find this argument convincing. The word "enforceable" does not appear in the Code's definition of "claim."

* * *

Whether Midland's assertion of an obviously time-barred claim is "unfair" or "unconscionable" (within the terms of the Fair Debt Collection Practices Act) presents a closer question. First, Johnson points out that several lower courts have found or indicated that, in the context of an ordinary civil action to collect a debt, a debt collector's assertion of a claim known to be time barred is "unfair."

We are not convinced, however, by this precedent. It considers a debt collector's assertion in a civil suit of a claim known to be stale. We assume, for argument's sake, that the precedent is correct in that context (a matter this Court itself has not decided and does not now decide). But the context of a civil suit differs significantly from the present context, that of a Chapter 13 bankruptcy proceeding. The lower courts rested their conclusions upon their concern that a consumer might unwittingly repay a time-barred debt. . . .

These considerations have significantly diminished force in the context of a Chapter 13 bankruptcy. The consumer initiates such a proceeding, see 11 U.S.C. §§ 301, 303(a), and consequently the consumer is not likely to pay a stale claim just to avoid going to court. A knowledgeable trustee is available. See § 1302(a). Procedural bankruptcy rules more directly guide the evaluation of claims. See Fed. Rule Bkrtcy. Proc. 3001(c)(3)(A); Advisory Committee's Notes on Rule 3001–2011 Amdt., 11 U.S.C. App., p. 678. And, as the Eighth Circuit Bankruptcy Appellate Panel put it, the claims resolution process is "generally a more streamlined and less unnerving prospect for a debtor than facing a collection lawsuit."

* * *

. . . The bankruptcy system, as we have already noted, treats untimeliness as an affirmative defense. The trustee normally bears the burden of investigating claims and pointing out that a claim is stale. See supra, at 1412–1413. Moreover, protections available in a Chapter 13 bankruptcy proceeding minimize the risk to the debtor. See supra, at 1413. And, at least on occasion, the assertion of even a stale claim can benefit a debtor. Its filing and disallowance "discharge[s]" the debt. 11 U.S.C. § 1328(a). And that discharge means that the debt (even if unenforceable) will not remain on a credit report potentially affecting an individual's ability to borrow money, buy a home, and perhaps secure employment.

* * *

To find the Fair Debt Collection Practices Act applicable here would upset that "delicate balance." From a substantive perspective it would authorize a new significant bankruptcy-related remedy in the absence of language in the Code providing for it. Administratively, it would permit postbankruptcy litigation in an ordinary civil court concerning a creditor's state of mind—a matter often hard to determine. See 15 U.S.C. § 1692k(c) (safe harbor for any debt collector who "shows by a preponderance of evidence that the violation was not intentional and resulted from a bona fide error notwithstanding the maintenance of procedures reasonably adapted to avoid any such error"). Procedurally, it would require creditors (who assert a claim) to investigate the merits of an affirmative defense (typically the debtor's job to assert and prove) lest the creditor later be found to have known the claim was untimely. The upshot could well be added complexity, changes in settlement incentives, and a shift from the debtor to the creditor the obligation to investigate the staleness of a claim.

* * *

For these reasons, we conclude that filing (in a Chapter 13 bankruptcy proceeding) a proof of claim that is obviously time barred is not a false, deceptive, misleading, unfair, or unconscionable debt collection practice within the meaning of the Fair Debt Collection Practices Act. The judgment of the Eleventh Circuit is reversed. . . .

(Dissenting opinion by Justices Sotomayor, Ginsburg, and Kagan omitted.)

(Citations omitted.)

NOTES AND COMMENTS

1. The Supreme Court granted certiorari on the *Midland Funding* case to resolve a split among the circuit courts regarding whether filing of a stale claim in a bankruptcy case can be a violation of the FDCPA. Midland Funding, LLC v. Johnson, 137 S. Ct. 326 (2016); *see also* Nelson v. Midland Credit Mgmt., Inc., 828 F.3d 749 (8th Cir. 2016) (filing of proof of claim on time-barred debt is not a violation of the FDCPA because the bankruptcy code provides protections for the debtor); In re Robinson, 554 B.R. 800, 806 (Bankr. W.D. La. 2016) (noting that Second, Eighth, and Ninth Circuits have held that FDCPA does not apply in bankruptcy cases, while Third, Seventh, and Eleventh Circuits have upheld use of FDCPA in bankruptcy cases on issue of filing stale claim). Justice Sotomayor noted in dissent that the nation's 6,000 debt collection agencies earned over $13 billion in 2016, and she suggested that attempts to collect stale debts is a business strategy rather than an innocent mistake. "For years, they have filed suit in state courts—often in small-claims courts, where formal rules of evidence do not apply—to collect even debts too old to be enforced by those courts." 137 S. Ct. at 1416. She further wrote "[a]s a wide variety of courts and commentators have observed, debt buyers

have 'deluge[d]' the bankruptcy courts with claims 'on debts deemed unenforceable under state statutes of limitations.'" *Id.* The majority noted that the bankruptcy trustee serves as a gatekeeper to protect the debtor. The dissent pointed out than an amicus brief filed by the United States on behalf of the bankruptcy trustees, the government stated that trustees "cannot realistically be expected to identify every time-barred . . . claim filed in every bankruptcy." Brief for United States as *Amicus Curiae* 25–26. Do you find the majority or dissent more persuasive, and why?

2. Who is harmed when a debt collector files a proof of claim on a stale claim in a bankruptcy case? Who does the FDCPA seek to protect?

3. In September 2018, California passed a new law, effective January 1, 2019, requiring debt collectors to let consumers know when collection of a claim is barred by the passage of time. For a claim that is time-barred but may still be reported to a credit reporting agency, the required communication provides that "[t]he law limits how long you can be sued on a debt. Because of the age of your debt, we will not sue you for it. If you do not pay the debt, [insert name of debt collector] may [continue to] report it to the credit reporting agencies as unpaid for as long as the law permits this reporting." For a claim that is barred and can no longer be reported, the communication is "[t]he law limits how long you can be sued on a debt. Because of the age of your debt, we will not sue you for it, and we will not report it to any credit reporting agency." Cal. Civ. Code §1788.14.

DECEPTIVE CLAIMS SOMETIMES MADE BY DEBT COLLECTORS

Debt collection is a lawful business, and not all debt collectors engage in deceptive conduct. Certain deceptive statements, however, are frequently used by debt collectors violating the law:

* *Paying off a debt in collection will improve a consumer's credit report.*
  o Unpaid debt remains on a credit report for seven years. Paying off a debt older than seven years will not be noted in a credit report. Even if the debt is less than seven years old, not all debt collectors provide payment information to Equifax, Experian, or TransUnion.

* *Paying off debts in collection will improve a consumer's credit score.*
  o Credit scores are derived from credit histories, and as mentioned above, not all debt collectors report payment information to the credit reporting agencies. Even if the information is reported, the debt payments may have little impact on a credit score, which is calculated on many other factors.

> • *Paying off debts in collection demonstrate a consumer's creditworthiness; or paying off debts in collection increase the likelihood that a consumer will be extended credit by lenders, and at more favorable terms.*
>   o Many creditors would weigh debt payment to a collection agency as less important than having generated and defaulted on the debt in the first place.
>
> *See* CFPB Bulletin 2013-08, July 10, 2013.

While creditors are required to file a proof of claim in most bankruptcy cases in order to participate in the bankruptcy distribution, what happens when a claim is not enforceable under state law? Recent cases have considered whether a creditor filing a claim for which the statute of limitations has run violates another federal law: the Fair Debt Collection Practices Act. The FDCPA provides that debt collectors must refrain from debt collection practices that are unconscionable. As you read the following two cases, consider how the traditional remedy of denying a claim may be bolstered by an FDCPA claim.

Dubois v. Atlas Acquisitions LLC (In re Dubois)

834 F.3d 522 (4th Cir. 2016)

FLOYD, Circuit Judge

Appellants Kimberly Adkins and Chaille Dubois filed separate Chapter 13 bankruptcy petitions in the Bankruptcy Court for the District of Maryland. Appellee Atlas Acquisitions LLC (Atlas) filed proofs of claim in their bankruptcy cases based on debts that were barred by Maryland's statute of limitations. The issue on appeal is whether Atlas violated the Fair Debt Collection Practices Act (FDCPA) by filing proofs of claim based on time-barred debts. We hold that Atlas's conduct does not violate the FDCPA, and affirm the bankruptcy court's dismissal of Appellants' FDCPA claims and related state law claim.

. . . The facts of Appellants' cases are similar. Adkins filed for Chapter 13 bankruptcy on August 29, 2014. Atlas filed two proofs of claim in her case. . . . It is undisputed that both debts were beyond Maryland's three-year statute of limitations when Atlas purchased and attempted to assert the debts in Adkins's bankruptcy case. See Md. Code Ann., Cts. & Jud. Proc. § 5–101. Adkins neither listed the debts on her bankruptcy schedules nor sent a notice of bankruptcy to Atlas.

Dubois filed for Chapter 13 bankruptcy on December 6, 2014. Atlas filed a proof of claim. . . . It is undisputed that this debt was also beyond Maryland's statute of limitations when Atlas purchased and attempted to assert the debt in Dubois's bankruptcy case. Dubois did not list the debt on her bankruptcy schedules nor did she send a notice of bankruptcy to Atlas.

Adkins and Dubois filed separate adversary complaints against Atlas. Both objected to Atlas's claims as being time-barred and further alleged that Atlas violated the FDCPA by filing proofs of claim on stale debts. Appellants sought disallowance of Atlas's claims as well as damages, attorney's fees, and costs under the FDCPA.

* * *

Before addressing the substance of Appellants' claims, we provide a brief overview of the relevant statutes in this case: the Bankruptcy Code (the "Code") and the FDCPA.

. . . A bankruptcy debtor must file with the bankruptcy court a list of creditors, a schedule of assets and liabilities, and a statement of the debtor's financial affairs. 11 U.S.C. § 521(a)(1). Scheduling a debt notifies the creditor of the bankruptcy and of the creditor's opportunity to file a proof of claim asserting a right to payment against the debtor's estate.

The bankruptcy court may "allow" or "disallow" claims from sharing in the distribution of the bankruptcy estate. 11 U.S.C. § 502. . . .

. . . Congress enacted the FDCPA to eliminate abusive debt collection practices and to ensure that debt collectors who refrain from such practices are not competitively disadvantaged. 15 U.S.C. § 1692(a), (e). The FDCPA regulates the conduct of "debt collectors," defined to include "any person who uses any instrumentality of interstate commerce or the mails in any business the principal purpose of which is the collection of any debts, or who regularly collects or attempts to collect, directly or indirectly, debts owed or due or asserted to be owed or due another." Id. § 1692a(6). Among other things, the FDCPA prohibits debt collectors from using "any false, deceptive, or misleading representation or means in connection with the collection of any debt," and from using "unfair or unconscionable means to collect or attempt to collect any debt." Id. §§ 1692e–1692f. The statute provides a non-exhaustive list of conduct that is deceptive or unfair (e.g., falsely implying that the debt collector is affiliated with the United States, id. § 1692e(1)). Debt collectors who violate the FDCPA are liable for actual damages, statutory damages of up to $1,000, and attorney's fees and costs. See id. § 1692k(a).

. . . Federal courts have consistently held that a debt collector violates the FDCPA by filing a lawsuit or threatening to file a lawsuit to collect a time-barred debt. Appellants contend that filing a proof of claim on a time-barred debt in a bankruptcy proceeding similarly violates the FDCPA. Atlas counters that filing a proof of claim is not debt collection activity and is therefore not subject to the FDCPA. Alas [sic] further argues that, even if the FDCPA applies, filing a proof of claim on a time-barred debt does not violate its provisions. These arguments are addressed in turn.

. . . Atlas does not dispute that it is a debt collector but argues that filing a proof of claim does not constitute debt collection activity regulated by the FDCPA. Instead, Atlas contends that a proof of claim is merely a "request to participate in the bankruptcy process."

Determining whether a communication constitutes an attempt to collect a debt is a "commonsense inquiry" that evaluates the "nature of the parties' relationship," the "[objective] purpose and context of the communication []," and whether the communication includes a demand for payment. Here, the "only relationship between [the parties] [is] that of a debtor and debt collector." Moreover, the "animating purpose" in filing a proof of claim is to obtain payment by sharing in the distribution of the debtor's bankruptcy estate. This fits squarely within the Supreme Court's understanding of debt collection for purposes of the FDCPA. Precedent and common sense dictate that filing a proof of claim is an attempt to collect a debt. The absence of an explicit demand for payment does not alter that conclusion, nor does the fact that the bankruptcy court may ultimately disallow the claim.

Atlas argues that treating a proof of claim as an attempt to collect a debt would conflict with the Bankruptcy Code's automatic stay provision. The automatic stay provides that filing a bankruptcy petition "operates as a stay" of "any act to collect, assess, or recover a claim against the debtor that arose before the commencement of the case." 11 U.S.C. § 362(a)(6). Atlas argues that if filing a proof of claim were an act to collect debt, then such filing would violate the automatic stay, "an absurd result."

Atlas's quandary is easily resolved as the automatic stay simply bars actions to collect debt outside of the bankruptcy proceeding. The automatic stay helps channel debt collection activity into the bankruptcy process. It does not strip such activity of its debt collection nature for purposes of the FDCPA.

Finally, Atlas argues that filing a proof of claim is not an attempt to collect debt because the proof of claim is directed to the bankruptcy court and trustee rather than to the debtor. However, collection activity directed toward someone other than the debtor may still be actionable under the FDCPA. Although a proof of claim is filed with the bankruptcy court, it is done with the purpose of obtaining payment from the debtor's estate. That the claim is paid by the debtor's estate rather than the debtor personally is irrelevant for purposes of the FDCPA. See 15 U.S.C. §§ 1692e, 1692f (prohibiting the use of deceptive or unfair means to collect "any debt," without specifying a payor).

Accordingly, we find that filing a proof of claim is debt collection activity regulated by the FDCPA.

. . . We next consider whether filing a proof of claim based on a debt that is beyond the applicable statute of limitations violates the FDCPA. Deciding this issue requires closer examination of the claims process in bankruptcy.

The Federal Rules of Bankruptcy Procedure specify the form, content, and filing requirements for a valid proof of claim. See, e.g., Fed. R. Bankr. P. 3001.

A properly filed proof of claim is prima facie evidence of the claim's validity, and the claim is "deemed allowed" unless "a party in interest" objects. 11 U.S.C. § 502. The bankruptcy trustee and debtor are parties in interest who may object. Indeed, the trustee has a statutory duty to "examine proofs of claims and object to the allowance of any claim that is improper." Id. § 704(a)(5).

If objected to, the Code disallows claims based on time-barred debts. See id. § 502(b)(1) (stating that a claim shall be disallowed if it is "unenforceable against the debtor . . . under any agreement or applicable law"); id. § 558 (stating that the bankruptcy estate has "the benefit of any defense available to the debtor . . . including statutes of limitation"). As previously noted, debts that are "provided for by the plan or disallowed under section 502" may be discharged. Id. § 1328 (emphasis added).

Appellants contend that the FDCPA should be applied to prohibit debt collectors from filing proofs of claim on time-barred debts.

Appellants argue that a time-barred debt is not a "claim" within the meaning of the Bankruptcy Code and that filing claims on time-barred debts is an abusive practice because such claims are seldom objected to and therefore receive payment from the bankruptcy estate to the detriment of the debtor and other creditors. Atlas, meanwhile, argues that a time-barred debt is a valid "claim" and that filing such a claim should not be prohibited because only debts that are treated in the bankruptcy system may be discharged.

. . . The Bankruptcy Code defines the term "claim" broadly to mean a "right to payment, whether or not such right is reduced to judgment, liquidated, unliquidated, fixed, contingent, matured, unmatured, disputed, undisputed, legal, equitable, secured, or unsecured." 11 U.S.C. § 101(5)(A). By using the "broadest possible definition," the Code "contemplates that all legal obligations of the debtor, no matter how remote or contingent, will be able to be dealt with in the bankruptcy case," thereby providing the debtor the "broadest possible relief." H.R. Rep. No. 95–595, p. 309 (1977); S. Rep. No. 95–989, p. 22 (1978).

> [W]hen the Bankruptcy Code uses the word claim . . . it is usually referring to a right to payment recognized under state law." Under Maryland law, the statute of limitations "does not operate to extinguish [a] debt, but to bar the remedy." Indeed, a stale debt may be revived if the debtor sufficiently acknowledges the debt's existence.

Appellants note that a debt must be enforceable to constitute a claim, citing the Supreme Court's statement that "[t]he plain meaning of a 'right to payment' is nothing more nor less than an enforceable obligation." However, we do not read the Supreme Court's statement to mean that a debt must be enforceable in court to be a claim. Indeed, the Bankruptcy Code treats debts that are "contingent" or "unmatured" as claims notwithstanding that such debts are not presently enforceable in court. 11 U.S.C. § 101(5)(A). . . .

It is also notable that while the Bankruptcy Code provides that time-barred debts are to be disallowed, see, e.g., 11 U.S.C § 558, the Code nowhere suggests that such debts are not to be filed in the first place. Indeed, the Bankruptcy Rules were recently amended to facilitate the assessment of a claim's timeliness by requiring that claims such as the ones at issue in this appeal be filed with a statement setting forth the last transaction date, last payment date, and charge-off date on the account. Fed. R. Bankr. P. 3001, advisory committee notes to 2012 Amendments (discussing filing requirements for claims based on open-end or revolving consumer credit agreements). This Rule suggests the Code contemplates that untimely debts will be filed as claims but ultimately disallowed. Lastly, excluding time-barred debts from the scope of bankruptcy "claims," and thus excluding them from the bankruptcy process, would frustrate the Code's "intended effect to define the scope of the term 'claim' as broadly as possible," 2–101 Collier ¶ 101.05, and thereby provide the debtor the broadest possible relief. Accordingly, we conclude that when the statute of limitations does not extinguish debts, a time-barred debt falls within the Bankruptcy Code's broad definition of a claim.

. . . Next, we consider whether filing a proof of claim on a time-barred debt violates the FDCPA notwithstanding that the Bankruptcy Code permits such filing. As noted above, the FDCPA has been interpreted to prohibit filing a lawsuit on a time-barred debt. The rationale has been explained as follows:

> As with any defendant sued on a stale claim, the passage of time not only dulls the consumer's memory of the circumstances and validity of the debt, but heightens the probability that she will no longer have personal records detailing the status of the debt. Indeed, the unfairness of such conduct is particularly clear in the consumer context where courts have imposed a heightened standard of care—that sufficient to protect the least sophisticated consumer. Because few unsophisticated consumers would be aware that a statute of limitations could be used to defend against lawsuits based on stale debts, such consumers would unwittingly acquiesce to such lawsuits. And, even if the consumer realizes that she can use time as a defense, she will more than likely still give in rather than fight the lawsuit because she must still expend energy and resources and subject herself to the embarrassment of going into court to present the defense; this is particularly true in light of the costs of attorneys today.

We note at the outset a unique consideration in the bankruptcy context: if a bankruptcy proceeds as contemplated by the Code, a claim based on a time-barred debt will be objected to by the trustee, disallowed, and ultimately discharged, thereby stopping the creditor from engaging in any further collection activity. If the debt is unscheduled and no proof of claim is filed, the debt continues to exist and the debt collector may lawfully pursue collection activity apart from filing a lawsuit. This is detrimental to the debtor and undermines the bankruptcy system's interest in "the collective treatment of all of a debtor's creditors at one time." Clearly, then, when a time-barred debt is not scheduled the optimal scenario is for a claim to be filed and for the Bankruptcy Code to operate as written.

Appellants complain, however, that trustees often lack the time and resources to examine each proof of claim and object to those that are based on time-barred debts. Debt collectors like Atlas purportedly take advantage of this by filing claims on stale debts in hopes that the claims will go unnoticed and receive some payment from the bankruptcy estate. When successful, these debt collectors reduce the amount of money available to legitimate creditors and may sometimes cause debtors to pay more into their Chapter 13 plans.

We appreciate the harm that can be wrought if time-barred claims go unnoticed. However the solution, in our view, is not to impose liability under the FDCPA that would categorically bar the filing of such claims, but to improve the Code's administration such that it operates as written. This may be accomplished, for example, by allocating additional resources to trustees or through action of the United States Trustee, who appoints and supervises all Chapter 13 trustees. 28 U.S.C. § 586.

Another consideration that counsels against finding FDCPA liability is that, for most Chapter 13 debtors, the amount they pay into their bankruptcy plans is unaffected by the number of unsecured claims that are filed. Chapter 13 debtors typically do not enter into 100 percent repayment plans; thus, their unsecured creditors receive only partial payment of their claims, with the remainder being discharged. As additional claims are filed, unsecured creditors receive a smaller share of available funds but the total amount paid by the debtor remains unchanged. Thus, from the perspective of most Chapter 13 debtors, it may in fact be preferable for a time-barred claim to be filed even if it is not objected to, as the debtor will likely pay the same total amount to creditors and the debt can be discharged.

Various other considerations also differentiate filing a proof of claim on a time-barred debt from filing a lawsuit to collect such debt. First, the Bankruptcy Rules require claims like the ones filed by Atlas to accurately state the last transaction and charge-off date on the account, making untimely claims easier to detect and relieving debtors from the burden of producing evidence to show that the claim is time-barred. Second, a bankruptcy debtor is protected by a trustee and often by counsel who are responsible for objecting to improper claims even if, as Appellants argue, they currently do not always do so. Third, unlike a debtor who is unwillingly sued, a Chapter 13 debtor voluntarily initiates the bankruptcy case, diminishing concerns about the embarrassment the debtor may feel in objecting to a stale claim. In sum, the reasons why it is "unfair" and "misleading" to sue on a time-barred debt are considerably diminished in the bankruptcy context, where the debtor has additional protections and potentially benefits from having the debt treated in the bankruptcy process.

* * *

We conclude that filing a proof of claim in a Chapter 13 bankruptcy based on a debt that is time-barred does not violate the FDCPA when the statute of limitations does not extinguish the debt.

* * *

(Citations omitted.)

Crawford v. LVNV Funding, LLC

758 F.3d 1254 (11th Cir. 2014)

GOLDBERG, Judge

A deluge has swept through U.S. bankruptcy courts of late. Consumer debt buyers—armed with hundreds of delinquent accounts purchased from creditors—are filing proofs of claim on debts deemed unenforceable under state statutes of limitations. This appeal considers whether a proof of claim to collect a stale debt in Chapter 13 bankruptcy violates the Fair Debt Collection Practices Act ("FDCPA" or "Act"). 15 U.S.C. §§ 1692–1692p (2006).

We answer this question affirmatively. The FDCPA's broad language, our precedent, and the record compel the conclusion that defendants' conduct violated a number of the Act's protective provisions. *See id.* §§ 1692(e), 1692d–1692f. . . .

Stanley Crawford, the plaintiff in this case, owed $2,037.99 to the Heilig–Meyers furniture company. Heilig–Meyers charged off this debt in 1999, and in September 2001, a company affiliated with defendant LVNV Funding, LLC, acquired the debt from Heilig–Meyers. The last transaction on the account occurred one month later on October 26, 2001. Accordingly, under the three-year Alabama statute of limitations that governed the account, Crawford's debt became unenforceable in both state and federal court in October 2004. *See* Ala.Code § 6–2–37(1).

Then, on February 2, 2008, Crawford filed for Chapter 13 bankruptcy in the Middle District of Alabama. During the proceeding, LVNV filed a proof of claim to collect the Heilig–Meyers debt, notwithstanding that the limitations period had expired four years earlier. In response, Crawford filed a counterclaim against LVNV via an adversary proceeding pursuant to Bankruptcy Rule 3007(b).

* * *

Section 1692e of the FDCPA provides that "[a] debt collector may not use any false, deceptive, or misleading representation or means in connection with the collection of any debt." 15 U.S.C. § 1692e. Section 1692f states that "[a] debt collector may not use unfair or unconscionable means to collect or attempt to collect any debt." *Id.* § 1692f.

Because Congress did not provide a definition for the terms "unfair" or "unconscionable," this Court has looked to the dictionary for help. "The plain meaning of 'unfair' is 'marked by injustice, partiality, or deception.'" Further, "an act or practice is deceptive or unfair if it has the tendency or capacity to deceive." *Id.* (quotation marks omitted and alterations adopted). We also explained that "[t]he term 'unconscionable' means 'having no conscience'; 'unscrupulous'; 'showing no regard for conscience'; 'affronting the sense of justice, decency, or reasonableness.'" We have also noted that "[t]he phrase 'unfair or unconscionable' is as vague as they come." *Id.*

Given this ambiguity, we have adopted a "least-sophisticated consumer" standard to evaluate whether a debt collector's conduct is "deceptive," "misleading," "unconscionable," or "unfair" under the statute. The inquiry is not whether the particular plaintiff-consumer was deceived or misled; instead, the question is "whether the 'least sophisticated consumer' would have been deceived" by the debt collector's conduct. The "least-sophisticated consumer" standard takes into account that consumer-protection laws are "not made for the protection of experts, but for the public—that vast multitude which includes the ignorant, the unthinking, and the credulous." "However, the test has an objective component in that while protecting naive consumers, the standard also prevents liability for bizarre or idiosyncratic interpretations of collection notices by preserving a quotient of reasonableness."

Given our precedent, we must examine whether LVNV's conduct— filing and trying to enforce in court a claim known to be time-barred— would be unfair, unconscionable, deceiving, or misleading towards the least-sophisticated consumer.

. . . The reason behind LVNV's practice of filing time-barred proofs of claim in bankruptcy court is simple. Absent an objection from either the Chapter 13 debtor or the trustee, the time-barred claim is automatically allowed against the debtor pursuant to 11 U.S.C. § 502(a)-(b) and Bankruptcy Rule 3001(f). As a result, the debtor must then pay the debt from his future wages as part of the Chapter 13 repayment plan, notwithstanding that the debt is time-barred and unenforceable in court.

That is what happened in this case. LVNV filed the time-barred proof of claim in May of 2008, shortly after debtor Crawford petitioned for Chapter 13 protection.

But neither the bankruptcy trustee nor Crawford objected to the claim during the bankruptcy proceeding; instead, the trustee actually paid monies from the Chapter 13 estate to LVNV (or its surrogates) for the time-barred debt. It wasn't until four years later, in May 2012, that debtor Crawford—with the assistance of counsel—objected to LVNV's claim as unenforceable.

LVNV acknowledges, as it must, that its conduct would likely subject it to FDCPA liability had it filed a lawsuit to collect this time-barred debt in state court. Federal circuit and district courts have uniformly held that a debt collector's threatening to sue on a time-barred debt and/or filing a time-barred suit in state court to recover that debt violates §§ 1692e and 1692f.

As an example, the Seventh Circuit has reasoned that the FDCPA outlaws "stale suits to collect consumer debts" as unfair because (1) "few unsophisticated consumers would be aware that a statute of limitations could be used to defend against lawsuits based on stale debts" and would therefore "unwittingly acquiesce to such lawsuits"; (2) "the passage of time . . . dulls the consumer's memory of the circumstances and validity of the debt"; and (3) the delay in suing after the limitations period "heightens the probability that [the debtor] will no longer have personal records" about the debt.

These observations reflect the purpose behind statutes of limitations. Such limitations periods "represent a pervasive legislative judgment that it is unjust to fail to put the adversary on notice to defend within a specified period of time." That is so because "the right to be free of stale claims in time comes to prevail over the right to prosecute them." Statutes of limitations "protect defendants and the courts from having to deal with cases in which the search for truth may be seriously impaired by the loss of evidence, whether by death or disappearance of witnesses, fading memories, disappearance of documents, or otherwise."

The same is true in the bankruptcy context. In bankruptcy, the limitations period provides a bright line for debt collectors and consumer debtors, signifying a time when the debtor's right to be free of stale claims comes to prevail over a creditor's right to legally enforce the debt. A Chapter 13 debtor's memory of a stale debt may have faded and personal records documenting the debt may have vanished, making it difficult for a consumer debtor to defend against the time-barred claim.

Similar to the filing of a stale lawsuit, a debt collector's filing of a time-barred proof of claim creates the misleading impression to the debtor that the debt collector can legally enforce the debt. The "least sophisticated" Chapter 13 debtor may be unaware that a claim is time barred and unenforceable and thus fail to object to such a claim. Given the Bankruptcy Code's automatic allowance provision, the otherwise unenforceable time-barred debt will be paid from the debtor's future wages as part of his Chapter 13 repayment plan. Such a distribution of funds to debt collectors with time-barred claims then necessarily reduces the payments to other legitimate creditors with enforceable claims. Furthermore, filing objections to time-barred claims consumes energy and resources in a debtor's bankruptcy case, just as filing a limitations defense does in state court. For all of these reasons, under the "least-sophisticated consumer standard" in our binding precedent, LVNV's filing of a time-barred proof of claim against Crawford in bankruptcy was "unfair," "unconscionable," "deceptive," and "misleading" within the broad scope of § 1692e and § 1692f.

Any contrary arguments mentioned in the briefs do not alter this conclusion. For example, we disagree with the contention that LVNV's proof of claim was not a "collection activity" aimed at Crawford and, therefore, not "the sort of debt-collection activity that the FDCPA regulates." As noted earlier, the broad prohibitions of § 1692e apply to a debt collector's "false, deceptive, or misleading *representation or means*" used "*in connection with the collection of any debt.*" 15 U.S.C. § 1692e (emphases added). The broad prohibitions of § 1692f apply to a debt collector's use of "unfair or unconscionable *means to collect or attempt to collect any debt.*" 15 U.S.C. § 1692f (emphasis added). The FDCPA does not define the terms "collection of debt" or "to collect a debt" in §§ 1692e or 1692f. However, in interpreting "to collect a debt" as used in § 1692(a)(6), the Supreme Court has turned to the dictionary's definition: "To collect a debt or claim is to obtain payment or liquidation of it, either by personal solicitation or legal proceedings."

Applying these definitions here, we conclude that LVNV's filing of the proof of claim fell well within the ambit of a "representation" or "means" used in "connection with the collection of any debt." It was an effort "to obtain payment" of Crawford's debt "by legal proceeding." In fact, payments to LVNV were made from Crawford's wages as a result of LVNV's claim. And, it was Crawford—not the trustee—who ultimately objected to defendants' claim as time-barred. Our conclusion that §§ 1692e and 1692f apply to LVNV's proof of claim is consistent with the FDC'PA's definition of a debt-collector as "any person who . . . regularly collects or attempts to collect, *directly or indirectly,* debts owed or due or asserted to be owed or due another." 15 U.S.C. § 1692a(6) (emphasis added).

* * *

Just as LVNV would have violated the FDCPA by filing a lawsuit on stale claims in state court, LVNV violated the FDCPA by filing a stale claim in bankruptcy court.

* * *

(Citations omitted.)

NOTES AND COMMENTS

1. The *Dubois* and *Crawford* cases highlight a circuit split regarding the issue of whether filing of a time-barred proof of claim constitutes a violation of the Fair Debt Collection Practices Act. Despite their differing conclusions, however, the two courts agree on many of the underlying aspects of the case. Identify those points of agreement and how each court followed from those points to differing conclusions.

2. The *Dubois* court suggests that filing of a time-barred claim may actually benefit the debtor by allowing the debtor to obtain a discharge of that debt. This is because the debt, though not collectable in a state-court proceeding, technically still exists after the statute of limitations expires. Consider this statement by the FTC, which was included in a part of the *Dubois* case not included in your excerpt:

   > Although the [debt] collector may not sue you to collect [a time-barred] debt, you still owe it. The collector can continue to contact you to try to collect. . . . [and] [i]n some states, if you pay any amount on a time-barred debt or even promise to pay, the debt is 'revived.'") (saved as ECF opinion attachment). Thus, under Maryland law, a time-barred debt still constitutes a "right to payment" and therefore a "claim" that the holder may file under the Bankruptcy Code.

   Dubois, 834 F.3d at 529, citing FTC, Time–Barred Debts (July 2013), https://www.consumer.ftc.gov/articles/0117-time-barred-debts

3. Review 11 U.S.C. § 502(a). Who could object to the proofs of claim filed by each of Atlas Acquisitions LLC and LVNV Funding, LLC? In both cases, the debtors objected to the claims or sought damages under the FDCPA. Why might another party object? Would those other parties also be entitled to bring an action under the FDCPA?

E. IMPACT OF CONSUMER PROTECTION LAWS ON BANKRUPTCY PROCEEDINGS

Many of the cases involving consumer protection laws in bankruptcy involve a consumer debtor alleging a creditor's failure to comply with creditor protection laws. However, the debtor or trustee can also be the party that must comply with consumer protection laws, as demonstrated in the following case.

In re White Crane Trading Co., Inc.

170 B.R. 694 (Bkrtcy. E.D. Cal. 1994)

KLEIN, Bankruptcy Judge

This motion seeks to revoke an order entered in this case authorizing a sale, variously termed "Chapter 11 Sale" or "Bankruptcy Sale" or "Cash Raising Sale", to be conducted on the premises of the debtor furniture retailer.

The controlling question is whether Judicial Code § 959(b), 28 U.S.C. § 959(b), prevents merchants from using bankruptcy as a screen for conducting financial distress sales of indefinite duration in a manner inconsistent with state consumer protection or deceptive trade practice laws.

A merchant operating as a liquidator has established a nationwide business of running financial distress sales, advertised as "Chapter 11 Sale" or "Bankruptcy Sale" or "Cash Raising Sale", for furniture stores. The merchant fends off local authorities by telling them that the Supremacy Clause prevents them from enforcing consumer protection and deceptive trade practice laws that prohibit false and misleading advertising.

I conclude that the mandate of section 959(b) requiring the trustee and debtor in possession to operate the debtor's business according to the requirements of the valid laws of the state in which such property is situated prohibits the use of bankruptcy as a ruse to circumvent applicable state consumer protection laws by those who continue to operate in the marketplace. . . .

Facts

White Crane Trading Company ("White Crane") began retail furniture operations in September 1992, claiming relation to the Levitz furniture chain. It commenced this bankruptcy case by filing a chapter 11 petition on February 12, 1993, scheduling $342,366.71 in inventory and $779,949.97 in unsecured debt and unpaid sales and employment taxes.

Seven days after commencing the case, White Crane, as debtor in possession, filed a motion for authority to enter into a postpetition "Bankruptcy/Liquidation Sale Agreement" with Planned Sales Promotions ("PSP"), a creature animated by Eugene Rosenberg and Gene Rosenberg Associates ("Rosenberg"). Under the agreement, PSP would conduct an on-going "cash raising" liquidation sale in which PSP would introduce and sell its own furniture in addition to, and in greater quantities than, the debtor's furniture. The sale would be authorized to last for 180 days and could be extended upon agreement. PSP would receive 10 percent of the gross sales of White Crane's inventory and PSP's sales personnel would receive an additional 5 or 6 percent. Net profits from sales of PSP's inventory, after commissions and operating expenses, would be split between PSP and the debtor. The movants said that their goal was to raise the capital necessary for the debtor to remain in the retail furniture business and propose a plan of reorganization.

The creditor's committee and the United States trustee supported the sale after PSP agreed to increase the debtor's share of the net profits. Nobody objected. The motion was granted subject to court-imposed conditions.

The first condition was the deletion of a proposed provision that would have authorized PSP to "conduct the Sale in the manner described herein without the necessity of complying with any federal, state, or local statute or ordinance regarding any licensing and/or permit requirements" that might otherwise apply. I refused to place judicial imprimatur on such a provision, expressing doubt about whether any such provision would be enforceable in light of section 959(b). Professing an intention to comply with otherwise applicable law, the parties deleted the provision.

The second condition related to proposed terms under which PSP would "be permitted to use names, phrases and concepts on all advertising, and at the Sale Location, like 'Bankruptcy Sale', 'Final Sale Days', and 'Going out of Business'" with the proviso that "the use of 'Going out of Business' type phrases shall only be permitted if the proceeding becomes a liquidating chapter 11 proceeding or a [c]hapter 7 proceeding." As a condition of approval, I also required that such phrases as "Bankruptcy Sale" or "Final Sale Days" and "Going Out of Business" could be used only to the extent permitted by applicable nonbankruptcy law, and that phrases such as "Going Out of Business" could be used only if the debtor were operating under a confirmed plan of reorganization that called for liquidation or if the case were to be converted to chapter 7.

PSP represented that no court order or decree of any federal, state, or local government authority existed that would impair consummation of the transactions contemplated by the agreement, and that the consent of any person or entity, other than the bankruptcy court, was not required.

PSP failed to disclose, however, the existence of a permanent injunction issued by a California Superior Court barring Rosenberg and his entities (including PSP) from participating in any furniture sale commonly associated with financial hardship or distress unless the sale is conducted in full compliance with all California statutes, the California Code of Regulations, and local California ordinances and codes governing such sales.

* * *

The sale was advertised in newspapers and on prominently displayed signage as a "chapter 11 bankruptcy sale" with representations that it was "court authorized". When, at a hearing on another matter in the case, I expressed concern that the phrase "court authorized" might inappropriately lend the prestige of the court in a manner that should not be permitted, an assistant district attorney for Sacramento County entered his appearance and noted that there were also issues regarding compliance with California consumer protection laws.

* * *

When the case was converted from chapter 11 to chapter 7 for cause, PSP asked that the sale be allowed to continue because, now that final liquidation was on the horizon, the public would "get serious" about buying. PSP's counsel explained how, consistent with the Rosenberg experience in other sales, the public was now being softened up for the final sale. Action was deferred on the request because the chapter 7 trustee needed to evaluate the situation.

The chapter 7 trustee discovered the undisclosed injunction and a hotbed of consumer protection issues and concluded that the sale was neither in compliance with state law, nor in the best interests of the estate. The trustee also concluded that the primary beneficiary of the sale was Rosenberg.

Pursuant to his discoveries, the chapter 7 trustee filed a motion to revoke the order approving the sale. He was joined by the California Attorney General. . . .

* * *

The primary question is whether a bankruptcy court may authorize a sale that is inconsistent with valid state consumer protection or deceptive trade practice laws.

The governing federal statute is section 959(b) of the Judicial Code:

(b) . . . a trustee, receiver or manager appointed in any case pending in any court of the United States, including a debtor in possession, shall manage and operate the property in his possession as such trustee, receiver or manager according to the requirements of the valid laws of the State in which such property is situated, in the same manner that the owner or possessor thereof would be bound to do if in possession thereof.

28 U.S.C. § 959(b).

The constraints of section 959 limit the debtor's authority to conduct business in the ordinary course and engage in the other transactions that are embodied in section 363. . . .

Section 959(b) has been on the books since 1887. It stands "for the uncontroversial proposition that a trustee must carry out his duties in conformity with state law."

* * *

Valid state consumer protection and deceptive trade practice laws qualify as "valid laws of the State in which such property is situated" for purposes of section 959, which applies to debtors who continue to sell goods in the retail marketplace.

* * *

The purpose of bankruptcy is not to permit debtors or nondebtors to wrest competitive advantage by exempting themselves from the myriad of laws that regulate business. Bankruptcy does not grant the debtor a license to eliminate the marginal cost generated by compliance with valid state laws that constrain nonbankrupt competitors. The Congress has thus required that every debtor in possession and bankruptcy trustee manage and operate the debtor's property and business in compliance with state laws—good, bad, and indifferent—that apply outside of bankruptcy.

* * *

State consumer protection laws recognized by section 959(b) focus on liquidation and going-out-of-business sales because of the widely-understood opportunities for exploitation of the gullible. The furniture industry, in particular, has been singled out for special attention.

Such phrases as "financial distress" or "going out of business" create consumer expectations about how long the sale will last and the nature of the bargains to be expected. Those expectations are easily exploited by merchants who are not really going out of business, who are not really financially distressed, or who are running the sale for an extended period. Thus, consumer protection and deceptive trade practice laws forbid misleading uses of such terms.

The California consumer protection and deceptive trade practice laws that apply in this instance are typical of many laws in many states. False and misleading statements in advertising are prohibited generally. Cal. Bus. & Prof. Code § 17500 (West 1993). And such statements are prohibited in the home furnishings business specifically. *Id.* at § 19150. Detailed regulations implement these statutes. Cal. Code Regs. tit. iv, art. 10, § 1300, et seq. (1993). Some California localities also have pertinent ordinances.

The introduction of new merchandise at financial distress sales is a suspect practice. In California, it is forbidden. Similarly, "special" sales, including liquidation sales, inventory sales, and overstock sales, must exclude new inventory. Here, approximately 70 percent of the furniture was new inventory brought in by PSP.

There is little doubt that the sale in question offended sections 1305 and 1312 of the California regulations for furniture sales.

* * *

Bankruptcy presents a classic distress scenario. Mere use of the word "bankruptcy" conveys essentially the same message as "financial distress" or "going out of business". The consumer has a sense of urgency and expects lower prices and greater bargaining power.

The genuine liquidation bankruptcy sale ordinarily poses no problem under consumer protection and deceptive trade practice laws because nobody is misled. Consumers' expectations comport with reality. But, when the bankruptcy sale is well-financed and extends over a prolonged period, it does have the capacity to mislead. At that juncture, state consumer protection laws become significant.

The problem is illustrated by the instant situation. The advertising created the impression that there were deadlines that compelled the merchant to accept low offers. For example, the July 12, 1993, advertisement invoked a July 18 deadline, saying: "This could be your last chance ever to buy at wholesale cost! . . . Our time is limited! WHOLESALE COST AND BELOW!" That deadline was purely artificial. The sale was authorized to continue for three more months and was extendable by agreement. The prices were higher than what PSP expected to get at the final going-out-of-business sale which it knew was inevitable once the debtor's "breathing room" in chapter 11 expired.

When the case was later converted to chapter 7, PSP admitted what it had been stringing the public along. It pleaded for permission to run an immediate going-out-of-business sale, confessing that the sales in preceding months were just part of the process of softening up the public for the final sale.

* * *

A judge's order approving a transaction cloaks the transaction with the prestige of the court. After such a cachet is conferred, it is susceptible of abuse.

"Court-authorized Bankruptcy Sale" in letters several feet high was emblazoned on the side of White Crane's building in plain view of a busy freeway. This was troublesome. Inside the building, a merchant was retailing furniture in a continuing business.

The language "court authorized" can convey a misimpression in consumers' minds that a court is supervising the activities within the store. This tends to lull consumers into a sense of security that they will not be cheated and that, if they are, the court will protect them from loss by ordinary restitution.

Permitting a merchant to trumpet court authorization amounts to entrusting the court's prestige to the care and custody of the merchant. It places that prestige at risk of being sullied by the actions of others. What if the merchandise is shoddy? Breaches of warranty? Dubious credit practices? "Bait and switch" tactics?

When a court recognizes that its name is being used in vain, it has an obligation to intervene sua sponte. *Cf.* Code of Judicial Conduct for United States Judges, Canon 2B (1992). Within several days after first seeing the sign on White Crane's building, I raised the issue in open court during a routine hearing in the case and suggested that the parties needed to persuade me that there was no problem. They elected, instead, to stop making references to court authorization.

* * *

It is also troubling that Rosenberg misrepresents the order to state and local enforcement authorities by suggesting that the order preempts consumer protection laws. The problem is that courts seldom consider such issues in connection with the order.

* * *

The Rosenberg strategy is to finesse section 959(b) and state consumer protection laws. Since section 959(b) admits no exceptions, the court cannot carve out an exemption from state law. A party should never present a court with a proposed order that would authorize the impermissible.

Some consumer protection laws, however, recognize an exception for sales that are authorized by courts. Thus, the requested order can make a difference and can serve to cure an otherwise doubtful transaction. The applicant for such an order, however, must be candid with the court and must unambiguously reveal that the sale that is being authorized would be troublesome under state law absent judicial imprimatur. If a proposed order would permit a merchant to operate outside the normal bounds of state law by virtue of the order alone, the court must be informed so that it may make a knowing and intelligent decision. Moreover, failure to give enforcement authorities notice hampers the court's ability to decide.

* * *

(Citations omitted.)

NOTES AND COMMENTS

1. Section 959 has been applied to a variety of federal, state, and local laws, and is particularly significant in the environmental law area. *See, e.g.*, Matter of Environ. Waste Control, Inc., 125 B.R. 546 (N.D. Ind. 1991) (the debtor-in-possession is required to complete an agency-ordered environmental cleanup); Matter of H.L.S. Energy Co., Inc., 151 F.3d 434 (5th Cir. 1998) (prohibiting bankruptcy trustee from abandoning property in violation of state law). However, courts have expressly rejected protections of § 959 in the context of rejection of executory contracts. *See, e.g.*, In re Old Carco LLC, 406 B.R. 180 (Bankr. S.D.N.Y. 2009) (refusing to apply dealer protection laws, such as waiting period for terminating franchise agreement, because Bankruptcy Code preempts state law by expressly allowing for contract rejection).

2. Does § 959 apply in a liquidation setting? *See* In re Valley Steel Products Co., Inc., 157 B.R. 442 (Bankr. E.D. Mo. 1993) ("Courts that have considered the question disagree whether 28 U.S.C. § 959 applies to debtors who have ceased operations and are liquidating their businesses"), *citing* In re Heldor Indus., Inc., 131 B.R. 578 (Bankr. N.J. 1991); In re Corona Plastics, Inc., 99 B.R. 231 (Bankr. N.J. 1989); In re Scott Housing Sys. Inc., 91 B.R. 190 (Bankr. S.D. Ga. 1988); Walsh v. West Virginia, 70 B.R. 786 (Bankr. N.D. Cal. 1987); In re Bourne Chem. Co., 54 B.R. 126 (Bankr. N.J. 1984) [each holding that trustee not required to follow non-bankruptcy law in liquidation setting]; In re Wall Tube & Metal Prods. Co., 831 F.2d 118 (6th Cir. 1987) and In re Stevens, 68 B.R. 774 (Bankr. D. Me. 1987) [each requiring trustee to follow non-bankruptcy law even in liquidation setting].

3. All states regulate the phrase "Going Out of Business" in conjunction with a sale and restrict the language to businesses that are actually liquidating. Read carefully the next time you see such an advertisement; some businesses not in liquidation try to skirt the law by hoping inattentive readers will not notice a sign that says "Going Out for Business." If a store is actually going out of business and you have a gift card for that store, remember that you will become an unsecured creditor unlikely to recover any money. Use your gift cards promptly, or risk the store going out of business and the gift card becoming valueless.

F. STATE LAW REMEDIES — ASSIGNMENT FOR THE BENEFIT OF CREDITORS (ABCs)

The states have a variety of bankruptcy-like alternatives that can often be less costly than federal bankruptcy cases. One of the common alternatives, known as an assignment for the benefit of creditors, allows a debtor to voluntarily assign its assets to a receiver in order to manage and distribute the assets to creditors. State laws regarding ABCs vary widely. Consider some of the provisions of Ohio law regarding ABCs.

Ohio Revised Code Commercial Transactions
Voluntary Assignment
1313.01 Assignee's bond

When a person, partnership, association, or corporation, makes an assignment to a trustee of property, money, rights, or credits, in trust for the benefit of creditors, within ten days after the delivery of the assignment to him and before disposing of any property so assigned, such assignee shall appear before the probate judge of the county in which the assignor resided at the time of executing the assignment, produce the original assignment, or a copy of it, cause it to be filed in the probate court, and enter into a bond, payable to the state, in such sum and with such sureties as the court approves, conditioned for the faithful performance of his duties. The court may require the assignee, or any trustee subsequently appointed, to execute an additional bond whenever the interests of the creditors of the assignor demand it.

1313.14 Notice of appointment

Each assignee or trustee for the benefit of creditors appointed on the failure of the assignee of a debtor to qualify, within thirty days after giving bond, must give notice of his appointment in some newspaper of general circulation in the county, for three successive weeks.

1313.21 Duties of assignee or trustee of insolvent debtor

An assignee or trustee for the benefit of creditors shall convert the assets received by him into money, and shall sell the real and personal property assigned, including stocks and such bonds, notes, and other claims as are not due and which probably cannot be collected within a reasonable time, at public auction, either for cash or upon such other terms as the probate court orders.

1313.32 Payment of liens

The probate court shall order the payment of all encumbrances and liens upon any property sold for the benefit of creditors, or rights and credits collected, out of the proceeds thereof, according to priority.

1313.44 Liens and securities

Persons who have performed labor in the service of the assignor within twelve months next preceding an assignment for the benefit of creditors, are entitled to receive out of the trust funds, before the paying of other creditors, the full amount of wages due for such labor not exceeding three hundred dollars. This section and section 1313.43 of the Revised Code do not prejudice or affect securities given, or liens obtained in good faith, for value, but judgments by confession on warrants of attorney rendered within two months prior to such assignment, or securities given within such time to create a preference among creditors, or to secure a pre-existing debt other than upon real property for the purchase money thereof, are of no force or validity as against such claims for labor, in case of assignment, to the extent provided in this section.

1313.45 Reports and settlements

An assignee or trustee for the benefit of creditors must file an account with the probate court at the expiration of eight months from his appointment and qualification, and as often thereafter as the court orders. Such account shall contain a full exhibit of all his doings as such, up to the time of filing, together with the amount of all claims remaining uncollected, and the amount thereof which in his opinion may thereafter be collected. Exceptions may be filed to the accounts by parties interested, in the manner provided in cases of accounts of administrators or executors. Such accounts shall be examined and the exceptions thereto heard by the court, in the manner provided for the settlement of the estates of deceased persons. Upon the filing of such accounts, the court shall fix a time for the hearing, and publish notice thereof as in the case of the filing of the account of an executor or administrator.

The following unreported case discusses some of the advantages and disadvantages of an Assignment for the Benefit of Creditors compared with a federal bankruptcy case.

Board of Trustees of UFCW Local 174 Pension Fund v. Jerry WWHS Co., Inc.

2012 WL 729261 (E.D.N.Y. 2012)

SEYBERT, District Judge

* * *

Plaintiff is the named fiduciary of the Local 174 Pension Fund (the "Fund"). The Fund is administered and maintained pursuant to collective bargaining agreements in accordance with Section 302(c)(5) of the Taft Hartley Act, 29 U.S.C. § 186(c)(5). Defendant and UFCW Local 342, the labor organization that for collective bargaining purposes represented the Defendant's employees, were the parties to one of those collective bargaining agreements (the "CBA"). Pursuant to the CBA, Defendant had a duty to make contributions to the Fund in accordance with the terms of the CBA as well as the terms of the Agreement and Declaration of Trust governing the Fund.

At some point in or before 2008, Defendant stopped making the required contributions and completely withdrew from the Fund, thereby triggering the imposition of withdrawal liability under ERISA § 4203, 29 U.S.C. § 1383. However, Defendant refused to make any withdrawal liability payments; so in June 2008, Plaintiff commenced a lawsuit in the Eastern District of New York seeking payment of the outstanding withdrawal liability. Defendant failed to appear or otherwise respond to that complaint, and in April 2009 Plaintiff was awarded a default judgment in the amount of $322,680.15.

Rather than seek to collect under the default judgment, on September 3, 2009, Plaintiff entered into a settlement agreement (the "Agreement") with Defendant. Pursuant to the Agreement, Defendant agreed to pay Plaintiff a total of $503,961.00 in periodic installments to settle the outstanding withdrawal liability. The Agreement also provided that, in the event of default, Plaintiff had "at its sole option and discretion the right to demand immediate payment of the entire $503,961.00, together with interest, liquidated damages, costs and attorney's fees." Defendant "expressly waive[d] any notice of the submission of a default judgment to the Court . . . and further expressly waive[d] any right to challenge, object to or defend against entry by the Court of such default judgment."

Defendant failed to make its scheduled payment on February 17, 2011. Then, on April 6, 2011, Defendant assigned all of its assets and liabilities to Douglas A. Pick (the "Assignee") for the benefit of all of Defendant's creditors. Defendant's estate is now being administered by Mr. Pick under the supervision of the New York State Supreme Court, Kings County (the "Assignment Proceeding").

After providing Defendant with a notice of default and an opportunity to cure, Plaintiff commenced the present action on July 14, 2011, seeking a judgment in the amount of $503,961.00 in accordance with the terms of the Agreement. . . .

On August 15, 2011, Defendant filed the pending motion to dismiss. It consists of an affidavit of the Assignee and accompanying exhibits. Defendant did not file a memorandum of law stating that one was not necessary because the motion to dismiss "does not present any novel issues of law."

* * *

II. Deference to the Assignment Proceeding

Defendant is also asking this Court to dismiss because "[w]hile there is no 'automatic stay' applicable in an assignment proceeding . . . , there is nevertheless a *de facto* stay and/or public policy under the Debtor and Creditor Law favoring the review and resolution of all liabilities and assets of an assignor in a single proceeding under the supervision of the assignee and the Supreme Court." Plaintiff refutes this argument, stating that "there is no case law or statutory authority which suggests that while the [state c]ourt is administering an [a]ssignment for the [b]enefit of [c]reditors, no causes of action may be brought against an Assignor or Assignee." Both parties are correct.

A general assignment for the benefit of creditors is an "assignment by a debtor transferring all of his or her property in general terms to an assignee in trust for all creditors of the debtor, or a voluntary transfer by a debtor of all his property to a trustee of his own selection, for administration, liquidation, and equitable distribution among his creditors." "A general assignment 'is distinguishable from a federal bankruptcy proceeding in that no discharge from the assignor's debts is obtainable in an assignment for the benefit of creditors.' "Because the assignor's debts are not discharged, "the creditor is not estopped from exhausting his legal remedies against the assignor." Accordingly, when an assignment proceeding is commenced, "New York law governing general assignments, unlike the federal bankruptcy law, does not impose an automatic stay on all litigation."

However, Defendant is correct that "public policy considerations tend to result in the dismissal of plenary actions in favor of assignments for the benefit of creditors." As one court explained:

> Where there is a special course of procedure, provided for a specific purpose, regulating certain proceedings, and adopted for the purpose of facilitating the disposition of matters cheaply and expeditiously, parties should be relegated to such method, and not be permitted a choice of tribunals, unless some substantial reason exists therefor, which should be specifically averred. In the case of insolvent assignments, the statute provides an expeditious and cheap method of procedure, where the rights of all creditors can be fairly protected, and the estate cheaply administered. Under such circumstances, the assignee ought not to be subjected to the vexatious trouble and burden of an action which leads, in the end, to an accounting, for which the statute provides, nor should the assigned estate be made subject to the costs and expense of an action and the inevitable waste which the fees of referees and other contingencies produce, as well as the costs of the action itself, unless there be exceptional grounds therefor; and such necessity ought to be clearly alleged.

Hynes v. Alexander, 2 A.D. 109, 37 N.Y.S. 527, 528 (2d Dep't 1896); *accord Abondolo,* 2011 WL 6012504, at *5.

"Nevertheless, whether to impose a stay or dismiss a claim in favor of an assignment proceeding remains a matter of judicial discretion." The Court again finds Judge Spatt's decision in *Abondolo* to be directly on point. In *Abondolo,* the petitioners commenced suit in district court to confirm an arbitration award in their favor for unpaid withdrawal liability. Judge Spatt held that public policy did not favor dismissing the federal petition in favor of the Assignment Proceeding because since "the [p]etitioners will still need to submit the claim for unpaid contributions in the Assignment Proceeding to effectuate judgment, confirming the award would not interfere with the 'orderly administration' of the estate." The same rationale applies here: Entering a default judgment against Defendant will not allow Plaintiff to circumvent the Arbitration Proceeding. Plaintiff will have to present any final judgment to the Assignee "who is obliged by law to accord that claim any priority to which it is entitled and, absent any priority, to distribute assets remaining after payment of priority claims ratably among the general unsecured creditors." Accordingly, the Court finds that public policy considerations do not require dismissal and hereby DENIES Defendant's motion to dismiss on those grounds.

* * *

(*Citations omitted.*)

NOTES AND COMMENTS

1. What factors contributed to the different results in the *Abondolo* case cited by the court and the *Board of Trustees* case?

2. How does the Ohio ABC statute compare to federal bankruptcy law? Consider the similarities and differences between the two schemes.

G. BANKRUPTCY IN PRACTICE

Assume that Diana never filed for bankruptcy protection. When she came to see you, she explained that the biggest issue she has been having is receiving calls from one debt collection agency at all hours of the night. They have called her ex-husband and even her employer! Draft a cease collection letter to the debt collection agency asserting Diana's rights under the FDCPA. The Consumer Financial Protection Bureau has sample letters to send to debt collectors on its website, including a request for more information, a denial of the debt, a demand to cease or narrow contact, or notice to contact an attorney. These letters are available at https://www.consumerfinance.gov/consumer-tools/debt-collection.

Table of Cases

Principal cases are italicized.

Index